ROUNDUP: *A Nebraska Reader*

ROUNDUP:

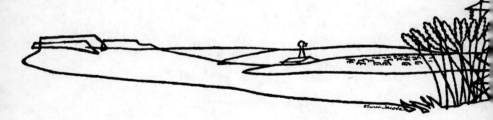

A Nebraska Reader

Compiled and edited by

Virginia Faulkner

Line Drawings by Elmer Jacobs

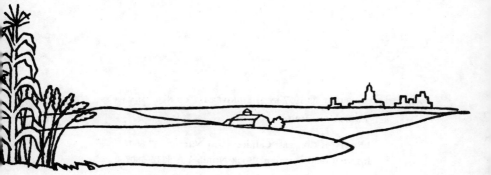

University of Nebraska Press

Lincoln & London

Fourth printing

Library of Congress Catalog Card Number 57-8597
International Standard Book Number 0–8032–5807–0

First Bison Book Edition: October 1974

Most recent printing indicated by first digit below:
2   3   4   5   6   7   8   9   10

Manufactured in the United States of America

FOR MORE THAN A CENTURY Nebraska has been an arena of adventure and achievement, the stage on which has been enacted some of the great American dramas of the mind and heart and spirit. Yet curiously enough, this 400-mile stretch of midland, this continental crossroads traversed yearly by thousands, has remained one of the least-known regions of our country. Nebraskans' awareness of the disparity between their state's solid significance in the national scene and its seeming invisibility to their fellow countrymen has been the animating force which has resulted in this book.

Acknowledgments

THE UNIVERSITY OF NEBRASKA PRESS wishes to acknowledge the kindness of the following publishers and authors in permitting the use of copyrighted material:

The American Mercury and the estate of Mrs. Gretchen Beghtol Lee for permission to reprint an excerpt from "Nebraska," January, 1925. *The American Mercury* and Dr. L. C. Wimberly for permission to condense "How a Dull Midwestern Town Takes on Class," July, 1934.

American Speech, the Columbia University Press, and Rudolph Umland for permission to reprint "American Cowboy Talk," February, 1942.

Appleton-Century-Crofts, Inc. for permission to quote from *A Lantern in Her Hand* by Bess Streeter Aldrich, copyright 1928 by D. Appleton & Co.; and to reprint a selection from *By Motor to the Golden Gate* by Emily Post, copyright 1916 by D. Appleton & Co.

A. S. Barnes & Co., Inc. for permission to extract from *Baseball's Greatest Pitchers* by Tom Meany, copyright 1951 by A. S. Barnes & Co., Inc.

Bartholomew House, Inc. for permission to extract from *A Treasury of Sports Stories* edited by Ed Fitzgerald, copyright 1955 by Bartholomew House, Inc.

Western Folklore and Dr. Louise Pound for permission to condense "Nebraska Rain Lore and Rain-Making," *California Folklore Quarterly,* Vol. 2, April, 1946.

Collier's and Bill Fay for permission to condense "Nebraska's 'Mr. Touchdown,'" October 6, 1951.

The Condé Nast Publications, Inc. for permission to reprint Robert Burlingame's "Nebraska on the Make," *Vanity Fair,* November, 1932, copyright 1932 by the Condé Nast Publications, Inc.

The Curtis Publishing Co. and Mari Sandoz for permission to reprint excerpts from "The New Frontier Woman," *Country Gentleman,* September, 1936, copyright 1936 by the Curtis Publishing Co. The Curtis Publishing Co. and Debs Myers for permission to reprint "The Grain Belt's Golden Buckle," *Holiday,* October, 1952, copyright 1952 by the Curtis Publishing Co. The Curtis Publishing Co., and the estate of Bess Streeter Aldrich for permission to extract from "Why I Live in a Small Town," *Ladies' Home Journal,* June, 1933, copyright 1933 by the Curtis Publishing Co. The Curtis Publishing Co. and B. F. Sylvester for permission to condense "Hoss Tradin'," *Saturday Evening Post,* January 6, 1934 and "Sandhills Paradise," *Saturday Evening Post,* June 14, 1947, copyright 1934 and 1947 respectively by the Curtis Publishing Co.

Thomas Y. Crowell Co. for permission to reprint excerpts from *Our American Music* by John Tasker Howard, copyright 1946, 1954 by John Tasker Howard.

Duell, Sloan & Pearce, Inc. for permission to quote from *Corn Country* by Homer Croy, copyright 1947, by Homer Croy.

Farrar & Rinehart and Stanley Vestal for permission to quote from *The Missouri,* copyright 1945 by Walter Stanley Campbell.

Wilfred Funk, Inc. for permission to extract from *Western Democrat* by Arthur F. Mullen, copyright 1940 by Wilfred Funk, Inc.

Harcourt Brace & Co., Inc. for permission to extract from *Bryan* by M. R. Werner, copyright 1929 by Harcourt Brace & Co., Inc.

Harper & Brothers for permission to present selections from *Inside U.S.A.* by John Gunther, copyright 1947 by John Gunther; *Incredible Tale* by Gerald W. Johnson, copyright 1950 by Gerald W. Johnson; and *Five Cities* by George Leighton, copyright 1938 by Harper & Brothers.

Houghton Mifflin Co. and the Executors of the Estate of Willa Cather for permission to quote from *O Pioneers!* by Willa Cather, copyright 1947; and *My Antonia* by Willa Cather, copyright 1918.

Johnsen Publishing Co. for permission to quote from J. R. Johnson's *Representative Nebraskans,* copyright 1954; and from *Sam McKelvie—Son of the Soil* by Bruce H. Nicoll and Ken R. Keller, copyright 1954.

Alfred A. Knopf, Inc. and the Executors of the Estate of Willa Cather for permission to reprint "Nebraska: the End of the First Cycle" by Willa Cather, Renewal copyright 1951 by the Executors of the Estate of Willa Cather; and for permission to quote from *Obscure Destinies* by Willa Cather, copyright 1950; *Youth and the Bright Medusa* by Willa Cather, copyright 1951; and *One of Ours* by Willa Cather, copyright 1953. Also for permission to quote from *Willa Cather Living* by Edith Lewis, copyright 1953 by Edith Lewis.

The estate of Charles G. Dawes for permission to extract from *A Journal of the McKinley Years,* copyright 1950 by Charles G. Dawes.

Life for permission to condense "Battling Bill Jeffers" by Ray Mackland, "A Nebraska Diplomat in Paraguay" by John Neill, and "The Thinking Machine Who Bosses NATO" by Robert Coughlan, copyright Time, Inc. 1943, 1941, and 1953 respectively. Also for permission to quote from "Four Seasons on the Farm," copyright Time, Inc. 1941.

The Lincoln *Star* for permission to quote from a story by Del Harding, November 10, 1956.

The Lincoln *Evening Journal* and the Sunday *Journal and Star* for permission to quote an editorial and extract from numerous feature stories.

The Macmillan Co. for permission to extract from *Them Was the Days* by Martha Ferguson McKeown, copyright 1950 by Martha Ferguson McKeown. Also to the Macmillan Co., the estate of A. G. Macdonell, and A. D. Peters for permission to extract from *A Visit to America* by A. G. Macdonell, copyright 1935 by A. G. Macdonell. Also to the Macmillan Co. and Mrs. George W. Norris for permission to quote from *Fighting Liberal* by George W. Norris, copyright 1945 by the Macmillan Co.

The Musical Quarterly for permission to extract from "Howard Hanson" by Burnet C. Tuthill, Vol. XXII, 1936.

The *Nation* for permission to reprint "Nebraska: the End of the First Cycle" by Willa Cather, copyright 1923 by The Nation, Inc.; and to condense "Norris of Nebraska" by Frederic Babcock, copyright 1927 by the Nation, Inc.

The Nebraska Alumni Association for permission to extract from "Louise Pound" by Hartley B. Alexander, *The Nebraska Alumnus,* October, 1933.

The Nebraska State Legislative Council for permission to quote from the *Nebraska Bluebook,* 1952.

Nebraska History, official publication of the Nebraska State Historical Society, for permission to reprint, condense, or quote from numerous articles.

Newsweek for permission to quote from "The Senate: 'I Could Use a Horse,'" May 10, 1954.

The Omaha *World-Herald* for permission to extract from numerous feature stories.

Popular Science Monthly for permission to reprint "They Torture Tractors" by B. F. Sylvester, May, 1954.

The *Prairie Schooner* for permission to reprint or condense numerous articles.

Reader's Digest for permission to reprint "The Town That Discovered Itself" by William S. Dutton, March, 1955, condensed from *Popular Science Monthly.*

The *Saturday Review of Literature* and the estate of William Allen White for permission to extract from a review of *Integrity: the Life of George W. Norris,* July 10, 1937.

Miss Ruth Sheldon for permission to quote from Addison E. Sheldon's *Nebraska: The Land and the People,* copyright 1931 by the Lewis Publishing Co.

Time for permission to reprint or extract from the following: "Nebraska's Howard," "Music Incubator," "War in the Corn," "Country Doctor, 1950," "One-Man Studio," "The Lady from Bar 99," and "NATO's General Gruenther." Copyright Time, Inc. 1928, 1940, 1945, 1950, 1952, 1954, and 1956 respectively.

The University of Colorado Press for permission to condense Walter Prescott Webb's "The Great Plains and the Industrial Revolution" from *The Trans-Mississippi West* edited by James F. Willard and Colin B. Goodykoontz, copyright 1930.

The University of Nebraska Press for permission to condense or extract from a number of its publications.

The University of North Carolina Press for permission to print a shortened version of Claudius O. Johnson's "George W. Norris" from *The American Politician* edited by J. T. Salter, copyright 1938.

The University Publishing Co. for permission to quote from *Nebraska Old and New* by Addison E. Sheldon, copyright 1937.

The Vanguard Press, Inc. for permission to quote from *Integrity: the Life of George W. Norris* by Richard L. Neuberger and Stephen B. Kahn, copyright 1937 by the Vanguard Press, Inc.

The Viking Press, Inc. for permission to extract from *Pioneer's Progress* by Alvin Johnson, copyright 1952 by Alvin Johnson. Also for permission to quote from *The American Democracy* by Harold J. Laski, copyright 1948 by the Viking Press, Inc.

We count ourselves fortunate to be able to include specially written pieces by the following authors: Lucius Beebe, Mildred R. Bennett, B. A. Botkin, Margaret Cannell, Jack Hart, Mamie J. Meredith, Bruce H. Nicoll, Col. Barney Oldfield, and Rudolph Umland.

We are indebted to Mari Sandoz and Mignon Good Eberhart for counsel and encouragement. Special thanks are due the staffs of the University of Nebraska Libraries and the Nebraska State Historical Society and Lincoln City Library, who bore up nobly under our constant and involved demands. We are deeply grateful to Professors Lowry C. Wimberly, James C. Olson, and Karl Shapiro, and Mr. John H. Ames, who read ROUNDUP in manuscript; and to Mrs. Rosalie L. Fuller, who typed it.

Among the persons to whom we are indebted for information, the loan of material, and other assistance, are: Stu Bohacek, the Wilber *Republican*; Ronald R. Furse, the Plattsmouth *Journal*; Nelle Greer, the Lincoln *Star*; C. Don Harpst, the Cambridge *Clarion*; Dick Herman, the Sidney *Telegraph*; Robert Houston, the Omaha *World-Herald*; Bill Lee, the Ord *Quiz*; Raymond A. McConnell, Jr., the Lincoln Evening *Journal*; George P. Miller, the Papillion *Times*; Arthur J. Riedesel, the Ashland *Times*; and Abel Green, *Variety*. Also to Larry Owen and Mrs. Shirley Wilkin of the Columbus Chamber of Commerce; Cletus Nelson, Secretary of the Holdrege Chamber of Commerce; Bob Thomas, Manager, WJAG, Norfolk; Captain James J. Brady, Deputy Chief, Public Information Division, Office of Information, Headquarters, Strategic Air Command; Professor J. H. Johnson, State Teachers College, Wayne; B. F. Sylvester, Omaha; and Victor E. Blackledge and Alan H. Williams, Scottsbluff. Also the following Lincoln people: Professor-emeritus Louise Pound, Professor James Sellers, Professor Mamie J. Meredith, Mildred M. Faulkner, Richard W. Faulkner, Merle C. Rathburn, and Burnham Yates.

Finally, we wish to express our special thanks to Mr. Morton Steinhart of Nebraska City, whose generous gift at a crucial moment enabled us to complete the research and preparation of the manuscript; and to the Cooper Foundation whose loan helped with the financing of the book.

Table of Contents

1923: Willa Cather's Nebraska

1932: Vanity Fair's Nebraska

VII. FAMILY ALBUM II

VIII. JUST PASSING THROUGH

1947: John Gunther's Nebraska

1957: The Nebraskan's Nebraska

1923

WILLA CATHER'S
NEBRASKA

Nebraska:
The End of the First Cycle

WILLA CATHER

THE STATE OF NEBRASKA is part of the great plain which stretches west of the Missouri River, gradually rising until it reaches the Rocky Mountains. The character of all this country between the river and the mountains is essentially the same throughout its extent: a rolling, alluvial plain, growing gradually more sandy toward the west, until it breaks into the white sandhills of western Nebraska and Kansas and eastern Colorado. From east to west this plain measures something over five hundred miles; in appearance it resembles the wheat lands of Russia, which fed the continent of Europe for so many years. Like Little Russia it is watered by slow-flowing, muddy rivers, which run full in the spring, often cutting into the farm lands along their banks; but by midsummer they lie low and shrunken, their current split by glistening white sand-bars half overgrown with scrub willows.

The climate, with its extremes of temperature, gives to this plateau the variety which, to the casual eye at least, it lacks. There we have short, bitter winters; windy, flower-laden springs; long, hot summers; triumphant autumns that last until Christmas—a season of perpetual sunlight, blazing blue skies, and frosty nights. In this newest part of the New World autumn is the season of beauty and sentiment, as spring is in the Old World.

Nebraska is a newer state than Kansas. It was a state before there were people in it. Its social history falls easily within a period of sixty years, and the first stable settlements of white men were made within the memory of old folk now living. The earliest of these settlements—Bellevue, Omaha, Brownville, Nebraska City—were founded along the Missouri River, which was at that time a pathway for small steamers. In 1855–60 these four towns were straggling groups of log houses, hidden away along the wooded river banks.

Before 1860 civilization did no more than nibble at the eastern edge of the state, along the river bluffs. Lincoln, the present capital, was open prairie; and the whole of the great plain to the westward was still a sunny wilderness, where the tall red grass and the buffalo and the Indian hunter were undisturbed. Fremont, with Kit Carson, the famous scout, had gone across Nebraska in 1842, exploring the valley of the Platte. In the days of the Mormon persecution, fifteen thousand Mormons camped for two years, 1845–46, six miles north of Omaha, while their exploring parties went farther west, searching for fertile land outside of government jurisdiction. In 1847 the entire Mormon sect, under the leadership of Brigham Young, went with their wagons through Nebraska and on to that desert beside the salty sea which they have made so fruitful.

In forty-nine and the early fifties, gold hunters, bound for California, crossed the state in thousands, always following the old Indian trail along the Platte valley. The state was a highway for dreamers and adventurers: men who were in quest of gold or grace, freedom or romance. With all these people the road led out, but never back again.

While Nebraska was a camping-ground for seekers outward bound, the wooden settlements along the Missouri were growing into something permanent. The settlers broke the ground and began to plant the fine orchards which have ever since been the pride of Otoe and Nemaha counties. It was at Brownville that the first telegraph wire was brought across the Missouri River. When I was a child I heard ex-Governor Furnas relate how he stood with other pioneers in a log cabin where the Morse instrument had been installed, and how, when it began to click, the men took off their hats as if they were in church. The first message flashed across the river into Nebraska was not a market report, but a line of poetry: "Westward the course of empire takes its way." The Old West was like that.

The first back-and-forth travel through the state was by way of the Overland Mail, a monthly passenger-and-mail stage service across the plains from Independence to the new colony at Salt Lake.

When silver ore was discovered in the mountains of Colorado near Cherry Creek—afterward Camp Denver and later the city of Denver— a picturesque form of commerce developed across the great plain of Nebraska: the transporting of food and merchandise from the Missouri to the Colorado mining camps, and on to the Mormon settlement at Salt Lake. One of the largest freighting companies, operating out of Nebraska City, in the six summer months of 1860 carried nearly three million pounds of freight across Nebraska, employing 515 wagons, 5,687 oxen, and 600 drivers.

The freighting began in the early spring, usually about the middle of April, and continued all summer and through the long, warm autumns. The oxen made from ten to twenty miles a day. I have heard the old freighters say that, after embarking on their six-hundred-mile trail, they lost count of the days of the week and the days of the month. While they were out in that sea of waving grass, one day was like another; and, if one can trust the memory of these old men, all the days were glorious. The buffalo trails still ran north and south then, deep, dusty paths the bison wore when, single file, they came north in the spring for the summer grass, and went south again in the autumn. Along these trails were the buffalo "wallows"— shallow depressions where the rain water gathered when it ran off the tough prairie sod. These wallows the big beasts wore deeper and packed hard when they rolled about and bathed in the pools, so that they held water like a cement bottom. The freighters lived on game and shot the buffalo for their hides. The grass was full of quail and prairie chickens, and flocks of wild ducks swam about on the lagoons. These lagoons have long since disappeared, but they were beautiful things in their time: long stretches where the rain water gathered and lay clear on a grassy bottom without mud. From the lagoons the first settlers hauled water to their homesteads, before they had dug their wells. The freighters could recognize the lagoons from afar by the clouds of golden coreopsis which grew out of the water and waved delicately above its surface. Among the pioneers the coreopsis was known simply as "the lagoon flower."

As the railroads came in, the freighting business died out. Many a freight-driver settled down upon some spot he had come to like on his journeys to and fro, homesteaded it, and wandered no more. The Union Pacific, the first transcontinental railroad, was completed in 1869. The Burlington entered Nebraska in the same year, at Plattsmouth, and began construction westward. It finally reached Denver by an indirect route, and went on extending and ramifying through the state. With the railroads came the home-seeking people from overseas.

When the first courageous settlers came straggling out through the waste with their oxen and covered wagons, they found open range all the way from Lincoln to Denver: a continuous, undulating plateau, covered with long, red, shaggy grass. The prairie was green only where it had been burned off in the spring by the new settlers

or by the Indians, and toward autumn even the new grass became
a coppery brown. This sod, which had never been broken by the
plow, was so tough and strong with the knotted grass roots of many
years that the home-seekers were able to peel it off the earth like
peat, cut it up into bricks, and make of it warm, comfortable, durable
houses. Some of these sod houses lingered on until the open range
was gone and the grass was gone, and the whole face of the country
had been changed.

Even as late as 1886 the central part of the state, and everything
to the westward, was, in the main, raw prairie. The cultivated fields
and broken land seemed mere scratches in the brown, running steppe
that never stopped until it broke against the foothills of the Rockies.
The dugouts and sod farmhouses were three or four miles apart, and
the only means of communication was the heavy farm wagon, drawn
by heavy work horses. The early population of Nebraska was largely
transatlantic. The county in which I grew up, in the south-central
part of the state, was typical. On Sunday we could drive to a
Norwegian church and listen to a sermon in that language, or to
a Danish or a Swedish church. We could go to the French Catholic
settlement in the next county and hear a sermon in French, or into
the Bohemian township and hear one in Czech, or we could go to
church with the German Lutherans. There were, of course, American
congregations also.

There is a Prague in Nebraska as well as in Bohemia. Many of
our Czech immigrants were people of a very superior type. The
political emigration resulting from the revolutionary disturbances
of 1848 was distinctly different from the emigration resulting from
economic causes, and brought to the United States brilliant young
men from both Germany and Bohemia. In Nebraska our Czech
settlements were large and very prosperous. I have walked about the
streets of Wilber, the county seat of Saline County, for a whole day
without hearing a word of English spoken. In Wilber, in the old
days, behind the big, friendly brick saloon—it was not a "saloon,"
properly speaking, but a beer garden, where the farmers ate their
lunch when they came to town—there was a pleasant little theater
where the boys and girls were trained to give the masterpieces of
Czech drama in the Czech language. "Americanization" has doubtless done away with all this. Our lawmakers have a rooted conviction that a boy can be a better American if he speaks only one
language than if he speaks two. I could name a dozen Bohemian
towns in Nebraska where one used to be able to go into a bakery and

buy better pastry than is to be had anywhere except in the best pastry shops of Prague or Vienna. The American lard pie never corrupted the Czech.

Cultivated, restless young men from Europe made incongruous figures among the hard-handed breakers of the soil. Frederick Amiel's nephew lived for many years and finally died among the Nebraska farmers. Knut Hamsun, the Norwegian writer who was awarded the Nobel Prize for 1920, was a "hired hand" on a Dakota farm to the north of us. Colonies of European people, Slavonic, Germanic, Scandinavian, Latin, spread across our bronze prairies like the daubs of color on a painter's palette. They brought with them something that this neutral new world needed ever more than the immigrants needed land.

Unfortunately, their American neighbors were seldom openminded enough to understand the Europeans, or to profit by their older traditions. Our settlers from New England, cautious and convinced of their own superiority, kept themselves insulated as much as possible from foreign influences. The incomers from the South— from Missouri, Kentucky, the two Virginias—were provincial and utterly without curiosity. They were kind neighbors—lent a hand to help a Swede when he was sick or in trouble. But I am quite sure that Knut Hamsun might have worked a year for any one of our Southern farmers, and his employer would never have discovered that there was anything unusual about the Norwegian. A New England settler might have noticed that his chore-boy had a kind of intelligence, but he would have distrusted and stonily disregarded it.

Nevertheless, the thrift and intelligence of its preponderant European population have been potent factors in bringing about the present prosperity of the state. The census of 1910 showed that there were then 228,648 foreign-born and native-born Germans living in Nebraska; 103,503 Scandinavians; 50,680 Czechs. The total foreign population of the state was then 900,571, while the entire population was 1,192,214. That is, in round numbers, there were about nine hundred thousand foreign Americans in the state, to three hundred thousand native stock. With such a majority of foreign stock, nine to three, it would be absurd to say that the influence of the European does not cross the boundary of his own acres, and has had nothing to do with shaping the social ideals of the commonwealth.

When I stop at one of the graveyards in my own county and see on the headstones the names of fine old men I used to know: "Eric

Ericson, born Bergen, Norway . . . died Nebraska," "Anton Pucelik, born Prague, Bohemia . . . died Nebraska," I have always the hope that something went into the ground with those pioneers that will one day come out again, something that will come out not only in sturdy traits of character, but in elasticity of mind, in an honest attitude toward the realities of life, in certain qualities of feeling and imagination. It is in that great cosmopolitan country known as the Middle West that we may hope to see the hard molds of American provincialism broken up, that we may hope to find young talent which will challenge the pale proprieties, the insincere, conventional optimism of our art and thought.

The rapid industrial development of Nebraska, which began in the latter eighties, was arrested in the years 1893–97 by a succession of crop failures and by the financial depression which spread over the whole country at that time—the depression which produced the People's Party and the Free Silver agitation. These years of trial, as everyone now realizes, had a salutary effect upon the new state. They winnowed out the settlers with a purpose from the drifting malcontents who are ever seeking a land where man does not live by the sweat of his brow. The slack farmer moved on. Superfluous banks failed, and money-lenders who drove hard bargains with desperate men came to grief. The strongest stock survived, and within ten years those who had weathered the storm came into their reward. What that reward is, you can see for yourself if you motor through the state from Omaha to the Colorado line. The country has no secrets; it is as open as an honest human face.

The old, isolated farms have come together. They rub shoulders. The whole state is a farm. Now it is the pasture lands that look little and lonely, crowded in among so much wheat and corn. It is scarcely an exaggeration to say that every farmer owns an automobile. I believe the last estimate showed that there is one motor car for every six inhabitants in Nebraska. The great grain fields are plowed by tractors. The old farmhouses are rapidly being replaced by more cheerful dwellings, with bathrooms and hardwood floors, heated by furnaces or hot-water plants. Many of them are lighted by electricity, and every farmhouse has its telephone. The country towns are clean and well kept. On Saturday night the main street is a long, black line of parked motor cars; the farmers have brought their families to town to see the moving-picture show. When the school bell rings on Monday morning, crowds of happy looking children, well nourished—for the most part well mannered, too—flock along the shady streets. They wear cheerful, modern clothes, and the girls, like the boys, are elastic and vigorous in their movements. These thousands and thousands of children—in the little towns and in the country schools—these, of course, ten years from now, will be the state.

In this time of prosperity, any farmer boy who wishes to study at the state university can do so. A New York lawyer who went out to Lincoln to assist in training the university students for military service in war time exclaimed when he came back: "What splendid young men! I would not have believed that any school in the world could get together so many boys physically fit, and so few unfit."

Of course there is the other side of the medal, stamped with the ugly crest of materialism, which has set its seal upon all of our most productive commonwealths. Too much prosperity, too many moving-picture shows, too much gaudy fiction have colored the taste and manners of so many of these Nebraskans of the future. There, as elsewhere, one finds the frenzy to be showy: farmer boys who wish to be spenders before they are earners, girls who try to look like heroines of the cinema screen, a coming generation which tries to cheat its aesthetic sense by buying things instead of making anything. There is even danger that that fine institution, the University of Nebraska, may become a gigantic trade school. The classics, the humanities, are having their dark hour. They are in eclipse. But the "classics" have a way of revenging themselves. One may venture to hope that the children, or the grandchildren, of a generation that goes to a university to select only the most utilitarian subjects in the course of study—among them, salesmanship and dressmaking—will revolt against all the heaped-up, machine-made materialism about them. They will go back to the old sources of culture and wisdom—not as a duty, but with burning desire.

In Nebraska, as in so many other states, we must face the fact that the splendid story of the pioneers is finished, and that no new story worthy to take its place has yet begun. The generation that subdued the wild land and broke up the virgin prairie is passing, but it is still there, a group of rugged figures in the background which inspire respect, compel admiration. With these old men and women the attainment of material prosperity was a moral victory, because it was wrung from hard conditions, was the result of a struggle that tested character. They can look out over those broad stretches of fertility and say: "We made this, with our backs and hands." The sons, the generation now in middle life, were reared amid hardships, and it is perhaps natural that they should be very much interested in material comfort, in buying whatever is expensive and ugly. Their fathers came into a wilderness and had to make everything, had to be as ingenious as shipwrecked sailors. The generation now in the driver's seat hates to make anything, wants to live and die in an automobile, scudding past those acres where the old men used to follow the long corn-rows up and down. They want to buy everything ready-made: clothes, food, education, music, pleasure. Will the third generation—the full-blooded, joyous one just coming over the hill— will it be fooled? Will it believe that to live easily is to live happily?

The wave of generous idealism, of noble seriousness, which swept over the state of Nebraska in 1917 and 1918 demonstrated how fluid and flexible is any living, growing, expanding society. If such "conversions" do not last, they at least show of what men and women are capable. Surely the materialism and showy extravagance of this hour are a passing phase! They will mean no more half a century from now than will the "hard times" of twenty-five years ago—which are already forgotten. The population is as clean and full of vigor as the soil; there are no old grudges, no heritages of disease or hate. The belief that snug success and easy money are the real aims of human life has settled down over our prairies, but it has not yet hardened into molds and crusts. The people are warm, mercurial, impressionable, restless, over-fond of novelty and change. These are not the qualities which make the dull chapters of history.

Reprinted from *The Nation*, Sept. 5, 1923

I. The Shifting Frontier

There was nothing but land: not a country at all, but the material out of which countries are made.

—Willa Cather, *My Antonia*

> *From the 98th meridian west to the Rocky Mountains there is a stretch of country whose history is filled with more tragedy, and whose future is pregnant with greater promise than perhaps any other equal expanse of territory.*
> —A. M. Simons, *The American Farmer*

West of 98°

1. The Great American Desert

JAMES C. OLSON

WHEN Major Stephen H. Long of the Army Engineers returned from his epochal expedition to the Rocky Mountains in 1820, he confirmed what many Americans had suspected all along—that most of the area between the Missouri River and the Rocky Mountains was a vast desert wasteland. "In regard to this extensive section of the country," he wrote, "I do not hesitate in giving the opinion, that it is almost wholly unfit for cultivation, and of course uninhabitable by a people depending upon agriculture for their subsistence." Dr. Edwin James, chronicler of the expedition, stated that he had "no fear of giving too unfavorable an account" of the region. It was "an unfit residence for any but a nomad population."

Lewis and Clark, along the Missouri in 1804–6, had suspected the same thing. Lieutenant Zebulon M. Pike, who went out along the Republican in 1806, had written of "barren soil, parched and dried up for eight months in the year," and had hazarded a guess that America's western plains would "become in time equally celebrated as the sandy desarts [sic] of Africa." Even Thomas Jefferson—who had never visited the West—shared the popular misconception, referring to the "immense and trackless deserts" to be found in the region.

With Major Long's scientific stamp of approval, the idea became well fixed, and by the end of the first quarter of the nineteenth century, most Americans shared the notion that the region between the Missouri and the Rockies was a vast, uninhabitable desert. It is little wonder that in the late twenties and the early thirties the suggestion that the area west of the Missouri be set aside as a permanent home for the Indians found ready acceptance.

11

There were a few who disagreed with the prevailing notion. As early as 1817, John Bradbury, the English naturalist, wrote that Americans were misled in their thinking about the Plains because they were accustomed to "a profusion of timber." He expressed a belief that the region could be cultivated "and that, in the process of time, it will not only be peopled and cultivated, but it will be one of the most beautiful countries in the world." Bayard Taylor, who went through the country in 1866, also disagreed with the common view.

By the time Taylor's book appeared in 1867, a great many people had acquired a vested interest in the land west of the Missouri. Nebraska had been admitted to the Union and was in the process of claiming its landed endowment; millions of acres had been or shortly would be withdrawn for the benefit of the Union Pacific and the Burlington railroads; speculators were busy locating large tracts which they hoped to turn at a profit; settlement by homesteaders was well under way. These people were gambling that the desert concept was erroneous. Experience on the wet prairies east of the Missouri had demonstrated that one doesn't need trees to grow bountiful crops of corn, wheat, and oats. A brief experience west of the Missouri had shown that this area, too, would produce good crops. The Missouri then was not the dividing line between farm land and desert. But where was it?

Nebraskans were a long time finding out. Indeed, a whole generation of them stoutly denied that it existed at all, and when in 1878 Major John Wesley Powell, chief of the Department of the Interior's Survey of the Rocky Mountain Region, stated that nonirrigable farming could not be carried on west of the one-hundredth meridian because the area had less than twenty inches of annual rainfall, a host—including Samuel Aughey, Professor of Natural Sciences at the University of Nebraska—denounced his findings as bureaucratic nonsense. Major Powell, of course, was not talking about a desert—he was talking about a region in which one would have to irrigate if he were going to farm safely and successfully over the years. There was a vast difference.

Though he was much and unjustly abused by his own generation for his pessimism about the West, Major Powell was, if anything, too optimistic—there were many areas *east* of the one-hundredth meridian where farming needed the aid of irrigation. In general, however, Major Powell's appraisal was correct. The Plains *did* present a problem to the American pioneer. Perhaps nowhere has the nature of that problem been better stated than by Walter Prescott Webb in *The Great Plains:*

> The Great Plains offered such a contrast to the region east of the ninety-eighth meridian, the region with which American civilization had been familiar until about 1840, as to bring about a marked change in the ways of pioneering and living. For two centuries American pioneers had been working out a technique for the utilization of the humid regions east of the Mississippi River. They had found solutions for their problems and were conquering the frontier at a steadily accelerating rate. Then in the early nineteenth century they crossed the Mississippi and came out on the great plains, an environment with which they had had no experience. The result was a complete though temporary breakdown of the machinery and ways of pioneering. . . .
>
> As one contrasts the civilization of the Great Plains with that of the eastern timberland, one sees what may be called an institutional *fault* (comparable to a geological fault) running from middle Texas to Illinois or Dakota, roughly following the ninety-eighth meridian. At this *fault* the ways of life and of living changed. Practically every institution that was carried across it was either broken and remade or else greatly altered. The ways of travel, the weapons, the method of tilling the soil, the plows and other agricultural implements, and even the laws themselves were modified. . . . [The problem] has been stated in this way: east of the Mississippi civilization stood on three legs—land, water, and timber; west of the Mississippi not one but two of these legs were withdrawn,—water and timber,—and civilization was left on one leg—land. It is small wonder that it toppled over in temporary failure.

Whether you accept Webb's ninety-eighth meridian, which enters the state at Niobrara and leaves it at Superior, or Powell's one-hundredth, which runs down the main street of Cozad, it is clear that a rather considerable portion of Nebraska is in this "problem area" of the Plains, and that much of the story of the state is a chronicle of man's adaptation to the Plains.

Condensed from *History of Nebraska,* University of Nebraska Press, 1955

2. The Frontier Machine

WALTER PRESCOTT WEBB

WHEN the advancing frontier reached the Great Plains and found its tools, technique, and institutions inadequate, there was a pause, a delay, a long interval of waiting until new ways could be devised, and new tools invented or adopted. Here a figure of speech may help make clear what happened. The frontier was a machine. It was a factory. Its function was to move across a primitive land, subdue the natives, mow down the forests, rear the cabins, turn the sod. The product of the factory was farm homes, which arose behind the moving machine like sheaves in the harvested fields. The machine was a complicated and clumsy affair built out of long experience. Its parts were guns, axes, plows, logs, rails, boats, horses, and wagons. Its operatives were men and women, boys and girls—the pioneers. It was powered by toil and directed by that restless spirit under whose urge civilization has always moved westward. When this dynamic frontier machine which manufactured farm homes reached the Great Plains, trouble developed, the parts broke; the machine refused to function, to move forward as it should, though the urge was as strong as ever in the pioneers. Now when the machinery breaks, the factory has to close down for repairs and overhauling. Sometimes it is necessary to close the plant and reorganize completely and install new machinery to meet new conditions. That is what happened when the frontier machine left the timber and came out in the open country of the Great Plains. It had been making woodland farm homes, but conditions had changed so that it discontinued this model and brought out a plains home.

There was, of course, a long interval of waiting while the overhauling went on. In the first part of this interval (1825–1860), the trails were thrown across the plains over which trickled the overflow of immigrants who were damming up along the timber line where the machine broke down. In the latter part of the interval (1866–1876), the cattle kingdom, with its origin in Texas, moved northward and westward and appropriated the whole Great Plains area. The cattle kingdom was something distinctly new in American life. It was a machine, too, but entirely different from the agricultural one undergoing repairs on the timber line. It was a plains institution, just as the broken machine was a woods affair; it was made for the plains.

By the time the cattle kingdom became well established (1875), the industrial revolution had come to the aid of the agricultural frontier, and patched up the machine, whereupon the farmers resumed their westward course. In response to urgent and imperative needs, the industrial revolution gave the plainsman a new weapon, the six-shooter; a new fence, barbed wire; a new water machine, the windmill; new farming implements; and a new method of farming.

The need for the six-shooter arose at the point where the Anglo-American pioneers came in necessary contact with hostile Plains

Indians. Three characters are necessary to the story: a Plains Indian, a Texas Ranger, and a Connecticut man named Samuel Colt.

The Plains Indians were nomadic, predatory, and extremely ferocious. The horse was the summation of all good to the Plains Indians: they moved on horseback, played on horseback, hunted on horseback, and fought on horseback. Moreover, they were the only horse Indians in America, the only Indians that the Anglo-American pioneers ever had to meet in mounted combat. It is not to be wondered at that when the meeting did take place, the pioneers found themselves in need of a new weapon, one that could be used on horseback.

The Texas Rangers were called into existence during the Texas Revolution and assigned the task of guarding the Indian frontier. Most of the forays came from the west and were made by the Comanches, a pure Plains tribe. So finally the Rangers were permanently stationed at San Antonio, on the margin of the Great Plains region, and from that strategic point scoured the country on horseback and held back the raiding Comanches. The accounts of the early Indian battles reveal that the Texans could not meet the Comanches on horseback, because their forest weapons were no match for the Indians' weapon in mounted war. But the Texans held the line with the long rifles and horse pistols until about 1840.

In 1830 Samuel Colt whittled from wood his first model of a revolving pistol. In 1835 he took out a patent in England and in 1836 in America. Although the manufacture of Colt's Patent Firearms on a considerable scale began in 1838, Colt could not induce the United States government to purchase the weapon, and private citizens did not buy it extensively. But for some reason orders began to come in from the far-off Republic of Texas, where the weapon had somehow found its way into the hands of the Texas Rangers. Colt named the first model the *Texas,* for obvious reasons, and brought out a second to meet the needs suggested by those guardians of the border.

The six-shooter revolutionized plains warfare. Colonel Richard I. Dodge expressed the change thus:

Then came the revolver, which multiplied every soldier by six, and produced such an inspiring moral effect on the troops, and so entirely depressing an effect on the Indians, that the fights became simply chases.

After the Mexican War gave the United States possession of the whole Great Plains region, the six-shooter spread rapidly westward and to this day is identified in folklore and literature primarily with the West. After the Civil War, it was adopted by the cowboys, who

looked upon it as their own special weapon. Its adoption, rapid
spread, and popularity through the Great Plains, the Indian and
cattle country, were due to a genuine need for a horseman's weapon.
It stands as the first mechanical adaptation made by the Anglo-
American people when they emerged from the timber and met a set
of new needs in the open country of the Great Plains.

The log cabin and the rail fence constituted the chief shield of
the American pioneer against the outside world for the first two centuries of American history. The one shielded the family: the other
guarded the crops that sustained it. Both were so much a part of
the life of the people that they became symbols of democracy, potent
ballyhoo for the politician. Together the log cabin and the rail
fence went west with the pioneer to the Great Plains, which they
could never penetrate. On the plains, the sod and adobe houses and
dugouts took the place of the log cabin, but there was nothing to
take the place of the rail fence. Without fences there would be no
farms: without farms the agricultural frontier ceased to advance.*
Words fail to describe the confusion that took place among the
farmers when they emerged from the timber into the plain, where
neither rails nor rock could be obtained for fencing. What alarmed
the people were the enormous cost of fencing and the increasing
cost in the West. In 1870 the Department of Agriculture prepared
a report on the fence question based upon an inquiry sent to every
state and territory. The government agent stated that a homestead
in the West that cost $200 in fees would cost $1,000 for fencing. An
analysis of the report shows that the cost of material, boards and
rails, ranged from 60 to 300 per cent higher in the plains states and
territories; the cost per rod ranged from 100 to 400 per cent higher;
and the cost of maintenance from 90 to 200 per cent higher!
The predicament of the prairie and plains people is further indicated by their efforts to find their way out of it, to find something
that would serve them, to escape from the trap. There were worm
fences, board, post-and-rail, Shanghai, leaning, bloomer, and osage
orange hedge. In Nebraska one-fourth of the fences were made of
an earth wall three and one-half feet high. For several years the
experiment and search for a practical and economical fence was carried on by farmers of the prairie region.

* Of course there were other factors that held the farmers back, such as lack
of transportation, the character of the Plains Indians, and the uncertain rainfall,
but none of these was more important to the farmer than fences.

It may be asserted, subject to qualifications, that Joseph F. Glidden, a farmer of DeKalb, Illinois, invented barbed wire. Glidden made his first wire in 1873 and sold the first piece in 1874. Others had invented it in some form, but Glidden "gave to it the final touch of commercial practicality." There is more than one story as to how the invention came to be made: One is that Mrs. Glidden wanted some flower beds protected from dogs. Her husband stretched smooth wire around the garden, which was of no avail, whereupon he placed short pieces of wire about the plain wire, forming crude barbs.

Glidden first made barbed wire by putting the barbs on a single strand of wire. The trouble with this method was that the barbs would not stay in place. One day, while thinking of this difficulty, Glidden picked up some tangled wires, which suggested that the barbs could be held in place, both as to lateral and rotary motion, by twisting two wires together. While trying to think of some way of twisting the two wires, "his eye lighted on the grindstone and he formed the idea of twisting the wire by means of the small crank on the grindstone. He asked his wife to turn the grindstone, which she did."

The Washburn & Moen Company of Worcester, Massachusetts, was at the time the largest smooth-wire manufacturer in the country. The company found so many and such large orders for wire coming from DeKalb that Charles F. Washburn was sent west to investigate. Washburn found the barbed-wire factories operating, and undertook to buy an interest in the business. He was unsuccessful, and returned east with samples of the new product, which were turned over to an expert designer of automatic machinery with instructions to design a machine that would fabricate barbed wire. Putnam got the assignment in August, 1875, had the machine working by October, applied for a patent January 20, 1876, and received the patent in February. Washburn, armed now with the machine and patent, went again to DeKalb, and in May, 1876, bought half of Glidden's interest for a cash and royalty consideration. By January 1, 1879, Washburn & Moen had made with the Putnam machines nine and one-quarter million pounds of wire.

In 1874 and 1875 the wire sold at $20.00 per hundred pounds, probably a half or a third of what the old fence would cost. The cost decreased yearly, reaching its lowest point in 1897 when it was $1.80 per hundred. It is safe to say that the industrial revolution, through barbed wire, cut the cost of fencing the Great Plains more than forty-fold, made fencing possible, and enabled the farmer to try his hand west of the ninety-eighth meridian.

The dominant note in the white man's history of the Great Plains has been the search for water. In the East the living streams and numerous springs furnished abundant water for the pioneer. If the supply was not sufficient, it could be augmented by shallow dug wells, but west of the ninety-eighth meridian there were few streams, practically no springs, and the groundwater lay far beneath the surface. The task of drawing water from a well one hundred feet deep was quite different from drawing or pumping it fifteen or twenty feet. When in drought the water had to be drawn for thirsty cattle and horses, the task became insuperable, as many a western boy can testify. Furthermore, many of the wells yielded little water and were easily exhausted. Something was needed to take the water from the well as it accumulated, some power other than tired human hands. It must be inexpensive, too. The windmill met all requirements as aptly as the six-shooter and barbed wire met theirs. The wind of the plains was very free and constant and of high velocity; the windmills could be bought, or they could be made of old wagon axles, Four X coffee boxes, and scrap iron at a cost as low as $1.50. The free wind drove the mills day and night, delivering the scant supply of water as it accumulated.

How the windmills found their way west is told by a veteran of the industry, Mr. H. N. Wade, as follows:

Way back in 1854, John Burnham, who was then termed a Pump Doctor . . . suggested to Daniel Halladay, a young mechanic of Ellington, Conn., that it would be a good idea if a windmill could be made self-governing as there was an abundance of wind all over the country that might just as well pump water and save the human energy expended.

Mr. Halladay was a man of an inventive turn of mind and he very quickly invented a windmill, which governed itself by centrifugal force. . . . These mills were first manufactured by the Halladay Windmill Company in 1854 in South Coventry, Conn., and a few were sold, but Mr. Burnham came to Chicago and decided that the real market for the windmill would be in the western prairie states.

About the time Mr. Burnham came west, the railroads were being built rapidly, and the promoter saw a market for windmills with which to supply water for the locomotives. He interested some railroad people and in 1857 organized at Chicago the United States Wind Engine & Pump Company, a sales organization for the eastern factory. Delays in shipping and high freight rates convinced the

Chicago company that it would be more economical to manufacture in Chicago; the result was that the Halladay Windmill Company sold out to the Chicago concern in 1862, and, in the words of Mr. Wade, "the manufacture of windmills was first commenced on what might be termed a large scale."

Barbed wire made it possible for the stockman to convert his range into a big pasture or a ranch. The ranchman could not, however, put in cross fences cutting off the highland or upland which had no water. The well drill and windmill made the next step in the evolution of the ranch when they brought the water to the upland and enabled the ranchman to cut up his ranch into small holdings. Access to the water front was no longer necessary. Not until this stage was reached was it possible in any sense for the agricultural classes to invade the Great Plains. They had to enclose small areas of land, and they had to have water, and, obviously, with streams fifty to a hundred miles apart—and dry in places for a large part of the year—they could not all own a water front. That is to say, in effect, that it was barbed wire and windmills that made the homestead law in any sense effectual in the arid region.

Farming in the Great Plains is as different from what it is in the Eastern Woodland as barbed wire is from a rail fence. The farm unit in the Eastern Woodland was small for several reasons. It was so heavily timbered that one man, even with numerous sons, could not clear a large farm in a lifetime. Before the invention of barbed wire, fencing was too laborious and expensive. The land was so rough, stumpy, and broken that machinery could not be successfully used. The foul vegetation set rigid limits to the size of the field; to let the weeds and grass "get ahead of the crop" was to lose the crop. Most important of all, however, was the fact that a small field was sufficient. The crop was sure to make, for the rains always came.

The farms expanded in size as they emerged from the Eastern Woodland onto the open plain. In the absence of timber there was no interval of clearing and log-rolling before plowing. There were no stumps or roots to retard the plow. Barbed wire solved the problem of fencing. The level surface and firm soil invited the invention and use of labor-saving machinery. The absence of foul vegetation and grasses speeded up the hoeing or dispensed with it. All these things made possible and encouraged the cultivation of large areas even in the Prairie Plains. In the arid portion men were compelled to cultivate more land than they had in the East. The crops were subject to drought, hail, hot winds, and grasshoppers. The farmer there became a gambler, staking a large and easily cultivated acreage against a probable failure. There were fat years and lean years.

Along with the enlargement of the farm unit went the increasing need for more manpower and horsepower, particularly in the harvest season. In response to this need came the big farm machinery. The reaper was the first machine to become important in western agriculture. Cyrus Hall McCormick invented his reaper in Virginia in 1831, the year after Colt invented the six-shooter, and there gave it a practical test. The way the machine moved west is told as follows:

> The ten years following the introduction of the first reaper were strenuous times for Mr. McCormick. He preached the gospel of the reaper without success until 1841 when he sold two for $100, the next year seven. In 1843 twenty-nine machines were made and sold, and fifty in 1844. About this time an order for eight had come from Cincinnati. It opened Mr. McCormick's eyes. He saw that the time had come to leave the backwoods farm, a hundred miles from the railway, so he set out on horseback for the western prairies.

For two years McCormick wandered around through Illinois, Wisconsin, Missouri, Ohio, and New York and sold in that time two hundred and forty reapers. "He then decided it was time to build his own factory at Chicago." This he did in 1847. By 1851 he was making a thousand reapers a year, and by 1859 he had made and sold in the United States alone fifty thousand machines.

Though the reaper may be rightfully considered the first improved farm machine used in the United States, it was followed soon by many other offerings of the industrial revolution, such as the riding or sulky plow, the disk plow, the multiple plow, the one- and two-row cultivators, and various other types of big farm machinery. Regardless of where these machines were invented, they have found their greatest usefulness in the Great Plains.

Big farm machinery has made dry farming possible and has made it profitable by enabling the farmer to work rapidly and to cultivate a large acreage. The tools used on the dry farm are not essentially different in construction from those on the prairie farm. Both are adapted to large-scale activities.

We have here only touched upon the most obvious aspects of a profound subject, the ramifications of which extend to all phases of western life, namely, the sweeping changes in the ways of life imposed upon the American people who crossed the ninety-eighth meridian.

Condensed from *The Trans-Mississippi West*, University of Colorado, 1930

The reports describing the Plains as an uninhabitable desert provided Congress with a solution to the problem of what to do with the Indians: remove them to the Plains, thus opening the land east of the Mississippi to white settlement and at the same time provide a haven for the Red Man. But by 1850 the Indian country was not outside the United States; it was right in the middle, a barrier that had to be removed.

On December 5, 1853, Senator Dodge of Iowa gave notice that he would "introduce a bill to organize a territorial government for the Territory of Nebraska." Dodge introduced his bill December 14. Senator Stephen Douglas' Committee on Territories reported the bill January 4, as a substitute, vastly altered. Instead of one territory, two were created: Kansas and Nebraska. The bill also provided that "all questions pertaining to slavery in the new Territories . . . are to be left to the decision of the people residing therein. . . ."

Without ignoring the profound ramifications of the sectional strife stirred up by the Kansas-Nebraska Act, the important consideration for the history of Nebraska—and for that of the nation—is that it set in motion the machinery that would open to settlement all that remained of the Louisiana territory acquired only a half century before.

—Condensed from Olson's *History of Nebraska*

It Took All Kinds

1. Pioneer Preacher

REV. GEORGE W. BARNES

(The author arrived in Florence—now a part of Omaha—in 1856. He had been born in New York State thirty-one years before.)

EVERYTHING was new in Nebraska. It had only been open for about two years. The first matter in hand was to get a place to put my family on their arrival. None could be rented, for the supply was far short of applicants, every stage bringing new additions to our

population. The exceeding high price of lumber, pine selling for
$95.00 per thousand and higher, and all building materials being
so very costly, and I having but little means, if any house was to be
had, it must be by my own hands. Securing a good location, I set
about building a dwelling.

Sunrise and sunset found me at the house, for my make was to do
with my might all I undertook. All the help I had was a carpenter to
"lay out" the sills, except in raising. The size was 15x25; front, two
stories, back part, lean-to, giving two rooms downstairs and one up.
In the latter part of October the house was so nearly ready my family
came out in company with Brother Alling. So tedious was the trip
for Mrs. Barnes, riding day and night in an overcrowded coach,
that she said, "I thought I should never get through alive."

Everything was in progress, nothing finished. Our house was some
like the Dutchman's who said his "was shingled mit straw." Ours
was plastered mit muslin. The whole inside was covered with heavy
unbleached muslin, drawn tight, tacked well to all the studding
and sized with flour paste. Then it was ready for papering, and made
a really comfortable house, looking well as plastered.

Our floor, however, was a fitting subject of history, and the source
of much merriment. In the morning of the day we were to occupy,
I sent a team to mill to bring boards for floor. They were sawed after
he came, from cottonwood logs nearly two feet through. This timber
has more water and will shrink more—they say end-wise also—and
twist more than any other I ever saw. They said there was a board
on a fence so warped that when a pig tried to get through into the
corn field, it came out on the same side it started in on. About three
o'clock the boards were laid loosely on the timbers, for it would have
have been folly to nail them. As the floor began to dry it shrank
and warped wonderously. Each board would cup so as to form about
the fourth of a circle. Hence walking the floor was amusement, and
danger. When you stepped on the edge, the board sprung up on
the other side like Jack-in-the-box. If someone else lighter happened
to be opposite, they were likely to be hoisted. Then there was a
constant clatter while passing around the rooms. When a certain
stage was reached, they were turned, to repeat the same half-moon-
on-its-back, the other way. After a long time when they seemed dry
and were nailed down, they shrank still, and left great seams between
that were filled with pieces fitted in.

As our things had only arrived in part, we borrowed a few, and
began housekeeping anew after months of separation, a happy family.

No place ever appeared better to the inmates than did our home in its roughness. Our table was the two sawhorses used in building with two boards atop, and some muslin for tablecloth; our seats were the trunks we brought. Kind friends had helped us in part to our first meal. The gratitude of our hearts was genuine as we invoked our Father's blessing upon that meal and at night dedicated the house to Him who loved us, and bought us with His blood. The fare was simple, perforce, for butter was seventy-five cents per pound, and every delicacy alike expensive.

The only house of worship was one put up for the M. E. church, a plain, neat, spineless building. We began our preaching in the dwelling of one of the brethren, also organizing ourselves into a church and electing one deacon, Brother S. P. Alling. He gave us the best sort of material for a deacon. He was kind, consistent, faithful, loving the cause and the Saviour with a full heart, delighting to use his means for the good of others, and to honor Christ. There were but few Christians among that varied population, and religion met only a left-handed favor. The great mass seemed in a terrible hurry to build their houses and push their various enterprises to success and wealth. A very large proportion seemed to have come to make a speedy fortune, then return east and enjoy the same. You could hear the whiz of the saw and the click of the hammer at all hours of day and night for the whole week. The Lord's day found only a very few who honored its claims.

Preaching was a real delight. The little room where we met in the fall was filled to the full, bed, boxes, and chairs out into the hall, so close as to leave me bare standing room. One time when preaching, standing behind one seated, in earnest gesticulation I brought my fist down thump on his head, to the general amusement. I wrote east to friends that "I possessed great advantage over most preachers for I can apply the gospel personally."

A Brother Blackley came among us who was of large help to me at this time. He was a Presbyterian preacher and physician, a man of good mind, well stored, and a real Christian. An argument had a peculiar attraction; he would leave a good meal for a regular set-to at it. Always kindly, no irritation. We had regular meetings every morning either at his or our house where, after a season of prayer, sermons or other topics of religious interest were talked over in a critical and helpful way.

Our preaching services were held the first winter in a vacant house, he occupying one part of the day, I the other. There were about as many Presbyterians as Baptists in town. The singing was led chiefly by Mrs. B. and Sister Alling, and it was good spiritual singing that could be enjoyed. A photograph of that room would sell well, it seems to me, and of all cold places, that was the one. It stood on the side hill, on upright sticks, one side near the ground, the other, two feet above, giving full sweep for the wind under. Not finished inside, the clapboarding warped so as to insure full ventilation; the floor laid of green elm had shrunk, leaving seams half an inch wide; this covered with Kentucky jean, which was laughed at by the winds as they lifted it in rolling waves from the floor. Rough boards fastened to the sides, some rude benches, and a few chairs furnished the seating conveniences, a box end-wise gave a place for the preacher, and a sheet-iron stove the heating apparatus. The whole service in cold weather was passed by the congregation in more or less of suffering. Yet we had fair attendance, with the best attention. There was earnest effort to give the people something warm inside, if the externals were so cheerless.

That winter was severely cold and stormy. As a family we had a narrow escape from great suffering. The cold began early in December. Our wood pile was exhausted, and a man with a team was secured to get a load from the woods a few miles away. As we started it began to snow some, kept increasing all day, so that when we returned about 4:00 P. M. the wind was high from the north, snow filling the air, and rapidly growing worse. For three days it was a regular blizzard, piercing cold, while about two feet of snow fell. Had we not obtained the wood that day, by no possibility could it have been the next, and our neighbors had none to spare. The Lord cared for us in a tender way, doing far better than we deserved.

We were more fortunate than some in regard to winter supplies. The amount raised was by no means equal to the population. I heard of a man below us who had some potatoes to sell, went at once, and bought enough at $1.25 per bushel. Flour could readily be had as a large stock was obtained by river in the fall. Butter kept so dear it was dispensed with and molasses largely used. Mrs. B. got so tired of this, that for a long time she could hardly bear to see it. All missed, especially the children, the supply of fruits, such as apples, etc. Dried fruits were all that could be had as a rule. At Omaha a few were found, and as mother peeled for use, the children would stand about to take the peels fast as they left the apple.

In the spring Brother Alling put up a two-story building for a storeroom and finished the upper part, seating it comfortably for meetings.

This was a real advance and free of cost to us all. The matter of a good brick meeting house was talked of, Deacon A. offering to stand back of the enterprise financially.

Coming in one day from calling, there was waiting me a thick-set, shortish, heavy Pennsylvania Dutchman from Cuming City, 20 miles above. In somewhat broken terms he wanted to know if I could come up there and preach, saying, "I talk of buying a claim there but will not unless someone can be had to give us Baptist preaching." He had taken that long drive to find a Baptist preacher before deciding to locate. I agreed to visit the place, several Baptists were found, and preaching was begun once every two weeks.

Subsequently we organized a church of fourteen members. I used to go up and back by stage. Our meeting place was a log schoolhouse. There was a very good class of people about Cuming City—the name was poetry, for not a half-dozen houses could be seen. It was very thinly settled as yet; long distances between claims.* The people generally came to meeting, and I enjoyed preaching to them. The first baptizing was done for me by Brother Taggert as I had not yet been ordained.

At this time, a most severe financial depression came upon the country, paralyzing business over the whole land. It was felt perhaps more severely in the new countries, as there were less moneyed facilities. The effect was sorely felt by my deacon at Florence. His project for a large mill was stopped. Also aid to our church building must be given up, so the matter fell through, for times kept growing worse. The place stopped growing, and some began to remove. At one time there were about 1,500 people in the place. The church made but little growth.

The vicious classes were not lacking among us; such are apt to float out on the current of emigration to new countries. Rum was plenty. That always augments and intensifies crime. One miserable drunken wretch was stabbed to death by another equally detestable scoundrel for intimacy with his wife. One day there was heard a loud hallowing, and great clatter of horses' feet, toward Omaha. Looking that way, quite a number of horsemen were seen riding at the highest speed and yelling like Indians. Several streets below, they came into

* Cuming City was located north of the present site of Blair. By 1857 it had become a place of bright promise, with 53 dwellings, three stores, two churches, a school, three hotels, and a number of saloons. Beginning in 1869, however, when Blair was established as a point of crossing for the railroad, Cuming City began to lose ground and eventually disappeared altogether. Most of the buildings were removed to Blair.

the village up one, and over another, when the report of pistols was heard, and the cavalcade stopped. It was a company from Omaha after a horse thief, whom they brought to a stand near the bank. He had stolen the horse in Iowa, and was delivered to those authorities. Horse-stealing was perhaps the most common crime. At another time two men were found hanging to a tree just beyond our village. They were in jail at Omaha for horse-stealing. A company of men went to jail, took them out, and hung them there. It was a frightful sight, and yet seemed but justice.

The son of one of our honored ministers in central New York was living in our place. He had a comfortable house, very nicely furnished, his wife an intelligent, sprightly woman. Indeed, they put on airs. As hard times came on, he tried to sell in vain. One night when both were absent at a ball in the town, his house was burned, under such circumstances that it was generally believed he fired it to obtain the insurance. The agent, however, would not pay, and he dared not sue for it, but left for Denver.

A peculiar trial to many was our high winds. Then, as now, they were severe and often did damage. Mrs. B. was sorely annoyed by them. Our house would rock very perceptibly, so much that she could not sleep. I could sleep anywhere. A great many times she awakened me to carry the bedding downstairs, where we would sleep on the floor the rest of the night.

My labors were regular between Florence and Cuming City. Our meetings at Cuming City were of good interest. In the spring of '58 the church there called me to ordination, asking that the Association meeting at Nebraska City attend to the services. This was the first ordination of a Baptist minister in the territory, and I am inclined to think the first of any.

Three years after the Reverend George W. Barnes was or-
dained, there occurred a gun fight at Rock Creek Station,
120 miles southwest of Florence, which—in the hands of
the myth-makers—established a man of considerable ill
will as the very model of a hero of the Old West.

The story told here, based on court records, state-
ments of reputable citizens, and the account of an eyewit-
ness, places James Butler Hickok in his proper niche—not
as a Homeric figure of the wild frontier where a good
horse was held in more esteem than human life, but as
one who lived to the ripe old age of thirty-nine only
because he knew no other code than "kill or be killed" and
never failed to take advantage of the main chance.

2. The Myth of Wild Bill Hickok

CARL UHLARIK

Jim, haven't we been friends all the time?"
"Yes."
"Are we friends now?"
"Yes."
"Will you hand me a drink of water?"
Jim Hickok turned to the bucket in the cabin and handed rancher
David McCanles a dipper of water.

McCanles drank and, as he handed back the dipper, saw something
inside the cabin which caused him to sidestep to another door. "Now,
Jim," he called, "if you have anything against me, come out and
fight fair." The answer came in a shot from a Hawkins rifle whose
roar was magnified by the intensity of the silence it shattered.

Hickok reappeared in the doorway with a Colt Navy revolver
and began firing at McCanles's nephew and a hired hand who were
running up from the barn following the shot. McCanles's twelve-
year-old son stood by his fallen father, horror and fright anchoring
him to the ground.

This, in a nutshell, is the documented account of what for ninety-
five years has been regarded as the greatest single-handed fight in
American history. It was the seed from which sprang the legend
of Wild Bill Hickok, the matchless Prince of Pistoleers, invincible
scout, plainsman, peace officer, and gambler who, by his own ad-

mission, had killed more than a hundred men before his own
brains were blown out by cross-eyed Jack McCall in a Deadwood
saloon.

James Butler Hickok was born near Homer, now Troy Grove,
Illinois, in 1837. He spent his formative years working on a farm
and left home at the age of eighteen when, by the standards of
the day, he was considerably more than a man. He turned up
first in St. Louis; two years later he was knocking about Johnson
County, Kansas; in 1858 he became a driver for the Overland Stage
Company. It was during Hickok's brief sojourn in Johnson County
that he reportedly killed his first man. However, there is not much
which can be authenticated about this period of his life: he was
merely one of thousands of obscure plainsmen until he captured the
country's imagination in a *Harper's Magazine* article of February,
1867. Its author, Col. George Ward Nichols, wrote that he'd had the
story of the McCanles Affair from Wild Bill himself. Since Hickok
never denied it, it brands him, *ipso facto,* a monumental liar.

David Colbert McCanles, on whose spilled blood the legend
was nurtured, was born November 30, 1828, near Stateville, North
Carolina. He attended an Episcopal academy for six years—a deal
of schooling in those days. At the age of twenty-three, he was
elected sheriff of Watauga County and was re-elected three times.
Fired by tales of gold in the Pikes Peak fields, he started west in
1859, but was discouraged by "busted" gold-seekers, homeward
bound. At Rock Creek Station, Nebraska Territory, six miles east
of the present city of Fairbury, McCanles gave up the quest and
fastened his hopes on the wild, unbroken prairie. He bought the
way station on the west bank of the creek and sent to Leavenworth,
Kansas, for a plow. With it he broke the first sod in what is now one
of the richest agricultural counties in the Middle West.

McCanles described the "land of promise" so glowingly in letters
that his brother Leroy came west with his own family and the wife
and five children David had left behind. David built a cabin on
the east bank of the creek for Leroy, and the families settled down to
harvest the fruit of the prairie paradise. With all his good qualities,
however, David McCanles was as rough and tough as the frontier
he sought to tame—hot-tempered, boisterous, bull-headed, and
afraid of no man.

By 1860 Leroy had moved away, and David contracted to sell
the East Rock Creek Ranch to Russell, Majors, and Waddell, propri-

etors of the Central Overland California and Pikes Peak Express Company, better known as the Overland Stage. The agreement called for one-third down and the balance in equal monthly payments. Overland sent out Horace Wellman and his wife as stationkeepers, and J. W. (Doc) Brink as stock-tender. Arriving soon after as assistant stock-tender—a glorified appellation for stable hand— was Overland's erstwhile driver, Jim Hickok.

The twenty-three-year-old Hickok had not evolved into the frontier dandy described by latter-day romanticists as "the finest example of frontiersman . . . [with] a fine, handsome face, a light mustache, thin, pointed nose, bluish-grey eyes with calm look, . . . a magnificent forehead, hair parted from the center and hanging down behind his ears in brown, wavy, silken curls." To those who knew him at Rock Creek, he was a horse-faced fellow, over six feet tall, moody, and hard to make friends with. He had not yet cultivated the mustache swooping gracefully around his mouth like the split tail of a swallow, offsetting thin lips which protruded so noticeably that the ranchers and farmers dubbed him "Duck Bill."

It is as "Duck Bill" Hickok that he is designated in the preliminary information filed against him in connection with the Rock Creek killings. Probably it will never be known why he permitted the derisive nickname to be formalized to "William" in other court records, but in the light of his subsequent notoriety it is not hard to understand how "Wild" came to replace "Duck."

There is no evidence to indicate that the quarrel which led to the Rock Creek slayings was any of Hickok's affair; on the other hand, there is every indication that the feud was between McCanles and Wellman over money due for the sale of the station. And there is ample reason to believe that the rifle ball which pierced McCanles's heart was fired not by Hickok but by Wellman concealed behind a calico curtain.

When McCanles came to collect the first deferred payment from Overland, Wellman told him the money had not yet arrived. It was the same story when the final payment fell due. McCanles then demanded payment in full or possession of the property. Wellman said he felt sure the money was waiting at Brownville, and he'd pick it up on a trip for supplies. McCanles's young son Monroe accompanied Wellman on the 200-mile round trip, which took ten days, and from which they returned about 4:00 P. M., July 12, 1861.

Monroe found his father, his cousin James Woods, and a hired hand named James Gordon at the near-by ranch of Jack Nye. When he learned that Wellman had brought no money, McCanles grabbed his son by the hand, and, with Woods and Gordon following, strode purposively toward Rock Creek Station. This was the entire "blood-thirsty M'Kandlas gang," and the only firearm in the group was Monroe's—a small-bore, double-barrelled shotgun he had taken on the trip to Brownville for bagging small game.

The fight version credited to Hickok in *Harper's* was prefaced by his statement that he had led a detachment of Union cavalry to Rock Creek and that an old friend, "Mrs. Waltman," ran out of the cabin to warn him that the "M'Kandlas gang" was out for his blood.

You see, this M'Kandlas was the captain of a gang of desperadoes, horse thieves, murderers, regular cut throats, who were the terror of everybody on the border. . . . He poked his head inside the doorway but jumped back when he saw me with the rifle in my hand. "Come in here, you cowardly dog!" I shouted. . . . M'Kandlas was no coward. . . . He jumped inside the room with gun leveled to shoot; but was not quick enough. My rifle ball went through his heart. He fell back outside the house where he was found afterward holding tight to his rifle. . . . I put down the rifle and took the revolver. . . . there was a few seconds of that awful stillness, and then the ruffians came rushing in at both doors. . . . I never aimed more deliberate in my life. One, two, three, four; and four men fell dead. That didn't stop the rest. Two of them fired their bird guns at me. And then I felt a sting all over me. . . . One I knocked down with my fist. . . . the second I shot dead. The other three clutched me and crowded me onto the bed. . . . I broke with my hand one man's arm. . . . Before I could get to my feet I was struck across the breast with the stock of a rifle, and I felt the blood rushing out of my nose and mouth. Then I got ugly and I remember that I got hold of a knife, and then it was all cloudy like, and I was wild, and I struck savage blows, following the devils up from one side to the other of the room and into the corners, striking and slashing until I knew that every one was dead. . . . there were eleven buckshot in me. . . . I was cut in thirteen places. . . .

Compare the eyewitness account of Monroe McCanles, substanti-ated in every important detail by court records and the statements of reputable persons who were contemporary with the principals. It is the account he was denied permission to relate at the trial, but which, years later, he wrote for George W. Hansen, pioneer banker of Fairbury.

Father and I stopped at the house and Woods and Gordon went on down to the barn. Father went to the kitchen and asked for Wellman. Mrs. Wellman came to the door and father asked if Wellman was in the house and she said he was. Father said "tell him to come out" and she said "what do you want with him?" Father said "I want to settle with him." She said "he'll not come out." Father said "send him out or I'll come in and drag him out." Now, when father made the threat . . . Jim (or Bill) Hickok stepped to the door and stood by Mrs. Wellman. Father looked at him in the face and said "Jim, haven't we been friends all the time?" [Followed the request for water and the rifle shot.] Father raised himself up to almost a sitting position and took one last look at me, then fell back dead. Woods and Gordon had heard the shot and came running up unarmed . . . and just then Jim reappeared at the door with a Colt's Navy revolver. He fired two shots at Woods, and Woods ran around the house to the north. Gordon broke and ran. Jim ran out of the door and fired two shots at him and wounded him. Just as Jim ran out of the door, Wellman came out with a hoe and ran after Woods, and hit him on the head with the hoe and finished him. Then Wellman came running around the house where I was standing and struck at me with the hoe and yelled "let's kill them all." I dodged and ran. I outran him to a ravine south of the house and stopped there. Mrs. Wellman stood in the door clapping her hands and yelling "kill him, kill him, kill him!" Father was shot from behind a calico curtain that divided the cabin in two . . . and was shot with a rifle that belonged to himself. He had loaned the gun to the station keeper for their protection in case of trouble with the many hard characters that were traveling the trail. . . . After Gordon had made his getaway, being wounded, the station outfit put the dog on his trail and the dog trailed him down the creek and brought him to bay about 80 rods down the creek. When the bunch caught up, the dog was fighting Gordon, and Gordon was warding him off with a stick. Gordon was finished with a load of buckshot from Dock Brink's gun. . . . When I made my escape, I ran to the ranch and broke the news to my mother. . . .

Consider the killing of McCanles: At the time he saw something suspicious in the cabin, he was reaffirming friendship with Hickok and was in the act of handing back—and Hickok was in the act of receiving—the water dipper. What, then, caused him to move to another door and ask Hickok to come out and fight fair? Was it some act by Wellman, the man he threatened to "settle with"? Fearing a thrashing, it's probable that Wellman dashed behind the calico curtain, or, already hiding there, reached out for the rifle.

As for Gordon and Woods, Monroe's statement that they were finished off later is supported by statements of neighboring ranchers who found the bodies. Among those who reached the bloody scene the following morning were the brothers Helvey: Frank, Thomas, and Jasper. They found the body of McCanles sprawled like a bag out of which the grain had spilled. Woods was around the corner of the cabin, his head crushed with a heavy instrument. Gordon lay south of the station, filled with buckshot. The Helvey brothers agreed that neither Hickok, Brink, nor the Wellmans showed a single bruise or wound which would indicate that they had been attacked and had killed in self-defense.

Leroy McCanles, farming in Johnson County, was informed of the tragedy and went to Beatrice in Gage County to swear out a complaint stating "that the crime of murder has been committed in the County of Jones and that Duck Bill, Dock and Wellman (their other names unknown) committed the same." Two days later, Gage County Sheriff E. B. Hendee made the arrests and claimed $5.50 as sheriff's fees. The only direct testimony produced or permitted at the trial was that of the accused men and Mrs. Wellman, wife of one of the defendants and an alleged accomplice to the crime. Upon a plea of self-defense, the three men were found not guilty.

The conclusion is evident that Hickok had no motive for killing McCanles. If, indeed, it was Wild Bill who pulled the trigger of the Hawkins rifle, then he was guilty of the basest treachery. As for Woods and Gordon, it is not inconceivable that in the frenzy of first blood-letting, Hickok grabbed his revolver and blazed away at them under the impression that they were running up to attack him and the Wellmans.

Now, to lay the ghosts of some of the other absurdities which still rise phoenix-like at any mention of the McCanles Affair and Wild Bill:

That McCanles was an outlaw leader of a gang of horse thieves.

David Colbert McCanles was the richest landowner in the county. He established the first school and made the first attempt at legal organization of the county.

That Hickok, notorious as a dead shot as early as 1857, could drive a cork into a bottle without breaking the neck by firing a pistol from the hip.

His shooting at Rock Creek was so wild that he missed Woods and merely winged Gordon.

That Hickok never backed down from a fight.

John Wesley Hardin, a Texas contribution to the art of gun-slinging, wrote in his reminiscences that he pulled the "road agent's spin" when Hickok, the Abilene marshal, demanded at gun point that Hardin surrender his pistols. Hickok thereupon said he had no intention of arresting Hardin and invited him to have a drink.

That Hickok was always on the side of law and order.

In 1869, while marshal of Hayes City, Wild Bill killed several Fort Hayes soldiers in a brawl, and General Phil Sheridan ordered him to be brought in dead or alive. Wild Bill hightailed it immediately after the killings and hid out. In Cheyenne, Wyoming, officials decided to rid the town of a "few of the worst criminals." They tacked notices on telegraph poles, listing a dozen names, headed by Wild Bill, giving them twenty-four hours to get out of town. Wild Bill cut up the notice with his Bowie knife and remained until he got ready to leave.

Some months later he went to Custer City and then to Deadwood and the rendezvous with death, a victim of his own reputation. The end came at 4:10 P.M., August 2, 1876, in a saloon on lower Main Street while Hickok was playing poker. Records of the coroner's jury stated that Jack McCall walked into the saloon, and when he was three feet back of his victim, raised his revolver, exclaiming: "Damn you, take that!" and fired. The cards which spilled from Hickok's hand as he crumpled to the floor were pairs of aces and eights—a spread which since that day has been known as the "Dead Man's Hand."

At his trial, McCall said he killed Hickok because Wild Bill had killed his brother in Kansas, while Hickok's friends claimed McCall was the hireling of jealous gunmen. After deliberating an hour and a half, the jury brought in a verdict of not guilty. Subsequently, McCall was arrested by federal authorities and taken to Yankton, South Dakota, where he was tried and convicted. He was hanged March 1, 1877.

In 1859, William H. Russell, of the freighting firm of Russell, Majors, and Waddell, conceived the then daring idea of a stage-coach express to the Pikes Peak region. Though his partners refused to join what they considered a wild scheme, Russell, with the aid of John S. Jones, went ahead, establishing the Leavenworth and Pikes Peak Express along the Republican-Solomon route. The "L. & P. P." was in financial difficulty from the beginning, and Russell, Majors, and Waddell bailed the enterprise out, transferring it to the Platte Valley route so that they could combine it with their Salt Lake mail service.

Meanwhile, Senator William M. Gwin of California had persuaded Russell to launch a pony express between St. Joseph and California. Russell's partners finally were induced to agree, and Gwin, in turn, promised to obtain a government mail contract for the Pony Express. On April 3, 1860, to the accompaniment of celebrations at both ends of the line, the first riders set out from Sacramento and St. Joseph. Riders, station-keepers, and ponies functioned with brilliant precision to bring the first mail through both ways in the scheduled ten days.

—Condensed from Olson's *History of Nebraska*

Stage-Coaching on the Great Overland

MARK TWAIN

FROM St. Joseph, Missouri, to Sacramento, California, by stage-coach, was nearly nineteen hundred miles, and the trip was often made in fifteen days (the cars do it in four and a half, now), but the time specified in the mail contracts, and required by the schedule, was eighteen or nineteen days, if I remember rightly. This was to make fair allowance for winter storms and snows, and other unavoidable causes of detention. The stage company had everything under strict discipline and good system. Over each two hundred and fifty miles of road they placed an agent or superintendent and invested him

34

with great authority. His beat or jurisdiction of two hundred and fifty miles was called a "division." He purchased horses, mules, harness, and food for men and beasts, and distributed these things among his stage stations, from time to time, according to his judgment of what each station needed. He erected station buildings and dug wells. He attended to the paying of the station-keepers, hostlers, drivers, and blacksmiths, and discharged them whenever he chose. He was a very, very great man in his "division"—a kind of Grand Mogul, a Sultan of the Indies, in whose presence common men were modest of speech and manner, and in the glare of whose greatness even the dazzling stage-driver dwindled to a penny dip. There were about eight of these kings, all told, on the Overland route.

Next in rank and importance to the division-agent came the "conductor." His beat was the same length as the agent's—two hundred and fifty miles. He sat with the driver, and (when necessary) rode that fearful distance, night and day, without other rest or sleep than what he could get perched thus on top of the flying vehicle. Think of it! He had absolute charge of the mails, express matter, passengers, and stage-coach, until he delivered them to the next conductor, and got his receipt for them. Consequently he had to be a man of intelligence, decision, and considerable executive ability. He was usually a quiet, pleasant man who attended closely to his duties, and was a good deal of a gentleman. It was not absolutely necessary that the division-agent should be a gentleman, and occasionally he wasn't. But he was always a general in administrative ability, and a bull-dog in courage and determination—otherwise the chieftainship over the lawless underlings of the Overland service would never in any instance have been to him anything but an equivalent for a month of insolence and distress and a bullet and a coffin at the end of it. There were about sixteen or eighteen conductors on the Overland, for there was a daily stage each way, and a conductor on every stage.

Next in *real* and official rank and importance *after* the conductor, came my delight, the driver—next in real but not in *apparent* importance—for in the eyes of the common herd the driver was to the conductor as an admiral is to the captain of the flag-ship. The driver's beat was pretty long, and his sleeping-time at the stations pretty short, sometimes; and so, but for the grandeur of his position his would have been a sorry life, as well as a hard and wearing one. We took a new driver every day or every night (for they drove backward and forward over the same piece of road all the time), and therefore we never got as well acquainted with them as we did with the conductors; and besides, they would have been above being familiar with such rubbish as passengers, anyhow, as a general thing. Still, we were always eager to get a sight of each and every new driver as soon as the watch changed, for each and every day we were either anxious to get rid of an unpleasant one, or loath to part with a driver we had learned to like and had come to be sociable and friendly with. And so the first question we asked the conductor whenever we got to where we were to exchange drivers, was always, "Which is him?" The grammar was faulty, maybe, but we could not know, then, that it would go into a book some day. As long as everything went smoothly, the Overland driver was well enough situated, but if a fellow driver got sick suddenly it made trouble, for the coach *must* go on, and so the potentate who was about to climb down and take a luxurious rest after his long night's siege in the midst of wind and rain and darkness, had to stay where he was and do the sick man's work. Once in the Rocky Mountains, when I found a driver sound asleep on the box, and the mules going at the usual break-neck pace, the conductor said never mind him, there was no danger, and he was doing double duty—had driven seventy-five miles on one coach, and was now going back over it on this without rest or sleep. A hundred and fifty miles of holding back of six vindictive mules and keeping them from climbing trees!

The station-keepers, hostlers, etc., were low, rough characters; and from western Nebraska to Nevada a considerable sprinkling of them might be fairly set down as outlaws—fugitives from justice, criminals whose best security was a section of country which was without law and without even the pretense of it. When the "division-agent" issued an order to one of these parties he did it with a full understanding that he might have to enforce it with a navy six-shooter, and so he always went "fixed" to make things go along smoothly. Now and then a division-agent was really obliged to shoot a hostler through the head to teach him some simple matter that he could have taught him with a club if his circumstances and surroundings had been different. But they were snappy, able men, those division-agents, and when they tried to teach a subordinate anything, that subordinate generally "got it through his head."

At noon on the fifth day out, we arrived at the "Crossing of the South Platte," *alias* "Julesburg," *alias* "Overland City," four hundred and seventy miles from St. Joseph—the strangest, quaintest, funniest frontier town that our untraveled eyes had ever stared at and been astonished with. For an hour we took as much interest in Overland City as if we had never seen a town before. The reason we had an hour to spare was because we had to change our stage (for a less sumptuous affair, called a "mud-wagon") and transfer our freight of mails.

Presently we got under way again. We came to the shallow, yellow, muddy South Platte, with its low banks and its scattering flat sandbars and pigmy islands—a melancholy stream straggling through the center of the enormous flat plain, and only saved from being impossible to find with the naked eye by its sentinel rank of scattering trees standing on either bank. The Platte was "up," they said—which made me wish I could see it when it was down, if it could look any sicker and sorrier. They said it was a dangerous stream to cross, now, because its quicksands were liable to swallow up horses, coach, and passengers if an attempt was made to ford it. But the mails had to go, and we made the attempt. Once or twice in midstream the wheels sunk into the yielding sands so threateningly that we half believed we had dreaded and avoided the sea all our lives to be shipwrecked in a "mud-wagon" in the middle of a desert at last. But we dragged through and sped away toward the setting sun.

In a little while all interest was taken up in stretching our necks and watching for the "pony-rider"—the fleet messenger who sped across the continent from St. Joe to Sacramento, carrying letters nineteen hundred miles in eight days! Think of that for perishable horse and human flesh and blood to do! The pony-rider was usually a little bit of a man, brimful of spirit and endurance. No matter what time of the day or night his watch came on, and no matter whether it was winter or summer, raining, snowing, hailing, or sleeting, or whether his "beat" was a level straight road or a crazy trail over mountain crags and precipices, or whether it led through peaceful regions or regions that swarmed with hostile Indians, he must be always ready to leap into the saddle and be off like the wind! There was no idling-time for a pony-rider on duty. He rode fifty miles without stopping, by daylight, moonlight, starlight, or through the blackness of darkness—just as it happened. He rode a splendid horse that was born for a racer and fed and lodged like a gentleman; kept him at his utmost speed for ten miles, and then, as he came crashing up to the station where stood two men holding fast a fresh, impatient steed, the transfer of rider and mail-bag was made in the twinkling of an eye, and away flew the eager pair and were out of sight before the spectator could get hardly the ghost of a look. Both rider and horse went "flying light." The rider's dress was thin, and fitted close; he wore a "roundabout," and a skull-cap, and tucked his pantaloons into his boot-tops like a race-rider. He carried no arms—he carried nothing that was not absolutely necessary, for even the postage on his literary freight was worth *five dollars a letter*. He got but little frivolous correspondence to carry—his bag had business letters in it, mostly. His horse was stripped of all unnecessary weight, too. He wore light shoes, or none at all. The little flat mail-pockets strapped under the rider's thighs would each hold about the bulk of a child's primer. They held many and many an important business chapter and newspaper letter, but these were written on paper as airy and thin as gold leaf, nearly, and thus bulk and weight were economized. The stage-coach traveled about a hundred to a hundred and twenty-five miles a day (twenty-four hours), the pony-rider about two hundred and fifty. There were about eighty pony-riders in the saddle all the time, night and day, stretching in a long, scattering procession from Missouri to California, forty flying eastward, and forty toward the west, and among them making four hundred gallant horses earn a stirring livelihood and see a deal of scenery.

We had had a consuming desire, from the beginning, to see a pony-rider, but somehow or other all that passed us and all that met us managed to streak by in the night, and so we heard only a whiz and a hail, and the swift phantom of the desert was gone before we could get our heads out of the windows. But now we were expecting one along every moment, and would see him in broad daylight. Presently the driver exclaims:

"HERE HE COMES!"

Every neck is stretched further, and every eye strained wider. Away across the endless dead level of the prairie a black speck appears against the sky, and it is plain that it moves. Well, I should think so! In a second or two it becomes a horse and rider, rising and falling, rising and falling—sweeping toward us nearer and still nearer, and the flutter of the hoofs comes faintly to the ear—another instant a whoop and a hurrah from our upper deck, a wave of the rider's hand, but no reply, and man and horse burst past our excited faces, and go winging away like a belated fragment of a storm!

So sudden is it all, and so like a flash of unreal fancy, that but for the flake of white foam left quivering and perishing on a mail-sack after the vision had flashed by and disappeared, we might have doubted whether we had seen any actual horse and man at all, maybe.

Extracted from *Roughing It*, Harper & Brothers, 1899

*A generation conditioned by more than a century of tech-
nological revolution finds it difficult to appreciate the
rapidity with which the transformation from wagon to
railroad took place on the Plains in the 1860's. But it was
a rapid transformation—and a far-reaching one. . . . It is
the central fact of Nebraska's territorial history.*

—James C. Olson, *History of Nebraska*

Hurrah for the Iron Horse

1. The View from Council Bluffs

GEORGE R. LEIGHTON

ON THE afternoon of August 13, 1859, two months before John Brown
made his raid at Harpers Ferry, an Illinois politician and railroad
lawyer stood on the Iowa bluff above the Missouri River and looked
across to a little village on the opposite bank. Some town lots in
Council Bluffs had been offered him as security for a loan of three
thousand dollars; he had come to inspect the lots himself. Presently
he left the bluff and went back to the tavern where he fell into
conversation with an engineer who explained why Council Bluffs
was the point where the much discussed transcontinental railway
ought to begin. The lawyer listened and, the next day, departed. He
made the loan. Less than a year later, supported by railroad promoters, abolitionists, manufacturers, and Free-Soilers, he was elected
President of the United States.

The lawyer was Abraham Lincoln. The little village that he saw
from the bluff was Omaha, the jumping-off place of the plains, that
Omaha which for more than a generation after meant to various
persons the gateway to the West—the West, that mystic country where
a man could try again, have another chance, become an empire
builder, grow up with the country, speculate in land, lend money
gathered up in Massachusetts and New Hampshire, get a start in the
world, escape the tyrannies of Europe, breathe once more, be a free
man, get a homestead for nothing, worship as he chose, and, incidentally, help to pay the interest on the foreign capital invested in
American enterprises. . . .

Already, in the fifties, railroads had reached the Mississippi from Chicago and were being pushed across Iowa. Among the promoters was Thomas Durant, a prairie physician turned Wall Street promoter, a gentleman fond of the ladies and a dispenser of shawls, diamonds, and yachts. He was interested not only in the Rock Island Railroad but also in another called the Mississippi & Missouri, partly built across Iowa, which Durant thought might be carried through to the Pacific. To further this plan he sent ahead his young engineer, Grenville Dodge, to make surveys and gather information.

The panic of '57 stopped railroad construction and stranded Dodge in Council Bluffs as a general storekeeper and small-time banker. There he dabbled in politics, sent letters to Durant's Wall Street office, and watched the wagon trains setting out for the West. The Omaha townsite speculators had rigged up a ferry to raft emigrants across the river. They didn't have much of a town, but they burned with enthusiasm. The settlement already had one case of delirium tremens and, along with Council Bluffs, talked about the railroad. Dodge had his facts in hand when the Illinois lawyer arrived to look over the town lots.

On the 4th of March, 1861, Lincoln took the oath. The issue was joined; it was up to the Illinois lawyer now. The war was imminent. . . . The Southerners were gone; a Pacific railroad was a certainty.

The Pacific Railroad situation was this: A group of California promoters, headed by Leland Stanford, Charles Crocker, Mark Hopkins, and Collis P. Huntington, had a railway started and wanted to build east. This road eventually became the Central Pacific. Various Eastern groups wanted to build west. Durant was the chief one of these groups; Grenville Dodge of Council Bluffs, famous later not only as a great engineer but as the most accomplished railroad lobbyist in America, was a minor figure in the Durant group. Every one of the railroad promoters knew that if a road was to be built the government would have to put up the money. The great question was: Who was going to get it? . . . But before any division of the spoils could be made, legislation was necessary. . . .

On July 1, 1862, the Pacific Railroad Act, providing for a hundred-million-dollar corporation, the largest capitalization ever known in the United States—was passed. The bill "to aid in the construction of a railroad and telegraph line from the Missouri River to the Pacific Ocean and to secure to the Government the use of the same for Postal, Military and other purposes" presented the promoters with

1. A right of way through the public lands, 200 feet on each side, for the entire distance.
2. The free use of building materials from the public lands.
3. The annulment of Indian titles.
4. Every alternate, odd numbered section of public land, to the amount of five sections a mile on each side.
5. A subsidy of $16,000 a mile on the plains, and from $32,000 to $48,000 a mile through the mountains.

Upon the completion of each forty miles, the subsidy, in the form of United States bonds, would be paid over to the railroad company. The bonds and the interest were to be redeemed at the end of 30 years and were to constitute a first mortgage.

Anybody in the country could have the subsidy. All you had to do was to build a railroad out to a point on the 100th meridian in the middle of the Nebraska plains. Whoever got there first received the subsidy on all that he had already built and the privilege of building the rest of the way. This left an open field for the various Eastern groups. The iron men had seen to it that the use of iron manufactured in America was obligatory.

Now the promoters and the bankers began to mull over the prospects. In the autumn of '62 Durant organized the Union Pacific Railroad Company and the subscription books were opened. The money didn't come in, despite all the fervor and publicity. The truth was that the subsidy wouldn't satisfy. Promoters wanted more. Finally, in the summer of '63, Lincoln sent for Dodge, who by this time was a general in the Union Army. They talked again as they had on that summer day in 1859 on the tavern porch at Council Bluffs. Dodge told him that it would take even better terms to make the promoters act; he advised him in the matter of fixing the eastern terminus of the road—at Council Bluffs, directly across from Omaha! Dodge had been constantly in correspondence with Durant and knew that Durant was determined to commence construction at Omaha. Would Congress loosen up? One could but try. The lobbyists were turned loose in Washington with a half-million-dollar expense account and Durant decided to waste time no further.

On the 3d of December, 1863, Durant's chief of publicity, the eccentric George Francis Train, arrived in Omaha to break ground for the great effort that was to unite East and West, all minds and hearts, into one indissoluble union. The feelings of the people in the village may be imagined. For so long all their speculative hopes, the very existence of their town, had depended on the moves in a

Wall Street poker game and the activities of lobbyists upon the Federal government. But now! "The great Pacific Railroad is commenced," Train told the assembled crowd at Omaha, "and if you knew the man who has hold of the affair as well as I do, no doubt would ever arise as to its speedy completion."

Extracted from *Five Cities*, Harper & Brothers, 1939

2. Promoter *De Luxe*

MARTIN SEVERIN PETERSON

DURING the years when the Pacific Railway was being built, there lived in Omaha a bushy-haired, voluble, dynamic man named George Francis Train. His principal job was that of chief of publicity for the new railroad, but in the comparatively short time that he was in Omaha he employed his talents in a dozen enterprises. He was a promoter in the grand manner, and the West may never look upon his like again.

The early life of this beady-eyed spellbinder could be used to confirm the stories of those Horatio Alger heroes who from humble beginnings soared to fame and fortune. He was born in Boston on March 24, 1829, and at the age of fifteen entered his uncle's shipping office in that city. There, true to the conventions of the Alger stories, he swept the floors early each morning and devoted the rest of the long day to running errands and doing odd jobs for the clerks in the counting rooms. Then things began to pick up. At the age of twenty our hero went to Australia, founded a shipping and commission house of his own in Melbourne, and in no time at all had an annual income of $95,000. But Alger would have disapproved of many of Train's subsequent adventures—particularly, perhaps, of his having been jailed seventy-five times during the course of his life. Although most of these visits to the cooler were the results of Train's firm belief in absolute rather than relative freedom of speech, he leaves something to be desired as an Alger hero.

In Melbourne, Train decorated his office with expensive tapestries, deep Brussels carpets, and marble panels. His office furniture was as sumptuous as that of a London club. In keeping with this scene of splendor, he adorned himself with clothes from Bond Street, which he set off by a gardenia worn in the lapel. Each day at noon, to all of his customers who happened in, he served champagne luncheons. The high point of Train's Australian career came when he was offered the presidency of that country. Since Australia was a crown colony at the time, and since the little revolutionary coup to replace the colonial government failed completely, no doubt the episode was also the signal for Train's departure.

It is somewhat difficult to follow Train's path for the next few years, but we do know that he was married in 1851, that he visited India and wrote a book about that mysterious land, and that he is credited with introducing street railways to Europe. It is certain that he capitalized the building of the first streetcar line between Liverpool and Birkenhead. He built three more in London, where he was jailed for a bland disregard of certain franchise restrictions. When the Civil War broke out, Train lectured up and down England in behalf of the Union cause and did much to prevent England's recognition of the Confederacy.

In 1863 Train returned to America. One of the first things he did on his return was to make the acquaintance of Thomas Durant, who was promoting a transcontinental railroad. Durant, Oakes Ames, and their Wall Street friends were quick to recognize a kindred soul, and Train was welcomed to the table over which there was eventually organized the Credit Mobilier of America and later the Credit Foncier—systems of credit based on personal property and law. According to Train's own account, it was he himself who discovered that the moribund Pennsylvania Fiscal Agency could be purchased by the Credit Mobilier for less than $30,000 and be used to sell stock in the new railway. The Pennsylvania Fiscal Agency enjoyed under its charter broad privileges and limited liability. Under this protection, Durant and his friends could sell the blue sky—not too inaccurate a description of Pacific Railway stock at this time. There may be some question as to whether Train suggested the idea, but it is on record that he did make the purchase of the Pennsylvania Fiscal Agency for slightly more than $27,000. "I think it is worth while," he remarked in his autobiography, "to call attention to the fact that this was the first so-called 'Trust' organized in this country."

But Train's services were not long employed in the legerdemain of early railroad financing. His talents were correctly ascertained to lie in the promotional field, and he was made chief of publicity for the road. Sent to Omaha to break ground for the first mile of railway track west of the Missouri, he arrived on December 3, 1863, and the same day made a speech forecasting the great development of Omaha and the Northwest. The Pacific Railway was

the grandest work of peace that ever attracted the energies of man. . . .
The President showed his good judgment in locating the road where the
Almighty placed the signal station, at the entrance of a garden seven
hundred miles in length and twenty broad. . . . Immigration will soon
pour into these valleys. Ten millions of emigrants will settle in this golden
land in twenty years.

For the next several years Omaha was his headquarters. One of
his first ventures was the purchase, at $175 an acre, of 500 acres of
land adjoining the town. This tract he divided into lots, which he
put on sale at $500 apiece. The subdivision, called Traintown, was
a distinct success and brought a handsome profit on the original
investment. But what might have been a full-time interest for another
man was almost a side issue to Train. He liked more dash in his
business deals.

One of the most characteristic stories of Train's life in Omaha
concerns his building of a "spite" hotel. The time was May of 1867,
and Train was breakfasting with friends in the dining room of the
Herndon House on Ninth and Farnam Streets.

The breakfast [writes Train in *My Life*] was a characteristic Western meal,
with prairie chickens and Nebraska trout. While we were seated, one of
those sudden and always unexpected cyclones on the plains came up, and
the hotel shook like a leaf in the terrible storm. Our table was very near
a window in which were large panes of glass, which I feared could not
withstand the tremendous force of the wind. They were quivering under
the stress of weather, and I called to a strapping Negro waiter at our table
to stand with his broad back against the window.

Allen, the manager of the Herndon, saw in the incident an assault on
the rights of the Negroes. He hurried over to the table and protested
against this act as an outrage. I could not afford to enter into a quarrel
with him at the time, so I merely said: "I am about the size of the Negro;
I will take his place." I then ordered the fellow away from the window,
took his post, and stayed there until the fury of the storm abated. Then I
was ready for Allen.

I walked out in front of the house and, pointing to a large vacant square
facing it, asked who owned it. I was told the owner's name and immediately sent a messenger for him post-haste. He arrived in a short time, and
I asked his price. It was $5,000. I wrote out and handed him a check for
the amount, and took from him, on the spot, a deed for the property.

Then I asked for a contractor who could build a hotel. A man named
Richmond was brought to me. "Can you build a three-story hotel in sixty
days on this plot?" asked I. After some hesitation he said it would be
merely a question of money. "How much?" "One thousand dollars a day."
"Show me that you are responsible for $60,000." He did so, and I took out
an envelope and sketched on the back of it a rough plan of the hotel. "I

am going to the mountains," I said, "and I shall want this hotel, with 120 rooms, complete, when I return in sixty days."

When I got back, the hotel was finished. I immediately rented it to Cozzens, of West Point, New York, for $10,000 a year. . . .

The foregoing episode was just an interlude in the life of Train. His real interest now lay in promoting the building of towns along the right-of-way, where on occasion it was a real problem to keep the bison off a certain area long enough for the surveyor's helpers to pound in the stakes.

The Credit Foncier, the land development corporation allied with the Credit Mobilier, had been given (according to a somewhat bilious contemporary) "nearly every power imaginable save that of reconstructing the late rebel states." Armed with these broad powers, it was no trick at all for Train to stand on the open prairie and talk a town into existence; he was, apparently, one of the most eloquent "boosters" ever to travel the West. Little did it matter to him that the towns he fostered were likely suddenly to pick up and move to a more advantageous location in a year or two. (Quite literally they did this. There is an authenticated story of a man standing at a station watching a long freight train loaded with houses, tents, fences, store fronts, and all the other properties of a town. As he stood there, a brakeman leaned out from a flat car, jerked his thumb toward the loaded train and said, "Sir, this here's Julesburg.") But it was Train's job to start towns; his contract did not call for his acting as anchor man in a tug of war to keep these towns in place. Had he been hired to do so, no doubt he could have achieved this also.

Train's last days in Omaha were not quite so zestful as his first ones. The boom which he had helped set in motion was rapidly losing its momentum, and he felt an urge to move on. "Move" is an inadequate word: in 1870 Train made a trip around the world in eighty days. It has been assumed that from this exploit Jules Verne derived the title and chief character for *Around the World in Eighty Days*. Train himself used to say, "Verne stole my thunder. I'm Phileas Fogg."

Eighteen seventy-two was a presidential election year, and in the political annals for that year the reader will find the name of George Francis Train as an independent candidate for president. Somewhat later in the seventies, Train ran afoul of Anthony Comstock and was jailed on a charge of printing obscenity: His publication *The Train Ligue* had included some passages from the Bible. He wished to plead guilty to the charge, adding to his plea the words "based on extracts from the Bible." However, the court refused to permit a conditional plea, and Train remained in the Tombs for five months. Eventually he was acquitted on the grounds of insanity.

Train was erratic, all right, but his mind was not unsound. His mentality was accurately described by a contemporary, who observed that Train had the brains of twenty men in his skull—"all pulling in different directions." A list of his inventions gives some notion of how restlessly at work his mind always was. He is credited with having invented eraser-tipped pencils, the perforations that separate postage stamps, retractable carriage steps, self-dumping wagons, and that badge of elegance, the gardenia worn in the coat lapel.

In the middle 1880's Train turned his attention to food fads. After a period in which he used himself as a laboratory, he came up with this daily regimen: fruit, peanuts, and chocolate. When he had given the diet a fair trial, he had a fling at fasting. The existing record was for forty days: Train fasted for twenty more. After a study of electricity, Train put forth the theory that human beings are electrically charged, either negatively or positively, and that should a positively charged person shake hands with one negatively charged, some of his precious electricity will flow across to the negative one and be lost. From that discovery dated Train's absolute refusal to shake hands with anyone.

George Francis Train died in New York City on January 19, 1904, at Mills Hotel No. 1, one of a series of hotels established for the indigent genteel on a pay-as-you-can basis. An autopsy revealed that his brain weighed 53.8 ounces, the twenty-seventh heaviest known. It is too bad that there is not some means of weighing the effect of Train's influence on that mystic force, "the spirit of the West." Without a doubt, he contributed to its creation.

Condensed from "George Francis Train, Promoter De Luxe," Prairie Schooner, Summer, 1942

*On August 7, 1864, Cheyennes, Arapahoes, and Brules
launched a concerted attack upon stage coaches, emigrant
trains, freight trains, stations, and ranches all along the
central and western stretches of the Platte Valley. That day
and the next they struck every stage station and ranch between Julesburg and Fort Kearny. Fortunately, few lives
were lost because a warning had been telegraphed from
Plum Creek where they hit first. The attack spread to the
valley of the Little Blue; here there was no telegraph to
warn the settlers and station-keepers, and the loss of life
was considerably greater. The entire Nebraska frontier was
thrown into a state of panic. Almost all the settlers in the
Platte and Little Blue valleys fled eastward, except the
Germans at Grand Island, who fortified the O. K. Store
and decided to entrench themselves.*

—James C. Olson, *History of Nebraska*

The Defense of Grand Island

Translated by H. L. WEINGART

This letter appeared in the Louisiana
Staats Zeitung, September 30–October 1, 1864.

Grand Island, Hall Co.,
Nebr. Terr. Sept. 10, 1864.

DEAR BROTHER:

Since mid-July we have been experiencing turbulent times here, as
the long-feared Indian War broke out in full fury by the first of
August. The red-skins began first in the far north in Minnesota and
Dacotah Territory; then in Kansas, on the Santa Fe Trail. The War
spread up here into Nebraska where finally by the beginning of
August strong bands of hostile Indians invaded the Platte River
region, after they had swept clean the trail from Leavenworth to Fort
Kearney. On the Little Blue they raged fiercely. On the Platte Route
from Omaha to Denver (on which we live) they have also made
attacks in several different places, murdered and scalped people,
burned down ranches and driven off livestock, especially horses.
East of Fort Kearney only two attacks have taken place, one seven,
the other thirty miles west of my farm.

Both attacks occurred on the south side of the Platte River, and it is especially noteworthy that to date no attacks have been made on the north side of the Platte. It is said that the warring Indians do not intend to disturb us, as we do not live on territory claimed by them but on a stretch of land which was purchased from the Pawnee. Most of the Indian tribes of the plains from Texas to the Canadian border have risen to wage war on the whites. No doubt you have read enough about it in the papers already. The Overland Express goes from Omaha only as far as Fort Kearney (40 miles west of us); from there to Colorado Territory all mail communication has ceased, and only large wagon trains heavily guarded by military escort are allowed to pass over this trail. All ranchers have fled from there or have been murdered.

At the outset of the war in this locality, all the Americans on Wood River fled to our settlement, that is, when the attack occurred 30 miles from here. The most horrible reports came in hourly. All the people gathered at my house and at the O. K. Store. My house was full of women, girls, and children, and the men lay around outside. The next morning the excitement lessened somewhat, and it became clear that most of the reports were only rumors, the truth being that only one man had been killed and some livestock stolen. Almost all of the people who, the night before, had left house and home in fear of their necks and heads, now went back home believing the whole affair to be a humbug.

I, however, induced several sensible people to help me put my old fort, which had been built over three years ago, in a better condition for defense. While all around us everyone was happy at his farm work, eight men and I were busy covering my castle,* which was enclosed in a 24-foot square, with three layers of sod, smearing it inside and out and armoring it all around with a thick wall of sod, improving loopholes as well as placing new ones on the corners. We also built an underground stable 12 feet wide and 80 feet long near to and on the south side of the castle in which to shelter our horses. The top and inside of this stable can be fired upon from the castle as well as having portholes of its own above ground and is connected with the castle by a trench. While eight men were taking care of this work, three more were busy making cartridges for the weapons, moulding bullets, and cleaning all the guns thoroughly. We have a nice well in the castle which has plenty of water.

* After building the sod protection for his home, Stolley used the word "Kastell" in referring to his fortified house.

About the time everything was completed, we got the following news: "The Indians have attacked and taken a large wagon train 17 miles below our settlement, killed all the personnel, and driven away all the draught cattle, after which the wagon was burned. Moreover, they have mortally wounded three persons seven miles above us, namely, a man and two grown sons, and left them in the belief that they were really dead." This news made everyone sit up and take notice. All the Americans above our establishment on Wood River and clear up to Fort Kearney packed up what they could on their wagons and fled, driving their livestock before them. These brainless fugitives had covered the trail for a stretch of 20 miles, and great clouds of dust showed where the greatest number having horses and livestock were to be found.

As the van reached our settlement I rode out to the trail and tried to stop the people, explaining to them that if the Indians really lurked along the trail, they were as good as lost because they were hurrying forward with wives and children planlessly and mostly without weapons, and that dust clouds naturally must betray them to the Indians. All remonstrances failed, however; the train continued well into the night; then it became quiet all around; the Wood River country was vacated.

The Germans were greatly startled by it and did not know what to do, and first this one and then that one asked, "But what now?" I said, "I am staying here, for I have no desire to let myself be scalped along the trail." "We have secured ourselves," I said to those who earlier had made fun of my fortifying operations and called me "cowardly." "As far as I'm concerned let the red devils come; we will take scalps instead of giving them up. For the rest, do better and secure yourselves, or you may soon suffer for it." Other cool-headed people also talked to the timid souls to the same end and now see! What foresight and reason could not do, fear soon did, and almost all the Germans in this region became united. Isn't it a wonder that Germans actually became united for once? A relative of General Lafayette, who had come here from Missouri with his family, took charge, and soon a regular fort made of sod was built two miles east of my house, the four corners of which were provided with lookout posts. The O. K. Store as well as adjoining buildings were completely enclosed with a strong wall and a trench. Meanwhile all the Yankees left. Everyone left who was able to, especially below our settlement, so that the Platte Valley was swept clean from Fort Kearney to a point 50 miles east of us—a stretch of 90 miles; only the Germans remained.

New trains soon came down from Fort Kearney and the upper Platte Valley, in which Fort they no longer felt safe because at that time not more than 60 cavalrymen on foot commanded by our old friend Captain Kuhl—who sends you his regards—were there. These retiring Yankees (some of them) soon visited the empty houses of their beloved countrymen on Wood River, slaughtered their hogs and poultry, drove their own livestock into their corn fields and bravely fed them deserted oat fields stubble. These conditions could not continue long, because communication with the western territories could not be held up for any great length of time or it would result in famine there. It was chiefly this fact that influenced those in this region not to leave.

General Curtis, in person, soon appeared with his troops also. He seemed to be astonished over the nice fort which had been built by the Germans and personally thanked them for their brave firmness and the fortification and left at the Fort as a tribute to their achievement a 6-pounder which is now fired on Sundays. The fort was named Fort Curtis. My fort also was inspected by the General and found to be excellent; nevertheless I called it "Castle de Dependence" for I had not received any cannon. General Curtis is on the whole a good-natured man who easily wins the liking of everyone. He gave us the assurance that the Indians would be thoroughly disciplined, for he said, "I have had enough of this war." Since then, the Yankees who fled the country have found their way back and are figuring up the cost of the trip and of what had been stolen from them, while they went on a pilgrimage to Omaha. In Omaha (150 miles east of here), the people were also filled with fear and anxiety. They set up outposts and sent out patrols in expectation of a raid on the city.

Instead of the 60 rifles and 1,000 cartridges promised by the Governor we finally received 16 old, bent blunderbusses on some of which the screws and locks were missing; the cartridges failed to appear altogether. A great many whites have fallen on the plain, under the scalping knife, even in the vicinity of Fort Kearney. Up until a few days ago, I have been sleeping with my people in our fort, which is well provided with victuals, water, and similar necessities, as well as with weapons. This Indian scare has set us back in our work, however, and we haven't put up anywhere near the amount of hay necessary for this winter. Leave unwholesome New Orleans and trade it for rough—it is true—but healthy Nebraska.

Your brother, Wm. Stolley.

Reprinted from *Nebraska History*, XVI (Oct.–Dec., 1935)

See Nebraska on Safari

IN 1871, the Burlington Railroad had completed its track from Plattsmouth to Kearney and its land department was carrying on an intensive advertising campaign in Europe as well as in America. The following poster, displayed in England, clearly was aimed at the de luxe tourist trade:

GRAND BUFFALO HUNT

A Grand Buffalo Hunt will be held in September next, on the prairies of NEBRASKA AND COLORADO, United States, and through the magnificent valley of the Republican River, the rich alluvial feeding grounds of the buffalo. The valley of the Republican River possesses some of the most varied and magnificent scenery in America, the wild pastures are rich in grasses, and it is most beautifully wooded and watered by clear streams and rivulets. The southern portion of Nebraska, through which the Republican Valley passes, will bear comparison either for climate, soil, or picturesque scenery with any country.

The Burlington and Missouri-River Railroad Company own some millions of acres of land. . . . and will aid and assist this Hunting Party in every way, in order that the Sportsmen of England may see the Western Country . . . Mr. Charles S. Dawson, who left England last April, has made arrangements with a corps of Western Hunters, Trappers, and Scouts, of the Western Frontier of the United States, for a Grand Hunt on the plains of Nebraska and Colorado, and in the valley of the Republican River, where Buffalo, Elk, Antelope, Red Deer, Beaver, Otter, Wild Turkey, Prairie Chicken, &c., abound in large numbers; the Buffalo in herds of from 3,000 to 10,000. THERE ARE NO HOSTILE INDIANS IN NEBRASKA WHATEVER; friendly chiefs of the Otoes, Pawnees, &c., will accompany the party.

Sportsmen will be provided with army tents and beds during the Hunt, and everything generally found in a first-class Hotel. There will be servants to take care of the horses, and in fact all arrangements have been made to give the Hunting party the greatest amount of pleasure with the least possible trouble. Wagons will be provided for the conveyance of any trophies of the chase, such as Buffalo Skins, Elk Horns and Antlers in limited quantity.

FARE—For the Round Trip of about Seven Weeks including every expense, except Wines, Liquors, Cigars, Guns, Rifles, and Ammunition, 90 guineas.

The arrangements will be such as to admit of Ladies joining the party, but the charge for Ladies will be 100 Guineas each.

For further particulars apply to

THE BURLINGTON AND MISSOURI-RIVER RAILROAD COMPANY

When Grand Duke Alexis of Russia, the fourth son of Czar Alexander II, visited the United States in 1872, the high spot of his trip (or so Nebraskans like to think) was his buffalo hunt in the Red Willow valley.

En route to North Platte, the twenty-two-year-old Imperial Highness stopped over in Omaha long enough for a reporter from the Omaha Tribune *to observe that "he is six feet two, [has] light golden side whiskers and a downy moustache," and that "his feet are immense." There was time, as well, for him to take dinner at the home of Governor Saunders. "Hardly had the dinner been completed when the public rushed in to meet the prince. All brought more or less mud into the house to the ruination of the beautiful carpets. Prince Alexis and General Sheridan shook hands with all who passed them in the front parlor. . . . The special train left for the west at ten minutes to three. The prince, standing on the rear platform, bowed to the spectators when a voice in the crowd cried, 'Goodbye, Aleck!' . . ."*

Buffaloes have vanished from the plains and czars are an extinct species, but up until a few years ago you could find many an old-timer out in southwestern Nebraska with vivid memories of—

The Famous Grand Duke
Alexis Buffalo Hunt

COLONEL W. F. CODY

ABOUT the first of January, 1872, General Forsyth and Dr. Asch of Sheridan's staff came out to Fort McPherson to make preparations for a big buffalo hunt for the Grand Duke Alexis of Russia. Learning from me that there were plenty of buffaloes on the Red Willow, sixty miles distant, they said they would like to go and pick out a suitable place for the camp. They also inquired the location of the camp of Spotted Tail, chief of the Sioux Indians, who had permission from the government to hunt the buffalo with his people during the winter, in the Republican River country.

General Sheridan's commissioner asked me to visit Spotted Tail's camp and induce about one hundred of the leading warriors and chiefs to come to the Alexis hunting camp so that the Grand Duke could see a body of American Indians and observe the manner in which they killed buffaloes. The Indians also would be called upon to give a grand war dance in his honor.

On the morning of the 12th of January, 1872, the Grand Duke and party arrived at North Platte by special train. Captain Hays and myself, with five or six ambulances, fifteen or twenty extra saddle horses and a company of cavalry under Captain Egan, were at the depot in time to receive them. Presently General Sheridan and a large, fine-looking young man came out of the cars and approached us. General Sheridan at once introduced me to the Grand Duke as Buffalo Bill, and said that I was to take charge of him and show him how to kill buffalo.

In less than half an hour the whole party were dashing away towards the south, across the South Platte and towards the Medicine, upon reaching which point we halted for a change of horses and a lunch.* Resuming our ride, we reached Camp Alexis in the afternoon. Spotted Tail and his Indians were objects of great curiosity to the Grand Duke, who spent considerable time in looking at them and watching their exhibitions of horsemanship, sham fights, etc. That evening the Indians gave the grand war dance which I had arranged for.

General Custer carried on a mild flirtation with one of Spotted Tail's daughters, and it was noticed also that the Duke Alexis paid considerable attention to another handsome red-skin maiden. The Duke asked me a great many questions as to how we shot buffaloes, what kind of a gun or pistol we used, and if he was going to have a good horse. I told him that he was going to have my celebrated buffalo horse Buckskin Joe, and when we went into a buffalo herd all he would have to do was to sit on the horse's back and fire away.

At nine o'clock next morning we were galloping over the prairies

---

* "While the Grand Duke was modestly dressed, some of the members of the party were appareled in gold and lace and all of the trappings of royalty, and these gorgeous Russian uniforms greatly impressed some of the colored troopers who were along to assist with the camp work. As the cavalcade moved south from the Platte, a colored sergeant ran his horse up to the head of the line and, saluting Buffalo Bill, said: 'Colonel, Ah begs leave to report, sah, dat another of dem kings has done fallen off his horse.' "—Bayard Paine, *Pioneers, Indians and Buffaloes* (Curtis Enterprise, Curtis, Nebraska, 1935)

in search of a buffalo herd. We had not gone far before we observed a herd some distance ahead of us crossing our way; after that we proceeded cautiously, so as to keep out of sight until we were ready to make a charge. The Duke became very much excited and anxious to charge directly toward the buffaloes, but I restrained him until, getting around to windward and keeping behind the sandhills, the herd was gradually approached.

"Now," said I, "is your time; you must ride as fast as your horse will go, and don't shoot until you get a good opportunity."

Away we went, tearing down the hill and throwing up a sandstorm in the rear, leaving the Duke's retinue far behind. When within a hundred yards of the fleeing buffaloes, the Duke fired, but unfortunately missed, being unused to shooting from a running horse. I now rode up close beside him and advised him not to fire until he could ride directly upon the flank of a buffalo, as the sport was most in the chase. We dashed off together and ran our horses on either flank of a large bull, against the side of which the Duke thrust his gun and fired a fatal shot. He was very much elated at his success, taking off his cap and waving it vehemently, at the same time shouting to those who were fully a mile in the rear. When his retinue came up, there were congratulations, and everyone drank to his good health with overflowing glasses of champagne. The hide of the dead buffalo was carefully removed and dressed, and the royal traveler in his journeyings over the world has no doubt often rested himself upon this trophy of his skill (?) on the plains of America.

On the following day, by request of Spotted Tail, the Grand Duke hunted for a while beside Two Lance, a celebrated chief, who claimed he could send an arrow entirely through the body of the largest buffalo. There was a general denial of his ability to perform it; nevertheless, the Grand Duke and several other witnessed, with profound astonishment, an accomplishment of the feat, and the arrow that passed through the buffalo was given to the Duke as a memento. On the same day of this performance, the Grand Duke killed a buffalo at a distance of one hundred paces with a heavy navy revolver. The shot was a marvelous—scratch.*

When orders were given for the return to the railroad, the conveyance provided for the Grand Duke and General Sheridan was a heavy double-seated open carriage drawn by six spirited cavalry

---

* According to Buffalo Bill's sister, Mrs. Helen Cody Wetmore, in her book *Last of the Great Scouts* (Partington Adv. Co., 1903), the Grand Duke shot eight buffaloes altogether, including the one "he thought he shot" with a revolver.

horses which were not much used to the harness. The driver was Bill Reed, an old Overland stage driver and wagon-master; on our way in, the Grand Duke frequently expressed his admiration of the skillful manner in which Reed handled the reins. General Sheridan informed the Duke that I also had been a stage driver in the Rocky Mountains, and thereupon His Royal Highness expressed a desire to see me drive.

In a few moments I had the reins, and we were rattling away over the prairie. When we were approaching Medicine Creek, General Sheridan said: "Shake 'em up a little, Bill, and give us some old-time stage-driving." I gave the horses a crack or two of the whip, and they started off at a very rapid gait. They had a light load to pull, and they fairly flew over the ground. At last we reached a steep hill which led down into the valley of the Medicine. There was no brake on the wagon, and the horses were not much on the hold-back. I saw that it would be impossible to stop them. All I could do was to keep them straight in the track and let them go it down the hill for three miles, which distance was made in about six minutes. Every once in a while the hind wheels would strike a rut and take a bound, and not touch the ground again for fifteen of twenty feet. The Duke and the General were kept rather busy in holding their positions on the seats, and when they saw that I was keeping the horses straight in the road, they seemed to enjoy the dash which we were making. I was unable to stop the team until they ran into the camp where we were to obtain a fresh relay. The Grand Duke said he didn't want any more of that kind of driving; he preferred to go a little slower.*

Condensed from *Story of the Wild West,* Historical Publishing Co., 1888

I recall a look I got when I was five at what was already history. My father was known as a good hunter, and often visiting hunters to the region sought him out when they were having bad luck getting wild game. One early fall evening, during a violent thunderstorm, a top buggy drew into our yard. Out of it came Buffalo Bill Cody and a friend of his from Alliance. Bill was a little under the weather,

* According to Helen Cody Wetmore, this was Alexis' comment on the ride: "I would not have missed it for a large sum of money; but rather than repeat it, I would return to Russia via Alaska, swim the Bering Strait, and finish my journey on one of your government mules."

and in the commotion I awoke and sneaked a look out into our kitchen. There, leaning against the closed door, was the handsomest man I had ever seen, wearing a fine beaded jacket, with beautiful flowing white hair that fell over his shoulders.

I was ordered back to bed, and the next morning, when breakfast was ready, Mother sent me to call Mr. Cody. I tapped on the door where he slept, but there was no answer, no stir, and I pushed the door open a crack. The bed was empty; Buffalo Bill was up and gone hunting for quail with my father, but on the bedpost hung that beautiful head of flowing white hair.

—Mari Sandoz

What the spirit of '76 was to the thirteen original states of the American democracy, the spirit of the 1870's was to the emerging state of Nebraska. "In those years," wrote Addison E. Sheldon, "was created the soul of Nebraska—characteristic mind, vision, and form of action. Soil and sun and wind, hardship and conflict, spirit, institutions, debates, and experiences shaped the type of man who still lives upon these prairies. The blendings of different racial stocks, begun then, still goes on. But the Nebraska type was created in the '70's. . . ."

Mont Hawthorne was nine years old when he first saw Nebraska. He had been born in 1865 on an old land-grant claim in Pennsylvania. The family moved to Virginia when he was five; they lived there for three years before moving on again to Nebraska. In its essential elements, the story of the Hawthorne family's journey and their first experiences as homesteaders is the story of hundreds of Nebraska families of the '70's. Mont Hawthorne's niece has recreated that story from the point of view, and in the words, of the boy who said of himself: "I done my learning on the plains."

The Road to Arcadia

MARTHA FERGUSON MC KEOWN

FATHER WROTE to the Union Pacific Railroad, telling them we wanted to move west and asking for information about a place to locate where they had real good climate with an even temperature. Well, they wrote right back and sent prices. It would cost about thirty dollars for him to go out alone. But they had a reduced rate for parties; when the time come for us all to go we could take one of them trains. But the first thing for Father to do was to come right on and get located. If he'd come clean to Grand Island, Nebraska, they'd bed and board him for a little while so he could take his pick of one of their good farms.

And they sent Father a book that said the Union Pacific Railroad was opening up 12,000,000 acres of the best farming, grazing, and

mineral lands in America in the state of Nebraska, and the territories
of Colorado, Wyoming, and Utah. The Union Pacific had got 1,037
miles of track laid out to Grand Island. It went right into the heart
of the best land in America, right into the valley of the Platte River.
Father said he didn't have to worry about the time of year we moved
on account of the good weather they had year around out in Nebraska. That was the part of that railroad book Mama liked best,
where it told about the climate in the Platte Valley. . . . "During
Fall and Winter the weather is usually dry. The heat of Summer
is tempered by the prairie winds, and the nights are cool and comfortable. The Autumns are like a long Indian Summer, extending
into the latter part of December. The Winters are short, dry and
invigorating, with but little snow. Cold weather seldom lasts beyond
three months, with frequent intervals of mild, pleasant days."

What we couldn't figger out was how them covered-wagon pioneers
had missed finding that valley. They'd kept on going clean to the
West coast, when right out there in the middle was the best country
in the world. By then the East coast was pretty well built up, and
the West coast was getting settled too. But, except for the railroad
and them covered-wagon roads, nobody knowed much about the
country in between. That must of been how they'd left that Great
Platte Valley empty all this time. . . .

We all went down to the train to see Father off to Nebraska, and it
wasn't long until we was getting letters from him telling about how
he'd hit some snags. You see, in 1869 when the railroads met out at
Salt Lake, the Union Pacific passed a ruling that they was only going
to open up the first 200 miles of the grant for settlement, and they
wouldn't open no more until what they had was settled because they
couldn't be hauling empty freight trains all along the line. So, as far
as the settlers was concerned, Grand Island was the end of the line.

The trouble was that Grand Island had first been settled in 1866
when the Union Pacific had made it a storage place for supplies while
the men building track moved on ahead. They figgered that it took
over three hundred tons of material for each mile of railroad that
they built. They'd had to have food, too, for their men and horses.
So, farmers had filled in close to town when the railroad family men
started sending back for their folks; and doctors, and teachers, and
preachers and other folks that go to make up a town, had moved in
too. The single fellows working on the railroad had got tired being
out there in front without nothing to come back to; so them other
kind of folks that helped them blow off steam come out there too.

For a while the saloon keepers and dance-hall girls had followed along as close as they could to the track builders. But when Father got there in 1873 the railroad building boom was over. A lot of folks didn't want to go back East, so they had stopped off in Grand Island and had filed on them homesteads around nearer the town. . . .

Father wrote Mama things was costing him more than he figgered, like the filing fee would be eighteen dollars instead of the ten they'd figgered on, but he only had to pay fourteen of it when he made the application. He said it was good country, and he'd kept going up the valley until he'd found a real good farm. It was close to the Middle Loup River and it had a spring on it. Of course it was the farthest one out beyond the twenty-mile railroad grant, because he'd had to keep going quite a ways until he found land close to the river that wasn't already homesteaded. He didn't have no wood for corner stakes, so he'd gone around on his quarter section and gathered up and piled buffalo skulls on each corner and put his name on them. He said they was as high as he could make them and he'd marked his name real plain on top of each pile, but he wanted to get out there before some squatter moved in and kicked them over so the grass would cover them. Anyhow he'd filed and he'd paid his fee at the land office in Grand Island and if we didn't get out there and settle within six months we'd never have another chance at a free farm as long as we lived. . . .

[Mr. Hawthorne returned to Virginia to collect his family and, in February 1873, they began the journey west.]

We shipped our stuff in boxes straight through to Grand Island by freight, and we said goodbye to the folks in the stores at Meherrin. When we got off the train in Richmond, we all followed Father over to where a fast-talking, promoting man, named G. B. Cady, was lining up families from a paper he had in his hand. While we was waiting, Aaron and Father and me walked over to the track where we got to see one of them new Pullman cars that was made with berths so that folks could undress and go to bed at night. But we didn't get to ride in nothing like that. Them railroad companies was using up the last of their oldest cars, with the slat seats and the bare floors, to take emigrant parties out West at a family rate.

All along the way the train would stop and another emigrant car would be hooked on behind ours. Most of them folks getting on hadn't never been out there, but they'd read that book and could hardly wait until they got located in that Platte River Valley. When they found Father had been there they all begun firing questions his way, and he told them about how pretty the land lay, and how it didn't have to be cleared, and how Nebraska had a herd law that every man must keep his own cattle in so that a man could start farming there without having to build no fences to keep cattle out. Father really believed in that country up where he had staked his claim. . . .

Omaha was a mighty big place with all kinds of folks crowded in at the depot. Mr. Cady told us we'd have almost a day's layover before our train left for Grand Island. Mama went into the women's room and she was gone a real long time. She sent the girls back to tell Father to call someone in charge there at the depot. The ticket agent went in and talked to Mama, then when he come back out again he said she'd found an old woman who was terrible sick and had told him to send for a doctor quick. After awhile Mama and another woman brung her out and they had the folks all clear away, then they stretched the old lady out on a bench and put her coat under her head.

It wasn't long after that until Father got back with a doctor who looked at the old lady and said she was critically ill with erysipelas and wasn't in no condition to travel; that it was a shame for us to be dragging her around like that when we ought to have her home in bed; that he had an emergency call; that since it was obvious that we was transients going through their city he'd like to have Father pay him his five dollars now so's he could be on his way. In no time he was gone and so was Father's money. Father went over to the ticket taker and asked him to pay back his five dollars. But that ticket taker got real mean and said he was running a depot and not a charity hospital.

The old woman was traveling all alone and she didn't have no money. She'd told Mama that the only kin folks she had was on ahead in a covered wagon. After they had left their home back East she had got to thinking about how she didn't want to die without seeing her daughter again. She knowed they was going to stop in Lincoln to pick up their mail, and she had figgered the train would get her there in time to catch them. We was too short of money ourselves to pay for her ticket, so the only thing we could do would be to take up a collection. The folks each took a side of the depot and started asking anyone setting there for money. They collected over three dollars but that wasn't enough to buy her ticket.

Then Mama set right down and she wrote out a paper because

she said she wasn't going out begging unless folks knowed what it was for. She wrote, "This money is to help an old lady to get to where she ought to be." Then she started up the main street with it. When Mama stopped two handsome, dressed-up stylish men who was walking by real fast, one of them says, pointing to the other fellow, "Don't bother this man, he's the governor of Nebraska, and he's in a hurry."

Mama says, quick, "Well, I've come to live in Nebraska, and I've got a right to know what kind of a governor we have. If he won't take care of his own people, he don't amount to much."

The governor picked up his ears and got sort of red. Then he laughed and says, "I guess she's right about that." Blamed if them two men didn't turn right around in their tracks and follow Mama back to the depot. She showed the governor the old woman laying there, still as death, and Mama says, "We haven't any money to spare but I'll take care of her on the train if you will get her passage and telegraph to the police in Lincoln so they will locate her family and meet us there."

Mama bossed that governor around just like he was one of us children, and she looked so handsome in her black alpaca suit, with her cheeks sort of flushed and her eyes real blue because she was excited and wanting her own way, that the governor, and Father, and everyone else around there was real happy to see she got it. He took time out to tell us his full name. He was Governor Robert W. Furnas, and she took time out to show him her children. Then he went over to the ticket man and he wrote out an order saying that the old lady with erysipelas was to have a free ride to Lincoln.

When he come back, he shook hands with Mama, and he says, "Mrs. Hawthorne, I hope you like our state. Nebraska needs women like you." Then he patted Father on the shoulder and says: "You're a lucky man. Take good care of her."

And Father looked real proud and says, "Most of the time she's taking care of us."

Then the governor and his friend said goodbye to us and we got on the train. Us children stayed close to Father until we got to Lincoln. The old lady was pretty weak by then but the police had located her kin folks where they was camped in a covered wagon out on the edge of town, and they had drove down to the depot and had a bed all fixed in the back of their wagon. Father helped lift her off the train, and they put her in the wagon, and she opened her eyes and seen her daughter was there, and she reached out and took her hand and said, "Mary." Then she dozed off again. We never knowed what happened to her. . . .

We was tired and glad to get off that train in Grand Island, but the Railroad House was small and the eating part so crowded that we waited a long time to get fed. Victuals come high. Mama priced everything first and then told the girl what we was to eat. While we was eating, her and Father talked about how we'd better get out to our homestead quick.

When Father was out there before, he'd stayed his first nights with James Michelson, who owned The Nebraska House. He said rooms was dear, but it was the only safe place he knowed to take us. Father told us about how Mr. Michelson had used his head when his wagon broke down when he was trying to ford the Platte River a piece from town. That had happened before the coming of the railroads, and he'd had to drop out of his wagon train right there. Because he'd been a blacksmith back East and had brung his tools along, he set up shop beside that ford. It wasn't long until he was sending back East for more equipment. He charged sixteen dollars to shoe a yoke of oxen, and them wagon trains was coming through there so thick that before long he had other men hired to help him.

Some other fellows come along and started farming in along the Platte River. Clean back in 1862, Henry A. Koenig and Fred Wiebe got tired of folks borrowing when the wagon trains stopped and so they opened the O. K. Store right on their farm. All them fellows made money. When the railroad come they moved up to town. In 1866 James Michelson took the money he'd saved blacksmithing and built The Nebraska House. And Henry Koenig and Fred Wiebe was doing a lot of business in their O. K. Store where we bought what provisions we had to have. Them boys was smart; besides the store, they'd put in the first mill, and they'd opened the State Central Bank of Nebraska in 1871, and because they didn't gamble or make fool loans, they was doing business all during that panic when folks back East was going under. Trouble was they was so careful we couldn't get no credit, and we didn't have much to eat along with us when we left town in our new wagon that was drawed by a team of green oxen that was the best Father could get with the money he had to spend. After we got our hand luggage loaded we set in the wagon and rode down to the depot to pick up our freight. Father walked alongside them oxen with his goad stick, but the rest of us got to ride. After we picked up our bedding and them other boxes from Virginia, Aaron and me just walked along in back of the wagon. Then when we rode over to Jim Cleary's store to get Mama's new Charter Oak stove that she'd been down and bargained for, and Father's plow and other farm implements that he just had to have, we seen we was up against it for room in the wagon-box.

So, Father drawed off to the side, and him and Aaron took a lot of the things out of the wagon, and they put the stove in the middle and up toward the front. Then they opened one of the boxes and we packed the oven and the firebox as full as they would hold. We seen we'd be lucky if we got all of our stuff in the wagon, and by then we knowed we'd all have to walk. The baby was too heavy to carry, so Father left a little place for her in back and to the right. He tied the load good so nothing would topple over or slide down and mash her. Mama said she'd walk in the right-hand wagon rut all the way so's she could watch her. . . .

We got to Noland's place about noon. By then us children figgered we ought to be about to our homestead, so we told Mr. Noland we was going to be his new neighbors. But he just looked at us, sad-like, and shook his head. Then he started talking to Father about the best places for us to make our all-night stops. That's the first time I realized we'd only covered six miles, and our homestead was over sixty miles from Grand Island on up the Middle Loup River. The good land along the Platte River had all been staked before Father got there, although nobody was living on a lot of the places. The Loup River was the largest river running into the Platte. The Middle Loup had looked the likeliest of any of them rivers he come to, so he'd followed up it and staked the first good claim with a spring. . . .

After dinner we started out again. Father set a slow pace because of them oxen and us children. By night we had only got as far as Noland's daughter's place. They was pleasant enough folks but I'd never slept in a sod house with a dirt floor before and I figgered they must be awful poor. When we got up the next morning it was snowing, but it let up a little and we made a late start. By keeping right at it, no matter how hard the going was, we made it to Dannebrog before night. Quite a bunch of Danes had come out there and filed on land all together. They called it the Danish Land and Homestead Company; their government and a bunch of their relatives up in Wisconsin had helped them get there. Mostly they lived back from the road in little dugouts, but Noland had told us to go see Lars Hannibal, who had the postoffice in his house, and to see if he wouldn't put us up. He spoke English some, but it was terrible broken. He said he couldn't put up all the strangers that come through Dannebrog, but Mama come around from her side the wagon, and he seen that the snow was caked thick in agin her hair at the edge of her 'kerchief. She says, "Could I buy some milk from you for my baby?"

He looked us all over standing there with the snow coming down on us and our stuff in that open wagon, and he opened the door for Mama and motioned us children inside. Him and Father put the oxen in with his. Father brung in some of the bakery stuff we had left to sort of pay our way, and we put our victuals in with theirs. His wife and Mama was real smiley with each other even if Mrs. Hannibal couldn't talk to her in English and Mama couldn't speak Danish. Then us children was bedded down with theirs along one wall. I was so tired I could hardly keep my eyes open long enough to see Mr. Hannibal and Father setting over by the fire drinking something steaming out of a couple of them big, tall steins, and Mama shaking her head at Father and wishing that he wouldn't.

Next morning we was snowed in. We stayed over that day, but it was plain to see that we had too many folks in that one cabin. No matter how hard we tried we couldn't keep out of each other's way. The second morning, early, we left. It had quit snowing and a couple of teams had been through and broke the road on ahead. We figgered the storm was over.

We made a good many miles that morning, but about mid-afternoon a blizzard struck. Father said there wasn't nothing to do but keep on going until we reached Loup City where some folks had been laying out a new town when he went through there on his way to locate our homestead. By that time we was all scared. We couldn't see six foot in front of us; the snow was about halfway to my knees. Father and Aaron was taking turns walking ahead, leading the oxen; the rest of us followed single file after one of the wagon wheels. Then the storm really hit us. One of the oxen stumbled and fell. We had trouble getting him up, and Father knowed they was through.

The baby was crying in the wagon. The girls was jumping up and down and blowing on their hands and a-screaming. Aaron run back and pulled me in under his coat to see if he could warm me a little. Father grabbed Mother by the shoulders and yelled, "Martha, can you make out while I try to go back for help?"

She said, "Sam, we'll be all right in under the wagon. Shovel part of the snow away. Get the featherbeds and pile them on the wind side, so we don't get buried by drifts."

Blamed if she didn't go right to work helping him. It wasn't no time until they had a place scooped out for us under the wagon. Mama handed the baby to Julia, because she was the oldest, and sent her in first. Then Sadie and me crawled in after her. Aaron's legs was as long as Father's, so they went back for help together, taking turns breaking trail. Before they left, they tied the oxen on the lee side of the wagon to protect them all they could from the wind.

That just left Mama to come in under the wagon with us. The wind was howling through there as she pulled the last of the feather pillows in after her. Us four children cuddled up to her like a bunch of little puppies, and before long I could feel my feet tingling and sort of coming to life again. Mama started right in talking to us about how we was within twenty-five mile of our new home and how it would soon be springtime out there on the prairie.

"I want you children to remember," says she, "that no matter how bad things may be for you some day, you can always be thankful that it's bound to be better than it was in '73." . . .

[Mr. Hawthorne returned, having secured the promise of help from a stranger who agreed to come with his team and a cart when the storm let up. The Hawthornes spent the night under their wagon. By morning the storm had blown itself out, and Mont, his mother and sisters went on to Loup City with the stranger, waiting there while his father and Aaron followed with their wagon. After another night in the Loup City hotel, they started on again.]

We put our stuff in the wagon and left right after breakfast. The snow was melting fast, and we could follow the ruts plain. The road followed along the bank of the Middle Loup River; the valley wasn't very wide in there and we couldn't tell much about it excepting that sandhills rolled back from each side and there wasn't much to see, no matter how hard we looked. Father said we only had fourteen more miles to go and we'd be home, so Mama and us children kept peering around the sides of the wagon as we went sloshing along through that melting snow trying to see all we could and still keep our feet in the wheel ruts.

When the oxen had to rest or the baby cried too hard, Father would stop long enough for Mama to feed her. Then she'd reach into our provisions and pass something out for us children so we could gnaw on it and half forget how the water felt running between our toes in them hard, old shoes we was wearing.

Father was walking out in front of the oxen, taking real big steps and looking proud of hisself, but us children was walking along in back thinking of how warm we'd been back in Virginia. By and by the going got harder. We didn't have no ruts to follow. The valley widened out until it was about three mile across. Down by the river we seen a log cabin with smoke coming out of it. Then Father stopped the ox team. We looked around the back end of the wagon-box, and there he was—off to one side, scratching around in the snow—looking at some old buffalo skulls. The girls and me just looked at each other. Why, there wasn't a thing to be seen around there but snow, and a clump of cottonwoods off a piece to the right, and we was all of a half mile from the Middle Loup River.

Then Sadie begun to cry about how she wanted a home 'stead of a homestead. Julia put her arms around Sadie, but Mama waded right out in the snow to stand beside Father. She took a deep breath, and us children seen her shoulders stiffen as she looked out over that big field of snow. Then she says, real slow, "Is this it, Sam?"

And Father stood real straight, and puffed out his chest.

"Yes, Martha, this is it! Yonder is the spring by them cottonwoods," he says, pointing at them few trees. "You'll have water handy to your kitchen, and there ain't no better ground outdoors."

He dropped down on his knees to scrape the snow away, then he come up with a double handful of rich soil. Mama pulled off her gloves and squeezed some of it between her fingers. After a minute she looked up, smiled, and says, "Yes, Sam, this is a lot better than we had back in Virginia." ...

II

It ain't no wonder Father bragged about that soil. Before the house was finished, the garden was up. I never seen things pop out of the ground like they done there that spring. Every night, after supper, we'd go past our sod corn to see how it was doing, and then we'd walk over to the garden to see how good it had growed that day; and, of course, Mama would have us take a few minutes to pull any weeds that had begun to grow. Father figgered things was doing so well that he could leave long enough to get things that we was needing, and to find out who'd give him cows on credit since we'd have to go in debt for them. Word got around that he was going and the neighbors give him their lists of what they had to have from Grand Island, and he took in the letters that had to be mailed and promised to pick up the mail that was being held there at the post office. Sixty mile was quite a ways to haul what groceries and other stuff we had to have. There was a store, fourteen mile away at Loup City, but they had to haul stuff by wagon theirselves and after they tied their money up in it and took the risks they sure wasn't giving it away.

By the time Father got back from that trip we wasn't even sure if it was him coming or not because by then we was used to seeing clouds of dust in the distance. Every day prairie schooners was stopping down by the spring, and women was visiting with Mama and washing out their clothes and talking her into selling them some of her good, homemade bread. And their men folks was inquiring around about the country on beyond. On each side of the railroads, wagonloads of folks was branching out along the streams looking for homesteads. The prairie was filling in. Father'd had enough trouble locating our claim when he was out in 1873, but by the spring of '74 things was getting plumb crowded in Nebraska. But them folks stopping at our place went right on because they was hoping to find springs and creeks and timber, and all them things they'd read about in them wore-out books they was carrying under their wagon seats.

Us children was over weeding in the garden when I looked up and seen Father driving up to our sod house. I lit out of there lickity-cut and when Father seen me he reached right down under the wagon seat, and he picked the blackest little kitten you ever seen right out of a box that was in back of his feet, and he give her to me! We took turns holding the kitten and helping Father get unloaded. He told us all about how we was going to buy fresh cows from a fellow named Stevens who was running a big herd of eighty head on farther down toward Grand Island. He said a good cow brung $16.00, but he was dickering for a special price because he was buying so many to eat up our hay. But when Mama got to asking about that part of it, and how was he figgerin' on taking care of the milk in hot weather, he sort of hemmed and hawed a little bit and I wasn't sure but what the sparks might begin to fly a mite, so I took my kitten and went on out to look at the garden again.

Golly, it was pretty. I never seen stuff growing as good as that in all my life. And Mama had brung some flower seeds along and Julia had planted hers to the right, and Sadie had planted hers to the left of the door at the house, and they'd covered some little rocks with white clay so folks couldn't walk into our flowerbeds. I felt sorry for them children that had just pulled out in a covered wagon from down by the spring. Why, we had as pretty a sod house as you could ever see, and before long we'd have cows giving milk, right there in our shed, and we had a garden with potatoes and other stuff just ready to eat, and sod corn almost growed. Excepting for money, we had just about everything a family could ever hope to have.

But while I was standing there looking over the prairie, I seen a little fire starting way off to the west. I started to run to the house to tell the folks about it, when I seen it wasn't a fire but a storm, because it was off the ground and coming towards us like a big cloud, and I run fast and started yelling that a snowstorm was going to hit us. It was a storm all right. In no time grasshoppers begun raining down on us. The air was so full of them we could hardly see. Mama give me the broom and told me to run for the garden and to beat them off the cabbage plants. Mama worked out there longer than I did, and I never give up until the sharp barbs on their legs had cut me so bad I was bleeding all over and had to go to the house. Sadie had pulled off her apron and throwed it over her little flower garden before she run out to try to help Mama. When they come back to the house, they seen that the grasshoppers had et clean through her apron and that the plants in underneath was gone. Julia and Father was down by the spring, carrying boards, trying to cover it over and save our water supply, but thousands of grasshoppers drowned in there, and before it was fit to use again Father had to take their bodies out by the bucketful. Aaron had run out to see about the sod corn, but he come in and said that every cornstalk was as thick as a man's upper arm with them grasshoppers.

By then we knowed that we was helpless to fight them, and that all we could do was to hole up in our sod house until the wind changed and they moved on some place else. Grasshoppers is like that. When the wind is blowing from the west, they light, and they don't go on again until the wind changes. . . . Over at Kearney they stopped the railroad train because them mashed grasshopper-bodies made the tracks so slick and oily that they couldn't get no traction. But, of course, we didn't know nothing about that then. We was all in the house, and Mama was using the elm bark salve as sparing as she could because she knowed it would never last to fix all them cuts on our faces and hands and feet and legs where them grasshoppers dug their sharp barbs into us.

And those of us that wasn't being doctored had to run around killing the ones that had got in the house and was jumping all over the place, and Father was using the broom and a thin board for a dustpan, scooping them up and dropping them into the fire where we'd hear them sizzle as the flames licked around that oil in their insides. And for days we had nothing to eat, nothing but some boiled wheat and boiled corn with nothing to put on top. Them was terrible days. I'm glad I'll never be coming over them again.

After the grasshoppers moved on and we opened the door and tried to start living again, we seen long lines of covered wagons coming back. Mama said we couldn't turn back like they was doing. They was still adrift. But we was anchored. We had to stay right there and toughy it out because there wasn't nothing wrong with our sod house—or with the land we'd built her on. . . .

Because the grasshoppers had got so bad they stopped the trains, they was news. Word got out about how folks in Nebraska was starving and was needing most everything, and the government voted money to send help, and all over the country folks started packing relief boxes and shipping them in. The boxes got there first. Waugh, who got hisself elected judge and then was put in charge of grasshopper relief, sent word up that he had appointed Father and Mama and Porter Brown as a committee to open and divide a big box of clothing that was for the settlers in our valley, and would they please come and get it and see that it was distributed. So Porter come down, and him and the folks went to town and got the box. There was a surplus of buckwheat somewhere else and so the government was sending it to Nebraska, and they was shipping in them old Civil War uniforms too that had been stored in warehouses ever since the soldiers had quit fighting.

When all the folks had gathered at our house, Father took his single-bitted ax and he struck right through the lid. He knocked off the iron bands and Mama stood up by the table and started taking the things out from inside. First, come a man's suit. It was made of black and white checks, real wide ones, and all the fellows let out a yell when she held it up because they'd never seen nothing as sporty as that. A man couldn't of wore it milking; them blamed checks was so loud they'd of scared the cows so bad they wouldn't give down no milk. That one suit was all they'd sent for men. There wasn't a single thing in the box for children. All the rest of the box was packed tight with the fanciest dresses I ever seen. They was made of real heavy silk, with nothing up around the top where a woman's shoulders sunburns bad, and they had all them trailers hanging down in back where she needs her clothes cut off floor length so's to have her legs loose for walking. When Mama got about half done with lifting them dresses out of the box she just quit and set down on a bench and cried like a baby. Porter Brown, trying to cheer her up, grabbed one of them big feathered hats that had been mashed down flat in the packing, and shoved the crown up enough to get his head in and says, "See, Martha, what I've got to wear plowing?"

Blamed if Mama didn't stop crying and start in laughing. Nobody could get her stopped for awhile, neither. But before long she entered into things and was having just as much fun as anybody there. The men and the women and us children got into them fancy dresses and we had a dance. No, sir, we never had so much fun in our lives as we did that night we unpacked the relief box that had come to us straight from New York. We laughed so hard at how folks looked in them dresses, that nobody minded having to go home without no refreshments. Them days, folks was used to cinching up their belts; and having that party done us all a lot of good.

The buckwheat come; we all got hives. No matter how hungry folks is, they can't get away with eating straight buckwheat.

So we planted most of our buckwheat to get a quick crop, but we kept enough back to keep everyone in the valley scratching all the rest of the summer. Of course, we had more prairie chickens than we could eat. They was in fine shape because they hadn't been eating nothing but grasshoppers. Even the fish we caught in the Middle Loup tasted like them grasshoppers. . . .

During the late fall, when the weather was too bad to work out in the fields, Charley Matthews got up gumption enough to ride all over with a petition for the government to establish a mail route up through our part of the state. It would run from Kearney on up to Loup City and then to where we was. That was about half way. Then he wanted it to go from there on up to a little settlement where he lived, sixty mile north of us. Him and a fellow named Oscar Smith had filed on some real fine mineral springs that bubbled up in Victoria Creek, close to where it run into the Middle Loup River. It was right at the edge of them Cedar Canyons, and they'd throwed up a store on Smith's place and put some sleeping rooms in above it. But they was a hundred and twenty mile from the nearest post office, and he wanted to see if something couldn't be done about it. He stayed at our place overnight, and the folks told him they liked the idea fine, only they didn't figger we had no more chance of getting that petition answered straight than we had of getting a fort built between us and them Sioux Indians. But when he asked right out if Mama would be willing to have the post office at our house, she was real glad to sign the paper saying she would. We never got our mail, them days, unless someone was going to Grand Island, and we couldn't hope for that more than maybe once a month.

We didn't have no name for our valley; up until then nobody had thought about needing one. But the paper had a place to fill a name in, so Mr. Matthews stayed around and him and Father rode all over to get the names on the petition and ask folks what they thought of Brownsville for a name. Rightly, the place should of been named for the McKellers, who was the first settlers, but they was so mean, nobody would have it. The Browns come next, so we sent in their name. After a long time a letter come back saying Nebraska already had a Brownsville, and it was up to us to pick another name. By that time Uncle Boone and his family was pretty well settled in their dugout. His wife, Aunt Sadie, was real fanciful and hadn't seen no grasshoppers nor nothing like that yet, so she says, "Why not call it Arcadia?"

It sounded real pretty, and it suited our valley, too. You couldn't ask for a better place to live when things was going good. We was just a piece from the river, where we could catch bass and catfish, while wild plums, gooseberries, grapes, choke-cherries, and blackberries growed thick along the banks of the creeks and up in the draws. And that ground in there can't be beat. Yes, sir, we figgered she was right, and that was the name we sent in, and that's what they call the town and the post office today. Them folks that bought Uncle Boone out, cut his homestead up into city lots, and then they subdivided our old place next. When I went back in 1924, after being away for forty-three years, I seen a big sign saying *Hawthorne's addition to Arcadia,* and I was real glad that Aunt Sadie, after looking out across that bare field where there wasn't another house in sight, says: "Let's call it Arcadia."

Condensed from *Them Was the Days,* Macmillan, 1952

I want to be a cowboy and with the cowboys stand,
Big spurs upon my bootheels and a lasso in my hand;
My hat broad-brimmed and belted upon my head I'd place,
And wear my chaperajos with elegance and grace.

The first bright beam of sunlight that paints the east with
red
Would call me forth to breakfast on bacon, beans and
bread;
And then upon my bronco so festive and so bold
I'd rope the frisky heifer and chase the three year old.

And when my work is over to Cheyenne then I'll head,
Fill up on beer and whisky and paint the d— town red.
I'll gallop through the front streets with many a frightful
yell;
I'll rope the staid old heathen and yank them all to h--l.

Quoted in *Folk-Song of Nebraska and the*
Central West by Louise Pound

The Real Cowboy

ROBERT STURGIS

FOR MOST PEOPLE the word "cowboy" conjures up the image of a swashbuckling, noisy, danger-loving fellow, who would rather fight than eat and who shoots to kill on the slightest provocation. This is the cowboy of fiction—a romantic figure, endowed with heroic qualities that the average man did not possess.

In reality the cowboy was just an ordinary human being doing an ordinary (to him) job in an ordinary way. It is true that he loved danger; it is true that he was sometimes compelled to kill; and it is true that his job was often a hazardous one. But he worked at it in exactly the same way as another man works at farming or engineering. It was a means of earning a livelihood.

The American cowboy owes his vocation to the Mexican. In 1821, when the first Americans began to drift into Texas, they found many Mexicans who owned large tracts of land and bred cattle for their personal use. They did not sell the cattle, because they were hundreds of miles from the markets. They simply allowed the herds to multiply, killing what they needed for food, and letting the rest wander where they would. The Americans captured some of these wild herds, added to them unbranded cattle stolen from the Mexican herds, and, after a few ineffectual attempts to find a market, settled into the easy-going ranching routine of their Mexican neighbors.

Then in 1869 came the railroads, providing the ranchers with a means of transporting their stock to the markets. The cattle industry grew to gigantic proportions and became the chief occupation in the territory between Central Nebraska and the mountains of the Pacific slope. It was in those rousing days that the cowboy first captured the country's imagination and became a hero to every American boy.

Cowboy dress was picturesque, but it was worn because it was functional, not because it was photogenic. Every item of the cowboy's apparel had its own especial use, and since it was designed for service rather than appearance, the style has never changed.

The broad-brimmed sombrero protected the puncher's face and neck from the burning sun and in wet weather served as an umbrella. It also was used as a drinking cup and, when rolled up, made a comfortable pillow. Often his "ten-gallon hat" was the finest article in a cowboy's wardrobe: it was by no means unusual for a puncher to spend six months' wages for a sombrero. To hold it in shape, there was a belt of adjustable length at the base of the crown. Most of these belts were leather, but in some sections, particularly in the Southwest, they might be woven of silver or gold wire. Leather belts usually were studded with ornamental nails or with "conchas"— flat silver or gold plates—which, if the owner's purse permitted, could be set with jewels.

The handkerchief which every cowboy wore about his neck was not an article of dress, but served as a mask to shield his face from the dust and biting wind of the prairies. While there was nothing distinctive about his shirt and pants, which were cotton or wool of a subdued color, the puncher's "going-to-town" vest of plush or shaggy wool often was brilliantly hued. His "ordinary" vest had many pockets for storing those various articles which the cowboy carried along with the "makings"—cigarette papers and a bag of Bull Durham.

Most of the men wore gloves when working, and some wore them during all their waking hours. Usually they were made of buckskin, with long, flaring gauntlets embroidered with silk thread or silver or gold wire. Tightly fitting leather cuffs of brown or black were almost always worn to protect the wrists.

The puncher's high-heeled boots were constructed of the finest quality of thin, pliable leather. They came up to the knee and were covered with fancy stitching. The two-inch heel prevented the rider's foot from slipping or becoming entangled in the stirrup, and the sole was quite thin so the rider could always feel the stirrup under his foot. Since vanity demanded that the boots fit tightly and the puncher considered it beneath his dignity to wear any other type of footgear, cramped toes and highly-arched insteps were physical characteristics of the cowboy throughout the range.

Spurs were another indispensable item of his attire: it is said that when a cowboy appeared in public he would as soon be without his trousers as his spurs. They were of far heavier make than those used anywhere else in the country. As a rule the blunt rowels were half an inch in length, and the wheels tipping them slightly more than an inch in diameter. However, the spurs imported from Mexico and used extensively in the Southwest had two-and-a-half-inch wheels with rowels of corresponding length.

Chaps, or to give them their real name, *chapejaros,* were skeleton trousers worn over the regular trousers to protect the rider's legs when he was thrown, or when riding through sage-brush, cactus, or chaparral. They were made of heavy leather covered with thick wool or hair. If the leather was free from hair, the chaps might be decorated with drawings of women's heads, frontier animals, and the like.

It is a popular fallacy that the cowboy always carried a gun. The truth is he went armed only when absolutely necessary: that is, when expecting a personal attack, when riding in Indian country or near the border, or when riding the range where he might meet injured or diseased cattle which would have to be shot. He also wore a gun when on a holiday visit to town or when he called on a girl. At such times the gun was as necessary for correct cowboy dress as a white tie is for formal evening wear.

The gun was the single-action Colt revolver of forty-four or forty-five caliber. It had an eight-inch barrel and weighed two and a quarter pounds. It was perfectly balanced by the long barrel, and aiming it was akin to pointing the finger. Usually the gun was carried in an open holster, swung low on the thigh, and fastened to the boot-top or near the knee with a raw-hide thong. The holster was attached to a wide belt, which hung around the waist and was looped for extra cartridges. Sometimes the gun was concealed and holstered on the breast, or attached to the end of a strap and carried in the coat sleeve. However, these deviations from the conventional were seldom favored by the cowboys, although much used by peace officers and outlaws.

To facilitate rapid firing, the majority of the punchers removed the trigger, firing the gun by pulling back the hammer and releasing it—"thumbing" the weapon. Another method was to fasten the holster to the gun belt by means of a swivel and fire by tilting the holster and thumbing the hammer. Since this eliminated drawing the weapon from the holster, it saved precious split seconds in getting it into action. Many of the cowboys were so quick on the draw that the eye could not follow the movements of their hands. Few would miss a target as large as a man at one hundred feet under any conditions, and many, at a moment's notice, could pour six shots into a two-inch circle at the same range.

Contrary to much fiction, the cowboy did not notch his gun. He was not a killer, and he disliked those who used this method of crudely recording and advertising the number of men they had slain. While the cowboy never avoided trouble, he did not look for it; and although when he shot, he shot to kill, he did it as a matter of self-preservation. In the early West the "bad men" were divided into two classes. There was the pseudo bad man who was an arrogant braggart and quickly faded at the first sign of trouble; and there was the genuine bad man who rarely said anything about himself and shot at the slightest pretext. As a general rule he did not last very long. The West wanted no part of him, and either forced him to move on or killed him.

Horse-stealing, cattle-rustling, murder, and robbery were the major crimes, but compared to horse-stealing, the latter three were rather minor offences. To a cowboy a horse thief was the lowest form of life, vermin to be shot or hanged on sight. There were two reasons for this attitude. A man who was deprived of his horse in wild country might die before he could reach help. Then, too, living a lonely life when on duty on the range, the puncher became deeply attached to his mount. Men who regarded sentimentality as an unforgivable weakness were not ashamed to pour their troubles into their horse's sympathetic ear. The average cowboy looked after the comfort of his horse before he did his own.

Literally he lived on his horse. The high-heeled boots made walking difficult, and if there were more than two hundred feet to be traversed the puncher got in the saddle. Most had learned to ride almost before they had taken their first steps, and they considered it undignified to walk. As a consequence another unmistakable mark of the puncher was bowlegs.

The cowboy's hours were from sunrise until his tasks were done, which often was long after dark. There were horses to be broken and trained and inspection trips to be made about the range—"outridings" as they were called—to locate and check on the condition of the scattered groups of cattle, and to drive them to better territory if food or water was found to be insufficient. There were strays to be driven back to the herd, and mired stock to be pulled at rope's end from the mud bogs. There was the need to keep a constant lookout for signs of thieves and predatory animals, and to set traps for any beasts that might endanger the herds. The daily round was a hard one, but it was a life which the cowboy probably would not change for yours.

The "roundups" were made in the spring and the fall. The spring roundup, often called the "calf roundup," was made for the purpose of branding the stock which had been born since the previous spring, and for computing how many head had been lost during the winter. The roundup in the fall, known as the "beef roundup," was made for the purpose of selecting stock for market, the selected cattle then being driven to the railroad. Necessarily a cattle drive was a slow affair: the cattle were driven in slowly so that they would not lose weight and decrease in value. Since the danger of a stampede was great on these drives, it was necessary to have one man to every two hundred and fifty cattle.

A cattle stampede was the most dreaded of all the dangers on the plains. An unusual noise, the sudden movement of a rider, and the herd would be off on a wild charge. The noise of their furiously pounding hoofs was like thunder, and nothing short of a solid wall could stop them. When a stampede occurred, the punchers would fire their guns and make as much noise as possible, and try through furious riding to draw the herd out in a long, thin line. Next they would force the ends of the line together into a U-shape, then drive the cattle together and close the gap, forming a circle in which the cattle would run about, or "mill," until they became exhausted. The danger of a stampede was greatest at night. Working in two- to four-hour shifts, cowboys would ride around the cattle, quieting them with ballads sung in a doleful voice.

Courage was the cowboy's dominant trait. Danger always rode at his side. He had to face the terrible blizzards of the North and the pitiless deserts of the Southwest. Broken bones and injury in the form of hernia received from bucking gave the average hand but seven years of active riding. After that he had to be content with less mettlesome mounts.

Cheerfulness was another trait he cultivated. If the food was bad he ate it; if the work was arduous he performed it. The axiom that nobody wants to hear about your troubles was a part of the philosophy of the range.

Reserve toward strangers also was a cowboy characteristic, and was due to the fact that he saw no one but intimates, and not even them for days at a time. Besides, the stranger might be an enemy and was regarded as such until he proved himself to be a friend; but when this reserve was broken down, a man could not wish for a better friend than a cowboy.

This suspicion of strangers was reflected in two customs. When a rider approached another rider he was bound not to change his course until he came up and spoke a word of greeting; and if approaching from the rear he was supposed to hulloa before coming within pistol shot. Similarly, a rider approaching a camp was supposed to come from the point from which he could be seen most easily. Failure to comply with these rules was regarded as an unfriendly act, for, as the saying was, "None came West save for health, wealth, or a ruined reputation."

Condensed from *Prairie Schooner*, Winter, 1932

The horse opera as an art form has been perfected in Hollywood, California—a place about as far from Nebraska as you can get without using a boat. But where, in real life, was the stamping grounds of a "passel" of the flesh-and-blood originals from whom Hollywood perennially derives its heroes and villains? Where but in—

Ogallala

1. Nebraska's Cowboy Capital

NORBERT R. MAHNKEN

GATEWAY to the northern plains—that was Ogallala from 1875 to 1885. At the little village on the Platte, Texas drovers during this decade delivered their trail herds of longhorn cattle by the thousands. Shrewd, hard-bitten Wyoming and Nebraska cattlemen met in Ogallala's hotel and saloons with the Texas cattle kings and haggled over prices to be paid for the longhorns. A quick handshake, a jovial round of backslapping, a nip at the bar, and bargains were sealed. Gold flowed freely across the tables, liquor across the bar, and occasionally blood across the floor as a bullet brought some unlucky cowhand to the end of the trail on the stained boards of "Tuck's" Saloon.

Ogallala's early history was singularly unspectacular. It was a by-product of the Union Pacific railroad and for its first few years seemed destined to be little more than a section house and water tank. Then, in the spring of 1868 there appeared three men whose fortunes are closely interwoven with the early growth of Ogallala: the two Lonergan brothers, Philip and Thomas, and Louis Aufdengarten.

The Lonergans came to do construction work for the Union Pacific, while Louis Aufdengarten arrived with the U. S. Army. A regiment of cavalry had pitched its summer camp here during the troublesome July of 1868 when Indian raids, real and imagined, were striking fear into the hearts of settlers as far east as the Blue River Valley. Aufdengarten, in business as a sutler, found his trade expanding when the first wave of professional buffalo hunters reached western Nebraska during that summer. Upward of a hundred hunters made this military post and Aufdengarten's "store"—it appears to have been a combination of dugout, soddy, and canvas tent —their base of operations. Buffaloes were plentiful, and Aufdengarten broadened his activities, buying up the hides for shipment east. The next year, 1869, saw him back at the same stand, his connection with the army severed and his interest now centered chiefly on furnishing supplies and equipment for trappers and buffalo hunters.

It was in this year that a number of large herds of longhorns were driven westward along the Platte to find their last range in Idaho, and in this year, too, that the first Texas cattle were brought into the region. After the Lonergan brothers and other outfits had successfully wintered herds along the river from near town to O'Fallon's Bluff, Ogallalans were convinced their community's future depended on the growth of the cattle trade.

During 1874 the step was taken which initiated Ogallala's career as a cowtown. Hoping to recapture the profitable trade it had enjoyed at Schuyler and Kearney, earlier shipping points for Texas longhorns, the Union Pacific constructed a cattle pen and landing chute just west of town. Ogallala's prospects were improved by two developments which at first might appear only indirectly related to the cattle trade. The truculent Oglala and Brule Sioux had been moved from their Platte River agency on the Nebraska-Wyoming border to the new Red Cloud and Whetstone agencies in northern Nebraska. The Republican River valley was closed to their hunting expeditions, and cattlemen could now move into that entire area with little fear of the marauding followers of Red Cloud. At the same time the westward surge of farmers along the rivers in Nebraska and Kansas was closing the trail to Abilene, Schuyler, and Kearney. Forced to seek new markets, trail bosses and ranchers began to realize that Ogallala might be the ideal site for a new cowtown.

The trail-driving business recovered rather slowly from the effects of the financial panic of 1873, and it was not until 1876 that the volume of cattle moving up the trail to Ogallala reached the high level it maintained thereafter. The increasing importance of Ogallala was partly due to the emergence of Dodge City as the leading Kansas cattle mart. A new trail, known as the Western or Texas Trail, gradually supplanted the earlier Chisholm Trail. For many longhorns and a few cowboys the end of the trail came at Dodge City, but for outfits handling younger stock cattle "Dodge" soon became only a point where man and beast could rest a few days before starting on the long road to Ogallala. With increasing frequency contracts signed in Dodge City required delivery of cattle at the Nebraska village. Similarly, an increasing number of drovers who failed to find a buyer on the Arkansas went on up the trail.

Before 1876 the only real demand for older stock in this area had come from contractors supplying the Indian agencies. The Black Hills gold strike unexpectedly added a second market for grass-fed steers; moreover, the call for younger stock was becoming insistent. Previously the North Platte River had marked the limits of the cattleman's domain in Nebraska and Wyoming: though most of the Sioux had been settled in the Red Cloud and Whetstone agencies by 1874, small bands of marauders still were common along the North Platte. But the campaigns of General Crook and Colonel Miles in 1876 ended this menace, and the region was thrown open to cattlemen. By 1878 dozens of new operators on scores of new ranch sites were demanding stock cattle at Ogallala, and the boom had begun—a boom which was to bring there from 75,000 to 125,000 Texas longhorns each season.

Ogallala in 1876 had changed little since its tank-town days. The town itself was but a block long. The stores were all south of the tracks, fronting what was popularly known as "Railroad Street." Louis Aufdengarten's general supply store was on the corner of the intersection of this street and the trail leading south to the Platte. Westward from his store extended the rest of the town, including the saloons and gambling establishments, operating under changing management, but generally carrying the same colorful names, the "Cowboy's Rest" and the "Crystal Palace." The last building in the row was the newly constructed hotel, the Ogallala House, run by S. S. Gast and later by his son-in-law Sam Rooney. One new building of note constructed during 1875 was "the most substantial jail west of Omaha." Its accommodations were soon to prove as inadequate as those of the hotel.

The tempo of living in Ogallala changed with the seasons. During the winter months life was dull and dreary, but with the coming of spring, bets were placed as to when the first herds would arrive, and the whole community took on an expectant air. Around the first of June, Ogallala came alive with a bang. The roundup conducted by the Nebraska cattlemen of the area generally reached town about that time, and June 10 soon came to be the date on which the first longhorns from the south were expected.

June, July, and August were bonanza months for saloonkeeper, storekeeper, and hotelkeeper. Ten or twelve herds, each of 2,500 head, could usually be located south of the town, a bawling mass carpeting the plains. The presence of a hundred or more trail hands meant that sleeping rooms were at a premium, and many visitors to Ogallala spent their first night napping on the "soft side of a walnut board." For a brief time in early summer the white tents of soldiers out after Indians were pitched close to the town. On their free nights, when the troops mingled with Texans in the saloons, many a near-riot started between the hard-fisted boys in blue and the lanky, hot-tempered drovers who not too long before had worn the grey. Loose talk about "rebels" or "Yankee bean-eaters" was enough to touch off a full-scale brawl.

The Ogallala House was the center of social activities for the townspeople and the big cattlemen. Parties and dances were held regularly there, but these gatherings were comparatively sedate—more restful certainly than the parties in the Cowboy's Rest. Frequently, the dancing lagged until "Old Number Seven" would chug in from the east, bringing Ed Hepner, a trainman with considerable finesse in handling the fiddle.

Activity in Ogallala continued at fever pitch until the end of August. By then the season's drives were ending, and the drovers who had chaperoned the herds up the trail were beginning to head back to Texas. Business revived briefly during the fall, especially in October, when the cattlemen brought their steers in off the grass for shipment east. By November, however, Ogallala had relapsed into a state of suspended animation which endured until the first thaws of spring set everyone to speculating about the extent of the year's drives.

Except for her sparse population, Ogallala differed only slightly from the other cowtowns of the prairies. In her saloons the clinking of glasses perpetually accompanied the shrill screech of the dancing-master's violin. Try as he would, this one-man orchestra—it was a great day when the first piano arrived—could hardly make himself heard above the stamping feet of booted cowmen partnered enthusiastically by painted ladies. Money changed hands quickly and in sizeable sums. Gold carefully counted out went into the pokes of cautious Texas drovers who had not yet accustomed themselves to using Yankee greenbacks or bank notes. By 1877, however, drafts on the more widely known banks were coming to be the accepted method of payment.

For its first few years as a major cattle market, Ogallala experienced little of the vicious lawlessness which brought fame of a sort to Wichita and Dodge City. Crime came to Ogallala in 1877 in the person of a nervous and acquisitive Texan, Joel Collins, who had delivered a herd of Texas cattle to purchasers in Nebraska. Intrigued by reports of the gold strikes in the Black Hills, Collins and his side-kick Sam Bass appropriated the money due the Texas cattlemen and hot-footed it for Dakota. When gambling losses and investments in unproductive mines left the pair with empty pockets, they recruited an assortment of kindred spirits and turned to the exciting but generally profitless business of stage robbery. The appearance of federal troops hastened their departure from the Hills, and about September 1 Collins and Bass turned up again in Ogallala. Over a corner table at the Crystal Palace they worked out the details of their next venture, which involved robbing the pay coach of the Union Pacific.

In the early morning hours of September 19, word came that the eastbound Union Pacific had been held up twenty miles west of Ogallala, at Big Springs station. A posse was hastily formed and rode out to trail the bandit crew, but found no trace of them.

News of the robbery created a furor throughout the Midwest. Not only was it the first time a Union Pacific train had been robbed, but the loot totalled $60,000, all in twenty-dollar gold pieces. The wildest guesses were tossed about as to the identity of the robbers. In Omaha, most people were convinced that either Jesse James and his gang or the remnants of the Younger gang had done the dirty work. But within a day or two after the Union Pacific officials posted a $10,000 reward for the arrest of the bandits and the recovery of the gold, it was known that Collins was one of the bandits. He was an acquaintance of a passenger on the train, Andy Riley of Omaha, who identified him positively for the railroad detectives.

Meanwhile, one of Ogallala's citizens, M. F. Leech, proprietor of a supply store, had been building up his own case against Collins and Bass. At the scene of the robbery he had picked up a piece of red, white, and black cloth which had been used as a mask by one of the bandits. Leech recognized it as material sold in his store, and also remembered that he had very recently sold a strip of this cloth to one of Collins' crew of Texans. Determined to obtain the Union Pacific reward, he saddled his best horse and started off to track down the train-robbers.

After camping on the Republican River for a day, the gang had split into three groups. Collins and his partner, Bill Heffridge, were trapped and both killed while resisting arrest at Buffalo Station, Kansas. Jim Berry, who was being closely trailed by Leech, met the same fate in Mexico, Missouri, shot down by officers who wanted to question him about the gold which he had carelessly deposited in banks in the area. Only Sam Bass and his crony Tom Nixon got their share of the loot safely back to Texas; they had traveled in the guise of land-seeking grangers. Ten months of notoriety were still ahead of Sam Bass. Then he too would be cut down by the bullets of Texas Rangers, but his fame would live on in the most celebrated of all cowboy ballads.

For Leech it had been a discouraging pursuit. Always he would catch up with one of his quarries, only to find him dead or in the hands of peace officers. Yet he received a warm welcome home, and shortly after his return was elected sheriff of Keith County. Ever since the office had been created, five years earlier, the turnover among job-holders had been very high. Six men had served at various times as sheriff, but none had relished the task of keeping the boisterous trail-hands in line. Leech was no exception: after a few months he resigned, to be succeeded by J. C. Hughes, a fearless old buffalo-hunter who could always be relied upon to take over temporarily after the elected officials "throwed up the job."

Until the election of 1879, law and order rested on rather unstable foundations in Ogallala. The low point came during the summer of 1878 when Barney Gillan was appointed sheriff. Gillan considered it his duty to protect the cowmen rather than the community. He became involved in the Custer County "war" between homesteaders and cattlemen, and for his part in the lynching of Mitchell and Ketchum, was arrested, indicted for complicity in the murder, and eventually tried along with other defendants in this most notorious trial in Nebraska's early history.*

William Gaslin, elected district judge for southern and western Nebraska in 1876, did as much as anyone to bring respect for the law into this stormy sector of the frontier. Judge Gaslin, who (so went the stories, anyway) at times mounted the bench armed with a Winchester as well as with the legal documents, soon was known as a fearless and ruthless judge.

A second major step in effective law enforcement came in 1879 when Martin DePriest was elected sheriff of Keith County. He was

* See page 91.

a Texan who had come up the trail in 1877, had settled in Ogallala, and opened a livery stable in connection with the hotel. Short, but stocky and wiry, DePriest had few equals in a rough-and-tumble fight. It was this ability, plus his coolness in the face of danger, rather than any unusual proficiency as a gunman which gained him the respect of troublemakers. DePriest understood the longing of the trail-hand for rowdy fun at the end of the drive, but when some drink-crazed or trigger-happy cowhand began using the water tower as a target or endangering life in the community, DePriest would take down and buckle on his Colts and call to his deputy, Joe Hughes, to grab up his shotgun or buffalo gun. The word that this duo was on the prowl would generally be enough to restore the peace.

Unexpected support for order—if not for law—came from Bill Tucker, the long-time proprietor of the Cowboy's Rest. Tucker, a lusty, boisterous character, had drifted over from North Platte as early as 1876. At the Cowboy's Rest, during his regime, the gaming tables were never empty, the bar never dry, and the ladies never too preoccupied but what the newly arrived cowhand found a welcome. Yet Bill Tucker disliked the sight and noise of guns, except for the shotgun he kept under the counter as the final arbiter in any dispute. On several occasions he rallied the support of Ogallala's citizenry to put the quietus on trail crews who were threatening to shoot up the town.

In spite of the efforts of Gaslin, DePriest, and Tucker, during Ogallala's ten years of fame seventeen violent deaths were recorded, a not inconsiderable number for a community whose permanent population was about one hundred. In Ogallala's Boot Hill cemetery were laid the bodies of those cowhands who had lost a debate with gamblers, refought the Civil War, or had found DePriest too much for them.

The cattle trade at Ogallala continued at a brisk pace from 1879 to 1884. By this time the stories of profits in the range cattle business were spreading throughout the eastern United States and to the British Isles as well. After 1879 eastern and English capital moved in, stimulating the incorporation of several great cattle companies capitalized at from five hundred thousand to a million dollars. Purchasing land sites, hiring expensive range managers, buying cattle at inflated prices and on the book count, these companies introduced a new speculative fever into the area. Their constant quest for young stock cattle kept the herds moving up from the south in spite of mounting costs and the increasing difficulties of trail driving. In the period between 1879 and 1884, between 100,000 and 125,000 cattle annually made their way through the Nebraska cowtown.

As the years passed, the herds from the south tended to pass more and more into the hands of a few purchasers. During 1882-83, many wise old pioneers of the range disposed of their stock at $30 to $35 a head for mixed range stock, yearlings included, that as late as 1880 would have brought only $20 or less per head. When the trail-driving business collapsed, its sudden end surprised everyone except these old-timers.

The last great drives of Texas cattle over the Western Trail into Nebraska came in 1884. No longer was the western part of the state the cattlemen's exclusive paradise. A succession of years during which the rainfall in western Kansas and Nebraska was unusually heavy convinced the venturesome granger that farming was profitable in these areas. Along the Republican River in Nebraska and the Smoky Hill and Arkansas rivers in Kansas numerous new settlements mushroomed. By cooperative action, the frontier farmers generally were able to turn aside the herds which might be driven over their lands, or could at least exact a sizeable cash payment for such passage. In June, 1881, Frontier County settlers constructed a corral near Stow post office, where cattle trespassing on their land claims were to be held until ransomed by their owners. As the despised "nesters" became more numerous, the drovers found it ever more difficult and more expensive to attempt to force their way through the settlements and on to Ogallala.

The Kansas state legislature under pressure from western settlers enacted a stream of laws designed to push the quarantine line against Texas cattle farther west. The law of 1884 moved the line west of Dodge City, while a more stringent measure of the next year closed the entire state to Texas cattle from March to December. This law, backed as it was by public opinion, forced those few cattlemen who sought to continue trail-driving to move northward through eastern Colorado.

While herds still made their way to the Platte in spite of settlers and quarantine laws, their number was small. Instead of cracking pistols and boisterous cowboy oaths, the noisy clatter of construction crews filled the Nebraska air. The advance guard of the farming frontier reached Keith County in the summer of 1884 and was followed by a great wave of settlers in 1885. When the Union Pacific began to push the sale of its lands along the South Platte, this further stimulated the migration, and within a few months Ogallala underwent a metamorphosis from cowtown to farmer shopping center. The population of the county, which in 1880 had been 181, had jumped to 700 at the end of 1884, while Ogallala itself, to judge by the columns of the local press, was approaching the 500 figure. Numerous new business houses were added, among them two newspapers, lumber and hardware stores, a millinery shop, and two land offices. Only three saloons were still operating, and they under the handicap of an $800 license fee which went into the school fund.

A fire broke out in one of the stores south of the tracks on August 6, 1884, and a good portion of the old business section burned down. A few days later Ed Whorley was killed in the Crystal Palace by a gambler named Lank Keyes: it was the last murder of the trail-driving days, and it might well have marked the end of Ogallala as a cowtown. The Lonergans were gone—Tom killed on a roundup down on Red Willow Creek, Phil to Colorado. DePriest sold out his livery stable in 1887 and the next year was relieved of his position of sheriff when he moved to Perkins County. Tucker sold his saloon after the 1885 season, went back to North Platte, and later drifted down into New Mexico in search of new wealth and excitement.

Soon after Ogallala's demise as a cowtown, nesters, adverse weather, overcrowding of the range, and inflationary and unwise financing brought an end to the most romantic phase of the cattle industry. Yet the industry was to emerge again in modified form, based on the firmer foundations of blooded stock, fenced pastures, and careful financing. Once again Ogallala was to become the center of the cattle industry in the Platte valley, but never again was it the lurid, hectic cowboy capital it had been from 1875 to 1885.

Condensed from *Nebraska History*, XXVIII (Jan.–March, 1947)

2. "They Went Thataway!"

JAMES H. CLARK

AMONG the men who participated in the gay life of Ogallala were some who became notorious characters of the west. One of these men went by the name of "Doc Middleton" on the ranges of the North. In Texas he was called by another name. I think it was in the spring and summer of the year 1876 that he and his brother, or half-brother, worked with the same trail herd I did, from Texas as far north as the Arkansas River. During the two months in which I saw Doc Middleton quite frequently, I failed to see that he was a first-class cowhand, that is, one whose first thought was the safety of a cow or a herd, and last the comfort and safety of himself. His brother, Joe, was the opposite. No nights were too dark, no rivers too wide for him to tackle when the safety of a cow or herd was at stake.

I met Doc Middleton on numerous occasions after I worked with him on the trail. He preferred gambling and other forms of recreation to trail-driving or ranch work. He did work for the Powers Bros. outfit near the place now called Bridgeport, on the North Platte River, but soon went to the town of Sidney to do some "shopping." While there he had a row with some soldiers and killed one or two of them. He escaped from the peace officers and soldiers who made an attempt to capture him. He joined a bunch of horse-thief outlaws, and not long after becoming their leader, he became famous as the greatest outlaw in the state of Nebraska. He was given credit for all of the crimes committed in the way of stealing livestock within the radius of five hundred miles of his hideouts in the sandhills of Nebraska. He was captured at last, after being wounded, and did time in the state penitentiary. After serving his sentence, he gambled and operated saloons. In the meantime he was married. Not long before his death, which occurred at Douglas, Wyo., when under arrest, he lived at Ardmore, South Dakota. His business there was running a saloon. He came to visit me in my home and told me some of his experiences after the time when we worked on the Texas cattle trail.

The following incident, which he related to me, illustrated a rather unusual phase of horse-stealing. He and three others, all of whom I knew, conceived the idea that they could go up into the country near the Red Cloud Indian Agency, where they thought the Indians would not feel that they had to guard their horse herds very carefully, and run off a big band of ponies, which they could turn over to some confederates in the country lying just north of North Platte city. They all had good horses and took no pack horse with them, but each man had an extra blanket and a little food, which he carried on his saddle horse. All of them were well armed. Three of them carried Winchester rifles. The other man carried a government "Long Tom needle gun" across his saddle.

When they arrived within a few miles of the Agency buildings, they discovered a large encampment of Indians on a creek named

Little White Clay near the Red Cloud Agency, now Fort Robinson, Nebraska. These Indians had a big band of ponies, but they kept a guard of several men with it night and day. Doc and his associates were concealed in the rocks and timber on an elevation where they could overlook the Indian camp and horse herd. They waited for a favorable moment when the herd was left unguarded. Food ran low, and the horse thieves were none too comfortable or safe from discovery by the Indians. One evening, Doc, who was watching the herd of ponies from his perch among the rocks, saw a fresh lot of Indians ride out of camp to night-herd the ponies. Acting on the impulse of the moment, Doc pumped a lot of lead out of his Winchester into the midst of the Indians' camp. Naturally the camp swarmed out after them. The only thing left for those enterprising horse thieves to do then was to make a very hasty departure.

They certainly did so, but in speeding over some open ground the horse ridden by the man who carried the long needle gun stepped into a gopher hole and turned a somersault. His rider was not injured much, so the moment he and the horse could get on their feet and the gun had been secured from where it had been thrown, all were off again for the land of safety. Not until they had ridden an hour or so from the place where the horse fell did they discover that the barrel of the long gun was bent into an arc and was a worthless impediment to their flight. They arrived safely in the white man's country, but that was their last venture in stealing a big band of Sioux ponies.

Another man whose face was familiar to people in Ogallala at one time, who later became one of the most notorious characters of the Southwest, was Luke Short. He was a gambler by profession, but at times he became interested in the Indian-pony-stealing business. I met him and became interested in him when I happened to see him doing some pistol practice one day on the banks of the South Platte River, about a mile from Ogallala. He could draw and fire a six-shooter more rapidly and accurately at short range than any other man I ever knew. After leaving Ogallala, he went to Arizona, and from there to Texas. In a gun fight there with Jim Courtright, a noted quick shot gunman of Texas, Courtright was killed. Short left Texas, and I never heard of him afterward.

Six other men who left their mark as desperadoes of the West were for a short time a part of the population of Ogallala. I think it was during the cattle season of 1877. At the time I happened to be in the town, and noticed a bunch of six men, with pack horses, ride into town. They made camp about one hundred yards west of the Rooney Hotel, as they had their camping outfit on pack horses. Soon after their arrival I met one of the men and recognized him as a cattleman I had met in one of the Kansas cowtowns. His name was Joel Collins. He remembered me and told me that he and the outfit of riders with him had just delivered a herd of cattle to some buyers up in the Black Hills country. I soon after met his outfit, and I spent some of my time with them in their camp. The names of these men were Jim Berry, Bill Heffridge, Jack Davis, Sam Bass and John Underwood.

Joel Collins was an inveterate gambler as well as being a cowman. One evening after having been playing Spanish Monte, he came to me and asked me to loan him seventy-five dollars for a day or two. I did so, although it was about all I had, as I had spent a goodly portion of my wages for an outfit of good clothes, a saddle, bridle, and blankets, such as I could well be proud of. For some reason Jim Berry and I took a liking to each other, although there was a great difference in our ages. Little did I imagine that the outfit of which he was a member would soon be engaged in a train robbery such as they pulled off at a little station located about twelve miles west of Ogallala.

Just prior to the time when they robbed that train, I was in the parlor of the Rooney Hotel with Joel Collins and some of his crew when some shooting began in the street, and a bunch of cowboys rode by shooting "high, wide, and scattering." Miss Gast and another woman or two came into the parlor, very much frightened. Joel Collins, who was a very gentlemanly man to meet, assured the women, in his low, kindly voice, that there was little danger. "The boys were just having a little play spell, and would harm no one intentionally."

I never knew the facts connected with the train robbery, other than that the robbers left their camp, robbed the train, and were back in their camp when the news arrived in Ogallala that a train had been held up and robbed. It was one of the best through passenger trains on the Union Pacific Railway.

During the days when Joel Collins and his crew of "cowboys" were camped in Ogallala and no doubt making their plans for holding up the overland train at Big Springs, a gent from somewhere arrived in town with an outfit for starting a shooting gallery. He secured a space between two of the buildings, and some old railroad ties, with which he built butts which would stop the bullets fired from the small-bore target rifles at the targets he used. He made a charge: six shots for a quarter, and if a certain high score was made by a patron, a prize of six cigars was to be given him. When he had everything ready, he began to call the attention of the numerous men on the street by shouting, "Right this way, gentlemen, and show your skill!" Joel Collins and some of his outfit, also Luke Short and several others, sauntered up to look at the "Gent's layout." Someone in the bunch remarked that he could "bust a bull's-eye" as he produced a Colts "45" from somewhere about his waistband and cut loose at a target.

The proprietor of the shooting gallery voiced a protest, but in a very short time after that first shot a dozen or more guns were brought into action, the result being that within a few minutes' time the entire shooting gallery was wrecked, rifles and all, including many boxes of twenty-two caliber cartridges. The owner was then invited to have a drink. Seeing that he had taken his wares to the wrong market, he had the good sense to behave and act the part of a good fellow by taking a drink of lemonade "with a stick in it" and then buying drinks for all thirsty shooters. He made such a good impression on the boys that a collection was taken up and he was paid the sum his outfit had cost him and his fare on the train back to North Platte city.

Although almost every farmer raised a few cattle, the cattle industry, in the strictest sense, generally was carried on by large-scale operators. Initially the ranchers simply ran their cattle on the public domain, for which privilege they paid neither taxes nor rent. This range, of course, was theoretically "open"; but the cattlemen generally were able to control it as they saw fit, keeping out any who tried to encroach upon it. Particularly obnoxious were the "nesters" who ventured into the range country to take quarter-section homesteads, build their little soddies, and fence their land, thus breaking up the open range. Wire-cutters became standard equipment for the cowboys, and when harassment would not drive the homesteaders away, some of the ranchers resorted to stronger methods, including, on occasion, outright murder.

—Condensed from Olson's *History of Nebraska*

Necktie Parties

1. The Mitchell and Ketchum Tragedy

S. D. BUTCHER

In 1877 a number of settlers located on Clear Creek, near the western border of Custer County, among them Luther Mitchell and Ami Ketchum. Mitchell, who came from Merrick County, was a farmer about sixty-five years old, and married. Ketchum, formerly a blacksmith, had decided to become a farmer, although he still did some work at his trade for the neighbors. He was unmarried and lived with the Mitchells.

One of the wealthiest men in Nebraska at that time was I. P. Olive, who lived on Plum Creek east of what is now Callaway and owned many thousands of cattle that grazed over the South Loup valley and the adjoining country. While he was generous and courteous to those with whom he was on good terms, he was an implacable enemy and a dead shot. His brother Bob had left Texas under indictment for two murders; on Olive's advice, rather than stand trial, he had fled to Nebraska, where he assumed the name of Stevens. It was as Stevens that he was known during his career in Custer County.

Like other ranchers, I. P. Olive had suffered heavy losses from the depredations of the cattle thieves and had become the prime mover in an attempt to drive them out. The confession of one Manley Capel, arrested on a charge of cattle-stealing, seemed to implicate Ami Ketchum. When information obtained from a man named McIndeffer, who acted as a sort of spy for the cattlemen, also seemed to point to Ketchum, the Olives determined to arrest him. Notwithstanding the enmity that was known to exist between him and Bob Olive, Sheriff Anderson of Buffalo County deputized Olive to make the arrest.

On November 27, 1878, in the company of two rough and reckless cowboys, Barney Armstrong and Pete Beaton, and with McIndeffer as a guide, Bob Olive started for Clear Creek. Arriving in the vicinity of the Mitchell place, three of the men remained concealed behind a small hill while the fourth rode on to the homestead and asked to have his horse shod. Ketchum explained that he and the Mitchells were about to go to a neighbor's to return a borrowed animal. If the stranger would come back next day, he would do the job then.

The "stranger" reported back to Olive that their ruse to separate Mitchell and Ketchum had failed, and the four men now rode boldly up to the settlers. Mrs. Mitchell already had taken her seat in the wagon; her husband and Ketchum were occupied in tying the animal to the hind axle. When a short distance away, the posse made a dash, four abreast, and Bob Olive shouted to Ketchum to throw up his hands in the name of the law, at the same time presenting his revolver. Ketchum threw up his right hand with a Colt .45 in it, and both men fired. Several shots were exchanged, one of which broke Ketchum's left arm.

As soon as the shooting began, the elderly Mitchell grabbed his Winchester and took deliberate aim at Olive, who cried out: "My God, old man, don't shoot!" But it was too late. Olive reeled in his saddle and only the cowboys prevented him from falling. Supporting him on his horse, they wheeled and galloped away, followed by bullets from Ketchum's Winchester, which was loaded for him by a step-daughter of Mitchell. One of the bullets cut in two a scarf around Beaton's neck; the next shaved off his hat brim; and another went through Armstrong's foot. The wounded Bob Olive was taken to a dugout farther down the creek. There he made his will and sent for his wife. He died three days later.

At the news of the shooting there was great excitement among the cattlemen and cowboys. That same night a large force returned to the Mitchell homestead to wreak vengeance on the two men. Finding them gone, they set fire to the house and burned up the roof, that being the only combustible spot.

Mitchell and Ketchum had fled to their former home in Merrick County. After Ketchum's arm had been seen to and they had found a place of safety for Mitchell's family, the two men started to retrace their steps to Custer County, intending to give themselves up. Passing through Loup City, they consulted an attorney, who advised them to proceed no farther as they would surely be lynched. Finally, they decided to surrender to Sheriff E. P. Crew of Howard County and went to a homestead on Oak Creek where Crew and Sheriff William Letcher of Merrick County met them and took them into custody. Since Crew and Letcher would not assume the responsibility of taking the prisoners to Custer County and handing them over to the cowboys, Mitchell and Ketchum were taken to Buffalo County and lodged temporarily in the Kearney jail, in charge of Sheriff Anderson of that county.

They were held at first without legal authority, as Olive had given the warrant for their arrest, issued in Custer County, into the hands of Sheriff Barney Gillan of Keith County. Olive also had offered a $700 reward, and all four sheriffs were anxious to collect the money. A dispute arose over the division of the reward, but Olive declined to pay a cent of it until the prisoners were delivered to Custer County. Mitchell and Ketchum, meanwhile, had engaged Thomas Darnell and E. C. Calkins as counsel.

At last it was arranged among the sheriffs that Barney Gillan should take the prisoners back. Not knowing Gillan's desparate character, Darnell and Calkins consented on condition they be notified of the departure in time to accompany their clients. Nonetheless, on the forenoon of December 10, Gillan removed the prisoners by stealth, hustling them aboard the westbound emigrant train just as it pulled out. As soon as he learned this, Darnell telegraphed to Gillan at a station en route, asking him to hold the prisoners at Plum Creek until the next train. Gillan replied that he would do so. Darnell also telegraphed to a Plum Creek attorney, Captain C. W. McNamar, to keep an eye on things until he could get there.

The train pulled into Plum Creek at three in the afternoon. Waiting at the depot were Olive and a party with wagons into which Mitchell and Ketchum were loaded, in spite of Captain McNamar's protests. Convinced that they intended murder, McNamar followed the wagon train. When they saw they were being followed, the wagons separated, but McNamar kept after the one containing the prisoners until it became so dark that he lost the trail among the hills.

The two groups of the Olive party kept on all night, meeting on the South Loup about five miles from the Olive ranch. There Sheriff Gillan turned the prisoners over to Dennis Gartrell, Pedro Dominicus and Bion Brown. After the transfer had taken place, Gillan and another Olive man, Phil Dufrand, walked away a short distance while the party left with the prisoners. Their destination was a place known as the "Devil's Gap," in a wild canyon about halfway between the Loup and Wood River valley, some five miles southeast of where Callaway now stands.

Olive and Gartrell drove the wagon with the prisoners under a small elm tree. A couple of ropes were passed over a limb. Gartrell tied one around Ketchum's neck, and Pedro Dominicus fastened the other around the neck of Mitchell. Ketchum was drawn up first. Olive then took a rifle and shot Mitchell, after which he was drawn up until he dangled beside his companion.

When they were found the next afternoon, the bodies were frightfully burned, that of Ketchum still hanging to a limb, while that of Mitchell was resting on the ground, the rope by which he had been suspended having been either broken or burned in two. The men were handcuffed together, one of Mitchell's arms being drawn up to Ketchum by the handcuffs, the other burned off to the shoulder.

It probably will never be known who burnt the bodies. After the lynching, the Olive gang rode about a mile toward the Olive ranch, where two of the men were given fresh horses for the return to Plum Creek. As they had to pass the scene of the crime on the way, it is generally supposed that these two, crazed with drink, resolved to put the finishing touches on the terrible night's work by emptying their liquor flasks over the hanging bodies and setting them on fire. It does not appear that Olive was a party to, or had any knowledge of, this part of the crime.

The whole state was horror-stricken at the sickening details of the tragedy, but the well known desperate characters of most of the Olive men made the question of apprehending them a very serious one. The Kearney paper declared that there was one man in Nebraska who would see that the criminals were brought to justice, and the man was Judge William Gaslin. And, in fact, Judge Gaslin adjourned court in Sidney and hurried to Plum Creek to do so.

I learned [he wrote later] that all the officials of Custer County either belonged to, or were under the influence of the Olive gang, and as they could not be moved against by, or through, any of the officials of that county, I left on the first train for Kearney to look up the law and see if I, as an examining magistrate, could not issue warrants for their arrest. I soon satisfied myself I had the authority. After I had made out the warrants, I offered them to Sheriff James of Dawson County and Sheriff Anderson of Buffalo County, and both declined to take or serve them on account of a fear of their lives, as they said.

Previously, a citizen of Kearney, Mr. J. P. Johnson, had told me that if the officers were afraid to arrest the criminals he would furnish the men to do it. I now turned to him and deputized them then and there. There were five or six in all, one being Lawrence Ketchum, a brother of the man who was lynched. In strictest secrecy it was arranged for one group of deputies to arrest those of the gang who were at the Olive ranch. Another group boarded a freight at Kearney about midnight, arriving in Plum Creek a little before daybreak. The railroad people, who were in the secret, halted the train outside Plum Creek; the officers walked into town and arrested all the gang who were there.

When the other party arrived at the Olive ranch they found that the men they were after had fled the country. Among them was the delectable Barney Gillan, sheriff of Keith County, who had delivered Mitchell and Ketchum over to the murderers, and who secured the $700 blood money paid by Olive.

All kinds of lawyers, good, bad, and indifferent, were employed by the defense, some for ability and legal lore, and some to insult and bulldoze the court—for which they occasionally got fined for contempt. The trial had not progressed long before the prosecuting attorney privately informed me that he had made a secret arrangement with one of the prisoners, Bion Brown, to turn state's evidence. Brown was in jail with the other defendants, heard and knew all their plans, and daily communicated the same to General Dilworth, the prosecuting attorney. He said at one time that they talked of having their friends, who were in disguise in the town, shoot General Dilworth and me and have horses ready for the prisoners, who would escape in the excitement. I then gave orders for no one to occupy the gallery opposite where I sat, and I had a large number of bailiffs, secretly heavily armed, scattered over the court room. One day it was reported that a number of the Texas friends of the prisoners were lurking in the hills near the Platte, armed to the teeth and provided with good horses with which to swoop down on the court and liberate the prisoners. Other things came to the knowledge of Sheriff Lewis Martin of Adams County which induced him to procure a company of regulars from Omaha: the soldiers were tented on the public square of Hastings, opposite the hall where the court was being held.

The trial commenced in Hastings in April. An indictment was found against I. P. Olive and eleven others for the murder of Luther

Mitchell, and he and Fred Fisher were put on trial for the crime. There were about 100 witnesses, among them Captain McNamar and Phil Dufrand, one of the defendants, who, along with Bion Brown, turned state's evidence. The case was given to the jury on the evening of April 16, and a verdict was arrived at before morning to the effect that I. P. Olive and Fred Fisher were guilty of murder in the second degree. Judge Gaslin sentenced them to the penitentiary for the rest of their natural lives.

Immediately after the sentence of Olive and Fisher, their friends began proceedings for their release. The following year their efforts were successful, the supreme court handing down a decision to the effect that the prisoners had a right to trial in the county where the crime with which they were charged was committed. This not having been done, the prisoners were sent to Custer County for trial. The following shows the disposition of the celebrated Olive case:

I. P. Olive, W. F. Fisher, in custody of Sheriff O'Brien, the court finding no complaint on county docket and no complaining witnesses, the court orders that the prisoners be discharged till further proceedings can be had.
This 17th day of December, 1880.
E. J. BOBLITS, County Judge.

The decision of the supreme court of course put an end to the proceedings against the other defendants, but in the meantime most of them had been allowed to escape from the various jails in which they had been confined, and as far as we know Olive and Fisher were the only ones that ever had to do any time in the penitentiary. Four years after his release, I. P. Olive and his son William were in Colorado. One evening young Olive had a quarrel with a stranger over a game of billiards and was shot dead. The next day, while the elder Olive was participating in a roundup of some cattle, he got into a quarrel and was instantly killed while trying to draw his revolver.

Condensed from *Pioneer History of Custer County* (Broken Bow, Nebraska) 1901

According to a biographical sketch of Judge William Gaslin contributed to the *Pioneer History of Custer County* by his court reporter, F. M. Hallowell, the Judge was born in Kennebec County, Maine, in 1827. His boyhood was a rugged one: he worked on his parents' "sterile, rocky farm," hired out by the month to cut lumber, and went to sea, at first serving as cook. In 1852 he entered Bowdoin College from which he graduated in 1856, "having paid his own way by teaching school and earning money at anything he could do." While he read for the law in the chambers of an Augusta, Maine, judge, he continued to teach school to support his mother and younger brother and sister. After being admitted to the bar, he began to practice on his own, but in 1865 a disastrous fire destroyed most of the business part of Augusta, including Gaslin's office and all its contents, and he decided to go west.

Gaslin arrived in Omaha in March, 1868, remaining there until 1871, when he took a homestead in Harlan County, opening a law office at Lowell the following year. Business was booming in Lowell: as well as being the location of the United States land office, it was the terminus of the Texas cattle trail and the outfitting post for southwestern Nebraska and northern Kansas. However, in 1874 when the land office was moved to Bloomington and the railroad extended to Kearney, "like Carthage, Babylon, Nineveh, and Sandusky, Lowell fell."

In 1875 Gaslin was elected district judge on the Republican ticket. So successful was he in clearing out desperadoes that when he ran for a second term "he had five more votes than the Republican and Democratic vote combined." When Gaslin was first elected, his district embraced Webster, Adams, Buffalo, Sherman, and Custer counties, the unorganized county of Sioux, which was attached to Cheyenne County for judicial purposes, and all the state west of these counties, comprising at least one-half the territory of the state. Yet despite the size of this district and the fact that he traveled by wagon to reach two-thirds of the counties in it, he held court less than one-third of the time.

Judge Gaslin contended that the way to put a stop to crime was by dealing out "speedy, sure, and severe punishment to confirmed and abandoned criminals," and he had the nerve, strength, and iron will to execute the law without fear or favor. "His clean-cut, unsophisticated, blunt, crisp way of running his court and disposing of its business without any frills made him many enemies among the lawyers." The first three years he was judge he presided over twenty-six murder trials, and during his full sixteen years of office, over a total of sixty-eight. "The felony cases would have to be numbered by the hundred—in fact, the warden of the penitentiary regarded him as one of his most reliable patrons."

His last three terms as judge, Gaslin was nominated by both

parties and elected without opposition. On leaving the bench in 1892, he went to live in Kearney where he continued to practice law until his death on January 14, 1909.

> *The Whiton Hotel, a blood-red stucco building on a corner of Bassett's sandy main street, is a relic of the days when the town was less sedate. Known then as the Martin Hotel, it was frequented by the fast-shooting, hard-riding, hard-drinking Pony Boys, a notorious gang of outlaws led by Kid Wade and David C. (Doc) Middleton. . . . In 1884 vigilantes caught Wade east of Bassett. . . .*
>
> —*Nebraska: A Guide to the Cornhusker State*

2. The Lynching of Kid Wade

T. JOSEPHINE HAUGEN

ON THE morning of February 8, 1884, the little village of Bassett, Rock County, Nebraska, awoke to learn that it had been host to a lynching party during the night: the body of Kid Wade had been discovered hanging from a whistling post a mile east of town.

For a number of years the Niobrara country had been infested by gangs of horse thieves, one of the most active being headed by Doc Middleton, who was captured and sent to prison in 1879. At this time, Albert (Kid) Wade, probably the most notorious of his followers, eluded the arresting officers, but the law caught up with him in Iowa some months later. Late in 1884 he was back again along the Niobrara, resuming operations near Carns, where twenty-five or thirty horses were stolen. This was too much for "Cap" Burnham's Vigilance committee, and from that day on events moved rapidly.

A number of the gang were captured in Middleton's Canyon on Holt Creek, but Kid and Eph Weatherwax escaped. Tradition says that Kid and his companion drove the stolen stock north to the Black Hills country, then followed the White River to the Missouri, continuing down the latter to the mouth of the Niobrara, where they started back west on the north side of the Niobrara through the Indian country. Until now Kid had kept all the horses, but when he turned westward he began selling them along the way, and it was this that led to his capture. Among the stolen horses was one having a split hoof, a mark easily detected. He sold the horse to a farmer, but evidently saw his blunder almost immediately, for he soon returned and bought the horse back. The farmer's suspicions were naturally aroused, and he followed a short distance after to see what happened. Kid and a helper drove the horse out a mile or so, shot and buried it. The farmer notified officers, who dug up the horse and identified it as one of those stolen near Carns. From the description given them, they recognized Kid Wade as one of the two men. Kid was traced to Iowa where he was captured near Le Mars a couple of months later.

The O'Neill *Frontier* of January 24 stated that Kid had been arrested and was being held near there; and a dispatch of February 3rd reported him in custody of the "Regulators" near Red Bird where he was giving away all that he knew. It had been generally accepted that he was guilty, but not believed that he would squeal. However, when he learned that others were passing the buck to him, he made up his mind to tell and take his chances with the law.

From Red Bird, Kid was taken to the north side of the Niobrara, then west in the direction of Carns. He was in the custody of Henry Richardson and two other Vigilantes when they stopped at my father's for lunch. The question has frequently been asked whether Kid displayed any apprehension as to his possible fate. My mother said that the prisoner showed no concern; he sat playing with the doorknob and laughed freely as he answered the cross-examination by Richardson. To one query of Richardson's as to his whereabouts in the past, he gave the significant reply, "Yes, I've had many warm breakfasts at your house." Had Kid known that his father had disappeared some weeks earlier, he would probably have shown less fortitude. But he had been a fugitive for several months, and the chances are that he never heard his father had also been taken by the Vigilantes. While the belief was general that the elder Wade had been put to death, nothing definite was learned until the following summer when his body was discovered in a ditch near Ash Creek.

After lunch the four went on to Carns where they again crossed the Niobrara. That evening three other men came to ask accommodations for the night. They too were seeking Kid, but whether or not they belonged to the same Vigilante company was not learned. Vigilantes were no more welcome than horse thieves, but pioneer hospitality shared with all.

This news item, taken from the Long Pine *Journal* and reprinted in the Omaha *Herald* of February 13, 1884, throws much light on the subsequent move of the Vigilantes:

On Tuesday afternoon our town was set agog when Kid Wade, the notorious horse thief, was brought in by one Kinney, a sort of lieutenant to Capt. Burnham. The Kid is a young man of less than 25 years, of rather slender build, and medium height, a shambling gait, a low forehead and massive jaws, and a face inclined to angular and sharp features, on which the beard scarcely yet grows; in fact the general makeup of the man, and especially the facial expression is one more fitting a levee loafer or sneak thief than one denoting the higher aspirations of a horse thief.

The object of the Vigilantes in bringing the prisoner before the public was to give the people an opportunity to question him as to his treatment since capture, and thus refute the charges that have been made against the Vigilantes as to their "holding up" their prisoners and extorting confessions from them at the rope's end. The Kid said he had been well treated, his appearance before us was voluntary, and any statements he made were wholly of his own free will; that he had not been intimidated by threats of violence, or influenced by promise of leniency—but it was the only means left him of retaliating upon numerous parties who had been "rounded up" by Vigilantes, and who invariably strove to throw all blame on him. He denies any knowledge of a regularly organized band of thieves as has been so extensively believed and reported; and his statements, if true, seriously implicate several heretofore prominent citizens of this county as being in complicity with the thieves, and measures will soon be taken that will establish their innocence or prove their guilt.

Tuesday night another party of Vigilantes, controlled by one Capt. O'Neill, arrived from Holt County and relieved Kinney of the prisoner, saying they should take the Kid to Holt County, where he would be held for trial, before the proper authorities, and on Wednesday forenoon left Long Pine with their charge. The prisoner was taken to Morris Bridge, fifteen miles northeast, and turned over to the sheriff of Holt County, Ed Hersheiser, who was in waiting there, and who, employing two men to accompany him, started for O'Neill, arriving in Bassett about 7:30 p.m., and putting up for the night at Martin's Hotel.

Kid preferred lying on the floor on a blanket, to going to bed, and was so disposed in the same room where the sheriff and several other men kept vigil. About 12 in the night, a band of some dozen masked men entered the room with revolvers drawn and ordered "All hands up." In this position Kid was roused up and marched off; but knowing full well the penalty he would soon pay, he begged piteously with his captors for mercy, promising to lead a better life, using his best powers of utterance to gain a respite from the inevitable and ignominious fate he felt he was fast approaching. Appeals were made to deaf ears. He was taken away, the masked party when leaving the hotel forbidding any one to follow them under penalty of death. The next morning Kid was found hanging to a railway whistling post.

It is interesting to observe the route followed by the Vigilante committee in taking Kid Wade on his last ride. The arrest was presumably made for stealing horses in Brown County, and the proper place for holding trial would have been at Ainsworth, the county seat. O'Neill is east and a trifle south of Long Pine. It has always been the consensus of opinion that the devious route taken from Red Bird was for the sole purpose of giving the Vigilantes every possible chance of preventing legal trial.

The question has been properly raised: Why, if the law-abiding citizens felt that the law should have been permitted to take its course, was no investigation made as to the lynching of the Wades? Two replies are given. First, the family had a bad name, yet whether it was merited by others than Kid is doubted by most. Second, the country was sparsely settled, and decent people were thankful at being permitted to go about their accustomed duties, hoping that if they attended strictly to their own affairs they would not be molested. Those familiar with local history have always maintained that both the Wades were put out of the way, not for stealing, but because they knew too much about some of the Vigilantes.

Condensed from *Nebraska History*, XIV (Jan.–March, 1933)

———————

Judge Lewis Cannenburg wrote the following account of events following the discovery of Kid Wade's body:

. . . the coroner at Ainsworth was notified by telegraph and came down by team before noon. The body of Kid Wade was then cut down and brought to the store and laid on the counter and there the inquest was held. The hands of the corpse were tied together, and a common halter rope around his neck. The corpse was frozen stiff and hard as a rock. After the inquest was over, the store people took the corpse and laid it on a pile of cord wood in front of the store. The coroner informed me by virtue of my office as justice of the peace and overseer of the poor he must leave the disposition of the body to me. . . . I applied to Mr. Martin for the privilege of taking the body to his house previous to burial, but he demanded $10, and as I had no authority to pay $10, I declined. There was then only my own house left, and as my better half was opposed, I requested Fred Kramer, the constable, to take the remains to my barn and watch over it until it was buried, which was done.

When the train arrived from the west the next morning, the passengers had a view of the dead outlaw, and all wanted a piece of rope he was hung with as a keepsake. The rope was cut in small pieces . . . and when that was all gone the boys took all the halter ropes and cut them up for relics. The next day the noted horse thief was buried on top of Bassett Hill.

—*Nebraska History*, XIV (Jan.–March, 1933)

July 4, 1874. On the train I met the once-notorious General O'Neill who led the great invasion of Canada which ended so suddenly in a most inglorious fizzle. O'Neill is a fine, handsome and very gentlemanly fellow of about thirty-five, and he is now engaged in the laudable endeavor to draw some of his countrymen from the temptations and poverty of eastern cities to the purer life and eventual comfort and plenty of homestead settlers in the Far West. An Irish colony under his auspices is expected to settle in Holt County, far up towards the sources of the Elkhorn.

—Edwin A. Curley, *Nebraska, Its Advantages, Resources and Drawbacks*

O'Neill

ARTHUR F. MULLEN

I FOUND the West in a long Nebraska twilight. A nine-year-old explorer, eighty years after Lewis and Clark had passed that way, I stood on the short-grassed hillock and saw for the first time the vast immensity of the wild, wide land spread out beneath a darkening blue sky that lifted into infinity. On the horizon hung the smoke of an Indian tepee. Under my feet ran the trail to the Black Hills. Before me, on that high plateau between the winding ribbon of the Elkhorn and the sharp cleft of the Niobrara, widened toward the rising sandhills a vista of utter, absolute space, miles and miles of limitless, unfettered prairie. No fences. A boundless empire, owned by no man and every man. The West!

O'Neill, I came to know later, was an outward sign of an inward urge. Every western town in the early eighties was a symbol of the desire of man for wider opportunity, for greater freedom. In O'Neill the desire was intensified by the racial elements of the little community. Directly founded in 1874 by General John O'Neill (no one called him anything else, although the Army records set him down as Colonel), the town in the Elkhorn Valley had some of the characteristics of that scholarly dreamer. It was, drunk or sober, always a little headlong. It was always essentially and preponderantly Irish; but its Celtic undertone always remained an undertone. Irish of birth or blood its people might be, but first, last and always they were loyal to the nation that promised and gave them the liberties which they or their ancestors had been denied.

They might, and did, stir to Irish causes. No town of General O'Neill's founding could do less than that. O'Neill had been associated with the leaders of the 1848 uprising in Ireland and had fled to the United States with Thomas Francis Meagher, afterward to be territorial governor of Montana. He had told his close friend President Andrew Johnson of his plans to lead a raid into Canada, conquer the Dominion, and hold it in order to force England to give freedom to Ireland. And O'Neill did have the satisfaction, at the battle of Ridgway, of seeing the backs of the red-coated Queen's Own as they retreated before his Feinians. But the expedition ended in defeat when the British ambassador served notice to the President that England would regard as cause for war the presence of American citizens in the Feinian army. Johnson had to threaten O'Neill with prosecution for treason, but he let him escape without punishment.

O'Neill then went on lecture tours to promote the freedom of Ireland, and out of his campaigning had come the Irish Colonization Society. He had come by wagon more than a hundred miles from the end of the railroad, and had located the town, first known as O'Neill's place, then as O'Neill City, finally as O'Neill. I never saw him, for he died of pneumonia in Omaha and was buried there before I was a part of his community; but the influence of his adventurous personality remained strong. But—not in spite of but because of—our boiling Irish blood, we children of immigrants were American. Better than those who had never known persecution for faith or for race, we knew what freedom meant.

In those earliest years we Mullens were a fairly self-centered, self-sufficient family. Although we inevitably had the sense of struggle that is part of all new country, we lived in comfort. Our house grew from a four-roomed cabin to a larger dwelling. Potatoes and turnips and other root vegetables stocked the cellar through the winters. Apples were plentiful. Mother's foresight kept us with enough fresh cows to provide us, even through the hardest winters, with milk and butter. Our clothing was homemade, but always warm enough or cool enough. In some respects, we were as comfortable as we had been in the softer civilization we had left. It was only in contact with the outside world of the prairies and the hills that we felt the force of our transplanting.

In time, as a boy does, I found the capacities for pleasure which a town can offer a country lad. We went to Mass every Sunday in decorous procession. When Mass was over, I explored the possibilities of the town as I waited for Father and Mother. It was a wide-streeted town of possibly less than a thousand inhabitants, as western as sage brush, swept by hot winds in summer and cold winds in winter, set on top of the world there on that high tableland, and endowed with that spirit which has made it one of the biggest little places in the West. I don't know whether men brought it to the place or whether the place gave it to men. To far more than to me, though, O'Neill has always been a strangely thrilling field of effort and adventure.

In my early teens life moved swiftly and violently. Desperadoes still rode through the streets. Vigilantes still sought horse thieves and cattle thieves. Murders were done on the wooden sidewalks. Sheriffs took their lives in their hands when they set out to do their duties. I was not above hoping to see some of these major excitements, but, waiting for them, I contented myself with minor but more permanent means of entertainment and listened to the town sagas of hotel and restaurant and drugstore.

O'Neill had a passion for information upon current events. The men who could read pored over newspapers, chewing the cud of reflection before they gave editorial pronouncement. Those who couldn't read found others willing to read for them. McKenna, the blacksmith, who was so deaf from the clanging on his anvil that he could scarcely hear, came out from his smithy night after night to sit, with cupped ear, listening to Jack Murphy. "Hi-hear," he would shout in approval or disapproval as Jack, with Irish deviltry, spun out yarns that had never seen print.

I found a gold mine of unbought and discarded reading matter down in the basement of the town drugstore. The record of events in the world beyond the horizon always fascinated me. Always, as I read, the bugles of that world sounded across the wide slopes of the cattle country.

Cattle pasturage the short-grass district was, and is again; but in the years we lived on the ranch beside the Blackbird, the home-steaders and other settlers strove to make it the kind of farm country they had known in the East. With the rest of our community we planted wheat and barley and rye, and waited for rains that came too seldom and grasshoppers that came too often. At Mother's in-sistence we had some cattle, thereby conforming to the real character of the land on which we lived and forestalling the disasters which sometimes overwhelmed the region. No one could miss, though, the destiny of doubt that was and is a farmer's life in the West; the long days and weeks and months of drought; the sky a great blue bowl of endless sunshine, the wind a never-ending roar. There were two kinds of years, two only, wet and dry, and the dry far outnumbered the others. Nothing, not foresight nor thrift, could provide against them. We were creatures of the sun and wind, fighting conditions which no man in his sober senses should have fought.

Our fight was not wholly in vain. If the land won back, in time, its old and elemental usage, we had in the meantime molded our own characters. If we couldn't raise wheat in that country, we could raise men, and by God, we did! It was cattle country—Holt County is still one of the first ten counties of the United States in cattle breeding—and cattle country, in the eighties, was the last great American frontier.

Bull trains to the Black Hills plodded over the road before us. There were three points of freighting to Deadwood, but the trail from Fort Pierre ran through hostile Indian lands, the trail from Sidney through Fort Robinson meant a longer rail haul from Omaha, and so the trail from O'Neill, longest of them all, remained the most used until that time when all trails closed with the building of the railroad into the hills.

Law came to the Blackbird long before enforcement officers appeared. In a land and a time of no fences, men of the cattle country had to guard their stock. When the outlaws began to band together for theft, the ranchers had to band together for their own protection. John Hopkins and John A. Robertson were both declared vigilantes, but neither of them ever attended any of the necktie parties with which the honest citizens sometimes defended law and order. Both Hopkins and Robertson were great constructive forces in the neighborhood, and Robertson was afterward one of the leaders of the Nebraska legislature. A big man, always black-shirted, with a bristling black moustache, he looked like all the pictures of all the western sheriffs. He could have taken on a gang of outlaws at any time; but the outlaws saw John coming and let him alone. In his home on the range he raised twelve children and acquired through them enough college diplomas to paper the walls, but his own accomplishment has remained an ability to shoot birds on the wing straighter and quicker than Buffalo Bill ever did at a moving target.

Thieves—cattle- and horse-stealers—were so common that almost any night we might hear their whistled signals to each other. That was, I think, why Mother hated to hear any one of us whistle. Too often she must have come close to danger when, in Father's absence, she went out at night to the barn. Fearful she must have been at times, but never, no matter what happened, did I ever hear her express fear. She was no born pioneer. Back in Canada all her interest had been in the gentler ways of living, but on the Nebraska prairie she met each day and night with high courage and an initiative which set herself and everyone else working at something. In time there were nine of us children. For every one of us she found a task and a way to interest us in it.

Every Sunday, rain, shine, snow—except in the week of the Great Blizzard—we drove, usually in the wagon, fourteen miles to church. Our mother went fasting—and Mass was at half-past ten and she'd been up for hours—and came home fasting. Even before O'Neill became consciously devotional, Mother observed all the feasts and fasts, the rules and regulations of our faith with the same exactitude she would have exercised in a grown city.

No task of the many hard labors on the ranch was ever too much for her. "I love the cattle," she would say. "There's nothing I wouldn't do for the men who take care of cattle."

Father bought and sold horses. Most of them were the wild horses brought in by the Flanigans and Wilcoxes from Nevada. All of them were devils, stamping, rearing, biting, snorting, roaring brutes which resisted breaking. They would rise on their hind feet so suddenly it was a struggle to hang on or to slide off in such a way as not to be killed. They would strike out at a thrown rider and kick at anyone or anything near them. But they were our means of livelihood, our means of locomotion, our way to a wider freedom, and we had to conquer them. There was hardly a lad in Holt County who couldn't do as well as the riders of the rodeo do now.

Southward and westward from O'Neill ran the sandhills; cattlemen had already found that the short grass, growing thick as moss upon its more sheltered surfaces, fattened the cattle as did no other grazing in the West. Year after year shrewd Texans had been driving their herds up the Chisholm Trail and from Ogallala into the valleys of the great sandy spaces which spread across Nebraska from the Platte to the Niobrara and from the Fort Robinson trail to the Elkhorn. Jim Dahlman, afterward mayor of Omaha, drove herds from El Paso.

Already the valleys within sight and sound of our claim were feeding thousands of cattle for the Chicago market. Great droves of cattle, beef to the heels, went toward the railroad. With them went cowboys, tight-lipped, grim-eyed, while duty held them, but ready to celebrate as soon as the job was done.

There were always saloons where whisky of all varieties might be bought and consumed. The West was won on whisky. Cattlemen, railroad builders, miners, freighters, all had to meet, as part of their lives, the high chance of death from violence of wind or weather or their fellow men. If they fortified their bodies or lightened their spirits by liquor, the frontier they were pushing forward neither abused nor excused them for the habit. O'Neill accepted the custom, and put the fallen brothers to bed.

Wilder revelry than any O'Neill countenanced went westward with the railway builders. The End of Steel was always a place of drinking and carousing. The railhead at the Thatcher Cut was, for the two years of its existence, as notorious throughout Nebraska and Dakota Territory as Dodge City was to Kansas or Virginia City to Montana. There desperadoes from all over the country, fancy women from Chicago and Omaha and St. Paul, deserting soldiers from farther forts, gamblers and tricksters, sought to take money away from the railroad builders. A tent city—its tents had no floors—it flourished while the builders sought to bridge the swift flow of the Niobrara. Murders were frequent. Once a gambler killed a woman in a tent saloon. Her body lay there all day till some of the boys from the railroad camp paid a man to bury her. Later her brother came to take her back to Chicago, but nothing was ever done to her murderer. Then one day steel ran from wooded slope to wooded slope of the river, and the settlement had gone like tumbleweed on the plains.

I used to walk, seven miles each way, to Eden Valley and back (arriving home at three A.M.) to be present at entertainments there. Hamilton Hall, who directed them as a sideline to his teaching, was establishing the sort of rural theater which is now a matter of wider experiment. He taught us our lines, devised costumes and make-up, and directed our performances.

There were sadder times, too, when we rode long miles. Death comes often on the frontier. Always strangely dramatic to us Irish, it must have struck those of us on the frontier with terrific impact; for, in spite of all the drinking there might be in the town saloons, I never but once saw any drinking in any place of death—and that was at the wake of a woman of ninety-three.

The Great Blizzard of 1888 marked the end of the heyday of the

cattle men. Stock, the staple of the Niobrara Valley, had been destroyed almost beyond belief. Ranchers who had been struggling toward a little profit were penniless. Although they held power on the
farther ranges beyond the turn of the century, their undisputed
sway had come to a crisis. Already in the sandhills they were putting
up fences against the coming of the homesteaders; but month after
month they kept coming northward and westward, pushing out upon
the ranges of the sandhill valleys, bringing in their wake schools and
churches and courts and law officers.

The metamorphosis of the town was Father Cassidy's work. He
found it one of the wildest settlements of a wild frontier. By force
of personality, fortified by ecclesiastical authority, he subdued tur-
bulence, established order, and substituted ambition for ebullience.
A tall, grave man always garbed in sober black, he walked the streets
of the town with a dignity which subdued his more pugnacious
parishioners and aroused the pride of his quieter ones. He was the
first priest in the country west of the Missouri to establish First
Friday devotions. He was a builder of brick and stone, but he was,
still more, a builder of men and women. His only other pastorate had
been Laramie, but his manner was that of places far from the frontier;
Richelieu never wore his red robe with more elegance than Father
Cassidy wore his black cassock.

We did not yet know in those days of our young endeavor that the
world of our childhood had gone. Already the valleys of the Elkhorn
and Niobrara had been peopled. Sitting Bull had gone from Fort
Randall to the Grand River and to death. No more ghost dancers
swayed on the Pine Ridge or the Rosebud. The eagle-bone whistles
sounded no more. No more bullwhackers popped their buckskin
whips over the heavy oxen of the bull trains. No more coaches went
to the Hills.

The Kinkaiders were still ten years away, but the old free range
was gone. Railroads spanned the rivers. The great herds from Texas
no longer darkened the hills. Cowboys no longer drove, singing,
from El Paso to Ogallala, from Ogallala to the Missouri. The half-
century of the cattle kings was ended, yet as the short but golden
age of Pericles influenced the culture of the world, so the fenceless
era of the American West had marked the minds of men. Fences
might now restrict western prairie and plain and valley, but no
fences yet restrained the horizon of the minds of the western men.

Condensed from *Western Democrat*, Wilfred Funk, 1940

II. Family Album I

The history of every country begins in
the heart of a man or a woman.
  —Willa Cather, *O Pioneers!*

"Native adults," Edwin A. Curley reported eighty years ago, "are scarce in Nebraska. It was unlawful to be born there before May 23, 1854, when the territory was first opened for settlement." . . . *But once the stork had received permission to land, the family doctor became an indispensable figure on the prairie scene.*

Prairie Doctor

1. The Doctor

FRANCIS A. LONG

ON JUNE 27, 1882, I came to Madison, Nebraska, a county-seat town said to have a population of one thousand, though it never seemed to me it had half that number of inhabitants. I had friends living there from whom I had learned that the place had but one physician, and this decided me. My colleague was the community idol; nonetheless, he was not anxious to have a competitor. Could he have foreseen how little competition my advent would bring, he would not have worried.

During my first summer's residence, a new brick bank building was erected, and I rented the old one for an office. There were three rooms, the rental being seven dollars a month. As soon as my income justified the expenditure, I purchased an adjustable office and examining chair—the latest model, ornamented with tassels. My armamentarium consisted of a pocket medicine case containing twelve remedies, namely: Bismuth, Dover's Powder, Morphine, Podophylin, Compound Cathartic Pills, Calomel, Mercury with Chalk, Bromide of Potassium, Tincture Aconite, Fluid Extract of Ergot, Tincture Belladonna, Tincture Hydrastis. I had a pocket case of instruments, a fever thermometer, and an obstetric forceps. An esteemed friend in town made me an oilcloth roll to wrap the forceps. My library consisted of seven medical books.

My father had promised me a young horse, but when I claimed it he substituted an old pony that I had once owned which was subject to heaves. Only the direst necessity forced me to accept the nag. I soon disposed of the pony and got a better one.

Practicing medicine pony-back or horseback required a pair of saddlebags. A saddlebag consisted of two leather pouches fitted with compartments for bottles, connected together with a heavy, broad leathern strap which fitted across the saddle and held the medicine pouches. After a year my saddlebag career ended, and I purchased an old open buggy from a liveryman. Gradually I acquired a second pony and drove a span. Prosperity of a sort! Eventually I owned two spans of horses and physician phaetons which I drove until the automobile age appeared.

Many times during the first years I would gladly have quit and taken any kind of a job if I could have paid my obligations and left honorably. In my third year I collected about a thousand dollars; the fourth year about twelve hundred; the sixth twenty-one hundred. One reason for this slow progress was that at one time there were five physicians in the town and business was much divided; but the principle reason for lack of clientele was, I suspect, inherent in myself. I was green, countrified, and without a practical knowledge of the world and its ways.

Just seven years after I located, the pioneer competitor moved to the Puget Sound country. My opportunity had come, and my business increased a thousand dollars during the next year. I had arrived!

The practice of medicine that prevailed in the early eighties presented many difficulties. Epidemics were prevalent, for there were no means of preventing them. The first autumn (1882), there was an epidemic of diphtheria, dreaded scourge of the pioneer. I was employed to care for several families, and fortunately my first patients recovered. I thought I had some pretty severe cases, but they may not have been so severe as I thought for I had never seen a case before. My competitor lost several cases. In desperation, on the theory that the new doctor could do no worse, several families changed physicians, so that before I realized it, I was busy in the midst of an epidemic.

Tracheotomy was an operation in vogue in laryngeal diphtheria. If the patient failed to breathe when the windpipe was opened, one of the things recommended in extreme cases was to lay a handkerchief over the wound made in the trachea and, with the lips, suck the secretions from the larynx. I did that once and succeeded in getting the patient to breathe. I told this experience to an Omaha surgeon, who said that one night he was taken out in the country to a similar case. He aspirated the trachea with his lips. On the way home he reflected on what he had done and was prompted to beg a chew of tobacco from the driver's plug and on reaching town he indulged freely in *spiritus frumenti* as an antidote!

Those were the days when sulphur and molasses was given as a blood purifier; when asafoetida was placed in a little bag and hung around the neck to prevent contagious diseases; when bacon rind or bread-and-milk poultice or possibly fresh warm cow manure as a poultice was used to "ripen" boils; when a red flannel or kerosene-soaked rag or fried onions was swathed around the throat for sore throat; when onion syrup was made for a cough, and so on.

The early settlers followed the water courses. Where streams were not near at hand, they dug open wells of a few feet depth for water. Those who came a little later had to take the upland prairie, and their wells also tapped the upper or surface streams of water. Typhoid fever, being for the most part a water-borne disease, became very prevalent. The cattle yards were close to the open wells for convenience, and surface contamination was inevitable.

In the later eighties the two physicians then occupying the field must have had seventy-five cases of typhoid to treat one fall. Whole families were stricken, one after another. I was in charge of one family consisting of father, mother, and ten children, all of whom contracted the fever except the mother and nursing babe. The father was one of the last to develop the fever, and as his was a mild case, he had much time for reflection and speculation as to the cause of the epidemic. A deeply religious man, he wondered why the Lord had visited this scourge upon his family. He asked me what could have caused this plague. I told him that his open well located by the cattle yard must be at fault. At first he could not believe it, but after he had recovered he cleaned out the well, bringing up rotten corn cobs and corn husks, dead rats and mice and a dead rabbit!

We had no quarantine laws and regulations, and the public knew almost nothing about contagion and infection. It was the custom of pioneers to go to the assistance of their sick neighbors. In the eighties the Odd Fellows had a provision in their by-laws that members, listed alphabetically, were called in turn to "sit up" with sick members. Thus a person ill with typhoid and perhaps in delirium had a different person "sit up" with him each succeeding night. A worse method of providing nursing care for the sick could not have been devised.

The fees in the early days were one dollar for town visits, day or night. Country calls were made on the basis of fifty cents a mile. Theoretically, one was supposed to charge something extra for visits, but this was rarely done. Confinements were cared for at the flat rate of ten dollars, whether in town or country; but instrumental or manual deliveries were charged extra. Physicians were rarely called to confinements in the country unless there was trouble in the delivery.

Very few physicians ever get overpaid or receive more than they charge. I have always cherished one exception. A young man and wife acquired 1,000 acres of land in the community, went there and improved it by the most extensive tree-planting program ever undertaken in the county. I attended the young woman in confinement, and when about to leave, the husband asked for the bill. I told him ten dollars. He said, "That is not enough," wrote out a check which I stuck in my pocket without looking at it. When, later, at home I looked at it, it read "Fifteen" dollars. This is perhaps a small thing to publish, but it made a lasting impression on me.

When a doctor was called to a patient, even though it was diphtheria, pneumonia, or typhoid, many persons expected the doctor to leave enough medicine to last for the cure. They would tell the doctor, "We will let you know how we get along." It took some argument to convince people that the patient needed daily attention.

Rural Nebraska, like the rest of the nation, had not become hospital-conscious when I came to the state to practice. The physician of the eighties had to be truly an all-around man. I remember the case of a man who was accidentally shot. The bullet entered above and to the outer side of the knee and lodged below the knee in the soft tissues of the posterior surface of the leg. The near-by physician first called was afraid to attempt removal of the bullet and advised leaving it. Not satisfied, the patient had me called to go some twenty miles to remove the bullet, an operation easily accomplished. The first physician merely lacked the nerve.

About 1883 or 1884, I assisted a railroad surgeon in a neighboring town in amputating a trainman's foot in the roundhouse. A table was improvised by using a door laid on blocks, and hot water obtained from the engine boiler. The foot, which had been caught under a car wheel, was amputated. The next day the surgeon put the patient on the train and took him to the home of his parents.

Without a doubt the very first operation for the removal of the appendix ever performed in north Nebraska was done by Dr. F. L. Frink of Newman Grove, Nebr., and myself on December 18, 1892, at a farm home sixteen miles in the country. I was called to see the patient, a sixteen-year-old girl, in consultation; a previously made diagnosis of appendicitis was confirmed, and operation advised and agreed upon.

The kitchen table was requisitioned for an operating table. Basins were scarce at the home, but several earthenware milk crocks were sterilized by boiling in a wash boiler. The instruments were sterilized by boiling. Sheets, towels, and gowns were sterilized by dry heat in the oven of the kitchen stove. Dr. Frink had been gold medalist in surgery in medical school, and naturally I supposed he would do the operation; but he insisted (no doubt in deference to my seniority in years) that I do it. He gave the anaesthetic and also assisted. The appendix lay under the incision made when the abdomen was opened—and this may have saved us some embarrassing moments, for has not one heard of cases of young surgeons hunting for the appendix in vain?

This case demonstrates a bit of courage of two frontier general practitioners at a time but a few years after the first operations were done by specialists in the larger cities. Emergency surgery had to be done in all kinds of homes, including sod houses, many of them under the most unsanitary conditions. But with it all, if operators were fairly well grounded in pathological anatomy and had some manual dexterity, the results were satisfactory—particularly when practical antisepsis was employed.

If we pioneer country doctors struggled along performing our surgery in homes, it should be remembered that even the larger cities had only meager hospital facilities at this time. Not only had the laity not become hospital-conscious, but early-day surgeons did not feel the need of hospitalization. That is a development which has come largely since the turn of the century.

2. The Doctor's Wife

MRS. FRANCIS A. LONG

THE PIONEER doctor in his frock coat and impressive beard was usually a young man—as were most of the pioneer settlers. After graduation, he selected a location, hung out his sign with the hard-won "M.D." attached, gave it an approving look, and waited for business.

Of course he had a best girl by this time, and he convinced himself that if he could persuade her of the great future that lay ahead of him in his profession, she might be willing to get married at once and share with him this dream of the future. The bride of that day usually brought to her new home the bedding, linens, dishes, the little silver her friends gave her, good clothes, and perhaps a little money with which to buy furniture. This was fortunate, for in many cases the doctor had not been able to repay the money he borrowed to put himself through college.

There were few families of means, and we shared what we had. We all had babies, took care of them ourselves, made their clothes, washed, ironed, cooked, baked, scrubbed, and had time to visit the neighbors. We knew everybody in town, exchanged patterns and recipes, taught in Sabbath school, attended church services, Missionary society, Aid society, held bazaars, and gave church dinners and dime socials. The doctor's wife was usually the center of all these activities. She was held in high esteem by all, and much was expected of her. The Germans addressed her as "Frau Docterin."

The first ten years for a pioneer doctor were years of pinching financially. I recall how ten days before the stork visited our home for the first time, we did wish someone would pay his bill so we could buy the necessary flannels for the little one. These had to come by mail from Omaha, over a hundred miles away! Finally a bill was paid. The flannels were ordered and arrived on a late train on Saturday evening. The child was born before five o'clock on Monday morning. If we never before believed in Providence, we learned to do so then.

A store building around the corner from our home was completed, and the church we attended celebrated by giving a big supper in this building on our first wedding anniversary. We did not have the fifty cents to pay for the supper, so we stayed home. The baby girl had been added to the family, and this gave us the excuse for not being there—"We could not take her out and we had no one with whom to leave her." I believe that was one of the hardest trials I ever had to face—married a year and not even fifty cents to pay for the church supper.

The office in the home in those early years was a necessity, for the wife could act as office girl—not that there was so much business, but to hang on to every bit of it. Families came to the office early in the afternoon, expecting to get attention at once and return to their homes in time to do the chores on the farm. The doctor might be out on a ten-mile trip. You knew he could not be home before five, but you told them to make themselves comfortable; he would be along about four. Custom demanded you stay at home with them—help to amuse the children, and keep the father from fretting too much because it was getting late. No doctor at four and none at four-thirty! By this time you had on hand a restless man and woman, and it was your job to keep them from going to the other doctor. Finally, after an hour of watching down the street, the doctor's team was seen driving toward home. Social obligations and house-work were forgotten in that hour, but you held the patient, only to learn they were a family that never paid!

My husband was the medical member of the Commission of In-sanity, and it was customary for the sheriff to bring such cases to the office. About ten o'clock one morning the sheriff walked in with a man and told me to "watch the man and not let him get away." Then the sheriff departed. I was dumbfounded. Two babies in the kitchen and an insane man in the office! We sat and talked awhile, then I suggested that he lie down and rest until the doctor arrived. He gave me a sharp look and said, "If you do what I tell you, then I will do what you want." My heart beat wildly. I had pre-viously locked the outside office door. I thought of those babies, then screwed up my courage and laughingly said, "All right, I'll do it, but I would like to get you a cup of coffee." When I brought the coffee he seemed to think he had played a great joke on me, drank his coffee and we chatted another half hour. It was an immense re-lief when I saw the doctor drive up in front of the house.

Occasionally people asked me for some of those "pink pills" they had been getting for fever. They thought all I had to do was to go to the medicine shelf and shake a few pills out of the bottle. But the only remedy I ever handed out was earache medicine. I knew where this was kept, because I often used it for our own children.

My husband and I realized that unless you got the money when a man came to pay, the bill might be forgotten, so from the very first I had access to the business records and could tell a man the amount of his bill in a few minutes. In the early days, foreigners hesitated to pay a woman, but as time went on they grew accustomed to American ways, and paid me without hesitation.

Operations were done in the patients' homes, and all laundry was brought to our home, surgical aprons, sheets, towels, and every-thing. Even if the operation occurred Saturday noon, the laundry had to be done that afternoon, regardless of previous plans, for it might be needed again before the regular Monday washday. More-over the soiled garments required attention at once. In case of a fracture, the bandages were laundered—ironed—and then yards and yards of bandages rolled over the knee on a clean towel. Later a small hand roller lightened the work.

Consultations with doctors from other towns were hailed as events. It was usually arranged for the morning so that the consultant could come back with the doctor for dinner. When possible the wife came along and the women enjoyed the visit together.

It was sometimes necessary for the doctor's wife to arrange to send out fresh teams to cross-roads to meet him to save driving to town and then back again over part of the same road. It was a wonderful day for us when rural telephones were installed, but at times it had its drawbacks. I recall one case in particular when my husband had a call to an obstetric case in which he was very much interested, for it was his first contact with that family. I called and called but got no response, for this family was on a party line. I could hear them discuss a new apron pattern, the setting of hens, and what they were preparing for dinner. Finally, when I was able to get my party, I was told he had gone four miles further north to see another case. Another doctor was called to the obstetrical case.

I think back on those days and wonder how a young mother could possibly do all that I did. In the midst of washing, ironing, baking, or cleaning, that office doorbell sounded, and everything was dropped. I smoothed my hair, straightened my apron, and dashed for the office to receive the patients. These constant interruptions delayed my housework, particularly on Saturday, when the farmers came to town. One of my daughters recalls many Saturday afternoons when she was bathed and dressed and placed upon the kitchen table away from mischief, while mother scrubbed the kitchen floor and watched the evening supper cook on the one-burner kerosene stove at the same time! That kitchen table was a treasure and could tell some tales of pioneer surgery if it would. It was six feet long and about two and one-half feet wide and had been the all-important piece of furniture in my husband's first office, where it served as operating table or patient's couch, etc., as occasion demanded. When he reached the stage of financial prosperity which enabled him to buy a proper office examination chair, I was only too glad to have this as an addition to my meagre kitchen furniture.

Condensed from *A Prairie Doctor of the Eighties,* Huse Publishing Co., 1937

3. Country Doctor, 1950

EVEN in the age of specialization in medicine, three-fourths of the people in the U.S. are born, live and die under the care of a general practitioner, their family doctor. In country districts the proportion is far higher. There, the relationship between the ailing and their doctors has not changed much since homesteading days. But there has been a great change in country doctors themselves.

Last week, the change was evident in the tiny (pop. approx. 1,000) crossroads town of Arnold, in the rolling sand-hill country of western Nebraska. Dr. E. (for Elmer) Howard Reeves and his partner, Dr. Robert A. McShane, received 300 patients in their office, made 40 house calls, delivered four babies, performed two operations. All the babies were born and both the operations were performed in Arnold's ten-bed private hospital. None of the cases was medically unusual, but this kind of service was the reason for the doctor's being. At 30, Dr. Reeves is the senior member of a two-man medical team which is responsible for the health of about 5,000 people scattered within 45 miles of Arnold.

Outwardly, the routine of Arnold's doctors is much like that of the traditional horse-and-buggy doctor. Up every day of the year by 7:30, Dr. Reeves takes time for a good breakfast with his pretty brunette wife Jean and their children, Steven, 5, and Pamela, 3. By 9 o'clock he is off to the partners' office on Highway 92, half a block from Main Street, where blonde Mrs. Audleye Nelson, receptionist and bookkeeper, gives him a list of the day's first house calls. These, with morning hospital calls, afternoon office hours and after-dinner calls, keep him busy until 11 P.M. And nearly every night he has to get up and dress to go to a patient's home or the hospital.

Also like the oldtimers' is Dr. Reeves's relationship with his patients. He knows most of them by their first names. (Nobody, not even his wife, now calls him anything but "Doc.") Born & raised on a farm near Madison in eastern Nebraska, Doc Reeves can talk with his patients about stock and crops, fodder and weather. In his office or at the hospital he can hear the shrill yipping of cowboys as they drive a herd of red Herefords through the middle of town to a feed lot. Many of his cases are cowboys with broken bones or farm boys with mangled hands.

Where Dr. Reeves and his partner, roly-poly Dr. McShane, 26, differ from oldtime physicians is in their methods. They carry few pills in their black bags, and rarely dispense medicine. (Their patients give the local drugstore $12,000 in prescription business a year.) In two years Dr. Reeves has never delivered a baby at home, nor performed surgery outside the little yellow stucco hospital on the edge of town.

As he sees it, the days of appendectomies on farmhouse kitchen tables are gone, and good riddance. "You can train the public to plan in advance and get to the hospital," says Dr. Reeves. "It's better for the patient and better for the doctor. In this day & age, there isn't much point in practicing under pioneer conditions."

To get farther away from pioneer conditions, Dr. Reeves has lent the hospital an electrocardiograph. Last week the partners installed a $5,000, hospital-sized X-ray machine to replace a portable model they had been using. Come spring, they will start building an office of their own to replace their present rented quarters (which replaced a wooden shack where Dr. Reeves had to practice at first). It will be big enough to serve as an out-patient clinic. In it will be still more modern equipment, notably diathermy and basal metabolism machines. ("With those," says Dr. Reeves, "we'll have all the essentials.") Finally, there will be facilities for a skilled laboratory technician to make the countless tests demanded by modern diagnostic methods.

Dr. Reeves's objective is clear: "We want to be able to practice medicine in such a way that fewer & fewer people will go to Omaha or the Mayo Clinic in Rochester. I want everyone in the community to have the advantages now limited to those who have the money to go to some distant clinic."

Husky Doc Reeves looks what he is: an ex-football player. Just short of six feet, he still has a lithe, athletic bearing, no trace of waistline bulge. To encourage high-school athletics, Dr. Reeves serves (without fee) as physician for the football and basketball teams. Graduated in 1946 from the University of Nebraska's College of Medicine in Omaha, Dr. Reeves served a year's internship at Southern Baptist Hospital in New Orleans, then cast about for a place to settle where he would feel at home. An advertisement in the *Journal* of the American Medical Association took him to Callaway, Neb., as assistant to a general practitioner. The young doctor had to make several calls in nearby Arnold, where a doctor had recently died. He liked the place, and within a few weeks moved in.

The first months were even busier than Dr. Reeves had expected.

Before a year had passed, he called in Dr. McShane, just graduated from his own old school, and made him a partner. Dr. Reeves hoped that a partner would cut down his 16-hour day, seven days a week. It helped, but he still has few chances to get away to the irrigation spillways to cast for bass, or onto the prairie to hunt for quail, or to the hills for antelope. Grinning, he sees a connection between last winter's blizzards (when he had to make farm calls by horse team or "weasel" tractor) and the heavy obstetrical practice in the last weeks of 1949: "The blizzards kept most people home, and we're just reaping the benefits now."

Materially, country doctors are far better off than they used to be. Though their fees are moderate ($50 for a delivery, an average of $125 for an appendectomy), Drs. Reeves and McShane are estimated to gross more than $20,000 a year each. And still, like old-timers, they give one-fifth of their service to those who cannot afford to pay.

Dr. Reeves believes that he could never be happy out of general practice. "I don't think a doctor should be a scientific automaton," says he. "He has to be a warm-blooded human being, capable of sympathy and understanding." And Arnold's general practitioner is resigned to the long hours: "A doctor ought to be busy; he can't be happy or proficient otherwise. But of course there is that matter of fishing. A man can go stale from too much work, so everybody ought to go fishing now & then."

Reprinted from *Time*, January 9, 1950. © Time, Inc., 1950

*For most Americans, the man with the plow symbolizes
the conquest of the plains. But in northwestern Nebraska,
victory depended on the man with the spade.*

Dutch Joe: Frontier Hero

A. E. SHELDON

MEN who risk their lives on fields of battle are justly held as heroes.
Those who risk and lose them in the cause of making human homes
in what was once a desert are no less deserving of the appellation.
Among them I write the name of Joseph Grewe.

"Dutch Joe" we called him. We were the homesteaders upon the
high tables and in the rich black valleys of the sandhills west of
Valentine in the eighties. We were upon the skirmish line of the
American advance, fighting to prove that American homes could be
made in the heart of the sandhills. We plunged into the deep canyons of the Niobrara and tore from their rugged entrenchments
thousand-year-old cedar trees, "snaked" them down the canyon,
split them into posts, hauled them forty miles to Valentine, and
traded them at six cents apiece for flour and bacon. We followed
the trail of deer and elk for a week to bring home a bit of fresh
venison. Pitch pine logs were our fuel. Water was our first necessity
and our greatest difficulty. From the rich, smooth grama grass table-
lands where most of us had built our cabins and staked our hopes
for a free American home, we could look miles away down the pine-
clad canyons of the Niobrara. At the bottom of the canyons ran
splendid, gurgling brooks of clear, cold water. Lazy settlers homesteaded there and built their cabins at the water's edge, where
there was no plow land. The high-table homesteaders hauled their
water in barrels, sometimes a distance of seven miles, while they
broke out their first fields and laid foundations for a real farm home.

The first experiments at digging wells on the high table were
failures. Some dry holes were sunk two hundred feet and abandoned.
It was then that Dutch Joe appeared on the horizon. His real name
was Joseph Grewe. He was born in Westphalia, Germany, in 1854,
came to Nebraska in 1879, and homesteaded in Cherry County in
June, 1884. He was a sturdy fellow of medium height, with a pleas-

ant smile, determined lips, and extraordinary muscular development. This was the man who undertook to prove that water could be obtained upon the high tables, and who dug his first wells more than two hundred feet through the hard, dry Niobrara chalk to the underflow of pure, cold water.

What a celebration was held when the first Dutch Joe well reached water upon the "German table"! It was a measuring rod by which each settler could calculate the cost of securing water upon his own homestead. From then on, Dutch Joe was in constant demand. Other settlers would do his farm work, break out prairie, and haul cedar logs for him while he dug their wells. In the next seven years he dug over 6,000 feet of wells, ranging in depth from 100 to 260 feet. There was no well-digging machinery in the region then, and the settlers were too poor to import any.

Dutch Joe's wells were large, round cylinders, straight as a gun barrel from the grama grass roots to the gravel underflow. Some of us who watched him work called him "The Human Badger." In a single day he was known to dig a well sixty-five feet deep. I have never seen a man who could strike his spade into the topsoil and sink out of sight in such an astonishingly short space of time.

One day in 1894 Joe had to go to the bottom of the first well he had dug in the sandhill settlement to clear out some obstruction. From the bottom of the well he gave the signal to hoist a bucket full of loose rock. When it was almost at the top, the bucket slipped from the steel catch holding it to the rope and fell 200 feet, crushing Joe's head. The steel catch was his own invention, made by himself, and designed to save time by quickly detaching the bucket from the rope for unloading. Many years' service had worn the steel catch, unnoticed, until it was ready for this last act in a frontier tragedy.

Condensed from "A Hero of the Nebraska Frontier," *Nebraska History and Record of Pioneer Days*, Vol. I, No. 1 (Febr., 1918)

Perhaps there are certain advantages for an artist grow-ing up in an empty country; a country where nothing is made, and everything is to be made. Except for some of the people who lived in it, I think no one had ever found Nebraska beautiful until Willa Cather wrote about it. A new convention had to be created for it; a convention that had nothing to do with woods and water-falls, streams and valleys and picturesque architecture. . . . There it lay; and it was as new, as unknown to art as it was to the pioneer.

—Edith Lewis, *Willa Cather Living*

Willa Cather of Red Cloud

MILDRED R. BENNETT

WHEN nine-year-old Willa Cather came from Winchester, Virginia, in 1883 to Webster County, Nebraska, she was already old enough to absorb material which she was to use in her first short stories at the University of Nebraska and later in *O Pioneers!, My Antonia,* and *One of Ours.* "This country was mostly wild pasture and as naked as the back of your hand," she said in a 1921 interview. "I was little and homesick and lonely, and my mother was homesick, and nobody paid any attention to us. So the country and I had it out together, and by the end of the first autumn, that shaggy grass country had gripped me with a passion I have never been able to shake. It has been the happiness and the curse of my life."

Catherton, the precinct in which the Cathers lived, had been named for George Cather, Willa's uncle, who had come to Nebraska ten years before and who had helped survey the county. A group of settlers from Virginia had formed a community called New Virginia; but Willa's closest neighbors were the Lambrechts who had come from Germany. Her first playmate was Lydia (Leedy) Lambrecht, a girl about her own age; and the children spent happy hours in the attic of Grandfather Cather's house where Willa's parents were living, trying on grownups' garments and pretending to be clowns or out in the tall grass snake-hunting with Lydia's brother Henry and his little dog.

In her play Willa (Willie) had no use for dolls and preferred to dramatize something grownups were doing; but she liked to leave the prosaic details of her projects for her playmates to accomplish. One of her greatest fascinations was the life of the foreign immigrants, and since the trail toward Red Cloud led past the Lambrechts' sod house, she often wandered over and into the kitchen, where she pestered Mrs. Charlotte Lambrecht with all sorts of questions. To this generous-hearted woman, the child's curiosity was something very commendable, and she would often stop her work to explain, or she would slowly demonstrate how foods were cooked or garments fashioned in the old country.

Willa saw with an exceptionally clear eye, experienced vicariously, and remembered. Her friendship of those early days flourished until death. To Mrs. Lambrecht, who had cared for Willa's mother during an illness with pneumonia, and to the girls "Leedy" and Pauline, Miss Cather sent gifts of handmade woolen sweaters, scarfs from abroad, and other beautiful and useful things. Particularly during the depression years she worried about these friends, regretting that she had recently moved into a more expensive apartment in New York, for she wanted to aid them financially when she felt the need. It was not so much that they needed what she could do, but rather that she derived great pleasure out of any opportunity to express her love for them. Repeatedly she wrote to Red Cloud merchants, giving detailed instructions and sending money to buy coffee, dried fruits, and delicacies to be dispatched to the Lambrechts. She knew what farming would be like in bad years, and although her friends, who were in some ways as reticent as Willa herself, would never write her of their struggles, she was sure that sometimes there wasn't enough money to buy the select brand of coffee roasted in Boston which Mrs. Lambrecht so greatly enjoyed.

Whenever the author returned to Red Cloud, no matter what the weather, she went out to Catherton, preferably by horse and buggy. (She returned to the Catherton locality in her last story, "The Best Years" in *The Old Beauty*.) On one occasion when the younger Lambrecht girls, Clara and Della, were preparing lunch, they set on the table a dish of wild plum jam. Their mother reproved them in German, saying it wasn't good enough for their important guest; but Miss Cather, familiar with German, understood and would not allow the dish to be removed. At lunch, to the delight of the girls, she ate several helpings of the jam. One time she was shown a quilt embroidered with all the state flowers. So much did Miss

Cather admire it that as soon as possible Mrs. Lambrecht and the girls made her a duplicate, which, she told them later, she used all the time as a counterpane on her bed in the New York apartment.

Willa liked to visit with Julius, the younger son, who raised purebred white-faced cattle and who faced life with such imperturbability that he was a challenge to her understanding. Her curiosity piqued her into spending as much time as she could out at the barn talking with him. In New York she kept track of events through the Red Cloud paper, *The Commercial Advertiser;* and if Julius sold a prize bull, she was certain to comment on it in her next letter home. If one of them had a crop failure, she managed to send a check—as a valentine, as a Christmas gift, as a birthday remembrance. Even after her death, the usual Christmas checks came to these intimate friends.

The impression that engraved itself so deeply on this youngster may have been more enduring because up to the family move to Catherton, she had been protected from seeing the actual struggle for life and sustenance. Into the sod houses and dugouts she went, watching the immigrant women, savoring their old-world background, sensing how unfitted many of them were for the rigorous life in the wilderness. H. W. Boynton in the New York *Evening Post,* November, 1915, quoted her: "I have never found any intellectual excitement more intense than I used to feel when I spent a morning with one of these pioneer women at her baking or buttermaking. I used to ride home in the most unreasonable state of excitement; I always felt as if they told me so much more than they said—as if I had got inside another person's skin. If one begins that early, it is the story of the man-eating tiger over again—no other adventure ever carries one quite so far."

Living in Catherton in 1883–84 was something like living at the crossroads of the world. Within a few miles of the Cather home were settlements of Russians, French, Irish, Norwegians, Germans, and Czechoslovakians, each with a rich heritage of tradition and superstition. Tragedy abounded, for many were too weak to survive the uprooting and replanting, and insanity or suicide was not infrequent. The bitter comment in some of Miss Cather's earliest stories is that after ten years on the divide, one is ready to commit suicide—a common practice of the Poles when they were too discouraged to shave was to keep their razors to cut their throats; but the Danes usually hanged themselves.

In the Norwegian settlement lived Yance Sorgensen, a bachelor who built up a very ample estate. His older sister had come first to Council Bluffs, Iowa, and worked until she could pay passage for Yance. Then the two had saved until they could send for the mother, the father, and the others. Finally Yance had his own house, not very well furnished by some standards. On several occasions Mr. Cather suggested that he should modernize his home: "Why do you live like this? It's shameful for you to go without a bathroom and heat."

Yance explained, "I'm so much more comfortable than I ever expected to be. When I first came here at nineteen, I had only my shirt and jeans." And not all the wealth Yance could ever acquire would cause him to change his ways.

When Miss Cather sent a copy of *O Pioneers!* to Carrie Miner Sherwood, she inscribed on the flyleaf: "This was the first time I walked off on my own feet—everything before was half real and half an imitation of writers whom I admired. In this one I hit the home pasture and found that I was Yance Sorgensen and not Henry James."

Once when Miss Cather returned to visit her home, she and her father went out to see the little church that Yance had rebuilt and had decorated. He hired a Czech named Ondrak to paint a picture at the front above the altar. Ondrak had gone to art school at Prague and Munich, and eventually drifted to America. He had done some rather crude murals as wall decorations of some Red Cloud homes, but as a rule, he just painted houses. Willa liked him because he talked about the old country, music, and culture, and he spoke excellent French. She once asked him to do some painting in the Cather home and invited him to lunch with her—a privilege he never forgot.

The painting he chose for the church was "Christ in the Garden." When Mr. Cather saw it, he hesitatingly pointed out to Willa the crudities of the work. She was furious. "Father, you know you don't know a thing about art!"

"But," he protested mildly, "look at that halo. Just like a ring of cheese."

Willa would not agree. To her any sincere effort was worthy. However much she might shun society and withdraw from people, yet, in her presence, humble sincere men like Yance and Ondrak always felt at home—appreciated.

Living at the edge of Catherton Precinct and over in the Bohemian settlement were the Czech families who were to be immortalized in *My Antonia*. When the Cathers moved to Nebraska, the father in one family had just killed himself. The tragedy was retold at every fireside, and Willa said later that the tale made such an impression on her that if she were ever to write anything, it would have to include that story.

When the girl from whom *My Antonia* takes its name first came to the Miners (the Harlings of *My Antonia*), she was about fifteen and had never done anything but hard field work. It is possible that she came through the suggestion of Grandmother Cather and Mrs. Grice, a woman who lived on the same section as the Bohemian family and who had always taken an interest in the girl. In any case, Willa had an opportunity to know Annie very well.

Knowing Annie and her never-failing energy was an inspiration. Although she had never tried before, she soon learned to cook and sew; and when Mrs. Miner gave her permission to use the machine, she made all the clothes—shirts, jeans, overalls, and husking gloves for her family. For herself, she fashioned everyday shoes with a cardboard sole and several thicknesses of suiting or denim, covered on the bottom with oilcloth. These she tied on her feet with black tape. Their flapping never delayed her in her breathless scurrying to do everything she could. In spare moments she picked out hickory nuts—it took a week to get enough—to make Hughie, the Miner boy, a special Sunday cake.

On their part the Miner children took Annie with them to opera-house performances and other diversions. She would work all day and dance all night if opportunity offered. She soon learned to copy any kind of dress and made herself duplicates of those she liked, much to the embarrassment of some of the society ladies. When, later, she went west to marry a brakeman, she had many beautiful clothes; but her happiness was short-lived. After a week her lover deserted her and Annie returned to Red Cloud.

When Miss Cather first conceived the story of Antonia, she had temporarily lost track of many of the "hired girls" and did not know how their lives had actually turned out. As it happened, however, the facts were much like fiction. Annie had married a Bohemian boy and mothered a large family of which she was justly proud. The girls were beautiful, and the boys couldn't be defeated in the county weight-lifting and boxing contests or the high-school basketball or football games. Annie's husband ("Neighbor Rosicky" in *Obscure Destinies*) was equally proud of his children. When neighbors told him that he should sell his cream, get more money, and buy more land, he and Annie agreed that roses in the cheeks of their children were more important than land or money in the bank.

There is a story that at one time Annie's husband went to the Hastings Hospital, and when asked something about himself, replied, "I am the husband of My Antonia." He is now buried in the little Bohemian cemetery in the northern part of the county—the cemetery which overlooks cornfields and rich sloping pastures.

After re-establishing contact with Annie, Miss Cather never failed to visit her whenever possible. She enjoyed the long table in the cheerful kitchen, the crowd of happy-faced children, the Bohemian cooking—kolaches and Annie's special banana-cream pie. Willa was particularly pleased with Annie's sons, one of whom won rapid military advancement in the recent war. All of them, according to Miss Cather, had the manners of children of a grand duke. Always sensitive to any change in the weather, Miss Cather carried an assortment of scarfs, capes, wraps; and when Annie's boys took her to the carriage at their farm gate, each one would have some garment draped over his arm, ready to help her into it or with a flourish lay it at her feet in the conveyance. The admiration was mutual; and after visiting this family, Miss Cather would be so breathless with excitement that she could scarcely speak, and she was completely exhausted.

Once Willa sent Annie a check for fifty dollars with instructions to buy herself something; but taxes were due and Annie paid them, never revealing that the money had gone for necessities. Too proud to admit any need, the family never asked for help; but Willa kept track of things. "Is Annie's oldest boy planting hybrid? If not, I shall see that he can afford it another year." Similarly, she sent money to provide seed wheat during the bitter drought years. Annie applied another gift check on a washing machine. When Miss Cather found out that the machine had cost more than the money she had sent, she wrote another check requesting that she be allowed to pay in full for the machine and that it be christened "Willie's Washer."

Annie's final years were alert and active, and filled with many friends. "I had a hard life," she used to say, "but now I have things easy and the children are so good to me." Having things easy in Annie's language did not mean idleness. Her cooking did not fail to please any guest who dropped in—and there were many of them from all over the country, especially after her picture and something of her story appeared in *Life*. And visitors were offered a choice of her crocheting or needlework, much of which bore blue ribbons from the county fair. She received many letters asking about

My Antonia, to which she replied with memories of the trip across Bohemia to Prague when she was twelve, of her first days in America, and of her work in Red Cloud homes. She even made a recording in Czech for the Voice of America broadcast.

In Annie's neat drawers and cupboards were gifts from Miss Cather: a set of Italian dishes, some prints from Czechoslovakia (a gift to the author from Thomas Masaryk), and a warm shawl sent after Miss Cather's death.* A small photo of her famous friend always stood on Annie's dresser and a packet of letters telling how much she enjoyed hearing from Annie and how during an illness these words from home comforted her.

However, it should not be thought that Annie lived in the past. She was concerned with world and neighborhood affairs and the latest movies. A Catholic, she would worship with any group—telling her beads, she said, within herself. One of her greatest pleasures was her yard in which were trees that she had started from peach and apricot pits. There was the cherry tree a son-in-law had planted, a rose bush given her by a son, and a bit of red clover "just like the old country."

On April 24, 1955, eight years to the day after the death of Willa Cather, Annie Pavelka died. "My work is all finished," she had told her daughter a few days before. "Finished and put away." But Annie and her work still live, and will live on so long as American letters endure, in the pages of Willa Cather's *My Antonia.*

She lent herself to immemorial human attitudes which we recognize by instinct as universal and true. . . . She was a battered woman now, not a lovely girl; but she still had that something which fires the imagination, could still stop one's breath for a moment by a look or gesture that somehow revealed the meaning in common things. She had only to stand in the orchard, to put her hand on a little crab tree and look up at the apples, to make you feel the goodness of planting and tending and harvesting at last. All the strong things of her heart came out in her body, that had been so tireless in serving generous emotions.

It was no wonder that her sons stood tall and straight. She was a rich mine of life, like the founders of early races.

Condensed from "Catherton," *Prairie Schooner,* Fall, 1949

---

* Many of these gifts may now be seen at the Willa Cather Pioneer Memorial in Red Cloud. Organized in March, 1955, its purpose is to keep alive the memory of the people and the places that Willa Cather loved.

"Nothing in the world," wrote Willa Cather, "not snow mountains or blue seas, is so beautiful in moonlight as the soft, dry summer roads in farming country, roads where the white dust falls back from the slow wagon wheel."

Among the old-time road traders, most likely there were many with an eye for this kind of beauty. But whenever they met a wagon on a country road, they found the animal pulling it far and away the most important object on the scene.

Road Trader

B. F. SYLVESTER

I SING OF the road trader, in whom horse-trading reached its apogee. Road trading was a vast, unorganized commerce grounded in the peculiar economics that often made a poor horse more valuable— to the trader—than a sound one. Most anyone could swap horses, but the road trader was an artist. The touch of the master was to trade and then to get back the twenty-dollar snide to use again and again. A snide was a good-looking horse with a hole in him—that is, with one or more major disabilities. Worthless as an animal, he was invaluable as a pawn, his loss a blow to the owner.

The range of the road trader was the Missouri Valley. It is no disrespect to New England and New York State to say that here were men who would have turned David Harum over to their herd boys for practice. The man who made a route from St. Joseph to the Canadian line and back each year could be said to have had the benefits of travel.

The Missouri Valley road trader began his season toward the first of May, when there was grass for the animals and reasonable warmth in the air. At that season, for forty years or so before the Model T, there was a stir in the covered wagon camps from Yankton, South Dakota, to Kansas City.

Ed Hilliker was the most celebrated of western road traders. His word was good. The man who said, "Ed, pick me out a team," was dealing with the Bank of England, but most of Hilliker's customers approached him with something to be got rid of. Then it was a horse trade. Hilliker was six feet, two and a half inches tall and weighed 285 pounds. He could hold a wild horse. When his first automobile failed to stop at his "Whoa! Whoa!" he pulled off the steering wheel. He broke the critter. On one hand in his later days he wore a four and a half carat diamond, on the other a ring with the Lord's Prayer engraved upon it. He paid fifty dollars for his Stetson hats, and as an eater was celebrated; his children say every day was Thanksgiving. During World War I, he and his partners sold 75,000 horses and mules to the armies. He spent and gave away a fortune.

At twelve he ran away from home at Red Oak, Iowa, after trading ponies with a preacher's son. His father, a blacksmith, ordered him to trade back. "No," Ed said. "It was a trade." He joined Hi Miller, then the greatest trader of all, and at sixteen had his own wagon and four horses.

In an Atlantic, Iowa, hotel, Hilliker, then about nineteen, overheard a man speak offensively to a girl employed in the restaurant —a girl Hilliker never had seen before. He dragged the man outside, gave him a beating, and returned to his wagon. The next spring he married the girl—sixteen-year-old Catherine Talty—and they went honeymooning in the covered wagon. The town thought it wasn't much of a match for her. For twenty years she went along, drove a wagon, bore children in camp, and when Hilliker quit the road, broke, he founded a fortune on $500 she secretly had saved.

Once Hilliker reached Council Bluffs with neither money nor food. Leaving his family in camp, he took a horse around to the barns to make a swap that would yield a few dollars. He tried all day and failed. When he returned to camp, supper was on and flour, bacon, and other supplies on hand.

"Kate, where did this come from?" he asked.

"Do you miss anything around here?" she countered.

"No, nothing except the dog."

"That's it," she said. She had made her own swap.

His chief diversion was poker. At Grand Island, Nebraska, an important war-horse-inspection point, there was a game that ran for eleven days, with large sums on the table most of the time. He played every night, sometimes all night, but by day he attended to business.

As Hilliker prospered, he built a barn a block long and an eight-room house across the street in Fremont, Nebraska. There was company all the time, but no servants. Mrs. Hilliker and her three daughters were equal to all domestic situations. Every tramp was fed, and visitors had to stay for dinner or all night.

At a time when his firm was making $1,000 a day on war-horse contracts, a real-estate agent suggested that a man of his means should live in a more fashionable district.

"No," he replied. "I wouldn't have a house where I couldn't smell the barn."

Traders were not in court as often as might be inferred. First, the losing swapper wasn't eager to advertise his defeat; second, the winner was skilled in talking his way out. Then, too, the horse sense of the justices of the peace was not always Blackstone.

A trader was summoned before a Nebraska justice on complaint of a dealer who said he had paid $175 for a balky team.

"Did you tell this man the team would pull?" asked the bench.

"No, Your Honor."

"What did you tell him?"

"I said, 'You'll be surprised to see them work.' "

The justice was seized with an attack of coughing and hid his face behind a law book. Presently he emerged and addressed the complaining party: "How long have you been trading horses?"

"Since I was seven, Your Honor."

The J. P. reflected upon this answer for a moment, then ruled: "The judgment of this court is that you better trade with somebody else."

Yes, the trader was a handy explainer. There was the old one about the farmer who complained: "One horse of that team I got from you is blind."

"No, he ain't really blind," the trader said.

"He's blind as a bat," the farmer insisted. "He runs into things. He runs into the fence. He runs into the barn."

"Well, he ain't blind," was the soft answer. "He just doesn't care."

Charley Mitchell, later to become wealthy with Hilliker in the horse-commission trade, tells of his kidney-dropper mare. The mare had a quick turn-over. Shown in harness, she seemed all right, yet the instant she was unhitched, she would lie down and roll. Thereafter she would raise herself on her front legs and sit. Mitchell, a huge man, could lift her the rest of the way by the tail, an advantage not owned by others. His customers sold back or traded back without haggling. The last thing they needed was a sitting horse.

The trader was a good actor. His wife and children were part of the setting. Not only did they lend verity to the idea that these were homesteaders on their way to a new location, but a wife's plea not to sell Ginger, her own property, or Nellie, the children's pride and joy, was disarming. Ed Miller had been a road trader out of Louisville, Nebraska, for years when he was taken in by this comedy.

"One of my team was a dummy," he tells, "making the other horse and me plenty of trouble. He wouldn't lead, he wouldn't pull. I passed another trader with a nice-looking young mare. I said would he trade. He said he might. The mare had an ankle bandage where he said a ringbone had been cut out, but she didn't seem to be lame any, and I thought if she could pull her half of that top wagon, there couldn't be anything wrong with her that I couldn't fix. But something told me to watch out, and I began backing away. That's when the old lady speaks up: 'Pa, you ain't goin' to trade off Hannah! Why, we raised her from a colt.' I thinks now maybe the mare's all right, so I trade. I'm not fifty yards down the road before she goes lame. The fellow had her hitched up and just standing there waiting for a sucker like me. I have to give her away."

The terminology of the trader was crisp. To "come back with the halter" was to be beaten in a deal. A man without money in the spring had been "winter-killed." "Shut 'em down" was to give temporary relief to windies and heavies or heavers. A bull-windy would go down at a little exertion. A windy was shut down by a sponge pushed up its nose. It then would breathe through the mouth. A string attached to a sponge permitted its removal. Another method, if the horse was being shown in motion, was a clamp over the nostrils, painted the color of the hair.

A wiggler, or bobby, had a spinal weakness that caused it to wabble behind. Such an animal would be hitched closely, traces and pole straps drawn up so there was no room to move. A freezer was one that couldn't back. A smooth-mouth was any horse past nine years old. That meant that the last dark cup in the teeth of the lower mouth—the cups disappeared two a year after five years— had gone. "Bishoping" or "cupping" was to drill small depressions in certain teeth and color them with sulphate of iron, depending upon how "young" the horse was to be. The trader could do a bit of face-lifting, making the sunken places above the eyes match the new teeth. A hat-pin incision would let in air and temporarily puff out the skin. If the horse were a grayhead, he would paint the eyebrows. The last touch was a rubber band around the base of an ear, so that the horse held it forward instead of letting it flop back.

A trader watched the eyes of another as a boxer does. Where he looked for defects in your horse was a good place to watch in his. A poke in the horse's ribs was revealing to a smart dealer. It could disclose bad wind, heaves, or a tendency to fits. The trader had the percentage in his favor. The other fellow might know how to detect one, but rarely more than one, of a dozen ailments to which horses are subject.

The trader had plenty of time. He hurried no deals, had no quotas, no pep talks. So far as known, no one tried to organize him. No congressman wept over his sad case. He got along well with others in the same line. Trading among themselves was largely accommodation. One needing a windy for a deal, another would help him out. All took care of their animals. A trader might have a poor coat for himself, but there was a rubber or canvas blanket to keep the rain off his snide.

Men made a side-line business of supplying snides to traders, a topsy-turvy traffic in which the buyer made the seller prove that the horse was no good. A balker would be hitched, and every trick exhausted to make it pull. A bull-windy must be demonstrated to be a collapser, not now and then, but always. Some horses got the idea and would drop at the tug of a halter.

Ed had a bleeder mule worth his weight, if not in gold, at least in silver. The mule was hauled from camp to camp in a wagon, but once in camp, would be hitched with a horse. As every horse-swapper sought matched teams, Hilliker's misfits were the signal for a trade. If he could get a modest boot, Hilliker didn't mind what sort of snide he got in exchange for his mule, knowing that the mule would never get more than 100 yards away; that was as far as the bleeder could travel under his own steam. Hilliker had another jewel, a big sorrel that couldn't be led to water or anywhere else. But where the trader's wagon led, the sorrel would follow without halter or tie rope, on the understanding that it was of his own free will. This self-respect was much admired by other traders to whom Ed would let the sorrel out on a percentage basis. One season his share was $200.

When cars began to be cheap and dependable, the road trader's decline set in. Roads were paved and no longer safe or comfortable to horse traffic. Tractors began to displace the horses and mules in the fields. Farmers were not so sociable. Once they had welcomed a chance to visit; now they had to be going somewhere in their cars. Boys were graduating from agricultural schools and appraising the trader's stock with a cold eye. There were laws against camping along the road. Water and grass no longer were to be found freely.

At the end, the road traders had just about what they began with. The business went into the hands of dealers who bought, sold, and shipped. Trading became negligible and confined for the most part to neighborhoods.

Charley Mitchell had seen what was coming and had interested some twenty horsemen, most of them road traders in the commission-sales business. A company was formed with Hilliker as president. It prospered, but when the wartime boom in horseflesh began in 1914 with the arrival of the first remount-buying details from the Allied armies, Mitchell, Hilliker, and Frank Simpson organized a new firm, and the business mounted dizzily until Armistice Day. Such as these made fortunes, but when the war ended, the commission-sales trade and the horseflesh boom deflated among the first, and there was no road trading to return to.

Ed Hilliker's last deal on a single span of mules, two weeks before he died in 1924. A farmer appeared at the house and told what he wanted.

"Chris," said Hilliker, "my days are about gone. I don't feel like any more business. But there's a team over at the barn I think would suit you. Cost you $400." The man paid the money and went for his sight-unseen team.

Condensed from "Hoss-Tradin'," *Saturday Evening Post*, January 6, 1934

In his history of the state, James Olson has remarked that "Early pioneers seem to have come to Nebraska in significant numbers for the express purpose of carving political careers for themselves. . . ." The tendency has persisted: in fact, some observers have maintained that the perpetual wind on the prairies is due less to the action of the elements than to the high incidence of politicians in the population.

Be that as it may, the state has long been recognized as a national guidepost of political trends and tendencies; and since 1867 gentlemen from Nebraska have been demonstrating to the country at large that democracy has no stouter pillar than the cracker barrel.

Politicians of the Old School

RUDOLPH UMLAND

1. Henry C. Richmond

YOU MEET his sort in the lobbies of hotels, on trains, in the galleries of legislative chambers; you recognize them by their courtly manners, their dignity, their dictatorial air. They are nearly always large men who smoke fat cigars and talk in a loud voice. The names of Mark Hanna, Champ Clark, and W. J. Bryan roll off their tongues smoothly as butter. There is something Pickwickian about them. Henry C. Richmond—Colonel Richmond, sir—of Nebraska, is one of these: a politician of the old school.

In 1912, Richmond, then Democratic candidate in Nebraska for state auditor, went to Washington, D. C., for a brief visit. As soon as he got into town, congressmen greeted him with smiles of recognition. They could not remember his name, they could not recall from what district or state he came, but they were quite certain that he had been in Congress and that they knew him. Colonel Richmond availed himself at once of the privileges of an ex-member. As he entered the floor of the House, a doorkeeper requested his card. "Ex-member, son," said Richmond with a lordly air, and breezed in. On the floor he had a bully time, greeting surprised acquaintances and others who thought they were acquaintances. Later, in the Senate restaurant, he met a solon who was full of reminiscences about Richmond's visit to Austin, Texas, years before. The fact that he had never been in Austin did not deter Richmond from contributing his quota of fond recollections of the visit.

Colonel Richmond was born on the Fourth of July, 1870, in Gentry County, Missouri. When he was still very young, the family homesteaded in Kansas and, when he was twelve, came on to a farm in Webster County, Nebraska. His first job was as country news correspondent for the Red Cloud *Chief,* and it wasn't long before he knew all there was to know about running a country weekly. In 1894 he became editor of the Red Cloud *Nation,* a seething red-hot Populist publication that was continually damning Wall Street and other eastern "special interest" groups for the hard times prevailing in Nebraska. The Colonel's editorials were reprinted throughout the state, and his trenchant pen won him the attention of many politicians. In 1897, after losing out for chief clerk of the House of Representatives in the state legislature, Richmond was offered a job by Richard L. Metcalfe on the Omaha *World-Herald.* He left the paper nine years later to become editor of the Fremont *Daily Herald,* a post which he obtained largely through the influence of Edgar Howard.

In 1908 Colonel Richmond gave up the editorship and served as clerk at the Democratic National Convention in Denver, which nominated William Jennings Bryan for the third time. Previously, in 1904, he had accompanied Bryan on a campaign tour. They wound up a day of busy speeches at the little town of Stuart, in Holt County. "I shall never forget a tall, gangling, dark-eyed young man of serious mien named Arthur F. Mullen who was running for county attorney," the Colonel says. "He was one of the best boosters our party had. That night in a hotel, Bryan, young Mullen, and I were assigned a single large room which had one bed and a cot. Bryan and I were to occupy the bed and Mullen the cot. I was mighty tired and I quickly skinned off my clothing and got into bed. A moment later Mullen donned his nightshirt and knelt to say his prayers. A little later Bryan did the same and then, joining me in bed, remarked, 'Henry, I guess you are the only pagan in the crowd.' Of course I had to come back at him in some way or other, so I said, 'Yes, but what of it? You fellows pray in opposite directions anyway.' Bryan laughed uproariously. You see he was Protestant and young Mullen a Catholic."

There are few Nebraska politicians and editors of the period from 1894 to 1940 about whom Colonel Richmond cannot tell some anecdote. Like most politicians of the old school, he will spin yarns by the hour, provided he has a liberal supply of cigars at hand.

Colonel Richmond tells the following one about Samuel McKelvie, governor of Nebraska from 1919 to 1923. Although McKelvie was thirty-seven, he looked so boyish he often was mistaken for a youth just old enough to cast his first vote. Shortly after his inauguration, he had business in Chicago. During his visit, he was guest of honor at a luncheon in one of the clubs. Directly across the table from Governor McKelvie was the prominent, but bibulous, mayor of a large Indiana city. One of Governor McKelvie's hosts greeted him and said: "I want you to meet our honor guest for today, Sam McKelvie, Governor of Nebraska."

The mayor fastened his wavering gaze on McKelvie, then turned to their host with an air of rebuke. "Look, friend," he said, "I'm pret-ty damn drunk, but not *that* drunk!"

The peak of Colonel Richmond's political career came during the years 1915–19, when he was serving as a member of the House of Representatives from Douglas County. In 1917 he introduced a bill which provided for the construction of a new capitol; and while his bill failed to become law, it started the movement which led to the building of the present State House. It also won for the Colonel the sobriquet which he relishes above all others—"Father of the Nebraska State Capitol."

2. Moses P. Kinkaid

EXCEPT in the deep south, there are few men who, once aboard the political merry-go-round, have displayed greater aptitude at latching on to the brass ring than Moses P. Kinkaid of O'Neill. His most noteworthy accomplishment during nearly ten terms of office (aside, of course, from getting re-elected) was in securing passage of the "Kinkaid Homestead Act." This legislation, originally formulated by Congressman William Neville of North Platte, permitted settlers in thirty-seven northwest Nebraska counties to take up 640 acres of land instead of 160 as provided in the original Homestead Act of 1862.

As a fellow townsman and a Democratic national committeeman, Arthur F. Mullen was uniquely well-qualified to report on Kinkaid's career. In his autobiography, *Western Democrat*, Mr. Mullen wrote:

Moses P. Kinkaid—his district called him Many Platforms Kinkaid—was one of the earliest and most successful of the Patent-Medicine School of Politics. He'd been district judge from 1897 to 1900, and had apparently become as stationary in O'Neill as the hitching post in front of the post office. Day after day he used to stand at a corner near the bank . . . chewing, spitting, spitting, chewing, eating crackers, drinking medicine from a bottle, shaking hands with every one, not once but every time he met him. Then, in 1902, he was elected to Congress, staying there until he died in 1922. . . .

His political strength was not in causes, not in eloquence, but in direct communication with the voters of his district. He sent flower and vegetable seeds, free, from the Department of Agriculture, to the wives of all the voters. He sent what he and they called literature, free documents of various governmental agencies, all posted under his frank. A lot of congressmen do that, and don't get far. Judge Kinkaid had a better system.

. . . He had classified his constituents by their ailments, rheumatism, asthma, bronchitis, heart trouble, sour stomach, biliousness, all the more ordinary ills of mankind. For each group he had a letter, similar in tone but different in recommendation. Each letter began, "You and I both suffer from the same trouble. I have found a remedy which has helped me, and I hope it will help you." Sometimes the remedies were efficacious. Sometimes they weren't—for anyone but Moses P. They always helped him to stay in office. And the nation has had lots worse representatives than he was, even though his adoption of the Neville Act just about changed the face of the West. For it brought in thousands upon thousands of homesteaders who couldn't cope with the conditions of life in the sandhills, and stirred up a lot of trouble before, in time, the cattlemen bought out most of the Kinkaiders.

It was lucky for him that typewriting had arrived before he went to Washington. He wrote so badly that once, when a man asked Doc Morris, the local druggist, to decipher a recommendation Kinkaid had written, Morris took it back of the counter, then returned with a filled bottle of dark liquid. "Seventy-five cents," he said, "and it's the best damned cough syrup I ever put up."

The value of the legislation associated with his name has long been a debatable point. However, the voters of the sixth district were sufficiently well impressed to send Kinkaid back to Congress until his death—in harness—in 1922. What some, at least, of his constituents thought of him was expressed in a song, "The Kinkaiders," which goes in part:

> Then let us all with hearts sincere
> Thank him for what has brought us here,
> And for the homestead law he made,
> This noble Moses P. Kinkaid.

3. Edgar Howard

IN 1895 the membership of the Nebraska legislature was made up mostly of Populists. There was a mere handful of Republicans, and only one simon-pure, unadulterated Democrat—Edgar Howard of Papillion, Sarpy County. When the legislature convened, hundreds of people from all parts of the state came to Lincoln by train and buggy to witness the opening of the session. Few of them had ever heard of Edgar Howard. He was just a country newspaper editor, newly elected. But before the day was ended, they were all talking about the drawling, long-jawed, long-haired young fellow from Papillion.

The procedure in electing legislative officials was for the presiding member to ask the parties in turn for their nominations for speaker. The Populist Party, which had polled the largest vote, was asked for its nominee first; then the Republican Party. Next both names were put before the house, and—as was a foregone conclusion—the Populist caucus nominee got the big vote.

"We will now proceed to the election of a chief clerk," announced the chairman.

"Mr. Chairman! Mr. Chairman!" came a shrill voice.

"For what purpose does the gentleman rise?" asked the chairman, who clearly did not know the member from Papillion.

"Mr. Chairman, before passing on to the election of a chief clerk, I suggest that you consider the nominee of the Democratic caucus which met at the Lincoln Hotel last night," said Howard. "We had a big meeting."

As a snicker started around the hall, the chairman grew suspicious. "How could that be with but one Democrat in the house? Who was nominated for speaker?"

"Edgar Howard," declared the member from Papillion. "He is a great Democrat and a great man. I second his nomination!"

Accompanied by roars of laughter, the name of Edgar Howard was then put to vote for speaker. There was one ringing "yea"— from the member from Papillion, and it was another show-stopper.

During a career in politics and journalism which covered sixty-eight years, Edgar Howard could be counted on to enliven any assemblage in which he played a part. Quick-witted, salty of speech, and unpredictable, as often as not he kept his colleagues on tenterhooks but never failed to delight newspapermen. According to an

article which appeared in *Outlook* in 1930, when Congressman
Howard was serving his sixth year in the House:

> The Nebraska Representative has many virtues. He bursts into song on
> the floor of the House, denounces lobbying ex-Congressmen who "spit in
> the face of the goddess of justice," ranks with Will Rogers as a favorite
> after-dinner speaker, and violates parliamentary canons almost daily with
> the encouragement rather than the disapproval of his good friend, Speaker
> Longworth. It was Howard who, fresh from a social function at which
> politically dry members drank deep from a "little green bottle," once
> delivered an allegorical address describing a visit to the House of Dreams,
> where hypocrisy assumed the guise of good fellowship. Wet-drinking, dry-
> voting members fidgeted wretchedly, but Edgar did not name names.
>   . . . While he served as probate judge, state legislator and lieutenant
> governor, his capsule autobiography in the *Congressional Directory* states
> that he "held contemporaneously the higher office of editor of a country
> newspaper." Senator Norris insists that journalism lost a great man in
> Howard. The loss is not complete. He still sends caustic editorials back to
> Columbus, Nebraska.

During the same year, *Time* summed up the career of "Nebraska's
Howard" as follows:

Born: at Osceola, Iowa, September 16, 1858

Start in life: a printer's devil

Career: aged 13, he went to work in a print shop in Glenwood, Ia. He
went to public school, worked his way through Western Collegiate Institute,
attended Iowa College of Law. He became a tramp printer, a wandering
newswriter, worked for journals throughout the U. S. Last subordinate
job: as city editor of the Dayton (Ohio) *Herald*. In 1884 he married
Elizabeth Paisley Burtch of Clarinda, Iowa, and settled in Nebraska. She
gave him one son, Findley, for the past five years financial adviser to Sal-
vador, and two daughters. He edited the Papillion (Neb.) *Times*. In 1891
he was already full of Democratic sentiments; William Jennings Bryan
took him to Washington (paying his expenses but no salary). This position lasted but a few months. Howard returned to Papillion, entered
politics. Only straight Democrat running against the American Protective
Association, Populist ("Demipop") and Republican candidates. He was
elected to the state legislature in 1895. From 1896 to 1900 he served as
Probate Judge of Sarpy County. He purchased the Columbus (Neb.)
Weekly Telegram, edited it. In 1917 he had one term as Nebraska's lieutenant governor, returned to journalism, made the *Telegram* a daily in
1922. In 1923 he was elected to Congress, sold control of the *Telegram,*
though he still writes for it daily and receives an editorial salary.

In Congress: most entertaining of representatives, but no clown, he is a
cogent contributor to the work of the committees on Public Lands, Territories, Indian Affairs, Coinage, Weights & Measures. He calls himself a

"Free Democrat," but is seldom not "regular." . . . He is one of the last of the old-school Democratic "statesmen." . . . Regarding foreign affairs, he describes himself as "an old-fashioned American," favoring isolation, the Monroe Doctrine.

Legislative hobbies: farm relief, protection of U. S. Indians, veterans' care. On the first two, at least, he is an expert along party lines.

In appearance, he tries to resemble Bryan, facially better resembles Benjamin Franklin. He is heavy-set, bobbed-haired, mild-mannered. He dresses in the traditional rusty-grey frock coat, the wide-brimmed black hat of Bryan and the old-timers, which helps distinguish him among the more babbity modern members. In the House his voice assumes a peculiar, almost clerical (but not monotonous) drone. Then he is meek, likes to remind his listeners that his mother was a Quaker. His own faith is the Episcopalian. He drives out of Washington for Sunday services in country churches. He smokes three cigars a day, does not chew, swears privately. His fraternal affiliations: Masons (32nd degree), Knights Templar, Shriner, Rotary, Odd Fellows.

Outside Congress: he lives with his wife at a modest hotel opposite the House Office Building. There almost nightly he holds a non-betting card game with such Congressmen as Garner of Texas, Ohio's Brand.* He likes to watch baseball games, horseraces. He says: "I am a natural sport." He bitterly opposes Sunday blue-laws, will not attend Sabbath sporting events. When in Nebraska he talks to farmers in their own language, and to the Indians in theirs, being particularly adept at Santee Sioux, with which he baffled stenographic reporters at the Interparliamentary Union in Paris.

Impartial House observers rate Edgar Howard thus: a fine example of what congressmen were in the last century, plus a pointed, ubiquitous sense of humor. An adept at floor strategy able to transcend House rules of debate by his witty, original methods, thus an insidious protagonist of minority measures. Perhaps the greatest "character" in the House and the most universally liked Congressman.

Despite his defeat in 1934 after twelve years in Congress, the "Old Roman"—as he had come to be known—continued to play an active part in state and national politics. He was an all-out supporter of FDR, but would not go along with Truman, saying that he could not support one of the Pendergast gang. His views on foreign affairs were considerably modified by the second World War: In 1942 *Life* quoted him as saying: "There will be no more isolationism after this war."

* He was not always a non-betting player. "There is a story (told on himself) that a few days before his marriage, Elizabeth Burtch's uncle gave them $500 as a wedding present. But he made the mistake of giving it to Edgar instead of Elizabeth. Edgar then slipped off to Omaha and lost it in a faro game but kept the news from her until after their marriage."—J. R. Johnson, *Representative Nebraskans*

Throughout his ninety-three years, Edgar Howard remained stead-
fastly unpredictable. He also managed to keep his thinking geared
to the times. According to one of his biographers, J. R. Johnson, in
1949, two years before he died, the long-haired "Patriarch of the
Prairies" ambled into Andy Mlinar's barber shop in Columbus and
got himself a crew-cut.

In 1935 appeared the most important piece of prose liter-
ature to come from Nebraska since My Antonia—*Mari*
Sandoz' Old Jules, *the biography of her father. During the*
previous year she had written a paper on pioneer women,
published in revised form in 1936, which included this
portrait of her mother.

The Wife of Old Jules

MARI SANDOZ

THE AMERICAN FRONTIER is gone, we like to say, a little sadly. And
with it went the frontier woman who followed her man along the
dusty trail of the buffalo into the land of the hostile Indian. Never
again will there be a woman like the wife of Marcus Whitman, who,
in 1836, looked out upon a thousand miles of empty West from the
bows of a wagon rolling up the Platte toward Oregon. But there was
a later, a less spectacular, and a much more persistent frontier in
America, a frontier of prairie fire, drought, and blizzard, a frontier
of land fights and sickness and death far from a doctor, yet with
all the characteristic gaiety, deep friendships, and that personal
freedom so completely incomprehensible to the uninitiated.

Among my acquaintances are many women who walked the virgin
soil of such a frontier and made good lives for themselves and those
about them. And when they could they did not turn their backs
upon the land they struggled to conquer. They stayed, refusing to
be told that they occupy the last fringes of a retreating civilization,
knowing that life there can be good and bountiful.

One of these frontierswomen is Marlizzie, living more than thirty
miles from a railroad, over towering sandhills and through valleys
that deepen and broaden to hayflats, with scarcely a house and not
a tree the whole way.

No matter when you may come, you will find her away somewhere:
chasing a turkey hen; looking after the cattle; repairing fence with
stretchers and staples; trimming trees in the orchard, or perhaps
piling cow chips for winter fuel. A blow or two on the old steel trap
spring that hangs in place of a dinner bell at the gate will bring
her—running, it seems to strangers, but really only at her usual gait,
a gait that none of the six children towering over her can equal.

She comes smiling and curious, shading her faded blue eyes to see who you may be, and eager to welcome you in any event. And as she approaches, you see her wonderful wiry slightness, notice that her forearms, always bare, are like steel with twisted cables under dark leather—with hands that are beautiful in the knotted vigor that has gripped the hoe and the pitchfork until the fingers can never be straightened, fingers that still deftly mix the ingredients for the world's most divine concoction—Swiss plum pie.

And while you talk in the long kitchen-living room, she listens eagerly, demanding news of far places—the Rhineland, not so far from the place of her birth; Africa, and the political games in the Far East. Apologetically she explains that the mail is slow and uncertain here. Her daily papers come a sackful at a time, and there is no telephone. Besides, the decayed old stock station thirty miles away is little more than a post office and shipping pens. News still travels in the frontier manner, by word of mouth.

And while Marlizzie listens, perhaps she will make you a pie or two or even three—for one piece, she is certain, would be an aggravation. Gently she tests the plums between her fingers, choosing only the firmest, to halve and pit and lay in ring after ring like little saucers into crust-lined tins. Then sugar and enough of the custard, her own recipe, to cover the plums to dark submerged circles. She dots the top with thick sweet cream, dusts it with nutmeg, or, if you insist—but it is a serious sacrilege—with cinnamon, and slips them into her Nile-green range, gleaming as a rare piece of porcelain and heated to the exact degree with corncobs. And as she works, her hair, that she had so carefully smoothed with water before she began the pies, has come up in a halo of curls, still with a bright, glinting brown in it, for all her sixty-nine years.

It is a little difficult to see in this Marlizzie, so like a timberline tree, but stanchly erect, the woman of forty years ago, delicate of skin, with white hands, and what was known as "style" in the days of the leg-o'-mutton sleeve, the basque, and the shirred taffeta front. She came hopefully to western Nebraska, with eight new dresses of cashmeres and twills and figured French serges in navy, brown, gray and green. One had a yard and a half in each sleeve, and one—a very fine light navy—had two yards of changeable gold-and-blue taffeta pleated into the front of the basque. Marlizzie got so many because she suspected that it might be difficult to find good tailoring, with good style and cloth, right at the first in this wilderness. It was, and still is; but she found no occasion for the clothes she brought, or the renewal of her wardrobe with anything except calico or denim. Gradually the fine dresses were cut up for her children.

Within three months of the day that she struggled with her absurd rosetted little hat in the wind that swept the border town and all the long road to her home in the jolting lumber wagon, Marlizzie had ceased for all time to be a city woman. She had learned to decoy the wily team of Indian ponies and had converted, without a sewing machine, a fashionable gray walking skirt and cape into a pair of trousers and a cap for her new husband.

Ten years later her children found the tape loops once used to hold the trailing widths of the skirt from the dust of the street. When they asked what the loops were for, she told them and laughed a little as she buttoned her denim jacket to go out and feed the cattle. She had married an idealist, a visionary who dreamed mightily of a Utopia and worked incessantly to establish his dream and forgot that cattle must be fed to stand the white cold of thirty-below-zero weather.

By the time the calluses of her hands were as horn, her arms gnarling, and she had somehow fed every hungry wayfarer that came to her door, she had learned many things—among them that on the frontier democracy was an actuality, and that, despite the hardships, there was a wonderful plenitude of laughter and singing, often with dancing until the cows bawled for their morning milking, or winterlong storytelling around the heater red with cow chips.

The six children of Marlizzie were brought into the world and into maturity whole and sound without a doctor in the house. Though sugar was a luxury and bread often made from grain she ground in a hand mill, they were fed. Despite the constant menace of rattlesnakes to bare feet, and range cattle and wild horses and the daredeviltry the frontier engenders in its young, not one of the children lost so much as a little finger.

Marlizzie learned the arts of the frontier: butchering, meat care, soapmaking, and the science of the badger-oil lamp, with its underwear wick speared on a hairpin. Stores were remote, even had there been money. Not for twenty-five years, not until she was subpoenaed on a murder case, was she on a train. Finally, in 1926, she was in town long enough to see her first moving picture. She stayed in the dark little opera house all the afternoon and the evening to see it over and over, and talked of it as she talked so long ago about the wonders of Faust.

During those years Marlizzie saw many spring suns rise upon the hills as she ran through the wet grass for the team or stopped to gather a handful of wild sweet peas for her daughter, who was tied to the babies and had little time for play. Often before the fall dawnings Marlizzie stripped the milk from her cow. It was far to the field, and she and her husband must put in long days to husk the little corn before the snow came.

In those forty years Marlizzie saw large herds of range cattle driven into the country, their horns like a tangled thicket over a flowing dusty blanket of brown. She saw them give way to the white-faced Hereford and the thick-skinned black cattle that crawled through all her fences. She saw the hard times of the East push the settler westward and the cattleman arm against the invasion. She helped mold bullets for the settlers' defense or listened silently, her knitting needles flying, to the latest account of a settler shot down between the plow handles or off his windmill before the eyes of his wife and children.

She knitted only a little more rapidly when it was her own man that was threatened, her brother-in-law that was shot. And always there was patching to be done when her husband was away for weeks on settler business and she could not sleep. In the earlier days, when there was no money for shoes, she made the slippers for the little ones from old overalls on these nights, making a double agony of it. Nothing hurt her pride more than the badly shod feet of her children.

She dug fence-post holes along lines of virgin land, hoed corn, fought prairie fires. She saw three waves of population, thousands of families, come into the free-land region, saw two-thirds of them turn back the next day and more dribble back as fast as they could get money from the folks back home, until only a handful remained.

Marlizzie still lives on the old homestead. With a hired hand she runs the place that she helped build through the long years with those gnarled hands. Now that her husband has planned his last ideal community, even the larger decisions are hers to make: the time for the haying, the branding and vaccinating of the cattle, the replacing of trees in her orchards. As the frontier women before her, she looks to the sky for the time of planting and harvest, to the earth for the wisdom and strength she yields to those who walk her freshly turned sod.

Extracted from "The New Frontier Woman," *Country Gentleman*, Sept., 1936

III. The Gateway

Omaha is one of the most masculine cities
in America. . . . It is full of dust, guts,
noise, and pith.
  —John Gunther, *Inside U.S.A.*

Omaha

DEBS MYERS

THE PEOPLE of Omaha believe the Almighty must have a particular fondness for Nebraska weather, because He furnishes such a sumptuous variety of it. The citizens were not unduly alarmed, therefore, one warm spring day when the skies suddenly blackened and the pleasant March breeze changed within half an hour to a fifty-five-mile-an-hour gale which blew ten windows out of a downtown department store and toppled a brick wall on an automobile. The calmness with which Omaha viewed this disturbance was not shared by a visiting businessman from the East who took refuge in a saloon and announced that never had he encountered a wind so powerful, and that he was leaving that night never to return. "Stranger, you should be ashamed of yourself," the bartender said. "Around here we don't pay much attention to the wind until we see a chicken coop or hog shed flying by. Even then we're not much concerned for ourselves—it's just that we know the crops and livestock across Nebraska to the west are catching hell and that's cause for worry."

To understand this random bit of philosophy—overdrawn but containing considerable wry truth—it is necessary to understand that to Omaha the farm land sprawling to the west is a wampum belt that keeps the city prosperous; a garden, feed lot, and granary supplying butter and eggs, corn and hogs which Omaha processes and sends across the world. When the farmers are happy, so is Omaha; when they are ailing, Omaha has a long face.

Even Omaha's most ardent boosters admit the climate is inclined to be skittish. The temperatures range from a record 114° above to a record 32° below, and it is not unprecedented on a spring day for the city to experience sunshine, rain, dust, hail, and snow, all within a few hours. This does not seem to faze Omaha a bit; instead, the city thrives on it. The climate has to be pretty good for all its eccentricities, the citizens reason, or the corn wouldn't grow so tall, the hogs get so fat, or human beings live so long.

This westward look is not a new thing with Omaha. The town was born in 1854 as a junction for steamboats coming down the Missouri River and wagon trains heading for Utah and Oregon. Stage coaches and teams of mules and oxen rumbled through the dusty streets; gamblers, gunmen, and claim-jumpers rubbed shoulders with honest men looking for a patch of land to plant a crop, and the clamor of the honky-tonks mingled with the street-corner exhortations of frontier preachers whose leather-lunged piety made even the mule-skinners take off their hats and marvel. It was a mule-skinner's town, tough as a bullwhip, and there was a saying that the devil himself, coming up from the nether regions to admire his handiwork, was scared away by the noise while still three miles underneath the Crystal Saloon. But even in those days the town, along with its more rambunctious characters, included a stubborn core of pioneer builders who believed that the prairies would be made into a farm empire and that Omaha, at the gateway to the West, someday would become big, rich, and respectable.

Today Omaha, with a population of 251,117,* is the largest city in Nebraska. It is known as the "Gate City to the West," "The City Surrounded by the United States," and, more elegantly, as the "Golden Buckle of the Corn Belt." Boiled down, this means that Omaha long ago has laid aside the bullwhip for the adding machine and become a comfortable, front-porch kind of place, proud of its parks, schools, and business buildings, admiring the famous paintings in the $4,000,000 Joslyn Memorial, but feeling, deep down, that there never will be a prettier picture anywhere than a straight furrow cut into the earth by a plow.

In appearance, inclination and habits, Omaha is stanchly midwestern. The city spreads out on the west bank of the Missouri River for twelve miles and rises far up on the hills to the west. Like most midwestern towns, it is sprawling and loose-jointed. When viewed from the top of the Woodmen of the World building, whose seventeen stories make it the city's tallest structure, Omaha looks bigger than it actually is. The people are neighborly, practical, and mind their own business. They have been through too much to be scared, or intimidated, by anything. In common with most prairie people, they have a deep strain of earthy individualism.

An illustration of this was overheard in a conversation in the lobby of the Blackstone Hotel, where a middle-aged man wearing a cowboy hat was describing to friends a parade of soldiers he had watched that day in downtown Omaha. "I'm standing there with my Uncle Ben," the man said, "and these soldiers are marching as good as I've ever seen soldiers march, never missing a step. And

* According to estimates of the Census Bureau and City Planning Department, on January 1, 1957, Omaha's population was 320,000.

I turn to Uncle Ben and say to him that that's what training and discipline will do for country boys, and I tell him it sure is a mighty fine sight. And Uncle Ben snorts and spits tobacco juice at the ground and he says to me: 'Yep, maybe so, but I'd like it better and it would be a sight more in line with the way this town grew up if a few of 'em were hollerin', raisin' a little hell and turnin' handsprings.'"

There is a belief among many people that Omaha's business well-being depends exclusively on agriculture. This is not completely true, although it is a fact that two out of every three dollars of Omaha's income are obtained from the processing or handling of foods. Omaha is also the fourth largest railroad center in the country, with ten trunk lines; it has more than thirty insurance companies, of which the Mutual Benefit alone employs more than 2,000; and it is headquarters for the Northwestern Bell Telephone Company, which operates in five states.

There are excellent department stores, shops, restaurants, and hotels. The Brandeis Department Store, ten stories high and a block long, is the largest department store in Nebraska and also does a prodigious restaurant business, serving more than 2,000,000 meals a year. Omaha has a dozen top-notch restaurants, most of which specialize in steak, and boasts one of the most cosmopolitan dining rooms west of the Mississippi in the Orleans Room of the Blackstone Hotel.

When pleasure-seekers set out to sample Omaha night life, they often wind up in South Omaha. In this section—a separate town during Omaha's early days—are located some of the town's less inhibited night clubs and saloons, as well as several excellent restaurants. South Omaha is chiefly notable, however, as the home of Omaha's vast meat-packing industry, probably the city's greatest single asset—it outranks Chicago as a livestock-marketing center. At the Union Stock Yards—including more than 160 acres of buildings, paved pens, and alleys—more than a million and a half dollars of business is transacted each working day. This tremendous volume of business is accomplished, incidentally, without written agreement, contract or down payment. The livestock is bought and sold on the basis of the spoken word or a nod of the head.

The best way to get an idea of how this is done is to follow a packing-house buyer through the yards. One of the best known of the buyers is a big, genial man named Grant Middaugh, with a reputation for knowing as much about beef on the hoof as any man around. On this particular morning a drizzling rain is falling and Middaugh, wearing boots, cowboy hat, and a slicker, walks from pen to pen, appraising the cattle, dickering over prices with the owners and trading small talk.

The buying of cattle is seldom a quick procedure; usually it is accompanied by haggling and robust insults, which are considered a mark of bargaining craftsmanship. At the first pen Middaugh shakes his head gloomily. "How much?" he asks. The farmer who owns the cattle sets a price. "At the price," Middaugh answers, "I would not buy them if they were the last of the barnyard species and I wanted to stuff them."

At his next stop Middaugh encounters a grizzled farmer sitting on a fence rail. Middaugh looks over the cattle with solemn deliberation. Neither he nor the farmer speaks. Finally, the farmer says, "Nice day." Not a man to side-step a ritual Middaugh answers, "For ducks." Middaugh sits on the rail next to the farmer and, after a pause, asks the price of the cattle. The negotiating begins. Middaugh walks away and the farmer walks after him, tugging at his slicker, lowering the price. Then the farmer climbs back on the rail and folds his arms in the manner of a man whose patience is exhausted. Middaugh raises his price and the farmer closes the deal with a brusque bob of his head. "It's mighty lucky," Middaugh says, "that my ancestors were Dutch and stubborn." The farmer sniffs. "For you to talk about your ancestors," he says, "is plain reckless."

When the morning is over Middaugh has bought six pens of cattle. In doing this he has haggled over prices with more than three dozen farmers and has walked more than five miles, which is about half the distance he walks on a day he considers really busy.

Most of Omaha's civic undertakings are linked to the outlying farms, and this is true of the unique organization known as Ak-Sar-Ben, which is Nebraska spelled backwards. During the depression year of 1895, a group of Omaha businessmen founded the organization in an effort to retain the state fair for the city, provide a shot in the arm for Omaha business, and co-ordinate the aims of the city and country people. These businessmen staged a series of parades, festivals, and entertainments which attracted thousands of rural dwellers into Omaha and garnished this hospitality with ritualistic fanfare which made it into a prairie version of the New Orleans Mardi Gras. Today Ak-Sar-Ben is a flourishing nonprofit civic organization with more than 15,000 members and an impressive plant six miles outside Omaha. The plant includes a race track, a coliseum, and excellent facilities for livestock shows and 4-H Club activities. The annual Ak-Sar-Ben ball is the major event of the Omaha social season.

Ak-Sar-Ben prides itself on its contributions to the public service, such as the occasion when it assumed the debt on two Missouri River bridges joining Nebraska and Iowa and made them both toll free. Fundamentally, though, Ak-Sar-Ben concentrates on helping Nebraska's rural farm and youth organizations. Ak-Sar-Ben leaders feel they know Nebraska farm youngsters as well as anyone, but occasionally they get surprised. There was the time at a livestock-judging contest when a fourteen-year-old farm boy was leading a bull into the ring to be judged and later sold. Two Ak-Sar-Ben officials were watching, and one said to the other: "You can tell this kid loves that bull and hates to sell it."

"Yeah," the other official agreed, "probably he'll break into tears."

Gravely the boy brought the bull into the ring and removed its rope. Then he kicked the bull in the hind quarters. "I'm glad to be seeing the last of you," the boy said, "you always have been an ornery —"

Omaha's foremost tourist attraction is not within the city limits, but ten miles to the west. This is the site of Boys Town, the home and school made famous by the late Rt. Rev. Msgr. Edward J. Flanagan. Riding the bus from Omaha across the rolling prairie to see Boys Town, I talked with a fifteen-year-old Negro boy. He grew up in the South, his parents were dead, he had been homeless two years, and now he was bound for Boys Town, and he was scared.

"I wonder how those white boys are going to treat me," he said.

The first sight of Boys Town is something people remember. This is not a collection of somber school buildings and dormitories, hinting of reformatory bleakness; instead, it resembles the campus of a college that takes pride in itself. The buildings are bright and modern, clustered on a hill, overlooking long acres of farm land.

The Negro boy, getting off the bus, was met by two white boys about the same age. One of them picked up the Negro boy's battered suitcase. The Negro boy was startled. "You mustn't do that," he said.

"Why not?" asked the boy carrying the suitcase. "You've had a hard trip." The three boys walked up the road toward Boys Town. The Negro boy was shaking his head. "Think of that," he said, "a white boy carrying my suitcase for me."

Boys Town is the "youngest" incorporated village in the country, with its own boy mayor, councilmen, and commissioners, its own post office, newspaper, schoolrooms, field house, carpentry shops, barbershop, chapel—in fact, a complete community.

Founded by Father Flanagan in Omaha in 1917 on ninety borrowed dollars, the institution today has an enrollment of nearly 1,000 boys of varied creed and color and covers 1,200 acres, more than half of which are in cultivation. The boys who live in the well-kept cottages surrounding the campus come to Boys Town from all over the United States. They are admitted between the ages of ten and sixteen, homeless and underprivileged, and some of them delinquent. At Boys Town they go to the church of their own choice, attend grade school and high school, and learn a trade.

Upon the death of Father Flanagan in 1948, the Rt. Rev. Msgr. Nicholas H. Wegner became the managing director of Boys Town. Father Wegner is a quiet-spoken native Nebraskan who turned down two major-league baseball contracts to study for the priesthood. On the wall above his office desk is a drawing by Cartoonist Percy L. Crosby portraying the youthful comic-strip character, Skippy, cap pulled down, hands thrust into pockets, chin lowered dejectedly. The caption states: "When you feel like this there's nothing like talking it over with Father Flanagan." Father Wegner points to the cartoon and smiles, "I can sum up my aims briefly," he says. "I am trying to follow in the footsteps of Father Flanagan."

Just as Boys Town is a mingling of races and creeds, so is Omaha itself. Of the entire population, 84.6 per cent is native-born white, but this does not tell how many thousands of its citizens are of foreign extraction. Large foreign-born groups include Germans, Italians, Poles, Czechs, Swedes, Irish, and Danes. Many of them have their own social centers and festivals, but this does not mean that they remain aloof from civic affairs. To the contrary, when the Omaha *World-Herald,* the city's only newspaper, sounds the call for any kind of civic improvement campaign, the foreign-born pitch in as readily as anyone.

Like all monopoly newspapers, the *World-Herald* is cussed by many of the citizens, but there isn't anyone who challenges the fact that it is a powerful force in the community. It was founded in 1885 by Gilbert M. Hitchcock, who served eighteen years in the United States Senate and House as a Democrat. The present boss of the *World-Herald* is Henry Doorly, who came to Omaha in 1900 as a draftsman for the Union Pacific Railroad, fell in love with Hitchcock's daughter, and married her. Hitchcock, wanting to bring his new son-in-law into the business, went to the managing editor, William R. Watson, and asked him to give Doorly a job.

"Sure, glad to do it," Watson said. "I'll start him out in the way I start all cub reporters, covering the night police beat."

Hitchcock fidgeted, "Look, Bill," he said, "you know me, and I'm not going to ask you any special favors. But if that boy is put to working nights, my daughter is going to give me unshirted hell."

Whereupon Doorly was made a day police reporter. After a year of this he went into the business department and is credited with furnishing much of the acumen which eventually drove out all competition and made the *World-Herald* a solid and prosperous property.

It is almost forgotten in Omaha, but the editor of the *World-Herald* for two years during the '90's was William Jennings Bryan. An old-timer who remembers Bryan during this period says of him: "He was more talker than writer, and I suspect not much of an editor, but, believe me, you forgot all that when you got into a conversation with him and he smiled. He had the biggest grin I ever saw—it looked as though he was whispering in his own ear."

Bryan helped to furnish the flavor of Omaha's early-day politics, which were gaudy and sometimes violent. The most colorful of Omaha's politicians was a former cowboy named James C. Dahlman who boasted that he grew up with a branding iron in one hand and a six-shooter in the other. He served five terms as mayor, starting in 1906, and there are still old men around who tell of how Dahlman in his first race for mayor outwitted an opponent who said that Dahlman was too uneducated to write a veto message.

"It's true that I haven't had much schooling," Dahlman told the voters, "but I know this is an independent-minded town full of unbranded mavericks like me, and if any ordinance comes up to me as mayor that takes one copper cent unjustly from the people, I'll get the biggest ink bottle and the biggest stub pen in Omaha, and I'll write across that ordinance as big as I can write, 'nothing doing,' and I'll sign it 'Jim Dahlman' and if there's any sucker who don't understand what that means, he ain't as well educated as I am."

During the town's infancy it had more than its share of rogues and swindlers, and the honest people had trouble driving them out. Finally they got the upper hand of these undesirable gentry—by lynching them, shooting them, ducking them into the cold waters of the Missouri River, or simply by scaring them.

The story still endures of a respected pioneer who became indignant over the conduct of a stranger in a trading post, tapped the man on the shoulder, and said to him politely: "I am Peter A. Sarpy, the old horse on the sandbar, sir. If you want to fight, I am your man, sir. I can whip the devil. If you want satisfaction, sir, choose your weapons—bowie knife, shotgun, or revolver."

Having disposed of these formalities, Sarpy drew a gun and fired at a candle on a table. The bullet—so the story goes—extinguished the candle and the stranger disappeared.

Omaha's more lasting memories are connected, not with its rambunctious beginnings, but with festivals and celebrations. One of the greatest shows in Omaha history was the Trans-Mississippi and International Exposition of 1898, which helped put Omaha on the map. It was a forerunner of other fairs to follow, and was replete even to a jiggily young woman known as Little Egypt, who danced with her clothes on—influenced possibly by the action of an unidentified reformer who roamed the fairgrounds one night smashing all the nude sculpture with an ax. Forty-one years later, in 1939, many of the same beaver hats, crinoline dresses, hoop skirts, and bonnets worn by Omahans during the exposition were dug out of trunks for a celebration known as the Golden Spike Days. Actually, it was a whopping publicity stunt to call attention to the premiere of a movie, Union Pacific, but it gave the city a chance to honor an esteemed partner in the community, the Union Pacific.

Omaha's affection for the Union Pacific is understandable. It hires 10,000 employees in the Omaha area, with an annual payroll of $26,000,000. The president of the Union Pacific is rugged, friendly Arthur E. Stoddard, who started in the railroad business at twelve as a water boy making twenty-five cents a day. Although not so colorful as some of his predecessors, Stoddard exerts an effective influence on the city's affairs.

Omaha also has one of the most impressive museums in the Midwest, the Joslyn Art Memorial. Located on top of a hill where the territorial capitol once stood, the building houses a wide variety of art and artcraft exhibits as well as serving as a lecture and music hall. The museum director is an energetic young man named Eugene Kingman, who has done a remarkable job of making the museum a part of the city's day-to-day life. One day Kingman was stopped in the entrance hall by a man who inquired: "Pardon me, but can you tell me the name of this mortuary?" Then and there, Kingman decided to popularize the museum with the town.

Much of Omaha's cultural impetus is furnished by its universities.

Omaha Municipal University is a school with an enrollment of more than 4,000. The campus, spread over fifty-two acres, is located in the middle of one of Omaha's best residential districts, bordered on the north by the Lincoln Highway. The university offers wide academic coverage, including the largest evening school of adult education between Chicago and Denver.

Creighton, Omaha's other major school, is a Jesuit institution with a pleasant campus on a hill overlooking part of the business district. Creighton is known throughout the United States for its courses in law and medicine: since the University of Nebraska also has a medical branch in Omaha, the city is one of the medical centers of the Midwest.

Whenever money is needed for a civic project, Omaha calls on W. Dale Clark, chairman of the board of the Omaha National Bank. In the bleak days of 1932, when banks were closing around the country, a line of depositors formed one day in front of the bank where Clark was working. Clark studied the line with concern. "Those people are hot and hungry," he said, and sent them iced tea and sandwiches. The depositors figured that any bank solvent enough to feed them when they wanted to take out money was in good shape—and the line quickly disappeared.

Another of Omaha's better-known businessmen is a husky six-footer named J. Gordon Roberts, president of the Roberts Dairy Company, who writes for the *World-Herald* a column of comment and opinion which he pays for at advertising rates. In these editorial essays he states his views on anything which he considers important to Omaha at the time. His subjects have included midget football, politics, philosophy, the rights of stockholders, free enterprise, and the Bible. Needless to say, Roberts took a strong position in favor of stockholders, free enterprise, and the Bible. Nonetheless, some of his friends at the outset considered him slightly daft for taking a chance on offending part of the public—this was something, they said, which a solid midwestern businessman simply couldn't do. To this Roberts answered in print: "Nuts. I have something to say and I'd rather be broke than a coward."

Today Omaha, rising far above the muddy waters of the Missouri River, is a scrapper come up the hard way, a city born in the prairie tradition with a faith in itself that comes from kinship with the soil.

There is a story about a New York City financier who once paid a visit to Mayor Jim Dahlman. Dahlman, as usual, was painting a bright picture of Omaha's future. "Your optimism is poorly taken," the financier said. "This city is a long way from the factories, production lines, and money markets of the East." Dahlman grinned, grabbed the financier by the arm, and said, "Come with me."

The two of them went to the banks of the Missouri River, climbed a bluff, and Dahlman waved toward the West. "There are our factories, our production lines, and our money markets, all in one big piece of land," Dahlman said, "created not by man but by the Almighty, and this town will do all right as long as the land is good, the hogs are fat, and we have the common gumption to keep our roots deep in the soil."

Reprinted by special permission from *Holiday*, Oct., 1952, copyright 1952 by The Curtis Publishing Company

People from other regions have not always understood the origin of breezy western manners, the love of horseplay and noisy fun characteristic of plainsmen. Yet it is a very old tradition, and . . . still seems a valid one.

In old times on the Plains, Indian enemies sneaked up in silence, but Indian friends always came yelling and making a loud noise. That was their custom. After firearms were brought in by traders, Plains Indians naturally made their peaceful salute by firing—and so emptying—their guns whenever they approached a friendly camp or fort or settlement. And their custom was, very naturally—and indeed of necessity—taken up by all traders, trappers, rivermen, and frontiersmen.

This, in fact, is the origin of that old cowboy custom of riding in at a high lope, whooping at the top of the lungs, and "shooting up the town."

—Stanley Vestal, *The Missouri*

Iron Horseplay

LUCIUS BEEBE

PERHAPS the most typical—certainly the most spirited and splendid—of all American jollifications during the nineteenth century was the railroad celebration. Other convocations and foregatherings of the people laid claim on the attention of posterity—barn-raisings, revival meetings, veterans' encampments, political rallies, peace jubilees, and the field days and musters of the Ancients & Honorables and the Fencible Light Guards. However, none approached the uproar, the barrel-broaching, the oratorical hosannahs, the fireworks, transparencies, and band music, the parades, barbecues, and square dances, the slugging, nose-pasting, and falling down in alcoholic swoons of entire populaces which accompanied the railroad celebration. Here the eagle screamed while hovering most gloriously visible over a people favored of fortune and providence. Here was the achievement of what was in actual fact the great American preoccupation and obsession throughout the seventies, eighties, and nineties. Here was salvation through the agency of the coefficient of ex-

panding steam, glory at the throttle, and wealth illimitable beckon-
ing down vistas of steel rails that led straight to the Shining
Mountains of Destiny itself.

The celebration that greeted the arrival of the first teapot locomotive, its thin and cheerful whistle coming in advance from far
over the prairie, took on aspects of religious ecstasy tempered with
Medford rum. Here were the politicians in plug hats and congress
gaiters to show their kinship with car tonk and gandy dancer. Here
the railroad presidents in wonderfully flowered waistcoats and gold
Albert watch chains and corporate titles all ending in the magic
word Pacific. Here the contractors and locomotive salesmen with
liberal expense accounts and all-Havana "seegars."

To know the incredible impact of the coming of the steamcars,
one must turn to the yellowing files detailing the jubilation at both
ends of the track and all intermediate points that greeted the in-
augural of service over the Western Railroad between Albany and
Boston. He should read of the epic convulsions along the right of
way that accompanied the first through train over the Erie from
Piermont on the Jersey shore opposite Manhattan all the way to
Dunkirk on Lake Erie, and enlisted the presence and oratory of the
godlike Daniel Webster himself. But the most significant of all
railroad celebrations, albeit limited in its immediate participants
while millions rejoiced elsewhere on the continent, was fated to be
held far to the west even of Lake Erie on a wet and windy upland
called Promontory Point, Utah Territory, on a day that will be
forever starred in the American record, May 10, 1869.

From earliest times, even before the completion of its tracks to
their eventual meeting with the Central Pacific at Promontory, Utah,
in 1869, the Union Pacific had been a favorite with western excur-
sionists, the pioneer railroad that opened limitless vistas to a nation
on the march toward continental destinies. As early as 1867 when its
railhead was still in mid-Nebraska and the Hell-on-Wheels that accompanied it was making night hideous far short of unborn
Cheyenne, an excursion was arranged out of New York to ride the
steamcars as far as the hundredth meridian at Platte City. Heading
out of Omaha in a train whose consist included five coaches, "the
Lincoln car and the sumptuous director's car of the Union Pacific,"
the expedition bristled with names that made the news of the day:
Thomas C. Durant and Sidney Dillon, vice-presidents of the railroad,
Grenville M. Dodge, its chief engineer, and Silas Seymour, consult-
ing engineer, George Mortimer Pullman, the Earl of Airlie and serv-

ant, the Marquis de Chambrun, the Hon. Rutherford B. Hayes, and a frock-coated gaggle of railroad presidents representing the Illinois Central, Burlington, Michigan Southern and Alton lines, all presumably digging their toes in the ballast and hefting loose sections of rail to see if the U. P. was living up to government specifications. There were also numberless womenfolk, two military brass bands, and Indians past counting.

The menus of the receptions, dinners, collations, and banquets arranged along the right of way by a Chicago caterer are a noble commentary on the capacities of the pioneers; and whenever things got dull the Indians could be counted on to provide a floor show with war dances and simulated attacks on the palefaces, causing the womenfolk to scream prettily and silk-hatted captains of industry to reach tentatively for the Remington .41 calibre derringers without which nobody in his right mind would travel west of Wabash Avenue in those days.

But although many a gaudy hurrah had accompanied the Iron Horse westward in the nineteenth century, it remained for Omaha in the latter nineteen-thirties to be the setting for the most epic of all railroad tumults, a civic convulsion at the memory of which a thousand elbows bend in ceremonial gesture, a reflex action delayed but still instinctive over the years. The occasion was the launching of a film called *Union Pacific,* devised for Paramount Pictures by Cecil B. DeMille and a supporting cast of experts, technicians, words artists, howdah bearers, and acolytes, of which demented congress the author of this brief chronicle was a member.

Conceived in the grand manner of all DeMille sagas, *Union Pacific* was a fairly realistic re-creation of empire-building days, into which there had been introduced a romance—compounded of suitable amounts of sentimentality, bathos, and hokum—between Mr. Joel McRae and Miss Barbara Stanwyck. The location company shot the vast panoramic scenes of railroad construction at Iron Springs, Utah, in the presence (among others) of William Jeffers, President of Union Pacific, and myself. On hand in advisory capacities, we saw whole tribes of imported Indians massacred by the United States Cavalry, trains wrecked, and frontier towns demolished by roistering extras. Nearly a year had been devoted to shooting the interiors and editing this nonesuch, and now the payoff was at hand, the world premiere at Omaha.

The effulgence of the launching of *Union Pacific* derived from a variety of circumstances. There hadn't been a big show of any sort in Nebraska in some years, not even the circus, and the countryfolk were spoiling for fun. Funds for this monster flag-raising were jointly raised from four impeccably solvent sources, the state of Nebraska, the city of Omaha, Paramount Pictures, and the Union Pacific Railroad. Together they contrived quite a bundle. The junket climaxed a long tally of similar expensive and charming follies which had translated Sunset Boulevard and Fifty-second Street almost intact to Dodge City, Kansas, Virginia City, Nevada, and Santa Fe, New Mexico. It was the heyday of the big film opening in a vaguely appropriate geographic locale. A million dollars was the sum most frequently mentioned in the bar of the Fontenelle Hotel to underwrite the gunfire that was even then resounding in the street outside, and the sum seemed not only probable but perhaps modest.

Sometimes it required half a year to get the communities favored with the full treatment in film premieres back in running order. Often the inhabitants simply found it more expedient to go elsewhere, leaving the ruins smouldering in the desert. That Omaha survived an invasion and pillage compared to which the sack of Babylon by Cyrus the Persian was the merest rehearsal for chaos is ample testimony to the durable qualities of the valley of the Platte.

I was present Thursday, April 27, 1939, at the opening of *Union Pacific* and have marks of Indian warfare on my person to prove it.

Signs and portents of an uprising near the Council Bluff of the Missouri had been perceptible in Chicago as long as three days before the actual outbreak of festivities. I had lunched with Chicago hotelman Ernie Byfield and Playwright Charlie MacArthur in the Pump Room, and MacArthur, fresh from the Coast, brought disquieting rumors of war parties assembling in Paramount's back lot. "Some of the lesser chiefs are off the reservation already," he reported. "The whisky smugglers have been selling a powerful lot of firewater, and they've got ball ammunition and breech-loading press agents. The word is that Bill Hebert did the Ghost Dance on a table at Chasen's night before last, and you know what that means. It looks like war."

Since Hebert was Mr. DeMille's personal publicity man, a maker of big medicine without whose counsel the Old Man undertook no major war party, I boarded the special train of Averell Harriman that night, reflecting that we might well be rolling westward into an ambush of cataclysmic proportions. On the platform two bands played "Garry Owen," the fateful tune to which Custer marched out of Fort Lincoln, Dakota Territory, bound for death and glory, and under the circumstances this seemed to me a singularly tactless bit of programming. But I was cheered on entering my stateroom to find that Mr. Harriman had thoughtfully sent each of his guests a magnum of Bollinger—to save wear and tear on the club car while they were dressing for dinner.

The arrival of the Harriman Special, nicely timed to meet the guests coming in on the DeMille Special as they were decanted onto the platform at Omaha, was the signal for dancing in the streets comparable to that which accompanied the Fall of the Bastille and the Relief of Lucknow. There was a cheerful blaring of massed bands and a master of ceremonies at the microphone who batted an even .1000 in misidentifying each and every celebrity to totter from the cars. Having breakfasted off rib steak and Dom Perignon '29, my morale was good, and, on the arm of an Illinois Central division superintendent who happened still to be wearing his dinner clothes of the evening before, I wandered into the rotunda of the depot.

Ten thousand schoolchildren had been corralled therein to sing "Crinoline Days" to welcome the august visitors; and the master of ceremonies, seeing our precedence in the procession and noting the conspicuously aristocratic attire of my companion, promptly announced over the public address system that I was W. Averell Harriman, chairman of the board of Union Pacific, "a public benefactor of conspicuous achievements and our honored guest today within the civic confines of festive Omaha." Thus invested with grandeur, I allowed myself to be conducted to the microphone, where I was given a generous hand, and was preparing to do Mr. Harriman proud in a brief address when the arrival of Mr. Harriman in his proper person caused me to be ushered politely, albeit swiftly and firmly, into a waiting carriage.

Of the hospitality that surged at times knee-deep through downtown Omaha for the next three days, what pen shall write justly, what lyric measures lend it immortality? There were colossi among those present—imperfectly visible, to be sure, through a thick protective foliage of false whiskers provided by a prudent management so that complete anonymity was achieved by several score of captains of industry who would never have cut loose as they did without crepe beavers and henna rugs. Who might know if it was indeed J. C. Penney who pushed a bystander through the plate glass window of Brandeis basement store, or Felix Warburg of Kuhn-Loeb & Company who charged into the bar of the Fontenelle Hotel with a rebel yell, the Stars and Bars in one hand, in the other a Colt's Frontier handgun with which he shot Steve Hannagan in the stomach? (Of course at this stage of the game all ammunition was blank, but still it could start a nasty brush fire in anybody's false beard.) Somewhere in the shuffle was Heber Grant, President of the Latter Day Saints; he alone was not suspected of any of the multiplicity of misdemeanors and minor outrages committed by heavily bearded strangers who always pointed to somebody else when the police arrived.

Who shall tell of the parades, the civic receptions, the unveiling of Golden Spikes, the speeches by Mr. DeMille, the speeches by William Jeffers, the speeches by governors, mayors, chamber of commerce coordinators, game wardens, and visiting dignitaries past all counting? The Hunkpapa Sioux gave a war dance; the Old Timers of the Union Pacific gave a dinner party for 6,000; and at all times limitless cheer radiated from a wonderful person whose memory, at this remove, is still green, an Omaha nabob named Otto Swanson. Mr. Swanson, splendid in a white beaver hat, lavender frock coat, spongebag trousers, and gambler's waistcoat, was a personage of mien at once menacing and enchanting. Wherever one encountered him, and that was everywhere, he was in a mood to set them up.

A notable characteristic of the film premieres of the 1930's, to which *Union Pacific* was no exception, was that none of them ever terminated on schedule. Special trains might depart, press agents might urge their valuable charges to cease and desist, but nobody paid any mind. The gala first showings of *Union Pacific* were held, the final oratory surged out of city hall and civic auditorium, the special trains left for the east and the west, the captains and the kings departed. But was the Fontenelle bar in any way abated of tumult or diminished of patronage? Think again. Two days after the festival was, in theory, over, Bill Hebert and I found ourselves leaning against that substantial structure still in the company of the indestructible Otto Swanson and a somewhat smaller dignitary in bright red Dundreary whiskers and a lemon-colored top hat, whose professional card announced that he was the official city coroner of Omaha and maintained a private practice in physic and surgery on the side. In the corner were the words "Gunshot Wounds a Specialty."

"I only had them run up special this morning," he announced in brisk medical tones. "So many slugs going around now you never know when you'll need a good doc."

As though in answer to the sentiment, a terrific burst of gunfire broke out at the other end of the bar, and a long panel of plate glass mirror leapt from its frame in approximately a million pieces.

"You see what I mean?" said the specialist.

Unwilling to suspend its merry-making just because most of the guests had gone home, Omaha was still abroad in frontier costume shooting glad salutes to nothing; but blank ammunition had run out in every hardware store and all that was available were ball cartridges. To the glory of the Old West it may be said that this fell circumstance did nothing at all to abate the party. Indeed it lent it a hitherto lacking cachet of authenticity. How much more satisfactory to shoot at the chandelier and have the fixture disintegrate and descend in a rain of crystal debris!

To add to the glad tumults of the day, a steam locomotive, a reasonable facsimile of gallant No. 119 that played the leading role opposite the Central Pacific's *Jupiter* at Promontory, had been emplaced behind the bar with live steam available to its whistle and whistle cords strategically spaced around the room for each to pull to his satisfaction.

I cherish doubts if in hell there will ever be such a tumult as the final day's demented symphony orchestrated to gunfire, the crash of glass fixtures of gratifying dimensions, the deafening whistle of a live steam locomotive, and the war cries of that resolute, nay, indomitable little band of Omaha frontiersmen who refused to admit that the party was over. Let us leave them there forever in the mind's eye, beards down among the beer pumps, boots and spurs entangled in the cuspidors, here and there a fallen soldier of the legion at peace on the floor while the tide of battle ebbed and flowed and the Anheuser Busch lithographs snapped their picture wires and the walls cascaded noisily into the picturesque debris of pioneers below. The Little Big Horn they depicted was nothing to the present reality of carnage.

Film openings at distant places are no longer in vogue. Railroad celebrations are history, but in a national periodical a few months ago I read a piece on Nebraska by Mari Sandoz in which she said that still embedded in the bar of the Fontenelle is a .45 caliber leaden slug. May it remain there in perpetuity, for it is a monument to the last of the Old West, to a golden week when there were giants abroad in the valley of the Platte.

Not all visitors to Omaha have carried away such lively memories as Mr. Beebe. For instance, Mr. Rudyard Kipling—a transcontinental traveler of 1889—seems to have been concerned chiefly with local burial customs.

Omaha Between Trains

RUDYARD KIPLING

OMAHA, NEBRASKA, was but a halting-place on the road to Chicago, but it revealed to me horrors that I would not have willingly missed. The city to casual investigation seemed to be populated entirely by Germans, Poles, Slavs, Hungarians, Croats, Magyars, and all the scum of the Eastern European States, but it must have been laid out by Americans. No other people would cut the traffic of a main street with two streams of railway lines, each some eight or nine tracks wide, and cheerfully drive tram cars across the metals. Every now and again they have horrible railway-crossing accidents at Omaha, but nobody seems to think of building an overhead-bridge. That would interfere with the vested interests of the undertakers.

Be blessed to hear some details of one of that class.

There was a shop the like of which I had never seen before: its windows were filled with dress-coats for men, and dresses for women. But the studs of the shirts were made of stamped cloth upon the shirt front, and there were no trousers to those coats—nothing but a sweep of cheap black cloth falling like an abbé's frock. In the doorway sat a young man reading Pollock's *Course of Time,* and by that I knew that he was an undertaker. His name was Gring, which is a beautiful name, and I talked to him on the mysteries of his Craft. He was an enthusiast and an artist. I told him how corpses were burnt in India. Said he: "We're vastly superior. We hold—that is to say, embalm—our dead. So!" Whereupon he produced the horrible weapons of his trade, and most practically showed me how you "held" a man back from that corruption which is his birthright. "And I wish I could live a few generations just to see how my people keep. But I'm sure it's all right. Nothing can touch 'em after *I*'ve embalmed 'em." Then he displayed one of those ghastly dress-suits, and when I laid a shuddering hand upon it, behold it crumpled to nothing, for

168

the white linen was sewn on to the black cloth and—there was no back to it! That was the horror. The garment was a shell. "We dress a man in that," said Gring, laying it out tastily on the counter. "As you see here, our caskets have a plate-glass window in front" (Oh me, but that window in the coffin was fitted with plush like a brougham-window!), "and you don't see anything below the level of the man's waistcoat. Consequently . . ." He unrolled the terrible cheap black cloth that falls down over the stark feet, and I jumped back. "Of course a man can be dressed in his own clothes if he likes, but these are the regular things: and for women look at this!" He took up the body of a high-necked dinner-dress in subdued lilac, slashed and puffed and bedevilled with black, but, like the dress-suit, backless, and below the waist turning into a shroud. "That's for an old maid. But for young girls we give white with imitation pearls round the neck. That looks very pretty through the window of the casket—you see there's a cushion for the head—with flowers banked all round." Can you imagine anything more awful than to take your last rest as much of a dead fraud as ever you were a living lie—to go into the darkness one half of you shaved, trimmed, and dressed for an evening party, while the other half—the half that your friends cannot see—is enwrapped in a flapping black sheet?

I know a little about burial customs in various places in the world, and I tried hard to make Mr. Gring comprehend dimly the awful heathendom that he was responsible for—the grotesquerie—the giggling horror of it all. But he couldn't see it. Even when he showed me a little boy's last suit, he couldn't see it. He said it was quite right to embalm and trick out and hypocritically bedizen the poor innocent dead in their superior cushioned and pillowed caskets with the window in front.

Bury me cased in canvas like a fishing-rod, in the deep sea; burn me on a back-water of the Hughli with damp wood and no oil; pin me under a Pullman car and let the lighted stove do its worst; sizzle me with a fallen electric wire or whelm me in the sludge of a broken river dam; but may I never go down to the Pit grinning out of a plate-glass window, in a backless dress-coat, and the front half of a black stuff dressing-gown; not though I were "held" against the ravage of the grave for ever and ever. Amen!

Reprinted from *From Sea to Sea; Letters of Travel,*
Doubleday & McClure Co., 1899

In the history of every town, there are certain happenings, seemingly of earth-shaking import at the time, whose significance diminishes with the passage of the years, yet which continue to bulk large in local lore. Such events usually are referred to as The This *or* The That, *as if each were the only one of its kind.*

In Omaha, there have been The Fair *and* The Kidnapping *and* The Tornado.

Omaha Newsreel

1. The Fair

GEORGE R. LEIGHTON

FROM June to November in 1898, Omaha held the Trans-Mississippi Exposition. What had commenced in the dark days of '95 as the mad scheme of a few Omaha men and other Western capitalists to help revive trade turned out to be a stunning advertisement of American business and returning prosperity. Only a few days before the fair opened, the war with Spain began. The admired sculpture of the time might have represented this at Omaha with an allegorical group: Triumphant business enterprise crowning itself with laurel and reaching for the sword at the same time.

Some Omaha businessmen looked cross-eyed at the idea of a fair. Where was the money to come from? But they didn't all feel that way, least of all Gurdon W. Wattles, a former Iowa banker who had come to Omaha on the eve of the panic of '93. Of all the promoters of the exposition, Mr. Wattles was the most ardent and the most vocal. He had gone through a strenuous youth on a poor Iowa farm and had accumulated a number of small-town banks before he sold out and came to Omaha. Investing a part of his accumulation in a bank, he set out to be an energetic citizen. He joined right and left, wore a mustache and a stiff collar, spoke at luncheons and did it all with a high moral tone. Not for him the bibulous habits of Count Creighton—who had received his patent of nobility from Leo XIII in '95—nor the raucous ejaculations of Bill Paxton. Those two worthies still lived, but the old-timers, the pioneers, were passing from the scene. The new types for the new era were in sight. Wattles was it; the twentieth century go-getter had arrived in Omaha and the Trans-Mississippi Exposition gave him the chance to show what he could do.

The main trouble was in raising the money, but Mr. Wattles and his colleagues could not be daunted. The Street Railway and the Gas Company chipped in ten thousand apiece and so did Mr. Kountze, the banker; the Stockyards Company and the New York Life Insurance Company were good for five thousand and so was P. D. Armour. "Influential citizens made frequent trips to New York, Chicago, St. Louis and elsewhere for the sole purpose of inducing officials of insurance companies, railways, packing houses, etc., to make subscriptions to the capital stock of the exposition." For a time the railroad people doubted the whole thing, but finally Mr. Holdrege was persuaded to go over to Burlington and see Mr. Perkins. Once upon a time a locomotive engineer on the Burlington bought his wife a silk dress. Mr. Perkins was outraged at the extravagance and denounced it. But the exposition was another thing. He put the Burlington down for a donation of thirty thousand dollars, and the other roads fell into line. Work on the exposition proceeded apace and the fair was opened on the 1st of June, 1898. It was a triumph and everybody in Omaha knew it.

During the worst of the hard times one could catch a streetcar on Farnam Street and ride out through a sad part of town filled with building lots which, after the real estate collapse of the eighties, had gone back to cornfields. Here in this tract, not far from the river bluff, a depression had been scooped out for a lagoon and round it were built, out of plaster of Paris and excelsior, a group of glittering white buildings. The architecture, "freely inspired by the classic and the renaissance," had no relation whatever to the life history of the plains and mountain country. Nor was it intended to have. More even than an advertisement of Omaha and the West, the fair was a reflection of the state of mind of its promoters. It was like a shot in the arm to leave the well-worn corner of Sixteenth and Farnam, with all the familiar feeling of everyday Midwestern existence, and step inside an enclosure half a mile long, all set about with "old Ivory" domes, sodded grass plots, flaming canna beds, and Corinthian columns. Flights of broad stairs looked down on a sheet of Missouri River water, dotted with gondolas and buttressed with dead-white balustrades.

The Fine Arts included Bouguereau's "Return of Spring"; "a life size figure of a young woman surrounded by cupids and flowers. The picture, valued at $50,000, came into prominence years ago when hung in an art loan exhibit in Omaha. At that time a young man, Cary J. Warbinton, threw a chair through the canvas, which was subsequently repaired." For the men, Little Egypt would shake that thing in the Streets of Cairo and Judge Dundy's gambler son, Skip Dundy, had the concession for the Infant Incubator. This experience was enough to send Skip to New York to build the Hippodrome, and Luna Park at Coney Island. But the chief place—after the pavilion of the Federal government was provided for—was reserved for the now politically impotent Agriculture.

Cass Gilbert, the young architect of St. Paul, was selected to design this mausoleum, "free Renaissance" also, with its garlands of wheat, corn, and fruit tinted in brilliant colors. To crown all, "the monotony of the sky line was relieved by statuary represented by a fine group— Prosperity—supported by Labor and Integrity." Where was the sod house now? . . .

"The mission of the exposition," said the acidulous Mr. Ingalls of Kansas, "is to communicate to mankind the impulses to which it owes its origin." Mr. Wattles certainly could agree to that. Fittingly enough, a conspicuous place was given to a huge plaster warrior in a chariot drawn by four lions and inscribed simply: OMAHA.

"Not a cloud marred the perfection of the cerulean vault, . . . all the cardinal and semi-cardinal points of the compass converged at Omaha" on that first of June. A platform had been set up at one end of the shimmering Grand Court and on it, facing the crowd, were the notables. All were waiting in the white, hot sunshine for Mr. McKinley to press the telegraph key in Washington. The message came; the parson prayed. Then Mr. Wattles took off his top hat and faced the crowd. "Fifty years ago," said he, "the larger part of the country west of the Mississippi River was . . . indicated on the map as the Great American Desert. No less than 80,000 miles of railroad have been constructed in the Trans-Mississippi country during the last fifty years at the fabulous cost of two thousand million dollars. . . . Great cities have been built and manufacturing has assumed enormous proportions. . . . This magnificent exposition, illustrating the products of our soil and mines and factories . . . will pale into insignificance at the close of the twentieth century. When the agricultural resources of this rich country are fully developed; . . . when the sugar as well as the bread and meat for the markets of the world shall be produced here and carried to the markets by the electric forces of nature; when the minerals in our mountains and the gold and silver in our mines shall be extracted and utilized by this same force; when our natural products shall be manufactured here, then this Trans-Mississippi country will support a population in peace and plenty greater than the population of any other nation in the world. This exposition . . . opens new fields to the investor, inspires the ambition of the genius, incites the emulation of states and stands the crowning glory in the history of the West."

Extracted from *Five Cities*, Harper & Brothers, 1939

While no doubt it is a distinction the city would be happy to do without, the fact remains that Omaha was the scene of the twentieth century's first nationally headlined kidnapping. What made the story sensational news in 1900 was the wealth and prominence of the kidnapped boy's family: Edward A. Cudahy, Jr., was the only son of a millionaire meat-packer, and heir-apparent to the Cudahy Packing Company. However, in recent years it is not the plutocratic lineage of the victim which causes newspapers to revive the story from time to time. To a generation which regards kidnapping as the most detestable of crimes, the real shocker is the verdict of the jury.

2. The Kidnapping

RUTH REYNOLDS

AT SEVEN P.M., on December 18, 1900, Edward A. Cudahy, Sr., asked his fifteen-year-old son Eddie to deliver a pile of periodicals to Dr. Fred Rustin's house. The young fellow walked briskly from the Cudahy's ornate home at 518 South 37th, in the heart of Omaha's "Gold Coast," to the Rustin's, about three blocks away. Having duly delivered the magazines, he declined an invitation to step in and get warm and set off again in the bright winter's night.

Along about nine o'clock Father Cudahy suggested that Eddie had found the Rustins so hospitable he was overstaying his welcome. But Mother Cudahy was uneasy, and at her urging Cudahy telephoned the Rustins. He was told that Eddie had left there almost two hours before.

Uneasiness changed to alarm. Eddie wasn't given to staying away

from home in the evening or to going places without first asking
permission. After a progressively nerve-wracking interval of waiting,
Cudahy called the police. By morning he had wired Chicago to send
out twenty Pinkerton detectives.

Omaha was rocked by the news that the only son of the town's
wealthiest man had disappeared. Police were called off their regular
assignments and sent to search resorts and gambling joints; and the
usual assortment of tips and false alarms began to pour into headquarters and the Cudahy home. At nine A.M. the Cudahy coachman
discovered a red flag fastened to a stick on the front lawn. Although
it must have been there most of the night, not one of the crowd of
police, reporters, and sightseers had noticed it.

Fastened inside the red flag were five pages of rambling, discursive
threats pencilled in a small, fine hand. The writer demanded $25,000
in gold, on pain of putting acid in Eddie's eyes if the money was not
delivered. Cudahy was told to start alone at seven P.M. and drive out
a prairie road until he saw a lantern tied with black and white ribbons. The money and the ransom note were to be left beside the
lantern.

The police persuaded the Cudahys to ignore the letter. They did—
until five P.M. Dodging the police, Cudahy reached the president of
the Merchants National Bank and arranged to get five bags of gold
in the specified denominations. Then he ordered his driving mare
hitched to his buggy and at seven P.M. was on his way. When he came
to the point where two transcontinental railroad lines converged,
the road turned into a cleft of two abrupt hills. By now Cudahy had
driven ten miles, and was half convinced that he was the victim of a
cruel practical joke. Then he saw the lantern several hundred feet
away. After making sure that it bore the black and white ribbons,
he dragged out the heavy bags of gold and piled them beside the
lantern.

It was nearly midnight when he got home. With his wife and his
attorney, he waited while the minutes ticked away. At half-past one
the men begged Mrs. Cudahy to lie down and try to rest. She was
insisting that she couldn't possibly sleep when they heard a footfall.
In a moment Eddie was in their arms.

The police were called, and he told his story. On his way back after
leaving the magazines, Eddie said, three or four doors from his own
home he was accosted by two men. Their hats were pulled down, and
he couldn't see their faces very well, but one was tall and one was
short. They addressed him as Eddie McGee, said that they were

police officers and that he was wanted for theft. He protested that he was Eddie Cudahy, but they hustled him into a carriage and drove away. They bound and gagged and blindfolded him and told him he was being kidnapped.

After about an hour's drive they took him into what seemed to be a two-story cabin. Although he couldn't see, he could tell from the voices that it was the short man who acted as his guard. The tall man kept going away and coming back and going away again. He seemed to be the short man's boss. They were both very good to him; and they both drank a lot. A few hours ago they had put him into the carriage again, driven for about an hour, then unbound him and put him out on the street. He took the bandage off his eyes and found himself only a few blocks from home.

In due course of time the police located the cabin where Eddie had been held. The owner was able to give some description of the two men—one tall, one short—who had rented it. A farmer, twenty miles away, remembered he had sold a mare to two men—one tall, one short. Another man remembered their buying a carriage from him.

The description of the tall man tallied perfectly with the description of a bad hat named Pat Crowe. As a young man he worked in his own Omaha butcher shop. Squeezed out of his business by the packers, he had taken a job at the Cudahy plant. He was dismissed for dishonesty, and had gone in for train robberies and roadside holdups. He once had boasted that he had "earned" as much as $700,000 by such activities. The description of the short man sounded like Crowe's less dangerous pal James Callahan, an ex-brakeman on the Union Pacific.

Crowe had disappeared, but Callahan was soon picked up and brought to trial in April, 1901. Although he virtually admitted his part in the kidnapping, he was tried only for robbery. Eddie testified that he recognized Callahan's voice as that of the guard at the cottage where he was held prisoner; the prosecution brought out that Callahan was on parole after serving one year of an eight-year sentence for highway robbery; neighbors testified to seeing Callahan about the kidnap hideout while young Cudahy had been missing.

The jury brought in a verdict of not guilty. Later, Callahan was tried for perjury. He was acquitted. Thirty-five years after the trial, Judge Ben Baker told a reporter: "There was no legitimate reason for Callahan's acquittal. The man was proven guilty. I can only account for it on the ground that the jury was prejudiced against wealthy people as represented by the Cudahys."

And where was Pat Crowe? Police learned he had sent a letter and a draft on an old debt to an Omaha attorney. The letter said he had gone to South Africa, had joined the Boer forces, was twice wounded, had been decorated for bravery, and was now done with crime. The news sent up official blood pressure. There was a $55,000 reward on Crowe's head: thirty thousand of it was offered by Cudahy, the rest by the city of Omaha. But they couldn't seem to lay hands on Crowe. At one point when he was negotiating surrender terms, the police tried to capture him at Butte. But Crowe hadn't built up his bad-man reputation for nothing. Three men were wounded; he escaped. In fact, not even his feelings were hurt: he went right on negotiating, his condition being that the reward be withdrawn. This time the Omaha police held out their arms and said "Come home. Almost all is forgiven."

The trial began in February, 1906. Crowe offered no real defense and, as in Callahan's case, did all but admit that he was guilty. The prosecution's ace in the hole was a letter written August 22, 1904, by Crowe to a priest in Vail, Iowa, the town of his birth. "I am guilty of the Cudahy affair," he wrote. "I am to blame for the whole thing. After it was over, I regretted my act and offered to return $21,000 to Mr. Cudahy, but he refused to take it."

After debating seventeen hours, the jury found Pat Crowe not guilty. And when the verdict was read, the courtroom rang with cheers. As soon as Judge W. W. Slabaugh could make himself heard, he expressed his displeasure in no uncertain terms. "This court," he thundered, "is very much surprised that a jury would pass a verdict clearing such a notorious criminal, that you citizens would make such a demonstration as this. You should be ashamed of yourselves."

Crowe was cheered again in the streets. Police had to clear a way for him through all his well-wishers. The Beef Trust, of which Edward A. Cudahy, Sr., was Public Member No. 1, was in disrepute with the common people, who paid high meat prices. They felt that if a man could bilk a packer of $25,000, more power to him.

For nearly thirty-five years, much of Pat Crowe's career consisted of attempts to cash in on his notoriety: he wrote, or at least was credited with the authorship of, three autobiographical books on the crime-does-not-pay theme; he was arrested countless times for drunkenness, vagrancy, and misdemeanors; and announced his "reformation" with the regularity of clockwork.

When Eddie Cudahy, Jr., was married, Crowe could not resist getting in the act again. He wired the bridegroom:

No one could wish you greater happiness in the hands of your new kidnapper than I do. Here's hoping you will cherish no ill will over our former escapade, and enjoy this one more.

In 1938, at the age of seventy-five, Crowe died a drunken bum.

Condensed from New York *Sunday News,* June 7, 1936

Compared to present-day weather bureaus, with their array of observational equipment and facilities for receiving up-to-the-minute weather data from all points of the compass, the bureaus of forty or fifty years ago operated on pretty much of a wet-finger-in-the-wind and crystal-ball basis. Nevertheless, then as now, the citizenry often gave vent to an irrational tendency to blame it all on the weatherman whenever the weather failed to perform as advertised or the elements suddenly got out of line.

On Sunday morning, March 23, 1913, readers of the Omaha Bee *noted that "PROF. WILLIS MOORE, CHIEF OF WEATHER BUREAU, RESIGNS." In view of what was to bust loose later that day, it could hardly have been a timelier move.*

3. The Tornado

AMY MITCHELL

THE greatest calamity in the history of Omaha was the big blow of Easter Sunday, March 23, 1913. Up until that time no tornado had ever occurred in the United States that was so destructive of life and property as this one; and although on prior occasions Omaha had been visited by atmospheric disturbances, the Easter Sunday twister surpassed in damage all of them combined.

About six o'clock in the afternoon the light grew strangely luminous, and in less time than it takes to tell it, a black funnel-shaped cloud materialized on the southwest horizon. With a mighty roar it swooped down upon Omaha, whirling diagonally across the city through the thickly populated residential districts to Levi Carter Park, where it crossed over into Iowa. In its wake it left a path one-fourth of a mile wide and seven miles long strewn with the bodies of

140 killed and 350 injured, and the debris of ruined homes—imposing mansions and humble dwellings—churches and schools. So sudden had been its descent and so swift its passage that people in downtown hotels were unaware of the disaster until it had been all over for an hour or more.

Fire broke out in the ruins, threatening Omaha with a general conflagration as hydrants were buried under the debris and masses of wreckage blocked many streets, making it impossible to get the engines and hose carts near the flames. The greatest damage was done in the vicinity of Twenty-fourth and Lake, where fifty or sixty persons were killed. When the rumor spread that a motion picture theater in that neighborhood had been levelled and everyone in the audience killed, people rushed to the scene from all parts of the city. The rumor was untrue, but the crowd further hampered the work of the police and fire departments. A heavy rain began about eight o'clock and continued for an hour. This aided the fire department, but it added greatly to the plight of the 2,500 persons who were homeless that night.

The tornado brought an abrupt end to a wedding ceremony in the German Lutheran Church at Twenty-eighth and Parker Streets. The organ and choir had just embarked on "O Promise Me" when the storm struck the building, carrying away part of the roof and the marriage license, which the minister was holding in his hand. The bride and groom hurried to an automobile, intending to start for home, but were compelled instead to seek shelter in the church cellar. The machine in which they attempted to flee was never found.

Three days after the tornado, another force of nature, Madame Sarah Bernhardt, announced she would give a benefit performance in Denver for the storm victims.

Omahans never forget that theirs is by far Nebraska's largest city, and sometimes tend to be a mite patronizing to their country cousins. But on the night the world's heavyweight wrestling championship was decided at old Rourke Park, the town belonged to a couple of—

Country Boys

HOWARD WOLFF

WRESTLING—from the schoolboy recess tussles to the lamp-lighted county fair matches for a three-dollar stake—has been as much a part of the Nebraska scene as the billowing grassy seas of the sandhills and dusty country lanes, the meandering Platte and the tawny Missouri.

The story of wrestling in Nebraska is the story of the Stechers. While there were many others—Farmer Burns, John Pesek, Pat McGill—"the boy in overalls," Joe Stecher of Dodge, and his shadow, Brother Tony, are the king-size figures.

The Stecher story begins with a celebration at Dodge in the spring of 1913. Brothers Tony and Joe had tested their developing muscles in almost daily wrestling matches behind the schoolhouse. They had made trips to the Fremont YMCA where they had been given formal instruction by volunteer tutors. In matches there, impromptu but deadly, the brothers had fought off all challengers.

Came then the fateful day when the champ, Frank Butler, was booked for an exhibition at Dodge. But Butler's fame had preceded him, and when promoters sought an opponent, there were no takers—until young Tony was offered the bout. He jumped at the chance. Although his successes had been confined strictly to amateurs and Butler was a seasoned pro, Tony threw him twice in jig-time.

The next day the brothers left home. Their father, Tony says, had "really laid me out" for wrestling for money. They landed at Atlantic, Iowa, on the first leg of an adventure that was to send them to the four corners of the world in one of the great success sagas of American sports.

"Joe and I hired out to a farmer near Atlantic," Tony recalls. "Just as at Dodge, Fremont, Hooper, and other towns near our home, Atlantic had its favorite wrestler. This was a young fellow named

Earl Caddock. Days, he delivered meat for the Atlantic butcher and at night took on all comers in matches at the livery stable."

A match was made with Joe, because his 200 pounds were nearer Caddock's weight than Tony's 165. Taking two of three falls, Joe collected the winner's purse which, Tony remembers, was four dollars. Seven years later, on January 30, 1920, Stecher was to beat Caddock again—this time in New York City with the world's championship on the line. The gate for that 1920 "return bout" was $85,452.

After six months as hired hands on the Atlantic farm, the brothers went home to Dodge to find that the welcome mat was out. Week by week Tony and Joe had been gaining fame, and by now Papa Stecher's neighbors were slapping him on the back at every meeting.

"Funny thing," says Tony. "Today when we think of a 'ringer' we think immediately of the racetrack, with a fast horse substituting for a slower one to bring off a betting coup. But in those early days of wrestling, many a tough pro was sent out of Chicago or Kansas City or Denver to pose as a home-town boy and await an eventual match with one of the Stechers from Dodge—and a killing for the city sharpies. But it never turned out that way. Joe and I beat every 'ringer' the smart boys sent at us. And our farmer friends took the gamblers, often betting 4 and 5 to 1 on a Stecher."

During this period Joe developed what probably is the most famous hold in wrestling—the leg scissors. "Joe had exceptionally long and powerful legs," Tony says. "He used to clamp those scissors on a full grain sack and then put on the pressure until the sack broke. Any wonder he nearly killed half a hundred wrestlers with that hold? Then, when he had developed the muscles and learned the proper pressure to rip the grain sacks, Joe shifted to the hogs in Papa's feed lot. That was the best kind of practice, because the pigs had a natural tendency to resist, so they worked very hard to break the hold."

January 5, 1915, marks another milestone in the Stecher story. It was on this date that a syndicate of Chicago-Kansas City-Omaha gamblers planted a ripe melon for a juicy carving. The melon was Ad Santel, a top-notcher of the time; and the carving was to be performed on the loyal farmer backers of scissors-expert Joe. Santel had slipped unobtrusively into Omaha as Adolph Ernst. He was "exhibited" in a half-dozen matches within a hundred miles of Omaha, never showing too much—just enough to convince the Fremont promoters that he'd be a good test for the undefeated Stecher.

The day before the match, the syndicate men fanned out to the towns where Joe was a hero. Licking their chops, the city slickers snapped up all bets on Joe, often getting as high as 10 to 1. Right up to the time Stecher and Santel stepped into the ring, the flood of cash continued. Telegraph wires had relayed the word to gambling establishments throughout the nation that Cuming County farmers were hellbent to give their money away, and runners at the ringside were armed with fresh ammunition from as far off as San Francisco. So successful were they in goading the farmers into making more bets that if Joe had lost that night many a Cuming County farm would have changed hands.

Not a farm was lost. Putting his scissors into devastating action almost at the outset, Joe won in straight falls at a minute and eleven seconds and seven minutes flat. The gamblers were flat too, but they hadn't had enough.

By now, Frank Gotch, the great world's champion from Humboldt, Iowa, had retired, and Charlie Cutler had inherited the title. This time, the sure-thing boys figured, there'd be no slip-up. A Cutler-Stecher match would bring back all that lost loot—with interest. Omaha promoter Gene Melady got the plum for July 4, 1915, at old Rourke Park. Once again the gamblers moved in for the kill—in fact, Cutler's manager, Billy Rochelle, came to Omaha early to make certain no stray Nebraska dollars would be overlooked.

Ed W. Smith, old-time Chicago sports writer and wrestling referee, gives us an interesting side light on this "shearing of the sheep." Wrote Smith:

When Rochelle went up to Fremont a week before the match to line up some bets on his boy he ran into Ed Reetz of Hooper, a strong Stecher backer. Rochelle told Reetz he'd like to bet three thousand dollars on his boy. "Why, I thought you wanted to make a bet," Reetz shot back. "I'll just take your three thousand and here's twenty-seven thousand more on Stecher." And Reetz produced thirty thousand dollars right under the nose of the bug-eyed Rochelle.

Later Smith reported that "it was probably the biggest clean-up in wrestling history. Once more the farmers put it over the smart chaps from the city." And Joe put it over Cutler without much trouble before 16,000 cheering fans. The scissors did the damage in both falls at 17:03 and ten minutes.

Reprinted from the Omaha *World-Herald*, May 23, 1954

Omaha has had many citizens whose careers have com-
manded the nation's attention and respect. But among
them—at least since frontier days—there has been only one
who, reputedly, was so tough that he broke half-dollars
with his teeth.

At the time the following profile was written, the late
William Martin Jeffers was serving the country as admin-
istrator of the wartime synthetic rubber program. News-
papers then referred to him as the "Rubber Czar." But
first, last, and always, William Martin Jeffers was a—

Railroad Man

RAY MACKLAND

BILL JEFFERS comes, specifically, from Omaha, Nebr., but his real
home stretches across 13 states, along the 10,000-odd miles of the
Union Pacific Railroad. Fifty-three years ago, at the age of 14, Jeffers
started working on that railroad, and he has been president since
1937. He is a big man, 225 pounds and almost six feet, who has been
around locomotives so long that he vaguely resembles one. Trained
in the tough school of one of the toughest U.S. industries, Jeffers
has settled scores of arguments with his fists.

Back in 1909, when he had just become superintendent of the
U.P.'s Mountain Division, where old-time railroaders liked to make
their own rules, he once asked a conductor in the station at Rawlins,
Wyo., where he was going.

"You may not believe it," the conductor answered, with more
insolence than Jeffers will take, "but I'm going to leave here on a
train."

"That's what you think," the new superintendent said, swinging
with his right. The conductor was still out cold on the station floor
when Jeffers' train left for Green River.

Though Jeffers did not become president of the U.P. until 1937,
he had been running the road since 1932. Railroads were harder
hit by the depression than almost any other industry, and many
went into receivership. But the Union Pacific stayed on a paying
basis and maintained its $6 dividend rate. The reason was Jeffers,

who boasts that with him the railroad always comes first. Because he feels that way, he was willing to make the decision to fire, demote, and cut temporarily the pay of thousands of U.P. workers. No one, including Jeffers, liked it, but for the success of the railroad it was necessary.

The tawny roadbed of the U.P., stretching from the midland plains to the California coast, is Jeffers' love. He has walked every mile of its main line and many of the branch lines to boot. He knows every depot, water tower, underpass, coal chute, and bridge on the system. Once he fired his own brother because he was not doing a good job for the U.P., and the two have been estranged ever since. Jeffers does not regret that action. "The Union Pacific," he says, "is greater than people or anything else."

He boasts, with reason, that he can fill any job from tracklayer to president on the railroad, and he has an intolerably sharp eye for detail. While riding past an obscure mountain station, he spotted a freshly painted elevation marker that read "8,014 ft." "Have that sign changed," he told his secretary. "It should be 8,013 ft." Another time, he was traveling on a U.P. passenger train when the engineer stopped a little too abruptly. Jeffers looked up, scowling, and dictated an order to have the engineer removed from passenger service and sent back for more training. In due time Jeffers saw to it that the engineer was restored to his job.

He prides himself on quick action. Once he was prowling through a women's car on the U.P.'s streamlined *Challenger* and asked a lady passenger how she liked the service. She said she liked it fine but objected to the cuspidors in the smoking compartment. "We smoke," she explained, "but we don't spit." This was at Cheyenne, Wyo. Jeffers wired ahead to the division superintendent at Ogden, Utah. During the night the cuspidors were replaced by standing ashtrays.

In 1868, a year before the celebrated golden spike was pounded into a laurel wood tie at Promontory, Utah, an illiterate Irishman, William Jeffers, emigrated direct from County Mayo to North Platte, Nebr., and took a tracklayer's job on the railroad. His peak earnings were $55 a month. Bill Jeffers was one of nine children. The family had enough to eat but not much more, and his sisters were the first girls to clerk in the stores of North Platte. Bill was a sturdy, freckled youngster who, when the town boys came to court his sisters, would entertain them by standing in the middle of the floor and singing "Billy with the Stunning Pair of Legs."

That period was very brief. "I can't remember when I was a boy,"

Jeffers sometimes says. "It seems I've always been a man, a working man." He quit school after a fist fight with his teacher—"it was a draw," he boasts—and at 14 went to work as janitor and callboy on the U.P. As callboy his job was to round up crews whose names were posted for runs. Older men liked this kid who took all the work they could give him and asked for more. They taught him telegraphy, and at 16 he was working as night operator in the way stations.

It was a telegrapher's duty to report every train that passed, and a boy of 16 had trouble staying awake all night. As insurance he invented an automatic waker. He suspended a coal scuttle over his head, with a string leading through the station window to the rails. When a train went by, it cut the string and the coal scuttle banged Jeffers on the head. The system worked fine except for one occasion when a locomotive stopped short of the string and the district superintendent found him asleep.

Steadily Jeffers climbed the U.P. ladder—from clerk to timekeeper to spare foreman. By the time he was 19 he was a train dispatcher, and had started courting Lena Schatz, the daughter of a Union Pacific blacksmith and sister-in-law of the sheriff of North Platte. Lena, who had gone to an academy at Salt Lake City, was a rural schoolteacher and dressed unusually well for North Platte. When he wanted to visit Lena, he could flag down a train for a ride into town. That was a more casual era of railroading when handcars were commonly used for hunting along the right of way or taking girls on dates to nearby towns. In June, 1898 the pair was married at 7:30 A.M., so that they could leave for their honeymoon on the 8:00 A.M. Portland express. This train had a great reputation of being on time, but on Jeffers' wedding day it was three hours late.

The honeymoon was Jeffers' only time off during his first forty years on the Union Pacific. He has relaxed a bit since then, and actually took two brief vacations in the last twelve years. The railroad is the sum total of Jeffers' interests, and any other pursuit seems dull by comparison. He couldn't understand a man who would rather loaf or play golf than work. Jeffers himself used to enjoy golf, but gave up the game when he decided that it was taking time that might be spent working. He likes to say that he has worked more than a hundred years for the Union Pacific. On the basis of an eight-hour day, this is literally true, because Jeffers habitually works twelve to sixteen hours, Sundays and holidays included.

Jeffers knows thousands of his workers by their first names, and he is "Bill" to the old-timers. But few employees would talk back to him like the stripling callboy whom he bumped into at Green River, Wyo.

"Why don't you watch where you're going?" the U.P. president growled.

"Why don't you whistle for the curves?" the U.P. callboy retorted.

Fear and respect are blended about equally in the U.P.'s attitude toward "the boss." Train crews say that anyone who "does business" doesn't have to worry. "The boss" will overlook one honest mistake, but not a second. A man does his job as Jeffers wants it done, or gets out. On the other hand, Jeffers never has had any labor trouble. He himself still holds a card in the telegraphers' union, and is described by labor men as a hard bargainer but a good man to do business with.

Though he has honorary law degrees from five colleges, Jeffers is strongly conscious of his humble origins and lack of education. In philosophical mood, it pleases him to remark that a college education isn't necessary, and that some of the most outstanding men in the world have little formal education. His intellectual interests are limited. He reads the newspapers, detective stories, and books about the West, but disdains any literature that he can't easily understand. Once a librarian asked him what books he had read when he was a small boy. "Then and now, the *Union Pacific Book of Rules*," Jeffers replied.

His closest friend—a Chicagoan named Joe Buker who always called him "Mr. Jeffers"—died two years ago, and since then his only intimate has been his assistant, John Gale, known along the U.P. as "Friday" or "Iron Hat," because of a fondness for bowlers.

On the rare occasions when Jeffers takes a hand in social functions, he likes to have them run the way he runs the Union Pacific. The 1937 dinner celebrating his promotion to president was planned to the finest detail. "You can't slip up on something like this," Jeffers explained. "It can be the biggest thing of its kind put on in the country. And not for me, remember. Presidents come and go, but the railroad goes on forever." There were 2,400 dinner guests from all the U.P. states, plus 4,000 non-dining spectators. Seating arrangements were planned by railroad engineers and special tables built from their blueprints. Every cup, plate and piece of silver was lined up with strings. Conductors and brakemen in freshly pressed uniforms served as ushers. Diners at the speakers' table were led out in platoons by blue-uniformed stewardesses from the U.P.'s trains.

A bugle blew mess call and 400 waiters, marching in military formation, served everyone in eighteen minutes flat.

Even bigger than the dinner was the coronation of Jeffers at the 1940 festival of Ak-Sar-Ben. In Omaha, a city still young enough to ladle out its social gravy to first-generation tycoons, Jeffers made a memorable king. Dragging a thirty-five-pound train, wearing black silk panties and looking a bit like Ole King Cole, he was crowned King Ak-Sar-Ben XLVI of the mythical Kingdom of Quivera. The setting was described by the ecstatic Omaha *World-Herald* as "a composition of ivory, aquamarine, and lotus pink, with moon and stars, fluted columns and glistening portals, silver curtains and green smilax." He was the first king who ever patted his queen (Gwendolyn Sachs) on the cheek while crowning her, and within ten minutes had his own crown tilted rakishly on the side of his head. Theoretically the identity of the Omaha royalty is secret, but Jeffers took no chances on that. He brought railroad men by special train from all over the country and invited Steve Hannagan, the master press agent, from New York. A battery of motion-picture cameramen and photographers frantically recorded the great event for posterity. Afterward, Jeffers gave a party. The style and scope of Jeffers' hospitality were so lavish that Ak-Sar-Ben decided to prohibit private parties in the future, lest new kings go bankrupt.

Jeffers makes no secret of his pride in his own career and his reputation as the world's greatest railroad manager. In their Omaha home his daughter keeps voluminous scrapbooks which tell of his rise in the world. One of these books has the revealing title, *Top Rung.*

Condensed from "Battling Bill Jeffers," *Life,* February 22, 1943. © Time, Inc., 1943

1932

VANITY FAIR'S
NEBRASKA

Nebraska on the Make

ROBERT BURLINGAME

THERE is no place like Nebraska." Twenty thousand voices regularly join in this paean of praise to a conquering Cornhusker football team after its accustomed victory in the Memorial Stadium on an autumn afternoon. For be it known that the pride of Nebraska is her gangling university on the flats of Lincoln, and the chief business of the university is the manufacture of championship football teams.

This business the university dispatches with regularity, barring a few untoward incidents, such as a 44 to 0 trouncing at the University of Pittsburgh in 1931. But the Pittsburgh boys were only iron puddlers and coal miners, who scarcely count. Out in the real America the Cornhuskers are kings, and lost is that October Saturday whose low descending sun does not find them proclaiming their royalty over the prostrate form of another corn-belt university. Best of all do the Lincoln boys love to pummel the high-hats from Iowa City, softened by their contact with the effete East—Illinois, Wisconsin, and even Ohio.

To the outlander beyond the Missouri or west of Scottsbluff, it may seem impious to open a Nebraska narrative in the university stadium, passing by such distinguished citizens as George Norris, the embattled liberal of the federal Senate, and Willa Cather, the chronicler of prairie life. But only thus can Ogallala and Wahoo and Broken Bow be made comprehensible, for the city of Lincoln and its university are practically the only forces that hold this hodgepodge state together.

The North Platte country, for instance, has always disliked the South Platte, and the South Platte retorts by expressing the pious wish that it may some day cast loose the North Platte millstone and make a more profitable alliance with Kansas. Omaha, with its back to Nebraska and its face turned east across the Big Muddy, is either a pariah or a rose in a cabbage patch, depending on whether the commentator lives outstate or in the city itself. The southeast section of the state is fat and middle-aged and prosperous; the north-

west has the sweep and rawness of Wyoming and the Dakota bad-
lands. Catholics jostle Lutherans and Mennonites elbow Orthodox
Russians, while the racial picture of the commonwealth is a contracted map of all Europe. In short, Nebraska is the product of the
later frontier and the work of the melting-pot when it was bubbling
its merriest.

Only the gilded capitol tower and the horseshoe-shaped stadium
a half-dozen blocks away bring some degree of unity out of these
discordant themes. And the stadium deserves a degree of precedence
over the $10,000,000 state house, because it takes the ranch-hand
from Cherry County, the sugar-beet laborer from the western panhandle, and the packing-house boy from South Omaha, and for
three months each fall makes them a crusading host for the defense
of Nebraska honor. During the dull months of spring the coaching
staff barnstorms the state, preaching to Rotary Clubs and Chambers
of Commerce the revealed gospel of higher football. Every Nebraskan
is pledged, by the head of the emperor, to assist in swelling the enrollment of the stadium courses at the university. Football has
given this school a hold over its entire constituency such as no other
state university approaches, with the possible exception of Wisconsin.

Each football victory, by a remarkable system of logic, serves to
convince the Nebraska citizen that his university is the equal of
Harvard, Oxford, Leipzig, and the Sorbonne, done up in one
package and with Cambridge and Stanford added for good measure.
His pride, however, does not touch his purse. He continues to complain like a stuck pig at the burden of the university appropriation,
and to applaud the legislature for heroically keeping the salary scale
of teachers below that of almost any other recognized university in
the country. The disarray of angular brick buildings strewn over
the campus does not trouble his aesthetic sense, for aesthetics is a
closed book to the Nebraskan. Only a smart-aleck easterner would
listen to the national fraternity secretary who dismissed Nebraska
with a reference to "its location on the endless plain, and a student
body of typical middle-class German people—who make good citizens
but offer little of special social life."

Nebraska boasts of Roscoe Pound and the *Prairie Schooner,* a
literary quarterly praised by so fastidious a critic as Henry Mencken,
but is content to send her children to one of the most inadequate
public school systems in America. Outside of Omaha Central High
School, where a true classicist wages a lone battle against his motor-
minded constituency, the state offers no adequate preparation for

college. Latin is displaced by Smith-Hughes agriculture, and if a hardy soul ventures into foreign language, he stops with two years of Spanish, which is vaguely thought to be helpful in a South American business career.

Sole rival to the university for the state's affection is Mr. Bertram Grosvenor Goodhue's extraordinary capitol, which is only now reaching completion after ten years of construction. A single-story limestone structure, two blocks square and surrounding a courtyard, it is surmounted by a tower that rises more than four hundred feet above the surrounding plain. Distinctly Egyptian or even Assyrian in line, it would seem as appropriate to a Mesopotamian setting as to Lancaster County. Groups of coatless farmers come in daily from Box Butte and Keya Paha counties, bringing their wives and children to see what God hath wrought. On pleasant Sundays the sightseers reach the proportions of a mob, whom a corps of university students escort from marvel to marvel, declaiming a carefully memorized speech on the costs of construction. One by one, the visitors sit in the governor's chair, caress the Italian marble pillars, and exclaim at the hundreds of kinds of wood in the Supreme Court bench. Only a few grumblers remark that the money might better have been spent on paved roads.

Except for the capitol and university, Lincoln is a smug middle-class town, conventional enough to satisfy the Methodist clergy and the Republican Party. Travelling men avoid Lincoln on weekends because of its rigid Sunday blue laws, which close theatres and all other places of amusement. Roadhouses are patronized only by university students trying to be devilish, and nightclubs do not thrive on a midnight curfew. A two-million-dollar bank robbery two years ago caught the police department unprepared for any crime more heinous than running through traffic signals; for several months the arm of the law bargained with the underworld for the return of the loot, a procedure that was not edifying to the state at large.

Churches, mostly Protestant, have hemmed in Lincoln with a fringe of suburbs, ranging from a Methodist community which has largely surrendered its purity to a Seventh Day Advent colony which eschews the devil by observing Sunday on Saturday and concealing the fact that women have ankles. The Protestant clergy occupies the same favored position which it held in Geneva under Calvin.

For a town that has not yet reached its three score and ten, Lincoln has a glamorous past. At one time in the early nineties, William

Jennings Bryan was teaching a Presbyterian Sunday School class, Charley Dawes was starting in the business world, and John J. Pershing was drilling university cadets. The Bryan legend is kept fresh by the Great Commoner's brother, now governor of Nebraska.

Divested of the skullcap which made him famous as Democratic candidate for vice-president in 1924, Brother Charley is serving his third term on a platform of low taxes and few frills. Verbose, domineering, and profane, the governor knows how to appeal to the Nebraska farmer in his own language. Unlike Bryan, Pershing figures in Lincoln society. His sister has long been a resident of the city, his son went through the Lincoln schools. On a memorial tablet in the nave of Holy Trinity Church, John J. Pershing's name heads the roll of parishioners who served in the World War. For the rest, Lincoln's aristocracy resembles the cave-dwellers of Washington, content with its own life along Sheridan Boulevard, its intermarriages, and its trips to Europe and the East. Like all of Lincoln, it is respectable, does its sinning and drinking quietly, and is not notable for public spirit.

Fifty-six miles east of Lincoln, over a new paved road, is Omaha, three times as large, ten times as cosmopolitan, but scarcely a part of Nebraska. A true Nebraskan feels ill at ease on its steep hills, which are entirely unlike the topography in the rest of the state. Omaha sneers at Lincoln as her country cousin, and Lincoln retaliates by lifting her eyebrows at the Sodom and Gomorrah of the packing-plants.

Omaha is a city; she has a beer racket, a political machine, and a night life, to say nothing of having furnished Lady Charles Cavendish, nee Adele Astaire, to Broadway. She is sophisticated but not intellectual, and she smiles in mild amusement at a $100,000 suit brought by one socialite against another for alienating the affections of a deceased husband.

Omaha's wealth is based on her location in the center of the western rail system, which makes the city a natural terminus for livestock and grain shipments. Cattlemen congregate at the Rome Hotel, as they once did at the old Paxton, and a remnant of the "line" still exists below Fourteenth Street for those who will have their fling at scarlet sin before returning to the country.

Omaha has lately gone artistic under the influence of a new municipal university and the three-million-dollar Joslyn Memorial, opened with great fanfare last November. It is the gift of Mrs. Sarah Joslyn out of a fortune which her husband amassed from the sale of newspaper boiler-plate and venereal-disease remedies. To direct her project Mrs. Joslyn drafted Professor Paul Henry Grumman from the state university. Professor Grumman enjoyed a local reputation for polite naughtiness in his course on Ibsen. The remaining cultural enterprise of the city is Creighton University, a Jesuit citadel, which was built from the proceeds of telegraph wire strung over the Rocky Mountain area by Count Creighton in the 1860's.

Lincoln and Omaha are Nebraska to all intents and purposes. Extending to the state line on the west are 450 miles of flat country, only occasionally broken by a town. Grand Island, "the third city," has a population of eighteen thousand, mostly conservative German burghers who like their beer, maintain a Turner Society, and appropriately call their city auditorium Liederkranz Hall. Columbus, on the Platte River, is predominantly Irish, while at Scottsbluff, on the western edge of the state, a large colony of Russians till the irrigated sugar-beet fields of the North Platte valley. Geologists work each summer among the buttes and escarpments of the Scott's Bluff region, excavating remains of a pre-Indian culture which once flourished there. To the north is Cherry County, five times as large as Rhode Island and abounding in vast cattle ranches that foster as vigorous a frontier spirit as survives anywhere in America.

The central part of the state is a drear waste, called the sandhills, with roads that must be tied down to keep them from blowing away and clusters of tiny lakes that provide excellent fishing. Just above the Kansas border, in the Republican River valley, the New England settlement of Red Cloud is the family home of Willa Cather, who has done the saga of the Bohemian immigrants in *My Antonia*. Ninety-five per cent of the names in Wilber are vowelless, like Brt and Srb, and until a few years ago beer-gardens existed, reminiscent of old Prague. Wilber is perhaps the only town in America which has publicly hanged and burned in effigy the leaders of the prohibition movement. This it did during a state campaign a generation ago. Sidney, tucked away in the southwest corner of the state, was once the end of the cattle trail, known far and wide as the "wickedest town in the West." An occasional sheriff is still shot there, just to keep old memories alive.

For a state that was settled by disappointed people who stayed only because they couldn't get farther west, Nebraska has done fairly well. Wind, drought, grasshoppers, and bad banks have inflicted on it most of the evils of man and nature, but in spite of them

George W. Norris sits in the Senate and Willa Cather writes her novels. The Methodists held prayer meetings for Al Smith's defeat in 1928, but eight hundred saloons paid license fees into the state treasury until the federal government undertook a great experiment. Choppy Rhodes and Monte Munn are more illustrious alumni of the university than all the Rhodes scholars since Jameson's raid, but Nebraska has been spared the dullness of her Anglo-Saxon neighbors by preserving the native flavor of the Slav, the German, and the Irishman.

IV. The Sower

When tillage begins, other arts follow. The farmers therefore are the founders of human civilization.

—Daniel Webster, *Remarks on Agriculture*

LIV. The Sower

"A scholar of high repute in the field of the social sciences, a novelist, editor of the New Republic, *a teacher, Director of the* New School for Social Research *in New York City . . ." So standard reference works describe the boy born on a farm near Homer, December 18, 1874.*

Education of a Nebraskan

ALVIN S. JOHNSON

1. Homer

HOME AGAIN, in my native Nebraska.

The westbound tourist, seeing Nebraska from the Pullman window, thinks, "Good Lord, how monotonous!" He acquired his sense of landscape from the romanticists, who needed mountain scenery as background to their cloud-topped heroes. The rational classic writers detested the mountains. In Latin literature the only comments on the Alps are, "horrid, miserable, detestable." The classics loved the sweet plains, fertile, homelike, and homemaking, the rich lands along the sluggish streams exuberant with harvests, and the gentle slopes above.

The Romans never laid eyes on such magnificent plains as those of Nebraska, and neither has modern man really seen them, his eyes blinkered by the literature of romance. For the Nebraska-born the gently winding streams with their flower-bedecked margins, the fertile bottom levels, the long swales of grassy hills, are quintessentially home, free and sunlit home.

Soon after arriving in Nebraska I visited the farm where I was born. There, on a grassy slope, was a small oak tree, perhaps six inches in diameter; it had been six inches in my earliest memory. It chose to live, not to grow. It was the tree to which my father tied up his horse when he came from Wisconsin, years before I was born. I looked out upon the landscape, with my father's pioneer eyes. Before me a descent to a stream; beyond, level ground covered with a plum thicket, rising to a green slope embraced by two hill spurs reaching forward from a long green range closing the horizon, with a saucy knoll coming forward between the embracing main hill arms. As I looked and contemplated, dusk came on, and over the range of hills the evening star appeared, dim at first and then a brilliant gem. I was back in my father's spirit. This is home. Home.

It was a country of recent settlement when I was a child. There were a few families that had come at the time of the Kansas-Nebraska struggle, intending to help hold the region against the Slave Power, without getting too close to the firing line. There was an old fellow who had set out from Maine in an oxcart to try his luck at California gold. He found the gold diggings packed with pistol-carrying ruffians and turned back for Maine. In our vicinity one of his oxen died, and he had to settle down.

Most of the settlers came with a rush at the close of the Civil War. There was a thick sprinkling of veterans, who had learned to hate work in the confusion of campaigning over the South. There was one man who had fought in the Confederate Army. My father stood up for him against the taunts of the Union veterans. What was wrong in fighting for one's own state? As my father had a better military record than most, and looked dangerous besides, Wigle was let alone. There was a man who had escaped the penitentiary in Sweden for poaching, that is, killing a deer that was destroying his garden, and eating it. Lindstrom, to my boyish way of thinking, was grand. He was blithe as a bird, singing Swedish lays in a rich baritone, dancing like a wild dream. He carried a big knife to settle accounts with any other Swede who dared to throw in his face his near-penitentiary record.

Lindstrom had a whole repertory of crafts: stone masonry and bricklaying, carpentry, furniture making. He was quick as lightning at farm work. Binding sheaves in my father's field, he did exactly three times the work of the next best man. But, alas, he had a wife twenty years older than himself, no doubt fair once but now a hag burning with jealousy. He ran away finally. America is large, and what was the use of abiding in the one spot that was hell? The hag remained with us, to make all the trouble she could by carrying tales.

We also had our local idiot. Gyp was an ape man—long arms ending in crooked fingers, sparse bristly hair all over his face, rolling eyes. His lower lip hung away from teeth sown broadcast. His only flight of speech was in the words, "Pass the 'lasses, hah!" His passion was for adolescent girls, and if he saw one passing on the road he would utter a sound, half growl and half obscene laughter, and start to pursue her. Nobody bothered about that. He was club-footed, and any girl could outrun him. As for the girls, they could pose as heroines if they had been chased by Gyp.

There was a philosopher from a German university, Winkhaus, held by the other settlers to be brain-broke. From a promising academic career he was dumped upon an inappreciative America by the abortive Revolution of 1848. He was deeply absorbed in the implications of a mathematical formula he had worked out, which proved to his satisfaction that time, space, matter, and the causal nexus were all different manifestations of the same thing, capable of expression in a single equation. He had the books of Kant and Hegel, Schopenhauer and Feuerbach, and could tell you precisely where each philosopher went wrong or fell short. The time he should have given to cultivating his corn or getting in his hay he spent in scribbling on the margins of his books or in the composition of a monumental treatise. His worried wife and daughters made shift to live on the scanty product of his weedy fields. A good husband and father he was, they said; pity that he was brain-broke.

My Uncle George, the only other educated man in the community, maintained that Winkhaus was no more brain-broke than any other German philosopher; that, in fact, he was a philosopher of powerful and original ideas. My uncle wanted me to cultivate Winkhaus. But I had enough to do in struggling with my nickname, Professor Frog, conferred on me for my long legs and my zeal for knowledge. I didn't want to be associated with brain-brokes.

There were two clusters of Danish settlement: one, a group of relations from my mother's island, Fyn, industrious and retiring folk, concealing their thought in a dialect not even my father could understand; the other, a group of emigrés from Schleswig, which had been annexed to Prussia and was therefore intolerable for Danes. They seemed a race apart, huge, noisy men, eager for a fight but dominated by their wives, who were prevailingly little.

There was a Little Deutschland of Germans who hated Bismarck but loved beer and a high voltage cheese, which they made by maturing it in jars at the center of a heap of green grass, whose fermentation would keep it warm for weeks. The result was something that made Limburger pap for babes and sucklings.

There was a community composed of new immigrants from the Emerald Isle, the men Paddies with snub noses and long upper lips, the women thin and crooked. On Nebraska food their boys were growing tall and handsome and irresistibly charming, their girls graceful and bright-eyed, proving the old German principle, *"Man*

ist was man isst." Too bad the pun can't be reproduced in English.
But one is what one eats.

There was a colony of real Americans who originated in "York
State"; good solid farmers, God-fearing men who kept their religion
in their great hearts and raised hell with nobody about his beliefs
or lack of beliefs. There was an inset of settlers who claimed origin
in Old Virginny, who had moved westward by generation stages. For
several generations they had moved through malaria country, and
the men were born tired. The Nebraska winds are intolerable to
the anopheles, and malaria could not survive among us. But the
malaria psychology is good for two generations, if not three. The
only man among them who amounted to anything was the illegiti-
mate son of one of the faithful wives of the tribe. He was industrious,
steady, ambitious. He set up in business as a cattle feeder and
proved the wisest and most skillful in the trade, made money, married a choice girl out of the rising upper class, got elected to a county
office, and would sooner or later have been in Congress. But, alas,
he got "inflammation of the bowels"—appendicitis, then fatal—and
died.

It was a discordant community. The Protestants disliked and distrusted the Irish—they were dominated by the priest, and the priest
took his orders from Rome. My father regarded all that as nonsense.
He had seen the priest, a tall, grave man, standing outside the door
of the saloon, saying nothing, but making it impossible for any
Irishman to go beyond a single glass. He almost made a Protestant
out of the saloonkeeper, whose business was shrinking to a mere
trickle. My father used to say he'd give all the preachers in the county
for that one priest. As for orders from the Pope, the Pope had his
own job to do, way off in Italy.

The chief butt of old American dislike was the Dane. He was
taking over the damn country. He lived on what the pigs wouldn't
eat. He was unspeakably gross in his disgusting broken speech.

At that time native American speech in the presence of women
was highly refined. It was an insult to pure womanhood to say at
dinner that you preferred the leg of a chicken. Refined folk said
"limb." You could not use the word stallion; you said "horse,"
with a peculiar intonation. But above all you could not use the
word bull. If a neighbor precipitately climbed your barbed-wire
garden fence and appeared with long rips in his shirt and pants he
complained, "Your gentleman cow chased me. Like to of killed me."
And suppose you told a Dane it wasn't decent to use such words.

His reply was, "Dat's Pjank" (nonsense). Now listen to that word Pjank. Is that a language?

There was a graver indictment of the Danes. Around the threshing machine, no women being present, it was the rule to express every obscenity known to man. The Danes did not contribute to the bawdy talk; therefore they must be deep in some kind of secret sin. For sound men talk bawdy.

I first encountered the prejudice against the Danes when, at four, I was taken by my sisters to visit the school. A tall girl of ten, named Hattie, took me by the hand and led me around. I was in a daze; for the first time in my life I experienced a sense of overwhelming beauty, Hattie's eyes, "nut brown pools of Paradise."

A big girl, Bertha, came up. "Hattie! Take your hand away from that nasty little Dane. He isn't fit to touch your hand."

Hattie squeezed my hand, let her lovely eyes shine upon me, and moved away.

I hadn't known that I was a Dane—only Alvin, a man child. Nasty? I looked at my hands. They were clean. Apparently that big girl didn't like me. But I remembered Hattie's wonderful eyes. I never got another good look at them, but two or three years later I saw just such two beautiful eyes in a calf, and I named it Hattie.

In this community my family lived in individualistic isolation. We were on speaking terms with a wide range of people, but of fast family friends we had few. My three uncles, particularly Uncle George Bille, stood first. William Holsworth, an exceedingly brilliant man, who could make a more effective speech than any I have ever heard except from William Jennings Bryan, was my father's closest friend; his sons, Charlie and Willie, were mine. Uncle Jesse Wigle, the ex-Confederate, illiterate, but a repository of the sweetest folk songs, stood high with us. Dibble, a man who had got his tongue inextricably tied through a medical course, in which he had to observe major operations without anesthetics or antiseptics, and had fled from the ghastly profession to the prairie, was our wisest friend, though we saw him seldom.

My friends among boys of my own age were few. I had no enemies to reproach me with my Danish origin, and that was because I had a redoubtable protector in Charlie Holsworth. He was six years older, and why he bothered to defend me I never could make out. No boy could twit or bully me without a fierce look from Charlie.

The old-fashioned farm home is itself an educational institution.

A child with open eyes learns the ways of plants and animals, domesticated and wild. He learns to distinguish the characters of people in the family and in the neighborhood. The data of his experience are set up with large blank spaces around them, offering opportunity for thought and appraisal. The talk of his elders, mostly tedious reminiscence or more tedious boasting of miraculous crops or marvelous fattened stock, does nevertheless float nuggets of wise old sayings, of unique situations, of legal maxims collected through jury service.

I was fortunate in living in a community of mixed origins. The difference in the status of the peasant or worker in Europe, as contrasted with the status of the American farmer, was vivid in the experience of the community. I was never to get over a sense of the wide difference between American liberty and the few acquired rights of the European working class, between the so-called classes of America, in which no ambitious youth expected to rest, and the rigid classes of Europe, which held their members secure, in default of a miracle. Above all I was fortunate in having natural educators for parents, and particularly the inspiration of my uncle, George Bille, who had a farm a mile away.

In the farm community there were only two fields offering scientific stimulus, geology and botany. On my father's farm the creek had cut a deep gully, and the erosion that preceded the plow that broke the plains had made many dry confluent gullies. There before your eyes was the record of some millions of years, if you could read it.

High on the hillsides there was a limestone outcrop which reappeared at the same level for a dozen miles. It was overlaid by a yellow earth the neighbors called clay, but which my uncle ascribed to the dust blown in from the southwest for thousands and tens of thousands of years. When my father opened his quarry my uncle taught me to read the geologic record. In the surfaces uncovered by my father's gunpowder were all kinds of shells, some like oyster shells, some rather like crabs—trilobites, I think—some of totally unknown character.

"You can see, Alvin," my uncle said, "this land was once ocean, shallow ocean, for there can't be many shellfish in deep water. These shells are millions of years old. There are none like them today."

Botany was more a matter of the here and now. There were no primordial plants to be discovered in our lime quarry. But the prairie was covered with plants for which there were no local names. My uncle asked me how many flowering plants I had seen. At least thirty, I thought. Then he brought me Gray's *Manual*. With Gray's *Key* I discovered the names of more than two hundred flowering plants, most of which I had never noticed. Without names you do not see things, or their differences. You call things gadgets, and let it go at that. By the end of our botanizing phase, I knew a hundred times more about plant life than I had known before. And I knew more about human life, for all flesh is grass.

> *For a man destined to become one of America's most distinguished educators, his first experiences at an institution of higher learning hardly could fail to remain a vivid and significant memory. Curiously enough, it was the Commandant of the Cadet Corps who made the deepest impression on young Alvin Johnson.*

2. Lieutenant Pershing

IT WAS A late afternoon in early November when my train arrived at Lincoln. I got out, a little stiff from the novel experience of sitting still a whole day. There was a trolley waiting, marked for a destination unknown to me, but it would no doubt go through the town. I asked the conductor how one got to the university. Get out at Eleventh Street and walk north two or three blocks.

There before me, as I got out of the streetcar, was University Hall, as it was pictured in the university catalogue. I walked up to the gate, where I was almost trodden down by students scurrying from the classrooms. The building before me seemed huge and majestic. It had four strata of windows, some of them lighted, under a mansard roof. The building was topped with a square tower. To the right were three other buildings of varying architecture, all handsome to my country eyes.

But night was approaching, and I needed shelter. I picked up my bag and walked about in the streets near the campus until I came upon a sign, "Boarders." I knocked and was admitted by an emaciated landlady, aproned and smelling of cooking. She led me to a room, about eight feet by twelve, with narrow bed, washstand, and table. Three dollars a week, room and board.

The next morning, having risen at five, I took a long walk to see the city and to kill the time until breakfast, served at the late city hour of half-past seven. I took another long walk to kill time until nine o'clock, when I surmised the offices would be open. What office? I did not know, but went to the campus and accosted a hurrying student. I said I wanted to enter the preparatory department.

"Oh, then you go to the registrar, Ma Smith. But say, you're awful late. She'll kill you. She nearly broke my neck because I was two weeks late. But you can try her. First floor, offices to the left." The student raced on.

Ma Smith was an elderly woman with thin gray hair done in a hairpinned bun at the base of her head. She was hauling an unlucky student over the coals, and the longer she talked the angrier she got. When I presented my modest request she almost frothed at the mouth. "Enter now, with the term half over? No sirree!" She turned her back on me. I retreated, not pleased but not crushed. I would try the chancellor.

Chancellor James H. Canfield was a robust figure, not tall but, in a friendly way, very imposing. His mobile face was well bronzed, his dark eyes were bright and understanding. I was able to put my case without embarrassment.

"My boy," he said, "you are too late. You can't make it. My advice is, go home to the farm and come back September fifteenth."

"That wouldn't work," I objected. "I can't go back to the farm to do nothing. I'd have to plant another crop of corn and I'd have to husk it. You know, you can't husk corn before the end of October. I'd be just as late next year."

The chancellor smiled. "As I said, you can't make it. At least I think you can't make it. But if you want to try it, the chancellor has no right to forbid you."

"Will you give me a note to Ma Smith?"

"*Miss* Smith," he corrected. "Yes." He wrote a note in his delicately perfect script, signed it with a flourish, and gave it to me. He offered his warm, cordial hand. "My boy, you'll make it."

In my senior year, when I counted Ma Smith among my best friends, she told me how near she had come to a "cat fit" when I presented the note from the chancellor. She said that in fixing up my program she tried to give me the toughest teachers on the faculty, of whom the very toughest was the "Lieut"—Lieutenant John J. Pershing, Commandant of Cadets, who taught elementary mathematics and studied law on the side.

Most of my teachers were very considerate and gave me more time than I needed to catch up. Not so Lieutenant John J. Pershing. I had been in his class one week when he ordered me to the board to work out a complicated problem in algebra. I asked to be excused on the ground that I had not had time to catch up with the class.

"You have been here a week," he said grimly. "Next Monday, be caught up."

I was.

Of all my teachers Lieutenant Pershing interested me most. I devoted myself more to studying him than to the progress of the class. He was my first experience of a professional soldier. Lieutenant Pershing was tall, perfectly built, handsome. All his movements, all play of expression, were rigidly controlled to a military pattern. His pedagogy was military. His questions were short, sharp orders, and he expected quick, succinct answers. Woe to the student who put a problem on the board in loose or slovenly fashion! Pershing's soul appeared to have been formed on the pattern of "Present—arms! Right shoulder—arms! Fours right! Forward march!"

The ladies of the city were crazy about him—so it was gossiped among us students. But their adoration was vain—so the gossip ran —for the Lieut was ambitious and could not use a wife who did not bring a fortune. There were no adequate fortunes in Lincoln.

I admired Lieutenant Pershing, as a soldier. But never in the whole year did he give us a single glimpse of the Pythagorean enthusiasm for mathematics as an incomparable weapon for subjugating even the unknowable. Where Pershing's abilities shone brilliantly was in his handling of the cadet battalion. He could take a body of cornfed yokels and with only three hours of drill a week turn them into fancy cadets, almost indistinguishable from West Pointers. The year before I came to Lincoln, Pershing had taken a body of his Nebraska cadets to a national cadet corps meet at St. Louis, and all but beat West Point.

The next year I was confronted with the problem of military drill. I was a proto-pacifist and would have been glad to see the cadet corps abolished. But there it was, a condition of certain grants from the federal government which the university needed. One could substitute gymnasium work if one had good reasons for doing so, such as having to work in the late afternoon for board and room. I had begun, in desultory fashion, to do odd jobs to replenish my purse, but I had no time schedule that would serve as an excuse. My friends urged me to go in for drill while still a prep. Thus I could get five years of it and be fairly sure of an officer's commission. But that was distinctly what I did not want. My pacifism took the peculiar turn of willingness to accept the training of a private but not of an officer. I couldn't explain the distinction; it seemed to me like a mathematical axiom.

If you were out for a commission you served one year as a private, one as corporal, and a third as sergeant. If you were any good at all you got a lieutenancy, or even a captaincy, the fourth year, and on graduation you got a commission in the National Guard—mostly a paper organization. Most cadets were dying to go up the promotion ladder and sycophanted the Lieutenant as intimately as they could sycophant that disintimate soldier. I looked on the whole process with equalitarian contempt.

At the end of the year I heard my name read out before the corps as one of the corporals for the next year. I wouldn't have it and went to Lieutenant Pershing to have my name taken off the list.

"Why?" he demanded in the first surprised tone I ever heard from him.

I tried to explain, but my explanation didn't get through to him. He frowned and said, "If you don't want it, there is another cadet who does."

About half a century later I met General Pershing at a party given by Bernard M. Baruch for the War Industries Board. "I think I have met you before, Doctor Johnson," said the great general.

"Certainly," I said. "You have met hundreds of thousands, who all remember you, but you can't remember the hundreds of thousands."

"Was it in Nebraska, when I was Commandant of Cadets?"

"It was."

"And you were the cadet who refused to be a corporal. I never did understand your reasoning."

Imagine such a memory! Caesar was said to have known the names of all the soldiers in his legions. Commanding an army of ten regiments, to correspond with Caesar's army, Pershing might have learned the names of his men. He had had more to command his attention in his brilliant military career, first as Black Jack in the Philippines and finally in command of the huge American armies in World War I.

Extracted from *Pioneer's Progress*, The Viking Press, 1952

Charles Gates Dawes, later to be vice-president of the United States, ambassador to Great Britain, and first president of the Reconstruction Finance Corporation, lived in Lincoln from 1887 to 1895. In the foreword to Dawes' A Journal of the McKinley Years, Bascom N. Timmons writes:

The nine Nebraska years, hard years most of them, were decisive in molding the sort of man Charles Gates Dawes was to be. They saw, too, the forming of two of the many great Dawes' friendships—those with William Jennings Bryan and John J. Pershing. . . .

The Bryan and Dawes families attended the same Presbyterian church and went to its Wednesday night prayer meetings. They were to live on the same street, their houses only two blocks apart. A modicum of prosperity came to Bryan first. He acquired a two story house and a one horse surrey, while Dawes still lived in an $18 per month rented cottage and had no horse and carriage.

The Pershing friendship began when Lieutenant Pershing came to the University of Nebraska as its military instructor. That close relationship continued the remainder of Pershing's life and led to the appointment of Dawes on the staff of Pershing as General Purchasing Agent of the A.E.F.

The panic and depression year of 1893 . . . marked the substantial beginning of a financial career which brought him eminence in his own country and, at one stage, pre-eminence in Europe above and beyond any American.

The Panic of 1893

CHARLES G. DAWES

Lincoln, Nebr., January 1. We are living in a "rapid" time. Changes in the business world are more numerous and portending than ever before. The tendency is toward consolidation and concentration of wealth and power into the hands of the few; and we are all striving with might and main to become one of the "few"—often at the entire sacrifice of all efforts looking toward a better condition of mind and morals. My own business as it grows, becomes more and more absorbing; and I feel that I ought to combat the tendency to occupy myself with it so entirely. But lack of attention generally means lack of success.

January 3. I have the north west corner of 13th and "O" streets constantly in mind—25 feet by 142 feet. It is held at $18,500. I am as sure of its rapid and permanent increase in value as I am that the day follows night. Would like to leave it to my children. Two little wooden shanties are on it now. My idea would be to improve it immediately if I purchased it.

January 7. Fearing that continued gold exports may cause a premium on gold—or, rather, that the gold exports will cause such a discussion of the question of the inadequacy of gold reserve in the U. S. Treasury to total circulation, as may excite distrust which might cause a premium on gold, I advised the teller [of the American Exchange National Bank] to increase his gold in vaults by paying out silver and silver certificates, and retaining all gold deposited.

January 23. Was roused out of sleep at 6 A.M. by a message from Dan Wing of the American Exchange National Bank that the Capital National Bank had failed, and to come down town at once. Went down, and found the word correct. While nothing definite can be learned as to the condition of the closed bank, it looks like a bad failure.

January 28. The week has passed without any flurry in banking circles other than that caused by the failure of the Capital National Bank—which seems a bad failure. By the assessment of stockholders the depositors may get out whole.

There is today in this State a great public grievance—exorbitant local rates on railroad freight. And yet, the leading men of the State and of this city pose as apologists for this robbery because they fear the robbers. They stand by, and see the proper internal development of the State retarded by these high local rates, and keep their mouths shut lest their annual pass takes wings and flies. The disproportion existing between the high local rates *in* the State, and the low (by comparison only) through rates from outside points *to* the State, shuts out the producers of interior Nebraska from dealing in their own home markets—the cities of eastern Nebraska—as against shippers three and four times the distance from these cities. The railroads make rates upon the "long haul" theory. They discriminate against those industries of interior Nebraska which have a tendency to produce for home markets those commodities upon which they can get a long haul from the East. They encourage only those industries producing commodities for distant markets upon which they can get a long haul. This plan prevents the development and diversification of the industries of interior Nebraska upon natural lines. It increases the burden the people are carrying. In the long run, it injures the railroads themselves; for the interest of the State and its common carriers are, from an industrial standpoint, identical.

February 4. Closed the purchase from Miss Maria Lillibridge of Lot 18 Blk 40 Lincoln—being the north west corner of 13th and O Streets—on joint account of Gen. J. D. Cox of Cincinnati and myself. I have long had my eye on this corner. For future increase in value I consider it one of my best purchases—if not the best.*

February 6. The Populists and Democrats combining, W. V. Allen was elected U. S. Senator from Nebraska by a majority of five. The people have gained a victory, and all the friends of good government ought to rejoice. Though a Republican, I am for honest treatment of the people's desires to have railroad domination in politics ended.

February 11. The export of gold at New York still continues; I cannot see how we can avoid having a premium on gold in this country in a very short time.

March 10. The monetary situation is not reassuring. The fact is that under our present methods of doing business, periods of tightness in the money markets are becoming much more frequent than ever before. The means of multiplying credit have themselves been so multiplied that credits become too extended in a very short time after a period of liquidation, and force a second liquidation sooner than formerly. The probabilities are, however, that the present situation is only temporary due to the demand for currency from interior points on money centers, and also to the gold exports which excite apprehension.

April 23. Almost a money panic prevails in the land owing to the long continued exports of gold which leads people to fear a premium on gold, and the consequent degradation of our currency. The $100,000,000 gold reserve has been encroached upon; but the banks are affording a relief by furnishing some gold to the U. S. Treasury in return for greenbacks. . . . Under our system of credits, financial panics generally follow a period of inflation in general business. There has not been a period of inflation preceding this stringency; but there has been an inflation (to a moderate degree) of currency by the operation of the Sherman Law which provides for the issue of Treasury Notes based on bullion deposits of silver.

---

* It was a good buy. For nearly fifty years "13th and O" has been Lincoln's main intersection—the center of the city. (Editor's note)

April 24. Attended a meeting of the Round Table Club at Congressman William Jennings Bryan's where we discussed a good supper as well as the silver question.

April 27. Many failures are occurring. Locally we are in comparatively good condition. Uncle Sammy is pretty hard up. His hands are tied by the Sherman Law which compels him to buy silver bullion, which is worthless for purposes of redemption, and issue notes which are inflating his currency and weakening public confidence in his financial ability to redeem them in gold on demand. His failure to redeem in gold on demand any portion of his currency, paper or silver, means a premium on gold, a contraction of credits, and a paralysis of business (perhaps temporarily only). Meanwhile, gold exports are likely which will still further diminish his gold reserve.

May 5. The Panic on Wall Street does not extend over the country. Stocks took a great drop and a few failures are announced. At the close of the market, however, there was a rapid advance over lowest prices. The time has long since past when a clique of gamblers can break this country; though there is no doubt that they do great harm—especially the grain and provision gamblers.

May 14. I fear the panic, for which I have been looking so long, and for which, thank heaven! I have been preparing my business, is at last upon us. The paper is full of failures—banks are breaking all over the country, and there is a tremendous contraction of credits and hoarding of money going on everywhere. As to what the consequences will be, will be determined simply by the duration of the money shortage. If it continues for a great length of time great disasters will result. The causes which have led up to the panic are many—one of the chief being the widespread discussion of the condition of the U. S. Treasury in connection with the silver question. When you set a nation to talking about money, you advertise very broadly the adverse side of national finances. Another cause is a deeper one—and that is that we have now reached another cycle. All over the world there is now going on the same trouble.

May 16. At the close of the day the Nebraska Savings Bank had only $2,000 cash on hand as against $120,000 deposits. The clearing house decided to bolster them up—times being too critical to allow a bank to break.

May 18. The big run on the Nebraska Savings Bank came today, and continued till evening. About $18,000 was paid out over the counters. . . .

May 21. I have the Chicago, New York and Omaha papers. The outlook seems to me to be growing darker all the time; and widespread trouble is, in my judgment, at hand—in fact, we are now passing through it. . . .

June 21. The financial situation is such in the city that it seemed something should be done to fortify the American Exchange National Bank against the liability of further withdrawals of deposits. The directors decided to send I. M. Raymond and myself East to arrange for $100,000 to be used if necessary.

Raymond announced that he could not go, and E. F. Brown and D. E. Thompson and myself were sent as a committee east. We took with us ten notes of $10,000 each signed by all the Directors present (ten) left blank as to payee and interest for us to fill in. We also took $130,000 good commercial paper belonging to the bank. While the bank is in good shape with 26% cash on hand, the situation is so critical in the city that we must get ready for bad times.

July 9. The country is passing through a great panic which, in its severity, has been approximated only by 1873. . . . The city and state are standing the strain wonderfully well,—especially the banks which are all in as good shape as could be expected. . . . The financial panic is a very interesting thing to study. Human nature asserts itself always, and once a crowd gets started, there seems to be nothing to do but to do nothing until they get over it.

July 15. One day matters seem better—the next worse. Men are being thrown out of employment, and the trade of retailers and wholesalers has almost come to a standstill. There is almost no money in circulation. It is very difficult to collect any rents. Banks are failing in Denver and Kansas City. The hoarding of money is still going on. Where things will end no one can tell. Money is all in the banks or in the stockings or in the safety deposit boxes.

July 20. Reports of bank failures all over the country continue to come in. There is much free silver talk, etc., all of which serves to render the public more uneasy, and to cause a feeling of apprehension which manifests itself in the continued falling off of bank deposits.

July 28. Panic in progress in New York. . . . It is with much reluctance that I prophesy a still worse condition of things in the future. Notwithstanding Congress is to meet and endeavor to outline a financial policy for the government, confidence will return very slowly. . . . You cannot legislate apprehension out of the mind of the masses.

August 12. Conditions of business over the country slowly improve. Deposits at the bank this week show a decided increase, and the worst of the times are certainly over. The heavy importation of gold and the increase in national bank circulation are having their legitimate effect in gradually restoring confidence. . . . The relief is, of course, first experienced by the banks, and soon will reach business men generally.

September 3. The recovery from "panic" conditions is very evident; but business of every kind is more or less stagnant. In the great money centers, the improvement in conditions is most marked. In this locality the feeling of relief comes from the disasters which have been avoided rather than from the condition into which we have emerged. As a general thing deposits are increasing. The packing house is running again. The repeal bill (repeal of Sherman Law for purchasing of silver bullion and issue of Treasury Notes thereon) is now being discussed in the Senate—the House has passed it by a very large majority.

October 13. . . . The chief effect of the panic here is now noticeable in the number of "good" men whom it has left hard up. It is an experience to go through; but "to him who over-cometh" there is a rich reward as a general rule. There will be widespread distress this winter which it will be the duty of everyone to try and alleviate.

October 29. The Senate of the United States will unconditionally repeal the Sherman Law. The events of the week in the Senate seem to settle the fact that it is impossible to bring the silver men together on any compromise measure.

Extracted from *A Journal of the McKinley Years*, Lakeside Press, 1950

It is easy to ridicule Bryan; he was often absurd, he was usually ignorant, and he had the narrow outlook of a man who has failed to sublimate inhibitions devoid of meaning. But when all is said against Bryan that can be said, his alliance with the silver interests, for example, the fact remains that he was the voice of the authentic American yearning that the forgotten man should be remembered.

—Harold J. Laski, *The American Democracy*

Bryan, Bryan, Bryan

1. The Voice

GERALD W. JOHNSON

WILLIAM JENNINGS BRYAN could speak to thirty thousand people in the open air and make every word heard at the fringes of the crowd without the aid of microphones and amplifiers or any other mechanical device. He was a big man, somewhat spindleshanked, but with a chest like a beer keg and a mouth that could have received a billiard ball with effortless ease. His head was thickest through the jowls, slanting to a relatively narrow ridge at the top, but in his youth he wore a great mane of black hair that gave the casual observer a contrary impression; his head seemed to be widest at the brow, a triangle standing on its apex. Even in his last days the hair still clustered thickly above his ears, and although a pointed, bald dome loomed up through it, most people still failed to note how the power of the head was concentrated in the mouth and jaws, with a comparatively small brainpan above them.

But when Bryan spoke nobody was interested in such details. In later years his voice acquired a note of stridency, but at the height of his powers it was a superb musical instrument with never a wolf tone through all the register. Even when in volume it rose to thunder, still it caressed the ears, a thirty-two foot open diapason, not a foghorn. This apparent ease was deceptive, of course; actually the man expended a terrific amount of energy in each of his orations, as is evidenced by the fabulous quantities of food he consumed on an active campaign without suffering any appreciable impairment

of his health. A man who ate like Bryan had to expend energy at a
furious rate; had he not done so, he would either have blown out
every gasket in his internal mechanism, or he would have ended
the tour weighing seven hundred pounds.

Yet at his most impassioned he seemed to be well within his limits,
with plenty of reserve power still untouched, and this gave an extraordinary effect of mastery to his utterance. To the common man
it seemed that whatever Bryan said had more behind it; at least
this was so in the early days and measurably so up until 1908. The
ironical fact that Bryan actually knew less than almost any other
man who figured prominently in public life at the time is beside
the point. He seemed to know. . . .

To do him justice Bryan had the answers to some questions that
seemed unanswerable then, to an astonishingly large number, in
fact. His trouble was that when he had the answer he almost invariably had it by the wrong end and so could not make it fit. His
knowledge was intuitive rather than empirical, which is to say, he
played hunches oftener than he thought things through; but because his hunches were usually good, he has made an indelible impression upon United States history, and is today a major prophet,
however he may have failed as a statesman.

Consider, as a shining example, the issue on which he first shook
the country, the free coinage of silver at the ratio of sixteen to one.
Modern schoolboys in the history class probably find one of the
dreariest moments in the whole course that in which they confront
the task of learning what was meant by "free silver" and "sixteen to
one." It is a dreary task because, as a matter of fact, they didn't mean
anything, being assertions that put effect ahead of cause. Yet in the
presidential campaign of 1896 these slogans occupied the attention
of the country almost to the exclusion of anything else, and Bryan
employed them so effectively that he almost shattered the Republican
party a full generation ahead of its fated moment.

Obviously, then, the people who participated in that campaign
thought that these expressions carried tremendous significance, and
the reasons why they thought so are more interesting than the fact.
One of the reasons was that Bryan had the answer, but had it by the
wrong end. In the course of the campaign he thundered against "the
Money Devil of Wall Street" and threw bankers, brokers, and in-
dustrialists into paroxysms of wrath and fear. The truth is, there
was a Money Devil, but his habitat was not Wall Street. His lair was
in the colleges and universities, in the textbooks on economics, in

the minds of farmers, businessmen and teachers, in the mind of Bryan himself. The devil of it was that we were trying to manage an elastic economy with a rigid currency. Every time the crops were harvested, money became tight and borrowers had to pay through the nose; every time business slacked off a bit, money lost value and lenders could get little or no return. This was true because the dollar represented, not a true economic value, but a certain weight of gold; since there was a fixed amount of gold in the world, there could be only a certain number of dollars, no matter how much the movement of business called for more money.

Bryan perceived the trouble plainly enough, but not the remedy. He had the idea that the recurrent economic crises were due to the fact that the dollar was stuck tight to the rare metal, gold, and that it could be relieved by attaching it in part to the relatively more abundant metal, silver. He therefore proposed to enact into law the principle that the number of dollars equivalent to one ounce of gold should always be equivalent to sixteen ounces of silver.

But the trouble, of course, was not that gold had been selected as the standard. The trouble was that the currency had no elasticity and could have none as long as it was rigidly bound to any metal in limited supply. Twenty years later we turned Bryan's answer around and then it was so beautiful a fit that the currency system sustained the shock of two frightful wars with almost no trouble.*

So it was with Bryan's chief issue in his second campaign, that of 1900. This time it was Imperialism that Bryan opposed, and again his opposition itself was correct, but again it was badly aimed. Imperialism lurked in the minds of some young and ebullient politicians, notably the Republican candidate for Vice-President in 1900, but that political imperialism was frank, aboveboard, and not very dangerous. The imperialism that made headway was the economic imperialism of men of a very different type—the elder Rockefeller, satrap of oil, Harriman of railroads, Baer of coal, Duke of tobacco, Morgan and his associates, the financiers.

They all had perceived the reality of economic power and had gathered it into their hands to an appalling extent. Bryan knew it, and he knew that in some instances they had achieved their ends by manipulating and perverting the power of the law, political power; so he decided that the way to halt them was to prevent the erection

---

* The device was the Federal Reserve note, based, not on gold, but on economic goods actually in existence. As the goods were consumed, the notes were canceled, to be issued again when more goods were produced. Thus the currency automatically expanded and contracted as the volume of business rose and fell.

of a political empire. Unfortunately for his theory, political imperialism was by no means indispensable to the creation of industrial
cartels, shipping agreements, and banking associations. So once more
Bryan had the answer to the problem, but had it by the wrong end.

But all this became clear only after many years. When the century began Bryan was the Voice that spoke the heart's desire of the
common man, the ancient desire that has driven him since history
began, the aspiration toward freedom from want and freedom from
fear. At the Democratic National Convention in Chicago, in 1896,
Bryan had adroitly seized the moment to stampede the Democratic
party into accepting the more important demands of the Populists.
He achieved it by an extraordinary oratorical effort that went down
in history as "the Cross of Gold speech" and that established him at
once as the greatest master of the platform in American politics.
But it did more. It made him also the leader of the disinherited—the
discontented, the disappointed, and the mentally incompetent, too,
but mainly those who had lost through no fault of their own. He
knew the problems that harassed millions, and persuaded them that
he knew the answers too, so for twenty years he was politically indestructible.

Extracted from *Incredible Tale*, Harper & Brothers, 1950

> July 9, 1896. *Went to Convention. Sat on platform. Heard
> my old friend, William J. Bryan, make his speech on the
> platform's silver plank. His oratory was magnificent—his
> logic pitifully weak. I could not but have a feeling of pride
> for the brilliant young man whose life for so many years
> lay parallel to mine, and with whom the future may yet
> bring me into conflict as in the past.*
>
> —Charles G. Dawes, *A Journal of the McKinley Years*

2. "A Good Many Votes on D Street"

M. R. WERNER

WHEN the Convention convened," wrote Bryan, "I felt as I always
do before a speech of unusual importance. I usually have a feeling
of weakness at the pit of my stomach—a suggestion of faintness. I

want to lie down. But this being impossible in the Convention, I got a sandwich and a cup of coffee and devoted myself to these as I waited for the debate to begin. . . ."

The setting as Bryan rose to speak was just the setting to put before an orator. The voices of the other speakers had not carried in the huge auditorium, but every one of the fifteen thousand in the audience heard Bryan's first words, beautifully modulated.

"I would be presumptuous, indeed," he began, "to present myself against the distinguished gentlemen to whom you have listened, if this were a measuring of abilities; but this is not a contest between persons. The humblest citizen in all the land, when clad in the armor of a righteous cause, is stronger than all the hosts of error. I come to speak to you in defense of a cause as holy as the cause of liberty—the cause of humanity."

He then traced very briefly the organization of the free silver forces, and he said triumphantly: "With a zeal approaching the zeal which inspired the crusaders who followed Peter the Hermit, our silver Democrats went forth from victory unto victory until they are now assembled, not to discuss, not to debate, but to enter up the judgment already rendered by the plain people of this country. In this contest brother has been arrayed against brother, father against son. The warmest ties of love, acquaintance, and association have been disregarded; old leaders have been cast aside when they have refused to give expression to the sentiments of those whom they would lead, and new leaders have sprung up to give direction to this cause of truth. Thus has the contest been waged, and we have assembled here under as binding and solemn instructions as were ever imposed upon representatives of the people."

Leading up from his introduction with a few careful words concerning the gentlemen who had preceded him, Bryan sailed into an offensive with these rolling words:

"When you [turning to the gold delegates] come before us and tell us that we are about to disturb your business interests, we reply that you have disturbed our business interests by your course.

"We say to you that you have made the definition of a business man too limited in its application. The man who is employed for wages is as much a business man as his employer, the attorney in a country town is as much a business man as the corporation counsel in a great metropolis; the merchant at the crossroads store is as much a business man as the merchant of New York; the farmer who goes forth in the morning and toils all day—who begins in the spring and toils all summer—and who by the application of brain and muscle to the natural resources of the country creates wealth, is as much a business man as the man who goes upon the board of trade and bets upon the price of grain; the miners who go down a thousand feet into the earth, or climb two thousand feet upon the cliffs, and bring forth from their hiding-places the precious metals to be poured into the channels of trade, are as much business men as the few financial magnates who, in a back room, corner the money of the world. We come to speak for this broader class of business men."

The audience rose to Bryan's eloquence in a manner which he described as "like a trained choir."

"Ah, my friends," he continued, "we say not one word against those who live upon the Atlantic coast, but the hardy pioneers who have braved all the dangers of the wilderness, who have made the desert to blossom as the rose—the pioneers away out there [pointing to the West], who rear their children near to Nature's heart, where they can mingle their voices with the voices of the birds—out there where they have erected schoolhouses for the education of their young, churches where they praise their Creator, and cemeteries where rest the ashes of their dead—these people, we say, are as deserving of the consideration of our party as any people in this country. It is for these that we speak. We do not come as aggressors. Our war is not a war of conquest; we are fighting in the defense of our homes, our families, and prosperity. We have petitioned, and our petitions have been scorned; we have entreated, and our entreaties have been disregarded; we have begged, and they have mocked when our calamity came. We beg no longer; we entreat no more; we petition no more. We defy them." There was a thunder of applause.

Then Bryan answered with generalities the general objections to silver offered by those who had spoken before him. "If they ask us," he concluded in this phase of his speech, "why it is that we say more on the money question than we say on the tariff question, I reply that, if protection has slain its thousands, the gold standard has slain its tens of thousands." Then he spoke of Mr. McKinley: "Mr. McKinley was the most popular man among the Republicans, and three months ago everybody in the Republican party prophesied his election. How is it today? Why, the man who was once pleased to think that he looked like Napoleon—that man shudders today when he remembers that he was nominated on the anniversary of the battle of Waterloo. Not only that, but as he listens he can hear with ever-increasing distinctness the sound of the waves as they beat upon the lonely shores of St. Helena." An "indignant people," Bryan thought, would visit their "avenging wrath" on a man who would "place the legislative control of our affairs in the hands of foreign potentates and powers." He then expressed his confidence that the Democrats would win, and described the two opposing theories of government: "There are those who believe that, if you will only legislate to make the well-to-do prosperous, their prosperity will leak through on those below. The Democratic idea, however, has been that if you legislate to make the masses prosperous, their prosperity will find its way up through every class which rests upon them." And then in mellow, resounding tones he uttered his famous peroration:

"You come to us and tell us that the great cities are in favor of the gold standard; we reply that the great cities rest upon our broad and fertile prairies. Burn down your cities and leave our farms, and your cities will spring up again as if by magic; but destroy our farms and the grass will grow in the streets of every city in the country.

"My friends, we declare that this nation is able to legislate for its own people on every question, without waiting for the aid or consent of any other nation on earth; and upon that issue we expect to carry every State in the Union. . . . It is the issue of 1776 over again. Our ancestors, when but three million in number, had the courage to declare their political independence of every other nation; shall we, their descendants, when we have grown to seventy millions, declare that we are less independent than our forefathers? Therefore, we care not upon what lines the battle is fought. If they say bimetallism is good, but that we cannot have it until other nations help us, we reply that, instead of having a gold standard because England has, we will restore bimetallism, and then let England have bimetallism because the United States has it. If they dare to come out in the open field and defend the gold standard as a good thing, we will fight them to the uttermost. Having behind us the producing masses of this nation and the world, supported by the commercial interests, the laboring interests, and the toilers everywhere, we will answer their demand for a gold standard by saying to them: You shall not press down upon the brow of labor this crown of thorns, you shall not crucify mankind upon a cross of gold."

All through his speech there had been spontaneous outbursts of applause, but when Bryan had finished, the convention went collectively insane. Men yelled, wept, shrieked, and marched, grabbing the standards of the various States and making for the seat of Mr. Bryan.

The effect on the entire nation was tremendous: "Through the nerves of the telegraph," wrote William Allen White, "that speech thrilled a continent, and for a day a nation was in a state of mental and moral catalepsy. If the election had been held that July day, Bryan would have been chosen President."

> September 4, 1896. (Chicago) William J. Bryan and his wife were at the Auditorium Annex. Called on them and had quite a talk. Bryan, somehow, imagines he has a chance to be elected President. He referred to our old silver debates and gave me a conditional invitation to visit the White House.
>
> —Charles G. Dawes, A Journal of the McKinley Years

THE TENSITY was greater than that of any election since the Civil War. In New York City the campaign had ended with the monster gold parade of Saturday. Sunday was a restless day full of suspense, and Monday seemed interminable. Early in the morning of Tuesday, November 3, men hurried to the polls, and the small boys began their bonfires. Toward evening huge crowds gathered in City Hall Park and around the newspaper buildings. Thousands of tin horns sputtered. . . .

In his house in Lincoln, Nebraska, Bryan was in bed. He needed rest badly. Downstairs in the library newspaper men gathered with Mrs. Bryan and received the bulletins, which she carried upstairs to the bedroom at regular intervals. "As the evening progressed," wrote Bryan, "the indications pointed more and more strongly to defeat, and by eleven o'clock I realized that, while the returns from the country might change the result, the success of my opponent was more than probable. Confidence resolved itself into doubt, and doubt, in turn, gave place to resignation. While the compassionless current sped hither and thither, carrying its message of gladness to foe and its message of sadness to friend, there vanished from my mind the vision of a President in the White House, perplexed by the cares of state, and, in the contemplation of the picture of a citizen by his fireside, free from official responsibility, I fell asleep." A stranger stopped Bryan's eleven-year-old daughter, Ruth, and asked her whether she thought her father would be elected. "I think he will get a good many votes on D Street, but I do not know about the rest of the country," she replied.

The final result of the election showed that McKinley received 7,035,638 and Bryan 6,467,946. In the electoral college the vote was 271 for McKinley, 176 for Bryan. A change of some 900 votes in California would have given Bryan that State's electoral vote, and a change of 142 votes would have given him Kentucky. A total change of 14,001 votes distributed in the proper States would have given him a majority of three electoral votes.

Condensed from *Bryan*, Harcourt, Brace & Co., 1929

March 3, 1897. *I took the train for Baltimore to meet the Presidential train from Canton. By a curious coincidence my old associates, Mr. and Mrs. W. J. Bryan, and their little daughter were on the same parlor car with us. I introduced them to Abner McKinley* and his wife and daughter, and had a long talk with them. Bryan did not express any disappointment. I had a talk with Mrs. Bryan. She talked very sensibly and pleasantly about "old times" and her husband. She believes that her husband will sometime lead to triumph in a presidential race the elements which stood for him in the last conflict.*

—Charles G. Dawes, *A Journal of the McKinley Years*

3. Mr. and Mrs. William Jennings Bryan (1900)

WILLA CATHER

WHEN I first knew William Jennings Bryan, he was the Democratic nominee for the First Congressional District of Nebraska, a district in which the Republican majority had never fallen below 3,000. I was a student at the state university when Mr. Bryan was stumping the state, which he had stumped two years before for J. Sterling Morton, now his bitterest political enemy. My first meeting with him was on a streetcar. He was returning from some hall where he had been making an address, and carried a most unsightly floral offering

* President McKinley's brother

of large dimensions, the tribute of some of his devoted constituents. The car was crowded, and the candidate had some difficulty in keeping his "set piece" out of the way of the passengers. A sympathetic old lady who sat next to him enquired: "Is it for a funeral?"

Mr. Bryan looked quizzically at his encumbrance and replied politely: "Well, I hope not, madam."

It certainly was not, for that fall he carried the Republican district by a majority of 7,000. Before that time Mr. Bryan had been a rather inconspicuous lawyer in Lincoln. He had come there in 1887 at the solicitation of his old college chum, A. R. Talbot, with whom he went into partnership. He was never a man who frequented ward caucuses, for he was an idealist pure and simple, then as now, and he had practically nothing to do with Nebraska politics until he stumped the state for Morton. Then he began to make a stir. His oratory "took hold," and his own nomination came to him entirely unsought. In those days Mr. Bryan used to have leisure to offer occasional good advice to university students, and I believe he drilled several for oratorical contests. He wrote occasionally for the college paper of which I was editor, and was always at home to students in his library in the evening.

The man's whole inner life was typified in that library. The walls were hung with very bad old-fashioned engravings of early statesmen, and those pictures were there because Mr. Bryan liked them. Of books there were many, but of the kind of books that are written for art's sake there were few. There were many of the old classics, and many Latin and French books, much worn, for he read them constantly. There were many lives of American statesmen, which were marked and annotated, schoolboy fashion. The works on political economy were mostly by quacks—men who were mentally one-sided, and who never rose to any true scientific eminence. There was much poetry of a didactic or declamatory nature, which is the only kind that Mr. Bryan has any taste for. In the line of fiction there was little more recent than Thackeray. Mr. Bryan used always to be urging us to read *Les Miserables* if we hadn't, and to reread it if we had. He declared that it was the greatest novel written, yet I think he had never considered its merits or demerits as a novel at all. It was Hugo's vague hyperbolic generalizations on sociological questions that he marked and quoted. In short, he read Hugo, the orator and impractical politician, not Hugo, the novelist.

The last ten years have changed Mr. Bryan very little personally. He is now, as he was then, a big, well planted man, standing firmly on the soil as though he belonged there and were rooted to it, with powerful shoulders, exhilarating freedom of motion, and a smile that won him more votes than his logic ever did. His prominent nose and set mouth might have belonged to any of the early statesmen he emulates. His hair is rather too thin on top and rather too long behind. His eyes are as sharp and clear as cut steel, and his glance as penetrating as a searchlight. He dressed then very much like a Kentucky judge, and I believe he still clings to the low collar and black string tie. I have seen him without his coat, but never without a high moral purpose. It was a physical impossibility for him to loaf or dawdle, or talk nonsense. His dining room was a forum. I do not mean that he talked incessantly, but that when he did talk it was in a manner forensic. He chipped his eggs to the accompaniment of maxims, sometimes strikingly original, sometimes trite enough. He buttered his toast with an epigram, and when he made jokes they were of the manifest kind that the crowd catch quickly and applaud wildly. When he was at his best, his conversation was absolutely overwhelming in its richness and novelty and power, in the force and aptness of his illustrations. Yet one always felt that it was meant for the many, not the few, that it was addressed to humanity, and that there should be a stenographer present to take it down.

There is nothing of familiarity or adroitness in the man; you never come any closer to him than just within the range of his voice. The breakfast room was always too small for him; he exhausted the air; he gave other people no chance to breathe. His dynamic magnetism either exhausted you or overstimulated you. He needs a platform, and a large perspective and resounding domes; and he needs the enthusiasm of applauding thousands to balance his own. The almighty, ever-renewed force of the man drives one to distraction; his everlasting high seriousness makes one want to play marbles. He was never fond of athletics. He takes no care of himself. After his own fashion he studies incessantly, yet his vitality comes up with the sun and outburns the street arc lights.

In his business relations, in his civic relations, in his domestic relations, Mr. Bryan is always a statesman, large-minded, clean, and a trifle unwieldy. If all this were not so absolutely natural to the man, so inseparable from him, it might be called theatric.

Mrs. Bryan's life is simply a record of hard work. She first met Mr. Bryan in Illinois when he was a college student and she was attending the "annex" of the institution. He graduated valedictorian, and she achieved a like honor in her class. Two such brilliant and earnest young people were naturally drawn to each other. It was a serious wooing. The days of their courtship were spent among books and in conversations upon dry subjects that would terrify most women. From the outset their minds and tastes kept pace with each other, as they have done to this day. Bryan never read a new book, never was seized by a new idea that she did not share. Away out west, where there are no traditions, no precedents, where men meet nature singlehanded and think life out for themselves, those two young people looked about them for the meaning of things. And the strange thing about these two people is that neither of them has lost that faith and fervor and sincerity which so often die with youth. It is not wholly practical, perhaps, but it is a beautiful thing to see.

Mr. and Mrs. Bryan were engaged when she was nineteen and he twenty, but they were not married until four years afterwards. They lived in Illinois a little time, then moved to Lincoln, Nebraska. There Mr. Bryan, a young man and a poor one, began to practice law in a country none too rich. In order to be better able to help him, Mrs. Bryan studied law and was admitted to the bar. She has never practiced law, but when her husband began to mingle in politics many of the duties of the law office fell upon her. To society she paid little or no attention. For there is such a thing as society, even in Nebraska. There are good dancing clubs and whist clubs, but she never found time for them. Except at political meetings and university lectures, and occasionally at the theater, she was seldom seen in public. Into one social feature, however, Mrs. Bryan has always entered with all her characteristic enthusiasm. She is a most devout club woman. She organized the Lincoln Sorosis and has been an active worker in the State Federation of Woman's Clubs. There is in Lincoln, as in all university towns, a distinct college clique, and in this Mrs. Bryan has always figured prominently. Mrs. Bryan is a wheelwoman, but she has never gone wild over it or made any "century" runs. She is an expert swimmer, and Wednesday mornings she and her friends used to go down to the plunge in the sanitarium and spend the morning in the water. But she carried none of these things to excess.

Before all else she is a woman of intellect, not so by affectation or even by choice, but by necessity, by nature. Eastern newspapers have devoted a great deal of space to criticizing Mrs. Bryan's dress. It is doubtful if she ever spent ten minutes planning the construction of a gown. But many and many an hour have she and her husband spent by their library fire talking over the future of the West and their political beliefs. In Washington they worked out that celebrated tariff speech together, line by line. When the speech was delivered she sat unobserved in the gallery and by signals regulated the pitch of her husband's voice, until it reached just the proper volume to fill the house. She knew every word of that speech by heart. Much of the reading, searching for historical references, and verification fell upon her. Several days before the speech which made Bryan famous was delivered, he was called upon to make a eulogy upon a dead comrade. Mrs. Bryan sat in the gallery and carefully noted what tones and gestures were most effective in that hall. They prepared that speech and its delivery as an actor makes out his interpretation of a role. At the reception given the Bryans, Mrs. Bryan did not appear in evening dress, and the couple stood about ill at ease until the affair was over. The people who work most earnestly do not always play the most skilfully.

The distinctive feature of Mr. Bryan's career is that he began at the top. At an age when most lawyers have barely succeeded in building up a good practice, he was the leader of one of the two great political parties of America. He attained that leadership quite without financial backing or an astute political impresario, attained it singlehanded. His constituents are controlled not by a commercial syndicate or by a political trust but by one man's personality. Behind this personality there is neither an invincible principle nor an unassailable logic, only melodious phrases, a convincing voice, and a hypnotic sincerity. During these last four years, instead of sealing influential allies to himself, he has been engaging in various crusades of sentiment. If he were struck dumb, he would be as helpless as a tenor without his voice.

He is an orator, pure and simple, certainly the greatest in America today. After all, it is not a crime to be an orator, and not necessarily ridiculous. It is a gift like any other gift, and not always a practical one. The Hon. William McKeighan was one of the first free-silver agitators in Nebraska and had gone from a dugout to the halls of Congress. When McKeighan died, Bryan came down to the sunscorched, dried-up, blown-away little village of Red Cloud to speak at his funeral. There, with an audience of some few hundreds of bronzed farmers who believed in him as their deliverer, the man who could lead them out of the bondage of debt, who could stay the drought and strike water from the rock, I heard him make the greatest speech of his life. Surely that was eloquence of the old stamp that was accounted divine, eloquence that reached through the callus of ignorance and toil and found and awoke the stunted souls of men. I saw those rugged, ragged men of the soil weep like children. Six months later, at Chicago, when Bryan stampeded a convention, appropriated a party, electrified a nation, flashed his name around the planet, took the assembled thousands of that convention hall and moulded them in his hands like so much putty, one of those ragged farmers sat beside me in the gallery, and at the close of that never-to-be-forgotten speech, he leaned over the rail, the tears on his furrowed cheeks, and shouted, "The sweet singer of Israel!"

Of Mr. Bryan's great sincerity there can be no doubt. It is, indeed, the unsophisticated sort of sincerity which is the stamp of the crusader, but in a man of his native force it is a power to be reckoned with. His mental fiber is scarcely delicate enough to be susceptible to doubts. It is failure and hope deferred that lead a man to modify, retrench, weigh evidence against himself, and Mr. Bryan's success has been uninterrupted.

It is scarcely necessary to say that he has no finesse. His book, *The First Battle,* is an almost unparalleled instance of bad taste. But his honesty is unquestionable. He favored the ratification of the treaty with Spain when his party opposed it. In the Kansas City convention he drove his party to the suicidal measure of retaining the 16-to-1 platform. He is the white elephant of his party, and yet they cannot escape the dominant influence of his personality.

Alphonse Daudet all his life made notes for a book he never wrote, a book which should embody in the person of Napoleon the entire race of the south of France. So I think William Jennings Bryan synthesizes the entire Middle West; all its newness and vigor, its magnitude and monotony, its richness and lack of variety, its inflammability and volubility, its strength and its crudeness, its high seriousness and self-confidence, its egotism and its nobility.

Reprinted from "The Personal Side of William Jennings Bryan,"
Prairie Schooner, Winter, 1949

At the turn of the century, the doings of a real live presidential-nominee and his spirited family undoubtedly were Lincoln's best entertainment. But those were the days, too, of the town's theatrical glory. "Players came to Lincoln," wrote E. P. Brown, "even before the railroad did. With the growth of railroads it became part of 'the road.' On that road toured the great ones of the stage and a lot of the little ones. Lincoln saw them all. . . . A list of the names of players who came to Lincoln in those days reads like a Who's Who of the American stage."

However, in the nineties the news that Nebraska's capital had been "pencilled in" could not always have been of unalloyed delight to touring artists. For the word had spread that Lincoln's leading dramatic critic, a Miss Willa Cather, wrote with "biting frankness" when performers failed to give their best.

If critics disagree on a production's merits, the show is said to have received mixed notices. *And judging by the reminiscences of Colonel Barney Oldfield, who covered all sectors of the Footlight Front in Lincoln during the twenties and thirties, this term would be a fair description of show people's reaction to the audiences they played to there.*

Mixed Notices

COLONEL BARNEY OLDFIELD

HER SERENE HIGHNESS Princess Grace of Monaco has never, so far as I know, been to Nebraska, but one of her relatives made it a few times and never got over it—or over lamenting about it. He was Walter C. Kelly, who travelled under the billing of "The Virginia Judge," and was one of vaudeville's greats. Great everywhere but Nebraska, that is. Audiences in the Cornhusker State watched his act with faces of stone and sat on their mitts. Invariably, on each of his engagements Kelly played to such thunderous silence that he may well have wondered if the curtain was up, yet elsewhere in the forty-eight he was rated as a top entertainer and one of the premier dialecticians of all time. This was in a day when dialect was standard comedy—before Hitler & Company had put the successors to Weber & Fields out of business.

Kelly carried his scorn of the Nebraska theater-goer to *Variety*, the show-business Bible, and wrote vitriolically therein of the apathetic hayshakers out where the Middle West ends. (He seemed to think it should have ended sooner.) However, although Nebraska never was considered an important sector of the road by vaudevillians or touring companies, it was one of the kindest in terms of loyal and lasting interest in the live performer. And in the late thirties, long after the great circuits had dwindled to nothing, Lincoln—despite Kelly's conviction that audiences there had predeceased vaudeville— had two competing houses offering a pit orchestra and a few acts as breathers between movies. But the legend that Nebraska theater-goers suffered from retarded uptake had spread through the trade, disseminated by men like Walter C. Kelly; and in conversations in front of New York's Palace—where "at liberty" artists gathered to boast, bleat, and boo, as the subject called for—the state received poor notices.

A sign backstage at the old Orpheum (now the Nebraska) in Lincoln indicated a reluctance to "give" on the part of the management as well as the audience. "Notice to actors," it read. "Please do not ask for passes. If your friends won't pay to see you, who the hell will?"

Actors who could get away with it reciprocated in kind. When Sarah Bernhardt played the state, she demanded—and got—her day's pay in cash before she went on. When, in the course of his innumerable farewell tours, Sir Harry Lauder came to Lincoln, he would never permit the box office to hang up the SOLD OUT sign. For every additional pasteboard sold, the Scotch star had them put another chair on the stage—and usually worked the last show with bare clearance for his kilts.

Scheduled for a matinee one time, Al Jolson came on and after a quick look out front—quick, but plenty long enough to enable him to count the house—told everyone to go on home and come back later, and himself went off to shoot some golf. Al was probably the brassiest actor ever to skip through the state. Each morning he used to hand the bellboy a dollar with instructions to "Page me every half hour. I won't answer, but people will know I'm in town."

It was largely, I believe, because of trade talk designating Nebraska as the Land of the Square that I became correspondent of the

New York daily *PM*, when Ralph Ingersoll started his great adless newspaper experiment in 1940. His theater editor, Cecelia Ager, wrote, asking me to do a weekly piece about what was going on in Nebraska, her reason being that there was no place in America likelier to register the far end of the pendulum swing from Broadway's sophistication! This in the face of the famous *Variety* headline STIX NIX HIX PIX, and the fact that hillbilly music was taking over Tin Pan Alley.

However, I dutifully wrote my weekly despatches, and Cecelia duly printed them. Of the many, the story which really sent her concerned one Jules Rachman, who had killed his two partners in a scramble over the till. He became booker, manager, entrepreneur, and sometime projectionist at the Nebraska State Penitentiary. Out of consideration for the guards who always chaperoned the lockstep set at his presentations, he, too, posted a sign: "If the cop gets shot in the picture, kindly refrain from laughing."

Although Lincoln was inclined to regard theater people as beyond the pale, it was big enough to elect one of its best-known managers, Frank C. Zehrung, mayor of the capital city. The dapper Frank, Nebraska's answer to New York's Jimmy Walker and undoubtedly Lincoln's best-dressed mayor, could deliver himself of a "welcome to our fair city" with an aplomb which compared favorably with that of the most accomplished of the monologists who sometimes worked for him.

Nebraska gave the circus world one of its best and best-liked managers in the person of the late Ralph J. Clawson, who died in 1956. And the Nebraska State Fair was the scene of a dramatic demise portending the end of the mightiest travelling show of them all—Ringling Brothers, Barnum & Bailey, which folded its tents forever in Pittsburgh, Pa., July 16, 1956. The prophetic episode occurred when the John Robinson Circus, of Dixie origin and a top favorite, played the State Fair as a grandstand attraction in September, 1930. Stowed aboard its long string of railroad cars at the end of the engagement, the show whistled out of town and into oblivion from Lincoln's Rock Island yards. It was the first of the big ones to be snuffed out completely, twenty-six years before the last stake would be pulled on these rail-borne monsters. Since John Robinson's performers had played at the Fair on bare rigging—they had no canvas up because the spectators sat in the grandstand—the symbolism of the prophecy was complete: the circus has literally lost its shirt!

Nebraska has given many personalities to Broadway and Holly-

wood, even if the state itself is not a popular place for the practice of
their art. Harold Lloyd made Burchard so proud that the town put
up a sign on the grain elevator proclaiming to all passers-by that he
was a favorite son. Just about the time Omaha's Marlon Brando and
Montgomery Clift were learning to walk, Robert Taylor and his
widow's peak were making the ladies palpitate from the Embarcadero
to the Bronx—quite a shake for a kid from Filley whose first performing venture was as one-third of an instrumental trio sponsored by a
fly spray account on KMMJ in Clay Center. And Henry Fonda had
left Grand Island and Omaha twenty-five years before Sharon Kay
Ritchie, the Third City's beauty, was to become Miss America of
1955.

Hoot Gibson (remember Hoot?) of Tekamah went west hunting
for the cowboys who were supposed to abound "out there" and kept
going until he hit Hollywood. The story was that he never rode a
horse until he got in front of a camera and when, for the first time,
he threw a leg over a saddle, he found himself facing the horse's
stern. But unfortunately the wildest-eyed press agent couldn't get
even Louella Parsons to buy that one!

Little Freddie and Adele Astaire, born Austerlitz, saw the first light
of day within easy sniffing distance of South Omaha's stockyards, but
they went off east, made the grade on Park Avenue as well as Broadway, and never looked back. Another Omahan, George Givot, assumed the title of "Greek Ambassador of Good Will" and won
plaudits from Walter Winchell at a time when WW was making
journalistic hay out of his "feud" with Maestro Ben Bernie.

That old-time palace of sweat, laughter, and tears, the tent repertory company, lingered on in Nebraska at Hebron. Every summer for
years the Chic Boyes Players would materialize from the canvas lofts
in Hebron. The company was remarkably versatile: it could, if need
be, change its bill twice a day for a week, all its offerings being about
one jump ahead of "The Perils of Pauline." In these days of easy
payments, government subsidy, and insurance against crop loss, the
dilemma of how to meet the mortgage payment may seem lacking
in drama; but in the tent show's heyday this situation would put the
audience in a state of suspense fit to make them pause at their popcorn and pray a little.

Speaking for myself, I always will remember Nebraska show business gratefully. Wages earned the hard way on a circus payroll paid
part of my first tuition at the University of Nebraska; and ushering
in the Paramount-Publix theaters of old helped pay my keep. To this

day I never pass the House of Murphy in West Hollywood without remembering how its owner, in his vaudeville days, used to give me fifty cents to run errands for him, at a time when four bits was 1/20th of my weekly take flashlighting customers to their seats.

On the many occasions that I saw Al Jolson before his death, I would always recall the time he was in Lincoln in 1930 with his ill-fated "Wonderbar." He was the first theatrical bigtimer I ever interviewed, and I approached his hotel door damp-handed and dry-mouthed: in a word, scared spitless. A booming "Come in!" responded to my knock, and when I stumbled through the door there he was, large as life, a big cigar in his hand.

"Who're you?" he asked.

"Al," I quavered, "I'm a newspaper man."

"Well, don't blame me," he said. "It's your own damn fault."

It was my stint in Lincoln reviewing films for the *Nebraska State Journal* and *Variety* that won me the dubious distinction of being named champion seer of motion pictures—more than five hundred a year for a five-year period. This landed me in Ripley's "Believe It or Not," John Hix's "Strange as It Seems," and on Cecil B. DeMille's Lux Radio Theatre; it also put me irrevocably in league with people in show business the world over. In war and in peace, in uniform and out, their fraternity and friendship have been worth a lot, a never-ending source of amusement and fun.

It is odd, though, how they remember Nebraska. In the spring of 1956, as Ringling Brothers, Barnum & Bailey was about halfway through its opening performance at Madison Square Garden, a man sat down next to me and said: "You Barney Oldfield?"

I nodded, peering at him in the dim light.

"My name's Rudy Bundy," he said. "I used to have an orchestra. You once gave me a bum notice when I played the Orpheum in Lincoln."

Shades of the memories of the Virginia Judge, Walter C. Kelly!

Although the University of Nebraska first opened its doors in 1871, its birth—on paper—was coeval with that of the city of Lincoln. Perhaps because they literally grew up together there always has been an unusually strong bond between the town and the university. While they acknowledge that it belongs to the whole state, Lincoln people have a proprietary feeling about Nebraska U: they take a special pride in it and have a special affection for it.

They feel much the same way about Nebraska's Dr. Louise Pound.

First Lady of Letters

1. Retrospective — 1957

B. A. BOTKIN

AM I BECOMING a professional patriarch?" asked Louise Pound, in her presidential address before the Modern Language Association of America, December, 1955. She was referring to the many commemorative honors heaped upon her since her retirement from the University of Nebraska ten years before—Lincoln Kiwanis Club medal in 1947; election as first woman president of the MLA in 1954; first woman to be named to the Nebraska Sports Hall of Fame, 1955. Was she not, rather, becoming a tradition, after the fashion of genuine folk songs, which, according to her definition, "have retained their vitality through a fair period of time" and "are not static but are in a state of flux"?

Like every tradition, she has her roots in a state of society, a region, and has never lost her feeling for these roots. Nebraska and the Middle West are written large all over her life and work. As her girlhood friend, Dorothy Canfield Fisher, has written of her, "It is not only that she is a first-rater, but that she stayed in Lincoln and became one." She was born in Lincoln, June 30, 1872, five years after Nebraska became a state and one year after the university was opened. From the Pound home at 1632 L Street, where she has lived for the past sixty-five years, the three Pound children—Roscoe, Louise,

Olivia—watched the town grow from raw prairie and frontier community to capital and university city. The Pound household was a microcosm of this developing society. Her father, Stephen Bosworth Pound, who had come to Lincoln from New York in 1869, set the children a high standard of character and achievement as probate and district judge and member of the city council, the first constitutional convention, and the first state senate.* Her mother, Laura Biddlecome Pound, who had taught in New York after graduating from Lombard College and was dissatisfied with the Lincoln public schools, was her only teacher until she was fourteen. In the family library, learning was an adventure instead of a chore and developed early habits of independent research and original thinking—habits which Louise Pound has in turn encouraged in her students.

Olivia Pound recalls that "When Roscoe and Louise were about twelve and ten respectively, they were offered a dollar each if they would read through Macaulay's *History of England*. They read together and tried to see who could get to the bottom of the page first. To prevent 'fudging,' they asked each other questions before turning the page. The tradition is that Louise read the faster, but Roscoe, who had a photographic memory, retained more of the facts."

Entering the two-year Latin or Preparatory School at the university, Louise went on to take two degrees and a diploma in piano and to make Phi Beta Kappa. In the "slightly radical" Literary Society she was associated with a group of young intellectuals, including Willa Cather and Hartley Burr Alexander. In 1894 she became an assistant instructor in English, and from then until her retirement in 1945 she has taught continuously in the department, except for a year at Heidelberg (where she took her doctor's degree *magna cum laude* in 1900, in two semesters instead of the usual seven) and summers at California, Yale, Chicago, Columbia, and Stanford—refusing all other offers.

With her, as with every great teacher and scholar, education and research are more than a profession; they are a way of life. This way of life had its roots in her Colonial Quaker heritage and in her family environment, with their stress on integrity, truth, service, and sociability. All these qualities she brought to her teaching, plus a simple, warm humanity, zest for life and learning, common sense,

* ". . . the young lawyer had so good a reputation for honesty, even in that early day, that a jury of six men refused to give a verdict against his client on the sole ground that three of the men declared it to be their unalterable conviction that Mr. Pound would not defend a case that was not absolutely correct and true."—*Collections of Nebraska Historical Society*, Vol. XVI

and a power of simple, clear expression. Her devotion and generosity to her students have been as heart-warming as their loyalty to her. "I believe the pleasantest thing that has happened to me is that I've had a number of books dedicated to me," she told a reporter on her retirement.

Her graduate students have testified gratefully to her "hundred per cent" support, her fertility in suggesting thesis and other subjects suited to them, her readiness, tact, and understanding in criticism and guidance. Women members of Chi Delta Phi, national honorary literary society, and men in the English Club recall cozy meetings in the Pound home, with its old-fashioned fireplaces, carved dark woodwork, stained glass windows, and the family cat on the Oriental rug. Many young writers were encouraged not only by her criticism but by opportunities for browsing in her library and study. She also instituted the pleasant custom of stopping in at Andrews Hall in the afternoon and taking a carful of English instructors and graduate students out to the suburbs for a coffee break.

On the lighter side, from 1917 to 1924, she was active in the Order of the Golden Fleece, an organization (named by her) of red-headed coeds on the campus. Twenty-eight shades were approved for membership, and prizes were given for the most fiery, abundant, or best-coiffured hair as well as for the most fascinating bob, freckles, green eyes, and so on. Louise Pound still wears her gleaming auburn hair in classic braids about her head.

A crusader for equal rights for women in higher education and graduate study, Louise Pound, combining brain and brawn, also pioneered in sports. She was a champion in golf and tennis, a medal winner in cycling (100 miles a day and 5,000 miles a year), introduced skiing in Lancaster County, and competed in figure-skating, swimming, riding, and bowling. "When I coached the girls' basketball team," she recalls, "I had three Phi Beta Kappas on the team. They kept their heads better. We played men's rules; we couldn't stand those sissy rules."

As a scholar she has been true to her midwestern, frontier, and regional heritage. About one-fifth of the two hundred-odd titles in her bibliography deal with literature, lore, language, and education beyond the Mississippi. Her first publication, in 1915, was a syllabus of *Folk-Song of Nebraska and the Central West*. Folk songs and folklore have continued to interest her as much for their reflection of the life of the people of the region as for the light they throw on problems of origin and diffusion. In *Poetic Origins and the Ballad* (1921), she demolished the theory of communal origins. But it is in philology that her pioneering leadership—"courageous and of a very high scholarly order"— has had the greatest influence and borne the most fruit. Her work in the Dialect Society and on *American Speech* (which she helped found in 1925) have, in the words of Mencken, "put the study of American English on its legs."

In matters of usage she has, in theory and practice, eschewed "gobbledygook," saying: "All is not literature that litters, but there is considerable litter about our official language as there is about professional jargons in general."

The remarkable career of this brisk, pleasant woman has for sixty-odd years continued, by their own admission, to "astonish a nation of scholars unused to the company of ladies who knew quite as much as they did." With her perennial youthfulness of mind and spirit, her wide range of interests and activities, she has broken records and precedents and shattered for all time the popular conception of the "lady professor" as schoolmarm, bluestocking, prig, or bookworm. Nor is there anything cloistered or stuffy about her personal life. Distinguished visitors to her house on L Street are as apt to find her in her work clothes—painting the green board fence, mending the roof, mowing the lawn—as in her party clothes. Male chauvinism hasn't a chance around Louise Pound, but masculine assistance—yes. "When a journalist interviewed her a few months ago on American folklore, he offered to shovel her snow-covered walks. She accepted gratefully: 'I was just going to do it myself,' she said."

The foregoing sketch has presented Louise Pound from the point of view of a former student, who has since attained national eminence in his own right as a folklorist and author. Concerning the author of the following "colleague's-eye view," Dr. Pound has written: "Many Nebraskans remember Hartley Alexander (1873–1939) as the University's most distinguished professor in the humanities division. A scholar, philosopher, lyric and dramatic poet, a teacher, a patriot, and a much-sought-for associate of architects of public buildings, he left a long list of printed works. His best books are perhaps his Mythology of the North American Indians, Truth and the

Faith, *and* God and Man's Destiny. *For the last-named,
the Commonwealth of California awarded him a medal.
France made him a Knight of the Legion of Honor for his
help in World War I. He furnished the inscriptions and
the art symbolism for the Nebraska State Capitol and for
many other buildings, including the Los Angeles Public
Library, the Fidelity Mutual Life Building, Philadelphia,
the Mutual Life Building, New York City, and for buildings at Rockefeller Center."*

2. *In medias res* — 1933

HARTLEY BURR ALEXANDER

WHEN LOUISE POUND first began to teach in the University of
Nebraska, she was already far better known to the majority of the
student body than many of the professors of that day. She had
graduated from the college not only with all the scholastic honors
(which came as a matter of course in the Pound family), but with an
athletic record such as no woman had approached and which, I
dare say, no Nebraska woman has since matched, and which for a
number of years continued to grow, with every type of trophy hers.
And these trophies were by no means local, for in '97 she defeated
the Canadian and our national champions in tennis singles and
later carried away palms in women's and mixed men's doubles. All
these things were of course known to the students, who are alive to
athletics, I suspect, before scholarship seriously excites them; and
they contributed not a little to a certain éclat which attached to the
name of Louise Pound well before her intellectual interests were
understood. Certainly it was a grand introduction for a young instructress, even if in a way somewhat deceptive.

Deceptive, I say, just for the reason that athletics was after all just
an incident in Louise Pound's personality, a lateral expression, if
one may so put it. Back of this devotion (as it appeared) to championships lay something much more significant, and puzzling. No
doubt to the student there appeared to be an incongruity in the
combination in one young woman of great athletic skill and clear
intellectual attainment. But this union in Louise Pound's case,
conspicuous as it was, by no means sufficed to explain the hold upon

imagination which she exercised. There was something enigmatical about her personality, almost cryptic, and I think that the feeling that here was an instructor whom no one could quite read was at the bottom responsible for a feeling akin to awe which touched the mind of many a youngster where she was concerned.

One factor which helped to give Miss Pound her half-mythical elevation was doubtless her quite striking appearance, for she was (and of course is) a person to be noticed in any assembly as a human being of distinction. This, however, is not merely a matter of physical gifts, but much more it is the result of a type of innerly contained and controlled expression quite out of the ordinary gamut. Most of us spend our lives half in the effort to read the countenances of our companions in life, and in the main this is not too difficult even for the most pokerset features. But Louise Pound here belonged to a category all her own. Few faces give more constantly the impression of alert and vivid seeing. It is the type of face which carries a dignity, and sometimes for others a discomfiture, which none but the dullest can fail to observe; and which, I suspect, partly accounts for the curiosity that attached to the instructress's powers and motives and attached to her description the adjective "hypnotic." I recall very well how in those days our mutual friend Derrick Lehmer informed me that he was going to Johns Hopkins to acquire a doctorate in mathematics, a beard, and dignity—the first of which materialized in due course. But when Louise Pound came back from Heidelberg with her doctorate in Germanic philology and a few overseas championships in athletics, to most of us these laurels seemed inconsequential: they had not been needed for any external purpose certainly. It was all clear that the title was less than a circumstance, as incidental as the athletic scores.

And in later years it has struck me that the same thing is true. All sorts of honors have come to Professor Pound, in America and abroad. But in the case of a real instructor, it is never the badges of scholarship that give that account of his personality or influence; and assuredly this is not the case with Louise Pound. As I have intimated, all such things are lateral, expressions and not cores of personality. No doubt they are excellent for college publicity, but after all what reading is so dry as Who's Who?

But for me the interest is quite other. It was a grand thing in the early days, as today it is a grand thing, to be counted as one of this instructor's friends, and the reason lies back of outward glamors. Of course I, with others, have thought about it—this unique impres-

sion of a famed Nebraska woman, not as famed but as a woman.
And while I hope that I have not come to any conclusion (which
God forbid in regard to any of my friends!), nevertheless as I look
back through certain years of association some things do stand out
as painting the character more clearly. For example, there were the
Carrollers. This society devoted to Alice in Wonderland and all
gorgeous nonsense was born in the Pound home, and it had more
than one life, too.

Am I not, then, ready to give the answer—what *is* the lady back
of the life? No; for truth is, I cannot. And indeed I am glad of it.
It is no part of honesty to wish to sound out the soul of a friend,
and of all manners the most ill is to pronounce a eulogy upon the
living!

But I will add one more type of incident. Some years ago the
English-literaturists of the country were under the spell of a biolog-
ical romance as to the origin of balladry, English and other. The
whole fictitious scenario was a solemnly accepted dogma, with ponderous books supporting. Turning aside from her real concern for
linguistic development, Louise Pound brought forth a book, *Poetic
Origins and the Ballad,* and the whole house of cards collapsed,
before a woman's singlehanded challenge. Not so very recently I
saw her review of the work of one who had been first in abuse of
her enterprise, but is now with no apology or recanting making
use of her results without credit—a sin of scholarship unfortunately
not unknown. Professor Pound, reviewing, merely complimented
the author upon seeing the light. Again, it was only an incident,
lateral to life. And I remember, too, my own dear lady once remark-
ing anent our mutual friend (it was in a day when "tatting" had
vogue), "I just cannot imagine Louise tatting." The nearest holiday
brought her a beautifully tatted handkerchief with Professor Pound's
compliments. Even in those first days, with which I started out, folk
used to inquire, "Is there anything Louise Pound cannot do?"

Condensed from *Nebraska Alumnus,* Oct., 1933

*Some years ago I was visiting an agricultural experiment
station in an out-of-the-way corner of England. My host's
face lighted up when I identified myself as from Lincoln,
Nebraska.*

"Ah, yes, Lincoln!" he exclaimed.

*I wondered if he was about to say something about hav-
ing seen pictures of our renowned capitol, or about Lincoln and William Jennings Bryan. But he went on,
"That's the place where you test tractors."*

—Editorial, Lincoln *Evening Journal*, August 4, 1956

The *"Supreme Court"* of *Tractors*

B. F. SYLVESTER

AT DAYBREAK, the sky-blue tractor was out on the 2,200-foot oval,
humming along at a steady $3\frac{1}{2}$-mile clip. For ten hours she rolled
that way without stopping—35 miles, 80-odd laps around the course.
When at last the driver turned off the motor, a small band of
observers, who had been waiting like expectant fathers for more
than a week, mopped their brows and hurried off to call long distance.

Test No. 500, a new Fordson Major diesel which had come 5,000
miles from England for just this purpose—testing by the world's most
important tractor laboratory, part of the Nebraska College of Agriculture at Lincoln—was over the hump. As the Fordson rolled off,
men busied themselves on the next track, readying it for the next
test. To L. F. Larsen, engineer in charge, Test No. 500 was merely
a part of the day's work. To Fordson, it was much more. A shipload
of other new Fordsons waited at a dock in New Orleans. They could
be delivered now. And Fordson dealers all over the world could
now assure their customers that their machine had been tested and
okayed at the supreme court of tractors. For that is the first thing
that tractor buyers all over the world want to know: Was it tested
at Nebraska?

For answer, observers from almost every country travel to this
sprawling midwest station. Thousands of others get the station's
meticulous reports on tractor performance. In some countries—India,

for example, and others in South America—a pass mark by Nebraska
is a prerequisite for sale. Foreign governments are attempting to
avoid tractor evils which beset this country about the time of World
War I, when power machinery began slowly to displace the horse.
In the general turmoil, many factories went out of business and
orphan tractors stood in the fields.

One victim was Wilmot F. Crozier of Osceola, Nebr., whose tractor
quit cold one day in the middle of his wheat field. Dealer and manufacturer had gone out of business. No service, no parts. Crozier said
there ought to be a law, and his neighbors agreed. They elected him
to the legislature and, by cracky, he put through a law. No tractor
could be sold in Nebraska without prior testing and provision by
the manufacturer for a supply of parts within reasonable shipping
distance. Result was the testing laboratory, set up in 1920. Fees,
paid by the manufacturers, support the program.

Tests cover two phases of performance: belt load—the power available for running such equipment as, say, a feed grinder or corn
sheller; and drawbar load—pulling power. In addition, careful meas-
urements are made of fuel and lubricating-oil consumption, extra
water used for cooling purposes, engine speeds and m.p.h. speeds
at different gears and under varying loads, radiator and air temperatures, and wheel slippage. Breakdowns, or necessary repairs or
adjustments, are also noted in the final report, as are minor misfunc-
tionings such as lube leakage.

First test of the series calls for a 12-hour warmup period, during
which the manufacturer's representatives may make any adjustments
they consider necessary. Fussy engineers have been known to take
four hours merely to set a carburetor, and in one case 75 hours
passed before the factory reps were satisfied that all conditions, including atmospheric, were exactly right. Muggy days are bad for
testing, and rain or even excessive humidity (90 per cent) will result
in postponement. But the day on which Test 500 was to begin was
perfect, weather-wise. The Fordson hummed like a happy top
through her 12 hours of limbering-up exercises.

Then fuel lines were attached and the tractor hooked up to the
belt. For over an hour, the engine was warmed up before being
connected with an electric dynamometer that would keep score. Now
followed a two-hour run at 100 per cent of maximum, throttle all the
way out and a dynamometer load on the belt to keep the engine
turning at the rated (manufacturer's recommended) speed of 1,600
r.p.m.

Next came a rated-load run, with 85 per cent of the first dynamometer load being placed on the belt. This is a somewhat better guide to performance, since the maximum may not be expected in the field, and not every tractor will attain the exact performance shown on the test. Then followed six runs of 20 minutes each with varying loads: no load, quarter load, half load, three-quarter load, rated load, and maximum load at full throttle.

Torque tests came next, to determine the horsepower obtained at different engine speeds. Torque is the twisting effect that turns the axles of the rear wheels.

At 5:30 next morning, the test crew and Fordson reps assembled on the track for the drawbar (coupled-weight) tests, in which the pulling power is measured. Since, in all, the drawbar tests call for 20 hours of driving and the average speed is about five m.p.h., each tractor covers 100 miles, or about 240 laps. The Fordson was hitched to a dynamometer car full of self-registering instruments, every aspect of performance being tested by gauges and a stylus which makes tracings on sensitized paper. Behind the test car was a tractor in gear, which provided a load of 5,000 pounds. The machine was tested in each of its six gears for speed, horsepower, slippage, the load pulled, and crankshaft speed.

Daylight the next morning saw the same little group out on the track for the big one: a continuous ten-hour run in one gear with a three-quarter load. Fordson reps chose the third gear for this as offering the best balance between horsepower and traction. Two other tests followed, but by now the worst was behind. Up to this point the tractor had carried ballast, iron weights of 1,292 pounds on each wheel. But now, Test J was run without ballast. Test K, the last one in the series, was run with the smallest tires recommended by the tractor's manufacturer.

That did it. The tractor had performed according to its specifications and claims, and this would be certified to the Nebraska Railway Commission which, in turn, would issue a sale permit. The laboratory does not tag any tractor as good, bad, or indifferent. It merely records and publishes its findings on a world-wide mailing list, sending out some 40,000 reports a year to farmers, county agents, teachers of agriculture, and others who write in.

There is a dedicated spirit out at the testing station. One crew with two John Deere tractors started at daybreak on a Friday. All day they plugged away, finishing up with the limbering-up tests after dark. Somebody said, "Let's keep going," and they started the belt test. They went all night until 8:30 Saturday morning. Saturday night looked like a fine night for more belt-testing, so they all came back and ran the test on the second John Deere, until it was finished at 8:30 Sunday morning. Then, because everybody still felt great, they started work on the track, packing it down for the drawbar tests, which would start on Monday. Monday night, they were still at it.

Reprinted from "They Torture Tractors," *Popular Science,* May, 1954

Reams of articles have been devoted to the pros and cons of intercollegiate sports, in particular football. Chiefly these discussions have demonstrated that there is a lot to be said on both sides.

In the Age of Pericles, the bays and laurels were not reserved only for the philosophers and poets and artists, the statesmen and generals. The stadia were thronged as well as the theaters. Courage and skill in the sports arena were admired and rewarded.

The University of Nebraska has been fielding an eleven for more than seventy-five years. The names of its pigskin "greats" are familiar not only to old grads, but to Nebraskans who have never set foot on the campus except on the way to the stadium.

We do not exalt an All-American halfback to the stature of a Shakespeare or an Abraham Lincoln or a Newton. But the emotions we, as spectators or participants, share at athletic contests are keen and valid. Take away the "big game" and we are deprived of an experience of drama and emotional community for which, it may be, there already are too few opportunities.

Nebraska's "Mr. Touchdown"

BILL FAY

A FEW MINUTES before the opening kickoff of the 1950 football game between Oklahoma and Nebraska at Norman, Oklahoma, the announcer on the public address system invited the 54,000 spectators to pay particular attention to a sophomore Nebraska halfback named Bobby Reynolds.

"There he goes!" the announcer declared, as a white-jerseyed Nebraskan grabbed a practice punt on the dead run. "That's Reynolds —Number 12—the nation's leading college scorer. Reynolds started the season with three touchdowns against Indiana . . . then kept right on rolling with two touchdowns against Minnesota . . . three against Colorado . . . three more against Penn State . . . one against Kansas . . . three against Missouri . . . three against Kansas State

. . . and one against Iowa State. That's nineteen touchdowns in eight games, and it's beginning to look like Nebraska's Mr. Reynolds can't be stopped. . . ."

Coach Bud Wilkinson's Oklahoma lads were unbeaten and untied in twenty-nine consecutive games and ranked No. 1 nationally in the Associated Press poll. By way of showing their disdain for Reynolds' reputation, they seized the opening kickoff and pounded 76 yards in ten plays for a touchdown. What's more, when Nebraska went on the offensive, the Oklahomans bounced Reynolds backward on three successive running attempts for a total net loss of seven yards. Having thus put Nebraska's sophomore phenomenon in his place, the Sooners slammed 65 yards for another TD and a 14-0 lead.

Then a red-jerseyed Oklahoma back fumbled, and Nebraska recovered on the Oklahoma 20.

Quarterback Fran Nagle called Reynolds' favorite maneuver—a slant off right tackle. Bobby scampered into the end zone. *Touchdown!* An exchange of punts later, Nebraska drove 40 yards to the Oklahoma 13. Nagle called upon Reynolds and Bobby scooted around left end. *Touchdown!* Five plays after that, the disconsolate Oklahomans fumbled again on their 16-yard line. Nagle called Reynold's signal. Bobby sliced off left tackle. *Touchdown!*

Eventually, Oklahoma's manpower overwhelmed Nebraska, 49 to 35, but Reynolds' three-touchdown blitz on this last day of the season (spectacularly executed within the span of thirty-three plays against 1950's national champions) made Bobby the highest intercollegiate scorer in more than thirty years. Averaging 2.4 touchdowns per game, he rolled up 157 points (twenty-two touchdowns and twenty-five conversions), for the biggest total since Jim Leech compiled the all-time high of 210 points for Virginia Military Institute in 1920.

Oddly enough, when Reynolds arrived on the Nebraska campus in 1949, he was ballyhooed not as a potential grid star, but as a great basketball prospect. There also was talk that the New York Yankees—impressed by Bobby's sand-lot baseball activities—had offered him a minor-league tryout. So far as football was concerned, Bobby had been a regular backfield performer at Grand Island High School, but had never come close to leading his team in scoring. Physically, young Mr. Reynolds scarcely resembled a high-scoring halfback. He was a pleasant blond nineteen-year-old, not skinny exactly, but on the slender side. He obviously didn't have enough power to run over tacklers, and he wasn't fast enough to run away from them, either.

Despite these deficiencies, in his first scrimmage against the varsity, Bobby squirmed loose for three touchdowns. "Maybe that kid doesn't have too much sustained speed on the straightaway," commented Nebraska's head coach, Bill Glassford, "but he's got a rocket start, and he doesn't slow down on the curves. Matter of fact, he runs around corners faster'n anybody I've ever seen."

Later, Glassford queried Reynolds' high-school coach, Jerry Lee, how come Bobby hadn't scored more touchdowns for Grand Island. "Well," Lee confessed, "I guess it was my fault for making him the quarterback. Every time we got close to the goal line, Bobby called somebody else's number."

Although Glassford saw to it that Nebraska's quarterbacks overcame Reynolds' reluctance to carry the ball for a TD, Bobby's record in 1950 did not result from an excessive number of easy scoring opportunities. Only four of his 22 touchdowns originated from inside the ten-yard line; the other 18 scoring dashes ranged from 11 to 80 yards (average 28.5).

Perhaps the most spectacular exhibition of Reynolds' zigzag touchdown technique took place against Missouri, when Bobby attempted to throw a forward pass from the Tigers' 33-yard line. Finding his receivers thoroughly covered, Bobby cut to the left to avoid three tacklers, then reversed his field and took for the right sideline. Still retreating rapidly, he straight-armed another tackler way back on Nebraska's 35-yard line. At that point, he was exactly 32 yards behind the line of scrimmage! Then Bobby turned around and jackrabbited through the whole Missouri team for a touchdown, evading (as movies subsequently revealed) a total of seventeen tacklers along his circuitous 65-yard route. Although the play went into the record book as a 33-yard advance, Bobby actually traveled almost 100 yards. During the course of the run, one frustrated Missourian had missed Reynolds three times.

A few moments later when Bobby got loose on another long run, teammate Charlie Toogood blocked Missouri's Dale Portmann, knocked him down, then rolled on top of the Tiger and held him down. "Lemme up," Portmann protested. "Reynolds is gone."

"I know," replied Toogood, "but you never can tell when he may come this way again."

As an interviewee, Reynolds definitely does not belong to the shucks-I-was-just-lucky school of bashful athletic heroes. Bobby is articulate and factual; he discusses his touchdown runs objectively. "A touchdown," he remarked recently, "is a chain of circumstances

involving 22 players. And very often the least important link in the
chain is the fellow who carries the ball across the goal line." As an
instance, he cited the situation in the 1950 Oklahoma game when,
after scoring twice, the Sooners fumbled and Nebraska recovered.

"In the huddle, our quarterback, Fran Nagle, picked a play on
which I was supposed to feint to the right, then cut back through
center. But as we came out of the huddle, Nagle noticed that Oklahoma's big eight-man line was bunched in close. So, Fran yelled a
warning signal—what we call an 'automatic'—which completely
changed my part in the play. Instead of cutting back through the
middle, I went wide outside the right end—and got loose. In other
words," Bobby concluded, "the difference between my running into
a mass of tacklers and going around end for the touchdown was
Nagle's alertness in detecting a defensive weakness and instantly
redirecting our offense to exploit it."

Of his 22 touchdowns, Reynolds recalls that six were scored on
Nagle's "automatics"—plays which were redirected a split second
before the center snapped the ball. Three other TD's followed re-
coveries of enemy fumbles ("You gotta get the ball before you can
score") ; and of course there was that all-over-the-field scramble
against Missouri (". . . which actually was a dumb play—I should
have passed that ball instead of fading back at the risk of being
tackled for a big loss"). As Reynolds reviews his 1950 activities, ten
touchdowns resulted from fortunate circumstances, and the other
twelve scores represented competent running jobs, aided and abetted
by solid blocking.

Regardless of his touchdown activities one thing is certain: Bobby
has a lot of fun playing football. If it wasn't fun, he wouldn't be
playing, because Bobby is that rarest of college athletic phenomena
—an unsolicited, unproselyted (and virtually unstoppable) halfback.
In the spring of 1949, a scout for a midwestern university who visited
Grand Island to engage Reynolds' basketball services was amazed
to learn that Bobby had already enrolled at Nebraska without even
inquiring into prospects for a scholarship. The scout pointed out
hopefully that his school provided skilled basketball players with
scholarships—and an ample monthly spending allowance. Bobby
thanked the scout for the kind offer, but explained that his grandfather already had provided for his education.

Bobby's late grandfather, Charles Olson, a rugged Swedish immigrant, settled in Wahoo, Nebraska, in 1882. Charles, who was 20
years old at that time, had 75 cents in cash and a notion that any

young fellow who worked hard at it ought to make a fortune in the construction business. This may or may not have been a sound theory; in any event, it worked for him. Once, commenting on his enormously successful career, Charles observed: "Just when I learned to call a yob a job, everybody else started calling it a praw-yack." By the time Charles learned how to call a praw-yack a project, he was a millionaire.

Five of Charles Olson's eight children were graduated from the University of Nebraska, including Bobby's mother, Blenda, who captained Nebraska's senior girls basketball team in 1925, the year she married Gil Reynolds, an Omaha paper salesman. Gil had been a third-string halfback on the Cornhusker football squad in 1923 and —to confound those who may believe that football ability is hereditary—never scored a touchdown. "There never was any question about where I was going to school," Bobby says. "Just about everybody in our family went to Nebraska."

Apparently that was true of the neighbors, too. Bobby was born in Omaha, right next door to Dave Noble, who still ranks as one of the most dangerous running backs in Nebraska's long and periodically brilliant football history. Veteran Cornhusker fans recall Noble as the halfback whose slashing runs paced Nebraska to upset victories over Notre Dame in 1922 and '23, the sophomore and junior years of an Irish backfield known to fame as "the Four Horsemen."

Bobby's first year on the Cornhusker squad saw Nebraska's first winning season (six victories, two losses, one tie) in a decade. Thanks to a tradition which decrees that sophomores must carry senior squad members' luggage, in one respect at least Bobby qualified as the hardest-working halfback in the United States. After the Penn State game, by which time Reynolds had scored eleven of Nebraska's fourteen touchdowns, tackle Toogood, a senior, observed: "I've heard of plenty of triple-threat backs, but I'll bet Bobby is the only quadruple threat in the country. He runs, punts, passes, and totes suitcases. . . . Yep, that Reynolds is a handy fellow to have around."

Condensed from *Collier's,* Oct. 6, 1951

After Nebraska's admission to the Union, March 1, 1867, the question of the location of the capital tended to overshadow all public problems. In the original bill the seat of government was to be known as "Capitol City." This unfortunate name was dropped when an Omaha senator, in an effort to draw South Platte Democratic votes away from the measure, moved the substitution of "Lincoln." The name still was anathema to many Democrats, but sectional loyalty overrode political considerations, and South Platte Democrats promptly approved the new name.

Having secured an outfit and employed a surveyor, Governor David Butler, Secretary of State Thomas P. Kennard, and Auditor John Gillespie made a cursory survey of all eligible sites. On July 29, 1867, they returned to the vicinity of Yankee Hill and Lancaster, on the banks of Salt Creek. At Lancaster "the favorable impressions received at first sight . . . were confirmed."

Omahans and many others living along the Missouri north of the Platte severely criticized the choice. "Nobody will ever go to Lincoln," prophesied the Omaha Republican, *"who does not go to the state legislature, the lunatic asylum, the penitentiary, or some of the state institutions." Founded on fiat, with "no river, no railroad, no steam wagon, nothing," it was destined for isolation and ultimate oblivion.*

—Condensed from Olson's *History of Nebraska*

Lincoln: Two Views

1. "The Best Known of All the Lincolns in the World" (1934)

LOWRY CHARLES WIMBERLY

FROM his travels abroad in 1932, a clergyman of Lincoln, Nebraska, brought back the following pronouncement, delivered by the Lord Mayor of Lincoln, England. "Your city is the best known of all the Lincolns in the world," said His Excellency. "Mail addressed to

Lincoln, unless it designates England, is always sent to Lincoln, Nebraska."

Whether or not the Lord Mayor knew what he was talking about or whether he was just talking, it is hard to say. But his pronouncement was at once laid hold of by the Nebraska capital. For it not only confirmed the city's private opinion of itself; it served to enlarge that opinion somewhat. Prior to His Excellency's statement, Lincoln had regarded itself as being the cultural hub of little more than the Midwest. But upon receipt of that statement, it felt not unjustified in taking in more territory still.

As a matter of fact, however, the Nebraska capital is near the heart or center of things in more ways than one. Were it a trifle farther south and west, that is, it would be the geographic center of the United States. And were it a bit farther east, it would be the population center of Nebraska. More specifically, as regards its situation, it is the principal city on Salt Creek, a small tributary to the Platte River, and is some fifty miles west of Omaha and about the same distance from the Kansas border. It is a typical prairie city, the country roundabout being of a slightly rolling, nondescript character—the sort of country that sends Lincoln people scurrying away to distant vacation grounds during the summer months.

Now and then an ungracious visitor to the town asks why the capital city happens to be situated where it is, or why the Lord ever put a town here at all. A proper answer to that question might well be that the Lord didn't. But such is not the answer that the average resident of the city would give. For Lincoln is strong in the belief that its destiny has always been a special concern of Providence. Its God is, to be sure, of the Republican faith and the Methodist persuasion. But is has served this God long and zealously, with the result, so it feels, that it has been the recipient of many divine favors.

These favors an active Chamber of Commerce is wont to catalogue year after year in some such wise as this: 98 churches, 21 of them Methodist; 11 office buildings, the highest towering 17 stories above the street; virtually no crime problem and not a single tenement house; three national banks and 12,000 college students; many famous men and women whose home is, or was, in Lincoln; the most beautiful capitol in America, and "one-fourth of the population of the United States within a radius of 500 miles."

The population of Lincoln itself is about 75,000—the female population exceeding the male by some 2,000. This preponderance of women, banded together as the women are in various sisterhoods, is said to account, in large measure, for the sanctity of the town—its Sunday blue laws, its expurgated movies and libraries, its clean alleys, and its general freedom from crime. There are enough lawbreakers, perhaps, to justify a small police force and a municipal court, but they are petty offenders—dog poisoners, traffic violators, and a few harmless drunks. Such major crimes as homicide, rape, and kidnaping are virtually unheard of. From 1927 to 1932, for example, not a single murder occurred in Lincoln, whereas in other American cities of the same size there was an "average of eight murders per year or a total of forty for the same five-year period." This is a remarkable record. And it is doubtless an enviable one, though a local wag did say that the foregoing statistics were not necessarily to the credit of the place.

But this same wag is happy, the chances are, to be living in Lincoln, and is as proud as the next man of its high-class citizenry, its financial strength, and its cultural attainments. And he is at one with his fellow townsmen in resenting any slurs on his home town. He resents, for example, the stupid opinion—held by certain Easterners—that Lincoln is nothing more than a "big country burg" or that it is merely one of a number of hinterland capitals, overrun with cowboys and Indians. He can appreciate, in this connection, the outraged feelings of Jeff Tidrow, one of the town's octogenarians. Jeff can usually be found selling papers at the corner of Fourteenth and O Streets. But last summer he took his savings and went back East to visit his brother in Philadelphia. Shortly after his return, we asked him how he had enjoyed his trip. He was speechless for a moment, then went off into a high treble of profanity. But after a bit he calmed down and told us what the trouble was. He said that the whole trip was spoiled because all that "Goddamned brother" of his wanted was to talk about cowboys and Indians. "I told him," Jeff said, spitting viciously toward the curb, "that I hadn't seen a Goddamned Indian in fifty years. I must of told him the same thing forty times, but it didn't do no good. So I cut my visit short and come on back."

Jeff's experience in the East is not, it appears, an uncommon one. And short of his profanity, he voices the general resentment of Lincoln toward Easterners who "low-rate" the town with their notions about Indians, sod shanties, and outdoor plumbing. It is true that the Chamber of Commerce stands always ready to give the lie to notions of this character. But if further evidence of Lincoln's modernity is needed, the city can bring forward its factories, airports, libraries, and schools. And it can call the roll of its famous citizens —General Pershing or Charles G. Dawes, for instance, or Louise Pound, Colonel Lindbergh, and Willa Cather. Strictly speaking, only one of these personages now lives in Lincoln, but the others have lived here in the not-too-distant past. Moreover, there is Guy Kibbee, well-known movie comedian, and Howard Greer, the celebrated Hollywood designer. Greer not only lived in Lincoln, he was born here. By his own admission, however, he heartily dislikes the town, and "avoids it, when crossing the country, by taking the southern route." His dislike is easily understood. When he was a boy the neighborhood gang poked fun at him for making doll clothes. On the contrary, Paul Swan, said to be the "most beautiful man in the world" and famous as a dancer and sculptor's model, professes to have only pleasant memories of his residence in Lincoln.

But no matter what these celebrities may think of the city, it makes a business of recalling them and of parading their names every now and then in the Sunday papers. Of late years it has even taken the Great Commoner to its heart, sings his praises unblushingly, and forgets that in the campaigns of 1896 and 1900 it bitterly opposed him for President. That it gave him a slight edge in 1908 was due solely to Bryan's making a special plea for the support of his home town. Bryan did succeed in impressing his ponderous morality on the town, but as a political prophet he was without honor, and he might well be consoled if he could know that his brother, Governor Charles Bryan, has for years hounded the city like a nemesis.

Nevertheless, the Nebraska capital, Republican stronghold though it is, owes a debt of thanks to the governor, for he has done as much as any man to keep the town in the public eye. Not only has he been thrice governor of his state; in 1924 he was his party's nominee for the vice-presidency. Oddly enough, Charles G. Dawes, a one-time resident of Lincoln, was the Republican nominee for the same office. So no matter how the 1924 election went, Lincoln was in a position to proclaim the vice-president as one of her citizens. The same may be said, moreover, of General Pershing. After all he did actually reside in Lincoln in the early nineties; hence, there is no reason to question the city's right to boom him for President twenty-five years later—in 1919, to be exact. The first Pershing for President club was organized in Lincoln. The boom came to naught; General Pershing, that is, was not interested.

Colonel Charles Lindbergh might well be gratified to learn that he, too, is a Lincoln celebrity. True, the colonel does not own a home there. He never did, in fact, but he did learn to fly there. He enrolled in 1922 as a flying student with the Nebraska Aircraft Corporation, took his training with great seriousness, and was regarded as something of a grouch by the other students. His instructors didn't, moreover, think highly of his ability, and wouldn't allow him to fly "solo," unless, that is, he would put up a $500 bond. Lindbergh felt that the demand was ridiculous; so in high dudgeon he left Lincoln to become a solo and stunt flyer on his own responsibility. But perhaps at this distant time the colonel has only kindly feelings for the place.

The slogan of the town is "Link up with Lincoln." And under this slogan the Nebraska capital has managed, in one way or another, to link itself up with a great many people of prominence. It established a rather unsavory connection, it is true, with the late Gus Winkler, big-shot gangster, shortly after the three-million-dollar robbery of the Lincoln National Bank and Trust Company. The robbery occurred September 17, 1930, and it was established that Winkler couldn't have taken part in it directly. Still, he was accused of engineering it, and the Lincoln authorities entered into an agreement to absolve him of any connection with it if he would aid in recovering the negotiable part of the loot. This he succeeded in doing, and turned back to the city $583,000 in securities.

But to take adequate note of all such personages as have lived, or still live, in Lincoln, or as have kept the town in the limelight, would be to write a book. A work of this sort would go far, however, to squelch all those who are inclined to high-hat the city. Generous space in such a history would have to be given to Roscoe Pound, a *bona fide* native son. Nor would Willa Cather go unnoticed. Miss Cather was graduated from the University of Nebraska in 1895. There is Dorothy Canfield Fisher, moreover. She spent some years in Lincoln when her father was chancellor of the university. And to this list of names they are now thinking of adding Stephen Crane's.

For it appears, on good authority, that Crane visited Lincoln in February, 1895. He had little more than landed in the town, though, when he was taken before a judge. With what he called his "eastern scruples" he had interfered in a saloon brawl, where a big man was pounding a rather small one. "But I thus offended a local custom," wrote Crane. "These men fought each other every night. Their friends expected it, and I was a damned nuisance with my eastern scruples and all that."

Crane came west to see the Mississippi, to see a cowboy ride, and to be in a blizzard of the plains. He found the blizzard in Lincoln. It is true that he could have done better farther west, but apparently he was satisfied with the Lincoln blizzard, or what he took for a blizzard.

Blizzards and tornadoes have a way of passing the town up, as do famines, epidemics, and Communists. Doubtless, the Republican and Methodist God still watches over it. But with Omaha, just fifty miles to the east, it is different. In 1913, for example, a tornado ripped that city up in good style. But Omaha—in the opinion of Lincoln, that is—is something of a hell-hole, casts a heavy Democratic vote, and disapproves pretty strongly of Methodist morality. So it was altogether right and proper that the tornado should pass over Lincoln and raise the devil with its big, wicked sister city.

Condensed by special permission of *The American Mercury*, July, 1934

2. The Prairie Capital (1955)

RAYMOND A. McCONNELL, JR.

A LOT about Lincoln is told in the exquisite Navajo hymn on the buffalo panel of the Nebraska capitol:

In beauty I walk. With beauty before me I walk. With beauty behind me I walk. With beauty above me and about me I walk.

From the time Bertram Grosvenor Goodhue's dream took reality in its midst, Lincoln has not been the same, nor Nebraska. You may say a mere building can't change a city or state. Its skyline perhaps, but not its character and spirit. But this building, the dominant new fact of the Lincoln of the past quarter century, has done so.

Self-expression always changes people, and for richer or for poorer depending on what is expressed. The capitol crowning Lincoln's skyline expresses Nebraska's pioneer faith and frontier hope, and the bold aspirations that sprout tall from the fertile Nebraska soil under the bright Nebraska sky. It symbolizes that which is noble in the spirit of the Plains. In so doing, it has served to reconfirm Nebraska plainsmen in that spirit. The person who has spoken his mind and heart, even though not wholly sure of his convictions or of where they might lead, knows that in the very expressing he has found a new and more sure self, a more certain sense of direction.

In the capitol, Nebraska spoke its unsure mind, eloquently. This in itself helped to make the mind up, and to shape a more resolute purpose.

That Nebraska's mind was unsure of itself twenty-five years ago is suggested by the fact that the Goodhue masterpiece, although conceived as an utterance of the spirit of the Plains, still had to win the acceptance of the Nebraska Plains people. It was all paid for but not all sold. Those who had paid for it wondered and argued over what they had bought. They wanted to know, sometimes querulously, disputatiously, what it meant. Goodhue's apostles told them, and the structure itself spoke in strong, true tones. Goodhue sensed what Nebraska people, once informed, would take pride in. Thus his creation spoke Nebraska's inner mind in its finest moments.

Twenty-five years ago Lincoln and Nebraska thought big thoughts, but except in football they lacked something in self-confidence. Now for twenty-five years Nebraskans with their capitol know that on their plains they can cultivate as fine a flower as any civilization can nurture. That knowledge, that new-found self-confidence, has permeated all of the life of Lincoln and Nebraska.

"A community like an individual has a work to do," says an inscription in the capitol, whose broad base symbolizes the material plane of prairie life.

Lincoln in 1930 thought its economic life broad enough. It called itself "Retail Capital of the Midlands" and "the most important commercial center between the Missouri River and the Pacific." It boasted the largest aircraft factories west of Dayton. With thirty-one home insurance companies it was "the Hartford of the West." The Security Mutual edifice ("Lincoln's only office building with marble corridors . . . and iced drinking water") advertised that its location at 12th and O was "in the center of Everything." The town had what it called a "Sound Economic Base," including "factories, offices, mercantile, industrial and business establishments . . . in the proper number."

Within a decade nationwide unemployment and regional drought —5,000 farmers marched on the capitol, demanding a farm mortgage moratorium, Nebraskans migrated with the Okies, abrasive dust some days cut down visibility to half a block—forced an agonizing reappraisal of the material base of a city heavily dependent on retail trade and servicing an agricultural area.

The diversification of the Lincoln economy through the wartime forties and into the fifties was equal parts circumstance and chance; Providence and the fates of war; and acumen of citizens who were convinced that the good old days weren't good enough. The circumstance was that for industries expanding for war, Lincoln offered a safe location and sane working populace. The chance was the casual remark of a business acquaintance of Bennett Martin's that the improbably named Elastic Stop-Nut Corp. of New Jersey was looking for another factory location. Martin knew the right spot. Sadly when the Stop-Nut scouts came, Salt Creek was flooding the site, but providentially there was an idle warehouse which Stop-Nut deemed suitable. Thus in 1942 Lincoln acquired war industry, a firm employing 1,500 and making a doodad that had 30,000 uses on a single bomber.

The product's merit was that it couldn't unscrew. With war's end, however, Stop-Nut came unscrewed from Lincoln. Fortuitously a Stop-Nut official mentioned the fact to an old college classmate, a top Elgin Watchman. Again, the sizeable Elgin operation—watch and ordnance mechanisms—which succeeded Stop-Nut at the once-empty warehouse, was sired by chance, out of local alertness. Meanwhile Western Electric—signal corps equipment—had moved into another begging building, and Goodyear—leakproof airplane gas tanks, later tractor belts and such—found the long-idle Patriot Aircraft factory to its liking. Local industry, like Charley Ammon's Cushman Motor Works—scooters—or Walton Ferris' National Manufacturing Co.—walking sprinklers—had evolved with military impetus into big operations. By 1955 Lincoln was a major manufacturing as well as a retailing, food processing, and insurance center. If it still wasn't quite the economic center of everything, the work its people had to do involved more nearly everything.

The prairie capital of the late twenties called itself the "Athens of the West." It remained for Goodhue's Parthenon, however, to give the Prairie Athens cultural stature. Like the Parthenon rising in the Athens of Pericles, it signaled the flowering of the arts. As with Athens, the flowering was sometimes disputatious. True, Bess Streeter Aldrich attained her greatest productivity in quiet dignity disturbed only when Hollywood brought to town its premiere of her *Cheers for Miss Bishop*. Lowry Wimberly each quarter nudged the *Prairie Schooner* to world literary repute without controversy. Emily Schossberger built the University of Nebraska Press into a recognized outlet of literature and scholarship with only occasional tribulation. But denunciation greeted expressions in the visual arts. When Keith Martin painted butterflies as big as cows over the Uni-

versity Club mantel, an outraged esthete quit the club. When the
Bryan admirers won assent to locate Rudolph Evans' statue of the
Great Commoner "temporarily" on the capitol's steps, there were
anguished cries. One critic said it looked like someone's forgotten
suitcase. The Bryanites stuck William Jennings "temporarily" fast
in concrete. When Kenneth Evatt, completing the rotunda murals,
painted a bull as ordered ("architectural in feeling . . . and . . .
nowhere realistic") , a state senator who had never seen a purple
cow complained that he had never seen a square bull. The furore
gave Nebraska's new designation as "The Beef State" the fillip the
cattlemen desired.

Despite attacks on its conservatism, the Nebraska Art Association
came to epitomize in its annual shows the whole range of modern
art, laid like the capitol on classical foundations, although again,
citizens found one show much too modern. The Lincoln Artists'
Guild's two annual shows, the exhibits of the Miller & Paine collection, plus one-man and group shows, brought art to the people.
Throughout the state Mrs. M. E. Vance took the University Extension Division's all-state art shows, bringing culture to the crossroads.

The Circlet Theater started, "in the round," later merging with
the Lincoln Community Theater and switching to conventional stage
—if the city bathhouse was conventional—before settling in a one-
time synagogue. New theaters had been fashioned on the Wesleyan
and Nebraska University campuses, meanwhile.

Founded in 1927 with twenty-five members and Rudolph Seidl
conducting, the Lincoln Symphony sharpened music appreciation.
Merging with an earlier concert course, it began bringing great
artists to town. By 1955 under the baton of Leo Kopp it was entertaining thousands in "pops" concerts at Pinewood Bowl—itself a
striking innovation of the quarter century. At the same Pioneers
Park site, the Singfest Committee was staging summer operas, and on
Sunday evenings Lincoln folks were gathering to sing hymns. Over
a succession of summers, on the downtown campus, Arthur West-
brook and David Foltz, starting with a handful of eager high school
students, had developed an annual fine-arts course of wide note. In
the thirties the remarkable John Rosborough had proclaimed Lincoln's fame throughout the land with his Great Cathedral Choir.
The cathedral dream faded. But Lincoln itself, a quarter century
later, had become in a sense a cathedral of all the arts, built by
many hands.

No portrait of the Prairie Capital in its metamorphosis from big small town to small big city would be complete without mention of its home life. For throughout the quarter century Lincoln has proclaimed that its greatest resource is its people, and that it is peculiarly a "city of homes." In the narrow sense this meant simply that since there was little down-town night life after the movies were over, such night life as there was in Lincoln was to be found in private homes. In a broader sense, it was a civic boast as to the character and quality—and quantity—of Lincoln's family life.

In the thirties, life at home was nothing like that of the pioneers. There were maids at three to five dollars a week, who gave the housewife some freedom. "Entertaining" meant a formal dinner served in courses, with the best linens and chinas and an elaborate centerpiece of fresh flowers. As times got tougher there were fewer maids and more modest preparations for parties. By the time the war struck, the maid had become Rosie the Riveter, and Lincoln women found themselves doing their own work, like their forebears. The pioneer sought and found a neighbor's help in putting out a prairie fire; the parents of 1955 were putting precisely the same system to work in finding baby-sitters.

The earlier Lincoln, and the Lincoln in transition, had been called "The Holy City." Sometimes this was in mild mockery of the peaceful co-existence of its active churches and its occasional rough-tough elements and civic smog. The city took the label unabashedly and in good grace, but the thirties were the years of choosing up sides, between "good" and "evil," black or white. In these agitated years, the houses of prostitution and more or less open gambling disappeared, and assaults on restrictions in the sale of liquor were beaten back. By the fifties the strident notes were less dominant, and a true, strong but not jarring, clear but not intolerant community tone had been set and fairly well settled upon. Sounding the pitch for this community tone was an augmented diapason of churches—123 in 1955, where in 1930 there had been 100.

The spirit of change was contagious. If the state could have a capitol without a dome and a legislature without chambers or parties, why couldn't the city have a city-manager form of government without a city manager? It could and did, replacing the mayor and four commissioners in 1937 with a seven-man council and dividing the managership into three parts—tailor-made for three extraordinary public servants, Theo Berg, Dave Erickson, and Cobe Venner. Eighteen years later it had seen the city through the pangs of war and postwar adjustment and the worst growing pains of a doubled population. Revision of an obsolete financial limitation in the charter in 1951 enabled city government to meet the community's mushrooming basic needs—for newer fire engines, more sewers, better streets. The water supply was expanded, a new viaduct negotiated, an auditorium begun. Cognizant that "political society exists for the sake of noble living," as it is said on the capitol, the city was getting around, also, to more of such niceties of life as swimming pools, libraries, and parks.

Two other innovations marked the Prairie Capital's quarter century. While staunchly opposed in principle to the growth of big government, it developed as a federal center of consequence. This began in 1929 when the business community put up $92,000 as come-on money for the Veterans Hospital, and reached a peak in the early forties when the Veterans Administration and the Soil Conservation Service set up regional shops, and the Post Office was doubled in size. Although fraternization was only tentative at first, the townsfolk discovered that the federal bureaucrats are people.

These townsfolk blinked a good deal in 1941 when a unique creature of Nebraska government called a public power district, and like the unicameral, bearing Norris' mark, took over the private utility in its quest for a firm market for Nebraska's hydroelectric power. But gradually they got used even to that—and barely in time, too. For in a mere fourteen years that same public power district was talking about smashing atoms in a nuclear power plant.

The city has spread broadly, now in orderly rectangles and massive businesslike horizontals, now in undulating residential plats, across the fruited plain. Geometric and white in its architecture, young in its ranchos, expansive in its spread, daring in its planning, the greater part of its face has changed in two and a half decades. In those twenty-five years Lincoln has become not quite an alabaster city—but it has acquired a lot of Bedford limestone, if not alabaster, and milk and honey flow fairly free. The city's population* and payroll are up, much. And over the years this city, which stands for a state, has found more and more a oneness about it—an integrity in which its culture and commerce, its town and gown, its art and its civic life have taken on some of the same oneness of spirit of "an house of state where men live well."

Condensed from *Seventy-five Years in the Prairie Capital*, Miller & Paine, 1955

* In January, 1957, according to the chairman of the City Planning Commission, Lincoln's population was 128,000.

V. The Weather Report

It's downright disgraceful that in most parts of the United States the climate is of foreign origin. Florida and California openly brag of their Mediterranean sunshine. The only place where one can get real, genuine American weather is on the Great Plains between the Mississippi and the Rockies.

—Paul R. Beath, *Febold Feboldson: Tall Tales from the Great Plains*

V. The Weather Report

The Seasons in Nebraska

Selected from the writings of
WILLA CATHER

I

Winter has settled down over the Divide again; the season in which Nature recuperates, in which she sinks to sleep between the fruitfulness of autumn and the passion of spring. The birds have gone. The teeming life that goes on down in the long grass is exterminated. The prairie-dog keeps his hole. The rabbits run shivering from one frozen garden patch to another and are hard put to it to find frostbitten cabbage stalks. All night the coyotes roam the wintry waste, howling for food. The variegated fields are all one color now; the pastures, the stubble, the roads, the sky are the same leaden gray. The hedgerows and trees are scarcely perceptible against the bare earth, whose slaty hue they have taken on. The ground is frozen so hard that it bruises the foot to walk in the roads or in the ploughed fields. It is like an iron country, and the spirit is oppressed by its rigor and melancholy. One could easily believe that in that dead landscape the germs of life and fruitfulness were extinct forever.

II

When spring came, after that hard winter, one could not get enough of the nimble air. Every morning I wakened with a fresh consciousness that winter was over. There were none of the signs of spring for which I used to watch in Virginia, no budding woods or blooming gardens. There was only—spring itself; the throb of it, the light restlessness, the vital essence of it everywhere: in the sky, in the swift clouds, in the pale sunshine, and in the warm, high wind— rising suddenly, impulsive and playful like a big puppy that pawed you and then lay down to be petted. If I had been tossed down blindfold on that red prairie, I should have known that it was spring.

III

The sun was like a great visiting presence that stimulated and took its due from all animal energy. When it flung wide its cloak and stepped down over the edge of the fields at evening, it left behind it a spent and exhausted world. Horses and men and women grew thin, seethed all day in their own sweat. After supper they dropped over and slept anywhere at all, until the red dawn broke clear in the east again, like the fanfare of trumpets, and nerves and muscles began to quiver with the solar heat.

IV

All those fall afternoons were the same, but I never got used to them. As far as we could see, the miles of copper-red grass were drenched in sunlight that was stronger and fiercer than at any other time of the day. The blond cornfields were red gold, the haystacks turned rosy and threw long shadows. The whole prairie was like the bush that burned with fire and was not consumed. The hour always had the exultation of victory, of triumphant ending, like a hero's death—heroes who died young and gloriously. It was a sudden transfiguration, a lifting-up of day.

*At reunions of old settlers there was one topic of debate
never, so far as is known, satisfactorily resolved by peaceful or other means. The question of the relative severity
of the Easter Storm of 1873 and the Blizzard of 1888
probably has disrupted more social gatherings of Nebraska's senior citizens than any other nineteenth-century
controversy.*

*The fact that an account of the latter storm is included
in this book is not to be regarded as a sign of partisanship.
It was chosen simply because, as it occurred later in time,
communication facilities were better developed, and the
reports on the storm are more comprehensive.*

The Blizzard of 1888

ORA A. CLEMENT

THE MERE FACT that on January 12, 1888, a storm crossed the middlewestern states, leaving a wake of suffering and death, may not seem
important to one who reads the statement nearly seventy years after
the event. The people of the plains have survived many disasters.
Why should one snowstorm be remembered more than others?

While it is true that the same area has known stronger winds, lower
temperatures, and heavier snows than those attending the famous
blizzard, there have been few, if any, other storms in which all these
elements were combined to attack an unprepared populace. The
old-timers who remembered the "Easter storm" of '73 may have recognized the threat of an unusually warm January day, but to the settlers
who had not yet learned the weather signals of the western plains,
the storm seemed to leap upon them out of nowhere, like some dia-
bolical thing. Its very suddenness was terrifying. As survivors tell the
story today, one detects a certain disposition to place the blizzard of
1888 in the realm of the supernatural, as something that had its
sources outside natural causes. Says one of them: "It was the wickedest thing I ever saw."

The blizzard of 1888 came at a strategic period in middlewestern
history. Free land was nearly all taken up. Many of the new settlers
had been lured across the Mississippi and the Missouri by agents of

railroad and land companies and some of them had been disappointed in what they found. Even the settlers who had been on their farms or in small villages for a considerable time still thought of their venture as being in the experimental stage. There was always more or less discussion as to whether they would stay or go "back East."

Their take-it-or-leave-it attitude of mind did not tend toward permanence. The man who was still undecided about the future did not take as good care of his buildings as the one who had already put down roots. This fact, too, is reflected in the reminiscences of the survivors. "The roof had not been repaired," says one. "We did not lose any stock because our sheds were good," says another.

The terrible experiences of teachers and pupils in poorly built and inadequately heated schoolhouses indicate that the pioneer school was also in an experimental stage. One man recalls that the little schoolhouse in his district was kept mounted on skids so it could be moved to the part of the district where the most pupils could be accommodated. At the time of the blizzard, many schools were without sufficient fuel; in other cases, what was on hand had been thrown on the ground outside the building and was soon buried beneath snowdrifts. Some of the tragedies of the storm were the direct result of insufficient fuel at the schoolhouse. The teacher had no choice but to try to find other shelter for her charges.

Because of its dramatic aspect, the blizzard was given wide publicity throughout the nation. How much this publicity injured the subsequent growth of the Middle West we do not know, but it could not fail to have its influence upon the easterners who had contemplated trying their fortunes "out West." The aftermath of unfavorable publicity must certainly have resulted in a defensive attitude on the part of the middlewesterners, who began to profess a confidence in and a loyalty for their adopted state or territory.

The general effect, then, of the devastating storm was to strengthen and solidify the states which had suffered the most because of it. It winnowed out the weaklings. The families who felt that they could not endure such experiences moved away. Those who remained made their decision to do so after consideration of all that was involved, and began to think in terms of permanence. This decision naturally led to home improvement and a growing community interest.

Parents who realized how easily their children might have become victims of the storm gave more attention to the comforts and conveniences of their district schools. Only a few weeks after the blizzard a letter went out from the state superintendent's office requesting that all rural schools in Nebraska have their winter fuel under cover on the school ground before cold weather began each year.

For such reasons as these, we maintain that the blizzard of January 12, 1888, had a peculiar historical and social significance which should not be lost to sight.

The cold front which moved out of the Canadian northwest first appeared in the United States on the nine P.M. map of January 11. It had by then passed southward into northwestern Montana. The next position is for six A.M. January 12, at which time reports indicated that the cold front had swept through Montana, entered the Dakotas, and was approaching the Nebraska Panhandle.

In the eight hours to two P.M. of that day the front of cold air had almost crossed Nebraska and extended along the western boundary of Minnesota to Sioux City, Iowa, and from there to the west of Crete, Nebraska, and curved southward over Kansas. The effect of the movement is shown at Valentine, where the temperature had risen to 30° by six A.M. and fell to —6° by two P.M., a drop of 36 degrees at a time when normally the greatest daily rise occurs. By nine P.M. the temperature at Valentine was —14°. Cold air continued to be transported southward, and the further fall during the next two nights brought temperatures of —35° at Valentine and North Platte. By the morning of January 13 temperatures were —20° to —30° in Montana. On the fifteenth, —26° was recorded at Omaha and —27° at Lincoln.

The snowfall in Lincoln is recorded at seven inches, which is more than other places where officially measured. At Omaha four inches were recorded. At North Platte snowfall was very light. From the available reports it appears evident that the snow in the air at the time of the blizzard was derived partly from snow that was on the ground before the storm began.

The blizzard was notable not simply because of the low temperatures, for other cold waves have been colder. Neither was the snowfall remarkably heavy, nor the depth on the ground unusual as compared with many other occasions. It was the combination of the three factors, namely, the gale winds, the blinding snow, and the extremely rapid drop in temperature from winter comfort level to well below zero which together made the blizzard most dangerous.

In Nebraska the morning of January 12 had been so mild that men were about in their shirt sleeves and cattled grazed in the field. The air was as soft and hazy as an Indian summer's day. In all parts of the state men and stock were out in the fields and school children played out of doors. Suddenly the wind changed to the north, blowing more furiously each minute thick blinding snow, first in large flakes and later in small ones with the impact of a bullet from a gun. There seemed no limit to the fury of the wind, while the driven snow fell more and more heavily. Men driving their teams could not see the horses' heads. The roads were blotted out and travelers staggered blindly on, not knowing where they were going. The storm and the intense cold which followed lasted three days and were almost immediately followed by another fierce storm. It was two weeks before the news from the farms and ranches began to trickle into the newspaper offices. Then it was learned that the storm was the greatest ever known in the West. In Holt County alone, more than twenty people lost their lives, and one-half of the livestock in the county perished.

Because in a great part of Nebraska it struck between three and four o'clock, just as the children were leaving school for home, the blizzard of 1888 is known as "the schoolchildren's storm." Hundreds of little ones were trapped, along with their teachers, in situations where their lives depended upon cool judgment and prompt action.

If many heroic deeds failed to receive proper recognition, there were others which were widely acclaimed. Best known, perhaps, is the Minnie May Freeman incident. Miss Freeman was teaching in a rural school called "the Midvale school" in Mira Valley, near Ord, Valley County, Nebraska. There were sixteen pupils present that day, several of them being nearly as old as the teacher, who was still in her teens. The schoolhouse was made of sod, and there was enough coal on hand to keep the group warm if it were found advisable to remain all night in the building. Before time for dismissal in the afternoon, the wind broke the leather hinges of the door and blew it in. The boys repaired the hinges and put the door in place. When it was blown in again they nailed it shut.

Soon a sudden gust of wind caught the corner of the tarpaper-and-sod roof and ripped it off, leaving a large hole through which the snow began to drift. Both teacher and pupils knew that they must now prepare to leave the building, for it would be impossible to keep warm with that hole in the roof. They expected the whole roof to be torn off at any moment. The sturdy, half-grown boys and girls were mostly Nebraska-born and were undismayed by the fury of the storm. They agreed to the teacher's plan to take the whole group to her boarding place, half a mile north of the schoolhouse, and assisted her in getting the smaller pupils through a south window and in lining them up for their march against the storm. Cheeks and fingers were frosted and it was hard going, but they struggled on and eventually reached their destination safely.

A few days after the storm the newspapers got the story of the trek, and a highly colored version of it was broadcast across the country. Miss Freeman found herself a heroine, the recipient of many gifts and congratulatory notes from unknown admirers from East to West.

A much sadder story is that of Lois May Royce who was teaching in District No. 32, near Plainview, Pierce County, Nebraska. Miss Royce had but nine pupils in school that day. Six of them went home at noon and did not return. Remaining with her were little Peter Poggensee, 9, Otto Rosberg, 9, and Hattie Rosberg, 6. There was not enough fuel to keep the building warm through the night, and Miss Royce decided to take the three children to her boarding place, which was at the farm home of Pete Hanson, about 200 yards north of the schoolhouse. Miss Royce, it will be noted, had no grown pupils to assist her. Leading her three little charges toward safety, she became hopelessly lost. The four of them were driven about by the fierce wind until they sank, exhausted, in a spot where a hay or straw stack offered some protection. Before daybreak all three children had perished, huddled close to the teacher's chilled body. With her own feet and hands frozen, the girl then crawled to the nearest farmhouse, which was but a quarter of a mile distant, to get help. She was given the best care possible, but both feet were amputated above the ankles, and one hand was permanently disabled.

Another tragic story which received much publicity is that of Miss Etta Shattuck, whose home was in Seward. Miss Shattuck was teaching in District No. 141, Holt County, near Emmet. Her pupils had all been taken home. (Some accounts of the incident state that she had no school that day.) She started out, alone, to reach the home of one of the directors to get a warrant signed. She became lost.

She wandered about until she found a haystack, where she decided to burrow in as best she could. When daylight came she was too weak to break her way out through the snowdrift that had covered the stack. Becoming weaker and more chilled as the hours passed, she lay there helpless from Thursday night until Sunday morning, when a farmer came to get hay for his stock and found her. For some time it looked as through her will to live might triumph over the severity of her injuries. Both legs were amputated below the knee, and although she survived the operation, she died a few days later.

In Dodge County, Nebraska, occurred the pathetic experience of

the Westphalen girls, 13 and 7, who were attending school near
Rogers. When the storm came up, the older girl asked the teacher to
excuse them so they might go home. The teacher was reluctant to
let them go, but the girls were so insistent, saying their widowed
mother would be terribly worried about them, that she finally gave
her consent for them to start out. The children never reached their
home and it was many days before their bodies were found in the
drifts. When discovered, the younger girl was wrapped in the coat
of her sister, who had, it seemed, made this great sacrifice for the
comfort of the little one in her charge.

Charles Gurnsey, only twelve years old, guided a group of children
home from a school in Loup County, Nebraska. The teacher dismissed school at four o'clock, without realizing the danger the children would encounter in attempting to reach their homes. Charles
took charge of a number of smaller pupils whose parents did not
come for them and personally delivered them to their parents, walking about two miles to accomplish the task.

While the daily and county press gave ample coverage to the storm,
there were many omissions and discrepancies in their reports because
of the difficulties of communication, especially during the days immediately following the blizzard. In 1888 telephones were in use only
in the larger cities, and the storm broke down the lines. Telegraph
wires and trains also were knocked out of commission. In favorable
weather the people in rural districts got their mail but once or twice
a week, and after the blizzard it was many days before some of these
communities could make any contact with the outside world.

An interesting controversy resulted from the various estimates of
the total deaths caused by the storm, which ranged from one or two
hundred to one thousand. The newspapers which inclined toward
the larger number accused their competitors of deliberately suppress-
ing the facts and of being the tools of the railroads and the land
companies whose interests were not furthered by stories of a disastrous storm in the territory they were just then promoting.

The spectacular heroism of the few resulted in much publicity, not
always favorable, for the part of the country visited by the blizzard,
but the unexploited courage and endurance of the majority have
been important factors in casting the mould for later generations of
middlewesterners.

Extracted from *In All Its Fury*, compiled by W. H. O'Gara,
Union College Press, 1935

> *The first question a stranger asks when he visits the Great Plains is "Does the wind blow this way all the time?" The native always answers "No, sometimes it blows harder."*
>
> —Paul R. Beath, *Febold Feboldson: Tall Tales from the Great Plains*

Cyclone Yarns

GEORGE L. JACKSON

ALTHOUGH this article is entitled "Cyclone Yarns," the title is misleading. The events mentioned herein are not "yarns," but are "gospel truths," each one being supported by authentic and scientific investigations. And although the term "cyclone" is used, this being the common terminology of the midwesterner, the true technical name for such an atmospheric phenomenon is "tornado."

On April 30, 1888, a cyclone passed over Howard County, Nebraska. This cyclone was not of the mass of windstorms but was a whirlwind with personality. The idiosyncrasy of this twister was its avidity for water. Every well, stream, and watering trough that happened to be in its path was sucked dry of its moisture and left as parched as if on the Sahara. Some wells were dry for weeks; the water in the creeks flowed into the dusty sands never to be seen again; even the cows for several days gave never a drop of milk.

On July 12, 1900, a cyclone with distinct uprooting proclivities passed near Onawa, Iowa. Trees, grass, corn, alfalfa, every form of vegetation in its path was uprooted and left, for the most part, in tangled heaps and windrows. Striking exceptions were noted. One old oak had been uprooted without a leaf or twig being injured, carried through the air, and balanced upright on the roof of a barn over two miles away. Twenty birds' nests were counted in the tree, but not an egg or a fledgling had been disturbed.

Near the end of a sultry afternoon on August 16, 1910, a tornado passed near Heartwell, Nebraska. An agent for a patented scrub brush was demonstrating a sample of his wares at the door of a farmhouse when the storm struck, whirling him high in the air and removing, with the exception of the house, every stick and straw from the premises. The last gust of the storm dropped the agent once more at the farmhouse door. "As I was saying," he began, "this brush is a regular cyclone. It sweeps clean and does a thorough job."

On June 6, 1912, a cyclone passed near Stillwell, Oklahoma. One of the early settlers in the community had dug a wide, deep well and had curbed the walls with pieces of native rock. Misfortune dogged the steps of the pioneer until the point was reached where the mortgage was due and he was about to be dispossessed, when the cyclone crossed his place. The "twister" pulled up the old well as a derrick would lift a straw and carried it several hundred feet, where it was left firmly planted but upside down near the farmer's barn. He plastered it inside and out and has used it ever since as a silo; from the old well gushed a geyser of oil. The farmer now has a summer home in the Adirondacks and a winter home in Palm Beach.

On July 13, 1913, a cyclone passed near Sweetwater, Nebraska. One of the members of the Ladies Aid Society was filling an ice cream freezer with the unfrozen constituents of that delicacy in preparation for the ice cream social at the church in town that evening. She had just clamped the lid down when the storm struck, whisking the freezer from her hands and hurling it aloft. The freezer was found on the church steps, filled with hailstones, and the cream frozen to a turn.

On the tenth of April, 1917, a very freaky cyclone devastated a section of the country near Mason City, Nebraska. At one place a farmer on the road with a wagonload of oats was picked up, wagon, team, and all, and carried to Arcadia, twenty miles distant, where he was set down, unhurt, team and wagon in good condition and not having lost an oat. At another place a woman owned a hundred prize-winning Black Langshan chickens from which the cyclone plucked every feather and pin feather from every bird in the flock. None of the birds was killed, but the fact that their experience had been horrifying in the extreme was attested by the further fact that the feathers which grew later were snow-white. At another place a farmer had just come in from a muddy field and was sitting with his feet in the oven of the kitchen range drying his socks and reading the daily newspaper. The cyclone blew the socks off the man's feet, carried the stove out the door and five miles over the hills, but left everything else in the house untouched, not even tearing the newspaper that he held spread before him.

Condensed from *Prairie Schooner*, April, 1927

Nebraska Land, Nebraska Land,
As on thy desert soil I stand
And look away across the plains
I wonder why it never rains.

　　　　　　—Chorus of a song popular in the nineties

Nebraska Rain Lore and Rain-Making

LOUISE POUND

WHEN the new and rather peculiar profession of rain-making arose in the late 1880's and 1890's, a profession that flourished especially in the Great Plains region, it did so with no little scientific or pseudo-scientific experiment behind it. Some of the efforts put forth were genuine endeavors to supplement or to replace the older reliance on prayer by reliance on science. Other efforts were associated with hocus-pocus and attempts to victimize the public.

Attempts to produce rain by human action began, of course, long before the nineteenth century, among primitive peoples in their incantations, rituals, and sacrifices to deities. Nearly every Indian tribe had the belief that its medicine man could produce rain. Civilized man, too, in all periods has called on divine powers for relief. Groups are still brought together now and then to pray for rain. On such group occasions the religious-minded take the lead, the skeptical remain a little apart; and sometimes rain comes.

In nineteenth-century America many theories of rain-making were advanced, and these brought in their wake various attempts to supply the rain which would end the drought and save the crops. Rain-makers appeared in the Plains region in the latter half of the century, reaching the Kansas-Nebraska region in the 1890's. Attempts were made over a period of years and in many places before it was conceded that theories of rain-making belonged not to the field of science but to that of lore, to which they are now relegated.

In 1870 Edward Powers of Delavan, Wisconsin, a civil engineer, published *War and the Weather, or the Artificial Production of*

Rain, the first elaborate treatment of an older idea. It was his conviction that rain could be produced by noise or concussion. In his
book he tried to demonstrate by means of statistics that great battles
are followed by rain. He failed to get Congress to authorize a test of
his theory, yet it proved long-lived and influential. It was his assumption that was responsible for most of the bombardment of the skies
and the general "foolish fireworks" of the 1890's. I heard several well
educated persons remark, during the rainy spring of 1945, "Surely
the war in Europe must have had something to do with our unusual
rainfall." On May 31 of that year, a newspaper story stated that Dr.
Benjamin Parry, chief of the United States Weather Bureau, had
said in reply to a telephoned question: "No, bombing and gunfire
have had nothing to do with a May rainfall. . . . If I kept a list of
the persons who ask me this question I would use up a lot of energy
and stationery, for the fallacy that gunfire causes rain is one of the
leading popular misapprehensions."

James P. Espy, whose theory published in his *Philosophy of Storms*
in 1841 brought him the title of "The Storm King" and who became
meteorologist to the United States War Department and to the Navy,
stated that "a very large prairie fire will cause rain." He held this
belief with great tenacity and in a special letter of 1845 proposed a
plan for the bringing of rain by means of fire. Edward Powers
repeated Espy's notion in stating, "It is well known that the burning
of woods, long grass, and other combustibles produces rain." This
idea, too, has passed into lore. Yet a statement which I heard in my
youth, "a very large prairie fire will cause rain," is still current on the
plains.

Major J. W. Powell's *Report on the Lands of the Arid Region*
included an article by G. K. Gilbert which furnished disproof of the
theory that the increased rainfall of the decade might be attributed
to the laying of railroad tracks and the installation of telegraph lines.
"When the railroads and the telegraph wires were first thrown across
the Plains they offered hope of increased rainfall. In this theory was
involved the idea that rain would be produced through the agency of
electricity in the wires and perhaps by the electrical current running
through the rails."

A folk belief current on the prairies was that smoke from the
chimneys and cabins of settlers might cause rain. And in 1892 Lucien
I. Blake of the University of Kansas had a dust theory for the artificial
production of rain.

A belief current in the decades when the rainfall seemed to be increasing was that the great increase in the absorptive power of the soil wrought by the cultivation of the soil and the growing of crops caused the greater rainfall and would cause it to continue. This belief was promoted by men of standing such as Professor Samuel Aughey of the University of Nebraska. Aughey's scientific prestige made the theory acceptable, and the railroads then existent (except the Union Pacific) took over enthusiastically the idea that the land had increasing agricultural possibilities. This belief was also encouraged by Charles Dana Wilber of the Nebraska Academy of Sciences, and by Orange Judd, editor of *The Prairie Farmer* published in Chicago. It was given circulation nationally and in Europe. Orange Judd was invited to speak at the Nebraska State Fair at Lincoln in September, 1885. He said confidently:

> When enough of the sod over a considerable region is brought under the breaking plow, a change comes over the entire country. Rains fall more frequently and more abundantly. Today in the cultivated counties rainfall is greater and more frequent than it was when they were first settled. As this goes on toward your boundary, the whole state of Nebraska will be in a new condition as to its rainfall and its fertility.

Yet officials of the United States Weather Bureau had warned people persistently for decades that climate is nowhere subject to permanent change either in temperature or in rainfall.

A belief held especially by the Latter Day Saints was that rainfall had increased and that it was a mark of special favor to them from the Divine Providence. Another belief of long standing was that the planting of trees would foster rainfall, though this is not borne out by the statistics of forestry. At the 1883 session of the Nebraska State Horticultural Society, Samuel Barnard of Table Rock stated, "The fact is well established that the cultivation of timber has the effect of equalizing the rainfall throughout the growing season by providing a porous surface to absorb the rain, by breaking the force of the wind, and by preventing the rapid evaporation from the surface." This idea still has wide currency on the Plains.

The most ingenious suggestion to produce rain by trees came before the National Irrigation Congress at El Paso in 1904. William T. Little presented a paper entitled "Tree and Plain." His reasoning was as follows: High winds on a level plain accelerate evaporation. Experiments have shown that evaporation is retarded on the leeward side of a grove of trees or windbreak. The higher the windbreak and the greater the velocity of the wind, the greater is the retardation. It was estimated that the retardation stood in about the ratio to the height of the obstruction as 16 to 1. Therefore a windbreak 30 feet high would benefit an area 480 feet wide. In the Great Plains the prevailing winds blow south and north. Therefore a series of board walls 30 feet high and 480 feet apart, built across the wind from Mexico to Canada, "from Gulf to British domain, could but be a solving." But since this may be impracticable, the same effect may be had by planting trees for windbreaks.

Basic for all these theories was the assumption that moisture in abundance exists in the sky. It is to be coaxed down by magic, incantation, or prayer, or to be jarred down by noise or concussion. Or it may be that oxygen or hydrogen, which in combination precipitate into rain, may be set loose by the proper combination of chemicals, helped perhaps by electricity, or even by fire or smoke or dust.

Theories and practical attempts at rain-making reached Nebraska in the last decades of the century. The dry years and crop failures of the late 1880's and early 1890's put an end to the roseate theory of increasing rainfall as the country grew more settled. In those years the long-suffering homesteaders might well have felt receptive to nearly anything that promised hope of relief.

In the panhandle of the northwest section of the state, the "Rain God Association" was formed in 1894 to raise—and it did raise—$1,000 to buy gunpowder. From Long Pine to Harrison on a hot July day, on high peaks known as "Rain God Stations," at the prearranged second, gunpowder was discharged in a steady cannonade. No rain fell.

Rain-making apparatus was set up not only in the Panhandle but in many other parts of the state, with cannonading leading as the rain inducer. Following are some illustrative items from regional newspapers.

July 2, 1894. O'Neill, Nebraska got a ton of dynamite to make the rain come. The dynamite was fired simulating thunder near town in hope that the jarring noise would cause rain. Two professional rainmakers came soon and were to have been given $1,000 if they "made" it rain. It rained hard a few hours after their time limit was up.

Special from Loup City, July 4, 1894: C. L. Drake, the local rainmaker, commenced operations in a blacksmith shop about 9 o'clock this morning and at 12:30 rain commenced. It came down in a steady downpour for an hour and a half. It was the first we had had for several weeks and farmers were becoming discouraged.

July 15, from Ravenna: The Ravenna News avers that five out of seven rainmaking experiments in that section proved successful.

July 26, from Hastings: The rainmakers are having a sorry time of it. The end of the five days in which they were to bring rain is approaching and prospects of the promised precipitation are not more flattering than before their arrival.

The four leading rain-makers who operated in Nebraska were Frank Melbourne, Clayton B. Jewell, Dr. W. F. Wright, and Dr. William B. Swisher. Melbourne, known as "The Rain Wizard" and later as "The Rain Fakir," was the most famous of the four and the one who operated most widely. He was also the man most obviously in his profession for revenue. Said to be an Australian, he came to Cheyenne in the autumn of 1891 and contracted to make the rain fall, taking money for it. The Cheyenne *Daily Leader* for September, 1892, stated: "The firm believers and the doubting Thomases were all forced in out of the wet, and those unable to find shelter were drenched to the skin." In the spring of 1893 he circulated a pamphlet, "To the People of the Arid Regions," giving testimony that he had produced rain in Ohio, Wyoming, Utah, and Kansas. He charged $500 for a "good" rain—one that would reach from fifty to a hundred miles in all directions from the place of operation. Associated with him was his "manager," Frank Jones. He seems to have operated in Nebraska as well as in Kansas and Colorado. A telegram to him from Bertrand, Nebraska, read: "Can you come here at once and prospect for rain. Wire conditions." Another telegram read: "Our money is raised. Name earliest date you can be here and await reply." From Grand Island, Nebraska, came another telegram: "Wire your price for one-inch rain." This was followed by: "Don't come until so ordered."

Ultimately Melbourne confessed that his claims were fraudulent. "The American people like to be humbugged," he declared, "and the greater the fake the easier it is to work." It was discovered that the dates he fixed upon were identical with those in the long-distance forecasts of Irl R. Hicks who made them from St. Louis for many years. Hicks published an almanac which had a large rural circulation, and his weather forecasts were believed to have a scientific foundation. If Melbourne went wrong on his dates, the prophecies of Hicks were responsible. Melbourne always announced that he kept his rain-making formula a secret. His method seemed to have involved burning chemicals on a raised platform in open country. His reign as the "King Rain-Maker" was not long. In 1894 or 1895 he was found dead in a hotel room at Denver. His death was attributed to suicide.

A second well-known rain-maker was Clayton B. Jewell, who came to be known, like Melbourne, as "The Rain Fakir." A Kansan, the chief train dispatcher for the Rock Island Railway at Goodland, Kansas, Jewell operated chiefly in Kansas and neighboring regions. After Melbourne's visits to Kansas, Jewell experimented in rain-making, believing he had discovered Melbourne's formulas, and for a time he seemingly had success. In the dry May of 1893 the officials of the Rock Island Railway placed at his disposal the electric batteries along the track from Topeka to Colorado Springs, for he thought electricity greatly helped in rain-making. The Rock Island also furnished him with balloons for trying the concussion theory. He lived in a freight car partitioned off as his laboratory. The trans-Plains railroads would have profited greatly by the success of rain-making endeavors, and it is not surprising that they financed the experiments.

Jewell and a helper experimented first at Goodland with chemicals valued at $250. In a few days their efforts were followed by a heavy rain throughout the county and, still later, by a more general rain. Next, the pair proceeded along the railroad, stopping at various places for experiments, some successful, some not. The boxcar in which they had started out was replaced by a car especially constructed for them by the railroad. A trip through Iowa and Illinois ending in "Kansas Week" at the World's Fair was planned, but Chicago was not enthusiastic over the prospect. No account seems to survive of his visit to the fair, if he made one. His experiments were free at this time, unlike those of Melbourne and those of the three rain-making companies that had been established at Goodland.

In the spring of 1893, experiments were begun by the Rock Island on a larger scale. It was intended that eventually contracts be made and successful rain-making be charged for. Three cars were started out by May, 1894. Jewell's methods were based chiefly on the hypothesis that volatile gases charged with electricity and sent high in the air would chill the atmosphere and bring a condensation of vapor. He used four generators in his work, making fifteen hundred gallons of gas an hour. Meantime opposition arose for various reasons. There was too much rain in some places. Some farmers complained of wind and cold weather. Others held that the dry weather was Divine punishment for man's impertinence in trying to take control of the rainfall. By the end of July, rain-making had died out, supplanted by increasing enthusiasm for irrigation.

One of the two leading rain-makers of Lincoln, Nebraska, was William F. Wright, usually termed "Doctor" Wright. The Lincoln *Journal* says of Wright that he claimed credit for 0.03 of an inch of rain after he had been trying to obtain rain for several days. The rainfall which he said his bombardment had brought on was so slight that it was of no practical benefit. After his first trial on a Wednesday night, he fired at intervals and on Friday was still firing. He had funnels on most of his guns in order to induce a spiral current when the shots were fired, but the funnels were blown away by the force of the concussion and were then discarded and the bases alone used. Wright is said to have tried unsuccessfully to obtain legislative aid. His plan was to "construct a huge gun or cannon of some sort, which would be shot into the sky." Recalling his activities some years later in an interview, John F. C. McKesson, a son-in-law of Dr. W. B. Swisher who worked with Wright, said that E. E. Blackman of the State Historical Society "once helped to carry a big black box up into a vacant barn." The box was supposed to contain rain-making material or equipment, and "to this day he does not know the magic which drew down rain within the specified 24 hours."

Wright was the author of a book, *The Universe as It Is,* the last section of which deals with "Artificial Rainfall." The book is well written and well printed and reads like the carefully prepared work of a thoughtful student. I cannot think that Wright was a fraud. Certainly he was no Melbourne. He placed his reliance, as did Dr. Swisher, on the explosion of gases rather than of gunpowder. He wrote in his last chapter:

It is not to be expected that one or two men operating at one point, with inadequate apparatus and a few chemicals, would be able to produce any very marked results. . . . A sufficient number of men, equipped with the right instruments and materials, stationed at proper intervals throughout the county and state, all working harmoniously under a well directed system, would soon remove all doubts as to the practicality and success of the undertaking.

The second Lincoln rain-maker was Dr. William B. Swisher, a surgeon in the Union army and later a pioneer doctor in Nebraska. His daughter, Dora Swisher McKesson, and granddaughter, Mrs. Hubert Walker, still live in Lincoln, and to them I am indebted for considerable information.

Of the three rain-making companies founded at Goodland, Kansas, after Melbourne's visit there the earliest formed was the Inter-State Artificial Rain Company, established in 1891. A central station was organized from which "rain-making squads" were to be sent out. The reported success of the Inter-State Company brought the formation of the Swisher Company of Goodland, chartered January 13, 1892, with a capital stock of $100,000; this company made contracts for doing business. The Swisher Company relied mainly upon chemicals with which Dr. Swisher had been experimenting. His success was reported to be equal to that of the Inter-State Company and his money reward to be good. The third company, the Goodland Artificial Rain Company, was chartered February 11, 1892. Contracts were made in many places and competition between the companies developed. At one time the Inter-State Company offered to furnish rain for the crop season for $2,500, the Swisher Company for $2,000, and the Goodland Company for $1,500. In a telegram from Lincoln, July 26, 1892, Dr. Swisher claimed: "Rain as per contract. Time 48 hours." According to A. E. Sheldon, Dr. Swisher was one of those "employed by the Rock Island railroad to travel in a special car fitted with rain-making apparatus. He was to operate in Nebraska and Kansas and to produce rain along the Rock Island right-of-way."

Dr. Swisher went back to Lincoln with his chemicals, where he made an agreement with a real-estate man, J. H. McMurtry, who owned a number of farms in the vicinity, to bring rain within three days. McMurtry promised to pay him $500 if one-half inch of rain fell. Shortly after the rain-maker began his work there fell a drenching rain of one-half inch. McMurtry claimed that it came from natural causes, but Dr. Swisher took the matter to the courts, and McMurtry was forced to pay the $500.

According to Swisher's son-in-law, McKesson, Swisher and Wright worked out their theory together and produced rain. Throughout the dry summer of 1894 they worked in various parts of the country and apparently with success. But "wind made results uncertain," blowing the gases elsewhere from the place where precipitation was desired. Moreover Dr. Swisher was religious-minded and "felt more and more that the plans of nature and Providence should not be tampered with. And so the black box was put away." The mysterious black box, said McKesson, "was merely a receptacle for two large earthen jars from Germany. As hydrogen and oxygen combined in the proper ratio produce water, we felt there was a deficiency in one or the other." They manufactured hydrogen and put it into the air to start a nucleus of water which might result in more. The first operations took place on Swisher's farm at Emerald near Lincoln. Two hundred people had subscribed to a fund for the work. Later, the two men operated elsewhere in Nebraska and in Kansas. McKesson stated to his interviewer that their efforts were "followed in every instance by rain."

Rain-making must have been a profitable profession while it lasted.

The largest profit came from selling the rain-making secret formula and the right to operate in a designated region. Whether farmers believed in any of the systems is a question. The contracts read always, "No rain, no pay." If it did not rain those who contracted for it were out nothing, and if it did rain they thought the benefit worth what was paid for it. Newspapers generally were skeptical. The rain-makers were accused of studying the weather forecasts and of being "out of chemicals" if the signs were not auspicious. And, in any case, the rain-makers were never brought in until there had been a long drought. After 1894 little is heard of rain-making. In the drought of the 1930's rain-makers did not reappear. Instead, came only occasional reversion to prayer and song.

Perhaps it should be added, in conclusion, that there is one method of rain-making that does not fail, according to current Nebraska folklore, and the saying is probably to be heard elsewhere in the central states: "Wash and polish your car and you may be sure rain will follow."

Condensed from *California Folklore Quarterly*, April, 1946

"Too thick to drink and too thin to plow"—that's the Missouri, the nation's longest river, 2,464 miles from Three Forks, Montana, to St. Louis. The man who knew the Missouri best, the late Lt. General Lewis A. Pick, of Pick-Sloan Plan fame, called it one of the wildest on earth.

As if aware that its unharnessed days were numbered, in April, 1952, the Mighty Muddy went on the loose again, perhaps for the last time. In holding back the most disastrous flood in the history of white occupation of the Plains area, the people of Omaha and their Iowa neighbors in Council Bluffs showed what may be expected of civilians in a crisis.

Men Against the River

B. F. SYLVESTER

BIG MO" was roaring drunk on a snow-melt cocktail which could have been mixed by Paul Bunyan. It was made in Montana and the Dakotas with eighty thousand square miles of deep winter snow which was one-third water, a chinook wind, and an almost total run-off over a layer of ice. This was poured into the main stem by the Milk, Knife, Heart, Bad, and Cannonball and downed all at once. An unprecedented volume of water rolled over towns and farms for a thousand miles, into a bottleneck at Omaha and Council Bluffs.

The river comes between the cities in the shape of a narrow question mark, tapering to a quarter mile at the Douglas Street bridge. Inside a ten-square-mile loop and against the stem on the Nebraska side were five thousand people, the Omaha airport, large industries, and the public power plant serving both cities. Under the bend on the Iowa side were eleven square miles, taking in two-thirds of Council Bluffs and thirty thousand people. The cities were protected by thirty-six miles of earth levees and a mile-long floodwall of concrete and steel, where Omaha industry crowds the river. These levees and floodwall were designed to protect against the greatest flood possible after upriver dams are completed—a stage of 26.5 feet, with a safety factor of five feet against wave action. The approaching crest was forecast at 26 feet, then 28.5, then 30, then 31.5. If not contained, the flood would bury large sections under fifteen feet of water.

Brig. Gen. Don G. Shingler of the army engineers offered technical help and called in fifteen hundred specialists, big and little river rats from Washington to Dallas, including General Pick. At Clinton, Mississippi, the engineers produced a small well-water flood in a concrete replica of the Missouri. At "Omaha-Council Bluffs" the tiny torrent was 3.5 inches high in a channel six to eight inches wide and tearing along so fast that one day's flood was reproduced in five and one-half minutes. The tests showed the levees would have to be raised two to seven feet in six days, and held. The odds, not counted at the time, were estimated later at ten to one against. Men and boys who finally numbered sixty thousand left their homes and went to the dikes.

Civil Defense had a skeleton organization and a plan in both cities. In Omaha, Director Sam W. Reynolds had medical and communication services, auxiliary police and firemen, and a file of material, equipment, and contractors. C. D. became the co-ordinating agency in evacuating the threatened area and raising 13.4 miles of levees. Reynolds' powers were not clearly defined, but when in doubt he interpreted the situation and put the legal aspects on file. He authorized the public power district to cross private property in building a $300,000 temporary levee around its plant behind the floodwall. He approved another levee which sealed off the switch tracks of six railroads. Probably no other chairman of a Nebraska delegation to the Republican Convention ever contravened so many federal regulations in three days. One-half million gallons of alcohol might have duplicated the 1951 flood-fire at Kansas City. Because of U. S. Treasury rules, it could not be moved, so Reynolds moved it. Interstate Commerce Commission regulations, limiting drivers to a sixty-hour week, slowed gas and oil deliveries to the levee. He suspended the regulations. Finally, he authorized the government, through the engineers, to lay explosives and blow up a section of the floodwall if the water got behind it.

James F. Mulqueen had been mayor of Council Bluffs one day, Kennard W. Gardiner acting city manager one day when the army engineers revealed the city's danger. Under Iowa law, Civil Defense was restricted to disaster from enemy action, as in fifteen other states. It had good elements in communications, auxiliary police, and equipment files. The mayor could take over and did. It required an hour and a half to change from defense against bombs to defense against flood. On a cold and rainy Good Friday, the mayor declared a state of emergency and government by proclamation. Including a county levee on the south, Council Bluffs had 29.69 miles to protect. To get to them, fifteen miles of roads had to be built over low and swampy ground. On Saturday the mayor issued the first of five evacuation orders and closed most business and industry to release manpower and trucks. Roads to the city were closed to keep out sightseers. Vehicles hauling dirt to the top of the levees were stuck in the mud. River stage, 22.6; mininum temperature, 35; precipitation, .27 inch.

Half the city had moved or was on the move Easter Sunday. Ministers held services, after which they evacuated their churches or turned them into shelters. The evacuation was in daylight, to avoid panic, from Saturday afternoon to Monday evening. It took in the west end and fringes of the business district, to within two blocks of the city hall. Under Red Cross, Harry C. Crowl, real estate man, directed 750 vehicles, volunteered by Council Bluffs establishments, farmers, Omaha stores which had suspended deliveries, and forty-eight towns. Besides trucks of all sizes, there were wagons and hay-racks drawn by horses and jeeps. Six winch trucks stood by to extricate them from the mud. Funeral homes removed 175 bedridden persons by ambulance. Novices moved out pianos and refrigerators. Some families took water heaters and furnaces. Sign on a house: "For Sail." Another: "I Shall Return."

The hill people took in the flatlanders until the district looked like a series of car parks. Between them and neighboring towns, only fourteen hundred went to shelters. Cadillacs were parked in the street, while garages, basements, and porches held furniture. Automobile dealers removed new cars to release showrooms. Furniture was stored in a dozen towns and finally in forty-six freight cars. Eighty-six families refused or failed to evacuate. The mayor called on the Reverend Denmore J. King, rector of St. Paul's Episcopal Church, who whittled the number to seventeen and tried again. A psychiatrist persuaded an expectant young mother to go to the hospital. A widow of ninety-six said her late husband had warned her to make no move without the advice of her lawyer. A retired sea captain, past eighty, was entertaining a young woman from Omaha and said to go away.

Nerve center of the fight was the city hall, which the mayor put on a twenty-four-hour basis, along with himself. He counted on an informed public as the first line of defense. Business houses gave up their telephones so the city hall could have sixty-five more lines. The radio station cleared the air instantly for the mayor. In many homes the radio was kept going. Mobilization was virtually total. Twenty-eight thousand registered volunteers went to the levees, not counting those who showed up on their own. A thousand were in the police auxiliary, and no one knows how many more were in other flood activities. There was one marriage, one divorce petition, and no other lawsuit. Doctors' waiting rooms were empty, and only the very old took time to die. Two leading morticians had no funerals. One obstetrician had no births, presumed the stork was flying patrol over the levee.

Manpower was dispatched from the basement of the city hall. Workers went out in trucks, clean, singing and laughing, and came back silent and covered with mud, to overflow cots and fall asleep on marble steps and floors. Volunteers came from ninety-nine towns, often in delegations headed by the mayor. One hundred Mennonite farmers were from Kansas. A thousand men came from Creighton University and the University of Omaha. A Jesuit priest, turned down as too old, waited around the corner for a dike-bound truck and was smuggled in. Five hundred were from the University of Nebraska, Midland, Dana, Iowa State, Grinnell and other colleges. Dr. O. E. Cooley, superintendent of the Council Bluffs district of the Methodist Church, who was throwing sandbags, met ministers from Atlantic, Cumberland, Macedonia, Oakland, Greenfield, and Centerville, which was two hundred miles away.

One hundred eighty radio hams flocked in from all over the country and reported to Leo. I. Meyerson, who had a communications center in his home, which handled eight thousand messages a day to and from the levees and other points. One hundred fifty members of the Civil Air Patrol from Oakland, Iowa, who patrolled the levees by air and on foot, had their daily briefings there.

The west end of the city was protected on the north by a levee anchored to a north-south bluff line two hundred feet high. It ran due west for a mile to the normal channel, then followed the river gently southwest toward Omaha. The water was highest there, five miles wide from bluff to bluff above the bend, fifteen miles wide upstream. The east end of this pocket was vulnerable for other reasons. The Chicago and North Western and Illinois Central tracks ran through it on a grade five feet from the top. The tracks had been torn out and the gaps closed with sandbags, but water seeped through the cinder and gravel ballast. This required careful watching by a group of old river men from Memphis and Vicksburg.

They were not concerned about ordinary seepage which was only the quiet weeping of the river, relieving pressure and doing no harm. This was even encouraged, almost as if one said, "Have yourself a good cry. You'll feel better." Relief wells on the land side brought up seep which flowed through the sand underneath the levee. This was stepped up by pumps which sent some water back to the river over the top of the levee and some onto the land where it made pools and lakes up to five feet deep. Pent-up seep was something else, violent and dangerous. Turbulent water, cutting and moving dirt, bubbled up in patches like a spring. The cry of "Sand-boil!" brought Memphis and Vicksburg on the run. They ringed 250 of these spots with sandbags, like a chimney, as high as the level of the river and let the water rise. One area, where the boils were cancerous and spread, had to be ringed with a levee that required 115 trucks hauling dirt for sixteen hours.

In two days of rain which made vehicle movement on top of the dikes impossible, engineer Tritt had been able to get less than a foot of dirt on the north levee. At two Sunday morning he got a dealer out of bed and ordered lumber to put up eight and a half miles of flashboard. This was a wooden panel, two and a half to five feet high, nailed to stakes driven into the top of the levee and reinforced by sandbags. A mile-long plank road for the lumber trucks was made on top of a muddy section of the north levee. In Omaha, engineer H. H. Nicholson went to flashboards and mudboxes, which were, in effect, a double flashboard with dirt between. River stage, 24.6; minimum temperature, 34; precipitation, .04 inch; wind, 18.4 miles.

At six Monday morning the nailing crews went to work. The story is told in one section the workers had lumber and nails but no hammers. A man went to get them and returned in half an hour to find three blocks of flashboard were up. A half mile of snowfence, weighted with sandbags, was put down on the river side of the north levee to guard against wave action. River stage, 25.6; minimum temperature, 36; precipitaton, 0; wind, 9.7 miles.

Meanwhile one-half mile below the north levee, Tritt was building a second and higher one. It was a mile and three-quarters long, over twenty-eight sets of switch tracks, and joined the north levee at the Illinois Central bridge. One hundred fifty dump trucks and twenty-six earthmovers wheeled their loads bumper to bumper twenty-four hours a day over the rising embankment. Little earthworms took twelve tons at a bite, middle-sized ones twenty-seven tons, and big ones forty-five tons. The levee took two and a half days to build, was finished at nine Tuesday night, losing a race to the flashboards which had been completed at two that afternoon.

Disturbing signs of saturation appeared Wednesday when the railroad fill sections of the north levee quivered underfoot. Saturation is the last stage before chunks of earth slough off and the structure melts away. Considerable water was coming under the fills. Sandboils spread until the danger was greater under the levee than on top. It was decided to build a third levee in a half moon to ring the danger area. It would impound the seepwater, put weight on the soft levee and, it was hoped, the seep would neutralize sandboils. The job took twenty-four hours. River stage, 28.3; minimum temperature, 33; precipitation, .01 inch; wind, 6.8 miles.

Thursday was the day of the expected crest. The water was sixteen feet higher than the land and up to eighteen inches on the sandbags. Volunteers and Fifth Army soldiers went along raising the levee one bag at a time, keeping ahead of the river. Water trickled between and under the sandbags, through cracks in the flashboard and over sandbag spillways on the land side. The dike fighters were to stay and pile on sandbags until the river washed them out. Fifty-two boats were ready at eleven stations, with eighty more standing by, to remove them. Planes waited to give the signal if the levees failed. The Council Bluffs alarm would be a siren; Omaha's a buzzing by day, flares by night. River stage, 29.4; minimum temperature, 49; precipitation, .17; wind 9.4 miles. Under carbide flares and electric lights the men watched the river rise slowly through the night. There were no discussions on what was holding it back. With a round oath, a boilermaker exclaimed, "I know the Lord is on this dike!"

The official crest at Douglas Street bridge was 30.2 at 4:00 A.M. Friday, though it was 32.5 on the north levee. A woman called up at 4:20 to ask if she could move back. It was hard to convince her that the crest would be constant for a day, and danger would be no less for two or three. This was proven on the Omaha side when a storm sewer exploded four hundred yards behind the levee at 7:00 P.M. Friday. It required nine hours to close the mouth, by dropping steel I-beams and nine hundred tons of rock from a barge.

The river was down to 29.5 feet by Saturday; 27.3 Sunday; and 24.3 Monday. The Dutch boys of 1952 took their fingers from the dike and went home. The evacuees returned under precautions. Now there was time for the two cities to look back. Thirty-five thousand persons had moved out of their homes and back with no injury and almost no damage to possessions. No home had been entered by water or pestilence and only two by looters. Except for one traffic injury in Omaha, there had been no major accidents.

In July, 1953, Omaha Civil Defense Director Reynolds received a Freedoms Foundation Medallion at the hands of President Eisenhower for his work in the flood. The era of community good feeling and the cooperation between Omaha and Council Bluffs continues.

VI. Look East, Look West

To the east, a cornfield that stretched to
daybreak; to the west, a corral that reached
to sunset; between, the conquests of peace,
dearer-bought than those of war.

—Willa Cather, "A Wagner Matinee"

The shaggy coat of the prairie . . . has vanished for-
ever. . . . One looks out over a vast checkerboard, marked
off in squares of wheat and corn; light and dark, dark and
light. Telephone wires hum along the white roads, which
always run at right angles. . . . One can count a dozen gaily
painted farm houses; the gilded weather-vanes on the big
red barns wink at each other across the green and brown
and yellow fields. The light steel windmills tremble
throughout their frames and tug at their moorings, as they
vibrate in the wind that often blows from one week's end
to another across that high, active, resolute stretch of
country.

—Willa Cather, *O Pioneers!*

The Mysterious Middle West (1934)

A. G. MACDONELL

I HAD GONE to catch a glimpse of the famous Middle West that has long been the bogey of Europe. If the United States Senate refused to ratify a treaty, we always ascribed it to pressure from the Middle West; if a new and super-efficient tractor began to undercut British tractors, it was always due to the mass production that was possible only in the illimitable Middle West; if the United States wanted its war debt repaid, it was owing to the ignorant clamour, we explained to each other, of the citizens of the Middle West who were so un-reasonable as to want their money back. In fact, we made the Middle West into a sort of Colossus, alternately illiterate and politically acute, alternately half-witted and shrewd, alternately turning its back and its telescope upon European affairs, alternately wrapped up in a loutish sleep and possessed of demoniac vigilance.

I motored out of Omaha with a banker friend to see something of this enigmatic land. We drove out by a curly, twisty road that was very unlike the great highroads that I had seen so far in the country. But its twistiness was historical like that of so many English roads, for it had once been the only trail westward out of Omaha, and in the days when that trail was first trodden by white men, it was more important to twist and curl under the skyline than to march arrogantly over hill and dale in full view of lurking marauders. One of the first villages we came to was called Elk City, and a huge notice-board on the outskirts announced its name and added, with very proper civic pride, "Population 42."

As we drew further and further away from Omaha, we were able to catch a glimpse or two of the countryside, and at last we got entirely clear of the billboards and were able to stop the car and have a look at the Nebraskan plains that lay before us in the sunlight. The country was not unlike the Somme country of France. There were the same gentle slopes and rolls of ground, the same dotted farmhouses, and the same wooded valleys. The difference was a difference of colour, for Picardy is white with chalk and its green is a dusty, chalky green, whereas Nebraska is black with the blackness of its soil, and its green is dark and rich, except where the winter wheat makes a lighter splash of colour. A great drought had just come to an end, and the landscape was checquered, light and dark, with the deep colour of the alfalfa crop and the brassy fields of corn that had been so scorched by the endless sun of spring, summer, and early fall that they were not worth the trouble of harvesting. In the distance the blue of the Elkhorn River made a cheerful patch between its tree-covered banks and with their oaks and lindens and walnuts, and here and there a cluster of cottonwoods added an almost Scandinavian touch of flaxen gold against the Elkhorn's blue. Far away, beyond the river, Nebraska stretched to the horizon and for many a hundred miles beyond the horizon.

Our objective, a farmhouse, was nearer at hand. It was a neat white building, with green shutters, of course, and a quantity of outhouses, and a clump of trees round about. It was forty miles from a city of no outstanding size, and entirely isolated from village, hamlet, or even neighbouring farm, and yet it was equipped with electric light, refrigerator, central heating, and telephone. What percentage of the farms within forty miles of London, the biggest city in the world, have any of those amenities, let alone all four of them?

Agriculture has never been a passion in my life; I was, therefore, rather at a disadvantage in listening to the agricultural talk of the farmer who greeted us as we alighted from the car. But in spite of my ignorance and Mr. Johansen's professional erudition, I learned some interesting things about the mysterious, Sphinxlike Middle West.

We went all over the farm, all the eight hundred acres of it. We saw the fat young calves that had come in that week from the Great

Sandhills—up Wyoming way—to be fattened for the Stock Yards. The calves had come from a ranch 350 miles away. With the strains of "Git along, little dogie," to which I had been dancing a night or two before, in my ears, I asked how many weeks it took to drive cattle 350 miles, in these days when the roads are jammed with traffic.

"I started on a Monday morning in my automobile," said Mr. Johansen, "and I got to the ranch that day. On Tuesday I selected my calves, and I got back on Wednesday just in time to get ready for them when they arrived in trucks."

It was several minutes before I tried any more of the taking-an-intelligent-interest stuff, and I gazed in prudently silent admiration at the chestnut-coloured son of the greatest Belgian stallion that ever came to America, and at the herds of cattle that were feeding at the corn-troughs while all the flies in Nebraska buzzed about trying to get the sugar out of the corn-canes. Then we got into Mr. Johansen's automobile and drove across the farm lands to see fat sheep that were pasturing in a wooded dell beside a stream; a group of grand-children of the Belgian stallion; an outhouse filled with up-to-date machinery; a group of men digging a well; and barns that were so bulging with corn that the boarding of the walls was bending outwards and a brick in the foundations had been dislodged by the pressure.

"Hey!" cried my Omahan companion, as he saw the sagging walls. "What's going to happen to that building if a high wind gets up?"

"Oh, it won't get up," said Mr. Johansen easily.

My banker friend was not so simply put off as all that. "But what will happen if it does?" he persisted.

"It will be all right," said Mr. Johansen with a big guffaw. "Some other part of Nebraska will get my corn, that's all. They'll gain what I lose."

The thought did not diminish Mr. Johansen's joviality, and he pulled his car off the track and drove it slap across a field so that I could see at close quarters the little purple flower which we call, I believe, Lucerne in Britain, but they call Alfalfa. Thence he steered briskly up a dried river-bed, shouting gaily that if we stuck in the sand we could always get a tractor to pull us out. That crisis did not arise, however, and we emerged on to a field that was completely bare. "This," said Mr. Johansen with some solemnity, "is my most important field. It is here that I am paid by the Government to raise nothing at all. That is called National Recovery."

This, of course, brought us to those two great conversational topics, Depression and the New Deal. Mr. Johansen had a lot to say about both of them and about a third that was mainly confined to the Middle West, the Long Drought.

"They come here," said Mr. Johansen, "and they offer me money not to do this, and they offer me money not to raise that, so I take their money. Naturally I take it. Why not? Anybody would. But I could get through the Depression without it. I'm not going bankrupt so long as I'm farming a Nebraskan farm."

"Plenty of banks have gone bankrupt," said my companion gloomily. "Seven hundred out of thirteen hundred in Nebraska alone."

"And a good job too," cried Mr. Johansen gaily, striking the banker an ox-felling blow on the back. "We are getting down to reasonable farm-finance at last. Why, in the good old days before Depression, we could mortgage our farms as wildly as we pleased, because we knew perfectly well that our next year's profits would be so enormous that we could probably pay the whole mortgage off in a year. We're more careful now, and when we do borrow, we borrow from the Federal Land Bank. And I'll tell you another thing," went on Mr. Johansen. "Depression has finished all the get-rich-quick notions that we used to have. When I was a kid, we used to arrange our futures very simply. Get over college and then make a million dollars. That was all."

"What college were you at?" I enquired timidly. That, at least, was a safe unagricultural question.

"Yale," said the farmer. "But that million-dollar stuff is finished. It's all small profits now, but steady ones. We've got accustomed to the English way of choosing a trade and sticking to it for life. In the old days we went into farming as a nice outdoor occupation for a few years while we made a fortune on the stock market. Now we're in it and we've got to stay in it, so we're learning our job at last."

"What about the Drought?" I asked.

"Well, the Drought was bad," said Mr. Johansen. "We've had droughts before, but never such a long one. Other droughts have been bad on one or two crops, but this one was so long that it was bad for all the crops. But it had a good side too. We had to sit down and think out ways of dodging it, new farming methods, new crops, new ideas. I've learnt more about farming during the last year than in all my life before."

"What will happen if you get another drought next year?" asked my companion.

"It will be bad, very bad," said Mr. Johansen. "But even another drought won't break us. Even N.R.A. can't break us. Look at that." And he swung his long arm in the direction of a hillside. "The longest drought on record, and look at that. After a few days' rain, the winter wheat is up, and strong as you like."

He swung his arm on a wider circle, embracing this time not his own 800 acres but the whole Nebraskan plain, or, wider still, the whole of the Middle West. "The valley of the Missouri River," he exclaimed, "is the richest in the world. Seventy-five years ago it was nothing but grass and saplings and bands of Indians. Look at the corn-lands now, and the cattle, and the farm buildings. Not a thing more than seventy-five years old. Do you think you can get that down with a silly little drought or two? Never. Your city-folk may talk of bankruptcies and ruin. Come and live on Nebraskan soil and learn what Nature can do in the way of recovery after a hard time. Nothing will worry you then.

"If you keep close to Nature," said Mr. Johansen, "you can't go wrong. Not in Nebraska, anyway. Of course if you like to plough up your cattle ranges and try to grow wheat as they did in South Dakota when wheat went to $2.20 a bushel during the War, then you deserve anything you get."

I asked what they did get.

"They got blown away," replied the farmer with a huge grin. "Yes, sir. There wasn't grass any more to hold their thin top-soil together, and it got blown away."

A herd of Hereford cattle came past, fat and sleek and healthy. "There's a link with old England," said the farmer. "Herefords. Best cattle in the world for us. Your Scotch Angus are good, but they're terribly wild. Talking of Scotch . . ."

The sun was setting over the Elkhorn River as we drove home along the old trail, and the population of Elk City was still 42. Purple clouds were trailing over the Nebraskan plains, and lights were beginning to shine in the windows of the lonely farms.

I learnt a lot of things that afternoon, besides such important agricultural facts as that you can bury your silage in Nebraska, whereas in Iowa and Kansas you have to put it into towers. For one thing I found that the Middle West is a long way from Europe. Even I, a European, felt incredibly remote as I stood on the banks of the Elkhorn River that afternoon. I was ten thousand miles further away than when I was in New York or Chicago, further away even than when I reached, later on, San Francisco. The whole outer world fades away. Nothing seems to be of any importance except the spring sowing or the fattening of cattle. What does it matter to you, as you stroll in the shadow of the cottonwoods, what the people of Memel think of the people in Lithuania? Would you leave your sheep beside the Elkhorn to go and fight for Latvia against Poland? Would you lie awake at night in your Nebraskan farm, worrying about the justice of awarding Eupen and Malmédy to Belgium?

What have wars, thousands of miles away, to do with this peaceful, eternal business of living on the soil, by the soil, for the soil? I used to think, as many others think, that the Middle West is supremely ignorant. I was wrong. The Middle West is supremely wise. It goes on its way, hating no man and fearing no man and saying, as Shakespeare's Corin said, "The greatest of my pride is to see my ewes graze and my lambs suck."

It knows very little about Europe, even though so many thousands of the farmers are first-generation immigrants from Scandinavia, and many thousands more are children of first-generation immigrants. "My father was born in Copenhagen," said Mr. Johansen, "but I am an American."

The Mississippi Valley takes them and makes them into Americans, because the Mississippi Valley is America. The cities of the East and of the long Pacific slope are important, but they are not the heart of the country. They talk more, but they mean less. They travel the world and broaden their minds, but when the ill winds begin to blow it is not the East and West that stand unshakable. It is that Valley in the Middle that cannot be conquered.

Extracted from *A Visit to America*, The Macmillan Co., 1935

The great, the upstanding prize was to get the county seat. The ways the towns went about this seem almost incredible. But there was a reason: if a town grabbed off that prize, it stood a chance to become the biggest in the county and the most prosperous. A county-seat town was tremendously important; its lots sold for more than lots in jackleg towns; the laws were made there and the taxes assessed and the political plums handed out. The town selected was usually the one nearest the center of the county; but not always. There were tricks. Sometimes a town several miles away, by some lucky stroke, walked off with the prize.

Two towns in Nebraska were fighting for the county seat. The matter was to be determined by an election at which every person in the county could vote. The people of Osceola did some thinking; then had stiff cardboard maps printed in the shape of the county. The voters were asked to balance these cutout maps on a pin, or a pencil, then look to see which town was nearest the balancing point. That settled it. Osceola won.

—Homer Croy, *Corn Country*

County Seat

ROBERT CHESKY

1. The Stolen Courthouse

THE MOST famous of all Nebraska county-seat fights, lasting considerably longer than the siege of Troy, raged in Saline County from the mid-seventies until as recently as 1927. Just as in the Trojan War, not strength but a strategem broke the back of the opposition, and, like its classic prototype, the struggle inspired bards and music-makers. A music-drama, "The Stolen Courthouse," was presented before audiences of the victorious Wilberians at the old Wilber Opera House.

The designation of Swan City, now Swanton, as the Saline County seat of government was merely a prologue to the drama. At the time —1867—it was the only settlement in the county. However, when the railroad by-passed it and population centers grew up farther east, there were demands for relocation. In 1871, after two county-wide elections, Pleasant Hill captured the prize from Crete and Dorchester, but its days of glory, too, were numbered. As new towns were born —among them Wilber, platted in 1873—there was again agitation for the county seat's removal, and by 1877 the race was wide open. No less than six localities were in the running, including a piece of real estate called "Center" which had no population but was in the center of the county (and also, presumably, the hands of a sharp operator). Two elections narrowed the field to Crete and Wilber, and finally, on the third go-round, Wilber won out by a 1,349 to 1,110 majority.

But the Cretans had not yet begun to fight. Alleging that signatures on the courthouse relocation petition were forged in some cases and void in others because signers hadn't been county residents long enough to qualify as electors, they obtained a temporary injunction against the scheduled moving of the records from Pleasant Hill to Wilber. The case went into the courts, all parties having agreed to accept the decision of Judge J. A. Weaver, who set January 28, 1878, as the day he would pronounce judgment from his home in Falls City.

The Wilberians at once arranged to have an emissary on the spot with instructions to telegraph the verdict in code to Dorchester, where a messenger would be waiting to carry the word to Pleasant Hill. When the fateful day arrived, the men of Wilber, three hundred strong, descended on Pleasant Hill with a hundred and sixty wagons. What happened after that is a moot point. According to one story, the Cretans, fearing violence by the Wilber mob, sent a message to Dorchester that the injunction had been dissolved. Another account casts S. S. Alley, a Wilber attorney and real estate promoter, in the role of the "crafty Ulysses." According to this version, Alley told the waiting crowd at Pleasant Hill that he would go and obtain the authority they needed to act. Having absented himself for a suitable interval, Alley came dashing back on his horse, waving a paper triumphantly. "It's all right, boys," he shouted. "It's all right!"

Barely pausing to cheer, the Wilberians forthwith stuffed the records into their wagons and departed for the new county seat. Nonetheless, the fact remains that Judge Weaver didn't dissolve the temporary injunction until January 31, three days after the removal of the records, and if anyone knows exactly what was on that slip of paper S. S. Alley carried, in the words of the poet, he ain't saying.

For forty years the issue smouldered; then in 1920 came more pyrotechnics. The old courthouse, built in 1879, was coming apart at the seams, and a new one was needed. Cretans figured this was the opportunity of a lifetime to secure the county seat once and for all. Meanwhile, however, state laws had been enacted providing that only two localities could compete in county-seat removal elections and that there must be a sixty per cent vote in favor of removal. Wilber, of course, would be one of the alternatives on the ballot, but there began to be some doubt about the other when a petition was circulated to locate the courthouse in that still-vacant cornfield in the center of the county. This development evoked loud cries of skulduggery from the Cretans. It was obvious, they said, that the wily Wilberians had instigated the movement just to keep Crete's name off the removal ballot. But the town on the Blue rallied its forces, and in a whirlwind campaign obtained enough signatures to beat the county center competition by a whisker.

The result of the ensuing election could hardly have been better calculated to increase mutual feelings of ill-will: although Crete won out in the balloting, it failed to gain the required sixty per cent majority. It was a crumb of comfort to the Cretans six years later when a bond election for funds to replace the old courthouse also failed to get the necessary majority. During these years Crete had carried its fight to the legislature and the courts, but without success, and bitterness between the towns had grown so great, one Wilberian remembers, that when he went to Crete to visit his parents he stayed strictly on home premises.

When peace came, it was in a way that foreshadowed the Geneva "conference at the summit" three decades later. At the urging of Crete businessmen, who felt the feud had gone too far, a series of meetings was held with representatives from Wilber and other county towns. The felicitous result was a peace resolution, signed and approved on neutral ground in Dorchester, June 7, 1927. At an election the next month, a thumping majority approved bonds for a new courthouse at Wilber, and the imposing structure—surely one of the finest courthouses in Nebraska—was dedicated two years, almost to the day, after hostilities ceased.

The fact that Crete is now the scene of the annual Saline County Fair, its location there being heartily endorsed by the Wilberians, may perhaps suggest how covenants of peace were arrived at.

2. Wilber

WHEN GENERAL John C. Fremont reached the Big Blue River on his Rocky Mountain expedition some hundred and fifteen years ago, he noted: "This is a clear and handsome stream, about 120 feet wide, running with a rapid current through a well-timbered valley." If he were to retrace his steps today, the handsome stream would still lie across his path, but in place of most of the timber he would find well-cultivated river valley farms. After trekking for not quite a mile from the river, across farm land flat as a table top, he would find the town of Wilber located on a slight rise above this fertile valley.

A serene, well-groomed little city, Wilber was in Willa Cather's mind when she wrote that there is a Prague in Nebraska as well as in Bohemia. Though Wilber is by no means exclusively Bohemian, and is becoming less so, an overwhelming majority of its 1,360 residents are of Bohemian extraction. You still hear the Bohemian language spoken on its streets; you still can see a Bohemian language movie once every two weeks in Wilber's only theater; and occasionally, still, an interpreter has to be used in Saline County Court for a witness whose best language is Bohemian rather than English.

Until a decade ago, Bohemian was taught in the schools, but English has become the dominant tongue. However, some of the richness of old Bohemia still remains in Wilber life and customs, imparting a special flavor to the town. One of the most durable of these customs is the dance which follows a wedding—the charivari (pronounced "shivaree"), in Czech, *kocicina*. The bride traditionally wears her veil until midnight, at which hour she ceases to be a bride and becomes a housewife. Her veil is thrown to the waiting girls, and the lucky one to catch it is supposed to be the next bride.

The Bohemian influence is reflected in Wilber's menus—in dishes like Bohemian potato dumplings, kolaches (a happy compromise between a cooky and a fruit tart), Bohemian rye bread, and the wieners and bologna that are the town's best-known products. There was a time, too, when the word Wilber was associated with foaming seidls of beer: there were eleven saloons in or near the town with a brewery to keep them supplied. But a crack-down came in the form of a lightning bolt which incapacitated the brewery, and the number of taverns has dwindled to five.

The local units of the national Sokol and ZCBJ organizations also testify to Wilber's European heritage. Zapadni Cesko-Bratrske Jednoty, or Western Brotherhood Fraternal Organization, began as a fraternal-insurance organization and the insurance aspect is now dominant. Sokol—the word means "falcon"—is primarily devoted to physical fitness. The organization originated in Prague, in 1862, signalizing the awakening of national spirit after two centuries of repression under Austrian rule. Its aims were equality, harmony, and fraternity: physical training for the body, training in patriotism for the mind. The movement spread to America, the first unit being organized in St. Louis in 1865. Best known of the many activities sponsored by Sokol are the *slets*—national and state festivals with mass gymnastic exhibitions and competition between Sokol units.

ZCBJ is a native Nebraska product, founded in Omaha in 1897. It has since spread all over the country, headquarters remaining in Omaha where the group publishes a monthly magazine in Bohemian and English. Both ZCBJ and Sokol lodges often are scenes of the festive wedding dances for which Saline County is noted.

Like most modern farm communities, Wilber has an economy that seeks a boost these days. Some townspeople are commuting ten miles to Crete or seven miles to DeWitt to work in manufactories and other establishments, and some work in Lincoln, forty miles away. Wilberians are watching with great interest the development of the atomic power plant at nearby Hallam. They feel their town will benefit from the plant during the construction phase, and perhaps later as well.

However, when boom days come, you won't find the people of Wilber throwing their money around. Bohemians have a great reputation for thrift, and Wilber's three healthy banks—an unusual number for a town of its size—plus the fact that Saline County consistently ranks with far more populous counties in purchases of U. S. Savings Bonds, are indices that the reputation is no myth.

Adapted from "Community Portrait," Lincoln *Sunday Journal and Star*, July 29, 1956

No such mundane matter as the location of the county seat touched off the feud between Shelby and David City. Aesthetic considerations—and maybe a little home-town pride —were involved in their display of local choler.

War in the Corn

DURING an August week in 1945, one fertile undulating corner of Nebraska produced a bumper crop of artistic excitement. David City and Shelby—18 miles apart—were each sporting a one-man painting exhibition by a native son. Both shows, first ever staged in these Nebraska towns, were smash hits. They were almost too coincidental for comfort. Almost before the ink was dry on the invitations, Shelbyans and David Cityans were hopping mad at each other. There was even talk of letting the artists settle their differences with pitchforks.

Shelby's painter was Terence Duren, frail, 40, ferocious lampooner of womanhood, an ex-Chicago Art Institute instructor, ex-Greenwich Village free-lancer. For the occasion, he dolled up his studio, a former mortuary off Shelby's Main Street, with bouquets of gladioli in milk pails. He also painted his potbellied stove azure and white.

To see his 32 paintings, 700 persons—more than the population of Shelby (627)—paid 50¢ each, stood two- and three-abreast in line, in their Sunday best. Among them was a blind woman with a seeing-eye dog, who had two friends describe the pictures to her.

The opposition (but not planned that way, insists David Cityans) was a showing of 28 oils by 41-year-old Dale Nichols, art editor of the Encyclopedia Britannica, and a nationally-known painter of Christmas-cardish Midwestern landscapes and Greyhound bus ads. Nichols' specialties are heart-warming red barns, picturesque blue snowhills, tree branches reaching to cobalt skies.

Both artists set out to show Nebraskans what their state looks like. Ranged on the walls of a David City municipal basketball court, Dale Nichols' pictures said it was a slick, sweet place. In Shelby's old mortuary, Terence Duren posted a tougher pictorial message. In his canvases, picnic wrappings were left on the ground, fat rolls and wrinkles decorated ladies' faces.

It was too much for Artist Nichols. Said he: "Some of these paintings disturb me. In *Art Heritage* * I suspect that Mr. Duren is looking with a critical eye upon my Nebraska friends and neighbors. If he is ashamed or bored or scornful of Nebraska life, may I clarify his erroneous thinking?"

Nichols further ventured that Duren should paint in a spirit which regards manure not as horrible filth but as a farmer's God-given instrument. Countered Duren: "I refer to manure but seldom. . . . I regard it as neither horrific nor as beautiful but merely as unimportant detail. Obviously Mr. Nichols finds it appealing."

Fellow-townsmen took sides. Little Shelby accused bigger David City (pop. 2,272) of stealing Duren's thunder with the Nichols show. The artists themselves took up prepared positions behind cornstalks and blazed away. Nichols: "I shall never be guilty of painting in the style or viewpoint of Terence Duren. Never! Never!" Duren: "It is easy to recognize that Mr. Nichols cannot draw people . . . save at the safe distance at which he conceals all lack of anatomical detail. I concur heartily: Mr. Nichols will never draw or paint like I do. Never!"

Reprinted from *Time*, August 20, 1945. © Time, Inc., 1945

* Three vacuous frumps depicted with an assortment of gimcracky "art objects."

What did you do before TV, Daddy?"

*To the generation whose birth was coeval with that of
commercial television, life without TV—and the radio and
motion pictures—must be almost inconceivable. Yet professional entertainment in the form of a "package show"
was available in pre-radio-and-TV days, even to farm families living so far out that their only regular outside contact was the bi-weekly visit of the R.F.D. carrier.*

*To view it required more exertion than twirling a knob,
but it was "live" entertainment and, what's more, there
was an "audience-participation" feature which at the very
least meant a picnic, and might even run to ten days of
camping out.*

We Liked Chautauqua

KATHERINE BUXBAUM

I WONDER how the historian of the future will deal with the Chautauqua movement, whose brief hour of success coincides with the
early years of this century. It has been the fashion to treat the Chautauqua assemblies as just another huge American joke, something
which gave gaping rustics a chance to enjoy second- or third-rate entertainment and persuaded them that they were absorbing culture.
I confess that this light treatment has never suited one midwest community where the Chautauqua was a going concern for nearly thirty
years. Or else we've shrugged a little and said, "Oh, well, maybe
that was your Chautauqua. Now, ours was different."

It was different. For one thing, it was what was known as an Independent. The talent was mostly hand-picked, and the picking was
good in those days. Jane Addams, for instance. There was nothing
shoddy about her. William Jennings Bryan was the man of the hour,
crusading always, it is true; but even if he and Billy Sunday and
Carrie Nation were the sensation of their day, they were vigorous
personalities, good to see and hear. Lecturers on movements such as
the Montessori system of education broke ground for contact with the
world of ideas. We heard them gladly.

Church-going folk being well represented among the stockholders of our Chautauqua, there were plenty of lectures that kept up the tone of the parent institution. For many years the day's session opened with a Bible lecture by a clergyman-professor, who would present a series of background studies for an understanding of Scripture; or, perhaps, a symposium of ethical teaching.

The Chautauqua booklets, those printed programs containing photographs of the talent, publicity notices, and advertisers' blurbs, make interesting reading now. I quote from the foreword of the very first one. The year was 1903:

> The Chautauqua goes back to first principles, and the schools are held in groves as Plato taught, walking among the trees. . . . It is a beautiful commingling of nature and art. Thus we may commune with nature and enjoy the feasts of reason that are prepared for us. . . .
> For a family outing Chautauqua is the most reasonable and decorous scheme yet devised. We learn a lot, and we learn it in the most agreeable way, by surrendering our think-tanks for an hour or two to some pleasing personality like Sam Jones, Booker T. Washington, or Hobson.

The merchants were frankly less concerned with such matters. Plato's noble brow and the think-tanks of the present did not impress them. One wrote his ad thus:

> Everybody and his girl will be going to the big Chautauqua picnic tomorrow, and you will want to be in it with the swells who are wearing the fashionable jewelry we sell.

"Chautauqua picnic" was not a figure of speech. The oak grove at the edge of town was ideal for camping. People pitched tents, laid in provisions, and lived for the ten days on the grounds. The little canvas town with the Big Top, which was the auditorium, in the center had a genuinely festive air. No wonder we whipped up the horses when we caught sight of it.

For a farm family like ours, it took some maneuvering to get to the morning sessions. Even the history lecture which followed the Bible hour was a hurdle for us. It meant unusually early rising, breathless haste with chores and breakfast, extra bathing and dressing, and packing the noonday lunch, for we were too thrifty to eat at the dining tent on the grounds. It meant hitching up the team, and then eight miles of jogging over a dusty road, facing the sun on a sweltering August day.

When we reached the tent, we had brief moments of envy when we tumbled, flushed and perspiring, into our seats on the bleachers. Down below us was the circle of chairs where the townfolk sat, looking very cool, very composed, in an atmosphere of serenely moving fans. The speaker would be talking of Napoleon or Bismarck; or he might have beguiled his hearers back into some antique world which seemed, for the moment, as real as their own.

I do not remember that the lectures ever dealt with contemporary affairs. For us, "history" concerned what was past. We had not learned to call it "social science." One series which the professor gave did, however, furnish a valuable perspective on our own day. It dealt with such great crises in history as the struggle for race supremacy; for independence; for constitutional sovereignty; for majority rule.

The program booklets furnish abundant evidence of shifting points of view. Even the cuts are edifying, with their record of changing fashions, the managers' sideburns and the towering pompadours of the women speakers giving way to smooth-shaven faces and bobbed hair. Lecture topics are eloquent of attitudes; the romantic view of war held the center of the stage until 1920. Of the Civil War veterans who addressed us, I remember best Bishop McCabe. I met with an accident the day he was there: just as I opened my mouth to take a bite of our picnic chicken, a honeybee flew in and stung me on the tongue. It took some eloquence on the part of the speaker to help me forget my pain, but the Bishop's did just that. He knew exactly how to play upon our emotions; and when he described the call Lincoln made for volunteers to end more swiftly the strife that was rending the nation apart, he climaxed his recital with the song that was the answer of the North: "We're coming, we're coming, Father Abraham, with three hundred thousand more!"

The War of '98 produced no hero more popular than Captain Hobson of osculating fame. We had him, of course. The 1905 program featured a man who spoke on "The Evolution of Firearms." Curiously enough, the publicity for this has a sprightly tone. It says: "This gentleman has made an invention which bids fair to revolutionize modern warfare," and adds that he and a colleague "will be on hand with a batch of machine guns." But after 1919 a new note appears. Private Peat and Norman Hall did not extol the glories of war. These young veterans chose subjects that showed the direction thought was taking then: "The Destiny of Democracy"; "America's Part in the World's Future"; "Secret Diplomacy and Sudden War."

Internal politics, being of perennial interest, got much publicity and drew good crowds. If two United States senators engaged in debate, that was no sham battle. In one of these, "Pitchfork" Tillman gave a performance that was up to his best, laying about him with words that stabbed like his chosen symbol. I do not remember what he was inveighing against. I only know that he was fighting mad. But Bryan, who addressed us three different seasons, gradually banked the fires of his political ardor. In 1921 he was still crusading, but this time in the interests of the other grand passion of his life. His topic now was "Brute or Brother?" and to this he addressed himself with all his old-time fervor.

One feature of the Chautauqua which was then decidedly novel as lecture material was the serious consideration of diet in relation to personal health. The subject was popularized by a contingent of food experts from the Battle Creek laboratories. How new and exciting their talk seemed then: "The Miracle of Digestion"; "Common Food Adulteration"; "How to Convert Labor into Health and Happiness." But although these people talked sense part of the time, we regarded them as food faddists, one and all. Try to make a farming community leave off eating so much meat and substitute things made of nuts!

The diet of lectures was spiced, of course, with lighter entertainment. On the days when the magician or the chalk-talk artist appeared, the gate receipts were sure to increase. Then there was the field which the colleges, abhorring the term "elocution," now designate so tamely as "speech." "Theater" with us was still a term of doubtful import. "Plays" we had, but it was understood that these were "home talent." But one must have theater, call it what you will. The Chautauqua, in those early years, called it impersonation. "The little elocutionist, famous for her Baby Cry act," was much in demand.

Really excellent bands, orchestras, and choruses introduced us to the classics. Airs from operas became, after a few seasons, as familiar as "Home Sweet Home." Welsh choirs that had taken prizes at the Eisteddfodd introduced us to a different type of music, beautiful and strange. The Negro choruses were something else again. Groups like The Dixie Singers, The Jubilee Singers, and quartets from Fisk University gave us our first glimpse of the artist soul of the black folk. Now for the first time we heard "spirituals" spoken of. Was it possible that the songs we had always treated as rather comic had such deep springs of emotion?

Yes, we liked Chautauqua. And although its usefulness came to an end with the dawn of the thirties, some of us were loath to give it up. After a while most people had a pole out by the garage and a boxful of tubes within the house from which they could draw more entertainment than they could find time to listen to; but, even so, some loyal patrons kept on coming to Chautauqua instead of staying at home with the new plaything. Nobody made any money from the enterprise. Money laid out for community welfare does not reappear in the profit column of the ledger. But in the bitter years that followed, when people found their "securities" scraps of paper in their hands, this investment in human happiness must have looked to those who paid for it positively gilt-edged.

Condensed from *Prairie Schooner,* Fall, 1944

*After two years of dust storms, of drought, of destroyed
crops, the writer drove more than two hundred miles
through farming country. It was one of the worst spring
days of those storms, impossible to see a hundred yards on
the highway, and yet old men and young men, blackened
with flying dust, were putting seed into the parched earth.
Many will not understand that. It takes a sublime faith
when hope seems so futile, a grandeur of spirit which
springs from the soil.*

—James E. Lawrence, *Review of Reviews,* June, 1936

Holdrege

ROBERT HOUSTON

IT WAS to be a gala evening for Holdrege. On that night in the mid-
thirties the great Stokowski and his Philadelphia Symphony, making
a tour of the nation's large cities, were to give a performance in this
"sticks" town of 3,000. The day had been hot and dusty, but late in
the afternoon the skies blackened and hail beat down, riddling the
roof of Holdrege's City Auditorium. After the hail came a pelting
rain.

But the concert went on. "Stoki" and his musicians were as game as
Holdrege's music lovers. Listeners brought their umbrellas and sat
under them all through the program. And Stokowski's harpist
strummed the strings while a stage hand held an umbrella over the
instrument. It was rather a black night for Holdrege, but it was
heartening too, and, in a way, symbolic. In those days of depression
and drought Holdrege had hit the depths. But the perverse elements
hadn't driven the people off the land, and couldn't keep the community from enjoying its favorite cultural fare—good music.

The little city was down but not out. From the depths, the only
way it could go was up; and today, thanks chiefly to irrigation in
Phelps County, Holdrege is husky and thriving. Its population grew
thirty per cent during the '40's, reaching 4,381 in the 1950 census,
and the expansion goes on. The town is still building close to one
hundred houses a year in an effort to catch up with the housing
shortage.

One of the things that Holdrege has attended to is the City Auditorium. Because of the community's tastes, such a building has meant far more than it does to the average small city. Holdrege's first opera house, with a seating capacity of 650, had been replaced in 1916 by an auditorium seating 2,300 persons. It was not pretty—in fact, it looked like nothing so much as a big barn—but such famed singers as Galli-Curci, Alda, Schumann-Heink, and John McCormack appeared there. Auto shows were held annually, but these were dropped as the depression deepened. However, in 1933—Holdrege's fiftieth anniversary year—the Chamber of Commerce named a ten-man group to promote auditorium activities. Its members called themselves the Sod Busters, and each put up a hundred dollars as guarantee money in obtaining talent. The Sod Busters brought in Stokowski, civic opera companies from New York and Chicago, the Navy and Marine bands, and leading dance orchestras.

Around 1943 the auditorium stockholders turned the building over to the city, and in 1948 the citizens voted a $125,000 bond issue for improving it inside and out. Since then Holdrege has had a Community Concert Association which brings five top-flight musical attractions a year. The Association membership has grown from 500 to 1,600, and Holdrege continues to be by far the smallest town on the itinerary of some of the musical groups. Although the Sod Busters organization dissolved, the name is carried on by a saddle club whose 60 members go on trail rides and picnics, take part in parades, and do what they can to boost their indomitable home town.

The original sod-busters came in to Phelps County back in the '70's. On arriving at the center of the county, just north of present-day Holdrege, a member of an immigrating party wrote:

As far as the eye could reach in any direction not a sign of human habitation was visible except about three miles southeast where [land agents for the railroad company] were building an Emigrant House and digging a well for the accommodation of the colonists. Nothing but miles and miles of level prairie burned black by the prairie fires. Hundreds of thousands of bleaching buffalo skeletons are scattered over the plains. . . .

But the settlers were undaunted by this bleak picture, and they broke the buffalo-grass sod.

Ten years after Phelps County was organized, Holdrege came into existence. It owed its founding to the Burlington Railroad and in particular to George Holdrege, for years the Burlington's general manager west of the Missouri. It was Mr. Holdrege who talked rail officials into extending a line into Phelps County. Rainfall wasn't great, and there was little surface water, but the soil was very rich.

The town was laid out in 1883, and late that year Burlington trains began bringing in settlers of Swedish extraction from the Galesburg area in Illinois. Until recently, people of Swedish descent outnumbered all others in Holdrege. Now only about forty per cent of the names in the phone book are Swedish. (However, there are ninety-one Johnsons and only seven Smiths.)

Until the last decade, Holdrege reflected the ups and downs of the farming community surrounding it. "You could almost gamble on a wet year every seven years," says one resident. "In between, rainfall was up and down. If you could hold out for seven years, you were all right." But the rich soil suffered as time went by because rainfall was insufficient to allow farmers to rotate legume crops with their corn and wheat crops.

In the dry '30's, Holdrege and the county faced a bleak future, as L. J. Titus, president of the Holdrege First National Bank, can tell you. Deposits in the bank, which had been started in 1888, had dropped to one million dollars in 1936.

"After graduating from college in 1935," Mr. Titus says, "I returned to Holdrege and worked in the bank for a year during those dust-storm days. Then I went to my Dad, who was president of the bank, and informed him that the town was going to the dogs. 'I can get a better job somewhere else,' I said. My Dad said, 'Son, wait a year, and if the irrigation project for Phelps County doesn't go through, I'll leave with you.' "

The Tri-County irrigation project in the Platte River Valley was assured in 1937, and the Tituses and a lot of others decided to stay. In 1946, the younger Mr. Titus took over the presidency, the third generation in his family to occupy that post, and now the bank has more than eight millions in deposits.

"I think I'm here to stay all right," says Mr. Titus with a grin.

The first waters from the Platte spilled onto farms in the north half of Phelps County in 1941. But under the water diversion laws, the Platte River watershed stopped about four miles north of Holdrege, and efforts of the county's residents to extend that area have failed. "We're ready to give up on that," says Mr. Titus, "and from now on, in the southern part of the county, farmers will drill more wells to provide irrigation water."

A campaign is being waged to cross-grid the county with natural gas lines, providing cheaper power for the water pumps. There were several hundred pumps at the start of 1954, and an estimated 600 more will be put down some 150 feet to tap the supply that runs under all but the two southwestern townships.

In 1941, when the first 13,000 acres were irrigated, value of crops totaled $1,841,650. Eleven years later crop values had soared to $11,711,122. In 1941, says Mr. Titus, there were only five cattle-raisers in the county, and the value of all the livestock was a little more than a million dollars. Now the value is in excess of six million dollars, and livestock sales annually gross better than $1,500,000.

This sudden increase in production has changed the looks of Holdrege: it has become a bulging grain storage center. The Production Marketing Association of Phelps County has close to a million bushels in storage. The Equity Exchange has 250,000 bushels of grain storage space as does the Holdrege Roller Mills. The roller mill, incidentally, has been operated by the Johnson family for more than 50 years. It manufactures flour and feed, and is one of the last "family flour mills ' left in Nebraska.

One of the fastest growing businesses has been the Holdrege Seed and Farm Supply Company, started in 1942. Its biggest line is farm seed, but the company supplies theaters from coast to coast with popcorn, and produces a line of fertilizer. Another thriving firm is the Nebraska Dairy Products Company, which sells milk to an area extending as far west as McCook and to a number of towns and cities to the east of Holdrege. The Phelps County Creamery is a large employer, with 85 persons on the payroll. Besides processing dairy products, the plant has an egg-cracking and -drying unit.

In line with the pattern of Nebraska's post-war industrial boom, Holdrege has a couple of small industrial firms, and most Holdrege businessmen agree that the city needs more. They cite the example of the Allmand brothers, who went into partnership some years ago in a garage and blacksmith shop. In 1947 they put up a $40,000 building where they turn out arc welders, stand-by generators, and other electrical products. The branch plant of the Platte Valley Tile Company of Scottsbluff and Fremont, employing 25, has been manufacturing tiles in Holdrege since 1948.

Almost half of the community's 134 business firms were started since World War II. Evidence of prosperity is the list of seven new car dealers, one of whom recently built an $80,000 plant. There are twelve automotive firms and seven farm implement dealers.

One of the city's largest employers is the Brewster Clinic and

Hospital, founded by Dr. Frank A. Brewster, once known as the state's first flying doctor. It is a 57-bed hospital and has 71 employees. On the medical staff with Dr. Brewster are his two sons and three other physicians. The doctor is one of Holdrege's most remarkable citizens. In 1951 he decided to retire, bought a farm, and had fun riding around on a tractor. But two years later there was a doctor shortage in Franklin, Nebraska, so Dr. Brewster set up a clinic in Franklin and now, at the age of 81, works there six days a week and checks in at the home clinic on Sundays.

One of his sons, Dr. Wayne Brewster, is president of the corporation which operates KHOL-TV, Holdrege's TV station, which was promoted by Holdrege and Alma investors. The Holdrege paper, the *Daily Citizen,* is only one year younger than the town. A daily since 1937, it moved into enlarged quarters in 1954.

Since the dust-storm years of the '30's, Holdrege has acquired a fine city hall housing all municipal activities, a $138,000 armory for the city's National Guard unit, two new grade schools which cost nearly a half-million, Memorial Homes, Inc., a non-profit home for the elderly, and such recreational facilities as one of the largest and most beautiful swimming pools in the state.

It was just 80 years ago that the first sod-busters looked out over the miles of blackened prairie, hitched up their britches, and fell to with the breaking plow. The present generation, it would seem, has not lost the knack.

Condensed from the Omaha *World-Herald Sunday Magazine,* June 6, 1954

Cedartown sits beside a great highway which was once a buffalo trail. If you start in one direction on the highway—and travel far enough—you will come to the effete east. If you start in the opposite direction—and travel a few hundred miles farther—you will come to the distinctive west. Cedartown is neither effete nor distinctive, nor is it even particularly pleasing to the passing tourist. It is beautiful only in the eyes of those who live here and in the memories of the Nebraska-born whose dwelling in far places has given them moments of homesickness for the low rolling hills, the swell and dip of ripening wheat, the fields of sinuously waving corn, and the elusively fragrant odor of alfalfa.

There are weeks when drifting snow and sullen sleet hold the Cedartown community in their bitter grasp. There are times when hot winds come out of the southwest and parch it with their feverish breath. There are periods of monotonous drought and periods of dreary rain; but between those onslaughts there are days so perfect, so filled with clover odors and the rich, pungent smell of newly turned loam, so sumac-laden and apple-burdened, that to the prairie-born there are no others as lovely by mountain or lake or sea.

—Bess Streeter Aldrich, *A Lantern in Her Hand*

Elmwood

BESS STREETER ALDRICH

THERE are fiction writers who would have us believe that just three types of people inhabit small midwestern towns. There are those who are discontented, wanting to get away; there are those who are too dumb to know enough to want to get away; and the rest are half-wits. Not qualifying for the first section, I must, perforce, belong somewhere down the line.

Our town is small. In fact, to speak of our "town" at all is rank hyperbole, for it is not even a town but is incorporated as a village. It is so small that, with the exception of Main, the streets are not called by their names, and you have to look on a map or an abstract to find out what they are. We glibly say "over by Clement's" and "down by the high school," and in the last few years have been putting on airs by saying "across the park" instead of "the meadow." It is so small that we have to go to the post office for our mail, where the postmaster knows everyone so well that a letter coming in one day addressed briefly to "Clara," minus any surname, immediately found its owner by the process of elimination. It is so small that whether you choose to or not you are obliged to hear the band practice every Monday night in the old G.A.R. Hall. Not that it is such a hardship. To be sure, its repertoire may not be so extensive as the late Mr. Sousa's and it may be top-heavy with brass, but it's a good little band at that.

"Tell me why you continue to live in a small town," wrote the editor. The question makes me stop and wonder. Perhaps it's just inertia—just small-town stagnation. But I do not think so.

It is true that I do not always stay here. Out of the twelve months of the past year, five of them were spent away—three on the West Coast and two in the pine-and-lake region of northern Minnesota. But my home is here. Good friends are here. I live and do my work here where the streets go unnamed, and the one train and one bus each way per day slip through town with few passengers, and the band lustily executes Poet and Peasant and Under the Double Eagle March.

No one and no circumstances are compelling me to remain. In the eight years since my husband's death, there has not been a day that I might not have packed the typewriter and moved to Lincoln or Omaha or to any big city east or west. Not that I depreciate the many advantages of living in one of them, but to me they are for visiting, and my little town for home.

It was just twenty-three years ago that as a young married woman with a two-month-old baby girl in my arms I arrived at the boxlike station and was met by my husband, who had preceded me by a few weeks. I had not wanted to come to Nebraska. My earliest recollection of hearing the name of the state was a picture of my mother sending me over to the church basement with some old clothes and dried apples which she explained were to be sent to the poor folks out in Nebraska. The impression persisted, so that when my husband and my sister's husband negotiated for the purchase of the bank here, I was not at all enthusiastic about the move. I did not want to wear old clothes, and I did not want to eat dried apples.

On the day on which we arrived there was a typical Nebraska dust storm of no modest or refined proportions under way. Si Mairs, whom the menfolks had hired to meet us, was at the station with a two-seated surrey and team to take the women of the party up to the cottage that my husband had rented. Because the wind was blowing so hard that I would not trust my baby out of my arms, my husband and my brother-in-law wheeled the empty cab up to the house, while my sister, mother, the baby and I rode in state with Si. Si was not sure which of three cottages at the end of the street was the one Mr. Aldrich had rented, but it did not take me long to pick it out, for through the blasts of dust I could see my best upholstered rocking chair, a wedding present, sitting on a little porch with an arm hanging limply down at its side, evidently broken in shipping.

Through the gusts of dirt we hurried up to the little cottage, and it was then that I had my first taste of Nebraska small-town hospitality. Si's sister had come in to get the dinner, which was all ready for us. On my stove and with my own dishes she had prepared a delicious meal for the strangers, that they might feel welcome.

I have experienced it a thousand times since—that warm-hearted hospitality, loyal friendship, and deep sympathy of the small town. And it is these characteristics and others of the better features of the small town and its people that I have tried to stress in my short stories and books. . . .

Once a story of mine, syndicated in a newspaper, carried in brackets an indulgent explanation from an editor that the writer "goes right down into small towns and mingles among the people for her material." Could anything sound more smug? As if I had gone slumming with drawn skirts. I have not gone small-townish for material. I *am* small-townish.

Of course, to be honest, I admit I would not choose this little place if I were driving across country seeking a town into which to move. I may have expressed something of that in the introduction to *A Lantern in Her Hand,* for, while the Cedartown of the story is fictitious, it is frankly located in this section of the country.

After all, it is contact and familiarity that help endear people and places to us. I came here in a happy day, and perhaps I am trying to cling to old happiness. As I write, I have only to glance outside my study window to see in the cement of the driveway the tracings of a fat hand with grotesque square fingers, a date of nine years ago, and the straggling initials C. S. A. I have one son who has always had a perfect obsession for leaving his footprints, not only on the sands of time but in every piece of new cement about the place. There are hands and feet of every size, width, and length on sidewalks, driveways, steps, and posts, all duly signed and dated. It would be absurd to say that the sight of that traced hand outside my study window holds me here, but it may readily be a symbol of all that does. It would not be possible for me to follow four young people with widely diversified tastes and talents out into the world—and to keep the home with its old associations means more to me than any advantage gained by moving cityward.

This is the home my sons and daughter knew in childhood, and I have a notion that in this rather hectic day of complicated life it is well for young people to have some substantial tie which still holds them to the anchor of unchanging things. You cannot break the radii of love which stretch out from the center of a good home. They are the most flexible things in the world. They pull at the hearts of the children until sometime, somewhere, they draw the wanderers all back into the family circle.

Small-town people are popularly supposed to be narrow. And yet are the realities of life narrowing? Birth? Marriage? Death? Small-town life is not artificial. It need not be superficial. Calvin Coolidge, in his autobiography, has expressed it in his simple, effective way: "Country life does not always have breadth, but it has depth." Small-town people are no longer mere isolated villagers. Although the whiskered farmer gent with the straw in his mouth is still the joy of the cartoonists, there is no character which adequately represents the Main Street man. Small-town people move about now, go places.

When I was a little girl, we used to drive six miles out in the country to an uncle's—jog . . . jog . . . jog over the country roads. And, incidentally, it had one advantage. It gave us time to see things—pink bouncing Bets at the side of the road . . . a meadow lark's nest . . . all the little wild things that we so easily overlook, now while the needle trembles toward sixty. From our small town, in far less time than those six miles used to consume, we drive on a paved road up to Lincoln; an hour in the opposite direction finds us in the still larger Omaha. Our physician and his wife recently took a Cuban trip . . . a young chap has just gone down to see South America for a month . . . my daughter's girlhood chum across the street studied music in Paris last summer. Even Heinie Mollen, the cobbler, put down his hammer last fall and went out to take a look at Hollywood to see if the stars really looked like the pictures tacked up on the walls of his shop.

A small town is a good place for a writer to live. Not only is he close to the people, and so close to life in the raw, but also it keeps him humble. For instance, if you are a professional writer, living in a small town, perhaps on the day on which you are coming home from the post office with a letter from the committee that a story of yours has been judged one of the best of the year and chosen for the O. Henry Memorial Award volume, you meet an old man who stops you and says: "Say, I just been readin' one of your stories." Ah, you think, everyone reads them—the O. Henry committee, young people, middle-aged, old men; babies cry for them. "Yep," he says, "it was the one in the—Well, I forget the magazine, but it's one my daughter takes." You overlook a little thing like that and wait for him to go on. "Anyway, the name of the story was—Say," he apologizes, "that slips me too." Oh, well, that's a mere bagatelle. What's a title? "Anyway," he brightens, "the story was about—" He takes off his cap and scratches his head. "Don't that beat you? I clean forget what the darn thing was about."

And there you are. If a story was not clean-cut enough for a nice old man to remember overnight, it wasn't very good.

Then there was the time I had received the annual report showing that a book of mine had been third in sales for the entire country for the year. With that rather pleasant bit of news uppermost in my mind, I went to a little social affair in my small town. When I sat down among the ladies, I made a remark about just coming home from Lincoln—that I had not been there in five weeks. A little woman looked up from her fancywork and said:

"Did you say you hadn't been there for five weeks? Well, isn't that queer! I was in Lincoln yesterday myself and stopped to buy some groceries. When I gave the groceryman a check he said, 'I see you're from the town where Bess Streeter Aldrich lives. I suppose you know her?' Now, will you tell me," she questioned earnestly, "if you hadn't been in Lincoln for five weeks, how that groceryman could have remembered your name all that length of time?"

Humble? I'll say they keep you humble. A prophet in her own village isn't a prophet at all, but just a woman who buys groceries. And isn't that as it should be?

Extracted from "Why I Live in a Small Town," *Ladies' Home Journal*, June, 1933 Reprinted by special permission. Copyright 1953 by The Curtis Publishing Company

Nebraska has been described as the state the west begins in the middle of. However questionable the syntax of this observation, it does point up the fact that in Eastern Nebraska the way of life is predominately middlewestern, while Western Nebraska—particularly the Panhandle region—is plain unvarnished western.

There is more to Nebraska's dual personality than meets the eye. The difference in point of view is a basic one. On a few occasions when there has been a collision between these views, the independent, plain-spoken Westerners have expressed their feelings about Eastern Nebraska by threatening to secede. But tempers cool, and the commonwealth remains intact. During times of truce, all hands agree that the East-West diversity is a beneficial, if sometimes unpalatable, tonic for the state.

Born with the twentieth century, the metropolis of Western Nebraska is the dynamic, optimistic, ambitious city of Scottsbluff.

Scottsbluff

ROBERT YOUNG

AFTER his unsuccessful attempt to nominate one Joe Smith for the vice presidency at the 1956 Republican Convention, Delegate Terry Carpenter of Scottsbluff was besieged with questions about the strangely anonymous candidate he had pulled out of his sleeve. If there was a Joe Smith, where did he live? What did he do? Mr. Carpenter, who has been variously described as a "one-man business boom" (Scottsbluff *Star-Herald*) and a "political cuckoo" (*Time*), obliged with the information that Joe lived in Terrytown—a housing development owned by Mr. Carpenter—and was "a retired fellow."

"Retired from what?" asked a reporter.

"From work," stated Mr. Carpenter, thereby making it crystal-clear to anyone remotely acquainted with Scottsbluff that Joe Smith existed only in Mr. Carpenter's imagination. A Scottsbluff man might retire from his job—yes, sure. But retire from work? Nonsense!

Less easily resolved is the question as to whether Scottsbluff people just happened to be born endowed with a double charge of
free-swinging energy, an extra supply of resourcefulness, and an
unusual aptitude for keeping their eye on the ball, or whether these
characteristics were developed in the course of the struggle to put
their town on the map. In any case it's apparent from the record that,
if not innately go-getters, they certainly qualified for the rating in
one hell of a hurry. In 1899 Scottsbluff was an alfalfa field. In less
than a decade it had overcome the johnny-come-lately handicap of
its proximity to two established trading centers—Gering, just across
the river to the south, and Mitchell, nine miles to the northwest—
and was firmly established as the leading town in Scotts Bluff
County. Before its fiftieth anniversary it was the principal city in
western Nebraska and eastern Wyoming.

It would be wrong, however, to infer that rivalry with neighboring
towns is the theme of the Scottsbluff story, and the attainment of its
present dominant position the pay-off. While they have remained
intensely competitive, the people of the North Platte Valley region
learned long ago to work in concert for the common good. The isolated location of this irrigated area four hundred miles west of
Nebraska's capital and centers of population, plus what valley inhabitants regard as indifference to their needs and ignorance of
their problems on the part of the legislature and the rest of the
state, have resulted in an uncommon degree of regional solidarity
and a strong feeling of community of interests. Moreover, as Scottsbluff's citizens are the first to admit—and as is true wherever commerce and industry are based on agriculture—the growth and
prosperity of a city only mirror the growth and prosperity of the
land around it.

Nebraska's historian, Dr. James C. Olson, summarizes the parallel
development of town and country in Scotts Bluff County this way:

In 1900 it had a population of only 2,552. By 1930, however, it had become the fourth most populous county in the state, and in 1940 it ranked
third and was first in density of rural farm population. By 1940 the city
of Scottsbluff, which in 1900 had been only a little huddle of tar-paper
shacks, ranked sixth in the state. In the value of crops produced, the county
ran well ahead of every other county in the state, with the margin being
greatly increased during dry years. The county's agricultural economy was
based to a large degree upon specialized cash crops—sugar beets, potatoes,
beans, and canning crops—grown under irrigation. In each of these it
ranked first in the state and produced a sizable proportion of the state's entire production—from about one-half to three-fourths. Irrigation farmers also

grew alfalfa, corn, barley, and oats for livestock feed. Other aspects of the economy reflected the high efficiency of the county's agriculture. In 1940 the county ranked third in manufacturing and third in retail sales. In freight shipments Scottsbluff was second only to Omaha.*

Since it is customary to account for Scottsbluff's jet-propelled rise by pointing to such factors as its strategic location in the heart of the valley, the irrigation ditches, its beet-sugar factory, and the demands created by the North Platte Valley agricultural empire, perhaps it also should be pointed out that in 1900 the location seemed more redundant than strategic, the ditches had yet to be dug, the factory had yet to be built, and if anyone had referred to the North Platte Valley as an agricultural empire, he would have been led gently away by a man with a net.

Scotts Bluff County had been organized in 1888, one of four created by the partitioning of Cheyenne County, which originally had comprised the whole southern half of the Panhandle. In 1889, after considerable acrimony and two elections, Gering, a centrally located town on the North Platte River, was named county seat. Eleven years went by—years signalized chiefly by the first real attempts to practice irrigation—and then along came Scottsbluff, riding on the back of the Burlington. The railroad having decided to extend its line through the North Platte Valley, the town-site was selected and laid out by a Burlington subsidiary, the Lincoln Land Company, and in mid-February, 1900, when the Burlington construction crews reached Scottsbluff, the curtain went up.

At once the scene exploded into activity. By March, the town had two store buildings (the first completed, Andy McClenahan's, was dedicated with a dance), a hotel, a church, and the beginnings of a post office, in the back part of which the newly appointed postmaster, Charles H. Simmons (whose son Robert was to be Chief Justice of the Nebraska State Supreme Court) installed his family while their Gering log house was disassembled, the roof sawed in quarters, the logs numbered for reassembly, and the structure carted across the river by team. In April, E. T. Westervelt of Gering, who

* According to the U.S. Bureau of the Census, 1954, Scotts Bluff County was first in Nebraska in sugar beets, fourth in the U.S.; first in the state in sheep and lambs, eighth in number and fifth in value in the U.S.; first in the state in potatoes, twenty-eighth in acreage and thirtieth in bushels in the U.S.; seventh in the state in cattle (numbers) and sixth (value), forty-first and thirty-first respectively in the U.S. According to the *Sales Management Survey of Buying Power*, May, 1956, in Gross Cash Farm Income Scotts Bluff County ranked seventy-sixth in the U.S., and in Nebraska was second only to Cuming County (sixty-sixth in the U.S.). The same source lists the present population of the city of Scottsbluff as 13,700.

had just finished a term as county sheriff, announced plans to publish a weekly paper, the *Republican,* and moved his family into
temporary quarters at the Presbyterian church while he built himself
a newspaper building.

May was a time of crisis and agonized indecision for Gering. The
land company was wooing Gering businessmen with offers of free
lots, and there was an evening when they agreed to move en masse
to the new town. Minds changed the next day—but not all of them,
and the exodus continued.

In June the town builders decided that to delay incorporation
would only delay needed civic improvements, and by extending the
proposed corporate limits to include a number of farms, jacked up
the population high enough to qualify Scottsbluff for village status.
On June 22, the petition to incorporate was granted and Frank
McCreary appointed chairman of the board of trustees, whose members barely took time out to inspect the town's first brick building,
Spry & Soder's saloon, before going into executive session over the
problem of how to tap the Mitchell Valley trade.

Some of the richest farms in the county were located there, but unfortunately to reach Scottsbluff these prospective customers had to
go a roundabout way through Gering, the result being they never
made it. A bridge affording a direct route was the board's recommendation, the voters forthwith approved a $6,500 bond issue to
finance it, the contract was let, and construction started promptly.
It stopped just as promptly when it was discovered that the board,
in its eagerness to start the ball rolling, had run the bond advertisements one issue short of the number required by law—a slight error
that made the bonds worthless. Buttonholing the contractors, eloquent board members, property owners, and merchants made a
succession of such persuasive pitches that work was resumed with
hardly the loss of a day. A new bond issue was authorized and the
Mitchell Valley bridge completed in time to make Scottsbluff's first
Yule a merry one.

Apparently most of the first-comers were equipped with a fair
complement of children: at any rate, about the same time they embarked on the bridge-building venture, the city fathers felt called
on to provide a school. For a community that could not have numbered two hundred persons to undertake two such projects simul-
taneously might well have overtaxed the nerves of a tribe of brass
monkeys, yet when it stubbed its toe on another legal stumbling
block, the board lost none of its *sang-froid.* Shrugging off the fact

that the legal bonding limit of the school district was $1,400 and the cost of the building $4,800, it issued warrants in the full amount needed, and John A. Orr bought them. The illegality of this procedure worried no one, least of all Mr. Orr. He knew he'd get his money in due time, and the town got its school immediately.

In their aggressive, unconventional handling of the bridge and school projects, and in their application of the principles of team play, Scottsbluff's businessmen had hit upon a formula for effective action which was to pay many a future dividend. For the time being, however, Scottsbluff was still losing out to Gering and Mitchell in the fight for the farmers' trade, was still the underdog, and pickings were slim.

Those were arduous years, but they were colorful, boisterous years too: the business of building a city did not go at such a frenetic pace that there was no time for fun. Almost as soon as there were nine people in Scottsbluff there was a baseball team; before very long its inevitable concomitant, a band. The women organized a library club which held regular meetings and staged art exhibits; there were Fourth of July celebrations, and dances at McClenahan's hall, and such gala affairs as oyster suppers and strawberry sociables, sponsored—unlikely as it may seem—by the Women's Cemetery Association to raise funds for the cemetery. There were cowboys still around in those days, clattering their cayuses up and down the board walks to the fury of the merchants, and on Saturday nights a fair amount of revolver ammunition was fired, but seldom at anybody. When the town voted dry in 1907, much of the rowdyism and some of the color disappeared with the saloons.

By then, the era of the big ditches was in full swing, and Scottsbluff was in the catbird's seat. In 1904 and 1905 thousands of men had come into the area to work on the Interstate and Laramie canals for the government reclamation service, and on the Farmers Canal for Heyward G. Leavitt's Tri-State Company. Thanks to fast footwork on the part of alert Scottsbluff businessmen, who got to the ditch contractors and superintendents first, Scottsbluff won the lion's share of their trade, and a real business boom started in everything from groceries to heavy equipment.

In 1910, before the ditch construction had begun to taper off, the Great Western Sugar Company built a beet-sugar processing factory in Scottsbluff. Coupled with the recent development of irrigation, this soon made the raising of sugar beets a great agricultural industry in Scotts Bluff and surrounding counties. For miles around, farmers hauled sugar beets to the Scottsbluff factory. They financed their crops, many of them, at Scottsbluff banks and did most of their trading at Scottsbluff stores. In proof that the town was keeping pace with its business growth, the 1910 census showed a population of 1,746, entitling it to replace the village board of trustees with a full-fledged mayor and city council. By now Gering had its railroad too, but Scottsbluff's second-fiddle days were ended for good and all. The arrival of the gasoline age helped consolidate its position as the principal trading center of the valley, bringing people from an ever-widening area to the stores on Main Avenue. And in 1916, having passed the 5,000 mark in population, Scottsbluff quietly advanced to the status of a city of the first class.

From then on its growth was unspectacular but steady. The 1920's saw its emergence both as a livestock marketing center and the hub of the state's potato and bean industries. Aided by the beet-sugar industry, with its feeding by-products of tops and pulp, the livestock industry had gained an impetus which was to make the North Platte Valley one of the principal beef and lamb producing areas in the United States, and to add a meat-packing plant to the array of Scottsbluff's industries. Wholesale houses started locating there about the time of World War I, and eventually it became the wholesale and warehousing center of western Nebraska and eastern Wyoming.

While their record of achievement had long held a high place on Nebraska's "we point with pride" list, a first taste of national publicity came to Scottsbluff and Scotts Bluff County in the thirties. It was then that Fred Attebery of Mitchell, already a legendary figure in the cattle-feeding industry, was heralded to the general public as America's No. 1 cattle feeder, and the name of Attebery and Scotts Bluff County became synonyms for fine beef. Attebery beef was featured by Swift & Company at the Century of Progress; on the menus of such hotels as the Palmer House and Hotel New Yorker (which displayed a neon sign: WE SERVE ATTEBERY NEBRASKA BEEF) and of such restaurants as Jack Dempsey's; by railroad companies and steamship lines. Attebery, who had begun to ship to the Chicago market in 1928, during a nine-year period sold 2,343 head of cattle at peak market price, establishing a new world record. For three years his cattle gave Scotts Bluff County the distinction of topping the cattle market more times than any other county in the U.S.

While the depression slowed business down a little, in the years that the state lost 64,500 persons, Scottsbluff's population grew from under 7,000 to 8,500; and although the number of banks was trimmed from five to two, deposits increased by something like thirty-three per cent. During the 1940's, as industry surged ahead under the forced draft of war demands, there was prosperity—bank deposits nearly doubled—and more building; and when its Golden Jubilee year rolled around in 1950, Scottsbluff could claim a population of 13,000, serving a trade area of more than 90,000 persons.

To anyone familiar with its early history, it should not be surprising that Scottsbluff today is a city of churches and schools and parks quite as much as it is a commercial and industrial center. In the post-World War II years alone, it has built seven new churches; and added a junior high school building, a stadium, a shop building, and improvements totalling more than $1,000,000 to its already excellent public school system. The community is justly proud of its junior college, which was founded in 1931 and has an enrollment of 260 and a faculty of twenty-eight, but it is perhaps even prouder that the Scottsbluff City Schools were the first in the state to operate a special education department for handicapped children. Originally financed by contributions from citizens and organizations and now maintained by the school board with the cooperation of parents, it was used as the "pilot model" in the 1949 legislation which established the present statewide special education program. The queen of the city's ten parks, another post-war development, is Riverside Park, twelve of whose acres are given over to the largest and most diversified zoo in the state.

Set in the midst of a region of great scenic and historic interest,* and with Scotts Bluff National Monument just across the river, for obvious reasons Scottsbluff is far more tourist-conscious than most Nebraska towns. Since it was proclaimed a national monument by President Wilson in 1919, the fame of the old Oregon Trail landmark, symbol of a heroic chapter in the conquest of the West, has attracted as many as 100,000 visitors in one year. During the 1930's a hard-surfaced highway was built to the top, and a historical and paleontological museum opened. A wing devoted to the work of William H. Jackson, pioneer artist and first photographer of the West, was added in 1949.

At the base of the towering bluff—not far from where, in 1828, a fur trapper by the name of Hiram Scott gained a certain immortality by perishing alone and deserted by his companions—the members

* For a description of Scotts Bluff, Chimney Rock, and other Oregon Trail landmarks, see Sir Richard Burton's account on page 389.

of the Scotts Bluff Country Club have built one of the most beautiful club houses in the Middle West. Naturally enough, at the unveiling of this opulent pleasure dome, it was bound to elicit comparisons with the more rudimentary and utilitarian structures, such as Andy McClenahan's store, that had been the scene of Scottsbluff's earliest clambakes. And inevitably there were those who felt that the change from shirt-sleeves to cummerbunds portended the end of an era—that Scottsbluff's do-it-yourself days were over and soon grass would be growing under its businessmen's feet. That was in 1948.

When the Blizzard of 1949 hit the Panhandle, stockmen and farmers were caught unprepared. Weather forecasts for the region came from the Kansas City District Station six hundred miles away, and because of delays in transmitting the blizzard warning, people died and hundreds of cattle were frozen and starved.

Before the end of the year there was a new United States District Weather Station serving the eleven counties of the Panhandle. And where do you suppose it was located? Yep; that's right—Scottsbluff.

Irrigation, paradoxically, is generally considered to be a dry subject. Yet its beginnings provided a chapter in the development of western Nebraska as dramatic at times as any in frontier history. The irrigation shovel more than once became a weapon. The land's lifeblood is water, and before there were laws regulating its use, farmers shed their own blood and died upon their headgates protecting their claim to it. As recently as 1935 Scotts Bluff County was declared under martial law when Governor Roy L. Cochran ordered out two companies of the National Guard to prevent farmers of the Mitchell Irrigation District from taking water out of the North Platte ahead of lower districts which had earlier water rights.

The earlier ditches were dug by the homesteaders themselves, with an incredible amount of hard work and very little money. The builders of the Winter Creek Canal ranged as far as eastern Wyoming collecting bones from the prairie to sell for money to buy scrapers. Others went into Colorado to "pick spuds" for a "grub stake," and on one trip discovered some worn-out and discarded Mormon scrapers along the roadside. Doing a quick right-about-face, they got teams and wagons, drove back after the old scrapers, and brought them home.

From the sublimity of the saga of these early canal builders, Nebraska irrigation history touched the ridiculous when central and eastern Nebraska factions, associating the idea of irrigation with desert regions, opposed irrigation legislation on the ground that it would be detrimental to the agricultural reputation of the state. The Democratic State Convention of 1889 even went so far as to declare, in a resolution, that there was "already enough arable land to glut the home market for nearly all farm products."

There were then only 9,000 acres under irrigation in the state, 2,700 of them in Scotts Bluff County. Fifty years later the Census of Irrigation showed 610,379 acres irrigated in Nebraska, of which—as before—nearly a third, or 200,468, were in Scotts Bluff County.

While some Scotts Bluff homesteaders had seen the light earlier, the major phase of irrigation started in 1887, when W. P. Akers, John Coy, and Virgil Grout came from Colorado, where irrigation had been practiced. They started the Farmers Canal Company as a private project, with a company of about eleven farmers. Although there were not yet laws regulating irrigation, in accordance with prevailing custom they posted a notice of appropriation of water on the bank of the North Platte about a mile below the Nebraska-Wyoming state line, and one of their group, Charles Ford, rode a hundred miles to Sidney to file the notice with the county clerk. By 1890 ten miles of canal, watering two sections of land, had been completed at a cost of $7,800. Then Akers and Company began to run out of money.

About this time, William H. Wright, a Weeping Water real estate man with well-heeled friends back east, came into Scotts Bluff County with an idea—namely, that irrigation on a large scale was needed, and that it could be made to pay for investors. As it turned out, he was fifty per cent correct: large-scale irrigation was needed, all right, but it has never paid investors. (Not long ago one of his sons, Judge Fred A. Wright, summed matters up with the comment: "You cannot separate water from the land. The farmers who own the land must also own the water that it needs.")

Wright and his stockholders took over the Farmers Canal in 1891, authorized a $450,000 bond issue, and started digging. During the next two years the canal progressed twenty miles, and $100,000 of the bonds were sold. Then came the financial panic of 1893, and Wright's flow of eastern capital suddenly dried up. Eventually, after a foreclosure sale and re-sale, a New Jersey corporation, the Tri-State Land Company, acquired title to the canal and by dint of spending more than $1,500,000 succeeded in constructing approximately eighty miles of canal, with three hundred miles of laterals, watering about 60,000 acres. Yet the enterprise couldn't make money for the simple reason that the irrigation charges were higher than the farmers could afford to pay. And in 1913 the canal came into the hands of the users, who, as the Farmers Irrigation District, issued $2,530,000 of bonds to buy it from Tri-State.

Although the Farmers Canal group was the first to post a notice of appropriation, the Minatare Canal and Irrigation Company was the first in operation. Begun in January, 1888—on sixty dollars borrowed from the wife of one of the members—by late summer of that same year the Minatare Canal was watering five hundred acres. There were other canals built during this period of individual enterprise and cooperative effort, but with the passage of the Federal Reclamation Act in 1902 irrigation entered a new phase. By putting the federal government in the irrigation business, it made possible irrigation on a scale that was beyond even the most ambitious private company or cooperative association.

The North Platte River often ran erratically; in the spring its banks were charged with more water than there was any use for, while in the late summer, when water was most needed, there sometimes was not enough to go around. The Reclamation Act provided for the building of huge reservoirs to hold back and store the spring flows, to be released as needed during the dry months.

An irrigation survey in 1904 led to the establishment of the North Platte Project, a system of dams and canals which has reclaimed 150,000 acres in Scotts Bluff and Morrill counties. The first unit to be built was the Pathfinder Dam, about forty miles southwest of Casper, Wyoming. In operation since 1913, it has a storage capacity of approximately 1,000,000 acre-feet.* An auxiliary channel reservoir, the Guernsey, one hundred sixty-eight miles downstream from the Pathfinder, was completed in 1927. With a net capacity of 61,000 acre-feet, it acts both as a supplemental storage and regulatory reservoir.

In Scotts Bluff County two beautiful little lakes, Lake Alice and Lake Minatare, with a combined capacity of 78,000 acre-feet, were completed in 1914. Two main supply canals, the Interstate and the Gering-Fort Laramie, for the irrigation of lands on the high terraces of the valley, also were constructed in the 1914-1927 period. A third canal, the Northport—an extension of the Farmers Canal—brought water to lands in Morrill County. The total cost of the North Platte

* An acre-foot is the volume of water required to cover one acre to the depth of one foot.

Project, including two hydroelectric power plants at Lingle and Guernsey and an estimated 1,600 miles of canals and laterals, was approximately $19,000,000.

Considerable legislating had to be done, and a fair amount of suing in the courts, before irrigation codes and practices became stabilized. The first legislation of any consequence was introduced in the Nebraska legislature in 1889 by Henry St. Raymor of Sidney, and established the appropriative doctrine of "first in time, first in right." In 1895, when statewide droughts had focused public attention upon the need for a sensible use of water, a more comprehensive water law was enacted. It provided for state administration and irrigation districts and, with minor changes, remains in effect today.

Shortly after the Pathfinder Dam was completed, it developed that the big reservoirs stored more water than was always needed in the government ditches. Therefore, in 1911 Congress passed an amendment to the Reclamation Act, known as the Warren Act, authorizing the sale of rights to excess storage capacity to other irrigation districts. Six such contracts were entered into by Nebraska districts: Farmers, Gering, Central, Chimney Rock, Brown's Creek, and Beerline. The effect of these contracts was to provide for the release of stored water during the growing season when the river flow was inadequate, and thus to stabilize the farm economy of the valley.

It has been said that the story of Scotts Bluff County is the story of the union of land and water. To those who have seen the gaunt and barren ranges transformed into a countryside of golden bounty, done in seventeen shades of green, it is a story more wonderful than the Arabian Nights.

Adapted from the Scottsbluff *Daily Star-Herald*, Aug. 2, 1950

The indiscriminate shooting of late prevalent in this town is becoming an intolerable nuisance and strong measures should be adopted to stop it. The offenders should be taught to respect the law if they won't respect themselves. The citizens of Sidney are mostly to blame in these outlaws not being brought to justice. An officer can not be in every nook and cranny in town, and where violence is done, it is the duty of every law-abiding citizen to inform the officers whom the parties are committing these crimes. Citizens, take this matter in hand, and in a short time revolver shooters will be scarce.

—Sidney *Telegraph,* January 4, 1879

Peace Officer

ROBERT HOUSTON

ONE OF THE surest-shootin' officers out west in Nebraska is Sheriff W. W. (Bill) Schulz of Sidney. He has never led a mounted posse chasing rustlers in the hills, but he's a whiz at shooting off a tire on a car he's pursuing at eighty miles an hour, and any fellows who think they can get away with something are hereby warned to stay away from Bill's home grounds.

Mr. Schulz is a western sheriff—modern style. Not for him an eight-gallon Stetson, levis, fancy boots, and a drooping moustache stained at the edges with tobacco juice. He's a good-looking, clean-shaven man who'd be taken anywhere for a well-dressed executive. And he spends his spare time in Boy Scout work.

Cheyenne County for a good many years was a place where a darned good sheriff was needed mighty bad sometimes. Sheriffs in these parts kinda figured they'd get shot at once in a while, and they were never disappointed. Fact is, Bill Schulz first became sheriff when his boss was fatally wounded in 1930.

"Jim Nelson was sheriff then," says Bill, "and I had been his deputy for less than a year. An inmate had escaped from the Hastings State Hospital and had been living in Sidney for some time. One night this man had a spell and attacked his dad, who farmed seven miles north of town. He walked him into town and made him sign a check for several hundred dollars. Then the old man got away and called the sheriff. Mr. Nelson finally spotted the son walking up a hill north of town. He drove up alongside and just had time to say, 'Hey—' when the fellow shot him through the head."

Three days after Mr. Nelson died, the County Board appointed 34-year-old Bill Schulz sheriff. That was twenty-seven years ago, and he's still in office. Although he's a Republican, the Roosevelt landslide in the '30's didn't bother him a bit, and he's been re-elected by a comfortable margin seven times.

"Sheriff Schulz has become a legend," avers Jack Lowe, editor of the Sidney *Telegraph.* "Everybody seems to like him. Why, I bet they'll still be voting for him ten years after he's dead."

While there isn't the turnover in sheriffs there used to be, Mr. Schulz has been a point-blank target on two occasions. "On New Year's Day, 1931," he recalls, "we got word that three men, all armed, had broken into a place in Kimball and were headed east toward Sidney. When we overtook them, like a fool I went between the two cars. My deputy went around on the other side. Just as the fellow on his side dropped his gun, the fellow near me fired. I'd put out my hand as I saw his gun come up, and the shot skimmed between two fingers. It tore off the glove, but I didn't even get nicked."

Luck was with the sheriff again a few years later when a man barricaded himself in his house with his fourteen-month-old child. Previously the house had been occupied by his estranged wife, who had custody of the child; he had slipped in one evening, and she had managed to escape.

Schulz and his deputies surrounded the house at 4:30 A.M., but had made no progress by three the next afternoon. "Then," says the sheriff, "we fired three bursts of gas into the house, and he started shooting. Thinking he had had a seven-shot weapon, a deputy and I went in as soon as he'd fired seven times. We went upstairs and searched all the rooms, but couldn't find him. I took the child outside and went back in. My partner and I were standing there, looking around, when a door at the other end of the room opened and the man started shooting again from the closet where he'd hidden. It turned out his was a nine-shot gun, but neither my deputy nor I was touched."

Something he learned in the early '30's, Mr. Schulz says, has helped sustain his morale as an officer. "In prohibition days we caught a still out in the country. There was sixty gallons of the finished product and ninety-five gallons of mash. When the alleged operator was tried, four witnesses testified that he had brought the still there and ran it. But the jury let him loose. After the trial I asked the judge what I'd done wrong. He said, 'Bill, you didn't slip up anywhere. It's just the way people feel about the liquor law. But you accomplished your purpose; you broke up the still.' Since then I've often consoled myself by thinking I've carried out an officer's purpose even though some fellow wasn't thrown in jail for a long stretch."

Boom towns are said to present extra police problems, and Sidney has been a boom town on several occasions. It was an early rendezvous for cowboys; in 1876 it was a jumping-off place for the Black Hills gold rush; and in 1904, when Congress passed the Kinkaid Act, it was thronged with homesteaders. Mr. Schulz, during his terms of office, has lived through a couple of booms himself. In World War II years, industrial workers poured into Sidney when the Sioux Ordnance Plant was built ten miles to the northwest; and in 1949 oil was discovered in Cheyenne County.

Since then, more than 150 oil and natural-gas wells have been brought in, in Sidney's immediate vicinity, and the population has jumped to around 9,000, double that of 1940. But Sidney has taken these developments in its stride. Gambling and drinking trouble, says the sheriff, has not been allowed to get a start in the county.

Following a visit to Sidney, an executive of a large eastern oil company remarked: "This is the quietest boom town I've ever seen." Which would seem to indicate that "peace officer" is no misnomer for Sidney's Sheriff Bill Schulz.

Condensed from Omaha *World-Herald Sunday Magazine*, April 15, 1956

The story of the Panhandle oil boom is one of friendly rivalry between Cheyenne and Kimball counties and their county seats, Sidney and Kimball. Cheyenne County was the first to feel the impact, because it was there, near Gurley, that the discovery was made. Between them the counties produced nearly eighty per cent of the state's oil in 1955, and Kimball took over the lead for the first time.

The boom changed the face and future of both cities. It has brought millions of dollars in leases and royalties, spurred tremendous business activity, and increased the population by thousands.

There is growth everywhere, jammed schools, and crowded living in some cases.

At the moment Kimball is probably the state's fastest growing city. A Chamber of Commerce census in March, 1955, put the population at 4,403 compared with an official 2,050 in 1950. The new population count included 1,482 persons living in 412 trailers outside the city limits but for all practical purposes a part of Kimball and served by its utilities. Since 1951, the city has spent nearly a million dollars in improving water and power services, streets, sewage disposal, and airport.

"Kimball is becoming a complete oil center for the whole area as far west as Torrington, Wyo., and as far south as the Colorado line (15 miles)," says Art Henrickson, publisher of the *Western Nebraska Observer*.

New businesses include many oil-connected enterprises. Depending on depth, the average well costs about $30,000 to complete and another $20-25,000 to put into operation. This is money which for the most part finds its way into local trade channels, whereas much of the royalties and other oil benefits do not.

Because oil was discovered inside the city limits, every property owner in Kimball gets his share of the royalties. The city is divided into drilling blocks of 150 lots each. An ordinance limits the number of wells to two for every forty acres. All but one block has at least one well, producing about one hundred barrels daily. The average lot owner gets about $6.25 in royalties for each lot, and the person on whose property a well is drilled receives a fee in addition.

The seventeenth well to be drilled inside the city was brought in one block from the site of excavation for a new grade school.

Schools, of course, are poppin' at the seams. Kimball built a new grade school in 1951, but it started bulging in two years. So another one's on the way. Total enrollment has shot from 588 in 1950 to 1,169 at the latest count.

"You can hear talk of the population going to eight, ten thousand," says Art Henrickson. "Perhaps more—if the oil keeps coming."

Condensed from an article by Harold Cowan, Omaha *World-Herald*, April 8, 1956

When the winter of 1948–49 brought what is probably the greatest blizzard in Nebraska's history, it required the world's largest bulldozer operation to dig the state out. Under the command of the late Lt. General Lewis A. Pick, 5,700 men of the Fifth Army used 1,800 bulldozers and 200 plows to open 185,000 square miles in Nebraska, Wyoming, and the Dakotas. All in all, Operation Snowbound dug out 200,000 people, some of whom had been isolated for more than two months, and opened up feed to 4,000,000 head of livestock.

While the Blizzard of January 2, 1949 may have been the biggest, nevertheless it is of far less significance in the state's history than an anonymous snowstorm back in 1879 which led to the discovery of a cattleman's paradise.

Hyannis

B. F. SYLVESTER

IN THE late '80's, Burlington Railroad officials laid out three towns within twenty-one miles in a bleak section of northwestern Nebraska and named them Whitman, Hyannis, and Ashby for their homes in Massachusetts. Whitman was the seat of Grant County, end of the line, had one store, seven saloons, and a new cemetery with tenant, the first man to arrive with five aces. In Buffalo, New York, a man who wanted to get away from it all asked for a ticket to hell, and the agent sold him one to Whitman. The line moved on, and eventually Hyannis became the county seat. Today, if you bought a ticket to Hyannis, population 449, you would find yourself in a place where everybody has a wonderful time doing what comes naturally.

On the surface, the Hyannis region is forbidding. Sand dunes, rolled up by westerly winds from the bed of an ancient sea, follow one another over 22,000 square miles. Mari Sandoz spoke of them as "endless monotony caught and held forever in sand." Less than seventy years ago, it was an unknown land where Indians would not go and where white men lost their way and died. Through it runs the Dismal River, named after due consideration.

In the heart of this, Hyannis sits on the side of a hill. Old frame buildings stairstep to the courthouse up Main Street, which is 88 feet wide and 500 feet long, with a heavy grade. The town has no civic cohesion or ambition to grow, doesn't care if it never gets to be 500. Save one, the roads are twisting, one-way trails that disappear in a sandstorm. The drugstore closes at 8:30, the pool hall at nine, the movie opens two nights a week.

Then why the complacent state of mind in Hyannis? The people are not the kind to brag, but will acknowledge in simple honesty that of the things promoting man's happiness, they have the mostest of the bestest. Elmer Lowe can cite Webster: "Paradise . . . A region of supreme felicity or delight." Widow Ellen Moran doesn't go that far and has a reservation: "It's a great country for cattle and men, but hell on horses and women."

There is not a real-estate agent, booster club, or luncheon club in the county. A notion prevails that parents are responsible for their young, and there is no juvenile delinquency. There is no crime. The law says there has to be a sheriff, and Calvin Rex serves on a part-time basis at sixty-six dollars a month. The last killing was forty-nine years ago, when the hotel clerk shot the saloon-keeper in a squabble over the saloon-keeper's wife. The law says, too, they must elect a county attorney, but they don't always do it, because sometimes there isn't any lawyer to take the job.

Everyone in Hyannis is a person, and each completes the sentence, "I like the sandhills because _____" with one word, "Freedom." The Bank of Hyannis has $3,000,000 in deposits. Back of Main Street are substantial landscaped homes. The twisting trails lead to great houses with air-conditioning, electric dishwashers, oil portraits of master and wife, and as many as sixty-four guests for dinner and bridge. In and around Hyannis are thirteen millionaires, most of whom once burned cow chips instead of oil and didn't always know what day was Christmas. From grass, air, and water, poor men have built an empire in which fifteen counties have 1,000,000 cattle—more than either Idaho or Arizona. Even a small ranch—say, 12,000 acres and 1,000 cattle—represents a quarter of a million dollars. Within fifty miles of Hyannis are seven outfits, each in excess of 90,000 acres.

Sandhills people admit there are places with better grass that produce heavier cattle but believe they have the best cow and calf country, and the most reliable, where 300 feet of sand has 100 feet of water, with never a failure of grass and hay. In the drought years, paraphrasing the inscription on the Statue of Liberty, they said to the stricken areas, "Bring us your tired, your poor and hungry critters, yearning to breathe our air and eat our hay," and the cattle came by the thousands from as far as Texas. They insist, too, that this is all that is left of the real cow country, with not one dude ranch. This is not to say that they don't like visitors. To their 2,000 lakes, thousands of city men come to retrieve ducks and masculinity. But cattle production is big business, and there is no place for the half-ranch-half-hotel. Furthermore, the cowboys do not sing. Sandhills cattle are well content and do not have to be soothed like the restive animals of some sections made nervous by the yip-yipping of rodeo cowhands. The only stampede was into the hills, not out.

This stampede was history on the hoof, the opening of the sandhills by a bawling, charging herd of 6,000 cattle. A line of riders stretching along the border north and west of the Niobrara River in March, 1879 were not land-hungry men waiting for a pistol shot, as in the run to the Cherokee Strip. They were hardy young fellows not afraid of man or beast, but no personal gain could have taken them across that line. They had known men who went into the mysterious trackless sandhills and did not return. The men in the line were cowboys of the E. S. Newman N-Bar ranch. Their job was to keep the cattle from breaking through in a blizzard that was coming up. The storm came, and at its height the cattle did break through. For years cattle had strayed into the hills and been charged off by the ranchers. Newman would not send his men after the N-Bar herd, but Cowboy Jim Dahlman, later to be mayor of Omaha, volunteered with eleven others. On April fifteenth, the expedition set out: they came upon rich valleys and wild native cattle as fat as ever they had seen, though it had been a terrible winter, and there was no other food than grass. They began finding their own, all thriving. In five weeks they brought out 9,000—the Newman herd plus 3,000 that had drifted in previously, hundreds of which had been there for years and gone wild.

The news that the hills would support cattle brought big outfits for summer grazing, among them W. A. Paxton, whose later struggles with the legislature in founding the Omaha Stock Yards led him to a definition: "An honest man is a so-and-so who will stay bought." In the middle '80's, Rufe Haney, Arthur Abbott, J. M. Gentry and Joe Minor came up from Kansas, the first of the small men who were to push out the big ones and become big themselves. Sixteen-year-old Jim Monahan and his mother came from Iowa, driving two Hereford cows. The first Peterson came alone, sent for his wife and seven children, who got off the train and waited beside the track for papa to come. Finally he showed up in a lumber wagon drawn by a horse and a cow.

Ellen McIntire came to teach school, married Rancher Sheriff Bud Moran and set up a tradition. Until the war, teachers' agencies practically guaranteed teachers would get husbands. Even in the last twenty-five years, sixty young women have come to Hyannis to teach school and stayed to marry. The Morans had a claim on Wild Horse Flats where mosquitoes were bad. They built hay and cow-chip fires, and their grateful horses would stand in the smoke all night. For fun on a Sunday, young Mrs. Moran would accompany her husband to a wild-horse breaking, where she helped the neighbors with the cooking. Ranch houses still are on the grub line, and anyone arriving around mealtime is expected to sit down with the family.

Eighty-nine-year-old J. M. Gentry tells you, "A group was invited to spend Christmas Day at Bert Proctor's, thirty miles south. Some went one day, some next. None had calendars. The Proctors didn't have a calendar, so we never did know who had the right date or if we were all wrong."

Sid Manning raced ahead of the great prairie fire of 1892 to save his twelve-year-old son George in their sod house. In the smoke he fell fifteen feet into a well, and from time to time put out fire in his clothing as blazing cow chips and hay were blown in. The fire passed, the father climbed out of the well, and the boy came out of the soddy unhurt.

What have the hills done to the man? This is the old homestead of free enterprise. From the day a calf is born in March, perhaps in a blizzard, it has no shelter but a friendly hill. It is the rancher's theory that range animals do best with the fewest man and man-made contacts. In the main, they feel the same about themselves and Washington. There is the Hyannis woman who has met with reverses, but all she will take from her well-to-do relatives is the regular fifty cents an hour for doing their washing. She holds her social position and her head high, perhaps a little higher for having proved herself in a community which labels self-dependence as top virtue. Times were hard in the '30's, even for the Abbotts, but they refused and continue to refuse $25,000 a year in government conservation checks for not using winter range in summer—which to a sand-hills rancher is like paying him not to commit suicide by overgrazing.

One rebel in that region gives his checks to the Republican Party. The county refused a new WPA courthouse, the village a $15,000 WPA water-works extension, doing the job itself for $8,000. It was decided the old courthouse would do: about all they use it for is to pay taxes in, the collection rate being 99.6 per cent.

The sandhiller is independent, but not indifferent. A rancher just getting started lost 700 tons of hay in a prairie fire. Doc Plummer at the Dumb Bell Ranch invited him to bring over his 400 steers to be his guests for the winter. An old-timer says men don't slug in business. He was asked, "Does that include land deals?" The reply was, "Now you are talking about the dearest thing to a cattleman's heart." At that, no rancher wants more than the place next to him.

Sam McKelvie, former governor, puts the sandhills' idea this way, "There was a peaceful lake in front of our ranch house. Why not have some geese to grace the scene while getting their living from the abundant food that grew in the lake? So my good friend, the late Dan Stephens, gave me a pair of fine goslings. I took them home and gave them a good feed at the barn, then drove them down to their future home about two hundred yards away. Did they appreciate that goose heaven? They beat me back to the barn. Moral: If you feed 'em out of your hand, they don't dive for it."

It is significant, perhaps the key to his character, that you can't tell a man from Hyannis. When Robert M. Howard, twenty-eight, came to be the new editor of the Grant County *Tribune,* he was full of fire and new ideas. Right off he suggested it would be a good idea to run a blacktop road to the Arthur County line. His editorial met with complete silence. Hyannis has two package-liquor stores, and one of its citizens says it drinks more and better whiskey per capita than any other place in Nebraska. On April second the town voted on the question of sale by the drink—without a word of comment from Editor Howard. He had learned fast. There wasn't even a story saying there would be an election—only the paid legal notice of same. The liquor interests kept hands off. The voters, making up their own minds, said no.

One thing that just about drove a preacher out of Hyannis was profanity, easy and unconscious, from long association with un-progressive cattle. A wife reproved her husband for a remark in the minister's presence, "You have embarrassed the reverend." The man was contrite. "The hell I did," he said, startled, and then apologized to the preacher: "Sorry. Didn't mean a damn thing."

The people look after their own affairs beautifully, but they are low on community spirit. The town has no sewage-disposal system, but it has some of the finest private cesspools in Nebraska. The courthouse has no restroom, rest being considered an individual and not a taxpayer concern. Even a community problem is met in an individual way. For twenty years the Hyannis Main Street was paved with materials which came from Bob Hayward's livery stable. Not altogether satisfactory, it was succeeded by soapweed, then blacktop. Even today manure topping is used on side streets in Whitman and on bad stretches in the country.

Hyannis is a credit town, with no unpaid bills except those of the doctor, who loses twenty per cent. The general store has had no loss in twenty years. A study of Federal Land Bank loans in the emergency-financing period of 1933-35 shows no losses in Grant or neighboring Hooker and Thomas counties. In the same section the Production Credit Corporation has had the same experience in twelve years of financing ranch operations.

The small businesses are mostly family owned and staffed. Except for the children of ranchers, there are few opportunities or inducements for young people, and they do not stay. Some of the townspeople level a finger here. There is almost no organized or commercial recreation. Ashby, population 155, has a dance hall open one night a week where village and ranch meet. Cowboys come in high-heeled dress boots, levis, two-tone gabardine shirts, and big hats.

There are thirteen woman's clubs. The Grant County Golf Club—sand greens—has thirty members, but the No. 1 men's club is the Hyannis Roping Club, limited to forty members. Its Sunday-afternoon exhibitions draw cheering crowds of 200. All concerned have a wonderful time except the calves, who become bored as the season wears on. The men used to have a Chuck Wagon Club with monthly dinners at which eastern guests were introduced to calf fries and tall stories. You can still hear tall stories at the Hyannis Hotel from Bill Renfro. Once, in a rainstorm, Bill left his double-barreled shotgun against a fence post, muzzle up, while he ran to a haystack. The rain roared right up to the fence, but there turned off toward Ashby, which needed rain. Bill crawled out of the hay to get his gun, and found the barrel on his side dry and the one on the other side full of water.

The hills have not changed, and you still can get lost. Recently an Omaha party wandered for hours. They came upon a beautiful white colonial house with acres of landscaped grounds and rose gardens. A gardener came out asking to be of service. They looked around for Cecil B. DeMille, but the man who bade them welcome was Wally Farrar, the most spectacular success in the sandhills. One item about the house twenty-two miles from Hyannis: it has two light and power systems, in case one breaks down, and an electrician to see that neither does. Farrar, a college student, married Helen, one of Joe Minor's three daughters—all wed to city men, who, under some contriving by Joe, have become ranchers. When the Farrars built their new home, they invited Joe to live with them. He looked over the vast expanse of rooms and asked, "Will you give me a bicycle, too?"

Minor could outfreeze any of his men. This means that he could take more weather. At seventy-six he still rode, and often took a hand with the work. In the early days he lassoed wolves, and once, after ten miles of the chase, his horse fell and died. He roped another horse, overtook the spent wolf, dragged it back and collected $150 bounty. Minor would not stay in his $28,000 residence at Alliance, preferring the old house on the ranch.

The most fun ninety-year-old Everett Eldred can think of is to ride out from his $65,000 house, an enlarged copy of a three-story flat-top he saw at the Chicago World's Fair, and contemplate 500 Herefords lying in two feet of grass.

Health is above average, along with sunshine—153 clear days a year—air—altitude, 3,748 feet—and water—they use it straight in car batteries. In thirty-odd years Dr. William L. Howell has found no mental breakdown from solitude. "When I came here," he says, "that was one of the things I particularly inquired about, and could get a history of only one case where the bullsnakes held conversation with a man."

Elmer Lowe has been everywhere, but found no place so beautiful or agreeable. On summer nights, he says, everybody has natural air conditioning as the breeze is filtered through the cool green grass and the wild flowers—spiderwort, ground phlox, prairie violet, wild sweet peas, niggerhead, prairie shoestring, aster, blazing star, Queen Anne's lace, sunflower, and goldenrod. The hills were even benefited by the dust storms, which added plant food.

How Lowe feels may be sensed from this testimony. He came out in the early '90's to hunt prairie chickens, worked it into a business of 50,000 birds a year, which he sent frozen to New York and Boston. He bought a ranch and did well, but got big ideas. He spent fifteen years in Denver with gold mines, oil wells, a truck factory, and went broke. At sixty he returned to his heavily encumbered ranch, and Ed Meyers lent him $200,000. Now, eighty-five, he has paid off all debts, and with his sons, Knight and Fred, operates 50,000 acres. Says Lowe, to whom the hills gave two chances, "A man can be as big as he wants to be." But he adds, "The day is past when a man can start a ranch on prairie chickens or wolf pelts. He would need at least $25,000 to start, with a minimum of 2,000 acres of range and hay land and a hundred cows."

Director of the vast Abbott enterprises—250,000-acre ranch, eight banks, and four stores—is 225-pound Christopher J. Abbott,* the richest man in Nebraska. Most of the time in the shipping season, August to December, Abbott is on a horse from 4:30 in the morning until 10:30 at night, sleeping on the ground in between, while Mrs. Abbott, keeping the same hours, brings meals to the outfit. They are Chris and Ethel to the help and everyone in the hills, and vice versa. Abbott is a director of the United States Chamber of Commerce and chairman of its agriculture committee. In the last year he has made twelve trips to Washington on cattle problems. He is president of Prairie Airways, Inc., which proposes a line from Miami to Nome, Alaska, and at fifty-six he has just learned to fly.

Though ranching is not a feminine trade, wives are active partners, and some on their own are among the largest operators. Ellen Moran has 17,000 acres. Mrs. Hannah Abbott is joint owner of the Abbott interests with her sons, Chris and Roy. Mrs. E. P. Meyers probably is the largest individual rancher, with 160,000 acres. She was Margaret Gorman, a clerk at Edholm's Jewelry Store in Omaha, where Meyers went to buy a diamond and got both diamond and wife. Mrs. Essie Davis was a milliner who married Arthur T. Davis. When he died she was left a four-month-old son and a small ranch, solvent, but $80,000 in debt. She paid off, has 30,000 acres, and her guests include Washington politicos. She is president of the Alliance Production Credit Corporation, where, a few years ago, ranchers sat, big hats in their hands, to borrow $100,000 or so.

The rich ranch women do not live in unmixed elegance. Cattle still are the basis of everything, and their needs come first. The June social season means going from one house to another on branding bees and helping cook for fifty neighbors. Between this and the other seasons—calving, haying, and shipping—they travel and buy jewelry and expensive clothes. Still, except for those in town, it is twenty miles to another house.

* Mr. Abbott was killed in a plane crash, January 10, 1954.

The men buy expensively, too—the leading horse thief of earlier days had his clothes made in Chicago—but perspective is not lost. When John H. Bachelor built the biggest house in Valentine, a piano seemed to be needed, so he went to Omaha, and the proprietor showed him the best. "How much?" asked J. H.

"That will be fifteen hundred dollars."

J. H. snorted, "There ain't nothin' worth fifteen hundred that can't have a calf."

The rancher has worries—income tax, scarce labor, blizzards, and some say the price of cattle, which may get too high for the housewife. They expect a dip sometime, but think they can take the downs with the ups.

Recently a rancher who owed $75,000 asked the lender to drop around and be paid off. He was fixing a fence when the man appeared. "Hello, Jim."

"Hello, Sam. I left that up the line. Want to walk up?"

They walked half a mile to where a vest hung on the fence. From the vest Jim pulled out the $75,000 in currency.

"Thanks, Jim."

"G'by, Sam."

Condensed from "Sandhills Paradise," *Saturday Evening Post,* June 14, 1947

The crew required in handling a trail herd consisted of a foreman, about eight riders, a horse wrangler, cook, and mess wagon. Most of the outfits from Texas carried no tents, the men all sleeping in the open. The distance traveled per day would be from five to twenty miles, depending on feed, water, and weather. At night the cattle were "bedded down," and the men stood night guard, divided into shifts. . . .

The cattle would commence to move at break of day. The men on last relief would wake the cook and then drift the cattle in the direction they were to travel. The horse wrangler would bring in the horses, all hands were called, and the day's work began—at daylight. When a river was reached, sometimes a mile wide after heavy rains, it was a matter of swimming the herd across. Men on horseback would swim by the side of the herd, guiding them. Many times the herd would split, some swimming across, others swimming back. This divided the outfit, and sometimes it would take several days and nights to get it together again. Cowboys would swim back and forth carrying food, and not a stitch of dry clothes or sleep until the work was done. The boys were stayers. Their slogan was loyalty and service, and they stuck to the finish.

> —James C. Dahlman, "Recollections of Cowboy Life in Western Nebraska," *Nebraska History*, X (Oct.–Dec., 1927)

Home on the Range

1. Branding Time in Nebraska

DON MUHM

WHILE other phases of animal agriculture have adapted themselves to changing, progressive times, the art of burning a neat brand on a sandhills range newcomer differs little from the process as performed by the ancient Egyptians. Pictures and inscriptions on tomb walls indicate that as long ago as 2000 B.C. it was a common practice to identify cattle with brands. Branding Nebraska-style—the Old West way—actually was copied from cattlemen in Old Mexico, where ranchers singed calves with replicas of family crests and coats-of-arms.

Brands may be briefer today, but the brands are made in a similar manner. Each spring sees millions of Nebraska-born calves sustain an imprint which unmistakably establishes their ownership. The business of branding is two-fold: There are the cowhands who do the job—round up the calves, chase them into a corral, and ready the branding irons. And there are the agencies which register and keep track of the brands—quite a chore, too, when you recall that there are nearly forty thousand of them on file at the State House.

A look at the ranching end can be taken in May or June, when a rancher like Don Hanna, Jr., of Brownlee, holds a "Branding Bee" with his neighbors the Pounds, the McLeods, and Harley Nutter. In the Brownlee area, branding is a community affair, and all those at the Branding Bee live within an eight-mile radius.

At the Hanna Ranch, the "Lazy H Triangle" brand is burned on husky Herefords in the old-style way. Each calf is roped, dragged to the branding area, where two "wrestlers" pin the animal to the ground. In moves the branding "backfield." In less than a minute the calf is branded, ear-marked (for quick identification in winter-time when hair might cover the brand), vaccinated, castrated, and bawling his way out into the grassy hills. According to some ranchers, burning a brand is not painful, and the bawling comes mostly from fear.

Although most brands are applied the hot-iron way—and contrary to popular belief, the irons are not "red-hot" but "grey-hot"—there are other methods. Some use electric branding, others acid branding. Brands like the "Lazy Triangle" are as individual as the ranchers themselves. Any kind of mark may go into a brand—just so long as there is no room for confusion as to ownership of the branded cattle.

To keep track of Nebraska brands is the job of the Brands and Marks Division of the office of the Secretary of State. This office and its duties often are confused with the workings of the Nebraska Brand Committee.

The Brand Committee is composed of five members, four of whom are cattlemen actively engaged in the cattle business. They are appointed by the Governor to serve four-year terms. The fifth member, and chairman, is the Secretary of State. The group meets about once a month to hear complaints, settle disputes, and decide ownership where confusion about various brands arises. When inspections are needed or cattle thefts reported, ranchers get in touch with the Secretary of the Brand Committee.

During the busy season when cattle are moved in large numbers, as many as 150 local, temporary, or permanent brand inspectors are at work. All cattle shipped into, or from, the "Brand Area" must be inspected. This area includes roughly two-thirds of Nebraska, and is located west of Cedar, Pierce, Madison, Platte, Nance, Howard, Hall, Kearney, and Furnas counties. However, Norfolk, Grand Island, and Kearney markets also are included in the area. At Omaha, which is an "open" market, there are inspectors who check all cattle destined for, or coming from, the "Brand Area." Both brands and numbers are checked, after which a clearance is issued and ownership declared. Cattle may be inspected at ranches for the same eight-cent-per-head fee.

Some of the cattleman's hatred for the rustler lingers on today as evidenced by the fact that writing a bad check for $45 would not draw the stiff penalty set for stealing a $45 calf. The minimum sentence for stealing cattle is two to five years in the state prison—the same as that for the branding of another's cattle or the defacing of a brand.

But there is none of the atmosphere of the Old West in the offices of the Brands Division at the state capitol in Lincoln. There, in a maze of paperwork, secretaries efficiently cross-file registered brands. The brand file is pure Greek—or ancient Egyptian—to the outsider. Brands are read from left to right, from the top down, and from outside inside. Some look like birds, boots, bells, bugs, bottles, chairs, ladders, lamps, leaves, forks, eyes, fish, flags, what-have-you. Then there are the "letter" brands, usually containing the rancher's initials (like the "Lazy H Triangle"). A letter partially over on its face is "tumbling." One on its face or back is, appropriately enough, "lazy." And there are "running," "flying," and "legs" letters.

Nebraska's forty thousand brands are renewed by law. A rancher pays a two-dollar fee to register his brand for four years. One-half of the brands must be renewed every two years, according to the new brands law. Up until 1941, brand inspections were conducted under the supervision of the Nebraska Stock Growers Association. Then a test case resulted in a ruling that the state could not delegate this function to a private organization, and the Brands Committee came into being.

A book of Nebraska brands is published every five years, but the

total number contained in the publication might be misleading.
Some farsighted ranchers take out brands for their children before
the youngsters are knee-high to a Hereford.

Condensed from Omaha *World-Herald Sunday Magazine*, Sept. 4, 1956

2. Nebraska Cowboy Talk

RUDOLPH UMLAND

MANY of the words used in the sandhill region date from Texas
Trail days and are common to cattlemen in all the western states.
A few, however, are local in origin. One such purely local word is
chipper, as applied to a rancher who is poor or who is in only
moderate circumstances. It is used chiefly by the more prosperous
cattlemen or by their hands in a slighting sense. If you ask them who
a certain individual is, they may reply, "Oh, he's an old chipper
living near Sandy Lake." Most of the poorer ranchers in the sandhills still gather cow chips (hence the word *chipper*) for their winter
fuel.

In the fall of 1940 I accompanied a couple of cowboys to some
abandoned ranch buildings in the sandhills of Arthur County.
While we were there we saw a herd of cattle being trailed toward the
abandoned buildings.

"Bet they're going to bring them right through here," said one
of my companions.

"Nope, bet they won't! There'd be too much chance of the cattle
spooking," said the other.

And a few moments later we saw the course of the cattle changed.
They were trailed away from the buildings across the hills so they
would not spook. The word *spook* in cowboy parlance means to
scare or fill with fright. Cattle that have been on pasture through
the summer are easily frightened. One animal will communicate
its fear to others, and the entire herd will spook and run. Anything
unusual, such as a tumbled-down soddy, washing on a line, or even
the sight of a man on foot, is sufficient to spook a herd.

A *fine cutter* is a horse with exceptional ability in *cutting,* or
separating cattle from a herd. Old hands still say *carving* or *chop-
ping* instead of cutting. Calves that have been cut from a herd and
counted are *dodged* out. The chute in which cattle are held while

being branded is the *squeezer* or *snapping turtle*. To *side-line* a steer is to tie two of its legs on the same side together; to *hog-tie* it is to tie three of its legs together. To rope a steer is to *put on a string*. A *waddie*, or cowboy, who is good at roping is said to *sling the catgut well*. When a waddie ropes a steer without having the rope fastened to the saddle, he *takes a dollie welter*.

Many of the words referring to roping or throwing a cow have become popularized by the rodeo. It's *fair ground* when a steer is roped around the head; then, while it is still running, the rope is allowed to slip over the steer's back to encircle its legs. When a waddie throws a calf by grasping the skin of its opposite flank while it's running, he *flanks* the animal; when he throws it by twisting its neck, he *bulldogs* it; when he throws it by giving its tail a sudden jerk, he *tails* it.

At the sandhill auctions one occasionally sees a cow with a *jingle-bob*, or ear slit its entire length with the pieces flopping. To *fork* a horse means to swing astride or get into the saddle. To *tooth* an animal is to look at its teeth in order to determine its age. The boss's house is often the *white house* to the hands. The *boss* is the ranch foreman or manager. The *big boss* is the owner of the ranch or outfit. The assistant to the manager or foreman is the *straw boss, top screw*, or *top waddie*. The man in charge of a herd on the trail is the *trail boss* or *ramrod*. A hand who rides along the fences and keeps them in repair is a *fence-rider*.

A sandhiller who shows a lack of judgment or is careless is said *not to have cow sense*. If he is a fool, he is said not to *know dung from honey*. To vomit is to *air the paunch*. Watching a card game is *sweating a game*. Hard liquor is *family disturbance*. Bacon is *overland trout*. When a sandhiller dresses well he *rags proper*. When he grows bold after taking on a few drinks he is *ready to go lion-hunting with a buggy whip*. When he leaves town or a neighboring ranch and starts across the prairie he *hits the flats for home*. A small town is *a wide place in the road*. Telling a tall tale is *telling a windy*. A sandhiller who is washing his face is said to be *washing his profile*, or *bathing his countenance*. A cowboy riding fast is *faggin' along*. When a green hand has acquired a little more experience, *he has taken a little more hair off the dog*. When something misfits, it is said to *fit like a hog in a saddle*. A waddie who has made a night of it is said to have *stayed out with the dry cattle*.

All the large sandhill ranches have a *weak, lame, and lazy pen*, or a pasture where sick animals are kept. Sheep are *woolies*. Horses used in drawing the hay sleds in winter are called *sled dogs*. The chore of milking is called *pailing cows*. Nearly every community boasts a *Monkey Ward cowboy*, a waddie who sports loud shirts, fancy trousers, fancy boots, and a big Stetson. The word *cows* may include cattle of both sexes. *She-stuff* means only females and is not always limited to cattle. I was standing on a street corner in Arthur, Nebraska, one day when a couple of girls passed. A waddie standing nearby remarked, "Some pretty fancy she-stuff, hey?"

Reprinted from *American Speech*, Febr., 1952

Commenting on the recent sprouting of "Sunday painters" over the state, Mari Sandoz wrote in a recent issue of Holiday:

"Perhaps, among outdoor men, the urge to paint is stimulated by the swift, subtle flow of blue hazes against the Nebraska hills, the yellow-greens, the tans, russets, and mauves of the rolling prairie, the patterns of the contoured fields, and the unsurpassed sunrises and sunsets over it all.

"'It's paint rags 'stead a pliers in my old ditty box now,' a gnarled cowman replied when I wondered about the easel beside him in the jeep out on the range. 'My boy down to the university drug me to look at some pictures Fair time. I seen right away I could do better.'"

Sandhill Sundays

MARI SANDOZ

OUT OF THE East and the South, God's country, came the movers, pounding their crowbait ponies or their logy plow critters on to the open range of northwest Nebraska. They exchanged green grass, trees, and summer night rains for dun-colored sandhills crowding upon each other far into the horizon, wind singing in the red bunch grass or howling over the snow-whipped knobs of December, and the heat devils of July dancing over the hard land west of the hills. No Indian wars, few gun fights with bad men or wild animals— mostly it was just standing off the cold and scratching for grub. And lonesome! Dog owls, a few nesters in dugouts or soddies, dusty cow waddies loping over the hills, and time dragging at the heels —every day Monday.

Then came big doings. Cow towns with tent and false-front saloons; draw played Sunday afternoons in the dust of the trail between the shacks; cowboys tearing past the little sod churches, shooting the air full of holes while the sky pilots inside prayed hell and damnation on them; settlers cleaned of their shirts by card-sharpers whilst their women picked cow chips barefooted and corn leaves rattled dry in the wind.

When the settlers got clear down in the mouth, the sky pilots showed up among them. The meeting-point of the revivals was most generally Alkali Lake, on the Flats. All Sunday morning moving wagons, horsebackers, hoofers, and a buggy or two from town collected along the bare bank. Almost every dugout or claim shack for twenty, thirty miles around was deserted. Everybody turned out to hear the walking parson.

From the back end of a buggy, the sky pilot lined out the crowd hunched over on wagon tongues, stretched on horse blankets or on the ground, hot with the glaring sun.

"You see them heat waves out there on the prairie? Them's the fires of hell, licking round your feet, burning your feet, burning your faces red as raw meat, drying up your crops, drawing the water out of your wells! You see them thunderheads, shining like mansions in the sky but spurting fire and shaking the ground under your feet? God is mad, mad as hell!"

Somewhere a woman began to moan and cry. The crowd was up like a herd of longhorns at the smell of fire. A swarthy ground-scratcher from down on the Breaks began to sing "Nearer My God to Thee," couldn't remember the words, and broke out crying, too. Others took up songs. "Beulah Land." Somebody broke into the popular parody and hid his face. "Washed in the Blood of the Lamb."

Two whiskered grangers helped the parson off the buggy. "Come to Jesus! Come to Jesus!" he sang as he waded into the already cooling water of the lake. The moaning woman was ducked first and came up sputtering and coughing. The crowd pushed forward, to the bank, into the water.

And when the sun slipped away and the cool wind carried the smell of stale water weed over the prairie, almost everybody was saved. Mrs. Schmidt, with eight children and a husband usually laid out in the saloon at Hay Springs, sang all the way home, she was so happy. The next week they sent her to the insane asylum. The youngest Frahm girl took pneumonia from the ten-mile trip behind plow critters and died. The lone Bohemian who scratched the thin ground on the Breaks strung himself up.

Talk of the big revival drifted back into the hills. "I wisht I coulda gone; it'd-a been a lot of comfort to me," Mrs. Endow mumbled when she heard about it. But one of their horses had died of botts, and her only chance of getting out now was in a pine box.

The nesters, well versed in drainage, were helpless against the drought. Each spring there was less money for seed, and Sundays were more and more taken up with the one problem, irrigation. Everybody threw in together here, the Iowa farmer, the New England schoolteacher afraid of his horses, and the worn-out desert rat, the European intellectual, and the southern poor white. There was no place for women at these meetings, and so they stayed at home, wrangling the old hen and chickens and watering the dry sticks of hollyhock.

Ten years later the drought, the cold, and too much buying on pump had driven out the shallow-rooted nesters and the sky pilots. A few hilltop churches took care of those who still believed in a benevolent God. The stickers took up dry farming, pailed cows, and ran cattle. But farming and milking meant long hours; ranching called for large pastures and consequent isolation. Night entertainment grew more common. First came literaries, with windy debates on Popular Election of Our Presidents and the British Colonial Policy, followed by spelldowns and a program—songs: "Love is Such a Funny, Funny Thing," "Oh Bury Me Not on the Lone Prairie"; dialogues; pieces: "The Deacon's Courtship" and "The Face on the Barroom Floor"; food. Then the long trails across the hills, dangerous at night, particularly along the gullies and river bluffs.

Eventually most of the communities settled upon dancing as the most conducive to all-night entertainment. Everybody went. If Old John was running the floor at the dance, there'd be a shapping match if he had to cuss out every cowhand or bean-eater there. He'd begin to look the crowd over while he was calling the square dances:

> Gents bow out and ladies bow under,
> Hug 'em up tight and swing like thunder.

—up on an old tub or bench, stomping his boots to hurry the fiddlers until the girls' feet left the floor and skirts flew. At midnight he'd help carry in the wash-boiler full of coffee, dip a tin cup among the floating sacks of grounds, and pour it back through the steam.

"Looks like your coffee fell in a crick coming over," he always bawled out.

With his cud of Battle Ax stowed away in a little rawhide sack he carried, Old John would sink his freed jaws into a thick slab of

boiled ham and bread as he helped pass the dishpans full of sandwiches and cake to couples lining the walls, sitting on boards laid
between chairs. And afterward, while he swept the dust and bread
rinds into little piles, he'd egg on the shapping match.

"Times ain't like they was," he'd complain, looking the crowd
over. "There ain't a feller here with spunk 'nuff to take a leatherin'
to git a purty girl."

Somebody who didn't bring a girl but would like to take one
home finally grinned and stood up; and somebody who was afraid
of losing his girl, or had a general prod on, got up too, and the
bargain was made.

A horsebacker's leather shaps are brought in and unlaced so the
two legs fall apart. Each shapper takes half and the crowd follows
them to the middle of the floor. Coats, if any, are jerked off, collars
unbuttoned. Norm and Al, the two shappers, sit on the floor, facing,
their legs dove-tailed, each with half a shap. Everybody crowds up,
the dancers first, then the older folks, and around the edge the boys
and dogs.

They draw straws from Old John's fist, and the unlucky one,
Norm, lies on his back and snaps his legs up over him. He takes
the horsehide across his rump with all the sting Al can spread on it.
Al's legs are up now; Norm gets his lick in on saddle-hardened
muscles. The crowd yells. The *whack-whack* of the shaps settles
down into a steady clockwork business, the legs going up and down
like windmill rods. After a while Al jerks his head and Old John
drags him out. He sits up, his face red and streaked as a homesick
school-ma'am's, only his is sweating.

"Norm's got two pairs of pants on."

The accused is taken out and fetched back. "Only one pair," says
Old John. The whacking starts again. Girls giggle nervously, their
men hanging to them. The crowd is taking sides. Two sprouts near
the edge take a lam at each other. Old John separates them. On the
floor the whacking is slowing up. He drags Al away again, the
puncher's head lolling, his face gray as window putty.

The crowd shies back. A pail of water is brought in. Al's face
is wet down with a towel. He grunts and turns over on his belly,
the sign that Norm's won. Who'll he pick? There's no hurry. He
can't dance any more tonight, and it's a long time until "Home,
Sweet Home." Everybody is talking. The fiddlers start:

> Honor your partner and don't be
> afraid

> To swing corner lady in a
> waltz promenade.

Sunday was spent in getting home and sleeping.

As the nesters pulled out, sheepmen bought in along the fringe of the hills. Here and there a settler who couldn't make a go of the newer farming or cattle took up woolie culture too, and then the coyote, up to now a raider of hen coops and scrub calves, developed into a killer. Wolf-hunts were organized. The regular hour for a hunt was about nine in the morning. A relay of shots started the horsebackers off on a fifteen-mile front, from Mirage Flats to Kepplinger's Bridge. Yelling, whistling, running any coyote that tried to break the line, they headed for Jackson's, towards a big V, made of hog wire, chicken fencing, and lath corncribbing, with a wire trap in the point.

Broad-handed women unpacked baskets of grub in the big barn now for the dinner. "Time they was rounding up a few coyotes," Mrs. Putney says, as she uncovers a roaster full of browned chickens. "Henry lost twenty-five sheep last week, just killed and let lay."

"They been having three, four hunts a year since '84 and all they does is make the critters harder to catch. They nearly never gets none," Mary Bowen, an old settler, commented. "Dogs or poison, that fixes the sneaking devils that gets my turkeys."

"But where's the fun in that?" asks one of the girls, climbing into the mow, late, but not dressed for work anyway.

By one o'clock the black specks are running over the Flats like bugs. Yells, commands, a cloud of dust. Horses tromping on each other's heels. A few shots. That's all.

Four rabbits, one badger, and two coyotes for two hundred hunters.

"Got sight of a couple more, but they musta snuck outa the lines. Not many-a the Pine Creek bunch showed up."

Now the dinner, dished up on long boards over barrels in the mow. Windy fellows talking about long-ago hunts, when there were real wolves, too smart for a mob. Cigars were passed by the local candidate for the legislature; an invitation to a hunt at Rushville two weeks come Sunday was read, and the hunt was over.

But the grass in the loose soil died under the sharp hoofs and close cropping of the woolies. The ranchers hated sheep and made it as hot for the woolie nurses as they could. At last most of the sheepmen pulled their freight. But just as the country was going back to cows, the Kinkaid Act was passed. The land rush put a shack on every section of land—easterners mostly, who established Sunday schools, with ladies' aids to meet Sunday afternoons because the horses must work on weekdays. Many of the newcomers objected to dancing and had play-parties instead. The soddies were small, and the Kinkaider chose his games accordingly. Charades, guessing games, or

> Tin-tin
> Come in,
> Want to buy some tin?

Perhaps

> Pleased or displeased?
> Displeased.
> What can I do to please you?

Foot races, pussy wants a corner, drop the handkerchief, or all outs in free on moonlit summer evenings. And endless songs, many of them parodies on popular tunes:

> Al Reneau was a ranchman's name,
> Skinning Kinkaiders was his game,
> First mortgages only, at a high percent,
> Jew you down on your cattle to the last red cent.

But no matter how much truck the Kinkaider grew, he couldn't turn it into cash profitably unless it could walk the thirty, forty miles to a shipping point. They must have a railroad. Once more the women stayed at home while the men gathered at the local post office, chewed tobacco, talked, wrote letters, signed petitions, and bought more machinery on pump, on the hope of a railroad that never came. Once more the shallow-rooted left, and the rest turned into combination farmers and stockmen. Sundays became ranch days, with a new crop of cowpunchers to show off before the native daughters at scratching matches.

The crowd is perched on the top planks, on the up-wind side of the corral. Here Monkey Ward cowboys strut about in bat wings and loud shirts. Riders that are riders sit on their haunches in the sun, dressed in worn shaps and blue shirts. In the corral several green hands are running a handful of wild-eyed colts around, trying for a black gelding. They snag an old sorrel mare, have to throw her to get the rope, try again.

"Why don't y'u do y'ur practisin' on y'ur bucket calves to home?" an old-timer laughs, nudging his straw-chewing neighbor. Dust, mix-up of horses and booted cowboys. They have the gelding, snub him short. Now for the blind and the leather. Red climbs on the last horse, the drawing card of the Sunday afternoon.

"Let 'er go!"

The corral gate flies back. The blind's jerked away. The black shakes, gathers into a hump, pushing Red up into the sky.

"Rip him open!"

The spurs rowel a red arc on the black hide. The horse goes up, turns, hits the dust headed north, and it's over. Red's still going south.

A hazer snags the horse, not head-shy, and brings him in. The fence hoots when Red gets up, dusts off his new hat, and walks away to himself. Not even hurt.

Lefty is prodded off the fence, not so keen now as he was a minute before Red lit. He climbs on. The black, instead of going up, spraddles out, sinking his smoke belly to the ground.

"Scratch him!" an old-timer shouts. Lefty does. The horse is off, across the prairie, bucking and running in a straight line. That's nothing. But he stops short, all four feet together. Lefty comes near going on.

"Fan him!" a tenderfoot shouts. An old rider spits. His guess is correct. There isn't time for fanning. The black leaves the ground, swaps ends, runs, swaps again. Lefty hangs on as best he can, but the turns come too fast. He's down on his shoulder, just missing the double kick the black lets out before he quits the country. Lefty picks himself up, his arm hanging funny.

"Collarbone's busted."

A couple of girls in overalls slide off the fence and fuss over Lefty. Any rider's a good rider while he's hurt.

"That horse belongs in a rodeo string," they comfort him.

The fence is deserted. "See you all at my place tonight!" Madge Miller shouts. The young people scatter down the valley, in little knots and couples. Some shag it over the chop hills, hurrying home to do the chores so they can go to the party at Madge's.

"Next scratching match at the Bar M week come Sunday," some-one reminds the riders.

"Hi!"

The country is scarcely grown up, and people are already building a tradition, a background. Old settlers and their children are suddenly superior to newer settlers and entitled to an annual barbecue as befits the honor. An old-time roundup dust hangs over Peck's Grove. Horses shy and snort at the smell of fire and frying meat. Cars are lined up by the signal stick of Mike Curran, who once prodded cows through the branding chute. Cowboys tear up, leading wild horses for the bucking contest.

"Hi!"

"Hi! Gonna ride that snaky bronc? Betcha two bits you can't even sit my old broomtail!"

Women hurry about, lugging heavy baskets, picking a shady place for the old settler's table. The men look over the race track, the horses, the new cars.

"Well, you son of a sand turtle! Step down and look at your saddle!"

Logan-Pomroy grins and gets out of his imported car. He shakes the hand of Old Amos, champion muskrat trapper, for this one day a year forgetting that he is owner of a ranch and three banks and that Amos is in dirty overalls, with gunny sack and baling wire for shoes. Today they are old cronies, the two oldest settlers.

"How's the meat hole coming?" Logan-Pomroy demands, and leads the way to the barbecue pit. Two sweating ranch cooks are turning quarters of browning beef with pitchforks or basting the meat carefully with a mixture of water, vinegar, salt, and pepper. The drippings sizzle and smoke in the red bed of ash-wood coals in the pit under the barbecuing racks.

"Come and git it!" a fat woman calls after what seems hours.

The men trail over to a table made of salt barrels and planks covered with white cloths. At the head Logan-Pomroy and Amos sit, with later settlers down the sides. Old settlers' daughters wait on them, passing huge platters of beef, mutton, and pork, followed by unlimited vegetables, salads, pies, cake, fruit, and several rounds of the coffeepot.

After the dinner there'll be contests. Fat men's, sack, three-legged, potato, and peanut races. For the women there is that old rip-snorter, a wagon race. Each contestant draws two horses, a wagon, and enough harness. First to drive around the track wins. The young cowboys with hair on their chests will show their guts in the bucking-bronco contest, twisting the broncs in approved style, and take part in the wild-cow, wild-mule, and surcingle races. But before that there are cigars and speeches and songs. Old Amos adds his rumblings to the "Nebraska Land":

> I've reached the land of drought and heat,
> Where nothing grows for man to eat.
> For wind that blows with burning heat,
> Nebraska Land is hard to beat.

About sundown the crowd scatters. Logan-Pomroy's motor roars up the hill. Without a good-bye Old Amos shuffles away through the brush down the river.

The big day is over.

But the sandhiller lives in the present also. The young folks take long car trips to dances that break up at midnight, by command of the law, and endeavor to spend most of the time until Sunday morning getting home. Sunday is a good day for those who need it to sleep off bad liquor. The more prosperous ranchers escape the cold by going south, the heat by going to the lakes. Some of these are old settlers noted for forty years of unfailing hospitality. Once their invitations, usually printed in the local items of the community paper, read something like this:

> Party and dance at Bud Jennet's, April 2.
> Dinner from one to seven.
> Beds and breakfast for all.
> Everybody welcome.

Seventy, eighty people would come in those days, some of them forty miles in wagons or on horseback. Next day the men slept between suggans in the haymow, the women all over the house. But that was when Yvette was a baby. Now she is home from college and formals as she calls them, and they have rounded up twenty guests for about four hours of housewarming in their new home. Some of them came a hundred miles, and it was worth the trip. There is an orchestra in the music room, with flowers from Alliance, and candles, Japanese prints framed in Chinese red, and tapestry panels.

"Such a beautiful home!" the guests exclaim to Mrs. Jennet.

And in three hours the maid has the muss all cleared away. There is no disputing the fact that the Jennets did well in cattle and potash.

The callers were all prosperous and charming. Not like the Jennets'
guests once were, when all who read the notice were welcome. Today
nobody ate with starvation appetite. Nobody had to be thawed out
at the hay-burner before he could sing "The Little Old Sod Shanty
on the Claim" or play "There'll be a Hot Time" on the fiddle or
the accordion. Nobody let habitual curses slip and surely none of
the guests today would ever think of singing:

> Just plant me in a stretch of west,
> Where coyotes mourn their kin.
> Let hawses paw and tromp the mound
> But don't you fence it in.

Reprinted from *Folk-Say*, edited by B. A. Botkin
University of Oklahoma Press, 1931

VII. Family Album II

With its ragged cottonwoods against the
sun, with its fogs whirling and cascading
by night over rustling fields of corn, with
the Old Timers still in the saddle, Nebraska is a place to dream of on a lazy
afternoon. Which explains, perhaps, why
you can never get it out of your blood—
why, on any night in May, the Burlington
station at Chicago is jammed with exiles
taking the 6:01 back to Ogallala, or Red
Cloud, or Bennèt.

—Gretchen Lee, "Nebraska,"
The American Mercury, Jan. 1925

Unlike a certain superabundant southwestern state (the one where purveyors of air-conditioned Cadillacs have been forced to post signs: "Sorry—only a dozen cars to a customer"), Nebraska is aware that there are forty-seven other states in the Union, many of which are good places to live, too. And if some of her sons and daughters choose to move for a time—or even permanently—to another part of the country, far from turning their pictures to the wall, she follows their careers eagerly, is delighted when they drop her a card, and saves the clippings when they get their names in the paper. As a result, her stack of scrapbooks reaches to the ceiling, for Nebraskans have gone forth and distinguished themselves in every area of national life—in the professions and the arts and politics, as builders of everything from bridges to nuclear reactors, as financiers and soldiers, entertainers and athletes.

Among the expatriate sons upon whom she has kept a proud eye is the man to whom Serge Koussevitzky once said: "The real beginning of American music was twenty-five years ago—when you came to Rochester and I came to Boston."

From Howard Hanson's Scrapbook

1. "An Unquestionably American Composer" (1936)
BURNET C. TUTHILL

AFTER-DINNER SPEAKERS and musical essayists have often seized upon the question, "What makes American music American?" But the final alloy has yet to come from the proverbial melting-pot of America, if ever one combination can be discovered that will represent our vast and diversified population as a single unit. How can we expect a unity of musical expression in the face of the continual struggle between the diverse economic and temperamental viewpoints of east and west, north and south, town and country, mountain and plain? To be sure, we live in an age of restlessness wherein a man seldom remains to pass his mature years in his natal town, but this only serves to mix and confuse the influences that are back of any creative work. To complicate matters further, there are the vestiges of national traits inherited from the lands whence we have come.

The music of Howard Hanson—an unquestionably American composer—bears telling witness to all of these influences. In the first place, he is but one generation removed from Sweden, where both his parents were born. His grandparents, Hans Hanson, Sr., and Per Munson Eckstrom, moved to the United States in the '70's, both families settling in eastern Nebraska. Here Hans Hanson, Jr., and Hilma Christina Eckstrom were married and made their home in the small Swedish Lutheran community of Wahoo, Nebraska, where their son Howard was born on October 28, 1896. Here he was brought up to the tunes associated with Martin Luther's simple and austere hymns.

But Wahoo is in the U.S.A. and close to Lincoln, as typical an American city of the open spaces as one can find. In the former, Hanson had the benefit of a normal boyhood, in which music was only one interest among many. Here his mother began his musical education. When he was seven, Howard entered Luther College, where in addition to the regular academic courses he studied piano and violincello, harmony and counterpoint, and at once began to set down musical compositions of his own. He was confirmed in the Lutheran Church and was seriously attracted to its ministry.

At fifteen, Hanson entered the University School of Music in Lincoln, where the Scandinavian influences began to lose their predominance in the larger life of an American city. Then on to New York to study piano at the Institute of Musical Art. A teaching fellowship at Northwestern University in Evanston, Illinois, led him westward again, and here, in 1916, he received his Bachelor of Music degree. In the autumn of that year, when still but nineteen, he was appointed Professor of Theory and Composition at the Music Conservatory of the College of the Pacific, and in 1919 became its dean. During his west coast stay, he composed the scores which led to his being awarded the Prix de Rome, giving him the first three-year fellowship at the American Academy in Rome.

Previously Hanson had conducted the Los Angeles and San Francisco symphony orchestras in performances of his own works. On his return to America in 1924 he was invited by Walter Damrosch to direct the New York Symphony in a first performance of *North and West*—a symphonic poem in which Scandinavian and American tendencies are juxtaposed. Later he visited Rochester to conduct the Rochester Philharmonic Orchestra in his *Nordic* Symphony.

On the podium he is vital yet poetic. He knows his scores, be they his own or those of others, and he brings to their interpretation a sympathetic understanding of the composer's ideas. His friendly and simple personality calls forth at once the full cooperation of the musicians. He has an uncanny sense of contrast and climax. Careful as a rehearser, he nevertheless gets his results quickly by drawing out the performers themselves rather than by seeming to impose his will upon them.

As a composer, he has shown himself a romanticist who lives in twentieth-century America, but who maintains a spiritual contact with his forbears in their rugged Scandinavia, and shares their firm belief in God. The music has a definite popular appeal from its own nature and not from any concession or calculated effort to make it so. The whole gives an impression of thorough sincerity, with no striving after effect for its own sake, no attempt to speak unnaturally merely in order to appear different. Here is the outpouring from the heart of a man among men, whose energy and obligations give him little time for seclusion. The music, like the man, is easily approachable. Behind both is an interesting and winning personality.

Howard Hanson stands as one of the first American composers, conductors, and leaders in music education. But above all he is an engaging person, friendly and generous of himself to a fault.

Condensed from *The Musical Quarterly*, Vol. XXII, 1936

2. Music Incubator (1940)

THE LATE George Eastman, onetime office boy, who founded, developed and headed the $177,000,000 Eastman Kodak Co., couldn't recognize a tune or tell one note from the next. But George Eastman wanted desperately to like music. In 1918 he founded a $17,000,000 school of music in Rochester. The Eastman School of Music flourished, and is today counted one of the most important music conservatories in the U.S.

As director for their music school, Eastman's executives in 1924 picked a boyish, bearded 28-year-old Nebraskan named Howard Hanson. Director Hanson's main interest was composition, and it was not long before he had turned Eastman's music school into a gigantic incubator for young U.S. composers. For them Director Hanson provided classes in counterpoint, a symphony orchestra, and even a ballet company to play their works. He installed a recording system, made phonograph records of students' lopsided sonatas and sway-backed symphonies, so that they could study their faults over & over again. Nine years ago Director Hanson held a Festival of American Music at which he conducted a bushel or so of new U.S. music. The festival was so successful that it has been repeated every year.

Director Hanson, who raised a goatee when he was studying in Rome because he thought young musicians attracted too little attention, still defends the young U.S. composer with crotchety vigor. No modernist himself, he personally dislikes the dissonant groanings and thumpings of the musical *Kulturbolschewiki*. But he will defend to the death their right to groan and thump.

"There is an enormous difference," explains Director Hanson, "between music that is well-knit and sounds like Hell, and music that doesn't sound the way the composer intended it to sound. The first is competent musicianship; the second is not. . . . A competent composer deserves at least one hearing before an audience."

Extracted from *Time*, May 8, 1940. © Time, Inc., 1940

3. "America's Gift of Music" (1946)

JOHN TASKER HOWARD

THROUGH THE American Composers' Concerts, which are now in their twenty-first season, and the annual Festival of American Music at Rochester, Howard Hanson has done more to encourage his fellow composers and to give new talent a hearing than any other individual or group in this country.

The most widely performed of his orchestral works have been the *Nordic* and *Romantic* symphonies, the latter commissioned by Serge Koussevitzky for the fiftieth anniversary of the Boston Symphony Orchestra, and two of his symphonic poems, *Lux Aeterna* and *Pan and the Priest*. Hanson's Fourth Symphony, which won for its composer the Pulitzer prize for musical composition, was first performed by the Boston Symphony, with the composer conducting, December 3, 1943. The work is dedicated to the memory of the composer's father, and consists of four separate movements which follow the plan of the Requiem Mass. As a whole, the symphony shows a significant departure from the romanticism of Hanson's early works.

His opera *Merry Mount* was produced by the Metropolitan Opera Company, February 10, 1934, with Tullio Serafin conducting, and a cast which included Lawrence Tibbett, Edward Johnson, Gladys Swarthout, and Goeta Ljungberg. The Metropolitan premiere was a tremendously successful affair, and, according to reporters, there were fifty curtain calls for composer, librettist, and performers. However, in spite of public acclaim, the critics were somewhat reserved in their praise.

But Hanson's importance to American music does not rest on any single work, nor, indeed, on any one phase of his activity. In spite of his devoted interest in the development of American music, Hanson is no chauvinist; he is not an advocate of a "nationalist" school. To him American music means music written by Americans. It makes no difference what their backgrounds may be, whether they are descendants of the settlers of Plymouth or the sons of immigrants newly arrived. His sole interest is that America contribute its gift of music to the world, that a rich creative musical life may flourish in this country, that some of the great ideals that are American may be transmuted into living tone.

Condensed from *Our American Music*, Thomas Y. Crowell Co., 1946

Some boys dream of being President of the United States and some of playing in the World Series. About the time a young Lincoln lawyer was, figuratively, packing his bags for the White House, a shaver out-state in St. Paul was pitching pickup games in the school yard, and his ambitions, too, were big league. The record books show that the young lawyer was a great competitor, but it was the St. Paul boy who made it.

Alexander the Great

TOM MEANY

1.

GROVER CLEVELAND ALEXANDER, the man who became a legend in his own lifetime, was his own worst enemy. He won more games than any other pitcher in National League history—indeed, only Cy Young and Walter Johnson ever won more major league games than Alex—but he never could win over himself. It is easy to moralize about Alexander, who died in semi-poverty in his native St. Paul, Nebraska, November 4, 1950; but Old Pete * himself was never one for moralizing. He never blamed his fondness for the bottle on anybody but himself.

It is doubtful if there ever was a smoother pitcher than Alexander. He worked without exertion while warming up, and when he went to the mound he pitched with the same easy motion. Alex threw three-quarters, scarcely seeming to stride and with no waste motion. There were no three-hour ball games when Alexander was pitching.

Tom Sheehan, now a Giant scout, recalls the first time he saw Alexander pitch in the tiny National League Park in Philadelphia, which

---

* "One day in Texas, shortly after he went up to the big leagues, he was tagged with the nickname 'Pete.' It was the off-season, and he set out with a couple of baseball cronies to do a little hunting and drinking. Riding on the back of a buckboard, filled with liquid cheer, he suddenly toppled off and landed flat on his face in a large pool of alkali and mud. When they finally got him back on the wagon, one of the ballplayers began to laugh, saying: 'Well, if you ain't old Alkali Pete himself.' "—"The Ups and Downs of 'Old Pete' " by Jack Sher

later came to be known as Baker Bowl. Sheehan was a rookie with the Athletics, and Joe Bush, another A's pitcher, took Tom to see the Phils perform on an off-day.

"I knew who Alec was and all about him," explained Sheehan, "because he had been a winning pitcher for the Phils for a couple of seasons, but this was the first time I had ever seen him. He certainly didn't look like much. He warmed up like a guy playing catch and then he went out and pitched the same way. He was six feet, but he kinda scrunched down so he didn't look tall. And he had a funny cap that didn't look like it fit him.

"I took one look at Baker Bowl, and I was glad I didn't have to pitch there. It looked like the right fielder was breathing down the second baseman's neck, and the stands were so close to the infield that there was no chance of catching a pop foul. Well, Alec goes to work on these guys and he murders 'em. He breaks curve balls off on their fists and he sneaks fast balls that don't look like fast balls right by 'em. I never saw such pitching in my life—and I haven't seen anything to beat it since. When it's all over, I turns to Bush and I says, 'Joe, how the hell do they ever beat this guy?'

"And Joe says, 'They don't—very often!'"

It is no wonder that his first look at Alexander left Sheehan bug-eyed in admiration at the artistry of his effort, for Alex was that type of pitcher. His pitching was founded on sheer skill, not brawn.

Another admirer of Alexander was Casey Stengel, who broke into the National League shortly after Alex and always considered Alexander the smoothest pitching machine he ever had seen.

"I remember in 1914 or thereabouts when I thought I had a way figured out to fool Alex," recalls Stengel. "He used to break his curve in on me—as he did on all the other hitters—and I figured that if I moved up four or five inches just as he was about to pitch, I'd be able to meet the curve ball before it broke. You had to move quick with Alex because he took hardly any windup, but I did it and I managed to pull the ball against the right field fence for two bases. As I rounded first, I saw the guys in our bull pen standing up amazed-like. Pulling Alexander! Why, it just wasn't being done.

"When I came back to our bench Uncle Robbie and all the boys are asking, 'What happened, Case?' and, 'How'd you do it, Case?' but ole Case ain't saying a thing but just giving 'em the big wink. Tell my secrets? Not me! Why, I'm the guy who's got Alexander the Great solved. At least that's what I thought until the next time I go to bat. Again I inch forward as Alex winds up. In comes the curve and smack!—right against my knuckles where I'm gripping the bat. Boy, it stung! I dropped the bat and commenced shaking my hands, just like a kid who's been rapped across the knuckles by teacher's ruler. And out on the mound, old Alex is grinning and shaking his finger at me as if to say, 'Naughty boy! Teacher spank.' Believe me, I never tried to get smart with that guy again.''

Although in one three-year span, the seasons of 1915, 1916, and 1917, Alexander won a grand total of 94 games for the Phillies and gave up the amazingly low total of 170 bases on balls in 1,153 innings—an average of lower than three every two full ball games— he is best remembered for his strikeout of Lazzeri in the 1926 World Series, which occurred after McCarthy had exiled him from the Cubs. McCarthy asked waivers on the veteran, and the Cards claimed him on June 22 for $6,000. Alex, who had a mediocre 3-3 record with the Cubs, won nine and lost seven for St. Louis as the Cards won their first pennant in history. It was a close fit with the Reds and Pirates for Rogers Hornsby's club, and the nine victories the 39-year-old Alexander had picked up were important.

After Herb Pennock had beaten Willie Sherdel 2 to 1 in the opener in New York, Hornsby called on Alex. The Yanks got two runs off him in the second, but after Earle Combs had opened the third with a single, Alexander shut up shop, retiring the last 21 Yankees in a row to win by 6 to 2.

When the Series moved to St. Louis, the Yanks won two out of three and came back to the Stadium faced with the pleasant prospect of merely splitting even to win the title. They might have made it, too, if it hadn't been for Alexander: he beat them 10 to 2 in the sixth game to even the Series at three-all.

It was here that legend began taking over the story of Alexander. Jesse Haines started the seventh game for the Cardinals on a chilly, misty, murky Sunday against Waite Hoyt. Babe Ruth got the Yanks off in front with his fourth home run of the Series in the third, but the American Leaguers fell apart behind Hoyt in the fourth, and the Cardinals got three runs. The Yanks nudged Haines for one in the sixth and really began to go to work on him in the seventh. Haines had a blister on the index finger of his pitching hand from the rigor with which he had been bearing down on every pitch. Combs walked to open the inning, and Mark Koenig sacrificed. Ruth was intentionally passed and forced by Bob Meusel, Combs reaching third. Hornsby took no chances with Lou Gehrig and ordered another intentional pass, filling the bases, bringing up Lazzeri and setting the stage for Alexander and myth.

One story is that Alexander had celebrated his second Series victory so thoroughly the night before that he practically needed a seeing-eye dog to guide him in from the bull pen; that Hornsby looked into his eyes to see if they were clear, handed him the ball and pointing to Lazzeri said, "There's no place to put him."

Here is Alex's version of what happened, told at the 1950 World Series in his visit to New York, less than a month before he died:

"I was cold sober the night before I relieved Haines in the seventh game," flatly declared Alexander. "After Saturday's game, Hornsby came over to me in the clubhouse and asked me not to celebrate, telling me he might need me in the seventh game. So I stayed in my hotel room all night.

"There were a couple of other fellows in the bull pen with me—Art Reinhart and Herman Bell—when the phone from our bench rang. Hornsby said he wanted me, even though the others had been loosening up and I hadn't." As far as Hornsby giving out any epigrams or instructions, Alex says there was none of that. "He was standing out by second base, and when I reached the mound, he just threw me the ball," said Pete. "That's all there was to it."

Actually, there was a little more to it than that—the matter of Alexander striking out Lazzeri to silence the last Yankee threat and then to hold them back in the eighth and ninth to preserve the 3-to-2 margin which gave St. Louis its first world's championship.

Alexander struck out Poosh-'Em-Up Tony on four pitches, and the second strike against Lazzeri was a ringing drive down the third-base line, foul by a few feet, which would have cleared the bases. Tony went down swinging.

Everything that Alex had done before that in baseball, all of his escapades since, have been forgotten. The strikeout of Lazzeri is the high-water mark of the old master's career, few caring to note that Alex fanned 2,227 major league hitters in his lifetime.

As glamorous as Alexander's record on the field was, his record off it was as sorry. After serving overseas in World War I, the great pitcher suddenly became subject to epileptic seizures. These were closely guarded secrets, and it was only in his later years, when he was found unconscious in the street, that his disability became generally known. Alex's drinking was always a private affair. As long ago as the winter of 1925-26, he entered himself into a sanitarium to cure himself of alcoholism, but it didn't last.

Aimee Amanto, whom Alexander married before he sailed for France in 1918, was the one person who could influence the pitcher, but even her influence didn't work always. They were divorced, remarried, and divorced again, and when Alex was found dead in his rented room, there was an unfinished letter to Aimee in his typewriter.

2.*

Grover Cleveland Alexander was born February 26, 1887, on a farm near St. Paul, Nebraska. There were 13 children in the family —twelve boys and one girl. His father was a farmer and the finest hunter in the community. Dode, as Alex then was called, did his first hunting with stones and rocks.

"He was always throwing at something," his mother once said. "When I wanted a chicken or a turkey killed, Dode would go out and bring it down with a rock, hitting it on the run."

Whenever he could, young Alexander would slip into town and get into a ball game. He pitched in pickup games on the schoolyard lot, using that awkward, funny, side-arm delivery that knocked down chickens on the run. None of the kids in the small Nebraska town could seem to get a piece of that ball that Dode whipped at them.

When he was 19, Alex took a job as a lineman for a telephone company. The linemen had a ball team and Alex pitched for them. His first time out, the big farm boy beat a team of "paid players" in Central City, Nebraska. He whipped them four games in a row. The telephone team didn't play often enough to suit Alexander, so he picked up with scrub teams whenever he could. One day when a game went into extra innings, Alex showed up late for work with the line gang. The foreman fired him.

The manager of the Central City team hired Alex at $50 a month. When the season ended in Central City, Alexander drifted to a county fair at Burwell, Nebraska, to pitch two games against a crack semi-pro team from Illinois. He won both games, and a shortstop named Miller, playing for the rival team, carried the news about "a young Nebraska kid who can pitch like a fool" back to the manager of a professional team in Galesburg, Illinois.

On January 12, 1909, Grover Cleveland Alexander signed his first contract as a professional ballplayer with Galesburg in the Class D

---

* The story of Alexander's early years has been condensed from "The Ups and Downs of 'Old Pete' " by Jack Sher in *A Treasury of Sports Stories* (Bartholomew House, 1955).

Three-Eye League. His salary was $100 a month. He won 15 games for Galesburg before he got slapped into the dirt, hit so hard it almost closed his career forever. During a hard-fought game, Alex, who wasn't much of a hitter, loped down to first on a scratch single. On the hit and run, he started for second, lumbering down the base-path in that comical, awkward way he always ran. The Galesburg batter hit a ground ball to the shortstop, who flipped it to the second-baseman for a force-out. The second-baseman wheeled and fired the ball toward first in an attempted double play. Alex came charging on, the ball struck him full on the side of the head, and he went down like a poled steer.

The big kid pitcher was unconscious for 56 hours. When Alex was able to sit up in the hospital bed, he saw two of everything: his eyesight had been affected by the blow on the head. He was told by the doctors that he might suffer from double vision for the rest of his life.

When they let him out of the hospital, Alex stubbornly insisted on getting back into uniform. Day after day, he tried to pitch. But he kept seeing two batters, two catchers. Finally, without revealing his ailment, Galesburg sold Alexander to the Indianapolis ball club, managed by Charlie Carr. Scared, heartsick, still seeing double, young Alexander reported to Indianapolis. He distinguished himself at the first practice by breaking three of Charlie Carr's ribs with the first ball he pitched. Carr sent him back home to Nebraska.

Pete should have been through. But he wouldn't quit. Day after day he would go into town, hunt up someone to catch for him, and keep on throwing at the two figures. He kept it up all through the long winter.

"I knew I was through, but I couldn't stop throwin'," he once said. "If I stopped, I knew I'd go all to pieces."

Alex couldn't believe it when the Indianapolis management notified him the following spring that he had been traded to Syracuse in the New York State League. Carr, who wanted a favor from the Syracuse manager, gave Alexander to that ball club for exactly nothing! "This Alexander is wild as hell," Carr told the Syracuse pilot, "but he's got plenty of speed."

And so Syracuse got, for free, the greatest control pitcher of all time.

Two or three days before Alex left to report to the eastern ball club, his vision returned to normal. It happened suddenly, miraculously. He was pitching to a friend in a schoolyard in St. Paul,

Nebraska. As he wound up, two catcher's mitts danced before his eyes and then, as the ball cracked into the receiver's glove, everything suddenly became one, clear and whole.

Into Syracuse like a windstorm came the tall Nebraskan with the freckled face, the shock of sandy hair, and the peculiar side-arm delivery. Straight from the farm, from hopelessness and despair, came the young pitcher who was to be called Alex the Great, who was to set mound records that would never be matched. Maybe he was greater in later years, but the Syracuse Stars thought that Grover Cleveland Alexander, pitching for them in 1910, was something of a miracle. Almost half of the 29 games he won were shutouts. He pitched 13 goose-egg ball games, this kid who couldn't see straight just a few months before!

The claw of a major-league club reached out, and the 22-year-old pitcher was purchased by the Philadelphia Phillies for the incredible sum of $500. He was promised $250 on the line every month, provided he made good. "It seemed like a stack of money," Alex told a reporter in later years, "so I tried extra hard." *

The rookie pitcher, with only one full season in the minors behind him, went on to win 28 games that year. Up went his first record, never to be touched. And late in the season, with the victories piled up behind him, Alexander faced the immortal Cy Young in what was undoubtedly the greatest pitchers' duel of the century.

It was Denton True Young's last game. Cy had won 511 ball games, which still sticks up there in the record book as the all-time high. He had won all those games and he still had it—the skill, the heart, all the ingredients that comprise greatness in a pitcher. Hurling for the Boston Nationals that day, the gallant Cy used every pitch he had learned in 22 years of baseball—sweeping curves, drops, the deceptive spitball. Inning after inning, the game wore on, neither side able to dent the matchless hurling of the fat, ancient veteran or the young rookie. Cy gave out in the 12th, the Phils pushed across one run, Alex held fast, and the game was his.

3.

Until his very last year in baseball, Alexander never had a losing season as a pitcher. Control as well as economy of pitching was the

---

* Compared to today's major league players, Old Pete worked for peanuts. The Phillies paid him $250 a month the year he won 28 games for them. The Cubs paid him $8,000 with a $1,000 bonus if he won more than 30 games. His all-time top salary was $17,000 from the Cardinals.

secret of Alexander's success. He pitched 90 shutouts in his career, a National League record, and holds the major league record for shutouts in a season, 16 in 1916. Twice Alexander pitched and won both ends of a double-header. He once pitched a game in 58 minutes and, although he never pitched a no-hitter, he did pitch four one-hitters in one season, 1915, something no other pitcher has done.

Although the dead ball employed before World War I undoubtedly was of great assistance to Alexander in the years when he was winning 30 and upward, it is revealing that he won 27 games for the Cubs in 1920 and 21 games for the Cardinals when he was over 40 years old. He never sought strikeout records but relied on getting the ball over the plate in such a manner that it couldn't be met squarely. In these days of the lively ball a batter can send a ball he doesn't meet properly flying into the seats. While Alexander won the great majority of his games in the dead-ball era, it is worth while noting that he continued to be a winning pitcher for a decade after the introduction of the jack-rabbit ball and a decade in which Alex didn't take the best care of himself, to put it mildly.

Alexander had such natural talent that he would have been a stickout under any conditions, yet oddly enough he wasn't figured as a regular when he first went south with the Phillies in 1911. The ease with which Alex pitched, the nonchalance which was to be his trademark, struck Dooin as being nothing but indolence. It was Pat Moran, Dooin's coach, who pleaded Alex's case at the Wilmington, North Carolina, training camp. "Let the kid come north with me on the second squad, Red," importuned Moran, "and I'll have a pitcher for you when we get back home."

When the two Philly squads reassembled in Philadelphia for the city series with the Athletics which preceded the regular season, Moran told Dooin he'd make no mistake counting on Alexander as a regular. "He's a pitcher if I ever saw one," declared Pat. Dooin, still wanting to be shown, pitched Alexander in one of the exhibition games against the A's. The kid from Nebraska turned in seven scoreless innings, and Dooin was convinced.

For the next twenty years nobody at all had to be convinced that Old Pete was truly Alexander the Great.

Condensed from *Baseball's Greatest Pitchers*, A. S. Barnes & Co., 1951

There is some dispute—says Lilian Fitzpatrick in Nebraska Place-Names—*as to the origin of the name Wahoo.
One explanation is that it derives from "euonymous" or
"wahoo," commonly known as the "burning bush." Another source says that it comes from "pahoo" which means
"not very bluffy." A third states that "wahoo" is an
Indian word for a species of elm.*

*There is no dispute, however, as to the origin of Darryl
F. Zanuck: he was born in Wahoo on September 5, 1902.
Nor is there any dispute as to what his name means in the
motion picture industry.*

One-Man Studio

AT THE far end of a lobby-sized green-and-gold Hollywood office, a
wiry, high-domed man gnawed a massive cigar, paced briskly back
& forth, and spewed memoranda in a loud Midwestern twang. Occasionally, hypnotized by his own train of thought, he ducked briefly
into an open anteroom behind his desk, to stalk an idea among the
stuffed heads of a water hog and an antelope, the skins of a lion and
a jaguar, the sawed-off feet of an elephant and a rhino. Working in
relay, three stenographers dashed into the huge office to scribble
notes, dashed out again to rush the words down through the hier-
archy of the 20th Century-Fox Film Corp.

His pale blue eyes hovering over everything from finances to
falsies, Darryl F. Zanuck was warming up to another 18-hour day
as production boss of 20th Century-Fox and pace-setter for the
U. S. cinema. In 142 lbs. and a carefully measured 5 ft. 6¾ ins., he
embodies what may be nature's ultimate attempt to equip the species
for outstanding success in Hollywood. Producer Zanuck is richly
endowed with tough-mindedness, talent, an out-sized ego, and a
glutton's craving for hard work. These qualities, indulged with endless enthusiasm, have not only sped him to the top but have somehow left him free of ulcers and in the pink of health.

As a trailblazer, Zanuck has no Hollywood equal. At Warners' he
played a key role in the industry's transition from silent pictures to
talkies (The Jazz Singer, The Singing Fool). He sired the cine-

musical (Forty-Second Street, Gold-Diggers of Broadway). He pioneered and developed the technique of snatching good movie plots out of the headlines (I Am a Fugitive from a Chain Gang), and injected memorable realism into the gangster cycle of the '30's (Public Enemy). He enabled Producer Louis de Rochemont to launch the semi-documentary (The House on 92nd Street). He set the postwar style of using authentic locations in foreign countries (Prince of Foxes), and, incidentally, melting Hollywood's frozen funds abroad.*

Most important, Darryl Francis Zanuck has gone further than anyone in Hollywood in breaking down resistance to serious, grown-up films with controversial themes. A man of courage, physical as well as moral, he insisted on producing such pictures in the teeth of angry pressure groups, and sometimes to the consternation of his own bosses in the New York office. He lost $2,000,000 on his biggest flop, Wilson (1944), which preached against postwar isolationism, and he fell short of a profit on 1943's The Ox-Bow Incident, a vivid anti-lynching movie which got critics' cheers. But with such films as The Grapes of Wrath (1940), Gentleman's Agreement (1947), The Snake Pit (1948) and Pinky (1949), he proved that stories based on such themes as unemployment, anti-Semitism, mental illness and the Negro problem could pay off on the screen.

For a tycoon of such solid accomplishments and recognition (two Oscars and two prized Irving Thalberg Awards), Zanuck for years cut a rather outlandish figure—even by Hollywood standards. He took sophomoric delight in playing such pranks as putting a trained ape into his executive chair, turning the lights down and summoning a new writer. He surrounded himself with court jesters, browbeat his oversubmissive underlings ("For God's sake, don't say yes until I finish talking"). His sycophants vied so earnestly in their assurances of devotion that one whimsical executive, putting an end to the contest, once volunteered: "When I die, I want to be cremated and have my ashes sprinkled on Mr. Zanuck's driveway so his car won't skid."

Zanuck's lack of formal schooling made for some conversational bloopers ("Betterment and correctment"), and gave him an oblique approach to culture. A restless traveler who keeps his retinue stepping, he once dogtrotted into the Louvre with the observation: "We

---

* Since this article was written Mr. Zanuck has done some more trail-blazing. In 1953, at a critical time in the industry, he was instrumental in introducing a third dimension to the screen—a development recognized as the most important innovation since the introduction of talkies.

gotta be outa this joint in 20 minutes." His enthusiasm for big-game hunting, duck shooting, riding and polo also provided sport for sniggering Hollywood humorists. But these furious pursuits were no joke to the animals whose remains now adorn his office, nor to his helpless subordinates who had to tag along. Though the polo team was at first sneered at as the only one "where the horses are better bred than the men," its intense, fearless little captain drove it to win the respect of its opponents and the hospitality of Pasadena's uppity Midwick Country Club. Meanwhile, headlong Darryl Zanuck became a two-goal player at the price of such injuries as a smashed nose and a broken hand.

More staid in his outside activities than he used to be, Zanuck, the one-man studio, still gives a 3-ring performance. In a story conference, where he plays all the roles of scenes in the making, the bristly mustache suddenly twitches and the face looks heavenward in horror. The jaw sags until the huge cigar droops from his lower lip; he leans back across the grand piano in his office; his voice becomes shrill and frightened. This is Zanuck impersonating a virgin in distress.

Zanuck's leather-lunged chatter during a conference rambles almost as much as his footsteps. He thinks in pictorial terms, does not fancy himself as a dialogue writer, intends his ad-libbing only as a guide. As an idea man, however, he is probably unsurpassed in Hollywood. His mind is a storehouse of plots, story angles and gimmicks, and with free-wheeling inventiveness, he works them endlessly into different patterns. He is also a merciless story critic. Respecting talent, he has a knack for channeling it, and knows when to leave it alone. For all his autocratic belligerence, he can quickly drop an idea of his own when someone else comes up with a better one.

Darryl Zanuck made his movie debut playing an Indian maiden on an early lot at $1 a day. That was just eleven years after his birth on Sept. 5, 1902 at Wahoo, Neb. (pop. 3,300). Worried about his health, his Methodist parents—Frank Zanuck, an Iowa-born hotel clerk of Swiss parentage, and Louise Torpin Zanuck, a Nebraskan of English stock—moved to Los Angeles when Darryl was six. His mother cut his early movie career short as soon as she caught sight of him in an Indian costume. Not long after their arrival in California, his parents were divorced. When his mother remarried unhappily, Darryl began spending his summers back in Nebraska with her father, Henry Torpin, a well-to-do grain processor and landowner who could spin eye-witness tall tales about an Indian massacre. In letters to his grandfather, the scrawny boy soon outdid the old man's stories with lurid imaginings of what might be seen from his train window.

Not quite fifteen, Darryl enlisted in the Nebraska National Guard after taking the braces off his teeth so that he could lie more convincingly about his age. He spent almost two years in service, on the Mexican border and in France, dispatching more letters * to his grandfather. A veteran at 17, he lost patience with school and determined to be a writer, like O. Henry. Meanwhile, he sold shirts and newspaper subscriptions, worked as a rivet catcher in the shipyards and a poster tinter in a theatre lobby. Writing furiously, he sold a story called Mad Desire to Physical Culture.

At 20 (and looking younger), unrestrainedly ambitious and insufferably cocksure, Zanuck set out to conquer Hollywood. He quickly became the nuisance of the Los Angeles Athletic Club, which was then home to such important personages as Charlie Chaplin, Mack Sennett and Fatty Arbuckle. Two of the club members, William Russell and Raymond Griffith, who were big stars of the day, treated Zanuck tolerantly. Thanks to a tip from Russell he made his first movie sale—to Universal for $525. He flourished briefly at selling his stories to the films until in 1923 the studios suddenly decided to buy only from writers with literary reputations. Getting nowhere, he turned for advice to Griffith, who casually counseled: "Do a book."

Zanuck did. In his first real stroke of Hollywood genius, he persuaded the manufacturer of a hair tonic called Yuccatone to pay for the job-printing of a volume called Habit, which is now a collector's item. Zanuck sent engraved cards to the studios announcing the publication of his "novel." Actually, Habit consisted of three of his rejected scenarios in narrative form, plus an elaborately disguised 100-page testimonial to Yuccatone.

---

* "The war started him off as a writer, although Zanuck didn't realize it at the time. All he thought he was doing was giving the home folks back in Wahoo, Nebraska, a thrill by writing them letters which were full of the pity and terror and glory of war, even though Zanuck had to invent most of it. These letters were printed in the local paper. . . . On his return he was met by his admiring public and also by one of his schoolteachers, who dampened the reception by inquiring icily when he was coming back to finish his schoolwork. There and then he announced that he was through with school and sick of people kicking him around because he looked too young. He'd show 'em, he would! So he headed for Hollywood. . . ." J. P. McEvoy, "He's Got Something," *Saturday Evening Post,* July 1, 1939.

Ever since Habit, there's been no stopping Zanuck. Though the long Yuccatone blurb somehow defied efforts to put it on the screen, the other three pieces were eventually filmed. He also used the book to impress petite Virginia Fox, an actress he met at about that time on a blind date. He sent her a copy the next day, followed it up daily for six months with flowers until she consented to marry him. Hollywood, pro- and anti-Zanuck, knows Virginia Zanuck today as an unusually gracious woman without airs, who has a strong influence for the best on her husband.

In 1924, Zanuck settled at Warners' as a writer assigned to Rin-Tin-Tin, the dog star. "He was the most brilliant bloody animal that ever lived," says Zanuck, who managed nevertheless to keep a jump ahead of the beast. Zanuck graduated finally to pictures with human stars, piled up 19 screen credits in one year until exhibitors protested that the Warners were charging too much for their movies when they had only one writer—"this Zanuck"— on their payroll.

One night in 1927 the Warners summoned him. Starting the next day, they told him, he would be the studio's executive producer, with a salary jump from $125 to $5,000 a week. Zanuck pampered his mustache, put more bite into his voice, began turning out flamboyant, exciting pictures at low cost. He had stuttered for years, but by 1930, as he grew into confident authority, the stutter disappeared.

Zanuck broke with the Warners three years later. He had committed the studio to restoring, by a certain date, a 50% industrywide pay cut. When the time came, Harry Warner insisted that he would not resume the full pay scale until a week later. Though his contract still had five years to run, Zanuck quit rather than to go back on his word. For advice on his next move, he went to canny Joseph M. Schenck, an industry pioneer and boss of United Artists. Before he left Schenck's apartment, they had written out a longhand contract to form 20th Century. In 18 months Zanuck made 18 pictures—17 of them successes. The bustling little company developed an earning power roughly equal to that of the huge Fox Film Corp., whose assets were nine times as large. While Zanuck hunted bear in Alaska, Joe Schenck bagged a prize at home: a merger creating 20th Century-Fox.

World War II matured Zanuck, both as a man and moviemaker, sent him back to the studio bursting to produce films of "real significance." As a lieutenant colonel in the Signal Corps, making training and combat documentary movies, he chafed under discipline and hostility, has since decided that "It was a great thing to get a kick in the pants at that stage of your career." The kick was sometimes well deserved, notably when he let himself be photographed in attitudes of bravery under fire in his Technicolor documentary of U.S. landings in North Africa. After service for which he won the Legion of Merit, he tore into his studio job again.

Zanuck begins a chain-smoking day with one of his eight-inch cigars—the first of 20—and a phone call on his private wire to the studio to find out how movies—his own and competitors'—are grossing around the country. After a shave by Sam ("The Barber") Silver, who comes out from the studio, Zanuck drives his green Cadillac ten miles to the lot, attacks production schedules, mail, memos and telegrams until 1 P.M. By 3:30 or 4 P.M., he darts to his projection room to look at rushes, wardrobe and make-up tests. By 4:30 he calls up his children—Richard Darryl, 15, Susan Marie, 16, and Mrs. Marrilyn Zanuck Jacks—for a fatherly chat. At 6 P.M., after a rubdown from the studio masseur, he takes a nap in a sound-proof chamber off his office. Awakened at 8, he dines at the studio, sometimes with Mrs. Zanuck or his French tutor (he has been studying French on the run ever since he was awarded the French Legion of Honor in 1936), sometimes alone, staring grimly at a television set. At 9, he is looking at more rushes or rough-cut complete films. Then he gives instructions to cutters, producers and directors who join him in relays into the night. He sees everything that is put on film at the studio, and the whole output of every major competitor. His working day ends sometime between 2 and 4 A.M.

Zanuck breaks up this grueling routine with three-day weekends, occasional flights in season to Sun Valley, where he skis expertly, and four-week vacations on the Riviera. Except during the summer, he weekends at his Palm Springs estate, where the Zanucks usually entertain 12 to 16 guests. Zanuck runs the weekend party with the same steely control he uses at the studio. He refuses to play any game at which he does not excel. Since being introduced to croquet, he has made it a cult, has turned his lawn into one of the world's best-kept croquet courts, complete with floodlights.

Insured by 20th Century-Fox for $900,000 (all it could get), Zanuck in 1949 signed Hollywood's longest-term contract: * ten years at his old salary of $260,000 a year. As the largest individual stock-

---

* Early in 1955, Mr. Zanuck resigned as vice-president in charge of production in order to produce his pictures independently, for release through 20th Century-Fox.

holder, he has 100,000 shares in the company, plus 30,000 in trust for his children (total current value: $2,616,250). In 1949 his income from salary and dividends, before taxes, came to $465,000. After taxes, it did not meet his expenses. Says Zanuck: "I manage only by going a few thousand dollars into my savings each year. I won't change my way of living to save a few lousy bucks. I have a philosophy about it: the only thing you get out of life is living. I'm not working as hard as I do to turn around and deprive myself." But for zealous Moviemaker Zanuck, the best part of living is his work: "Actually, nothing has ever given me the genuine satisfaction of taking pictures, seeing them through and then getting wonderful reviews. I love what I'm doing."

*When you know that this U.S. Envoy Extraordinary and
Minister Plenipotentiary was Edgar Howard's son, it will
not surprise you that he was a diplomat with a difference.*

"El Ministro Cowboy"

JOHN NEILL

April, 1941, Asuncion, Paraguay

Findley Howard has gone home. He packed his trunks, bade farewell to a host of friends, and departed for his native Columbus,
Nebraska. Paraguay grieved to see him go.

Findley Howard has been, for the last five years, U.S. Minister to
the Republic of Paraguay. A widower, he made the Legation a single
man's paradise. In accord with tropical custom, the Minister frowned
on serious drinking before noon, and during the morning confined
himself to a pink liquid identified by some visitors as pink gin, by
others as Lavoris. Whatever it was, he found it very tonic and
restorative.

In food, the Minister had a one-track mind. His dish, day after
day, was canned tongue imported from the U.S. Howard employed
a good cook and set a varied table for guests. As for himself, he
didn't care much about eating, and when he was alone it seemed
simplest to settle on tongue.

It gets steaming hot in Asuncion, and when the weather became
too much for him, Howard was wont to discard clothing as a needless
bother. Another odd habit which impressed guests was his morning
game of solitaire. After breakfast the Minister would proceed in state
to the Legation bathroom where there was set up a card table with
a deck of cards and a glass of the invariable pink liquid. Here the
Minister would while away an hour before undertaking the arduous
duties of the day.

When Howard, the son of a Nebraska newspaper publisher, first
blew into town, his midwestern breeziness soon had the Paraguayans
holding their hats. Some dignified citizens were jarred by his habit of
strolling into the pompous Union Club and clapping them on the
shoulder with a genial "Hi ya, Toots." But as they came to recognize
his keen business sense, his straight-shooting, and his political under-

standing, they decided that if this was Yankee style, they liked it.

What really won the Paraguayans was the Minister's fantastic personal courage during a Paraguayan revolution. As the story is reported, Howard donned his white linen suit and sun helmet and insisted on going himself through the bullet-whistling streets to the cable office to report to Washington. He refused to let any married member of the Embassy staff accompany him, saying of himself, "Hell, as far as my kids are concerned, with insurance I'm worth more dead than alive anyway." He added, grinning: "Mind you, nobody is a greater coward than Findley Howard; but nobody is a braver man than the U.S. Minister." He strolled down the main street toward a spitting machine gun, which miraculously missed him, turned it to one side with his walking stick, and said: "Sonny, you'll hurt somebody with that thing, and wouldn't it be embarrassing if it were the U.S. Minister?"

At the cable office, they told him that no outgoing cables were permitted. "I'm the U.S. Minister," began Howard, sitting down very firmly, "and I'm going to send my cable to Washington." With repetition, suasion, threats, and general carryings-on, he finally tired them out. His was the only diplomatic cable accepted.

One great success was his annual Fourth of July party. The entertainment fund of such a ministerial post as Asuncion is less than $1,000 a year, and Howard quickly decided that was just enough for one good party. His choice of July Fourth was particularly happy because that happens to be a great holiday in Paraguay too, and many of his guests took it as a special compliment to their country.

Howard never allowed his conviviality to interfere with his work and could stick to iced tea when he had to. Many officials, furthermore, found that a few Scotch-and-sodas with Howard at the Union Club had more effect on their tongues than on Howard's ears. "I often thought," mused one of them, "that he sometimes pretended a mellowness which had no basis in fact."

Howard was a close friend of Colonel Jose Felix Estigarribia, the hero of the Chaco War who became Paraguay's great president. Those in the know feel that the Chaco Peace Conference, which the U.S. and five other nations sponsored at Buenos Aires, would never have been such a success had it not been for the work Howard did behind the scenes. The Paraguayans, cocky at military successes, reputedly would not accept the very generous offer of the arbitration commission until Howard got Estigarribia's ear. Estigarribia, rushing to Buenos Aires and replacing a negotiator by himself, forced the settlement. Later Howard played the major role in getting from the U.S. unlimited credit for Paraguay that helped cushion the shock of post-Chaco War demobilization.

His influence was reputedly resented by the German Embassy, so strongly indeed that Estigarribia got the notion (probably quite unfounded) that the Germans were "out to get" Howard. Estigarribia passed the word that if Howard had an "accident," 200 Germans would have similar ones.

Paraguay had a change of government seven months ago, and the new crowd, which does not have the same dislike for the Germans that Estigarribia had, showed antagonism toward Howard. Probably this had something to do with his leaving Paraguay. If he was sorry to go, he was nevertheless glad of the prospect of getting back with his two children, a boy 17 years old and a girl 13, who have been staying with an aunt in Columbus. Howard lives for these kids, whose mother died when they were small children, and does everything for them so that, as he gruffly states, they will be better persons than he is.

There are many hundreds of Paraguayans of every class, from cabinet ministers down, who sincerely miss "El Ministro Cowboy." Said one: "He was an odd man, but we accepted him as he was and grew to love him. And Paraguay owes more to him than Paraguay could ever with dignity admit."

Extracted from "A Nebraska Diplomat in Paraguay," *Life*, April 14, 1941.
© Time, Inc., 1941

"First things come first," Mari Sandoz told the New York firemen who recently found her guarding a large wooden box on the fire escape of her walk-up flat in Greenwich Village. She had managed to get her hoard of more than 200,000 index cards to the escape, determined to save them at all cost. The firemen soon extinguished the blaze and carried the box back for the intrepid author to resume her writing on the fifth of her series on the high plains—the story of the cattle industry.

—The Brand Book, Fall, 1956

Mari Sandoz

MAMIE J. MEREDITH

ONE DAY in 1933 Mari Sandoz received a letter from Little, Brown and Company, the publishers to whom she had submitted a book called *Old Jules,* the story of her father's life. For five years she had devoted every available moment to the book—three years of research in old newspaper files and courthouse records and in the four thousand letters and papers in her father's boxes; then two years for the writing. She had entered the book in the Atlantic Monthly $5,000 prize non-fiction contest, and now, after eight months of waiting, the news came that her manuscript had been rejected.

Mari wrote back a letter predicting that her book would be remembered after the judges of the contest were dead and forgotten. Then she began carrying out the stories that she had been writing, rewriting, and sending to editors during the dozen years she had lived in Lincoln. There were eighty-five of them, and she watched them burn in an old galvanized iron washtub behind the apartment house. A few friends, watching with her, protested. But Mari said, "They were not good enough." Her face pinched and greenish-yellow from one of her frequent migraines, she got together her few belongings for the trip back home to the sandhills—to the ranch which she had left twelve years before for Lincoln, the state university, and a career in writing.

The eldest of six children, Mari had been born and reared on a homestead in Sheridan County, in northwestern Nebraska near the Niobrara. Her parents were Swiss immigrants, and when she started

to school at the age of nine, she spoke only a few words of English—
"with an equal smattering of Polish and French mixed into my
mother tongue, Swiss German." In all, she went to school less than
five years: "I went . . . when I could, but with father being crippled,
a community builder, and a conversationalist, mother had to do
much of the outside work and I looked after the younger children.
I also learned to run father's trap line when necessary and to skin
anything from a weasel to a cow."

At sixteen she passed the examinations for rural teachers, and
taught for five years in the sod-house school in which she had been a
pupil. Then, in 1921, when she was twenty-one, she had entered the
University of Nebraska as an "adult special," despite considerable
opposition from the administrators because she had not attended
high school. For the next eight years she went to classes part time,
meanwhile supporting herself as she could—working in the laboratory of a wholesale drug house, reading proof nights on a newspaper,
and acting, for a year and a half, as assistant to an English instructor.
Her literary ambitions had been stimulated and encouraged during
these years by her friends and teachers on the campus—in particular
by Louise Pound, who urged her to write of the sandhills and in
her personal style, by John Hicks, with his luminous understanding
of pioneer life in America, and by Melvin Van den Bark, who could
help her with problems of technique.

Some recognition had come: In 1924 Mari had won an honorable
mention in an intercollegiate writing contest conducted by Harper's,
and her work had appeared in a few national and regional publications including the *Prairie Schooner,* whose first issue—January,
1927—had opened with her story "The Vine." * Now, however, with
the rejection of her book by the Atlantic judges, she expected to
give up writing and go home. Nebraska was hard hit by the depression; Mari did not see how she could hang on in Lincoln any longer.
At least at the ranch there would be food and shelter.

On her return to the sandhills, she was pressed into the fall work
of the ranch, dehorning and vaccinating steers, holding the animal
down with her knee on his back while she pushed the needle behind
the shoulder blades. No one there had any thought of her physical
unfitness after those years of sedentary work in offices and libraries,
much of the time with not enough to eat. But proper food and outdoor life revived her desire to write. Her mother gave her permission

---

* It was signed with the pen name "Marie Macumber."

to use a small shack near the house; and within a month of her return, with a Topsy stove for heat, she set about writing what she described as "the story of a will-to-power individual turning every honest, good, and beautiful thing about her to her end."

In this winter of 1934, she also wrote "Pioneer Women," a paper commissioned for a paltry sum by a woman's club in eastern Nebraska. Two years later a reworking of this article appeared in *Country Gentleman*.* Those who condemn Mari for the jaundiced view of pioneer women in *Slogum House*—the novel she wrote in the winter of her defeat—might well modify their judgment after reading this piece. The "Marlizzie" whom it sketches was drawn from life— was in fact Mary Elizabeth Fehr Sandoz, Mari's mother. Her father, of course, lives unforgettably in the pages of *Old Jules*—which at last, in 1935, was named winner of the Atlantic prize.

It was only after her father's death that Mari, who had started to write when she was nine, finally was released from the constraint placed upon her by his pronouncements when she was a child. Fiction, he said, was "fit only for maids and stable boys"; and "writers and artists are the maggots of society." Just before his death he had asked her if she was still writing. And when Mari admitted that she was, Old Jules said, "Why don't you write the story of my life?" So it became her duty as well as her desire to write of her father as he had been, a bundle of paradoxes but also a builder of communities and "The Burbank of the Sandhills."

The winning of the Atlantic award marked a turning point: it gave Mari leisure to write; it permitted her to live in the east near research libraries and in closer touch with her publishers. In the twenty-odd years since, honors have been many: in 1950, her alma mater conferred the honorary degree of Doctor of Literature, and in 1954 she received the first Distinguished Achievement Award of the Native Sons and Daughters "for her sincere and realistic presentation of Nebraska as it was."

Not unmindful of the encouragement given her in difficult times, for several years Mari has awarded three cash prizes for unpublished short stories to University of Nebraska students. She has taught at summer writers' conferences, and the past eight years has conducted regular courses at the eight-week session of the University of Wisconsin, making it possible when she can for her students to continue their work by means of fellowships.

* See page 145

Mari's best-known books, in addition to *Old Jules,* are those in her series dealing with the trans-Missouri region, among them *Crazy Horse, Cheyenne Autumn,* and *The Buffalo Hunters. Crazy Horse: The Strange Man of the Oglalas,* second in the trans-Missouri series, appeared in 1942. This Sioux chief was perhaps the most magnificent fighting man that the Indian race has produced. He was a leader during the critical period (1855–75) when the Plains Indians were being deprived of their homes, subsistence, and freedom and forced into living on reservations. Mari had known and liked the Sioux since childhood, and in this book she modeled her style upon their speech. *Cheyenne Autumn* (1950), third in the six-book study, is the epic account of how a band of 278 half-starved Northern Cheyennes fled from the Oklahoma reservation to their homeland some 1,500 miles away. Pursued by 10,000 men under General Custer in the winter of 1878, only a remnant reached their home on the Yellowstone. *The Buffalo Hunters: The Story of the Hide Men* (1954) shows in sweeping panorama the slaughter of four great herds of buffalo, numbered in the millions, in about fifteen years (1867–1883). The Indian wars treated in the two preceding books are seen here as a result of the extinction of the buffalo—the Indians' source of food, clothing, and shelter. Famous frontier characters like Buffalo Bill and General Custer appear in this book, and Indian leaders like Sitting Bull and Spotted Tail.

During the past twenty years four novels have alternated with the volumes of history, and they too deal with the region with which Mari is emotionally identified. *Slogum House* already has been mentioned. *Capital City,* "a microcosmic study of a unit of modern democratic society selling itself into fascism," evoked angry protests from dwellers in capital cities of Nebraska and surrounding states, but Mari answered that in studying public records she had found the same graft and corruption in all. *The Tom-Walker* was written from a four-year study of postwar society in America after the Civil War and two World Wars; and *Miss Morissa, Doctor of the Gold Trail* is a novel of the changing Nebraska frontier of the 1870's, following the discovery of gold in the Black Hills and the breaking of the Sioux.

At present Mari is working on a fifth volume in the trans-Missouri series, the story of the cattle industry. An "oil book" will follow, undertaken after 1960—"if I'm still in the running." After that, a last book is planned—though chronologically it is the first—to complete the account of how man "is shaped by and shapes his world": the coming to this region of the Stone Age Indian.

Mari does not know just when she thought of writing this series. Before she left the sandhills, she had considered the question: *what happens to modern man in a stone age region?* In a personal letter, written in 1936, she said:

I've always been interested in man and his way of life upon this earth and felt a strong urge to clarify my conclusions in writing. Early I saw that Old Jules and his community were by far the most promising material of my experience.

And looking at Mari's work as a whole, one can see that she has remained true to her purpose of revealing universalities in the language of the common man.

VIII. Just Passing Through

This region, which resembles one of the immeasurable steppes of Asia, has not inaptly been termed the great American desert. . . . It is a land where no man permanently abides.

—Washington Irving, *Astoria*

No early visitor surveyed the Nebraska landscape with a keener or more cosmopolitan eye than Sir Richard Burton. An orientalist and explorer, he is best remembered now as the translator of the "Arabian Nights," but in the 1850's he won renown for his African explorations and his discovery, with Speke, of Lakes Tanganyika and Victoria Nyanza. As a sort of sequel to his pilgrimage to the Holy City of Mecca, he came to America during the summer of 1860 to visit the "City of the Saints," and en route to Great Salt Lake passed through Nebraska.

Nebraska Panorama (1860)

SIR RICHARD BURTON

The Valley of the Little Blue, 9th August

Issuing from the Big Sandy Station at 6:30 A.M., and resuming our route over the divide that still separated the valleys of the Big Blue and the Little Blue, we presently fell into the lines of the latter, and were called upon by the conductor to admire it. Averaging two miles in width, which shrinks to one-quarter as you ascend, the valley is hedged on both sides by low rolling bluffs. As the hills break off near the river, they show a diluvial formation; in places they are washed into a variety of forms, and being white, they stand out in bold relief. In other parts they are sand mixed with soil enough to support a last-year's growth of wheat-like grass, weed stubble, and dead trees that look like old cornfields in new clearings. One could not have recognised, at this season, Col. Fremont's description written in the month of June—the "hills with graceful slopes looking uncommonly green and beautiful." Along the bluffs the road winds, crossing at times a rough projecting spur, or dipping into some gully washed out by the rains of ages. All is barren beyond the garden-reach which runs along the stream; there is not a tree to a square mile—in these regions the tree, like the bird in Arabia and the monkey in Africa, signifies water—and animal life seems well-nigh extinct. As the land sinks towards the river bottom, it becomes less barren. The wild sun-flower—it seldom, however, turns toward the sun—now becomes abundant.

Changing mules at Kiowa, about 10 A.M., we pushed forward through the sun to Liberty Farm, where a station supplied us with the eternal eggs and bacon, a dish constant in the great West. The Little Blue ran hard by, about fifty feet wide by three or four deep, fringed with emerald-green oak groves, cottonwood, and long-leaved willow: its waters supply catfish, suckers, and a soft-shelled turtle, but the fish are full of bones, and taste, as might be imagined, like mud. The prairie bore signs of hare and antelope: in the valley coyotes, wolves, and foxes, attracted by the carcasses of cattle, stared us in the face, and near the stream, plovers, jays, the blue bird, and a kind of starling called the swamp or redwinged blackbird twittered a song of satisfaction. We then resumed our journey over a desert, waterless save after rain, for twenty-three miles; it is the divide between the Little Blue and the Platte rivers, a broken tableland rising gradually towards the west, with, at this season, a barren soil of sand and clay. As the evening approached, a smile from above lit up into absolute beauty the homely features of the world below. Strata upon strata of cloud-banks, burnished to golden red in the vicinity of the setting sun, and polished to dazzling silvery white above, lay piled half way from the horizon to the zenith, with a distinct strike towards a vanishing point in the west, and dipping into a gateway through which the orb of day slowly retired. Over- head floated in a sea of amber and yellow, pink and green, heavy purple nimbi, apparently turned upside down—their convex bulges below, and their horizontal lines high in the air—whilst, in the east, black and blue were so curiously blended that the eye could not distinguish whether it rested upon darkening air or upon a lowering thundercloud. We enjoyed these beauties in silence, not a soul said "look there!" or "how pretty!"

The Platte River and Fort Kearny, August 10.

After a long and chilly night—extensive evaporation making 40°F. feel excessively cold—lengthened by the atrocity of the mos- quitoes, we awoke upon the hill sands divided by two miles of level green savannah, and at 4 A.M. reached Kearny station, in the valley of La Grande Platte, seven miles from the fort of that name. The first aspect of the stream was one of calm and quiet beauty, which, however, it owed much to its accessories: some travellers have not hesitated to characterise it as "the dreariest of rivers." On the south is a rolling range of red sandy and clayey hillocks, sharp towards the river—the "coasts of the Nebraska." The valley, here two miles broad, resembles the ocean deltas of great streams; it is level as a carpet, all short green grass without sage or bush. It can hardly be called a bottom, the rise from the water's edge being, it is calculated, about 4 feet per 1,000. Under a bank, from half a yard to a yard high, through its two lawns of verdure, flowed the stream straight towards the slanting rays of the rising sun, which glittered upon its broad bosom and shed rosy light over half the heavens. In places it shows a sea horizon, but here it was narrowed by Grand Island, which is fifty-two miles long, with an average breadth of one mile and three-quarters, and sufficiently elevated above the annual flood to be well timbered.

Without excepting even the Missouri, the Platte is doubtless the most important western influent of the Mississippi. The Canadian voyageurs first named it La Platte, the Flat River, discarding, or rather translating after their fashion, the musical and picturesque aboriginal term, "Nebraska," the "shallow stream": the word has happily been retained for the territory. Springing from the eastern slope of the Rocky Mountains, it has, like all the valley streams westward of the Mississippi, the Niobrara, or Eau qui court, the Arkansas, and the Canadian River, a declination to the southeast. From its mouth to the junction of its northern and southern forks, the river valley is mostly level, and the scenery is of remarkable sameness: its singularity in this point affects the memory. The Platte is treacherous in the extreme, full of quicksands and gravel shoals, channels and cuts, which shift with each year's flood. It is a river wilfully wasted by nature: its great breadth causes a want of depth which renders it unfit for the navigation of a craft more civilised than the Indian's birch or the Canadian fur-boat.

Hugging the right bank of our strange river, at 8 A.M. we found ourselves at Fort Kearny. We left Kearny at 9:30 A.M., following the road which runs forty miles up the valley of the Platte. It is a broad prairie, plentifully supplied with water in wells two to four feet deep; the fluid is cool and clear, but it is said not to be wholesome. Along the southern bank near Kearny are few elevations; on the opposite or northern side appear high and wooded bluffs. The road was rough with pitchholes, and for the first time I remarked a peculiar gap in the ground like an East Indian sun-crack, the effect of rain streams and snow water acting upon the clay. Each succeeding winter lengthens the head and deepens the sole of this deeply gashed water-cut, till it destroys the road. A curious mirage appeared, doubling to four the strata of river and vegetation on the banks. The sight and song of birds once more charmed us after a desert where animal life is as rare as upon the plains of Brazil. After fifteen miles of tossing and tumbling, we made "Seventeen Mile Station" and halted there to change mules. About twenty miles above the fort the southern bank began to rise into mounds of tenacious clay, which, worn away into perpendicular and precipitous sections, composes the columnar formation called O'Fallon's Bluffs. At 1:15 P.M. we reached Plum Creek, after being obliged to leave behind one of the conductors, who had become delirious with the "shakes."

About Plum Ranch the soil is rich, clayey, and dotted with swamps and "slews" by which the English traveller will understand sloughs. The drier portions were a Gulistan of bright red, blue, and white flowers, the purple aster, and the mallow, with its parsnip-like root, eaten by the Indians, the gaudy yellow helianthus—we remarked at least three varieties—the snowy mimulus, the graceful flax, sometimes four feet high, and a delicate little euphorbia, whilst in the damper ground appeared the polar plant, that prairie compass, the plane of whose leaf ever turns towards the magnetic meridian. This is the "weed-prairie," one of the many divisions of the great natural meadows; grass prairie, rolling prairie, motte prairie, salt prairie, and soda prairie. It deserves a more poetical name, for

> These are the gardens of the desert, these
> The unshorn fields, boundless and beautiful,
> For which the speech of England has no name.

Buffalo herds were behind the hills, but we were too full of sleep to follow them. The plain was dotted with blanched skulls and bones which would have made a splendid bonfire. Apparently the expert voyageur has not learned that they form good fuel; at any rate, he has preferred to them the "chips" of which it is said that a steak cooked with them requires no pepper.

12th August.—We cross the Platte.

Boreal aurora glared brighter than a sunset in Syria. The long streamers were intercepted and mysteriously confused by a massive stratum of dark cloud, through whose narrow rifts and jagged chinks the splendours poured in floods of magic fire. Near the horizon the tint was an opalline white—a broad band of calm steady light—supporting a tender rose colour, which flushed to crimson as it scaled the upper firmament. The mobility of the spectacle was its chiefest charm. The streamers either shot out or shrank from full to half-length; now they stood like a red arch with steadfast legs and oscillating summit, then, broadening at the apex, they apparently revolved with immense rapidity; at times the stars shone undimmed through the veil of light, then they were immersed in its exceeding brilliancy. After a full hour of changeful beauty, the northern lights slowly faded away with a blush which made the sunrise look colder than its wont. It is no wonder that the imaginative Indian, looking with love upon these beauties, connects them with the ghosts of his ancestors.

At the Upper Crossing of the South Fork there are usually tender adieux; the wenders towards Mormonland bidding farewell to those bound for the perilous gold regions of Denver City and Pike's Peak. We crossed the "Padouca" at 6:30 A.M., having placed our luggage and the mails for security in an ox cart. The South Fork is here 600 to 700 yards broad; the current is swift, but the deepest water not exceeding 2.50 feet, the teams are not compelled to cross diagonally.

We had now entered upon the outskirts of the American wilderness, which has not one feature in common with the deserts of the Old World. In Arabia and Africa there is majesty in its monotony. Here it is a brown smooth space, insensibly curving out of sight, wholly wanting "second distance," and scarcely suggesting the idea of immensity; we seem in fact to be travelling for twenty miles over a convex, treeless hill-top. At 12:45 P.M., travelling over the uneven barren, and in a burning Scirocco, we reached Lodge-Pole Station, where we made our "noonin."

As we advanced, the horizon, everywhere within musket-shot—a wearying sight!—widened out, and the face of the country notably changed. A scrap of blue distance and high hills—the "Court-house" and others—appeared to the northwest. The long, curved lines, the gentle slopes and the broad hollows of the divide facing the South Fork changed into an abrupt and precipitous descent, "gullied" like the broken ground of subranges attached to a mountain chain. Deep ravines were parted by long narrow ridges, sharp-crested and water-washed, and, after passing Lodge-pole Creek, which bears away to the west, the rocky steps required the perpetual application of the break. Presently we saw a dwarf cliff enclosing in an elliptical sweep a green amphitheatre, the valley of our old friend the Platte.

Past the Court House and Scott's Bluffs, August 13th

At 8 A.M., after breaking our fast upon a tough antelope-steak, and dawdling whilst the herdsman was riding wildly about in search of his runaway mules—an operation now to become of daily occurrence—we dashed over the Sandy Creek with an *élan* calculated to make timid passengers look "skeery," and began to finish the rolling divide between the two Forks. We crossed several arroyos and "criks" heading in the line of clay highlands to our left, a dwarf sierra which stretches from the northern to the southern branch of the Platte. The principal are Omaha Creek, more generally known as "Little Punkin," and Lawrence Fork. The latter is a pretty bubbling stream, running over sand and stones washed down from the Courthouse Ridge; it derives its name from a Frenchman slaughtered by the Indians, murder here, as in Central Africa, ever the principal source of nomenclature.

After twelve miles' drive we fronted the Court-house, the remarkable portal of a new region, and this new region teeming with wonders will now extend about 100 miles. It is the *mauvaises terres,* or Bad lands, a tract about 60 miles wide and 150 long, stretching in a direction from the northeast to the southwest, or from the Mankizitah (White Earth) River, over the Niobrara (*Eau qui court*) and Loup Fork to the south banks of the Platte: its eastern limit is the mouth of the Keya Paha. The term is generally applied by the trader to any section of the prairie country where the roads are difficult, and by dint of an ill name the Bad lands have come to be spoken of as a Golgotha, white with the bones of man and beast. American travellers, on the contrary, declare that near parts of the White River "some as beautiful valleys are to be found as anywhere in the far West," and that many places "abound in the most lovely and varied forms in endless variety, giving the most striking and pleasing effects of light and shade."

The Court-house, which had lately suffered from heavy rain, resembled anything more than a court-house; that it did so in former days we may gather from the tales of many travellers, old Canadian voyageurs, who unanimously accounted it a fit place for Indian spooks, ghosts, and hobgoblins to meet in pow-wow. The Courthouse lies about eight miles from the river, and three from the road; in circumference it may be a half a mile, and in height 300 feet; it is, however, gradually degrading, and the rains and snows of not many years will lay it level with the ground. In books it is described as resembling a gigantic ruin, with a huge rotunda in front, windows in the sides, and remains of roofs and stages in its flanks: verily potent is the eye of imagination! I saw it when set off by weather to advantage. A blazing sun rained fire upon its cream-coloured surface—at 11 A.M. the glass showed 95° in the wagon—and it stood boldly out against a purple-black nimbus which overspread the southern skies, growling distant thunders, and flashing red threads of "chained lightning."

Shortly after "liquoring up" and shaking hands, we found ourselves once more in the valley of the Platte. The road, as usual, along the river-side was rough and broken, and puffs of Simoon raised the sand and dust in ponderous clouds. At 12:30 P.M. we nooned for an hour, and I took occasion to sketch the far-famed Chimney Rock. The name is not, as is that of the Court-house, a misnomer: one might almost expect to see smoke or steam jetting from the summit. Like most of these queer malformations, it was once the knuckle-end of the main chain which bounded the Platte Valley; the softer adjacent strata of marl and earthy limestone were disintegrated by wind and weather, and the harder material, better resisting the action of air and water, has gradually assumed its present form. Chimney Rock lies two and a half miles from the south bank of the Platte. Viewed from the southeast, it is not unlike a giant jackboot based upon a high pyramidal mound, which, disposed in the natural slope, rests upon the plain. The neck of sandstone connecting it with the adjacent hills has been distributed by the floods around the base, leaving an ever-widening gap between. This "Pharos of the prairie-sea" towered in former days 150 to 200 feet above the apex of its foundation and was a landmark visible for 40 to 50 miles: it is now barely 35 feet in height. Around the waist of the base runs a white band which sets off its height and relieves the uniform tint. Again the weather served us: nothing could be more picturesque than this lone pillar of pale rock lying against a huge black cloud, with the forked lightning playing over its devoted head.

After a frugal dinner of biscuit and cheese, we remounted and pursued our way through airy fire, which presently changed from our usual pest—a light dust-laden breeze—into a Punjaubian duststorm, up the valley of the Platte. As we advanced, the storm increased to a tornado of north wind, blinding our cattle till it drove them off the road. The gale howled through the pass with all the violence of a Khamsin, and it was followed by lightning and a few heavy drops of rain. The threatening weather caused a large party of emigrants to "fort themselves" in a corral near the base of Scott's Bluffs.

"Scott's Bluffs," situated 285 miles from Fort Kearny and 51 from Fort Laramie, was the last of the great mark formations which we saw on this line, and was of all by far the most curious. In the dull uniformity of the prairies it is a striking and attractive object, far excelling the castled crag of Drachenfels or any of the beauties of romantic Rhine. From a distance of a day's march, it appears in the shape of a large blue mound, distinguished only by its dimensions from the detached fragments of hill around. As you approach within four or five miles, a massive medieval city gradually defines itself, clustering, with a wonderful fulness of detail, around a colossal fortress, and crowned with a royal castle. Buttress and barbican, bastion, demilune and guardhouse, tower, turret, and donjon-keep, all are there, and, that nothing may be wanting to the resemblance, the dashing rains and angry winds have cut the old line of road at its base into a regular moat with a semicircular sweep, which the mirage fills with a mimic river. At a nearer aspect again, the quaint illusion vanishes: the lines of masonry become yellow layers of boulder and pebble imbedded in a mass of stiff, tamped, bald marly clay; the curtains and angles change to the gashings of the rains of ages, and the warriors are metamorphosed into dwarf cedars and dense shrubs, scattered singly over the surface. Travellers have compared this glory of the *mauvaises terres* to Gibraltar, to the Capitol at Washington, to Stirling Castle. I could think of nothing in its presence but the Arabs' "City of Brass," that mysterious abode of bewitched infidels, which often appears at a distance to the wayfarer toiling under the burning sun, but ever eludes his nearer search.

Scott's Bluffs derive their name from an unfortunate fur-trader there put on shore in the olden time by his boat's crew, who had a grudge against him: the wretch in mortal sickness crawled up the mound to die. The politer guide-books call them "Capitol Hills": methinks the first name, with its dark associations, must be better pleasing to the *genius loci*. They are divided into three distinct masses. The largest, which may be 800 feet high, is on the right, or nearest the river. To its left lies an outwork, a huge detached cylinder whose capping changes aspect from every direction; and still further to the left is a second castle, now divided from, but once connected with, the others. The whole affair is a spur springing from the main range, and closing upon the Platte so as to leave no room for a road. The sharp, sudden torrents which pour from the heights on both sides and the draughty winds—Scott's Bluffs are the permanent headquarters of hurricanes—have cut up the ground into a labyrinth of jagged gulches steeply walled in.

Presently we dashed over the Little Kiowa Creek, forded the Horse Creek, and, enveloped in a cloud of villainous mosquitoes, entered at 8:30 P.M. the station in which we were to pass the night. It was tenanted by one Reynal, a French creole, a companionable man, but an extortionate: he charged us a florin for every "drink" of his well-watered whiskey.

Our host, M. Reynal, was a study. The western man has been worked by climate and its consequences, by the huge magnificence of nature and the violent contrasts of scenery, into a remarkable resemblance to the wild Indian. He hates labour as the dire effect of a primaeval curse; "loaf" he must and will. His imagination is inflamed by scenery and climate, difficulty and danger; he is as superstitious as an old man-o'-war's man of the olden school; and he is a transcendental liar, like his prototype the aborigin, who in this point yields nothing to the African negro. I have been gravely told of a herd of bison which arrested the course of the Platte River, causing its waters, like those of the Red Sea, to stand up, wall fashion, whilst the animals were crossing. In this age, however, the western man has become sensitive to the operation of "smoking." A popular Joe Miller anent him is this:—A traveller, informed of what he might educe by "querying," asked an old mountaineer, who shall be nameless, what difference he observed in the country since he had first settled in it.

"Wal, stranger, not much!" was the reply; "only when I fust come here, that 'ere mountain," pointing to the tall Uintah range, "was a hole!"

Condensed from *The City of the Saints*, Longman, Green, Longman, and Roberts, 1862

Phileas Fogg, hero of Around the World in Eighty Days, *traveled with a valet to help ease the hardships of the journey, but even so his train trip across Nebraska was not without its inconveniences. There was, for example, an attack by a hundred Sioux who "jumped upon the steps without stopping the train" and had to be fought off until the train reached Fort Kearney station and soldiers of the fort were "attracted by the shots." The Indians "had not expected them" and fled, "disappearing along the banks of the Republican River." Unless the Republican was running some seventy-five miles out of its course, those travelers were a sharp-eyed lot.*

Unfortunately, the redskins had managed to make off with some of the passengers, including the valet Passepartout; and although Mr. Fogg rescued them with commendable alacrity, on his return to Fort Kearney he found the train had gone on. Here a Mr. Mudge—presumably a local man—takes the spotlight. Nebraska winters often being severe and snow-plows scarce, Mr. Mudge had devised a contrivance which enabled him to get around regardless of road conditions. In no time at all a deal was arranged, and the Fogg party caught a snow-boat to Omaha.

Crossing Nebraska by Rail and Sail

(1872)

JULES VERNE

MR. FOGG EXAMINED a curious vehicle, a kind of frame on two long beams, a little raised in front like the runners of a sledge, and upon which there was room for five or six persons. A high mast was fixed on the frame, held firmly by metallic lashings, to which was attached a large brigantine sail. This mast held an iron stay upon which to hoist a jib-sail. Behind, a sort of rudder served to guide the vehicle. It was, in short, a sledge rigged like a sloop. During the winter, when the trains are blocked up by the snow, these sledges make extremely rapid journeys across the frozen plains from one station to another. Provided with more sail than a cutter, and with the wind behind them, they slip over the surface of the prairies with a speed equal if not superior to that of the express trains.

Mr. Fogg readily made a bargain with the owner of this landcraft. The wind was favourable, being fresh and blowing from the west. The snow had hardened, and Mudge was very confident of being able to transport Mr. Fogg in a few hours to Omaha. Thence the trains eastward run frequently to Chicago and New York.

At eight o'clock the sledge was ready to start. The passengers took their places on it and wrapped themselves up closely in their travelling-cloaks. The two great sails were hoisted, and under the pressure of the wind, the sledge slid over the hardened snow with a velocity of forty miles an hour.

The distance between Fort Kearney and Omaha, as the birds fly, is at most two hundred miles. If the wind blew good, the distance might be traversed in five hours; if no accident happened the sledge might reach Omaha by one o'clock.

What a journey! The travellers, huddled close together, could not speak for the cold, intensified by the rapidity at which they were going. The sledge seemed to be lifted off the ground by its sails. Mudge, who was at the rudder, kept in a straight line, and by a turn of his hand checked the lurches which the vehicle had a tendency to make. All the sails were up, and the jib was so arranged as not to screen the brigantine. A topmast was hoisted, and another jib, held out to the wind, added its force to the other sails. Although the speed could not be exactly estimated, the sledge could not be going at less than forty miles an hour.

"If nothing breaks," said Mudge, "we shall get there!"

The prairie, across which the sledge was moving in a straight line, was as flat as a sea. It seemed like a vast frozen lake. The railroad which ran through this section ascended from the southwest to the northwest by Great Island, Columbus, an important Nebraska town, Schuyler, and Fremont, to Omaha. It followed throughout the right bank of the Platte River. The sledge, shortening this route, took the chord of the arc described by the railway. Mudge was not afraid of being stopped by the Platte River, because it was frozen. The road, then, was quite clear of obstacles, and Phileas Fogg had but two things to fear—an accident to the sledge, and a change or calm in the wind.

But the breeze, far from lessening its force, blew as if to bend the mast, which, however, the metallic lashings held firmly. These lashings, like the chords of a stringed instrument, resounded as if vibrated by a violin bow. The sledge slid along in the midst of a plaintively intense melody.

The sledge flew fast over the vast carpet of snow. The creeks it passed over were not perceived. Fields and streams disappeared under the uniform whiteness. The plain was absolutely deserted. Between the Union Pacific road and the branch which unites Kearney with Saint Joseph, it formed a great uninhabited island. Neither village, station, nor fort appeared. From time to time they sped by some phantom-like tree, whose white skeleton twisted and rattled in the wind. Sometimes flocks of wild birds rose, or bands of gaunt, famished, ferocious prairie wolves ran howling after the sledge. Passepartout, revolver in hand, held himself ready to fire on those which came too near. Had an accident then happened to the sledge, the travellers, attacked by these beasts, would have been in the most terrible danger; but it held on its even course, soon gained on the wolves, and ere long left the howling band at a safe distance behind.

About noon Mudge perceived by certain landmarks that he was crossing the Platte River. He said nothing, but he felt certain that he was now within twenty miles of Omaha. In less than an hour he left the rudder and furled his sails, whilst the sledge, carried forward by the great impetus the wind had given it, went on half a mile further with its sails unspread.

It stopped at last, and Mudge, pointing to a mass of roofs white with snow, said, "We have got there!"

Arrived! Arrived at the station which is in daily communication, by numerous trains, with the Atlantic seaboard! Phileas Fogg generously rewarded Mudge, whose hand Passepartout warmly grasped, and the party directed their steps to the Omaha railway station.

Extracted from *Around the World in Eighty Days*, Street and Smith, 1891

"... from the high wagon-seat," wrote Willa Cather, "one could look a long way off. The road ran about like a wild thing, avoiding the deep draws, crossing them where they were wide and shallow. And all along it, wherever it looped or ran, the sunflowers grew; some of them were as big as little trees, with great rough leaves and many branches which bore dozens of blossoms. They made a gold ribbon across the prairie."

From his "observatory on the top of a fruit-waggon" in an immigrant train, Robert Louis Stevenson, too, saw the sunflowers. But their brightness did not warm him; and his magical fancy, which created a whole galaxy of marvelous, many-colored worlds, found no enkindling spark in "so bare a playroom" as the Nebraska plains.

The Plains of Nebraska (1879)

ROBERT LOUIS STEVENSON

IT HAD thundered on the Friday night, but the sun rose on Saturday without a cloud. We were at sea—there is no other adequate expression—on the plains of Nebraska. I made my observatory on the top of a fruit-waggon, and sat by the hour upon that perch to spy about me, and to spy in vain for something new. It was a world almost without a feature; an empty sky, an empty earth; front and back, the line of railway stretched from horizon to horizon, like a cue across a billiard-board; on either hand, the green plain ran till it touched the skirts of heaven. Along the track innumerable wild sunflowers, no bigger than a crown-piece, bloomed in a continuous flower-bed; grazing beasts were seen upon the prairie at all degrees of distance and diminution; and now and again we might perceive a few dots beside the railroad which grew more and more distinct as we drew nearer till they turned into wooden cabins, and then dwindled in our wake until they melted into their surroundings, and we were once more alone upon the billiard-board. The train toiled over this infinity like a snail; and being the one thing moving, it was wonderful what huge proportions it began to assume in our regard. It seemed miles in length, and either end of it within but a step of the horizon. Even my own body or my own head seemed a great thing in that emptiness. I note the feeling the more readily as it is the contrary of what I have read of in the experience of others. Day and night, above the roar of the train, our ears were kept busy with the incessant chirp of grasshoppers—a noise like the winding up of countless clocks and watches, which began after a while to seem proper to that land.

To one hurrying through by steam there was a certain exhilaration in this spacious vacancy, this greatness of the air, this discovery of the whole arch of heaven, this straight, unbroken, prison-line of the horizon. Yet one could not but reflect upon the weariness of those who passed by there in old days, at the foot's pace of oxen, painfully urging their teams, and with no landmark but that unattainable evening sun for which they steered, and which daily fled them by an equal stride. They had nothing, it would seem, to overtake; nothing by which to reckon their advance; no sight for repose or for encouragement; but stage after stage, only the dead green waste under foot, and the mocking, fugitive horizon. But the eye, as I have been told, found differences even here; and at the worst the emigrant came, by perseverance, to the end of his toil. It is the settlers, after all, at whom we have a right to marvel. Our consciousness, by which we live, is itself but the creature of variety. Upon what food does it subsist in such a land? What livelihood can repay a human creature for a life spent in this huge sameness? He is cut off from books, from news, from company, from all that can relieve existence but the prosecution of his affairs. A sky full of stars is the most varied spectacle that he can hope. He may walk five miles and see nothing; ten, and it is as though he had not moved; twenty, and still he is in the midst of the same great level, and has approached no nearer to the one object within view, the flat horizon which keeps pace with his advance. We are full at home of the question of agreeable wall-papers, and wise people are of the opinion that the temper may be quieted by sedative surroundings. But what is to be said of the Nebraskan settler? His is a wall-paper with a vengeance—one quarter of the universe laid bare in all its gauntness. His eye must embrace at every glance the whole seeming concave of the visible world; it quails before so vast an outlook, it is tortured by distance; yet there is no rest or shelter, till the man runs into his cabin, and can repose his sight upon things near at hand. Hence, I am told, a sickness of the vision peculiar to these empty plains.

Yet perhaps with sunflowers and cicadae, summer and winter, cattle, wife and family, the settler may create a full and various existence. One person at least I saw upon the plains who seemed in every way superior to her lot. This was a woman who boarded us at a way station, selling milk. She was largely formed; her features were more than comely; she had that great rarity—a fine complexion which became her; and her eyes were kind, dark, and steady. She sold milk with patriarchal grace. There was not a line in her countenance, not a note in her soft and sleepy voice, but spoke of an entire contentment with her life. It would have been fatuous arrogance to pity such a woman. Yet the place where she lived was to me almost ghastly. Less than a dozen wooden houses, all of a shape and all nearly of a size, stood planted along the railway lines. Each stood apart in its own lot. Each opened direct off the billiard-board, as if it were a billiard-board indeed, and these only models that had been set down upon it ready made. Her own, into which I looked, was clean but very empty, and showed nothing homelike but the burning fire. This extreme newness, above all in so naked and flat a country, gives a strong impression of artificiality. With none of the litter and discoloration of human life, with the paths unworn, and the houses still sweating from the axe, such a settlement as this seems purely scenic. The mind is loth to accept it for a piece of reality; and it seems incredible that life can go on with so few properties, or the great child, man, find entertainment in so bare a playroom.

Reprinted from *Across the Plains,* Chatto and Windus, 1892

Oscar Wilde loves Nebraska canned corn.

—Omaha *Daily Republican*, March 25, 1882

Oscar Wilde in Omaha (*1882*)

CARL UHLARIK

MILKING the placid and bulging-uddered American cow always has been a favorite means of revenue for various literary and artistic folk from across the seas, so it was not strange that Oscar Wilde should try his hand at such milking, too. "I have nothing to declare but my genius," he told the customs men on landing in January, 1882. He left for home in July richer by about one thousand dollars —a pretty fair take, considering that he was a youth fresh from Oxford with little more than a volume of poetry and a certain notoriety in mannerisms and dress to commend him.

The people of Omaha knew of Oscar Wilde and his preachments on *aestheticism* long before they had any intimation that he would appear in their city. American journalists were prodigal in their use of *aesthetic, sunflower,* and *lily*—Wilde's trademarks—and in the Omaha papers one saw dead-pan references to *Paddy McGuire's aesthetic cow,* the *aesthetic guano combine,* and the *aestheticism* of a local paperhanger's trial for murder in a sporting house. Individuals were called *sunflowers* and *lilies* derisively.

It was on the first day of spring, appropriately enough, that the exponent of the sunflower and lily gave the West its first glimpse of an English aesthete. Bundled in an overcoat and accompanied by his valet and business manager, Wilde hurried through the raw March day directly to the Withnell House on 15th and Harney Streets. There, lolling at ease and puffing a cigarette, he received his callers dressed in dark trousers, a black velvet jacket, and leather gaiters faced with yellow cloth. A handkerchief dainty enough to be drawn through a lady's ring fluttered over the breast pocket of his jacket, and a maroon silk scarf was tied at his throat. The *Daily Republican* for March 22 spoke of ". . . his physiognomy, a long face looking out from a pretty 'long head'—the hair, darkly brown, voluminous and long, divided near the middle and thrown back in wavy masses on either side." His hair-dress alone elicited no wide-eyed comment, for Omahans were familiar enough with Buffalo Bill and other characters whose hair covered their ears and hung to their shoulders.

Since time immemorial, visiting celebrities had been asked The Question, and Oscar Wilde, too, bowed gracefully under the sweet burden of fame. When asked by a writer for the *Weekly Herald* how he liked Omaha, Wilde replied: "You have not the lower orders of the eastern cities. I find less prejudice and more simple and sane people. The western part of America is really the part of the country that interests us in England because it seems to us that it has a civilization that you are making for yourselves—not the complimentary echo of British thought." (Since his dash from the station to the hotel comprised his whole experience of Omaha, Oscar obviously got the feel of a place fast.)

About one thousand people were at Boyd's Opera House that evening. Members of the Social Art Club, sponsors of the lecture, were there in full body. These westerners, hardly over the pioneer stage, these merchants and soldiers, sod-breakers and track-layers, were to hear a young man from the Old World lecture to them on art and its relation to the decoration of the home.

Introduced by Judge Savage—lawyer, orator, and erstwhile groomsman at the wedding of Chester A. Arthur—Wilde was a bizarre enough sight to evoke Philistine jeers from the gallery. He wore black velvet knee-breeches, black silk hose, and low pumps with shiny metal buckles. A white tie of delicate fabric concealed his shirt front; a flowing handkerchief was tucked in one of his lace cuffs; and there was a large gold seal ring on the hand that placed a sheaf of manuscript on the reading desk. But the aesthete's pale features were composed, and when at last he began to speak the impatient rustling and stirring died away.

After some general remarks on the nature of art and the honor due the handicraftsman, Wilde pitched into American domestic architecture and interior decoration. Most American houses, he said, were "horrors"—badly designed, decorated shabbily and in bad taste, filled with furniture that was not honestly made and was out of character. Then after declaiming against the glaring billboards and muddy streets, he pointed out that America was filled with such "horrors," but that in England the artist and the handicraftsman were brought together to their mutual benefit. That if decoration was a fine art, all the arts were fine arts. That the real test of the

workman was not his industry or his earnestness but his power of
designing. That the surroundings of the handicraftsmen in America
were meaningless architecture, and sombre dress of men and women,
and the lack of a beautiful national life. At the conclusion of his lecture he gave many practical suggestions on household decorations
and art studies and urged that the lives of boys be made joyous and
that they be taught to love the beauties of nature. "Physical beauty,"
he said, "is really, absolutely the basis of all great and strong art. All
true art must be wrought by healthy and happy men and women."

The Social Art Club paid Wilde $250.00 for the lecture and netted
$150.00 for itself, and had it not been for the desire of certain social
lights to touch the robe of the disciple of aestheticism, the further
taint of commercialism would not have marred this advent of art
and culture in an artless western city. After the lecture, Judge Woolworth and his wife sent Wilde an invitation to dinner at their home.
Wilde sent a polite note of acceptance with, however, the stipula-
tion that Judge Woolworth make out a $50.00 sight draft to Wilde's
order.

When the news leaked out, people who until then were favorably
impressed by Wilde saw him not as a whole-souled disciple of
beauty but as a rude, grasping snob whose only concern seemed to
be the harvesting of good American dollars. Those who jeered at
him from the beginning became more vitriolic. After deriding them
for their "horrors," muddy streets, and glaring billboards, they said,
he added insult to injury by demanding a price to grace the table of
a generous couple.

Whether Wilde was culpable it is hard to say now. Apparently no
one took into account the business manager in the background. In
any case, Wilde escaped the hot comments. He entrained for San
Francisco at noon of the day following the lecture.

Condensed from *Prairie Schooner*, Spring, 1940

*Narcissa Whitman and Eliza Spalding, two preachers'
wives, in 1836 became the first white women to make the
trip over the Oregon Trail. No less intrepid, in its way,
was the journey made seventy-nine years later by a lady
who has devoted much of her life to fighting the good
fight for gracious living and whose word is gospel wherever white ties are worn.*

Next Stop, North Platte! (1915)

EMILY POST

NORTH PLATTE might really be called "City of Ishmael." For no reason that is discoverable except its mere existence, every man's tongue
seems to be against it. Time and time again—in fact the repetition
is becoming monotonous—people say to us, "It is all very well, of
course, you have had fine hotels and good roads so far, but wait
until you come to North Platte!"

Why, I wonder, does everyone pick out North Platte as a sort of
third-degree place of punishment? Why not one of the other names
through which our road runs? Why always set up that same unfortunate town as a target? It began with Mrs. O. in New York, who
declared it so dreadful a place that we would never live through it.
Her point of view being extremely fastidious, her opinion does not
alarm us as much as it otherwise might, but in Chicago, too, the
mention of our going to North Platte seemed to be the signal for
people to look sorry for us. Now a drummer downstairs has just
added his mite to our growing apprehension.

"Goin' t' th' coast?" he queried. "Hm—I guess you won't like th'
hotels at North Platte over much."

"Do you go there often?" I returned.

"Me?" he said indignantly. "Not on your life! No one ever gets
off at North Platte except the railroad men—they *have* to!" That is
the one unexplained phase of the subject, no one of all those who
have vilified it has personally been there.

Just as I asked if he could perhaps tell me which of the hotels
was least bad, a fellow drummer joined him. The usual expression
of commiseration followed. "Well," said the second drummer, "it's

this way. Whichever hotel you put up at, you'll wish you had put up at the other."

Of all the bogey stories, the one about North Platte is the most unfounded! Instead of a rip-roaring town, rioting in red and yellow ribaldry, it is a serious railroad thoroughfare, self-respecting and above reproach and the home of no less a celebrity than Mr. Cody—Buffalo Bill. Of course, if you imagine you are going to find a Blackstone or a Fontenelle, you will be disappointed, but in comparison to some of the other hotels along the Lincoln Highway, the Union Pacific in North Platte is a model of delectability!

It is an ocher-colored wooden railroad station, a rather bare dining-room and lunch counter, and perfectly good, clean bedrooms upstairs. You cannot get a suite with a private bath, and if you are more or less spoiled by the supercomforts of luxurious living, you may not care to stay very long. But if in all of your journeying around the world, you never have to put up with any greater hardship than spending a night at the Union Pacific in North Platte, you will certainly not have to stay at home on that account. There are no drunkards or toughs or even loafers hanging about; the food is cleanly served and good; the rooms, although close to the railroad tracks, are as spotless as brooms and scrubbing-brushes can make them.

Across Nebraska from the last good hotel in Omaha to the first comfortable one in Denver or Cheyenne is over five hundred miles. At the prescribed "speed" of about seventeen miles an hour average, it means literally a pleasant little run of between thirty and forty hours along a road dead level, wide, straight, and where often as far as the eye can see, there is not even a shack in the dimmest distance, and the only settlers to be seen are prairie dogs. If between Omaha and Cheyenne there were three or four attractive clean little places to stop, or if the Nebraska speed laws were abolished or disregarded *and it didn't rain,* you could motor to the heart of the Rocky Mountains with the utmost ease and comfort.

In May, 1915, the road by way of Sterling to Denver was impassable; all automobiles were bogged between Big Springs and Julesburg, so on the advice of car owners that we met, we went by way of Chappell to Cheyenne. It is quite possible, of course, that we blindly passed comfortable stopping-places, but to us that whole vast distance from Omaha to Cheyenne was one to be crossed with as little stop-over as possible. Aside from questions of accommodations and speed laws, the interminable distance was in itself an unforgettably wonderful experience. It gave us an impression of the lavish immensity of our own country as nothing else could. Think of driving on and on and on and yet the scene scarcely changing, the flat road stretching as endlessly in front of you as behind. The low yellow sand banks and flat sand islands scarcely vary on the Platte, which might as well be called the Flat, River. The road does gradually rise several thousand feet, but the distance is so immense your engine does not perceive a grade. Once in a while you pass great herds of cattle fenced in vast enclosures, and every now and then you come to a group of nesters' shanties, scattered over the gray-green plain as though some giant child had dropped its blocks. At greater intervals you come to towns, and you drive between two closely fitted rows of oddly assorted domino-shaped stores and houses, and then on out upon the great flat table again. For scores and scores of miles the scene is unvarying. On and on you go over that endless road until at last far, far on the gray horizon you catch the first faint glint of the white-peaked Rocky Mountains.

Perhaps you may merely find dullness in the endlessly flat, unvarying monotonous land. But steep your sight for days in flatness, until you think the whole width of the world has melted into a never-ending sea of land, and then see what the drawing close to those most sublime of mountains does to you! And afterwards, when you have actually climbed to their knees or shoulders and look back upon the endless plains, you forget the wearying journey and feel keenly the beauty of their very endlessness. The ever-changing effect of light and shadow over that boundless expanse weaves an enchanted spell upon your imagination that you can never quite recover from. Sometimes the prairies are a great sea of mist; sometimes they are a parched desert; sometimes they are blue like the waves of an enchanted sapphire sea; sometimes they melt into a plain of vaporous purple mystery, and then the clouds shift away from the sun and you see they are the width of the world, of land.

But however or whenever you look out upon them, you feel as though mean little thoughts, petty worries, or skulking gossip whispers could never come into your wind-swept mind again. That if you could only live with such vastness of outlook before you, perhaps your own puny heart and mind and soul might grow into something bigger, simpler, worthier than is ever likely otherwise.

Extracted from *By Motor to the Golden Gate*, D. Appleton, 1916

There was no buffalo hunt in honor of these Russian visitors, but then, unlike Grand Duke Alexis, they weren't here for fun. Nevertheless they seem to have had some anyway.

The Moscow Express (1955)

JACK HART

THERE WAS no indication in the summer of 1955 that the Kremlin bosses considered a visit to Nebraska in the same category as a Soviet-styled trip to Siberia. So it can be assumed that a dozen Russian farm experts spent three bustling days in the Cornhusker State, not because they had violated Communist precepts, but in a genuine effort to improve themselves and their nation.

The Soviet agriculturists obviously liked what they saw. Apparently they have since put their Nebraska knowledge to good use in their homeland. For soon after his return, the leader of the delegation, Vladmir Matskevich, was named Soviet Minister of Agriculture. The Russians' enthusiasm for Nebraska agriculture showed even through the language barrier. It was apparent in an incessant flow of questions. It was acted out as they scribbled furiously in thick notebooks. They investigated much of what makes the state's agricultural machine tick—the latest in irrigation equipment at Columbus, the world-famed tractor-testing laboratory in Lincoln, a watershed conservation project south of Wahoo, hybrid seed corn in the making near Fremont, a turkey farm at Venice, and a steak dinner in Omaha.

But it wasn't Nebraska's bountiful crops that impressed the Russians most. Nor was it the friendliness and good humor with which Nebraskans greeted them, though admittedly they were overwhelmed by their reception. It wasn't even the sight of scores of B-47 jet bombers which unfolded in their full view as they passed the Lincoln Air Force Base.

No, it was the weather—Nebraska's irresponsible, delightful, miserable, unmatchable weather. Like a small boy trying too hard to be noticed, Weather was an unforgettable show-off from the time the

Russians stepped out of their air-conditioned bus into its 102-degree greeting.

Not until the guests had suffered sufficiently from its deviltry did Weather show its angelic side. That came when Delegation Chief Matskevich, with Yuri Golubach and Andrei Shevchenko, sought refuge from the heat in a flying trip to the sandhills, their first visit to an American ranch.

Standing knee-deep in grass at the By-the-Way Ranch south of Valentine, with a gentle breeze drifting across a placid lake, Matskevich could not contain his emotions.

"They ought to sell the air from out here by the pound in New York," he exclaimed.

"Our prize for two weeks of hard work," he called it.

For Shevchenko—whose appearance, mannerisms, and ready humor had earned him the title of "Russia's Will Rogers"—it was too much. Throwing his inhibitions and outer clothing to the breeze, he deserted an inspection of a purebred cattle herd and leaped as far as he could into Big Alkali Lake. Nebraska Weather had won a friend.

As they prepared to rejoin their comrades in eastern Nebraska, Matskevich made one last irresistible observation: "What wonderful air! What a wonderful smell! What sun!"

Nebraska is not pretty and easy to like. Its colors seem to change abruptly all at once. Actually they don't. In spring the prairie is all bright fresh green. But while the corn is still young and green, the wheat and oats are already yellow. If the summer is too dry, the land gets baked and gray. But in a good summer, the countryside looks soft. The corn rustles and shows the silvery underside of its leaves. The heavy-headed wheat waves peacefully.

In late summer, earth and sky seem yellow. When the locusts get tired at summer's end and stop their dry din, the chattering blackbirds take up where the locusts left off. The few trees and the brambles turn bright. The air fills with the strong smell of weeds. The tumbleweeds bounce across the harvested fields and pile up at the fences. Winter, like summer, is violent. Sometimes it blusters and the fierce winds bring only small flurries of snow. Sometimes, very quietly, the sky opens and three feet of snow lies smooth on the white prairie.

—*Life,* March 3, 1941

Nebraska Not in the Guidebook

RUDOLPH UMLAND

March 18. Hotel Sullivan, Spalding, Nebraska. To most travelers, Nebraska means merely a one-night's stop on the way to some place else. After the tourist has expended a roll of film on the capitol at Lincoln, the state has no architectural marvels, no overpowering scenic wonders, no famous historic shrines to detain him. Yet in my own journeys within Nebraska's borders I find many places of interest and even some of beauty. My work has carried me back and forth over its roads many times, and several days of each week for the past six years have been spent living out of a suitcase and putting up at small hotels.

Some of the hotels where I've stayed have given me the impression of antedating statehood—perhaps because at the time I was a guest they still were furnished with iron bedsteads and the unmoored kind of plumbing. I believe it's quite possible I've even slept at

"The Blue Hotel" of Stephen Crane's story: at a junction-town, on his visit to Nebraska in 1895, Crane glimpsed from his railroad car a frame hostel painted blue, and the color so impressed him that he wrote a tale of the dire happenings he imagined must have taken place within its walls. Many nights, listening to the wind rattling the windows, I have been led to similar conjectures.

Many times, too, in small town hotel lobbies I've had rewarding encounters with old-timers. At Lexington's Cornland Hotel I was once entertained by a senior citizen whose father had taken him by buggy to Broken Bow, and on the way had pointed out the cottonwood on which "them squatters Mitchell and Ketchum" had been hanged by cattlemen in 1878.

June 25. Hotel Ord, Ord, Nebraska. Last month when I was at Ord I noticed an old man sitting on a stool in front of the bank reading aloud from the Bible. This afternoon when I arrived at Ord and got out of my car, I heard the drone of his voice still continuing and found him sitting at the same spot as if he hadn't moved during the thirty days intervening.

I am occupying Room Five in the hotel tonight and am curious about the frame of a picture hanging on the wall. While the picture is a banal tinted photograph of a lake scene with a man paddling a canoe, the wooden frame has a bone five inches in length embedded in it. The more I study this odd ornament, the more curious I become. Is it the bone of a fowl or the small upper arm bone of a murdered child?

August 7. Koster Hotel, Niobrara, Nebraska. I have no doubt that this is the oldest hotel building still in use in Nebraska. It is a two-story frame structure with sagging ceilings, bulging walls, and sloping floors. The original portion of it was built in 1873 and operated as a hotel by Herko Koster. After the flood of 1881 the building was moved to the new location of Niobrara, and moved again in 1911 to its present site on Main Street. The building has been enlarged by several additions and has been owned and operated continuously as a hotel by members of the Koster family. The present owner and manager, Florence Bell Koster, is seventy-one and the widow of George Koster, son of the original owner. The story is told that Kid Wade, the outlaw, was staying in the hotel one night during the early 1880's when the vigilantes came for him. Herko Koster refused entrance to them and protected his guest all night, sitting in the door with a loaded shotgun across his knees. Sometime before morning, the Kid departed by a back window.

October 11. Burwell Hotel, Burwell, Nebraska. When I drove into Burwell this evening, I met a pretty cowgirl on a horse loping out of town. Burwell's center is a square full of business houses. Surrounding the square, and fronting it on all four sides, are other business houses. The unique thing about the plan is that all four streets entering the square enter at the center rather than at the corners. Most of Nebraska's county-seat towns are laid out around a square with the courthouse and a memorial to the civil war dead in the middle. Some, like Broken Bow, are laid out around a square with a bandstand in the middle and the courthouse stuck elsewhere. They are built with straight streets bordering the square and entering at the corners. The majority of little towns in Nebraska weren't laid out at all but just grew, with their business houses strung along the main wagon route; and today they remain one-street towns. Even the smallest of them used to have at least one hotel. Now many towns have none, the number of hotels dwindling each year, their business lost because of speedier transportation and, since World War II, the rapid growth of motels.

October 26. Hotel Hartington, Hartington, Nebraska. It was a beautiful Indian summer day with the thermometer reaching 82 degrees in the afternoon. I met an old German resident of Bow Valley who told me about the "Shootzenfest" which used to be held in that locality. "Hundreds und thousands of people used to come," he said, "mostly Germans, to shoot at der vooden bird und see who would be king of *das Schuetzenfest.* Ach, from as far avay as Chicago und St. Louie die shooters come!" I have heard from others about the great Bow Valley *Schuetzenfest.* A commercial traveler told me that once, years ago, when he was staying overnight at Hartington, some friends took him to Bow Valley. They found several thousand people milling around a pole that rose about fifty feet in the air to which was nailed a wooden bird. He said that, once in the crowd, every time you moved or turned, a frau or fraulein would thrust a platter of food at you or hand you a foaming stein of beer. Each shooter got to fire a certain number of shots from a twenty-two-caliber rifle, the object being to shoot the bird from the pole. The one who succeeded in accomplishing this feat became king of the *Schuetzenfest* and was privileged to select the queen. The commercial traveler said the gaiety and hospitality of the affair made it seem as if you had stepped suddenly out of the Nebraska landscape into another country and another century.

November 3. Arrow Hotel, Broken Bow, Nebraska. A pretty night with a half-moon and stars hanging in a black sky over the city square. A lot of cowpokes, ranchers, and cattle-buyers in town for a big cattle show and sale. It was only by luck that I got a room at the hotel.

At the town of Pleasanton today I was given a demonstration of water witching by a well-driller who uses one-eighth-inch steel welding rods cut thirty-six inches long with five inches bent to form a handle. Grasping a pair of these rods in his hands and holding them level before him, he advanced into the yard near his shop. As he advanced, the rods crossed, an indication that there was no underground water flow. He continued to advance across the yard until suddenly the rods swung apart and away from each other in an arc as far as they could. This indicated an underground water flow. I then took the rods in my hands and walked over the same area. The rods performed in the same fashion for me. They swung apart as if by magnetic force. It's a puzzling thing. The well-driller says, "I don't believe in them but I use them. I don't believe in them because there is no sensible explanation for their behavior. I use them because they are nearly always right."

November 17. Stockman Hotel, Atkinson, Nebraska. I drove eighteen miles up the Calumus River northwest of Burwell to visit a rancher this morning, and accompanied him in his jeep out over his range to feed pellets to his cattle. He has a nice herd of one hundred and ten head of white-faced Herefords with about the same number of calves. On his range is some of the grass known as Poor Joe. Cattle don't like Poor Joe; it isn't nutritious. It invaded the sandhills range after the Kinkaiders had moved in and broken up the native grassland. The Kinkaiders gave up the struggle and moved away, but Poor Joe now grows on land which once was excellent range.

Driving through the sandhills from Burwell to Bartlett this afternoon, and noticing the contour of the hills, made me think of the missionary in Somerset Maugham's story *Rain* who had neurotic dreams about these "mountains of Nebraska" because they resemble female breasts. Early cowboys were aware of this resemblance too and named one of the mounds near Chadron "Squaw's Tit."

December 22. Hotel Golden, O'Neill, Nebraska. Winter officially started about three o'clock this morning; the sun rose in a clear sky about eight o'clock. I hear roosters crowing, hundreds of sparrows chirping in the canvas awnings, and some cows bawling when I walked from the hotel to the cafe for breakfast in Atkinson this morning. The weather was mild, and during the afternoon the thermometer reached sixty degrees. It was more like corn-planting weather than the first day of winter. I drove thirty miles to visit a farmer near Mariaville and found him engaged in hauling fourteen scattered alfalfa stacks, each containing about seven tons of hay, a distance of a quarter-mile or more to his farmlot with a tractor and an underslung rack. To load a stack, one side of the rack was propped up by means of two blocks so that the other side rested on the ground next the stack; the stack was next encircled at its base by a long chain which was hooked onto a cable attached to a winch on the tractor; the tractor was then driven forward, the chain tightening and pulling the entire stack upon the rack. It is a startling sight to see a large haystick moving across a field or coming down a road. This system of transporting an entire stack of hay came into use in the late 1930's and is a great time-saver for farmers and ranchers.

January 14. Lincoln, Nebraska. Returning home from Chambers this afternoon, I stopped at the Public Power building in Columbus just to see if my old friend Aquabella was still there. She wasn't, and I didn't succeed in finding anybody who could tell me what happened to her.

Aquabella was the bust of a maiden, sculptured in terrazzo by Floyd Nichols (brother of Dale Nichols, the artist) of David City. The bust was set in a drinking fountain in the lobby of the Public Power building, and from the lips of the upturned face bubbled a continuous flow of cool water. The fountain was actually designed to be controlled by an electric eye, so that when one bent over to take a drink, the water would gush on. However, Aquabella created such a furore in the community that this intended feature probably never was added. Bashful farmers were loath and embarrassed to stoop over Aquabella's upturned face to sip a drink from her lips. Even those who weren't bashful admitted they had an uneasy feeling. "She's so real," they said, "that you get the feeling she's offering more than just a drink."

The most serious objections to the fountain came from women: "She may be a work of art, but she doesn't belong in a drinking fountain!" . . . "A corruption of the young!" . . . "I don't want to catch my husband drinking from her lips!" The controversy evidently grew too much for officials of the power district, and Aquabella had to be removed.

1947

JOHN GUNTHER'S NEBRASKA

Inside Nebraska[*]

JOHN GUNTHER

FORMER GOVERNOR Dwight Griswold let me ride by highway patrol from Omaha to Lincoln and we spent most of a day together. I admired "O" Street which is part of US 34 and which runs sixty-nine miles without a turn, and so is called the longest and straightest street in the world. I admired the state capitol also. Like that in Bismarck (also Baton Rouge) it is a skyscraper, and, rising out of the wide green-tawny flatness of the plains, it is strikingly dramatic. A story goes with it too. It cost eleven million dollars and took eleven years to build, since it was paid for, year by year, by a special property tax calculated to yield exactly a million dollars annually. The doughty Nebraskans don't believe in debt, and they built, penny by penny, as they got the money. The portals of the building bear the legend, THE SALVATION OF THE STATE IS WATCHFULNESS IN THE CITIZEN, and atop the dome is a large statue of the "Sower." This too shows what Nebraska thinks about.

Griswold, who was one of the best governors in the nation, left office in January, 1947. He had previously been beaten in a run for the Senate by Hugh Butler, an extreme diehard.[**] What defeated Griswold was the British loan—mostly. Butler, a fierce isolationist who not only voted against the loan but against selective service, Lend Lease, and Bretton Woods, made isolation the chief issue. Griswold, a liberal Republican of the Stassen school, took a strong internationalist line, and lost three to one.

Let me write about Dwight Griswold briefly as an example of a modern Great Plains-corn-belt chief executive. He was a "sand hill" boy; his parents were homesteaders who settled in western Nebraska before the railroads came. That, in high school, he won a $100 prize for an essay, "How to Lay the Foundations of Good Government," shows how character patterns may be forecast in childhood. Except while governor, he has lived in a small town called Gordon since 1901, and is chairman of the board of the local bank and publisher of

---

[*] Of the 920 pages of text in John Gunther's *Inside U.S.A.*, a total of 5½ are devoted to Nebraska. They may be found under the subhead "Addendum on a Great State, Nebraska," at the end of the chapter on the Dakotas.

[**] Both Governor Griswold, who was elected to the Senate in 1952, and Senator Butler died in office in 1954.

the Gordon *Journal,* with a tiny but important circulation. Griswold's tough independence reminded me to a certain extent of Sumner Sewell, who was then governor of Maine, though he isn't so rambunctious or iconoclastic. He is a stubborn man; he had to run for the governorship three times before he made it. Then he was re-elected twice. Once he recorded 74.8 per cent of the total vote cast, and once 76 per cent, an all-time record for Nebraska. He was one of the few Republican governors to "go along" with FDR on foreign policy, and his secretary was a registered Democrat. The international question was not the exclusive cause of his defeat. He had had three terms as governor and people thought that this was enough public office for the time being. Nebraska is a fickle state.

What runs Nebraska is—the weather! I do not mean this as a wisecrack. The state differs markedly from its neighbors South Dakota and Kansas in that it has no mineral wealth, and there are few foaming, power-producing rivers in the interior. All Nebraska has to live on is its eight- to twelve-foot-thick rug of soil.

On this it lives quite well—provided the weather smiles. It is the thirty-second state in population, and yet the sixth in production of food stuffs; what supports it is, in other words, export of corn, wild hay, wheat, alfalfa, feeder cattle, feeder hogs, butter, eggs. It is, after Wisconsin and New York, the third dairying state. More than a billion dollars are invested in the 181,000 Nebraska farms, which are tended as carefully as lawns in Connecticut. These farms average 191 acres in size incidentally—more than twice that of farms in the country as a whole—and they are mechanized 61 per cent more than the national average.

Driving back to Omaha I looked at some farms and decided that my synonym for the word "rich" hereafter would be corn growing in southeastern Nebraska. But not all of it is so lush and fertile. The state is half West, half Middle West. The western half is dry ranch and sand hills country, with thousands upon thousands of acres that have never seen a plow.

No wonder weather is such a preoccupation. It can almost literally be a matter of life or death. I saw the clouds burst open one day; out of sunshine came water that was three inches deep in half an hour. The first copy of the Omaha *World-Herald* I picked up had three weather stories on its front page, and the local radio broadcasts weather news all the time. Incidentally an Omaha hotel is the only one I have ever known with radios in the elevators. Out in the country, the fact that there are comparatively few trees, no big stands of timber, and no mountains for a windbreak, makes the impact of the weather more dramatic; nothing screens you from what may be elemental violence. The summers are as brutally hot as the winters are brutally cold. The drought of the middle 30's hit here just as it did in the Dakotas; nobody has forgotten the "black blizzard" dust storms. Of course, as in all agrarian states, weather equals politics and bad weather equals radicalism. James E. Lawrence of the Lincoln *Star* went east in 1936 to do a series of articles on Alf Landon's chances. When he left, the corn was green. When he returned it was black. He knew then that Landon's chances were gone with the corn, "fried out."

The name Nebraska means Flat Water; the Otoe Indians called it this, for the Platte * and its famous characteristic of flowing "bottom side up." Originally the state was a Louisiana "orphan," being in that part of the Louisiana Purchase which Congress first set aside as Indian country. The first homestead in the United States (1863) was in Nebraska, at a town named Beatrice, pronounced Be-*at*-rice. There were two main streams of settlement. First, Civil War veterans who sought homesteads. Nebraska, unlike Kansas, had no slave problem. There is scarcely a county seat today without the imprint of the Grand Army of the Republic. Second, German, Scandinavian, and to a somewhat smaller degree Czechoslovak settlers. These had an enormous yearning for land, their own land; they cared little for cities, and pushed straight out into the flat wilderness. Some early villages were so small that, for a time, each had only one church; Catholics and Protestants worshiped in the same room, with half the pews facing an altar at one end, half a pulpit at the other.

This was all sturdy stock. It believed in health, hard work, and education. Anybody who has read the early novels of Willa Cather knows what the circumstances of life were. Today, Nebraska has more folk of German extraction than any state except Wisconsin, and about 11 per cent of the total population is of Czechoslovak origin. Most of the Scandinavians are Swedes, though both Norwegian and Danish communities exist. Some counties are almost solidly Czech,

---

* "Colorado, Wyoming, and Nebraska have been at each other's throats for a quarter of a century, arguing in courts about disposition of water from the North Platte; each of the three states, by long-established 'filings' gets its 'take' of North Platte water. Colorado says: 'We've been here for seventy years. We make the prairie bloom. We turned sagebrush into sugar beets. We did all this when Nebraska and Kansas were nothing but territory fit for jackrabbits.' Wyoming, too, bitterly resents what it calls Nebraska's 'grab.' But by a recent Supreme Court judgment Nebraska is to get 75 per cent of North Platte water, with Colorado and Wyoming dividing the remainder."—*Inside U.S.A.*, page 215.

and Czechoslovak is spoken almost as commonly as English; one county is half Czech, half Swede. The Germans are largely Lutheran, and their political affiliation varies. Woodrow Wilson, I heard it said, made Republicans out of them; then prohibition made them Democrats; during World War II they were divided. There was no discernible disloyalty among the Nebraska Germans,* though plenty were strongly isolationist, in 1941–45; the Bund was not a problem. In World War I many Germans had thought well of the Kaiser, but Hitler alienated Lutherans, Catholics, Jews and all. During World War I when the German newspapers were a real power in the state, a law had to be passed proscribing foreign language schools and papers. This wasn't necessary in World War II. In a sense, the old German Turnverein and similar societies, which had played a sub-stantial role in Nebraska for well over a generation, never regained their former influence after 1919. A striking point—the American melting pot does melt—is that even after Lidice, Germans and Czechs in the same Nebraska town got on perfectly well together.

Nebraska is, like most western states, exceptionally hospitable and friendly. The atmosphere is quite different from that in some parts of Iowa where, if a stranger passes, the suspicious citizenry assemble to discuss him. A hotel in one western Nebraska town has a big sign on the door, HUNT AND FISH AS YOU DAMN PLEASE. WHEN THE BELL RINGS COME IN TO DINNER.

Any innocent traveler from the East who thinks that Nebraska is a stick-in-the-mud politically will get some surprises.** Somehow the illusion exists that it is overwhelmingly Republican and conservative, which is absurd. Simply recollect that this is the state not only of George W. Norris but of William Jennings Bryan. It had a series of Populist governors, Roosevelt carried it twice, its leading newspaper is Democratic (though strongly anti-New Deal) and Democratic and Republican governors have tended to alternate. Except for Butler and the loud-mouthed Wherry (the other senator) it has scarcely ever elected an outright reactionary to public office. It

* ". . . formidable numbers of Middle Westerners are of German background, and many of these had German sympathies. Again, the region is full of Scandinavians, who were traditionally isolationist, even in Europe itself. One should not, however, draw too sweeping conclusions about this. Nebraska is a strongly German state, and Kansas has scarcely any Germans at all, yet Kansas was much more isolationist than Nebraska."—*Inside U.S.A.*, page 288.

** On page 238, *Inside U.S.A.*, Mr. Gunther says that North Dakota, Minnesota, Nebraska, and Wisconsin are "traditionally the chief repository of progressivism in the United States." On page 248, he adds: "The Great Plains states do still produce radicals, of course, but mostly they move out. . . . Nebraska has a big export of radicals."

dislikes Republicans with a Wall Street flavor, and it is the only state ever to have elected a federal senator (Norris) as a nonpartisan. On the other hand it has recently shown a strong antilabor tinge, and in 1946 it was one of three states to adopt a constitutional amendment outlawing the closed shop.*

In the old days what ran Nebraska was the railways. This was inevitable, in the pattern the reader knows well: the railways got the land, then populated it, then exploited it. For many years, the Union Pacific and the Chicago, Burlington & Quincy divided the state between them; the UP was always supposed to elect one senator, the Burlington the other. One thing that broke down railway dominance was the direct primary. Another lively factor was the growth of the automobile, which made free railway passes less valuable and desirable. A chief minor weapon of the railways everywhere in the nation was, for many years, the free travel with which they bribed legislators and practically anybody else.

The chief uniqueness of Nebraska today is that it is the only state with a unicameral legislature. Largely George Norris was responsible for this. Senate and assembly were abolished in 1934, and a one-house system with forty-three members came into operation. Norris developed the idea when, in Washington, he saw bills dear to him killed in committee or hopelessly weakened by compromises; he thought that the "special interests" would have less room in which to operate in a single chamber. I found people in Nebraska somewhat divided on this subject. Most agree that the unicameral idea, as it has worked out, makes for a higher class of legislator (since fewer are to be elected) and greater efficiency and economy generally; some thought however that the system, by giving the lobbyist a single target to aim at, and by eliminating the possibility that special interest legislation which manages to pass one chamber will get stopped by the other, has not been so effective as Norris would have hoped.

The Cornhusker State has plenty of other political distinctions. The legislature (like that of Minnesota) is elected on a nonpartisan basis; a man does not stand as a Republican or a Democrat, and there is no division in the chamber itself on party lines. Another important reformist item is that debate on all bills must be public; this I believe something unique in the nation; Nebraska has no "executive sessions" (where so much bad legislation is worked

---

* The others: South Dakota and Arizona.

out in other states) or private committee meetings. Once again, we see western ideals of democracy demanding expression in concrete form. The *people* insist on running things. All judges and educational officers in Nebraska (as in California) are also elected, like the legislators, on a strict nonparty basis. Another singular factor is that the constitution limits the bonded debt to $100,000; Nebraska cannot undertake expensive public works without specific authorization from the people. Sometimes the passion for pure democracy and complete control of the procedures of government leads to picturesque exaggerations: for instance, the Omaha ballot in November, 1946, was thirteen feet long and contained 26,000 words. One proposal on this ballot was that the state should contribute $40 per year to the support of every child in the public schools.

Recent big issues have been (a) prohibition and (b) public power. A referendum to make the state dry was beaten three to one in 1944; Nebraska has many do-gooders, but it is not dominated by them as, for instance, Kansas is. As to public power, a subject of cardinal importance, the simplest thing to say is that Nebraska has it. Behind this "simple" sentence are years of struggle, violent affrays with the utility companies, convoluted maneuvers by Electric Bond and Share, an irresistibly expanding sentiment for rural electrification, pressure by the Securities Exchange Commission, establishment of people's power districts like the PUD's in the Northwest, and finally the transfer to public ownership of the Nebraska Power Company, one of the great old-time behemoths. The result is that Nebraska (not Washington or Oregon which might claim the distinction, or Tennessee which does claim it) is the first public power state in the nation.

Extracted from *Inside U.S.A.*, Harper & Brothers, 1949

IX. The First Hundred Years Are the Hardest

Troubles we had none, as I look back now. I suppose I must mention the county-seat fight, the meanness of the railroad company in refusing us a station house, blizzards, droughts, prairie fires (one fire destroyed our young nursery), and the grasshoppers, but what were they in the course of sixty years of good things?

–Ada Gray Bemis, "My Own Biography," *Nebraska History*, XIV (Oct.–Dec., 1933)

> *. . . I have discovered that, in the minds of many people,*
> *Nebraska has really changed very little from 1854. There*
> *was a time when Nebraska was the state of Senator George*
> *Norris, and, depending upon the observer's politics, was*
> *a region of great acumen and progressiveness, or of dan-*
> *gerous radicalism. But since the death of the great Sena-*
> *tor, Nebraska is usually characterized as "that long flat*
> *state that sets between me and any place I want to go."*
>
> —Mari Sandoz, "The Look of the West—1854,"
> *Nebraska History,* XXXV (Dec. 1954)

A Norris Portfolio

1. "Very Perfect, Gentle Knight"

CLAUDIUS O. JOHNSON

TRAITOR, Pro-German, Copperhead, Pacifist, Socialist, Bolshevik, predatory politician, demagogue, agitator, meddler, reformer, idealist, major prophet, monopoly-hater, Wall Street-baiter, friend of the common man, statesman unafraid, a living, perambulating Declaration of Independence—these are only a few of the terms which have been used in characterizing Senator George William Norris. Independent of party, he has held office for fifty years in a country which perfected the party system. Scorning almost every device which practical politicians have considered indispensable, he has remained in public life as others have fallen, often the stupid victims of their own orthodox practices. In a country and a period which definitely prefer young men, he won his most signal victory at the polls when seventy-five; and in a country which expects quick performance, he had passed three score and ten before he started winning major victories for his principles. Here is a man who placed his principles above himself and whom the people placed above his principles, even above their own principles.

Norris's earliest years fit into any American success story. He was born in Sandusky County, Ohio, July 11, 1861. His parents, who had come to Ohio from the eastern seaboard, were poor in everything but offspring, for George (called William at home) was the youngest of twelve children. After the death of his father and elder brother, to help support his mother and sisters, George worked for farmers in the summer and attended school in the winter. With a meager public school training he taught for a few years to earn money to continue his education. He wanted to become a lawyer and eventually completed his legal studies at Valparaiso University, passing the bar examination in 1883.

Once more he taught school, this time in Washington Territory, near Walla Walla, for the purpose of securing means to purchase a law library. After seven months, he left the Territory and went back to the Middle West, to Beaver City, Nebraska, a little town in the south-central part of the state. There, in 1885, he hung out his shingle. Some years later he moved to McCook, a few miles farther west. His law practice grew slowly, and he was glad to make the race for county prosecuting attorney in 1899. He won the election, and he has been holding elective office ever since.

As a young attorney, George Norris married Pluma Lashley in 1890. This marriage was an entirely congenial and happy one. Mrs. Norris died in 1901, leaving the future senator with three daughters. Two years later, he married Ella Leonard, who had been principal of one of the public schools at McCook. Since 1903, they have lived quietly in Washington during the sessions of Congress. They shun Washington society; the Senator occasionally ridicules it. During recesses they enjoy their home and friends at McCook. In the summer they often motor to Wisconsin, where they live in a little forest cabin of which the Senator is the architect and builder. The Norrises enjoy motoring in their inexpensive car, and on the road they give every appearance of being just one of many hundred thousands of plain couples on limited incomes who are out for a little recreation and pleasure. The Senator enjoys doing the odd jobs about his yard such as trimming trees and mowing grass. This work and simple living doubtless go a long way to explain why he has enjoyed such good health.

The Norris library is well stocked. Leisure time means to the Senator time to read and study. He loves stirring poetry, which he often reads aloud, and, as would be expected of a man so modest, he associates the triumphal lines with the deeds of his friends rather than with his own accomplishments. The greater part of his reading is on economic and social problems. It includes not only books and magazine articles but dry-as-dust reports. All of these he carefully analyzes, and on occasion he comes into the Senate with neat diagrams and charts, which he inserts in the record for the benefit of the few who will trouble themselves to look at them.

He has never been affiliated with any church, nor has he ever professed any kind of religion. He does not play to the religious groups by occasional church attendance and scriptural references in his speeches. On occasion he has been known to jest on the floor of the Senate that overly optimistic senators are using too much Christian Science. He says he is "one of the followers of the religion proclaimed by Abou ben Adhem . . . who loved his fellow men." A prominent minister in Nebraska wrote Norris that the "good" people of the state were ashamed of him, particularly for his support of Smith in 1928. Norris wired for advice on how he should vote on a naval armaments bill then before the Senate. The minister was for it. Norris replied: "It may be that the way to save the heathen people is to do it by backing up our prayers with a big navy and with armed marines and flying machines dropping bombs upon the homes of innocent people. You, being an educated teacher of religion, perhaps know more about this than I do, but I hope you will pardon me if, in my sinful way, I cannot see your viewpoint."

Not a backslapper, not a hail-fellow-well-met, the Senator nevertheless has always had his friends. In the days when he was considered regular in politics and sound in economics, he may have had a greater number of the garden variety of friends, but if his heterodox ideas have limited the number of his friends, they have strengthened the remaining friendships. Perhaps the strongest friendships he has ever had were those he enjoyed with Senators Robert M. La Follette, Sr., of Wisconsin and Harry Lane of Oregon. In La Follette he found a man whose views on railroads, banks, and other business concerns he frequently shared and a man whose broader and longer experience in public life made him something of a teacher. There is no doubt that La Follette greatly influenced the Senator from Nebraska.

Generally a warm supporter of President Franklin D. Roosevelt, often his adviser, he does not hesitate to say that the President is guilty of the sin of ingratitude when he thinks he is, and the President "takes it" from his "Uncle George." So do the Senator's associates. An unspotted record for integrity over two generations has given him the right, tacitly conceded by all, to pronounce harsh judgments.

Ordinarily he is mild, soft-spoken, unobtrusive. In his office, he

receives all who have any good reason to demand his time. Smoking
a cigar or pipe (seemingly his only "bad" habit or extravagance),
he just converses, exploring a question or problem. Often he lets
the visitor do the greater part of the talking. He never pounds his
desk, makes a grand declaration, or gives an oracular utterance.

If the Senator's relations with newspaper publishers have not been
altogether cordial, there has been compensation in his association
with the newspaper correspondents. Sick of senatorial bombast,
pomposity, and insincerity, these men love to talk to Norris, for
whom they have profound respect and admiration. Norris tells them
what he thinks, and he gives them the status of any question before
the Senate unless a rule of that body binds him to secrecy. He may
object to such rules, but he feels honor-bound to abide by them.

The occasional unreasonable suspicions and unjust judgments
of the Nebraska senator arise not from a suspicious and severe character but rather from his great dominant interest in the plain people, the relatively inarticulate masses. By nature he is not suspicious
or harsh or bitter, but trusting, charitable, and kindly. Having devoted his life to farmers and wage-earners and having so often
found their representatives break faith with them, as he sees it, he
is eternally vigilant to protect the masses from the laws which may
hamper them and from men who may discriminate against them.
Yet, aside from remarks in the heat of a debate, there is nothing
personal in the Senator's criticisms of men who represent corpora-
tions rather than the people. Indeed, even in debate he often makes
this clear. But once, while speaking he is reported to have said of
Coolidge, "He thinks he is a little Jesus Christ," a remark which
a tactful clerk entered in the *Congressional Record* as "He thinks
he is the embodiment of perfection."

Political independence is one of the outstanding qualities in the
mature statesmanship of Senator George W. Norris. As the orthodox
view it, the Senator has tried many times to commit political suicide,
but he misses or the bullet penetrates a non-vulnerable spot or
strikes such a tough spot that it bounces off. Or to put it in other
terms, the other politician's poison is his political medicine. This
is Norris since about 1910. As we look back, we can now discover
a few indications of a growing independence in Congressman Norris
during Theodore Roosevelt's administration, but on the whole he
was a good enough party man to praise the protective tariff and
use such expressions as the "magic wand of Republican encouragement and enthusiasm," and mean them. Within three months after

he took his seat in the House, he committed a little offense against party rule. On Washington's birthday, a Democratic member had moved that the House adjourn in tribute to the Father of the Country. Freshman Congressman Norris thought that this was a perfectly proper proposal, and he voted for it, the only Republican who did so. Leaders indulgently but gravely explained to him the impropriety of a Republican's supporting even such a patriotic resolution when introduced by a Democrat. Norris still could not understand why he should not vote for measures which he approved. A few months later he made a speech against his party's bill increasing the pay of an officer of the House, thus beginning a long and unbroken record against the spoils system.

Despite such lapses in party regularity, Norris meant to be a good Republican, and he naively thought that voting and speaking his convictions was perfectly sound Republicanism. He did not change his course upon learning that the masters of the party disagreed with him most positively. They gave him no patronage, which according to their political axioms would end his career. The innocent member from Nebraska had never thought of patronage as essential to a public career. In any event, he did not ask for or receive the privilege of naming even one man for an appointive position during the ten years he served in the House. The Senator thinks this is a record, and in all probability he is right.

Not only does the Senator scorn the restraints of party, he scorns every other type of restraint which men may attempt to impose upon his judgment and conscience. In March, 1917, as the country was entering the World War, one of Nebraska's senators, Mr. Hitchcock, led in the movement, while Norris, politically speaking, tied himself to the mouth of a cannon in opposing American participation in that war. As Congress approached adjournment, he and his close friends, La Follette and Lane, and eight other senators, prevented from coming to a vote the bill which was to have authorized the arming of American ships against German submarines. This was the "little group of wilful men, representing no opinion but their own," who rendered "the great Government of the United States helpless and contemptible." Articulate elements in Nebraska denounced Norris as few men have ever been denounced, and a few weeks after the memorable contest in the Senate, he went to Lincoln to explain his action. His speech was scheduled for Monday night, and he arrived in Lincoln Sunday morning. That Sunday was the darkest, most lonely day of the Senator's life. Few people came to see him, and nearly all of them advised him to leave town in order to escape violence. The only person who encouraged him was a young reporter who slipped in after dark.

Grim and determined, Norris stepped out on the platform that Monday night, a lonely figure, and faced a large and ominously silent audience. Serving as both chairman and speaker, he began, "I have come home to tell you the truth." Almost at once the realization that George Norris never told anything but what he firmly believed to be the truth seemed to spread over the audience. They listened attentively as he outlined the developments which were leading us to war. Presently they applauded and shouted, and they stood up and yelled when he denounced the newspapers for not giving the full story. His triumph was complete.

Norris has never been a radical, unless that term should be applied to anyone who opposed the status quo. He was not even a good progressive until he was near the half-century mark. After thirty years of warfare he is still a progressive. Many of the progressives of 1910 were quite through "progressing" in 1918 or 1920, but Norris has never wearied. In Franklin D. Roosevelt's words, he has "preserved the aspirations of youth" as he has "accumulated the wisdom of years," and he "stands forth as the very perfect, gentle knight of American progressive ideas."

Extracted from "George W. Norris," *The American Politician,* edited
by J. T. Salter, University of North Carolina Press, 1938

Not until he read the following article, written ten years after the event, did Senator Norris realize that the "young reporter" who had encouraged him on his "darkest, most lonely day" had become one of America's most distinguished newspapermen.

2. "A Homespun Man"

FREDERIC BABCOCK

I AM on the downhill slide—sometimes, I think, traveling rapidly. The end cannot be very many years in advance. I think I have, to a great extent, run my race. If I can do some good while I am traveling over the balance of the road, I want to do it, because I realize I am going over it for the last time.

"I am not conscious of having a single selfish ambition. Neither money nor office holds any enchanting allurements. There have been times in my life—and I presume it is true of most public men —when ambition, and I think an honorable ambition, caused in my heart great concern about such things. But I have lost all that. I have received all the honor I can ever expect. I should like to repay the people by an unprejudiced and unbiased service in their behalf. I have no other ambition."

Those two paragraphs, contained in an intimate and informal letter to a personal friend, reveal, much better than could any outsider, the character of George William Norris, senior Senator from Nebraska. They tell why the liberals of America have been drawn to him as they have been drawn to few men in modern times.

It is difficult for me, a self-expatriated Nebraskan, to give an accurate view of George Norris. I admit I am prejudiced. He was my boyhood idol. I have worshiped him ever since the day, at the height of the war fever, when it seemed that the whole country had joined Woodrow Wilson in denouncing him and his associates as "that little group of wilful men," and when he came home, told the truth, confounded his critics, and emerged unscathed.

A homespun man is Norris, a man entirely lacking in political, personal, or intellectual vanity. He is quiet in his manner. His face is open, frank, almost sad, but friendly. Structurally, he is strong, deep-chested, with wide shoulders.

"I have battled, battled, for everything I ever got," Norris once told an interviewer. The slow tragedy of dull poverty and toil was his in his younger years. He knew what it was to fight for a living. His whole life has been a record of modest triumphs. He has fought his way inch by inch. But it is axiomatic that if things had come easier for him he probably would not be where he is now. In his manner, in his processes of mind and his mode of living he is still as simple, as plain, as direct, and as unassuming as when he was on the upward climb. He knows more, of course, than he did then. His mind is more mature and has broadened. His convictions, however, for the most part are based on what he has personally known and seen, rather than on deductions from wide reading. He is not afraid to think and do for himself.

He first appeared on the national scene in 1903 as a member of the House. And he first had the spotlight thrown on him when, in the Sixty-first Congress, he led the fight for the overthrow of Cannon and Cannonism. He has been an insurgent since there has been any notable insurgency in the House. From the start, he declined to become one of those glorified political peons that are lightly worked, carefully clothed, highly paid, and accorded every privilege save that of independent thought and action. He did not rebel against the authority of the Cannon group because of sentiment in his home district. It was the other way around. At that time, as in a number of more recent instances, he has had to educate his constituency to accept his views.

"I saw men on either side of the political fence follow blindly the dictates of their machines," he says. "Even when there was no question of party fealty concerned, they would vote as their bosses ordered, dumbly, stupidly, like a lot of sheep or geese. I believed in the absolute freedom of thought and action, and, cherishing feelings of this sort, it did not take me long to become an objector—an insurgent."

The war came along, and with it hysteria. In the Senate, Norris voted against the armed-neutrality legislation demanded by President Wilson, and later braved the condemnation of most of the country by voting with others of the "wilful" group, against the resolution of war. The storm of denunciation centered on the West; the full force of it swooped down upon La Follette and Norris. The pseudo-patriots and the "stand-by-the-President" boys licked their chops and prepared for the killing.

Norris outmaneuvered them. Before they could get to him, he offered to resign. He called upon the Nebraska Governor to ask the legislature to provide for a special election to choose his successor. "If the verdict is against me," he told the Governor, "I shall at once place my resignation in your hands."

While the matter was still being debated, he left Washington and came to Lincoln. There was no welcoming committee at the station. As I recall it, he was left almost alone. A raw reporter, I called on him at his room in the old Lindell Hotel. He gave me all the time I wanted, answered fully every question I put to him concerning his extraordinary actions at Washington—and he told me plenty. The following day he addressed a joint session of the legislature, and that night he hired the city auditorium, introduced himself to the throng—and once more told plenty.

But a peculiar thing took place at that night meeting. The thousands present did not ask him for any explanation of what he had been up to or why he had defied the President. They did not wish any explanation. They showed him when he first appeared on the platform, and all the time he was speaking, and at the close of his address, that they would stand by him. Again and again they rose to their feet and cheered.

Norris went back to his duties in the Senate, and the talk of forcing him out of office became less than a whisper. The common people, the people among whom Norris was raised and still moved, had convinced the politicians that it was no use, that they would never stand for his being betrayed. They have been repeating the performance at intervals ever since.

His record since the war is fresh in the minds of American liberals. They remember gratefully, among other things, his fights for the preservation of Muscle Shoals; against the water-power combine; for a constitutional amendment doing away with "lame-duck" congresses; to abolish the electoral college and for the direct election of the President and the Vice-President; for the exploited farmers of the West and the rights of the oppressed throughout the country; for a recognition of the aspirations of the underdogs of other nations; his refusal to bow to the rule of patronage; his amazing attempt to defeat the Vareism of his own political party—all these are at last known to the public.

It has been his wish for years to assume some day the leadership in a movement for the reform of state government. He favors a one-house legislature of about twenty-five members, the consolidation and cutting down of state elective office, the appointment of all employees on a strictly civil-service merit basis, and the nomination and election of the legislature and the officials on a nonpartisan ticket. What a Utopia! But what a man to bring it about!

Extracted from "Norris of Nebraska," *The Nation,* Dec. 21, 1927

In May, 1931, the members of the Pulitzer award committee did an unprecedented thing. They gave the prize for the previous year's outstanding editorial to a denunciatory discussion of a living American. The title of the winning editorial, which appeared in the November 7, 1930, issue of the Fremont, Nebraska, Daily Tribune, *was "The Gentleman from Nebraska." Its basic thesis was that Nebraska continually re-elects Norris, not because of any appreciation of his ability or character, but to assert*

*through him its contempt for the cultural, social, and
political institutions of the East. The Fremont paper said
the aged Senator was held in lower esteem in his own state
than in any other part of the Union. Three years later
this prize-winning theory was given a blow in the solar
plexus when the Senator stumped Nebraska alone against
the opposition of press and politicians and persuaded the
voters to change the form of their state government by the
adoption of the unicameral legislature. . . .*

*Charles S. Ryckman still believes the portrait is a true
one, but his opinion is not shared by the country at large.*

—Richard L. Neuberger and Stephen Kahn,
Integrity: The Life of George W. Norris

3. The Gentleman from Nebraska

CHARLES S. RYCKMAN

SENATOR GEORGE W. NORRIS, never lacking a mandate from the people of Nebraska in the course he has pursued as a member of the United States Senate, now returns to Washington doubly assured of the unquestioned approval of his state and its people.

The senatorial record of Mr. Norris, with all its ramifications, has been endorsed in as convincing a manner as anyone could wish. Many reasons have been advanced as to why such an endorsement should not be extended to him. The opposition to Mr. Norris has been conducted as ably and as thoroughly as any group of capable politicians could do the job. The candidacy of as fine a statesman as Nebraska ever produced has been presented to the state as an alternative to that of Mr. Norris, and has been rejected.

Acceptance of the situation is therefore a matter without choice. To continue the argument is to waste words. The opposition to Senator Norris has been so completely subdued and so thoroughly discredited that further jousting with the windmill is more quixotic than Quixote himself.

There is not even good reason for being disgruntled over the result. For the purpose of the Nebraska political situation, 70,000 people can't be wrong. The will of the state is seldom expressed in so tremendous a majority, and it must be taken not only as an endorsement of Mr. Norris but also as at least a temporary quietus upon his critics and opponents.

The state of Nebraska has elected Norris to the United States Senate this year, as it has many times in the past, mainly because he is not wanted there. If his return to Washington causes discomfiture in official circles, the people of Nebraska will regard their votes as not having been cast in vain. They do not want farm relief or any other legislative benefits a senator might bring them; all they want is a chance to sit back and gloat.

Nebraska nurses an ingrowing grouch against America in general and eastern America in particular. The state expects nothing from the national government, which it regards as largely under eastern control, and asks nothing. It has lost interest in constructive participation in federal affairs, and its people are in a vindictive frame of mind.

This grouch is cultural as much as political. Nebraska and its people have been the butt of eastern jokesters so long they are embittered. Every major federal project of the last half-century has been disadvantageous to them. The building of the Panama Canal imposed a discriminatory rate burden upon them. Various reclamation projects have increased agricultural competition. Federal tariff policies increase the cost of living in Nebraska, without material benefit to Nebraska producers.

Nebraska voters have long since ceased to look to Washington for relief, and they no longer select their Congressional representatives with relief in view. Neither George Norris nor any of his Nebraska colleagues in Congress have been able to combat this hopeless situation. If Norris were forced to rely upon what he has done in Congress for Nebraska, he would approach an election day with fear in his heart.

But Senator Norris has found another way to serve Nebraska. By making himself objectionable to federal administrations without regard to political complexion and to eastern interests of every kind, he has afforded Nebraskans a chance to vent their wrath. He is, perhaps unwittingly, an instrument of revenge.

The people of Nebraska would not listen to George Norris long enough to let him tell them how to elect a dog-catcher in the smallest village in the state, but they have been sending him to the Senate so long it is a habit. If he lives long enough and does not get tired of the job, he will spend more years in the upper house of Congress than any man before him. Death, ill health, or personal disinclination—one of these may some day drive him out of the Senate, but the people of Nebraska never will!

The state asks little of him in return. It gives him perfect freedom of movement and of opinion. It holds him to no party or platform. It requires no promises of him, no pledges. He need have no concern for his constituency, is under no obligation to people or to politicians. He can devote as much of his time as he likes to the Muscle Shoals power site, and none at all to western Nebraska irrigation projects. He can vote for the low tariff demanded by cane sugar producers of Cuba, while the beet-sugar-growers of Nebraska are starving to death. He can interest himself in political scandals in Pennsylvania, and be wholly unconcerned over the economic plight of the Nebraska farmer.

He can do all these things and be as assured of election as the seashore is of the tide. He could spend a campaign year in Europe, and beat a George Washington in a Republican primary and an Abraham Lincoln in a general election.

And yet George Norris is not a political power in Nebraska. The people of other states believe he is revered as an idol in his own state. As a matter of fact, he is probably held in lower esteem in Nebraska than in any other state in the Union.

His endorsement of another candidate is of no real value. He could not throw a hatful of votes over any political fence in the state. He gave his tacit support to La Follette as a third-party presidential candidate in 1924, and the Wisconsin senator could have carried all his Nebraska votes in his hip pocket without a bulge. He came into Nebraska in 1928 with a fanfare of Democratic trumpets and of radio hook-ups, stumped the state for Governor Smith—and Nebraska gave Herbert Hoover the largest majority, on a basis of percentage, of all the states in the Union.*

As far as the people of Nebraska are concerned, George Norris is as deep as the Atlantic Ocean in Washington, and as shallow as the Platte River in his own state.

The explanation of this fascinating political paradox is to be found, not in an analysis of Norris, but of Nebraska. As a senator, Norris has given Nebraska something the state never had before. He has put the "Gentleman from Nebraska" on every front page in

---

* Neuberger and Kahn point out that this is an error. Hoover's vote in Nebraska was 63.2% of the total ballot, whereas he received a larger percentage in the following states: Kansas 72.2%, Michigan 70.5%, Maine 68.6%, Washington 67%, Vermont 66.5%, Pennsylvania 65.2%, Delaware 65%, Ohio 64.8%, Colorado 64.7%, Idaho 64.7%, California 64.1%, Oregon 64.1%, Wyoming 63.6%. "That so glaring an error of fact should have been overlooked . . . tends to substantiate the *New Republic*'s insinuation that some of the Pulitzer judges were desperately anxious to berate Senator Norris."—*Integrity*, (Vanguard Press, 1937) page 364.

America and has kept him there. A resident of Nebraska can pick up the latest edition of a New York daily or of an Arizona weekly and find "Norris of Nebraska" in at least three type faces.

But the publicity Norris gets for Nebraska is not the whole story. His real strength in Nebraska is measured by the antagonisms he stirs up beyond the borders of the state. His people take delight in setting him on the heels of the ruling powers, whether of government, of finance, or of industry. The more he makes himself obnoxious to a political party, to a national administration, or to Wall Street, the better they like him.

Nebraska is not interested in the smallest degree in what progress he makes or what he accomplishes. It has been said of Norris that he has cast more negative votes against the winning causes and more affirmative votes for lost causes than any other man in the Senate. But every time he succeeds in pestering his prey until it turns around and snarls back at him, the chuckles can be heard all the way from Council Bluffs to Scottsbluff.

The summary of it all is that Nebraska derives a great deal of pleasure out of shoving George Norris down the great American throat. He has been an effective emetic in Republican and Democratic administrations alike, has worried every president from Taft to Hoover. His retirement from the Senate, whether voluntary or forced, would be welcomed in more quarters than that of any of his colleagues.

The people of Nebraska know this and enjoy it. Every time Norris baits the power trust or lambasts the social lobby, Nebraska gets the same amusement out of his antics that a small boy gets out of sicking a dog on an alley cat. When he shies a brickbat at a president, Nebraska has as much fun as a kid pushing over an outhouse.

You have to know the isolation of the hinterland to understand why this is so. Nebraska has sent many men to the Senate who were more capable than Norris, as his predecessors and as his contemporaries. It has had other senators who have done more for the state and for the nation than he has.

But it has never had another senator who let the whole world know there was a "Gentleman from Nebraska" in the manner he has succeeded in doing. Nebraska could send a succession of great men and good men to the Senate, and the East and West and South would never know there was a state of Nebraska or that such a state was represented in the Senate. But Norris lets them know there is a Nebraska, and Nebraska does not care how he does it.

There is an instinctive resentment in the hearts of these people of the states between the Mississippi and the mountains against the failure of the far East to understand and appreciate the Middle West. It crops out in politics, in religion, even in sports.

Nebraska is one of the richest of all the agricultural states, and yet the wealth of its industries exceeds that of its farms. It has given such names as Gutzon Borglum, Willa Cather, John J. Pershing, Charles G. Dawes, William Jennings Bryan, and a hundred others of prominence to the nation. It has unsurpassed schools, progressive cities and towns, people of intelligence and culture.

And yet the rest of the nation persists in regarding Nebraska as provincial, its people as backward. If the East thinks of Nebraska at all, it is as a state still in a frontier period. The national conception of a Nebraskan is that of a big hayshaker, with a pitchfork in his hands, a straw in his mouth, a musical comedy goatee on his chin, a patch on the seat of his overalls, and the muck of the barnyard on his boots.

Nebraska has resented these indignities, but has given up hope of avoiding them. Its only hope is to pay back in kind. In the days of the real frontier, it vented its wrath on the occasional luckless tenderfoot from the East. Now it sends George Norris to the Senate.

Norris does not represent Nebraska politics. He is the personification of a Nebraska protest against the intellectual aloofness of the East. A vote for Norris is cast into the ballot box with all the venom of a snowball thrown at a silk hat. The spirit that puts him over is vindictive, retaliatory. Another senator might get federal projects, administrative favor, post offices, and pork barrel plunder for Nebraska, but the state is contemptuous of these. For nearly two decades Norris has kept Nebraska beyond the pale of federal favor, but his people consider him worth the price.

George Norris is the burr Nebraska delights in putting under the eastern saddle. He is the reprisal for all the jokes of vaudevillists, the caricatures of cartoonists, and the jibes of humorists that have come out of the East in the last quarter of a century.

Reprinted by permission of the Fremont *Daily Tribune,* Nov. 7, 1930

*At seventy-six, George W. Norris had just been returned
to office for what proved to be the last time when another
famed midwesterner, the Sage of Emporia, reflected on
the Senator's long years of public service, his character
and achievements, and posed what still remains—*

4. The Norris Riddle

WILLIAM ALLEN WHITE

PROBABLY no other man in the United States Senate since it was
founded has more actual, constructive work to his credit than has
George Norris. Yet his name, compared with that of Blaine, Clay,
or Calhoun, among other famed senatorial statesmen, is much less
glorious in his own generation. Whether his name will live as theirs
have lived, revived and nurtured by the story of his real ability and
worth, no one can know. His is the story of a brave, wise, honest
man in public life who never compromised with himself and so had
no temptation to dally with ambition or treat with his enemies.
His instinctive modesty, which makes it impossible for him to dramatize himself, makes it hard for his biographers to picture him
exactly either as a hero or as a victim. His career, by its very monotony of selflessness, lacks climax, and except as a study in a
monotone of decency, it has no drama. Yet no other senator of his
time has such a line of real achievement in American politics.

George Norris was one of the ablest, most efficient advocates of
four Constitutional amendments, the one providing for the income
tax, the one providing for the direct election of United States senators, the one providing for votes for women, and the last—which
was adopted almost solely because he wrote it and engineered its
passage—for the inauguration of a president and the assembling of
Congress immediately after election instead of three months later.
All of these amendments were democratic amendments. The three
political amendments gave the electorate a more direct control over
government, and the income-tax amendment was and is an obvious
instrument in democratizing the national income. Under the
income-tax amendment it is possible to use taxation as an agency
of human welfare.

But these amendments are not the major achievement of George
Norris. When he came to Congress he was an ordinary congressman
from the high plains, a Republican by tradition, with no record
back of him that was not duplicated by a hundred of his fellow congressmen. In the middle of the first decade, he joined the insurgent
group in rebellion against Speaker Cannon and the oligarchical
control of the House of Representatives. They won their fight at
the end of the decade, Cannon was shorn of much of his power, and
control of the lower house passed in Taft's administration more or
less out of the regular Republican organization.

George Norris's work in the House was not conspicuous. He was
one of a dozen young progressives there who made their mark and
did their work, and most of the others passed into a decent oblivion.
When Norris went to the Senate, he took with him a profound
conviction that government is something more than a policeman.
His senatorial career has been based upon the theory that government is a policeman and a social worker with a talent for super-
engineering and a lust for justice.

In the Senate he became one of the leaders there who took control of the Senate out of the hands of his party and placed it in
an independent senatorial bloc, nominally Republican but actually
far removed from the Republican way of thought, with aims entirely foreign to those of the Republican tradition and leaders of
his day. This bloc, of which George Norris was the most intelligent,
the most capable, and the most intransigent member, was in effect
a new party. Its roots sank back into the Roosevelt policies, through
Bryanism into Populism and thence went deeper, even into the
Granger movement and the Greenback Party of the seventies. The
senatorial group which Norris joined had been forming while Norris
and Murdock were fighting the Cannon machine in the Taft administration. In the Wilson administration the Progressive Senatorial group devoted themselves to introducing and pushing through
Congress the pledges, not of the Democratic platform, but of the
Bull Moose platform. They stood for the law establishing the Federal Trade Commission, the Tariff Commission, the Federal Reserve
Bank, the direct election of United States senators, the income tax
law, legislation directed against the monopolies, and the Adamson
law regulating the hours of service on the railways.

Curiously, though Norris had every other quality that makes for
a successful senator, he has never taken dramatic leadership. He is
too modest, or perhaps he is instinctively a lone worker. He has not

been checked by his political vices, for he has no political vices. He does lack charm. He is not socially inclined. He makes few friends but is loyal to those he has. He is passionately earnest but never politically self-righteous. He gives no impression of being holier than his colleagues, certainly does not think he is: an essential gentle humility is the inner Norrisness of George Norris. Perhaps he lacks imagination to cast himself as a hero, and he may be too modest to see what he has achieved and how glorious is his achievement.

No biographer will be able to paint George Norris in raw colors. His portrait will have to be done in mauves and beiges, in heliotropes and lavenders. It will be such a book as Henry James or George Meredith might have written, sophisticated, deeply discerning, and in the end full of affection and pride.

For George Norris is one of the really great and profoundly enigmatical figures of his day and time. The riddle which he presents to his generations may be stated thus: Why has a man of so many solid qualities, a man of such diligences in his business, such an intelligent conscience, so modest a courage, and such sweet and self-effacing honesty, never become a hero to the American people? Why has he never even aspired to the highest offices in the Republic? Why has George Norris left the mark of no distinctive glowing personality in the government he served so selflessly for a generation? Perhaps the sphinx of time will answer its own riddle.

Condensed from *The Saturday Review of Literature*, July 10, 1937

The establishment of the Rural Electrification Adminis-
tration, the object of which was to carry electricity to the
farms of America, was an undertaking that had my deep-
est sympathy and interest. . . . From boyhood, I had seen
the grim drudgery and grind which had been the common
lot of eight generations of American farm women. I had
seen the drudgery of washing and ironing and sewing
without any of the labor-saving electrical devices. I could
close my eyes and recall the innumerable scenes of the
harvest and the unending punishing tasks. Why shouldn't
I have been interested in the emancipation of hundreds
of thousands of farm women?

—George W. Norris, *Fighting Liberal*

The Kitchen Frontier

MARGARET CANNELL

WHEN the first pioneer women crossed the Missouri into Nebraska, they might well have lost heart had they seen beyond the cotton-woods and oaks along the river bank to the miles of dusty prairie awaiting them. But if they could have looked into the future, into the lives and homes of their granddaughters and great-granddaughters, surely they would have felt a surge of pride at their roles in a drama which for thousands of Nebraska families has turned out so well.

On one of the oldest farms in southeast Nebraska lives Eloise, whose husband's grandparents came to the county in the early sixties. Their deed required that they "defend the land from the Indians," and some of the guns of those days are still treasured on the farm. From her kitchen window Eloise can see the clump of ash trees and tangle of wild gooseberries that mark the corner of the family cemetery where her children's great-grandparents lie buried. Beyond the bend of the creek are the remains of the limestone foundation of the first house on the place. Her own two-story frame house, built by her husband's father, dates from a time when several good corn crops warranted a bathroom and central heat in the new house—innovations which even people from town used to come out to admire. Its wide front porch and double living room, big kitchen and roomy upstairs have made it a comfortable home for her growing family. The golden oak and mission furniture has almost all been replaced through the years, and electricity supplies servants to take the place of the "hired girl" who came in to help at canning or harvest time when the house was new. One by one the vacuum cleaner, the washing machine, the ironer, the dishwasher have come to make life easier.

As Eloise works at her sink, glancing out now and then at the woods beyond the farmyard, she thinks of the women who preceded her on this family farm. She remembers stories about the earliest pioneer mother who took her baby and drove with a load of grain to the grist mill at the river town to have her wheat ground into flour; of her long wait for her turn in the line of wagons while the baby alternately cried and slept; of her fright on the return trip when she met a party of friendly Pawnees, her relief when she reached home with her baby safe and flour enough for the winter, and a quantity of bran and shorts as well. Now Eloise goes to the same river town and sometimes she has to wait in line, not for flour and bran, but for an order of frozen cherries which she will bring home to her own deep freeze. Looking over the supplies of frozen fruits from her own and nearby orchards, peas and beans from her garden, steaks and chops and chickens, she thinks of the food which once stocked the larder on this same farm—the wild plums and grapes and gooseberries gathered from thickets and roadsides and preserved for winter use, sometimes with molasses and honey for sweetening; the salt pork and smoked meats; the endless corn dishes —hominy, cornbread, corn cakes, corn pudding, cornmeal mush, corn dodgers.

Family tradition tells that the first organ in the neighborhood belonged to the great-grandmother who liked to play and sing "The Red River Valley" for visitors. Was it from this willing performer that her children inherited their proclivity for public appearances, Eloise wonders, as she helps them load the French horn, the clarinet, and the saxophone into the station wagon and chauffeurs them to band practice; and as she goes about her kitchen dodging the twirling baton of the thirteen-year-old, who hopes to become drum majorette. She imagines that some of her older daughter's talents come from the grandmother who had the first really good sewing machine in the county, a marvel with foot treadle and drop head, on which she could make everything from men's work shirts to tucked and ruffled christening robes. Now her granddaughter fashions school clothes and dressy suits on an electric sewing machine and carries off prizes at the state and county fair. Helping to plan her daughter's play outfits with shorts and blouses, slacks and formals, Eloise sees the ghost of an earlier young girl struggling to carry out her duties as wife and mother, carrying water, building fires, lifting heavy iron kettles for washing and soap making, and dressed always in calico and heavy work shoes.

Thankful as she is for her modern conveniences, Eloise wonders if she has any more leisure than the women who went before her. The heavier jobs are gone, but the number of duties has increased. She hurries through her housework so that she can meet with her extension club and pass on the directions for upholstering, which the home agent from the university has given her. There are new tricks with draperies, too, which her neighbors are waiting to learn. Then she must meet with the group to discuss plans for study sessions on child psychology, and it will be her job to write to the State Library Commission for needed books. With three of her children in the high school band, she has become an active Band Mother and must work on menus for fund-raising dinners: new gold and green uniforms for state Band Day are as important as the music. Because she has a college degree, the local school board has turned to her in emergencies, and for a month during a teacher's illness she has substituted in the elementary grades.

There is too much bustling about, she often thinks, and she is constantly trying to find for herself and her children a little quiet time—something of the peace their forebears knew as they sat under the old maples and watched thunderheads pile up in the evening sky or gathered around the dining-room table to crack walnuts and read aloud on frosty nights.

Almost four hundred miles across the state from the corn and fruit of this half-section farm, a six-thousand-acre ranch extends along the Lodgepole, its alfalfa and hay fields lying beside the creek, its range going back for miles into the rolling hills. There is a local story that the ranch buildings are on the site of an Indian camp ground; now the ranch is something of a show place, with its arched gate displaying the 2Bar V brand between electric lanterns and its tree-bordered tar road leading to the cluster of buildings on either side of the creek. Across the little bridge lie the old bunk house and barn, whose stone walls are still solid after sixty years, and the three trim bungalows which are the homes of the permanent helpers, married couples who have been on the ranch for years. On a little rise beyond them, safe from the Lodgepole—which can rampage as wildly as the Missouri—stands the modern ranch house, its picture windows framing views of the fenced lawn bordered with flowers, of alfalfa fields, of grazing cattle and billowing hills.

As Carolyn, the mistress of the house and garden, works among her flowers or manipulates the dials and switches controlling the equipment in her kitchen, she remembers when she came to the ranch as a bride almost thirty years ago. Living then in the little house which is now a guest cabin, she seemed nearer to the founders of the ranch. She knows that she herself was not really a pioneer, but there were not many conveniences in that first little house. In those earlier days she could not even have imagined her present domain: the kitchen with its automatic stove, wall ovens, dishwasher, mixer, refrigerator, and deep freeze; the utility room which has a sewing corner as well as washing, drying, and ironing equipment; the central heating and cooling plant so sleek and streamlined that it is almost decorative. The 2Bar V has seen great changes in the years she has dwelt there, and nothing has changed more than the daily life of the woman who is its mistress.

Now there is no sense of isolation on the ranch. In the past there had sometimes been empty days when Carolyn brooded over the story of a woman from the tree claim beyond the hills who used to wander away looking for a baby dead years before, and who had to be taken at last to the State Hospital, a victim of loneliness and sorrow in a harsh new land. But there was always the Ford if she needed to go to town, and now there are the telephone, the radio, and television, besides the ranch intercommunication system, which lets her talk to her husband in the barn or the women who are her friends and helpers in the bungalows. Now she can entertain easily and often, sometimes at luncheon in her pine-paneled dining room, oftener, on summer evenings, at outdoor dinners when the yard is floodlighted and ranch steaks are cooked over charcoal grills and french fries come sizzling from her electric frier.

With her children grown she is finding new interests. For months she has been helping with plans for a community hospital, working for funds, going over architects' drawings, taking responsibility for furnishings. She has recently been elected to the county high school board, and getting acquainted with enthusiastic young teachers has given her year a new zest. She loves the life on the ranch, knowing the young people who come and go as guests of her college son and daughter, the friendships with people in both town and country. She is keenly aware that it is a life of violent contrasts—the opulence of her home and the wildness of the hills that lie behind it; the ease within the house and the hardships that are still faced by the men and cattle in times of blizzard or drought; even the appearance of her children—the son riding the range in felt hat and levis and greeting his guests in white dinner jacket and cummerbund; her daughter in blue jeans and plaid shirt driving a tractor in the hayfield, later glowing like a young princess in a satin evening gown. Carolyn has noticed lately how many things are described as "fabulous," and thinking of all that has happened within her own memory she decides that nothing was ever more fabulous than her home under the cottonwoods on Lodgepole Creek.

For many Nebraska farmers' wives, Carolyn's life on the 2Bar V would seem a fairy tale, and even Eloise's more modest home a thing beyond dreams. Most of them have electricity, but the bathroom, the automatic stove, the deep freeze will not come until there are several really good crop years or the price of cattle and hogs is right. Some of them live in square or T- or L-shaped farm houses which defy efforts to incorporate modern decorators' ideas. The houses were planned, it seems, according to whim by an absent-minded carpenter. They waste space where staircases open on large useless hallways. They lack closet room, since wardrobes were in fashion when they were built. Their windows are small and arranged at random. But their owners do not give up; they have ideas for remodeling and rebuilding. They collect plans and suggestions from magazines and advice from home agents. They have visions of knocking out partitions and cutting new windows, of building family rooms and installing showers. They know about storage walls and baking areas and sewing centers, and they are as full of hope and energy as the women who first came west to make homes in Nebraska. They may need five years or even ten, but when the time comes they will be ready to transform old homes into new.

Those who must pump water and carry wood are becoming fewer and fewer on Nebraska farms. Electric lines are bringing power to remote homes; and whether they live in the Panhandle, along the Platte, the Republican, or the Niobrara, farm people are finding work lighter than it was a generation ago. But the pushbutton which simplifies life in some ways has made it more complex in others. Modern communication has brought the farm family into a larger group, and social and community life have become more demanding. The present-day farm woman must not only learn to operate her new equipment but she must undertake a variety of new duties. As she serves on neighborhood projects, plays a responsible citizen's part in local government, plans for schools and libraries, she is not without a sense of enterprise and high adventure akin to that of her forebears. Like those pioneer women of a century ago, she gladly devotes all her strength and ingenuity to the quest for a more bountiful life for her family and her children's families to come.

It is noteworthy that Governor David Butler (1867–1871) advocated women's suffrage in a special message to the legislature, but this was defeated. The legislature, however, passed what was known as the "Married Women's Property Act," which . . . gave a woman the right to sell and dispose of her real and personal property, to engage in any separate trade, business or employment on her own account, free from the control of her husband, and allowed her to sue and be sued in her own name. This was pioneer legislation.

—Othman A. Abbott, *Recollections of a Pioneer Lawyer*

The Lady from Bar 99

1.

IN THE U.S. Senate's 165-year history, it has had just seven women members. Last week an eighth name was added to the list. To fill the vacancy created by the death of Republican Dwight Palmer Griswold, Nebraska's Governor Robert B. Crosby appointed Mrs. Eva Bowring (rhymes with now ring), owner and operator of an 8,000-acre ranch at Merriman, 315 miles northwest of Omaha.

The new Senator is a remarkable woman. Married at 19 to a blacksmith, she was widowed at 32 with three small sons. To support them, she became a traveling saleswoman, for more than four years fought her way over muddy and rutted Nebraska country roads selling bakery supplies. In 1928, she remarried, and moved on to her husband's Bar 99 ranch in the Nebraska sandhills. She was told then that grass and trees would not grow in the sand, but her sprawling white ranch house now stands in a grove of hackberry and willow trees and on a velvet green lawn. Inside are her collections of Early American glass, beer steins, colonial furniture and needlework.

Since her second husband, Arthur Bowring, died in 1944, Mrs. Bowring has bossed the ranch. Equally at home in a western saddle or as the hostess at a formal dinner, she is up at 5 A.M. with the hands, often helps with branding, haying and riding the range. Last month, she missed the Nebraska Republican Founders' Day ceremonies because a sudden snowstorm came up and she was helping to drive some of her 700 Herefords 10 miles to a feed lot. Her philosophy: "I've not been one who thought the Lord should make life easy; I've just asked him to make me strong."

Mrs. Bowring's interest in politics came from her second husband, for many years a county commissioner and a state legislator. (He once was appointed to the state legislature to succeed Dwight Griswold.) She was a Republican precinct worker for 20 years, then county chairman; since 1946 she has been vice chairman of the Nebraska Republican State Central Committee. To get to political meetings on the western Nebraska plains, she has traveled by plane, car, snow sled and on horseback. Says she: "I've gone to those meetings in everything but a manure-spreader."

When Governor Crosby announced her appointment, he said that he had spent two days trying to persuade Mrs. Bowring to take it. At a press conference in the governor's office, she confirmed his statement: "He kept talking about the honor. But I told him it would be just a burden. I think that what really convinced me was myself. I've been saying for years that women should get into politics, and so when I got the chance, I just didn't feel I could turn it down." The way she plans to use that chance: "The Eisenhowers, Ike and Mamie, deserve all the support we can give. Nevertheless, I reserve the right to make some decisions myself."

A handsome, erect woman ("My grandmother always told me: 'Stand tall and spurn the earth' ") with a weather-tanned face, popular and respected Eve ("Everyone calls me 'Eve' ") Bowring flew back to the ranch after the announcement "to kiss the cattle goodbye." Said she, with a characteristic twinkle: "They're about the only ones interested in kissing me any more." For her introduction to Washington, she adopted a rancher's formula: "I'm going to . . . ride the fence awhile . . . until I know where the gates are."

Reprinted from *Time,* April 26, 1954. © Time, Inc., 1954

2.

Mrs. Eve Bowring of Merriman, Nebraska, the nation's newest senator, was quickly caught up in the official and social whirl of Washington. No sooner had the swearing-in ceremonies been completed last week than she had to answer her first quorum call. "In almost the twinkle of an eye a citizen was made into a senator," she marveled.

Two days later, after being assured there would be no vote on the floor, she ducked out early to attend a reception of Republican women. Shortly after her arrival, an urgent phone call summoned her back for a vote. "That taught me not to figure on being able . . . to accept any invitations until about 6 o'clock," she said.

After spending an hour standing on marble floors at one official reception, Senator Bowring, who runs a 10,000-acre cattle ranch back home, complained good-naturedly: "I'm doing fine. But I sure could use a horse."

Extracted from *Newsweek*, May 10, 1954

3.

When she was appointed to the U.S. Senate two months ago, Nebraska Rancher Eve Bowring adopted a rancher's formula. Last week Senator Bowring found a gate and rode through at full gallop.

A few hours after the Senate Agriculture Committee voted 8-7 to continue high, rigid support of basic farm-crop prices (the House Agriculture Committee had already voted 21-8 for the same policy), Republican Bowring rose then on the Senate floor to make her maiden speech. She knew that freshman senators are supposed to be quiet, she said, but "I feel that the hour is crucial, and that the circumstances demand that I make my position known." Her position: the congressional committee majorities were dead wrong; the flexible price-support plan backed by Secretary of Agriculture Benson and President Eisenhower "will best serve the future of the nation and its agriculture."

Said Rancher Bowring: "In the long run, rigid price supports take from the farmer more than he receives. They encourage him to deplete his soil. They saddle the markets with surpluses which give him no opportunity to realize full parity. They destroy the normal relationship of feed and livestock prices. They encourage the development of competitive synthetics. . . . They place farmers in such a position that they lose much of their freedom to make management decisions."

When the new senator had finished, eight of her colleagues rose to compliment her. Among them was one of the oldest hands in the Senate, North Dakota's cantankerous Bill Langer, who thought she had done a fine job of presenting her case but hoped "that before adjournment she will have changed her mind." Mrs. Bowring stood her ground.

Reprinted from *Time*, July 5, 1954. © Time, Inc., 1954

Nebraska has tended to benefit from the national trend toward the decentralization of industry. The state has been active, through a division of resources, in the promotion of industrial development adaptable to its agricultural economy.

—*Nebraska Blue Book,* 1952

Columbus

WILLIAM S. DUTTON

THOSE old plaints about little business not having a chance and of machines robbing men of jobs are louder than ever. Before the gloom gets too thick, however, let's visit Columbus, Nebraska.

As World War II drew to a close, the outlook of this town's 8000 people was as bleak as its prairie winter. Platte County, of which Columbus is the seat and center, was losing population. Farms established by homesteaders were being merged, machines were doing most of the farm work, and the young folks were leaving. Columbus saw itself becoming a mere signal stop in a vast mechanized corn patch. Signal *tower* describes Columbus better today.

Young men, faced with carving futures elsewhere, have devised more than 100 improvements for use on the robots that elbowed them off the farms. Out of these have grown eleven new factories employing upward of 1000 persons. Nearly half a dozen small plants have moved in. Total payrolls from the burgeoning industries exceed three million dollars yearly. This added wealth has created another 1200 jobs in stores, service stations, repair shops. Retail sales in Columbus are five times what they were before the war. The population is pressing toward 11,000. Seventy-six blocks of new streets, four schools and 869 homes have been built. Pawnee Park on the edge of town now has night-lighted football and baseball fields, a swimming pool, bathhouses, picnic areas. Yet, while the town's budget has more than doubled, the tax rate has been halved.

Columbus was much like many rural county seats until 1945: pleasant but somewhat of a dead-end headquarters for lawyers, county officers, and those who served or supplied the farmers. But when the war ended, sons in uniform came home to find that there were few farm jobs; employers in town were laying off help, not taking on. At this point, a group of town leaders met to take a hard look at what was ailing. The diagnosis was that machines had changed the face of the Midwest, yet Columbus was hitched to the horse age. "We came to an inescapable conclusion," Phil Hockenberger, one of the leaders, told me. "Towns are what their people make them; the responsibility for our future was our own."

The men formed a corporation, Industries, Inc. An abandoned tract of land was bought and laid out in small factory sites served by electric power, natural gas and a railroad siding. "We set out to do what towns in our fix usually do: to try to bring in outside industries," said Mr. Hockenberger. "Yet our first applicant for a site was young Walter Behlen, who had grown up right here on a Platte County farm."

Walter, Gilbert and Mike Behlen, and their father Fred, no doubt would be tilling their own small farms today if machines and mergers had not shoved them off the land. Walt had found work in town driving an express truck for $25 a week. Gib worked in the express office. Mike was still in school. "None of us ever got to college," Walt relates. "Our only assets were that, like most farm-bred boys, we had good strong backs and were handy with tools."

When a chance popped up to buy a little manufacturing business for $600, Walt, his brothers and father each put $25 into a down payment and signed notes for the rest. Their new shop was fitted with tools and dies for making corn hooks. Farmers had used such hooks for centuries in hand-husking corn from the shock—surely this would be a safe product to invest in. Not until they began trying to sell the hooks did Walt find they had been hooked. Mechanical harvesters that picked the corn and husked it in a single operation had invaded the Corn Belt. In two years the hand-husker was out of date.

Walt took over the notes and was five years paying them off. But he still had the shop, and in his mind he formed a resolve; whatever he undertook to make next was going to be *ahead* of what others made. He began looking at things with a new eye, the eye of an inventor. As an expressman Walt handled many cases of eggs in shipment. The lid clamps could be better, he believed. Nights in his shop or summer evenings under an apple tree where he had a forge, he experimented with a better clamp. It wasn't long before he had one. In 1941 he sold all the clamps he could make and had enough advance orders to quit his job on the express truck. He took in his father as a partner; they called themselves the Behlen Manufacturing Co.

Walt next studied a major problem of the Midwest corn grower.

Fall rains often prevented feed corn from drying sufficiently in the field, which caused it to mold later in the old wooden corn cribs. For years farmers have required a cheap, dependable method of crib-drying. Walt hit on a simple scheme: he rolled strips of stiff mesh wire into tubes, built a motor-driven blower to force dry air through them, then placed them among ears of corn in a crib. This crib-drying scheme proved so effective that corn could be harvested before the rains or as quickly as it matured. Overnight the tiny Behlen company was leading a small revolution in harvesting practices. Soon the Behlens and others adapted the idea to the bin-drying of wheat, rye, oats, barley, shelled corn. An all-metal storage bin, which may be air-sealed after the grain is dried, was their next step, and such bins are standard in the Midwest today.

Walt's one-man shop had grown into a booming venture in several rented downtown buildings when, in 1945, his two brothers joined the partnership. By 1946 they applied to Industries, Inc. for a factory site. They were employing some 100 men. When they got the site, they borrowed $140,000 from the Reconstruction Finance Corp., built a factory of glass and steel, and paid off the loan in jig-time.

This set the whole town to talking.

Walter Schmid, a nearby farmer, was bothered with a sore back. "It's time somebody built a tractor seat that doesn't ride like a bucking steer," he told his cousin, Ivan Schmid, and his brother-in-law, Leonard Fleischer. They went to work. Result: a tractor seat fitted with a hydraulic shock absorber and adaptable to any farm tractor. Later a universal joint was built into the seat to iron out the lurches on rough ground. In 1947 the Fleischer-Schmid Corp. sold 25,000 tractor seats, and their new factory rose near the new Behlen works.

A sore neck started the Kosch Manufacturing Co. Howard, one of Farmer Kosch's seven grown sons, complained one evening that his neck hurt from looking backward all day at the cutter bar on the field-grass mower. "There's no sense in having that bar behind the tractor wheel," he said. "It ought to be in front, like it was on our old horse-drawn mower."

"That's a good idea," nodded Farmer Kosch. "Why not do something about it, like Walt Behlen?" Howard, Max and Joe Kosch, late of the Army and Navy and now surplus hands on a mechanized farm, soon had a shop where they were turning out ten front-suspended cutter bars daily.

Allen Hanner, a 20-year-old ex-Marine, took a homemade soil-mover that had been used in scooping out irrigation ditches, added some ideas of his own, and in partnership with his mother and sister organized the Soil Mover Co. Before long he was making 50 of his ditchers per month.

Carl Siefken, former Richland farmer, opened a shop for making his idea of a better corn-blower, an attachment that cleans the ears of bits of husk and silk as they are mechanically picked and husked—and now shelled, too—right in the field.

All of these ventures have adopted the basic Behlen policy: never get caught behind the times. As one of the men puts it: "By keeping a jump ahead of the big fellows, we make sure that nobody is going to trample us underfoot." At the Behlen plant—now grown to 225 employees—they will show you a mesh-welding machine, used in making metal corn cribs, that cost less than a tenth of the best price quoted by a big machine-builder. The mesh-welder was built from scratch by local boys.

Since the lesson of the corn hooks, the Behlens have introduced 19 other improvements in farm equipment, most of which have been successful. One of the ideas hatched in casual talks around Walt's desk, the biggest, brought out in 1949, is still a cause of wonder wherever it is seen. Explaining its inception to me, Walt took a sheet of letter paper and stood it on edge on the desk-top. The sheet promptly fell down. Then he pleated it into an accordion effect. It stayed upright. On that principle he built the first commercially feasible frameless building made wholly of aluminum sheets.

Townspeople invited to view the building were flabbergasted. The interior was 50 by 200 feet, and not a supporting pillar or girder or partition was in sight—just empty space. Walt swung 14 farm tractors from the ridgepole to prove that he had calculated every stress and strain. Not until a full-scale storm hit the area, however, were folks convinced that the structure was safe. A nearly finished frameless building, its most exposed end open to the elements, stood the full force of the 80-mile wind without damage! Since then, 125 of these buildings have been erected in more than a dozen states. They are being used as factories, warehouses, barns, churches and, at Wood River, Nebr., as a public school. The largest, 100 by 552 feet, is a warehouse at the Union Stock Yards at Omaha.

So confident has Columbus become that its inventors will have new wonders every year, that the Chamber of Commerce has leased a lot at the Nebraska State Fair for an annual Columbus show. The sensation for 1954 was an improved hay loader developed by Marvin Preifert and a research group headed by Dr. Frank G. Johnson. On a modern farm, machines bale hay in the field. The bales, left in rows on the ground, are heavy and awkward to handle, so loaders of the escalator belt type are widely used. Some of these loaders have a serious fault, however: they won't pick up bales without human assistance. Preifert, whose prairie farm is 30 miles from Columbus, observed that clods of earth caught on the tread of his tractor wheel went around with it, usually dropped off near the top. Suddenly he saw those clods as bales of hay. Building a wheel loader to fit his vision, he called in Dr. Johnson's research staff for technical help.

At the 1954 fair, Nebraska farmers saw a loader that resembled a small Ferris wheel. It was mounted on a wheeled frame that could be pulled easily by a farm truck. Instead of seats for riders, this Ferris wheel had sets of steel prongs spaced regularly along its rim. As the wheel is drawn forward the prongs slip under and pick up the bales in the wheel's path. When hitched beside a farm truck, the wheel, canted at a 45-degree angle, overhangs the truck's loading space. Bales slip off naturally at the top of the turn and drop into the truck's body. Tests have indicated that this bale-loader works in any sort of farm field, and enables two men to do the work done by six men using older methods. So another new factory will soon be scheduled for Columbus's abandoned tract, now known as the Industrial Site.

That area, a corn field ten years ago, is now almost filled with busy industries. A second vacant tract has already been marked on the municipal plan as Industrial Site No. 2. At the Chamber of Commerce, Manager Doane L. Fessenden will tell you with no little pride that America has discovered Columbus. Actually, Columbus discovered itself first.

Reprinted from "The Town That Discovered Itself," *Reader's Digest,* March, 1955

Seventeen-Gun Salute

1. NATO's General Gruenther

As NATO's first Supreme Commander in Europe, Eisenhower and his towering prestige rallied and heartened Europe's terrified nations and gave them confidence that the thing could be done. His successor, General Matthew Ridgway, was a blunt soldier who demanded more troops than the Europeans were willing to supply, stepped on many toes, left no happy memories. In a time of peace-mongering, Gruenther has inherited the demanding and delicate job.

Few men have been so superbly fitted to fill their time and place in history as General Alfred Maximilian Gruenther. Admits one French newspaper: "A commander less flexible and informed on European politics would have brought great peril not only to the military organization but to the Atlantic alliance itself." Said able NATO Secretary-General Lord Ismay, who as personal chief of staff to Churchill in World War II has seen many: "General Gruenther is the greatest soldier-statesman I have ever known."

In the present crisis of indifference, Gruenther understands that no alliance is stronger than the will to support it. With a cascade of facts drawn from an incredible memory, an inextinguishable smile and a dry Nebraska lucidity that is the admiration of every statesman in Europe, Al Gruenther expounds to everyone who will listen—to groups of manufacturers, parliamentarians, schoolgirl choirs—the necessity, importance, and stature of NATO.

Last week Gruenther rushed off to Belgium to talk to the Premier, have an audience with young King Baudoin, lunch with the Defense Minister, and deliver a lecture to the royal military school. He never made the mistake of publicly reproaching the Belgians for failure to contribute more than they do. But in his conversations with King, Premier and top officers, he demanded not the politically

458

impossible but tried to demonstrate with typical well-informed cogency, with figures on coal production and production indexes, what more was possible. Back in Paris, he took off again for London, in the face of a heavy fog, for the sole purpose of giving his pep talk to a gathering of Britain's public-relations men. "We can stand criticism, but we cannot stand indifference," he warns, and for a moment the smile fades.

NATO's indispensable man has been described as a human IBM machine, the perfect staff officer, the smartest man in the U.S. Army, the most factual man of his times. His extraordinary talents were so much in demand as a staff officer that until he became NATO's supreme commander, he had never commanded anything bigger than an artillery battalion. Eldest of six children of a small-town newspaper editor, Alfred Maximilian Gruenther was born 57 years ago in Platte Center, Neb. "A skinny kid with an extra good head on him," young Al took a memory course by correspondence when he was 13, later added a course in public speaking. When he discovered that every rising young officer should play bridge, he sent for an instruction book, soon became the Army's best bridge player and eked out his Army pay by refereeing public matches, including the famed Culbertson-Lenz match of 1931. He graduated fourth in his class, but he was stuck for 17 years in the grade of 2nd lieutenant, teaching at West Point.

During World War II, Gruenther proved himself a planner without peer. He planned the North African invasion, the Fifth Army landings in Italy, the arduous campaign in Italy's mountains. Says Mark Clark: "On every efficiency report I ever turned in on Gruenther I wrote: 'Highly qualified to be Chief of Staff of the Army at the appropriate time.'" Dwight Eisenhower, with an admiration matching Clark's, has been heard to remark: "Al Gruenther would make a good President of the U.S."

When Ike was called from the presidency of Columbia University to become NATO's first Supreme Commander in Europe, his first and only choice as his chief of staff was his old friend and favorite bridge partner, Al Gruenther. Gruenther stayed on under Ridgway. In mid-1953, Ridgway left to become the Army's Chief of Staff, and Eisenhower made Gruenther Supreme Commander.

The nerve center from which Al Gruenther commands NATO's 4,000-mile front is a low, many-winged building, 40 minutes from the Ritz bar, in the President of France's official hunting preserves. Through its halls hustle 800 professional military men of 15 nations, comprising the unique multilingual command staff called SHAPE (Supreme Headquarters Allied Powers in Europe).

On a typical day, the commanding general is driven up in his black Buick at exactly 9 A.M.; he glances at the flags fluttering from 15 tall flagpoles at the entrance, and trots briskly up the steps. His working day had begun almost an hour earlier, when his French aide reported to his breakfast table to brief him on the day's news in the French press (Gruenther had already whipped through the Paris edition of the *Herald Tribune*). At his desk, Gruenther hands a secretary six or seven Dictaphone records filled with instructions and answers to letters that he had dictated at home. Gruenther moves through the prepared pile of papers with the efficiency of a high-powered threshing machine. Each paper gets a flash of concentration that is complete and immediate. He raps out his decision and flips the paper to a waiting aide without looking up.

These chores over, Gruenther browses through six British newspapers (flown over every morning), and several U.S. and other weeklies.

Soon a steady stream of Gruenthergrams—paper slips bearing orders, queries or demands—is rocketing from his desk. The Gruenthergrams range as far and wide as the general's far-ranging mind. Samples: "Please investigate the scratching and meows on the roof." "It seems to me that about a year ago I sent to G-2 a study dealing with Soviet concepts of strategy. I'd like to use it over the weekend." "I hear your sergeant-major had a baby yesterday. Boy or girl?" (The general will write a letter of congratulation.) Gruenther's insatiable demands for information keep his staff in a state of palm-sweating nerves all day long. But they accord him a rare loyalty and devotion, tending him like some dangerous but tremendously precious machine which must be kept running at all costs.

A demanding perfectionist, Gruenther seldom is more than gruff to erring allied officers. He saves the rough side of his tongue for his U.S. aides, a painful process known as being "Gruentherized." It consists of a detailed itemization of all the unfortunate officer's weaknesses, punctuated by explosive cuss words. Few escape.

Mindful of his mission, Gruenther lets no group that might influence opinion pass through Paris unnoticed. In 1955, he personally briefed 175 visiting groups totaling 7,000 people. Outside his office is a card file of visitors, noting the time of their last visit, a brief biography, whether it is "Mr. Fairfield" or "Jack." Once, flying to Britain for a meeting with Members of Parliament, he had aides get out photographs of the 120 M.P.'s who had visited SHAPE and thumb-nail biographies of each. Said an awed Englishman: "When he walked into Parliament, he knew every damn one of them, greeted them by name, adding remarks like 'How's your new daughter?'"

Such talent for detail, priceless in a staff officer, can be disastrous in a commander, and some senior NATO officers were worried that Gruenther would let details distract him from broader thinking. "But we found that he is able to clear his mind and his desk with lightning speed," says one SHAPE officer. "He never abandoned the detail; he simply operates brilliantly on two levels instead of one."

How would the free world stand if there were no NATO? Gruenther's answer is short. NATO's failure would be a staggering blow to the West. How long could small nations like Denmark or Greece stand against Russian threats? Or unstable nations like France against Communist subversion? NATO's other justification for being, and by no means a secondary one, is as peacetime weapon of the cold war. It reduces fear and restores hope to Europe, by providing a shield—a shield that is visible, and visibly American. In its seven short years, NATO has created a community powerful enough to deter its enemy, healthy enough to survive the family squabbles so far, binding enough so that no member has wished to withdraw.

And for NATO's present solidity and good repute, the free world has reason to be grateful to General Al Gruenther.*

Extracted from *Time*, Febr. 6, 1956. © Time, Inc., 1956

2. Nebraska's Al Gruenther

ROBERT COUGHLAN

THE east central part of Nebraska, in which Gruenther's home town of Platte Center is situated, was settled largely by Irish immigrants. Gruenther's mother was Mary Shea, a country schoolmarm, the daughter of local farmers. After the Irish, the Germans—mostly from the southern, Catholic sections—arrived in great numbers and among them were Gruenther's paternal grandparents. Thus Alfred was a

* On his retirement in December, 1956, General Gruenther became President of the American Red Cross.

typical product of this particular corner of the Middle West: German and Irish, a descendant of farmers, a Catholic.

Today Platte Center has a population of about 500, with several dozen pleasant-looking clapboard houses set in big, leafy yards along dirty streets. Except that it has lost about 10% of its population, it is very much the same as when Alfred Gruenther was born there on March 3, 1899, in a small white clapboard house with gingerbread trim, set far back on a big lawn.

In this village, entertainment was not something that happened but that had to be planned, and young Alfred's bent toward organization had a chance to develop early. The neighborhood baseball games took place in his yard, with Alfred playing all positions indiscriminately. In the classroom at St. Joseph's school his favorite sport was to put a pin in the toe of his shoe and prick the bottom of the pupil in the desk ahead of him, looking up with bland surprise when the victim yelped. He was alert, mischievous and dissembling, and on top of it got reasonably good grades in school without seeming to do much work. He acquired the nickname "Simp," from Simpleton, because, his schooldays' friend, Harold ("Stump") Gleason, recalls, "He was so outlandishly clever."

But there were few pranks at home. Mary Shea Gruenther, who is in her late 70's now, still full of energy and country sense, says of her household, "We belonged to the old school. By the time you got your chores done and ate your supper, it was time to march off to bed. In our house there was a boss, and that was Mr. Gruenther. I like to think I added something, but I don't want to take anything away from Mr. Gruenther. Alfred got everything from his father."

By every account Christopher Gruenther was an extraordinarily able and virtuous man. He had learned hard work and self-reliance when his mother died and his father went to Oregon, leaving him with relatives. He made his living as a farmhand and put himself through a year of college. Afterward, with more hard work and frugality, he saved enough to start a weekly newspaper, the Platte Center *Signal* (circulation 300). He was a tall, good-looking man, full of energy and good humor, and in that time and in that part of the country it was inevitable that he go into politics. He became clerk of the district court, managed two successful campaigns for U.S. Senator Gilbert Hitchcock and was state manager during two of William Jennings Bryan's presidential campaigns.* However,

* "The Bryan Volunteers had for officers only a president, a vice-president and a secretary. The president, myself, did all the field work. The secretary, Christian

politics was neither a vocation, except incidentally, nor an avocation with him. He was an old-fashioned patriot, who approached his political tasks with strong convictions and a sense of moral obligation; and he took his parental responsibilities with equal seriousness. He was an affectionate father and entered into the front yard ball games with enthusiasm. But he was also a strong disciplinarian who expected exact obedience and refused to allow his children to give anything less than their best, and who punished laziness and bad behavior with righteous wrath.

Alfred was the oldest. Homer, Lester (who died at 11), Leona, Louis and Veronica arrived in descending order. Chris seemed to concentrate his particular attention on Alfred. He supervised his schoolwork, paid him a bonus for good marks, talked to him about the value of knowledge, drilled him in "knowing the problem," taught him checkers, not as a game but because it was "good mental exercise." Mary Gruenther says, "His ideas conformed to his father's." By the time Alfred was 13 and ready for high school, Chris had become clerk of the district court at Columbus and was also a leading land auctioneer. Mary Gruenther was in charge at the *Signal*. With their combined income Alfred's parents were able to send him to boarding school, and as Chris already had formed the idea that he should eventually go to West Point the school he chose was St. Thomas Military Academy, a Catholic prep school at St. Paul.

Alfred was not then particularly ambitious. But "to fail would have been to grieve my father," he has said. "He was so pleased when I did well, and he took it *so* hard when I didn't." So he took a memory course—the beginnings of that minute memory that is so impressive to his colleagues now. But his grades still were not brilliant, and Chris, taking no chances, sent him to the Army and Navy Preparatory School in Washington to prepare him for the West Point examinations. When the time came, and Senator Hitchcock made him an appointee, he passed the examinations handily. Classmates at West Point remember him as a grind, and one of them

M. Gruenther, did all the headquarters work. Untiring in labor, stanch in democracy, zealous in devotion to Bryan's leadership, Gruenther instituted and carried on the mechanics of party organization.

"It seemed incredible to me then and still does that Bryan, when he was Secretary of State, should have refused the one request that Gruenther made of him. Gruenther asked Bryan to endorse his application to become Collector of Internal Revenue. Bryan refused insultingly, basing his refusal on the grounds that Gruenther had supported Harmon for the Populist nomination in 1912. He said that even Gruenther's children would live to regret their father's course. . . ."
—Arthur F. Mullen, *Western Democrat*

has said, "He was a little mousy. You wouldn't have said he had capacity for leadership or that he could impose his personality on others." He graduated fourth in his class on Nov. 1, 1918, 10 days before the Armistice. In 1920 he found himself at Fort Knox.

Here he met and fell in love with Grace Crum, a Jeffersonville, Ind., girl who was working at Knox as a secretary and sometime hostess at the officers' club. His mother remembers, "His father worried a good deal about it, but then he thought, 'If he's in love and wants to marry, it will be on his mind and harm him in his work, so maybe it will be better if he goes ahead and marries.' So Mr. Gruenther wrote and gave him his permission."

Less than a year later Chris Gruenther was fatally injured in an automobile accident. His oldest daughter, Leona, remembers, "Al got there before Daddy died. He took charge of everything, made all the arrangements with that complete efficiency. And then, when it was all over, he broke down and cried like his heart would break. In a way it was worse for him than for any of us."

Soon afterward Alfred and Grace and their baby son Donald left for the Philippines (a second son, Richard, was born there). In 1927 he returned to West Point as an instructor in chemistry and electricity and stayed for five years, until 1932. They were important years for him. The same classmate who had thought him "a little mousy" as a cadet was there also and was interested in watching him change. "I think it began with the realization that he was a damn good teacher. There was a gradual development of confidence. With that he began to show qualities of leadership. I think he found himself at the academy."

It was not until 1935 that Gruenther made captain, and four more years elapsed before he got his first field command. In that period he became one of the youngest of his class at the Command and General Staff School and the Army War College, a fact that persuaded Gruenther he eventually would gain at least fairly high rank. Since ranking officers often were called upon to speak in public Gruenther enrolled for an evening course in public speaking; he also began to collect—and index—the anecdotes and jokes which enliven his talks. This ceaseless self-improvement extended to his relationships with others. He had been a "pretty serious young man who missed a lot of the fun of life" when he started out, his wife remembers. But the surface aspects of that changed too, and Gruenther came increasingly to resemble Chris in warmth and humor of personality.

In 1939 Captain Gruenther was given command of the 15th Field Artillery Battalion at Fort Sam Houston. When he called on Major General (later Lieut. General) Walter Kreuger to pay his respects, Kreuger, a bluff soldier, declared that Gruenther had spent far too much time at West Point and far too little in the field and would be worthless as commander of an artillery unit or, for that matter, anything else. Gruenther's first intimation that the general had mellowed came more than a year later when Kreuger suddenly asked him to become one of his aides.

In 1941 Gruenther was sent to Washington to serve at General Headquarters under Lieut. General McNair. Also on McNair's staff was a young brigadier general named Mark Clark who, as it happened, was a good friend of a colonel named Dwight Eisenhower, chief of staff to General Kreuger, now commander of the Third Army. On Clark's recommendation, and with Kreuger's strong endorsement, Eisenhower made Gruenther his deputy. "It was love at first sight," Eisenhower has recalled. "I was intrigued by the little devil. He always had a joke or wisecrack, he had all the answers at his fingertips, and he never got tired."

When Eisenhower was sent to London, he at once asked for Gruenther. Things were happening very fast just then. Gruenther had to leave for London unbriefed on Operation Torch, the invasion of North Africa. His first day there Eisenhower told him a little about the invasion and added that Gruenther would be chief planning officer for it. That night he was notified to appear at a meeting the next morning. When he arrived, he found himself among 30 ranking British officers.

To Gruenther's horror, everyone turned expectantly to him. The British had come to hear the American plan for Torch. With acute embarrassment Gruenther explained that he was just in and didn't feel qualified to speak. The British politely asked when he might do so—that being Monday, would Friday be convenient? Gruenther wanly agreed. He had had very little practical experience in planning, but he pulled together a small staff and on Friday had a preliminary plan ready. Within six weeks the whole operation was planned in detail. "It was sink or swim," Gruenther says. "I managed to swim, and in the process I learned the art of planning and I've spent most of my time at it ever since."

As the youngest four-star general in the Army, Gruenther probably could be pardoned some self-congratulations. But conceit is not in his temperament, and nature in this case is ably assisted by Grace Gruenther, founder and president of the Anti-Gruenther Society. The idea for this organization came to her as a bride, when she found herself a newcomer among what seemed to her to be innumerable Gruenthers. She was the only member until Homer married, whereupon his wife was admitted, and all subsequent spouses of Gruenther children and grandchildren have automatically become members. (The two Gruenther sons, Don and Dick, both are West Point graduates, now respectively a major and a captain.) A principal objective of the society is to keep General Gruenther from assuming that his four stars carry any weight outside the Army or, indeed, that he is touched with divinity in any way.

After 30 years Grace has become reconciled to Gruenther's addiction to work, but she does not approve of it. As he never has digestive troubles, sleeps well, is cheerful and considerate around the house and shows every sign of splendid health, she has no very effective arguments to make him slow down. So she makes the best of it by seeing that he is supplied with plenty of steaks and chops, by insisting that he eat an egg for breakfast and by keeping the household running smoothly. Both the Gruenthers and the anti-Gruenthers are agreed that she is "a wonderful homemaker," and as such she exercises her rights with good humor but with firmness. It is perhaps the ultimate test of Gruenther's ability to analyze the problem and to learn from experience that he never tries to infringe on them. "Oh, I consult him about things," she says, "even the shade of green when we're doing a room over, and he's always interested, or at least acts like he is. But unless I ask him, he doesn't interfere. He knows it wouldn't do much good if he tried. I'm the commanding officer around here."

Extracted from "The Thinking Machine Who Bosses NATO,"
Life, June 1, 1953. © Time, Inc., 1953

*On the site of the Council Bluff—sixteen miles north of
Omaha—where Lewis and Clark held council with the
Indians, once stood Fort Atkinson, the first United States
fort in Nebraska. Built in 1819, it was a large, strong fort
with fifteen cannon, garrisoned by several hundred men
of the Rifle Regiment and the Sixth Infantry under the
command of Colonel Henry M. Atkinson. Besides the
soldiers, there were teamsters, laborers, hunters, trappers,
and Indians, making a town of nearly a thousand people.
Here was established Nebraska's first school and the first
library in the Missouri region; here the first journal was
published. Roads ran in all directions from Fort Atkinson,
for it was the most western army post in the United States.*
—Condensed from A. E. Sheldon's *Nebraska Old and New*

First Line of Defense

A SCORE or so of miles below the spot where Fort Atkinson stood
lonely guard on the Missouri's west bank now stands the headquarters of the nation's most powerful military force, the Strategic Air
Command. For just as it did in the 1820's, the United States again
faces a problem of security for its people.

Nebraska began its association with the Strategic Air Command in
November, 1948, when General Curtis E. LeMay, SAC Commander-
in-Chief, moved his headquarters from Andrews Field, Washington,
D.C., to Offutt Air Force Base (old Fort Crook), eight miles south of
Omaha. SAC had been organized two years previously as a strategic
air force with a global responsibility as a counter to the growing
threat of long-range aircraft and nuclear weapons in the hands of
hostile nations. Omaha, near the geographical center of the United
States, is an ideal location for the headquarters, for Nebraska also
lies at the center of the command's far-flung operations in the Pacific,
the Caribbean, the United Kingdom, and North Africa, and at Air
Force bases in Alaska and Greenland.

The locating of the headquarters at Offutt and the activation of
Lincoln Air Force Base in 1954 have given Nebraska an essential
role in SAC's world-wide operations and have added to the state a

revenue of nearly $50 million annually. SAC's investment at Offutt exceeds $71.2 million, of which $38.3 million has been spent on property, construction, and improvements. Base inventories, administrative aircraft, and equipment account for the remainder. No combat aircraft are stationed at Offutt, which functions only as support for SAC headquarters. The presence of two combat wings at Lincoln, whose B-47 jet bombers, KC-97 tankers, and other equipment are valued at more than $265.3 million, brings SAC's total investment in the base to over $350 million.

The United States' total investment in the Strategic Air Command is valued above $15.5 billion. About $8.5 billion is invested in inventories, aircraft and equipment, and real property. The remaining $7 billion is the value the command places on its most important asset—the professionalism of its men, the end-product of years of training and actual combat experiences in Korea and World War II.

Should war ever come, SAC is capable of completing its war mission within hours. Its bombers can fly against an enemy anywhere in the world and return nonstop, leaving devastated targets in their wake. Every crew knows what target, under any given condition, it would strike, and it knows by what routes it would reach the target and return. Support forces are equally trained in their war mission. Everything that will help put a SAC bomber over an enemy target has been planned in detail, and practiced until accomplishment would be little more than routine.

SAC was still a fledgling command when it moved its headquarters to Nebraska. It had only 22 active bases manned by 52,000 men. About 1,000 aircraft of assorted types, almost all veterans of World War II, made up its combat inventory. In the eight years since, the Strategic Air Command has been built into the most powerful air force ever developed. It now operates a vast network of more than 40 air bases, its aircraft inventory has nearly tripled, and almost 200,000 men and women are assigned to the command. From the beginning, SAC's men and planes have worked on a wartime schedule which today keeps 10-15 per cent of its aircraft airborne around the clock. During the last ten years command aircraft have accomplished more than 20,000 ocean crossings in more than $6\frac{1}{2}$ million flying hours. In the past eight years there has not been a day when some SAC units were not on duty at forward bases overseas.

From his Offutt Field headquarters General LeMay directs the global air operations of SAC through three numbered air forces in the States and three air divisions overseas. In December, 1956, a new $8.5 million building was completed to house SAC operations headquarters. Constructed of heavily reinforced concrete set on a slab-type foundation, the control center has three stories above ground and three below. Communications are handled by more than 2,500 telephones, and a closed-in circuit television set-up enables staff members to "attend" conferences without leaving their offices.

Heart of the underground headquarters is a huge U-shaped chart room. It is refrigerated the year around because of the heat from 130 spot and floodlights needed when chart room proceedings are televised. Eight electronic clocks, accurate to within 1/1000th of a second, show the time in the various zones around the globe. Charts containing tactical information—including weather reports and the location of SAC aircraft—are affixed to sheet metal and structural steel panels, mounted on tracks and manually operated.

Administration of the command equals the efficiency of SAC combat crews who regularly fly ten-hour missions over thousands of miles to seek out and destroy specified targets as part of a realistic training program which occupies 43 hours of a crew's time each week. Only three per cent of SAC's nearly 200,000 men and women are assigned administrative jobs; the remainder work in direct support of the command's mission of convincing hostile nations of the futility of starting a global war.

Condensed from *Nebraska on the March*, Sept., 1956

Offutt Field is located on the outskirts of Bellevue, Nebraska's first permanent continuous settlement and for many years its largest community. The drama of Bellevue was played out in the pre-territorial years, culminating in her brief reign as the first territorial capital.

"Bellevue aspired to greatness," wrote William J. Shallcross, "and she was blessed with much in her favor. Her pioneers recognized the richness of her soil, the beauty of her prospect, the possibilities of her location near the confluence of the Platte. But all these failed to gain for her the coveted prize of pre-eminence among the cities of her state. When Trader's Point, landing place of the first ferry across the Missouri, washed down the river, Bellevue little realized that with it floated away her hopes. Omaha snatched the Capital . . . outbid Bellevue in her bid for the terminus of the Union Pacific, and in a manner browbeat her way to gain the location of the first Nebraska bridge to span the Missouri. From that day on, Bellevue was the forgotten village, the quaint, sleepy little old Rip Van Winkle place which no one dreamed would ever awaken."

The construction in 1942 of the Martin Bomber Plant at nearby Fort Crook saw the beginning of her revival, and the designation of Offutt Field as SAC headquarters continued and augmented Bellevue's wartime boom. Quickened into new life, at the end of Nebraska's first century the state's oldest community could also boast that it was its fastest-growing one.

For the gambler and the speculator who counted upon a few turns of the cards or plow to bring them wealth for a lifetime, nature indeed must appear capricious: too much one year; not enough the next. Yet it was this very uncertainty that prompted them to gamble and speculate. If they wished to try their luck, nature was willing to spin the wheel. All she asked was that the house rules be observed, rules by which only a few won while many lost. If they wished to tear her grasslands with their plows, let them try. They would learn the price by trying.

But nature's plan was not contrived for gamblers. It was made for the steady, humble, and courageous ones, those willing to sow and reap with the seasons. The rules of nature operated in favor of those who, like nature herself, were more interested in the fulfillment of needs than in clever manipulations for profit.

—Bruce H. Nicoll and Ken R. Keller,
Sam McKelvie—Son of the Soil

Wheat Farmer

ROBERT HOUSTON

IN THE Nebraska Panhandle, they call Morris Jessen the wheat king. It's a title he deserves. Morris was broke when he came to Sidney in 1916. A year later he planted eight acres of spring wheat on prairie ground he had broken. Today the Jessen wheat domain covers about 28,000 acres in four states, and the expansion is still going full speed ahead. But no longer is it a one-man realm: it has become a family empire.

Morris Jessen is of Danish parentage but considers himself a German immigrant. And if he had been the eldest son, he might never have left the family farm near Flensburg in German-held Schleswig-Holstein. "The eldest son inherits the farm, and the younger sons must either work for him or seek their fortune elsewhere," says Mr. Jessen.

So in 1907 at the age of fifteen, Morris Jessen left home. He followed to America an uncle and an older brother who had settled on

land near Bloomfield, Nebr. When he had turned twenty, Morris
started farming there. "I went into hogs pretty heavy," he recalls. "I
lost them all to cholera. The next year I had cattle, and the cornstalk disease took them. I was wiped out."

In 1916 he went to Sidney where he worked on a farm for $30 a
month and on a bridge gang for $2.50 a day. By wheat-harvest time
he had acquired four head of horses, and he harvested crops on
absentee owners' holdings. By 1917 he was able to buy a quarter
section of prairie land; it was the start of the family empire. He
broke eight acres and planted them to wheat. "That fall I broke
out one hundred acres more and put in winter wheat. I built a 12-by-
16 foot granary, and that was our first home. During a snowstorm
we'd put our clothes under the bed to keep them dry, then sweep the
snow out of the shack. I hauled water three miles."

That breaking of the tough prairie in the fall of 1917 was a
measure of Mr. Jessen's vitality and dogged determination. "I've
always been able to get by with little sleep," he says. "I bought a
second-hand Mogul tractor, and I'd run it twenty-four hours one
day and twenty-one hours the next. Every other day I'd catch three
hours sleep. I had to hurry, for the breaking season for prairie turf
was short—in dry weather, plowing it was impossible. I had a lantern
out in front of the tractor at night, and when I was close to neighbors'
land, they cussed about the noise. I used to put out more work than
three average men."

Mr. Jessen's land-buying soon brought him to grief. "After the
1920 depression, I owed $30,000. I had 560 acres and rented ad-
ditional land on which I had broken the ground." But he hadn't
yet learned caution. "In 1926 I lost a splendid section after paying
$10,600 on it. I learned then not to go in over my head on mort-
gages."

But the land he had bought at '20's prices kept him in financial
hot water during the '30's. For more than a decade he barely beat
one foreclosure after another. "In my spare time I did just about
everything under the sun, like hauling corn to Wyoming and hauling back coal and selling the coal to my neighbors. I bought old iron
and shipped it out by the carload, shipped in coal by the carload.
I was in the oil business until 1952, when two of my sons went into
the armed forces."

Finally he caught up and went ahead; and since then, Mr. Jessen
has been smiling. "I've had nineteen good crops in a row," he says.
"That's not a bad record."

How does he do it in an area where occasional drought years are expected to cut into or wipe out the crops? Mr. Jessen gives the credit to summer tilling. There is not enough moisture to insure a wheat crop every year. The ground lies fallow every other year, and this idle ground is tilled to hoard the moisture. "I've got two months in the spring to plow wheat stubble into the ground. I keep it clean during the summer. After a rain, I break the ground crust and mulch the top by pulling straw from underneath the ground up on top."

This helps account for some of the good crops. In 1946 his land averaged forty-six bushels. But how does the Jessen family manage to farm close to 30,000 acres? In all their realm, they keep only nine hired men the year around.

The wheat king and his four sons and two sons-in-law are great time-study men. They have always bought the largest and fastest machinery obtainable. They can tell you what their cultivators can do in terms of acres per hour, or what harvesting machines can do in terms of bushels per minute. They "improve" farm machines to suit their own purposes.

"We can build anything in our shop," says Morris, "and it looks just like it came from a factory." He pointed to the Jessen rout weeder, which cultivates fallow ground. The weeder has a twelve-foot rod which is dragged below the ground surface, upending the roots of weeds. "We hook seven of them in a line, and one tractor pulls them. They weed an eighty-four-foot strip, and we can cover forty acres in an hour. We take the best parts from rout weeders made by a couple of companies, put them together, and reinforce the parts which take the most stress."

The Jessen family owns fourteen combines for harvesting and keeps four of them on the home place. Some years ago, Jessen combine crews used to start in Texas and work north during the wheat-harvesting season.

Mr. Jessen regards wheat-farming as an easy way to make a living. "You only work a few days in the summer," he says, "but you do work hard then."

Mr. Jessen and his Berlin-born wife like to travel, and in recent years they have found the time for it. Mr. Jessen was widowed during the '20's. He met Ilse Frey on a visit to Berlin, and they were married there in 1927. In the last dozen years they have been steadily transferring title to their land to twenty-two others in the Jessen clan. Morris and Ilse now share the ownership with four sons, three daughters, two sons-in-law, twelve grandchildren, and Mrs. Jessen's mother.

Hale and hearty at sixty-four, Morris ostensibly has been retired since the close of World War II. He now owns only about 5,000 acres, but he might be said to hold a position as "chairman of the board." Says he: "I'm retired, but I work anyway. I'm pretty cheap labor. I work for nothing and board myself. And I'm still tough. I like to dance, and I can dance all evening and not get tired."

The Jessen home eighteen miles south of Lodgepole hasn't a horse, cow, pig, or chicken on the place. But it does look like the site of a grain elevator. There are a 40-by-120 foot quonset and a score of round bins crammed with 125,000 bushels of wheat. From the two-hundred-bushel crop harvested by Mr. Jessen in 1917, the family's wheat production has spiralled ever upward. This year on slightly less than 11,000 acres they harvested 350,000 bushels. With wheat selling now for two dollars a bushel, that's a gross of more than $700,000.

Over the years, as Mr. Jessen picked up more and more wheat land, he could find no more large holdings in southwestern Nebraska, so he turned to Wyoming, Colorado, and South Dakota. This fall he and his son Ray took over 3,680 acres near Martin, S.D., which was obtained in late summer for $224,000. Two weeks ago the family acquired another 2,240 acres near Pine Ridge, Wyo.

Why has Mr. Jessen bought so much wheat land?

"If you had money, where would you go with it?" he asked. "If you do your own farming, you get all of the income from it. And besides, the money came out of the land and I wanted to put it back in."

Condensed from Omaha *World-Herald Sunday Magazine*, Oct. 28, 1956

1957

THE NEBRASKAN'S NEBRASKA

Nebraska Is Here to Stay

BRUCE H. NICOLL

TEN YEARS ago John Gunther passed through our state gathering material for his book *Inside U.S.A.* He concluded, seriously, that the weather runs Nebraska. His observation is understandable. We don't talk about the weather. We *discuss* it—with an uncommonly dedicated interest. Anytime. Anywhere. With friends or strangers.

You pause at a street corner, waiting for a car to pass. You turn to the fellow standing beside you. "Pretty day!" you say. The fellow glances at you. Then he squints upward to the brilliant blue sky. He says, "Yes, sure is." You know he is a Nebraskan if he reflects a moment and then adds soberly, "But we could stand some more rain."

This is a critical point in the conversation. You can be un-Nebraskan and nod in agreement, stifling the conversation. Or you can accept the challenge and remark, "Well, maybe so. But the wheat needs more weather like this. The harvest will be getting started in a week or two."

"The wheat's made!" the fellow exclaims. "No use worrying about that. It's the corn. The subsoil's too dry. If we have a summer like the last one, the corn will need plenty of subsoil moisture."

You are now ready to *discuss* the weather. In depth. And we usually do.

But when visitors are puzzled or amused by our obsession with the weather as conversational fodder, many of us become inarticulate. We just smile self-consciously and shrug our shoulders. We know it's been this way for a long time, and we feel we came by the habit honestly. We can't quite believe the weather runs Nebraska, but we'll admit that its caprices have profoundly influenced us.

Weather and our concern about it are rooted deeply in Nebraska history. Out here, history is not yet the exclusive pursuit of the archivist. Our past is still near us in the living memory of many.

Slightly over one hundred years ago, the first big wave of pioneers crossed the Mississippi, forded the Missouri, and plunged into the expanse of land which separated them from the riches of Oregon and California. Part of this land-obstacle was Nebraska, hence a place to be traversed in the shortest possible time. In this respect our state, or what was to become a state, commended itself to the immigrants: it was an excellent highway. Some of the Forty-Niners settled in Nebraska, but the major settlement came later, in the years immediately following the Civil War and in the 1880's.

The pioneers had no Baedekers. What did they know of Nebraska? There were the forbidding tales of the explorers and travelers, of Lewis and Clark, and Zebulon Pike, and Major Long; and there were the railroad advertisements promising them a lush and fertile land. Neither picture was wholly true nor wholly false; and neither could prepare them for what they found—a storehouse of agricultural wealth in a realm of natural violence. The new frontier was without a counterpart in their experience.

There was the grass, a vast ocean of it washing endlessly over the prairie, the horizon unobscured by the comforting outline of trees, nowhere an object the eye could fix on. The familiar sound of settlement—the ring of the woodman's axe—was stilled in the silence of the grass. The pioneers did not understand the significance of the prairie grass. They had yet to learn that the tall grass of eastern Nebraska bespoke a sub-humid climate where precipitation is always something less than in the humid forestlands of the East; that the mid-grass of central Nebraska told of an even drier region; that the short grass farther west indicated an almost arid climate. And everywhere the grass had another, broader message: it can exist (where other vegetation fails) in long periods of normal or abnormal wet weather followed by extended periods of drought.

There was the weather—that, too, had to be learned about. And to be learned about it had first to be lived through. Hailstorms, unique to the Great Plains, would slash out of purple thunderheads, in an instant battering to bits a promising crop. And the perpetual wind: nowhere in the interior of any continent were the winds so persistent, one moment caressing the land, the next doing it violence. The blizzard, as the pioneers described snow driven straight before a strong north wind, meant incredible suffering for many, death for some. Almost as dreaded were the hot south winds of drought periods, blasts from a fiery furnace, searing the face of the prairie, leaving destroyed fields in their wake.

Finally, there was the soil—the hidden treasure resting beneath the grass, a triumph of Nature's patient husbandry during countless millennia. The tall grass, the mid-grass, and the short grass had each developed a rich soil from the gravel, sand, silt, clay, volcanic ash, and potash brine washed down upon the Nebraska flood plains from the melting glaciers or blown in by the ceaseless winds. Here beneath the grass the pioneer found his reward. And in eastern Nebraska he possessed a fertile soil unequaled on the earth.

Yet his was indeed a frustrating predicament: a soil that would produce bountifully when nature smiled—as it often did—and a soil that lay barren when nature frowned—as it often did. Three tides of migration washed over Nebraska's prairie before the farmer established a firm foothold, each wave contributing something to man's attempt to subdue the wild land. It was a unique phenomenon, this struggle to adapt to and master the Great Plains environment. In many respects it was heroic.

Consider the white man's innovations: the sod house carved from the treeless prairie; buffalo chips for fuel where there was no wood; the steel plowshare which was the only tool rugged enough to turn the tough sod; the windmill, even in the names of its models—Go-Devil, Jumbo, Battle Axe—flinging defiance at that region of much wind and little water; new kinds of crops to replace the failures from seeds brought from the humid east; new cultivation practices, known as dry farming or dryland farming, to save every drop of moisture.

It's nearly a century since we became a state—since plows broke the prairie sod and longhorns moved into our ranges. But what a time—oh Lord, what a really rough time—we've had getting our agriculture squared up with its environment.

We've licked the grasshoppers, which once descended on our fields in clouds and devoured everything that grew. The tractor and the multitude of machines which followed it have reduced enormously the labor required to farm and have transformed agriculture into a somewhat complex technological endeavor. The machines are reducing the number of farms and increasing their size and at the same time driving more workers from the rural areas into our villages and towns. We have adapted our crops so that they are capable of yielding in quality and abundance. (Our winter wheat, for example, draws premium prices because it makes into one of the finest baking flours in America.) We have worked hard at tillage practices (like summer fallowing, stubble mulching, and crop rotation) to make the best use of our soil and water. We are improving our marketing standards and practices to reward those who strive for high-quality products. We have made great progress in our perennial battle with the insects. We have discovered ways to add more meat, of better quality, to the carcasses of our meat animals—at greater profit to the rancher and livestock feeder.

Now, all this is very heartening; yet the fact remains that we are still frustrated, perplexed, dismayed, and deceived in our farming enterprise, and most of these grievances can be traced to the basic trinity of our agriculture: weather, water, and soil.

Since our beginnings in Nebraska, we have enjoyed four long periods of normal or above-normal precipitation—and, brother, when the elements cooperate, our soil will grow practically anything—in quantity. Each of these halcyon times has been interrupted by droughts of varying intensity: one of the worst blighted our state from 1932 to 1940, and we are now in the midst of another which began in 1952 and is still with us in 1957.

Drought is a grim spectacle, and some measure of our anxiety about it is found in rain-making experiments. During the drought of the 1890's, the rain-makers did a thriving but unsuccessful business; now in the 1950's, they are with us again—this time backed up by substantial scientific fact. The new rain-making devices—dry ice and silver iodide—do work, but only under conditions within the cloud mass normally required for rain. Let us not kid ourselves— the Nebraska skies will remain a wild and unpredictable realm, and drought will remain a characteristic of our weather.

We have been more successful in making better use of the water after it falls.

Our main source of water lies beneath the surface. We have a marvelous underground storage system. Precipitation in the sandhills soaks downward, then percolates slowly (some of it is 50 years old before we use it) southeastward across the state. This "reservoir" of groundwater supplies all of our municipal water systems except Omaha's, and we have little fear of exhausting it, since at any given time it holds roughly a billion acre-feet of water.

In the past twenty-five years we have found another use for groundwater. Pump irrigation is growing by leaps and bounds. Powerful pumps are now watering about a million acres of crop land. And the growth continues. There is some justifiable concern that we will overdevelop our groundwater resource in some areas, and here again we are faced with the problem of innovating. Our surface water law, there is reason to believe, does not precisely fit the groundwater use problem. Debate will soon be joined. In our own way and in our own time public policy for groundwater will be evolved. The current fear is that our groundwater resource may be abused before we arrive at a decision.

Our interest in gravity irrigation—this is the kind that flows over the land in ditches supplied by reservoirs on rivers—has blown hot and cold, depending upon the weather. The drought of the 1890's spurred interest in the arid western part of the state and resulted in a Bureau of Reclamation project on the upper North Platte. It transformed the valley there into an ever-abundant agriculture. In the 1930's, the drought provoked a renewed interest in irrigation in central Nebraska. New dams were built on some of our rivers, and additional uncertain cropland was assured of a constant water supply. In 1944 the Congress enacted a flood control act which has come to be known as the Missouri Basin Development Program, under which our reservoirs have been built. Thirty-three more are planned. The program contemplates adding 1,600,000 acres of irrigated land in Nebraska.

Nebraskans are responsible for another innovation, less than a decade old, which will help us control and conserve our water. This is the small watershed program designed to hold water on the land or in small reservoirs upstream before runoff swells creeks and streams to destructive size downstream. The program operates in the small watersheds which comprise the much larger river basins. The Salt-Wahoo Creek program in eastern Nebraska was a national pilot project. Twenty small watershed organizations have been organized in Nebraska. The program is spreading to all parts of the nation.

These programs ultimately may bring a fourth of our cultivated land under irrigation, help us conserve water upstream before it becomes a flood, and partially free us from the ups and downs of production caused by our wet-dry cycles. Our farming will become more diversified and more productive.

We have used and abused our soil. Fifty per cent of our land has suffered only slight erosion. The remainder has had moderate to severe erosion. Our profligacy is worst in eastern Nebraska where our richest soils lie. Here over seven million acres have been stripped of 75 per cent of the topsoil—and that's the part we live on.

Except in the sandhills and adjacent grazing areas, we have plowed up the prairie grass and with it the best soil conservation system ever devised. Listen to the plea of Prof. C. E. Bessey, a world-famous botanist at the University of Nebraska, writing in 1902:

The planted crops may be ever so good and successful, yet they may not warrant the destruction of that wonderful grassy covering which now adorns our hills and valleys. The wild grasses are disappearing not only because of cultivation of the soil but also on account of too heavy and injudicious grazing. We have been as wasteful of our natural grasses as our fathers were of the forests of the eastern states.

Well, we went right ahead with the plow, and in the 1930's the folly of our ways became painfully apparent. We became a part of the "Dust Bowl." The fact is we had the living daylights scared out of us: some believed the land would never recover from its desert condition.

When the federal soil conservation program began in 1936, we were johnny-on-the-spot. Soil conservation districts were organized under a state law enacted in 1937. Our first district was one of the nation's first, and we were the first state west of the Mississippi to include all its land under soil conservation districts. *Contouring, terracing, strip cropping, crop rotation, gully control, grassed waterways, stubble mulching, shelterbelts,* and *windbreaks* are now familiar words. We have come a long way in our struggle to save the topsoil, but there is a king-size task still ahead. Nebraska now has 3,500,000 acres of land unsuited for cultivation and another 1,500,000 which shouldn't be farmed. Year after year, wind and water continue to erode the topsoil of the naked land. The destruction is man-made. Perhaps the Plainsmen will devise a remedy— in time.

Those who came to the Great Plains and settled in Nebraska were the restless, the ambitious, the discontented, and the poor. They saw in the West a new chance to make a place for themselves, to build, to acquire wealth, to win power. For the Europeans there was, as well, the bright promise of political liberty.

All that the pioneers sought was attainable. But this was rugged, unfamiliar country, and the conditions it imposed for success were tremendous. Some failed to grasp the meaning of the new land; they were the ones who gave up and got out. Not all those who stayed understood the total significance of the new frontier, but they were resourceful enough to absorb the shocks and husband the gains. The land and the climate influenced them profoundly, but not exclusively. There were other shaping forces—economic, political, social, of national and international origin—from which they could not and did not escape.

Certainly the circumstances of life in Nebraska, which obliged the settlers to devise new ways to earn a livelihood, played an important part in molding their social and political character. With the past still so close to the present in our state, we who live here believe we can see how the Plains environment came to breed a distinctive type of political innovator. In the 1890's, for example, there were grasshoppers and there was a drought. Both were regional, and disastrous. There were ruinously low prices for whatever we were lucky enough to grow or raise. That this was a consequence of a glutted world agricultural market was something we didn't know. Our misfortunes, we earnestly believed, had resulted from the machinations of the trusts and vested interests of the East. So we revolted. The Grange movement, bitterly demanding a fair shake for agriculture, blossomed into a political party which was appropriated by W. J. Bryan and came near to putting its candidate into the White House. And although the Populist Party's life was short, its progeny were numerous—Progressivism, the Non-Partisan League, the Farmers Alliance, the Farm Holiday Association. Moreover, the issues raised in 1892 were to be issues again in 1932, with social and political consequences not yet measurable.

The farmers' anguished outcries often have been the prelude to both local and national innovations. Nebraskans played leading roles in amending national homestead laws which made the basic land unit adequate to support the family on the Great Plains. Nebraskans did the political agitating necessary to organize the western states in support of a federal program of reclamation and irrigation. Nebraskans substantially reinforced the demands which led to Theodore Roosevelt's federal forestation program and which would mean so much to the treeless prairie. Nebraskans figured prominently in the revolt which led to the federal soil and water conservation programs, and emergency farm relief inaugurated in the distressing 1930's.

Agricultural crises and the resulting social unrest have inspired innovations within our own borders. Among them are movements which culminated in abolishing price abuses perpetrated by the "big-line" elevators, in ending arbitrary intra-state rate-making by the railroads, in delegating more legislative power to the people through the process of initiative and referendum, in providing the direct election of nominees for political office, in establishing the one-house legislature, in converting all power-generating facilities within our borders into a single publicly owned system.

Much that has happened in Nebraska can be explained in terms of a frontier society, for our state *was* a frontier for nearly half its politically organized existence. Much that has happened can be explained in terms of traits we inherited from the pioneers. Much also is explained in terms of new influences, developments of the past quarter-century.

The growth of small industries in our state has been great, and their wealth is rapidly approaching our agriculture's. Our population gains are occurring in the towns and cities. Broad ribbons of concrete and asphalt, supporting streams of trucks and automobiles, tie us closer together. Food, clothes, furnishings, gadgets, all the paraphernalia of living appear in our stores at virtually the same instant they reach the consumer in Brockton, Mass. Main Street in Nebraska has the same neon-lit, plastic-and-glass-front look as Main Street everywhere in the U.S.

Books, magazines, motion pictures, radio, and TV bombard the Nebraskan—as they do the eastern suburbanite—with the good and the bad of our mass culture, be it the NBC Symphony or Elvis Presley, Arnold Toynbee or Mickey Spillane, Olivier's *Richard III* or Proctor and Gamble's "Life Can Be Beautiful." Communication has bridged the distances—physical and psychological—which once separated us from the main stream of America. It has made us more conscious of America and its place in the world community. It has made us aware that while agriculture is an important factor in our national life, it is not the single most important factor. It has dramatically changed our *conditions* of life.

The unifying forces have not yet become leveling forces. This is important to us because we believe that a most significant aspect of Nebraska life remains, as it was in our earlier years, a robust individualism. We show it most in state and local politics which are tough on politicians and a morass of frustration for those who seek a common unity in attacking our problems.

We are a people of diverse interests and attitudes. Agriculture is our largest single economic interest, yet within it the corn-grower and the wheat-raiser and the dryland farmer and the irrigator and the cattle rancher and the livestock-feeder go their separate ways. The worries of our growing industrial enterprise are not always those of the agriculturist. Historical and not-so-historical rivalries flourish between regions, counties, towns, and neighborhoods. These offer formidable obstacles to innovations which, viewed in broad perspective, would benefit the whole.

Local conflicts of interest are not unique to Nebraska. They can be found everywhere in America. Yet, in Nebraska they are more meaningful, more virile, more intense, more personal. We take stubborn delight in expressing our individualism; and our society is so constructed that we can be heard.

Despite automobiles and planes, distances are still imposing—from Omaha to our western border is roughly the same distance as from Chicago to Pittsburgh, or from Washington, D.C. to Boston—and those who "stump" our state find it an arduous task. Further complicating matters for them is the fact that Lincoln and Omaha are our only cities with metropolitan areas. Thirty-nine other cities have populations between 2,500 and 25,000. The remaining 495 are under 2,500, and most of these are less than 1,000. About a third of us live on farms and ranches, another third in small towns and villages, and the rest of us in the larger towns and cities.

No prevailing force—local political machines, political leader, newspaper chain—binds us together. At times we suffer for our parochialism, our refusal to look at the statewide picture, our lack of a voice that speaks for us all. At other times the idealists and innovators rise among us to be heard. We listen and follow. From our achievements and disappointments we have acquired a social conscience which is cautious but not perverse, conservative but not bigoted, responsive but not gregarious. Our need to be "thoroughly sold" on a new idea and on those expounding it derives in large part from our predominately small-town life.

We lead a "showcase" existence in our towns. We do not build high fences and hedges to separate us from our neighbors. We find it hard to understand those who wish to withdraw from our midst into a private world of their own. We share not only the housewife's cup of sugar but our joys and sorrows, hopes and ambitions, successes and defeats.

We are unabashed boosters. We want to build, to improve, to grow. We are not embarrassed if our starry-eyed idealism must sometimes yield to hard-headed practicality, because ours is a man-made world unsupported by mineral bonanzas. When a man runs a good farm or a good ranch or a good business, we tell him. But when we do his inward satisfaction is balanced by an outward embarrassment. We covet the esteem of our neighbors, but we like to be known as common folks. We take an inordinate interest in our children because all the children of our communities are an integral part of our lives. We hope they will succeed us on our farm, in our business.

Here we are Somebody; we are an Event when we are born and when we die. Here is an intensely personal world, a world where "they" are people with faces and first names. In our home towns we find a comfort and a security in the familiar which we wouldn't trade for all the variety and novelty and urban glitter of the eastern metropolises.

Thousands of Americans hurtle across our state each year, pausing only long enough to gas up and gulp a hamburger. They have heard that there is nothing spectacular or super-colossal here: for them, as it was for the Forty-Niners, Nebraska is a land-obstacle to be traversed in the shortest possible time. But we are not disturbed at this brush-off. We do not pluck at their sleeves to detain them. We have a proud record behind us and a spacious future ahead. We know what has been done and what can be done to make our agriculture more productive, while still conserving and protecting our water and soil. We think it remarkable that our community of small industries should be rapidly growing, even though many of them must import raw materials and export their finished products.

We believe we have done a pretty fair job of ordering our society without forfeiting our sometimes too-individualistic approach to solving our problems. We believe we are headed for bigger things and better ones, and we fondly cherish the hope that our children will do a better job than we.

We find a satisfying beauty in our state—in the precise rows of towering corn stalks, the freshly turned earth, the grandeur of a thunderstorm, the awesome loneliness of the sandhills grass, the well-kept yard.

We Nebraskans understand the conditions of life here. With good humor and serious purposefulness, we accept them—and like it.

On the edge of the prairie, where the sun had gone down, the sky was turquoise blue, like a lake, with gold light throbbing in it. Higher up, in the utter clarity of the western slope, the evening star hung like a lamp suspended by silver chains—like the lamp engraved upon the title-page of old Latin texts, which is always appearing in new heavens, and waking new desires in men.

—Willa Cather, *My Antonia*

Sources Not Acknowledged Elsewhere

FOR FEAR of cluttering the text too much, many sources of interpolated material were not identified by footnotes. Following is a listing of all material not acknowledged elsewhere, tabulated under the heading of the selection in which it appeared.

It should be noted also that footnotes citing sources were, in nearly every case, omitted from condensed and excerpted articles.

I. THE SHIFTING FRONTIER

The quotation on the divider was taken from *My Antonia* by Willa Cather (Houghton Mifflin Company, 1918), 7.

The second paragraph of the introduction to "The Myth of Wild Bill Hickok" by Carl Uhlarik was extracted from the original article.

The Burlington & Missouri poster in "See Nebraska on Safari" is in the Nebraska State Historical Society collection.

In the introduction to "The Road to Arcadia," the Addison E. Sheldon quotation may be found in his *Nebraska: The Land and the People* (Lewis Publishing Company, 1931) I, 579.

The quotation introducing "The Lynching of Kid Wade" was taken from *Nebraska: A Guide to the Cornhusker State* (Hastings House, 1939), 311.

II. FAMILY ALBUM I

The quotation on the divider may be found in *O Pioneers!* by Willa Cather (Houghton Mifflin Company, 1947), 65.

The quotation which ends "Willa Cather of Red Cloud" may be found in *My Antonia* (Houghton Mifflin Company, 1918), 353.

In the introduction to "Road Trader," the lines quoted from Willa Cather occur in the story "Two Friends," *Obscure Destinies* (Alfred A. Knopf, Inc., 1950), 212.

Outlook's comments on Edgar Howard appeared in the issue of April 23, 1930. The *Time* biography was published in response to readers' requests in the "Letters" section, July 28, 1930.

III. THE GATEWAY

In "Omaha Newsreel," the material on which Ruth Reynolds based her account of the Cudahy kidnapping was supplied by B. F. Sylvester. The account of the 1913 tornado was derived in part from Arthur C. Wakeley's

Omaha: The Gate City (S. J. Clarke, 1917), 448–451, and Alfred R. Soren-son's *The Story of Omaha* (National Printing Company, 1923), 644–645.

In the introduction to "Railroad Man," John Gunther's *Inside U.S.A.* (Harper & Brothers, 1947), 255, was the source for the statement about Mr. Jeffer's reputed ability to break half dollars with his teeth.

IV. THE SOWER

In the introduction to "Education of a Nebraskan," the quoted descrip-tion of Alvin S. Johnson was taken from *Current Biography 1942* (H. W. Wilson Company, 1942), 421.

Willa Cather's profile of the Bryans appeared originally in *The Library*, July 14, 1900, under the pen name "Henry Nicklemann."

In the introduction to "Mixed Notices," E. P. Brown's description of early theatrical activities in Lincoln is quoted from *Seventy-Five Years in the Prairie Capital* (Miller & Paine, 1955), 39.

V. THE WEATHER REPORT

"The Seasons in Nebraska" was selected from the following writings of Willa Cather: I. (Winter)—*O Pioneers!* (Houghton Mifflin Company, 1947), 187–188. II. (Spring) and IV. (Fall)—*My Antonia* (Houghton Mifflin Com-pany, 1918), 119–120 and 40. III. (Summer)—*One of Ours* (Alfred A. Knopf, Inc., 1953), 158.

In "The Blizzard of 1888," the paragraph beginning "In Nebraska the morning . . ." was taken from Addison E. Sheldon's account in *Nebraska Old and New* (University Publishing Company, 1937), 352–353.

The introduction to "Men Against the River" was derived in part from the article by B. F. Sylvester in its uncondensed form.

VI. LOOK EAST, LOOK WEST

The quotation on the divider may be found in Willa Cather's *Youth and the Bright Medusa* (Alfred A. Knopf, Inc., 1951), 222. That introducing "The Mysterious Middle West" was taken from *O Pioneers!* (Houghton Mifflin Company, 1947), 75–76.

"Scottsbluff" was based on the following sources: (1) The Golden Jubilee Edition of the Scottsbluff *Star-Herald*, August 2, 1950, compiled and mostly written by Robert Young, and containing contributions by Nadine Ander-son, Lola Banghart, Mrs. Elizabeth Thies, Walt Panko, Bob Franson, and Dean Razee. (2) A brochure, "Scottsbluff and the North Platte Valley," compiled by Thomas L. Green and published under the auspices of the Scottsbluff Golden Jubilee Celebration Committee (Star-Herald Printing Company, 1950). Articles were contributed by Robert Young, Harold J. Cook, H. J. Wisner, T. L. Green, Winfield J. Evans, Charles S. Simmons, Phil Sheldon, Robert G. Simmons, J. C. McCreary, Maynard S. Clement, L. L. Hilliard, Elizabeth Hughes Thies, Lester A. Danielson, and A. T. Howard. (3) Information supplied by Victor E. Blackledge and Alan H. Williams. (4) *History of Western Nebraska and Its People,* edited by

Grant L. Shumway (Western Publishing & Engraving Company, 1921), II, 444–511.

In the introduction to "Hyannis," material pertaining to "Operation Snowbound" was obtained from an article by B. F. Sylvester in the New York *Sunday News,* January 17, 1949.

The quotation introducing "Sandhill Sundays" is extracted from "Nebraska" by Mari Sandoz, *Holiday,* May, 1956.

VII. FAMILY ALBUM II

The anecdote introducing "Mari Sandoz" was related in *The Brand Book* of the New York Posse of The Westerners, a national organization of people who write about, draw, paint, or photograph the Old West.

VIII. JUST PASSING THROUGH

In the introduction to "The Plains of Nebraska," the lines quoted from Willa Cather may be found in *My Antonia* (Houghton Mifflin Company, 1918), 19.

The introduction to "Nebraska Not in the Guidebook" was extracted from "Four Seasons on the Farm," *Life,* March 17, 1941, copyright Time, Inc., 1941.

IX. THE FIRST HUNDRED YEARS ARE THE HARDEST

The description of the new Strategic Air Command Headquarters in "First Line of Defense" was based on a news story by Del Harding appearing in the Lincoln *Star,* November 10, 1956.

In the same article, the passage quoting William J. Shallcross appears in his *Romance of a Village: The Story of Bellevue* (Roncka Brothers, 1954), 229.

CLOSING QUOTATION

These lines are from Willa Cather's *My Antonia* (Houghton Mifflin, 1918), 263.